alone with god

alone with god

BIBLICAL AND LITURGICAL
MEDITATIONS FOR EVERY DAY

BY

JULES HEYRMAN, S.J.

Translated and Edited by
Thomas Heyrman, S.J.

VOLUME ONE

alba house   DIVISION OF THE SOCIETY OF ST. PAUL
STATEN ISLAND, N.Y. 10314

REVISED EDITION

NIHIL OBSTAT: Father A. Ferrero, S.S.P., *Regional Delegate*

IMPRIMI POTEST: Father Crick, S.J., *Praep. Prov. Ranchiensis*

IMPRIMATUR: ✠ Most Rev. L. Raymond, *Bishop of Allahabad*

die III Julii MCMLXI

First printing, April 1963
Second printing, September 1964
Third printing, December 1965
Fourth printing, June 1967

Library of Congress Catalog Card Number: 63-14571

© Copyright, Society of St. Paul

Title of the Dutch Edition, "Alleen Met God"
Published by Desclee De Brouwer, Belgium.

Published by special arrangement with
St. Paul Publications, Allahabad, India.

Printed and bound by the Pauline Fathers and Brothers,
Society of St. Paul, Staten Island, New York 10314.

FOREWORD

The title of this book clearly expresses its purpose: to leave the soul alone with God, as quickly as possible. Such was the purpose of all those who wrote meditation manuals to be used by others, and this was the aim of St. Ignatius in his *Spiritual Exercises*. The Saint was aware that in this matter some guidance may be indispensable, but he desired that the guide display great discretion. It is his business to help the soul, to set it going on the right road, to keep it there, to give sound advice; but let him be careful to allow the Creator to deal directly with His creature, and the creature with its Creator and Lord. The Saint said: "He shall carefully propose to the exercitant the subject matter of the meditation, going through the points briefly, and with a short explanation. When the person who contemplates takes the true groundwork of the history, discussing and reasoning by himself, and meeting with something that makes the history clearer and better felt (whether this happen through his own reasoning, or through the enlightenment of his understanding by divine grace), he thereby enjoys greater spiritual relish and fruit, than if he, who gives the Exercises, had minutely explained and developed the meaning of the history. For it is not to know much, but it is to understand and savor the matter interiorly that fills and satisfies the soul."

The matter has been distributed in distinct "points"; but St. Ignatius directs that, "if in a certain point the soul finds what it desires, it shall not proceed further until it is fully satisfied".

These are directions emanating from a wise and experienced spiritual guide, and they should be followed by those who use this book, which is nothing more than a means to an end. "Let each one use it as long as it makes him advance towards the goal; and let him lay it aside whenever it fails to help, or becomes an obstacle."

However, most people, especially beginners and such as are endowed with a lively imagination, and also those that lead a very busy life, find out by experience that they need the help of a book.

St. Teresa of Avila told her Sisters: "During more than fourteen years I was unable to make a meditation without the help of a book." And she added: "Many may have had the same experience, and there are those who, even when helped by a book, are unable to meditate, and can say only vocal prayers. While praying thus, they experience fewer distractions" (*The Way of Perfection,* 17, 4).

We may follow the counsel of Jesus, "enter into thy chamber, and having shut the door, pray to thy Father in secret" (*Matt.* 6, 6), but we soon find how difficult it is to control our imagination, and to keep our mind fixed on God. A poet said he would follow Jesus to the mountain; but there was none so high, that there he could find Jesus alone; and however high he ascended, still the world kept pursuing him. Is that not our own experience?

A meditation manual can render service in several ways. For instance, if circumstances or our actual dispositions do not suggest a subject for the next morning's meditation, a manual will assist us to prepare the subject matter for the next morning— the last but by no means the best preparation. The most effective preparation for praying "in our chamber" is our life away from it. We shall easily find God in prayer if we meet Him and love Him in our work,, and if, with a pure intention and a single heart, we seek Him, and Him alone, in all things. When the soul listens, all things speak to it about God. "By two things is man lifted above earthly things, viz., by simplicity and purity. Simplicity must be in the intention, purity in affection. Simplicity aimeth at God, purity taketh hold of Him and tasteth Him" (2 *Imit. of Christ,* 4, 1).

There is another and even more efficacious method of preparing the soul to pray, viz., that we create in ourselves those dispositions from which prayer naturally springs: a lively sense of our spiritual misery and of the needs of our soul will place us in the attitude of a suppliant. "Rabboni, that I may see!" (*Mark* 10, 51); "If thou wilt thou canst make me clean!" (*Mark* 1, 40); "Lord, save us, we perish!" (*Matt.* 8, 25.) The great and crying needs of the Church, and of the souls dear to us, or entrusted to our care, will urge us to fervent prayer. A more contemplative prayer calls for more profound inward silence, for greater detachment from earthly things, and for complete and self-forgetting dedication to the service of God and of neighbor. These are conditions for, and also fruits of, contemplative prayer.

*   *   *

The subject matter of these meditations is borrowed mostly from the liturgical texts, as they are found in the daily Masses of the ecclesiastical year, mostly from the Gospels and the Epistles, offering us Christ our Lord as the enduring object of our love and devotion. We constantly try to keep looking on Jesus "the author and finisher of our faith" (*Heb.* 12, 2), on Him that was to come, and about whom the Father said, "Hear him" (*Luke* 9, 35). Against the disadvantage of that system which excludes the following of a systematic order, militates the great advantage that the Gospel every day places a concrete image before our eyes, and that there is a close relation between our meditation and the daily sacrifice of the Mass.

In a few cases an attempt has been made to take certain prayers as subject matter for meditation. This method, says St. Ignatius, "consists in considering the significance of each word of a prayer." The Our Father, which is the very substance of the prayer of our Lord, can be easily treated in this manner.

A few meditations have as subject matter some striking feature in the life of certain Saints who are specially venerated by the faithful.

* * *

The subject matter of each meditation is divided into distinct headings or "points". This may contribute to a better understanding of the subject. Let them be "starting points", whither we can return when we have wandered away from the subject; and they may help to keep the matter clearly before the mind, when attention and devotion begin to flag. But, as mentioned above, we shall find the best starting point of our meditation, not in a book, but in our own soul, its present needs and its longings. Therefore the preparation of the meditation should consist, not in the hurried reading of the "points", but in an effort to become aware of our needs, and an attempt to apply the points to the present conditions of our soul.

* * *

Formerly too much stress seems to have been laid on practical applications and on resolutions, so that one gathered the impression that contemplation, even of the most sublime mysteries, had to crystallize as quickly as possible into practical conclusions, and had to yield place to examination of conscience. This way of thinking seems to have arisen from the mistaken interpretation of a direction of St. Ignatius, who at the end of his points of meditation says, "and then to reflect thereupon, in order to derive profit from each of these things" or "to obtain some fruit". The meaning was that we should allow the mystery, which we have contemplated at leisure, to impregnate our soul and to influence our life. Does one hang apples on the branches of a tree? They must grow naturally, fed and matured by the sap that is the life of the tree. Intense interior prayer and contemplation have a deeper influence on our lives than many resolutions, "that become scorched because they have no root and wither away."

The principle of St. Ignatius, quoted above, may be helpful here also: "Not by many resolutions, and practical applications does the soul make progress in virtue, but by interiorly feeling and tasting the Lord." The best practical applications are those that flow spontaneously from a deeper insight into, and a clearer personal understanding of, the divine mysteries. However, for those who find it hard to apply themselves to contemplative prayer, and also for others who grow dizzy on the lofty peaks whither their imagination carries them, so that they lose hold of the real facts of life, some of the most obvious practical applications have been suggested in the book.

* * *

There is a meditation for every day of the year. However, the more intimate and richer our spiritual life becomes, the less we stand in need of subject matter and change. The day comes when curiosity, or even the simple desire to know, has yielded place to the longing for that "Beauty, which is always old, and yet ever new." It is advisable for all—taking, however, into account the character, dispositions and needs of each person—to repeat a meditation that has made a special impression on the soul, or that, contrary to expectation, utterly failed to stir the heart. One of the clearest proofs of spiritual progress is the profound desire for greater unity and more simplicity. Says the *Imitation of Christ*: "He, to whom all things are one, who referreth all things to one, and seeth all things in one, may be steadfast in heart, and abide in God at peace. O Truth, my God! make me one with Thee in everlasting charity. I am oftentimes wearied with reading and hearing many things; in Thee is all I wish or long for. Let all teachers hold their peace, and all created things keep silence in Thy presence; do Thou alone speak to me."

* * *

A great scholar, who was also a saintly man, had spent his entire life writing a treatise on the Person of our Lord Jesus Christ. The conclusion of the book ran thus: "The writer had only one thing in view, and that was to make the Person of Jesus Christ better known.... Such books have value only in so far as they lead men closer to the Source. When he has reached so far, let him who thirsts fall on his knees and drink deep draughts." *Si parva magnis....* If it is permissible to set small things by the side of great ones, then let this book lead all those who will use it, closer to "the fountain of living water, springing up unto life everlasting."

J. Heyrman, S.J.

PREFACE TO THE SECOND EDITION

That these meditations should be reprinted so soon after their first publication in July 1961, that in less than one year 3,000 copies have been sold, is ample proof that "Alone with God" answers a real need. Many priests and religious have indeed expressed their appreciation for these meditations which happily combine a time-honored method with all that is fresh and wholesome in the liturgical revival, so characteristic of our modern times.

The author is a man of rich experience. He has spent nearly sixty years of his life in the mother-house of the Jesuits of the Northern Belgian Province, at Drongen, near Ghent, as a teacher, as a spiritual guide of the young as well as seasoned religious, and as Rector. He has preached scores of retreats and recollections to priests and nuns. His wise experience he shares now on a larger scale with all those who look for a sure companion to guide them in their life of prayer.

The text of this second edition slightly differs from the first edition in a few places where a better rendering of the original text was desirable. For the facility of the reader, several references have been added to the titles wherever possible.

THE EDITOR

Ranchi, June 15, 1962

Biblical texts are quoted from the *"Douay-Rheims"* translation from the Latin Vulgate; except for a few quotations taken from other versions, when necessary for a better understanding of the context.

1974

CONTENTS

FOREWORD   5
PREFACE TO THE SECOND EDITION   9

First Week of Advent

SUNDAY: Nov 29 Silent, Hopeful Longing   19
MONDAY: The Second Coming of Christ   21
TUESDAY: "I Have Lifted Up My Soul"   23
WEDNESDAY: A Perfect Prayer   25
THURSDAY: Waiting   27
FRIDAY: Crying For Salvation   30
SATURDAY: Heaven's Golden Portal   32

Second Week of Advent

SUNDAY: Nov 6 The Precursor   34
MONDAY: "Stir Up Our Hearts, O Lord"   36
TUESDAY: The Mystery of the Incarnation   38
WEDNESDAY: The Immaculate Conception   40
THURSDAY: "And Blessed Art Thou That Hast Believed"   42
FRIDAY: Joseph, Mary's Spouse   44
SATURDAY: "Drop Dew, Ye Heavens, From Above"   46

Third Week of Advent

SUNDAY: Dec 13 Christian Joy   49
MONDAY: "The Peace That Surpasseth All Under-
       standing"   51
TUESDAY: Jesus, the Unknown   53
WEDNESDAY: Cooperation With Grace   55
THURSDAY: The Great Things Done to Mary   57
FRIDAY: Hallowed Silence   60
SATURDAY: Holy Mass   62

Fourth Week of Advent

DECEMBER 17: O Sapientia   64
DECEMBER 18: O Adonai   66

79-127
127-192

DECEMBER 19:	O Radix Jesse	68
DECEMBER 20:	O Clavis David	70
DECEMBER 21:	O Oriens	73
DECEMBER 22:	O Rex Gentium	75
DECEMBER 23:	O Emmanuel	77
VIGIL OF CHRISTMAS:	Tomorrow You Shall Witness His Glory	79
CHRISTMAS DAY		82
DECEMBER 26:	The Virginal Motherhood	84
DECEMBER 27:	Saint John	86
DECEMBER 28:	The Holy Innocents	89
DECEMBER 29:	The Master's First Public Lesson	91
DECEMBER 30:	The Preface of Christmas Time	93
DECEMBER 31:	To Praise and to Thank God	96
JANUARY 1:	Octave of the Nativity of Our Lord	98
JANUARY 2:	The Holy Name of Jesus	101
JANUARY 3:	"Do All in the Name of the Lord"	103
JANUARY 4:	To Pray in the Name of Jesus	106
JANUARY 5:	Bethlehem, the Palace of Peace	108
JANUARY 6:	The Epiphany of Our Lord — I	110
JANUARY 7:	The Epiphany of Our Lord — II	112
JANUARY 8:	Virtues Practiced by the Wise Men	114
JANUARY 9:	"They Offered Him Gifts"	117
JANUARY 10:	The Adoration of the Magi — Mary's Place	119
JANUARY 11:	The Flight Into Egypt and the Return	122
JANUARY 12:	Concluding Meditation on the Mystery of Christmas	124
JANUARY 13:	The Baptism of Our Lord	127
JANUARY 14:	The Marriage at Cana — I	129
JANUARY 15:	The Marriage at Cana — II	132
JANUARY 16:	The Holy Family	134
JANUARY 17:	The Hidden Life at Nazareth	137
JANUARY 18:	The Progress of Jesus	139
JANUARY 19:	Jesus Found in the Temple	142
JANUARY 20:	Jesus Leaves Nazareth	144
JANUARY 21:	The Christian Ideal of Life — I	147
JANUARY 22:	The Christian Ideal of Life — II	149
JANUARY 23:	The Christian Ideal of Life — III	152
JANUARY 24:	The Christian Ideal of Life — IV Perseverance in Prayer	154

Nov 1

JANUARY 25: The Christian Ideal of Life — V
Sympathy 156
JANUARY 26: The Christian Ideal of Life — VI
Humility 158

Third Week after Epiphany

SUNDAY: Christ Cleanses the Leper 161
MONDAY: Christ Cures the Centurion's Servant 163
TUESDAY: "Lord, I Am Not Worthy" 165
WEDNESDAY: "God's Eye and God's Hand" 167
THURSDAY: "Be Not Overcome by Evil" 169
FRIDAY: God Has Overcome Evil 171
SATURDAY: Mary Has Overcome Evil 173

Fourth Week after Epiphany

SUNDAY: Christ Stills the Tempest 175
MONDAY: The Church in the Storm 178
TUESDAY: The Whole Law 180
WEDNESDAY: Jesus Preaches at Nazareth 182
THURSDAY: The People of Nazareth Are Scandalized 184
FRIDAY: Christ's Failure at Nazareth 187
SATURDAY: The Prayer of St. Nicholas von Flue 189

Fifth Week after Epiphany

SUNDAY: The Parable of the Cockle 192
MONDAY: God's Policy 194
TUESDAY: Remember Thy Last End 197
WEDNESDAY: Thanking God Through Christ Our Lord 200
THURSDAY: Christian Behavior 202
FRIDAY: Our Wavering Wills 205
SATURDAY: The Unwavering Heart of Mary 207

Septuagesima Week

SUNDAY: "Pre-Lenten Dispositions" 210
MONDAY: The Laborer's Hire 212
TUESDAY: God's Infinite Goodness 215
WEDNESDAY: "Not I, But the Grace of God With Me" 218
THURSDAY: No Unemployment in the Kingdom of God 220
FRIDAY: A Prayer of St. Thomas Aquinas 223

SATURDAY: "Root of Jesse, Gate of Morn, Whence
                   the World's True Light Was Born"   226

Sexagesima Week

SUNDAY: The Parable of the Sower — I   228
MONDAY: The Parable of the Sower — II   231
TUESDAY: The Parable of the Sower — III   233
WEDNESDAY: Privileged Knowledge   235
THURSDAY: Saint Paul on the Defensive   238
FRIDAY: Saint Paul Weak and Yet Strong   240
SATURDAY: The Word of God in the Most Pure
                   Heart of Mary   243

Quinquagesima Week

N or 8

SUNDAY: Worthless Performances   245
MONDAY: "A More Excellent Way"   248
TUESDAY: "Charity Never Falleth Away"   250
ASH WEDNESDAY: Dust and Ashes — Life Eternal   252
THURSDAY: "Thy Father, Who Seeth in Secret"   255
FRIDAY: The Preface of Lent   257
SATURDAY: Fasting: True and False   259

First Week of Lent

SUNDAY: The Fast of Our Lord   262
MONDAY: Our Lord Is Tempted   264
TUESDAY: The Separation of the Sheep From the Goats 267
WEDNESDAY: Safe in God's Hands   270
THURSDAY: The Woman of Canaan   272
FRIDAY: Before the Face of the Lord   274
SATURDAY: "Who Is My Mother?"   277

Second Week of Lent

SUNDAY: The Transfiguration of Our Lord — I   279
MONDAY: The Transfiguration of Our Lord — II   282
TUESDAY: Jesus and the Pharisees   284
WEDNESDAY: True Penance   287
THURSDAY: God's Mercy   289
FRIDAY: Jesus, "A Friend of Publicans and Sinners" 292
SATURDAY: The Prodigal Son   294

Third Week of Lent

SUNDAY: Children of the Light 297
MONDAY: "Blessed Are They That Dwell in Thy
House" 299
TUESDAY: "If Thy Brother Shall Offend" 302
WEDNESDAY: Honor Thy Father and Thy Mother 304
THURSDAY: Jesus and the Sick 307
FRIDAY: Jesus and the Samaritan Woman 310
SATURDAY: Christ and the Woman Taken in Adultery 312

Fourth Week of Lent

SUNDAY: The Second Multiplication of the Loaves 315
MONDAY: Jesus Casts the Sellers Out of the Temple 317
TUESDAY: "My Doctrine Is Not Mine" 320
WEDNESDAY: Jesus Gives Sight to the Man Born Blind 322
THURSDAY: Two Resurrections From the Dead 325
FRIDAY: The Raising of Lazarus 327
SATURDAY: The Solicitations of God's Grace 330

Passion Week

SUNDAY: The One, Great Sacrifice 332
MONDAY: Jesus, Source of Living Water 335
TUESDAY: The Agony at Gethsemane 337
WEDNESDAY: Jesus Is Apprehended 340
THURSDAY: Jesus Publicly Humiliated 342
FRIDAY: Our Lady of Dolors 344
SATURDAY: Jesus, Though Innocent, Suffers Patiently 347

Holy Week

SUNDAY: Jesus' Triumphal Entry Into Jerusalem 349
MONDAY: Jesus Suffers With Humility and Dignity 352
TUESDAY: Jesus Treads the Winepress Alone Yet,
He Was in Touch With All Mankind 354
WEDNESDAY: Jesus Obedient Unto Death 357
THURSDAY: The Institution of the Blessed Sacrament 359
FRIDAY: Vexilla Regis 362
SATURDAY: With Mary, the Mother of the Lord 364

Easter Week

SUNDAY:	The Resurrection of Our Lord	367
MONDAY:	Apparition to the Disciples of Emmaus	370
TUESDAY:	Apparition to Peter	372
WEDNESDAY:	Apparition by the Sea of Tiberias	375
THURSDAY:	Apparition to Mary Magdalen	377
FRIDAY:	Apparition to the Apostles	380
SATURDAY:	Jesus Appears to His Holy Mother	382

First Week after Easter

SUNDAY:	Apparition to Thomas and the Other Apostles	385
MONDAY:	Preserving the Easter Graces	387
TUESDAY:	Our Faith Overcometh the World	389
WEDNESDAY:	Easter Joy	391
THURSDAY:	The Vows of Religion, Sources of Joy	394
FRIDAY:	The Religious Life, a Source of Happiness	396
SATURDAY:	Mary, "Cause of Our Joy"	399

Second Week after Easter

SUNDAY:	The Good Shepherd	401
MONDAY:	"I Know My Sheep"	404
TUESDAY:	"And Mine Know Me"	406
WEDNESDAY:	Intruders, Hirelings, or Pastors	408
THURSDAY:	"I Am the Door"	411
FRIDAY:	"One Fold and One Shepherd"	413
SATURDAY:	"The Good Odor of Christ"	415

Third Week after Easter

SUNDAY:	"A Little While and You Shall See Me"	418
MONDAY:	"It Is Expedient to You That I Go"	420
TUESDAY:	"I Go to the Father"	423
WEDNESDAY:	"My Peace I Give Unto You"	425
THURSDAY:	"A New Commandment I Give Unto You"	428
FRIDAY:	The Influence of a Holy Life	430
SATURDAY:	Our All-powerful Intercessor	433

487-end

Fourth Week after Easter

SUNDAY: Supported by Faith   436
MONDAY: "Of One Heart and One Will"   438
TUESDAY: The Father, Fountain of All Good   441
WEDNESDAY: Gradually   443
THURSDAY: "My Father and Your Father"   446
FRIDAY: "Wondrous Exchange"   448
SATURDAY: A Prayer to Mary   450

Fifth Week after Easter

SUNDAY: "Doers of the Word"   453
MONDAY: True Piety   455
TUESDAY: "Ask in My Name"   458
WEDNESDAY: Our Lord's Priestly Prayer   460
THURSDAY: The Ascension of Our Lord — I   463
FRIDAY: The Ascension of Our Lord — II   465
SATURDAY: With Mary in the Cenacle   468

Sixth Week after Easter

SUNDAY: The Service of the Divine Majesty   470
MONDAY: The Heart of Jesus in His Farewell
               Discourse   473
TUESDAY: The Last Question and the Last Answer
               Before the Ascension   475
WEDNESDAY: Before All Things, Have a Constant
               Mutual Charity   477
THURSDAY: Persecuted, Not Scandalized   480
FRIDAY: Our Frail Nature at the Right Hand of
               God's Glory   482
SATURDAY: Need and Desire   485

Pentecost Week

SUNDAY: The Descent of the Holy Ghost   487
MONDAY: The Gift of God   490
TUESDAY: The Holy Ghost as Purifier   492
WEDNESDAY: The Spirit of Light   494
THURSDAY: The Holy Ghost as Bond of Union   496
FRIDAY: The Spirit of Fortitude and Meekness   498
SATURDAY: The Soul's Most Welcome Guest   501

MEDITATIONS FOR FEAST DAYS

Nov 15

DECEMBER 3:	St. Francis Xavier	504
JANUARY 18-25:	The Church Unity Octave	506
JANUARY 25:	Conversion of St. Paul	509
JANUARY 29:	St. Francis of Sales	512
FEBRUARY 2:	The Purification of the Blessed Virgin	515
FEBRUARY 11:	Our Lady's Apparition to Bernadette	517
MARCH 7:	St. Thomas Aquinas	521
MARCH 19:	The Feast of St. Joseph, Spouse of Mary	523
MARCH 25:	The Annunciation of the Blessed Virgin	526
MAY 1:	St. Joseph the Worker	529
MAY 31:	The Queenship of the Blessed Virgin Mary	531

Nov 22

FIRST SUNDAY OF ADVENT

SILENT, HOPEFUL LONGING

1. The best way to begin all our Advent meditations is to look at Mary. She was the first to experience the sacred feelings of the season of Advent, and with what sublime fervor! We behold her, in prayer or at work, her soul ever intent on adoring the Savior, who has become man in her womb. With awe and wonder we gaze at her, while we pray fervently.

2. *Petition*: That through her intercession we may obtain those dispositions that are fitting during the holy season of Advent.

I. Silence and Longing

Holy Church every year sets aside four weeks to prepare her children for the solemn feast of Christmas; that is Advent, *His coming*. In order to put us in the right disposition, she quotes the words of those prophets who, through many centuries, expressed the profound longing of the chosen people, for the coming of the promised Messiah.

This longing sprang from the promise, made by God when Adam was driven from paradise, and often confirmed and renewed to the House of Israel: One day a Savior would appear, a Deliverer, the Messiah.

This intense longing for deliverance also sprang from that deep sense of weakness and spiritual need, which was characteristic of the Israelite soul. Surrounded by nations that served manifold idols and that fell victims to the allurements of the flesh, they kept conscious of being bound to worship the one true God and Him alone, and to abide by His stern law.

The Church desires that we too entertain a profound conviction of our spiritual poverty. As St. Catherine of Siena said, "We must first feel athirst; then the soul opens itself to the grace of God." By so doing we shall cease to lead that merely superficial existence, wherein things external completely possess us so that we have no perception of the profound needs of the soul.

The season of Advent is a time of recollection and of inward silence; thence prayer flows, as it were, naturally.

II. Hopeful Longing

Throughout the centuries the Jewish people felt comforted by its hope for a Savior. "And, as I gaze into the distance, I behold the Power of God, coming closer; and a cloud overshadows the whole earth. Hasten to meet Him, and cry out: Tell us whether Thou art He that is to rule Israel. And ye, inhabitants of the earth, and children mine, rich and poor together, hasten to meet Him" (First Responsory, Matins of this Sunday).

We Christians know that *He has come,* and that His Kingdom has been inaugurated. Yet, every day of Advent we implore: "Come, O Lord," and every day of the year we repeat the words He has laid on our lips: "Thy Kingdom come." Thus will the Church ever pray until the end of time. For Jesus can always enter deeper into our hearts, and His grace can always penetrate our soul more intimately. And externally God's Kingdom can always extend more widely among the nations of the earth. We should always pray that the light may shine in the darkness.

"All my heart goes out to Thee, my God, deceive Thou never the trust I have in Thee, let not my enemies boast of my downfall; can any that trust in Thee be disappointed?" (Offertory of the Mass.)

III. Firm Confidence

The Christian soul knows that the Savior has come, and yet that He is still coming. Thence flows that silent, humble, subdued gladness which is characteristic of this season of Advent. Though Advent is a penitential season, the feeling is not that of Lent, when we commemorate the sufferings which Jesus had to bear that He might enter into His glory. Now we await Him as a Child, a dedicated victim to be sure, as the Church expresses it in the Hymn of Advent, but coming forth fresh and bonny out of the shrine of the Virgin's womb.

We experience a silent, deep, intense gladness, when we are waiting for a joyful event that irrevocably draws nearer, and such must be our disposition during Advent too. In order to achieve it we must foster a deep awareness of our own spiritual necessities, and of the crying needs of war-torn, peace-craving humanity. This demands recollection and silence. Advent is the most appropriate time of the liturgical cycle to cultivate that hallowed, dedicated, inward silence of the soul.

Prayer: Invoke Mary as we see her during that first and most fervent Advent, which she spent at Nazareth.

"O God, who makest us rejoice year by year, in the expectation of our redemption; grant that we, who gladly welcome Thine only-begotten Son, as He comes to redeem us, may gaze on Him without fear when He comes to be our Judge; our Lord Jesus Christ, Thy Son, who liveth and reigneth with Thee" (Collect of the Vigil of Christmas).

MONDAY: FIRST WEEK OF ADVENT

THE SECOND COMING OF CHRIST

1. Our Lord used solemn words and images to describe the last coming of the "Son of Man": "then they will see the Son of Man coming in a cloud, with His full power and majesty" (This Sunday's Gospel). Thus did Michelangelo behold Him, with threatening mien, descending from on high; close to Him, in the attitude of supplication, appeared His Mother, who is our Mother also.

2. *Petition*: That we may always maintain towards God that attitude which befits our nature; an attitude of filial fear as well as of filial love.

I. The Two Advents of Christ at One Glance

Holy Church, in the liturgy of Advent, strikingly connects the Lord's second coming with the first, for which latter we are just now preparing our souls. With the Church, as with the Lord, "one day ... is as a thousand years, and a thousand years as one day" (2 *Peter* 3, 8). In the same glance she beholds the first coming of the Savior in the utter poverty of Bethlehem, and the last coming of the Judge in power and majesty. Indeed, on the plane of eternity, things transitory and changing are of no account. "This, therefore, I say, brethren. ... It remaineth that ... they that use this world, use it as if they used it not. For the fashion of this world passeth away" (1 *Cor.* 7, 29-31).

Yet, even though our sojourn on earth be short, it determines what our eternity shall be. "Therefore, whilst we have time, let us work good to all men" (*Gal.* 6, 10).

II. The Coming of the Savior

The coming of the Savior fills us with joy; the coming of the Judge strikes fear in our hearts; both feelings have a share in determining our attitude towards God, and in molding our spiritual life.

God irresistibly draws us to Himself. "Thou hast so made us that in our hearts there is a longing for Thee, nor can the soul find repose until it rests in Thee." Thus prayed St. Augustine in the first lines of his *Confessions*.

Jesus has revealed God unto us as a Father. We therefore are His children, and our home is where our Father dwells. That Father sends us His Son; the Son of God, become through Mary the "Son of Man", and through His human nature our Brother.

God is infinitely powerful, infinitely good, infinitely wise, infinitely beautiful; our soul was created to possess Him, as the eye has been made to see the light. The soul of man is athirst for the fullness of truth and of beauty. And now we are preparing ourselves for the feast of His coming in our midst. "A child is born to us, and a son is given to us," in all things like unto us, sin excepted, in whom dwelleth, veiled and hidden, the whole Godhead.

Indeed God said truly, "I will draw them with the cords of Adam, with the bands of love" (*Osee* 11, 4).

III. The Coming of the Judge

One day this same Son of Man will come as a Judge. "And they shall see the Son of Man, coming in the clouds of heaven (the symbol of His lofty throne), with much power and majesty" (*Matt.* 25, 31).

For in His divinity He is "God of Infinite Majesty". He is the All-Holy, whose eye endures neither spot nor uncleanness, before whom Powers and Principalities tremble. Shall I, a mere creature and a sinner, not tremble before the All-Holy? Not only in the Old Covenant, but in the New Dispensation as well, we find that all the Saints fostered those alternate feelings of love and fear, which complement each other; love that rushes forward to the divine embrace, and fear that draws back. "Depart from me, for I am a sinful man, O Lord," said Peter when, after the miraculous draught of fishes, he discovered that the Divinity dwelt in his Master. He begged Jesus to depart; he himself did not depart, but stayed close to his Lord.

And when, after the Multiplication of the Loaves and the mysterious announcement that His flesh would be to them the Bread of Life, "many of his disciples went back... Jesus said to the twelve: Will you also go away? And Simon Peter answered him: Lord, to whom shall we go? Thou hast the words of eternal life" (*John* 6: 67, 69).

Because He is the Supreme Good, our souls are irresistibly drawn to God; and yet, when we cast a glance at our wretchedness, we experience the pangs of fear. In this manner we preserve, as long as we are on earth, that reverential love that must ever remain the solid foundation of our spiritual life. Thus, in all sincerity, we can pray "Lord, I am not worthy", and with these words on our lips advance to the Holy Table.

God grant that this childlike love, and this reverential fear may always fill our hearts. They are the mighty pillars on which we can safely build the edifice of our spiritual life.

Prayer: Fill us, O Lord, with a lasting love, as well as fear of Thy Holy Name, for we shall never be deprived of Thy guidance if Thou hast thoroughly trained us in Thy love. Through our Lord (Collect of the 2nd Sunday after Pentecost).

Mary, Mother of fair Love, after this our exile, show us the blessed Fruit of thy womb, Jesus.

"I HAVE LIFTED UP MY SOUL"

1. We may behold Simeon, "a just and devout man, who was awaiting the consolation of Israel". We see him filled with ecstatic joy, as he receives the Savior into his arms, and lifts up his soul to God (*Luke* 2, 25).

2. *Petition*: That our soul may be released from all earthly bonds and, in glad expectation, be lifted up to God.

I. I Have Lifted Up My Soul (Introit of the Mass)

These words occur frequently in the Psalms and elsewhere in Holy Writ. They refer to the eyes, the voice, the hands, the soul, man's whole being that strives to rise aloft and possess God.

This is the cooperation which God requires from man. Our
human nature feels the attraction for lower things; it is drawn
downwards, not seldom engrossed in things of the earth. Sinful
attachments may be the reason the soul "no longer relishes
the things of the spirit"; or in our ascent to God we may feel
encumbered by discouragement, distrust, mental dissipation, the
worldly spirit, inordinate affections, spiritual sloth.

Brethren, says St. Paul in the Epistle of today's Mass, you know
"that it is now for us the hour to rise from sleep". We rise from
sleep when we free our soul from the shackles that prevent her
from hastening to the embrace of the Redeemer who is to come.

Only too often do we feel that we are unable to break the chains
that fetter us; then God comes to our rescue and maybe hacks
them to pieces by means of painful trials, or delivers us by
gentler means in answer to our prayer so well worded in the
Postcommunion of the Mass, "Grant, O Lord, that Thy healing
hand may gently deliver us from our perversities." His aim is
always to make us belong to Him unreservedly.

II. "To Thee, O My God"

To the Father, who is in heaven, but who is also close to me,
deep down in my soul; who searches the reins and the heart;
who knows my great weakness, and is pleased with my generous
dispositions and holy desires. He has compassion on me. He
gazes upon me with love, even before I turn my eyes towards Him.

He says to me, "Thou wouldst not seek me, if thou hadst not
already found me." We could not lift up our hearts to Him, nor
long for Him, if we did not already hold Him, not yet with face-
to-face recognition and forever, but across the veil of true faith.
"We see now through a glass in a dark manner, but then face to
face," says St. Paul (1 *Cor.* 13, 12). Gradually our hearts are
purified and our spiritual insight waxes keener; gradually our
souls are cleansed of earthly dross, and then the veil becomes
thinner, and the soul's spiritual sight penetrates to loftier heights
and profounder depths. We have God's promise. "None of them
that wait on Thee shall be confounded" (*Ps.* 24, 3).

III. God Draws the Soul Aloft

To free the soul from carnal bonds, to lift her on high, that is
God's work far more than ours. He draws us unto Himself, for by
our own strength we cannot raise ourselves to Him. The grace of

God is at the root of our every effort to get closer to Him; and the strength to persevere unto the end, too, is the gift of His bounty. Through death He draws us to His embrace.

It is our firm belief that God's grace is always at work in us; in all that befalls us, we must see the Lord's hand, stretched forth to lift us out of our remissness, perhaps ready to strike a sharp blow so as to rouse us from sleep, or refreshing us with its gentle touch, when we are tired and heavy-laden.

In His ineffable love, so that He may draw us unto Himself "with the cords of Adam, with the bands of love" (*Osee* 11, 4), the Father is now on the point of sending us His own Son, through whom He will draw us unto Himself; for Jesus said, "No man can come to me, except the Father, who hath sent me, draw him" (*John* 6, 44).

Prayer: With Simeon: "May my eyes see thy salvation which thou hast prepared before the face of all people" (*Luke* 2, 30-31).

And with Mary (for no other creature ever lifted its soul to God in such ineffable transports). At first "she was troubled at the word of the angel"; then she spoke her humble *Fiat* as the handmaid of the Lord; but in her final *Magnificat* she sang forth her gratitude in the most sublime accents ever uttered by human lips.

WEDNESDAY: FIRST WEEK OF ADVENT

A PERFECT PRAYER (Ps. 24)

1. A man wrapt in prayer may be represented in two ways: either with eyes lifted up to heaven, adoring God and imploring divine help; or, deeply recollected, with eyes closed, head bowed. Such was Mary, when she uttered her *Fiat*, and when she sang her *Magnificat*.

    Psalm 24, from which is taken the Introit of the Mass of the 1st Sunday in Advent, is an example of perfect prayer, a lifting up of one's soul to God.

2. *Petition*: "Lord, teach us to pray," as the Church, guided by Thee, prays during this holy season of Advent.

I. Humble Prayer

He, to whom the soul lifts itself up in prayer, is the God of mercy. "Remember, O Lord, Thy bowels of compassion, and Thy mercies that are from the beginning of the world" (*Ps.* 24, 6). And the soul cannot forget its sinfulness: "The sins of my youth and my ignorances do not remember. According to Thy mercy remember Thou me, for Thy goodness' sake O Lord" (*Ps.* 24).

When we seek a man's favors we proceed in a wholly different manner. We avoid any allusion to the offenses we have committed against him. With God we act in another way. We do not appeal to our merits, because before God we have nothing that is our own. Nor do we try to hide our shortcomings; the only thing we pray for is that He should have mercy on us.

The more a man grows in holiness, the more keenly he feels the need of confessing his own nothingness when he approaches the Almighty in prayer. God is the Supreme Good, man is naught. God is infinitely holy, man is a sinful creature.

II. Supernatural Prayer

The Psalmist prays for light that he may see the right way. "Show, O Lord, Thy ways to me, and teach me Thy paths. Direct me in Thy truth and teach me" (*Ps.* 24, 4-5).

We do know the right way; the highway, by which all men must travel, is the way of God's commandments. But God does not lead all men in the same manner along that road. To some He shows shortcuts, others He calls quickly to Himself. Therefore the Psalmist says, "Show, O Lord, Thy ways to me, and teach me Thy paths." And of these ways God Himself says, "My ways are not your ways."

How does God show us His ways? By the inward promptings of His grace, and by the external dispositions of His Providence. We cannot hear the inner voice of God, calling us unto Him, unless silence reigns in the soul, with an ardent desire to hear Him. We cannot discern God's guiding hand in the events of daily life, unless we have faith and confidence. God's ways with man are often inscrutable and bewildering to our puny minds. Let us pray, "Lord, grant that I may walk in Thy truth." Thy ways are always the best, the safest, the shortest.

"Per tuas semitas duc nos quo tendimus, ad lucem quam inhabitas." By Thy ways lead us to our goal, the light eternal in which Thou dwellest.

III. Persevering Prayer

During many centuries the chosen people lived in expectation of the Messiah; with sighs and ineffable longings they awaited His coming. In Psalm 24 the soul expresses its firm confidence; it awaits the coming of the Redeemer, and knows it will not be disappointed. "My eyes are ever towards the Lord, for He shall pluck my feet out of the snare" (*Ps.* 24, 15).

During these four weeks of Advent the Church unceasingly directs our attention towards the Savior, whose coming is imminent. The greater the consciousness of the need we have of Him, the more readily do we think of Him. Which are the great needs of my soul? How sorely does it need a Savior?

Throughout the day we have many opportunities of fostering this sense of expectation. We may begin our meditation every day by greeting Mary; all her thoughts and feelings, the whole of her being, are concentrated on the great event that is a-coming. The recitation of the Rosary and of the Angelus should transport us to that region of awed silence and of hallowed expectation, which is peculiar to the season of Advent. With humility, and courage, and perseverance, let us make a new beginning every day.

Prayer: "Hail Mary, full of grace, the Lord is with Thee; blessed art Thou among women." Thou wert the first to know that the days were accomplished and, more than any other, thou hast contributed to the coming of the Savior. Thou wert the first to live in the constant expectation of His Advent. Holy Mother of God, allow us, we beseech thee, to stay close to thee. Arouse in our soul the ardent desire that was in thee at Nazareth. Turn thine eyes of mercy towards us, and show us the fruit of thy womb, Jesus.

WAITING

1. Behold Mary, in the holy house of Nazareth, absorbed in prayer or engaged in simple household duties, in perfect peace, ardently longing and awaiting the coming of the Savior.

2. *Petition*: The grace that like Mary, we may keep all our thoughts and feelings intent on the coming of the Lord at Christmas.

I. Waiting

We all know that state of tense expectation when the soul is waiting; the hour draws closer and closer, when we shall receive the visit of one we long to see, or when we shall be home again in the midst of those we love. If ever we have struggled through a long sleepless night, tossing about in pain on our sickbed, then we know the pangs of waiting for daybreak, when the doctor will come to soothe our sufferings. Or think of the prisoner, impatiently awaiting the day of his release.

Release! It is his first thought on awaking and his last before he falls asleep; it abides with him every moment of the day, whatever he may be doing; it consoles, it stimulates, it gives strength to bear all things and overcome all difficulties.

II. The Waiting of Advent

What does the feast of Christmas signify for the Church and for every Christian that shares the Church's life of liturgical prayer? For many souls the earth is still plunged in darkness; the Church, loving these her children, longs for the Light that will soon shine forth. So many of her children are ailing and spiritually weak; she expects the coming of Him that will heal their infirmities. So many of her children are laden with the heavy burden of sin; the Redeemer is about to come.

St. Bernard, who was familiar with the dark dungeons of the Middle Ages, in heartfelt words describes our impending release: "I was aware that the Son of the Great King was passing by my prison, and at once I cried out and moaned louder and louder: Son of God, have mercy on me! And the most merciful Prince asked, 'Whence come these cries and these moans?' And they said to Him, 'It is the voice of Adam, the rebel. Thy Father commanded that he be cast into prison, until it be decreed what manner of death he deserves.' On hearing this, what do you think He will do, He who is perfect Goodness, who spares the sinner and whose mercy endureth forever? He went down into the dungeon and broke the bonds of the prisoner." This parable gives us a faint idea of the true purpose of the coming of God's Son among us.

In order that a man may desire to see the light, he must be endowed with eyes made to see the light. The eyes of our soul have been created that they may see the marvellous Light that is God. On Christmas day, "through the mystery of the Incarnation of the Word, the brightness of the Divine Light will enlighten the eyes of our soul."

We shall not feel an ardent desire for the coming of our Redeemer, unless the burden of our sins weighs us down and the sense of our weakness makes us faint. The Church supposes that we are thus distressed, when she prays, "We pray Thee, O Lord, show us Thy power by coming to our aid, that through Thy protection we may escape the dangers that threaten us because of our sins and, having been set free by Thee, may attain salvation, Who livest and reignest. . . . (Collect, 1st Sunday of Advent.)[1]

III. "The Armor of Light"

If we want to prepare ourselves for the coming of the Savior, we must, as St. Paul bids us in the Epistle of the Mass, "abandon the ways of darkness and put on the armor of light". For our salvation is already achieved; already it bears fruit in our souls, and must bear more abundant fruit in the souls of all men throughout the world.

"The armor of light" is sobriety, purity of life and brotherly love. St. Paul puts it briefly: "Put ye on the Lord Jesus Christ" (*Rom.* 13, 14). The Lord is on the point of appearing among us, in our human nature, with which Mary has clothed Him. Now we shall be able to "put on" Jesus Christ. A vesture is not part of our being; we put it on; it is put on us from without. In the same way the supernatural life, the partaking in the divine life is not a thing that pertains to our nature. It is given to us by Jesus Christ, the God-Man and the Son of Man. This life is bestowed on us from outside, but it does permeate our whole being and make us "new creatures." And thus, our souls having put on the Lord

---

[1] Note that this Collect, which dates from the earliest times, is addressed to the Son. Yet the old rule was: At the altar every prayer is addressed to the Father. The most ancient manuscripts show that in the beginning this Collect was addressed to the Father; and that it had the usual conclusion: through Christ our Lord. In course of time some liturgists began to regard the Advent collects as addressed to the Son, and so they changed the conclusion to: Who with God the Father . . . livest and reignest. . . .

Jesus Christ, and being inwardly regenerated, shines with the armor of light, purity and brotherly love.

The Savior, whose Advent we long for, bestows these things on us.

Prayer: Holy Mother of God, thou didst put on the Lord Jesus Christ more than any other creature, and thou hast clothed Him with thine own human nature. Obtain for us the grace duly to prepare ourselves for His coming, as thou didst in silence and recollection long for His coming.

FRIDAY: FIRST WEEK OF ADVENT

CRYING FOR SALVATION

1. Last Sunday, in every church and chapel, a cry for salvation ascended to heaven. In the name of the faithful, the priest, standing before the altar, raised his hands and prayed, "We pray Thee, O Lord, show Thy power by coming to our aid."

2. *Petition*: The grace to see the great needs of our own soul, the needs of the Church and of all other souls, so that we may pray with greater fervor.

I. "O Lord, Show Thy Power"

How dare we thus address God Almighty, as if He needed counsel or advice from us? God needs no urging from us. And yet, how often do we hear the Psalmist addressing similar words to God!

"Arise, why sleepest thou, O Lord? Arise, and cast us not off to the end. Why turnest thou thy face away and forgettest our want and our trouble? For our soul is humbled down to the dust; our belly cleaveth to the earth. Arise, O Lord, help us and redeem us for Thy name's sake" (*Ps.* 43, 23-26).

Do we perhaps labor under the impression that the Father in heaven dwells far away from us? Does St. Augustine not tell us that "though most hidden, God is most intimately present to us", and therefore, "He is the most mighty, yet the most discreet"? And then, from the depth of our misery we cry out, "O Lord, show Thy power." In this cry there is not the faintest trace of irreverence, but only the profound consciousness of our need and childlike trust in the Lord. We humbly confess our destitution and bear witness to His power and His goodness. These are the feelings that befit the creature.

Throughout Advent this cry recurs again and again in the liturgy; lest it be mere empty sound, we should realize the needs of our soul. It is wise and salutary often to ask ourselves the question, What am I seeking? Which are my spiritual needs? And that other question, so characteristic of the genuine Catholic, do I remember the crying needs of the Church? Am I praying that the Lord should come to her aid? The greater the need, the more fervent must be our prayer, "O Lord, show Thy power!"

II. "And Come"

We can long for Him, we can prepare our soul to receive Him, we may run to meet Him; but He, out of sheer goodness and mercy, has to come down to us.

This He has done. "And the Word was made flesh and dwelt among us" (*John* 1, 14). In the hymn of Advent we say, "Thou, who from the shrine of the Virgin's womb comest among us to atone for the sins of all men, Thou proceedest like the innocent lamb to the altar of the cross."

Daily He comes to us, in Holy Communion, and through the workings of His grace. We, however, are in duty bound to receive Him hospitably; we must beg Him to enter ever deeper into our heart; we must surrender our whole being to Him, and allow Him to mold our soul according to His will.

With a sincere and ardent desire, we shall say to Him, "Come, O Lord." That prayer one day will be our last, as it is the last word in St. John's Revelation and of Holy Writ: "Come, Lord Jesus."

III. "To Save Us"

Salvation from the besetting dangers of sin, salvation through pardon of sin; that is what mankind stood in need of; that is what we still need today, the more so as the sense of sinfulness has grown sadly blunted in many souls.

Those that desire greater purification, and that strive to live by the Gospel more perfectly, will pray more earnestly that His help and His salvation may be granted to them and to Holy Church, and to all men.

The words of the Collect are: "We pray Thee, O Lord, to

show Thy power, by coming to our aid; that through Thy protection . . . we may deserve and attain salvation." Can we deserve it? We can, through Christ, who has merited it, not for Himself, but for us. To the extent that we are united with Him, that we accept and appropriate what He has deserved for us, and offers us, to that extent we can deserve to be set free and attain salvation.

Prayer: Every hour of the divine office begins with the words: "O God, remember to come to my aid; O Lord, hasten to my assistance." Make sure that these words express a sentiment that exists deep down in your heart.

Reverently we unite ourselves with Mary, whose whole being is wrapt in longing prayer.

SATURDAY: FIRST WEEK OF ADVENT

HEAVEN'S GOLDEN PORTAL

1. It is natural that we should see in imagination the little house of Nazareth as the place where we make our meditation on the advent of Jesus. Let us greet Mary, stay close to her, and pray with her.

2. *Petition*: That through Mary, who is the gate of heaven, we may draw closer to Jesus.

I. "In the Beginning of His Ways"

Mary, because she had been chosen to be the Mother of God the Son made man, had from all eternity her special place in the plan of the Holy Trinity. "The Lord possessed me in the beginning of his ways, before he made anything from the beginning. I was set up from eternity, and of old before the earth was made. . . . When he prepared the heavens I was present" (*Prov.* 8: 22, 23, 27). These words refer to God's wisdom, but the Church applies them to Mary. "A lily blossomed forth, in the depths of God's thoughts."

When, after the fall of Adam, God in His mercy promised a Redeemer, He mentioned a woman from whom the Savior would be born. She (or her seed) would crush the serpent's head (*Gen.* 3, 15). Here Mary is shown to us as most intimately participating in the mystery of our salvation. She is present at the dawn of creation and at the beginning of the work of our redemption, never alone by herself, but at the side of her Son: He the First, she ever next to Him.

II. Fashioned and Adorned by God

In the unfathomable counsels of divine Wisdom, which prepared the Savior's coming, we are shown several prototypes of the Messiah and of His Mother; Judith who delivered her nation from its enemies, Esther, etc. . . . Mary herself was the last and the most perfect type of Him that was to come. She was the serene dawn, inevitably followed by the radiant sun itself.

On her the Creator lavished all the treasures which His omnipotence could bestow, to make her worthy to be His Mother. She was to be the hallowed abode of God's Son, who would not disdain to inhabit a virgin's womb.

Mary was a Jewish maiden, of lowly estate; but she was conceived without sin, full of grace, and determined to preserve her virginity, though she was espoused to a man called Joseph. She was indeed highly favored by God, who in a wonderful manner "had regarded the humility of His handmaid".

Conceived without the stain of Adam's sin! The Almighty would not allow the faintest shadow of a stain to tarnish the soul of His Mother. Full of grace! No divine gift was too valuable to be bestowed on her who was to be in all truth, the Mother of God, and would bear the Son of Man. This fullness of grace made of Mary God's most perfect instrument in the most divine work of Redemption. It was right that the Holy Ghost should favor her, and guide her, in an exceptional manner. She vowed her virginity and yet she espoused Joseph, the just man. In this way Joseph became the witness and the guarantor of the virgin birth.

"He that is mighty hath done great things" to her! My soul is filled with awe; I believe: I thank the divine mercy.

III. Blessed Expectation

Never was a mother in a more hallowed state of expectation. All these wonderful ways of God with her, Mary pondered and kept in her heart. Even before the power of the Most High had overshadowed her, the angel had proclaimed her full of grace. But from the time Mary conceived the Son of God in her soul even more truly than in her womb, this fullness of grace grew and increased in a marvellous manner. Now she was the living, adoring, tabernacle of the Divinity. For her the Advent of Christ lasted nine months. Her heart felt and expressed all the ardent longings of Israel, all the supplications of suffering mankind which craved for peace and deliverance. According to some Fathers of the Church, Mary's spotless purity and profound humility hastened the coming of the Redeemer.

Prayer to Mary: We might recite the Angelus, which is particularly the prayer for the season of Advent. At this time we should recite it with greater devotion.

SECOND SUNDAY OF ADVENT

THE PRECURSOR

1. God chose Mary to be the Mother of His Son made Man; in silence and humility she introduced Him into our human race. He chose John the Baptist to fulfill a like function with regard to the public ministry of Jesus. As Precursor it was his privilege to make straight the way of the Lord, and to bear witness before Israel that Jesus of Nazareth was the new Prophet, the last and the greatest of all. And then John, confessing that he was neither Elias, nor *the* Prophet, vanished into obscurity. Yet after Mary he was closest to the Lord, and the humblest of men.

2. *Petition*: That we may admire and follow the ardent and most unselfish zeal of the Baptist.

I. John's Manifestation

John was not like Mary conceived without original sin, yet unlike any other saint, he had been sanctified even in his mother's womb. God had appointed him to prepare the way for the Messiah, to administer unto Him the baptism of penance, to bear testimony to Him before Israel. He was still a child when he withdrew to the desert, as the ancient prophets had done. There he led an austere life, and by prayer and penance prepared himself to accomplish his mission.

A few months before Jesus left Nazareth, John had emerged from solitude. In fiery accents he preached repentance of sin and the baptism of penance. A mighty Prophet had arisen in Israel. Jesus said of him, "there hath not arisen among them that are born of women a greater than John the Baptist" nor one that is more humble (*Matt.* 11, 11).

II. His Message

He speaks the truth boldly, sparing not even the great. "Ye brood of vipers," he says to the Pharisees, "who hath showed you to flee from the wrath to come?" (*Matt.* 3, 7). The Jews gladly welcome his message and understand it, for John follows in the footsteps of the seers of old. "And there went out to him all the country of Judea, and all they of Jerusalem and were baptized by him" (*Mark* 1, 5). Even King Herod had to hear the truth, for John spared no one but boldly admonished all alike. Yet his words neither offended nor angered any guileless soul, because all knew that he sought not himself, but only God's glory. He was transparently selfless.

May all those whose office it is to speak in the Lord's name learn a lesson from John. When it is their duty to blame or reprimand, let them be utterly selfless, seeking God's glory only, as did the Baptist, and Christ his Master.

III. He Bears Testimony to Another

This Prophet, whom Israel is ready to follow, remains faithful to his mission. He is the Precursor, the servant who prepares the way for his Master, the voice of one crying in the wilderness. He bears testimony to Another. "There shall come one mightier than I, the latchet of whose shoes I am not worthy to loose" (*Luke* 3, 16). And when they asked him "Who art thou?" he confessed "I am not the Christ. The same is he that shall come after me" (*John* 1: 20, 27).

In the presence of all the people Jesus receives the baptism of penance at his hands. Christ had as yet no disciples, nor did He show Himself to the Jews, like John, "in the spirit and power of Elias". Then, when John saw Jesus after His fast coming along the banks of the Jordan he sent two of his disciples to follow Him. A little later, when it was whispered by men of little faith that this Jesus, whom he had baptized, might be a rival, John did not hide the truth, but gave testimony saying, "I am not Christ, but I am sent before Him. He that hath the bride is the bridegroom; but the friend of the bridegroom who standeth and heareth him, rejoiceth with joy because of the bridegroom's voice. This my joy therefore is fulfilled. He must increase, but I must decrease" (*John* 3, 28-30).

John will decrease indeed and pass into the night, dying a martyr's death, a bright example of a wholly selfless, self-sacrificing, faithful witness and apostle. His austere life and his stirring eloquence had earned him prestige with the multitudes, and he used his power to turn the people's eyes from himself and to show them the One that was to come. And so the Master increased whilst the servant gladly decreased and passed out of sight.

Prayer to St. John the Baptist: Great Saint, of whom Jesus said, "there hath not risen among them that are born of women, a greater than John the Baptist;" who with great power and humility hast announced God's message; who didst confess that a greater than thyself was to come; obtain for us a share of thy nobility of soul and of thy zeal in the service of the Lord.

MONDAY: SECOND WEEK OF ADVENT

"STIR UP OUR HEARTS, O LORD"

1. The Collect of the Mass of the 1st Sunday of Advent was addressed to the Son of God, which is rather unusual in the ancient liturgy. We prayed that He might "show His power by coming to our aid". This Sunday's Collect is addressed to the Father, whom we request that He "stir up our hearts that we may prepare the way for the coming of His Only-Begotten Son". Remember that, in the work of sanctification and grace, the very beginning is a sheer gift of God, but we must co-operate in the work of our salvation and prepare the way for the Savior's coming.

   The image used by God Himself, to describe His workings in our soul, may be helpful in this connection: "Behold I stand at the gate and knock" (*Apoc.* 3, 20).

2. *Petition*: The grace to be aware of God's knockings at our hearts and to respond to them.

I. The Knockings of God's Grace

God's grace generally touches our souls in the gentlest of ways. God Almighty will not use coercion with His free creatures. He stands at the gate, and knocks for admittance. He does not gate-crash, but waits patiently till we open to Him. Every day, every hour the inspirations of His grace invite us to greater generosity in His service, to cheerful detachment from the world, to humble service, to the practice of considerate fraternal charity, to a life of deep recollection....

"It is characteristic of divine grace," says St. Ignatius, "that its inspirations fill the soul with spiritual joy and profound peace." In the Introit of the Mass we say, "The Lord shall let you hear His glorious voice to the delight of your heart." But if our soul is asleep, or if the din of the world clatters around the gate where the Lord is standing, then our attention may have to be awakened by hard blows, coming from outside, that is, by trials manifold. In which case we may find it hard to be convinced that these blows are struck by God's loving hand, and that their only purpose is to stir up our hearts, so that we may prepare the way for the coming of the Only-Begotten Son of God.

Then we must bring ourselves to say, "This is the Lord's doing, and it is wonderful in our eyes" (*Ps.* 117, 23).

II. The Ways of the Only-Begotten

We know the ways by which the Only-Begotten comes to us, and by which we must go to Him; the way of humility and the way of purity.

The Only-Begotten, who "being in the form of God ... emptied himself, taking the form of a servant.... He humbled himself becoming obedient unto death, even to the death of the cross" (*Philip.* 2, 6-8). And He assumed the form of a servant through the instrumentality of a pure Virgin-Mother.

Concerning the ways of the Lord, Isaias spoke in prophecy, "Prepare ye the way of the Lord, make straight his paths. Every valley shall be filled and every mountain and hill shall be brought low; and the crooked shall be made straight, and the rough ways plain" (*Luke* 3, 4-5). This straight road, even and broad, without steep ups and downs or sudden turns, along which the King comes to us, and by which we must hurry to meet Him, is the road of humility, uprightness, purity.

By that way, further than any other creature had ever travelled,

Mary went to meet Him, till the very limits of the Divinity, as
a great theologian dares to express it. In Mary, God met our
human nature in its humblest, purest, most gracious form. Along
that straight way He came to us.

From Mary we may readily learn how to prepare the way for
the coming of the Only-Begotten into our hearts.

III.   "That We May Be Enabled to Serve Him With Pure Minds"

Our final aim is always that we may serve God. He, whose
coming we long for, is Himself "the servant of Jahve", the chosen
instrument in the service of the Father, obedient unto death,
even to the death of the cross.

That was the lesson which, by word and example, He taught
us throughout His life on earth. Let us "serve with pure hearts",
which abhor all sin and petty self-seeking.

Prayer: Stir up our hearts, O Lord, that we may prepare the
way for the coming of Thine Only-Begotten Son, that, by His
coming, we may be enabled to serve Thee with pure minds:
Who liveth and reigneth. . . . (Collect, 2nd Sunday of Advent).

TUESDAY: SECOND WEEK OF ADVENT

THE MYSTERY OF THE INCARNATION

1.   Mary, who "kept all these words in her heart" passed the
whole time of her Advent in the prayerful meditation of the
great mystery of the Incarnation, in which she played such an
important role. Her faith never wavered; her heart was filled
with awe and gratitude. Whether she was engaged in formal
prayer, or busy with her lowly household duties, she always
dwelt on the great mystery. We beg that we may walk close
to her, and unite our prayer with hers.

2.   *Petition*: That we may join Mary in the contemplation of
this sublime mystery of God's love, a mystery that surpasses
all human understanding.

I.   The Mystery

"God became man." It is impossible to express this historical
event more simply, more tersely, more correctly. But our mind

can neither grasp nor fathom the fact itself; we can only marvel in awe-struck silence, and adore divine Wisdom.

St. John says, "And the Word was made flesh," and St. Paul, "Who being in the form of God... took the form of a servant" (*Philip.* 2, 6-7). Both Apostles seem to be at a loss to find words and contrasts that might express that abysmal humiliation, to which the Son of God was moved by His love.

The Divine Word, made man, is "true God and true man". "In Him dwelleth all the fullness of the Godhead corporeally," says St. Paul (*Col.* 2, 9). The one Person of the Incarnate Word possesses both the divine nature, which is infinite, and the human nature, which is limited. The angel had said to Mary, "No word shall be impossible with God" (*Luke* 1, 37). Mary believed the word of the angel, and Elizabeth proclaimed her blessed because she had believed. But even Mary did not understand.

With Mary we believe, and adore, and offer thanks to God.

II. The Reason Why

The mystic writer Ruusbroeck points out, "The reason why God became man was his incomprehensible love, and all men's dire need."

"His incomprehensible love!" The final and complete explanation of all things must be sought in God Himself, in His love which is as incomprehensible as He Himself. God's love is creative love. It differs from man's love, which is called forth by something outside himself, by a thing that appears desirable and deserving of affection. God's love is purely a love that gives, gives all things, desires nothing in return, gains nothing. Out of love God gave being to what was not.

Still more incomprehensible is the love, which prompted God Almighty to go in search of His erring, rebellious creature, and for that purpose to become man. In her Easter liturgy the Church, in an ecstasy of love, thus proclaims her wonder, "O inestimable condescension of Thy goodness, O untold excess of love, that to redeem a slave Thou didst deliver up Thy Son!" He loved us, not because we were worthy of love, but because He is God, because He is love, love incomprehensible.

III. "All Men's Dire Need"

Not because of our merits did God become man, but because of our need, of the extreme need of all men.

Faith tells us that God created man to His own image and likeness, and that the human heart can find no rest except in God. Moreover, it is revealed that, because of the sin committed in the beginning by our first parents, mankind lay under a heavy debt to God, which it had no means of paying.

The Jewish nation was deeply conscious of man's need of Redemption; and even in the souls of the rest of mankind the prevalent idolatry had not utterly wiped out the awareness of it. All men stood truly in extreme need, and out of sheer benevolence and mercy, God came to the assistance of destitute mankind. "When the fullness of time was come, God sent his Son" (*Gal.* 4, 4), i.e., at the moment His inscrutable Wisdom had appointed.

"All men's utter need": The sinner needs God, who has mercy and grants forgiveness. Still more than the sinner, the Saint needs God, for more than the sinner he is aware of his weakness, and his need of God leaves him no peace. "I long to be dissolved and to be with Christ," cried St. Paul. What is it that will draw down upon us the manifestation of God's incomprehensible love? Not our merits—for, what do we have that we have not received? —but the humble confession of our wants and of our conscious need for grace and forgiveness.

Prayer: Be appeased, we beseech Thee, O Lord, by our humble prayers and offerings, and although we have no merits with which to support our pleas, grant us Thy aid and assistance. Through our Lord (Secret of the Mass, 2nd Sunday of Advent).

WEDNESDAY: SECOND WEEK OF ADVENT

THE IMMACULATE CONCEPTION

1. On December 8, 1854, in St. Peter's at Rome, Pope Pius IX, surrounded by hundreds of Bishops and thousands of Catholics, who had assembled in the Eternal City from every part of the world, solemnly and infallibly proclaimed that Mary's Immaculate Conception is a dogma of the Catholic faith, revealed by God. In imagination we may assist at this glorious ceremony, remembering meanwhile how the angel appeared to Mary, in the humble house of Nazareth and called her "full of grace".

2. *Petition*: The grace to be moved to joy at the homage paid to our Lady, to thank God with her, and to acquire firm confidence in her powerful intercession.

I. "Saved in a More Sublime Manner"

Mary was a daughter of Adam and Eve, and therefore liable to the penalty that had befallen all Adam's descendants. In the genealogies, which we read in the Holy Bible, many sinners are mentioned, both men and women. Mary, like ourselves, stood in need of Redemption—and Redemption by the one and only Redeemer, her Son Jesus Christ. But, as Pius IX wrote in the bull proclaiming the dogma, "by a special grace and privilege, in view of the merits of Christ, Savior of the whole human race, Mary, from the first moment of her existence, was preserved from all taint, so that she was saved in a more sublime manner. She was so close to the Sun, that no shadow at all could fall upon her." She was "full of grace", the "all-beautiful", the "glory of our race". These favors were not bestowed on her because of any excellence or merit of her own, but on account of her Son and through His merits. No one was better aware of this than Mary herself; for in her Magnificat she proclaimed, "He that is mighty hath done great things to me."

It was because she had been saved in so sublime a manner that she was so abysmally humble.

II. "For the Honor of Mary"

"To the honor and glory of the Virgin from whom He was born," says the papal bull. "God has loved her, and adorned her; has vested her with a splendid garment." Love feels the need of adorning and embellishing the object of its affections. In the case of Mary, He that loved was all-powerful. The omnipotent Son would make His Virgin-Mother all-beautiful. He would make her worthy to mold His sacred Humanity, Body and Soul, into "the Son of Man". He would preserve her from the faintest breath or shadow of sin. He endowed her with the fullest measure of grace which a creature can receive.

All this grace and spiritual beauty was hers, when in the humble house of Nazareth she awaited the coming of the Divine Child. But all this beauty was interior, quite hidden to the eyes of the simple folk, who saw in her no more than the spouse of Joseph, the village carpenter.

III. "In Honor of the Holy and Undivided Trinity"

These are the opening words of the papal bull, defining the dogma of the Immaculate Conception. All the three Persons of the Blessed Trinity bear a part in the creation, the redemption, the forming of Mary. The more complete and sublime her redemption was, the greater was her holiness; and therefore the greater the glory she gave to the Father, to the Son, and to the Holy Ghost. No creature ever stood in such unique intimate relation to each of the three Persons of the Blessed Trinity.

"The Holy Ghost shall come upon thee, and the power of the Most High shall overshadow thee. And therefore, also the Holy which shall be born of thee shall be called the Son of God (*Luke* 1, 35).

Human words, even our loftiest figures of speech, are too carnal and too gross, to express adequately the mysterious relation that exists between Mary and the Father Almighty, Mary and the Word Incarnate, Mary and the Holy Ghost. An old Latin hymn tried to express it as follows:

> Thee made the Father, Who knows no beginning;
> On thee lay the shadow of the Father's only Son;
> Upon thee came the Holy Ghost;
> Thy whole being, O Mary, is related to God.

Prayer: O God, who didst prepare a worthy dwelling for Thy Son by the Immaculate Conception of the blessed Virgin; we beseech Thee, who didst preserve her from all stain in view of the death of Thy Son, to make us through her intercession so pure as to be admitted to Thy presence. Through our Lord (Collect, Feast of the Immaculate Conception).

THURSDAY: SECOND WEEK OF ADVENT

"AND BLESSED ART THOU THAT HAST BELIEVED"
(Luke 1, 45)

1. The angel had told Mary that her cousin Elizabeth had conceived. Mary, "rising up went to the hill country" to visit her relative. When she entered the house, Elizabeth greeted her as "Mother of my Lord", and declared her blessed—the very

first beatitude in the Gospel: "Blessed art thou that hast believed, because those things shall be accomplished that were
spoken to thee by the Lord" (*Luke* 1, 45). What impression
do these words make on Mary? We reverently gaze upon her
and seek to understand her feelings.

2. *Petition*: The grace to live our faith, as Mary did, and to find
therein peace and joy.

I. Mary's Faith

It is evident that Mary was enlightened by the Holy Ghost
in a wonderful manner, and that, deeper than any other Saint,
she had penetrated into the divine mysteries. But even for her,
faith had not yet given way to sight, and she had to believe, as
we have to. Surrendering her intellect and whole being, she had
to hold as true what she did not, and could not, understand:
that, while preserving her virginity, she would bear a son, and
that the Child born of her would be the Son of God.

St. Therese of Lisieux writes pertinently: "Preachers love to
dwell on the unparalleled privileges of the Blessed Virgin. They
should not fail to remind us also that she practiced humble virtues
which we too must practice; they should remind us that she
lived by faith as we do, that she too was of those of whom the
Gospel says, 'And they understood not the words He spoke unto
them'."

Such an unexpected and awesome intervention of God into
the laws of human nature, as the angel had announced to her,
Mary "kept pondering over in her heart", but she understood
not its mysterious operation. Yet, "God is greater than our heart"
(1 *John* 3, 20), even than the heart of Mary. So, she never har-
bored the least doubt—not because she understood everything,
but because she gave credence to whatever God had sent the
angel to say.

God grant that, following Mary's peerless example, we too
may more and more live by faith, firmly adhering to whatever
God teaches us through Holy Church and those who speak
to us in His name.

II. "Blessed Art Thou That Hast Believed"

What happiness! The Messiah who had tarried so long is
a-coming, and she is His Mother! The realization of it had overwhelmed her, but she could not—and she thought she should not

—reveal it to anyone, not even to Joseph. God alone was entitled to manifest the fact.

But when the words of greeting her cousin show her that God has indeed made it known to someone, she pours forth the abiding exultation of her soul in her *Magnificat*. The grandiose prospects conjured up by the angel's words arise before her mind: "He hath showed might in His arm and hath scattered the proud in the conceit of their heart. He hath put down the mighty from their seat and exalted the lowly. . . ." Ah! She will keep all these things in her heart through countless afflictions, of which the angel had not spoken, through the long years of humble toil at Nazareth, and even as she stands by the Cross on Calvary. She did not know beforehand all the things her divine motherhood entailed, but by her *Fiat* she has surrendered herself unreservedly to God. Meanwhile, "her spirit rejoices in God her Savior, because He that is mighty has done great things to her. . . . And all generations shall call her blessed."

Blessed art thou that hast believed.

III. Faith, the Source of Our Joy

St. Paul affirms this in the epistle of the 2nd Sunday of Advent: "(May) now the God of hope fill you with all joy and peace in believing" (*Rom.* 15, 13).

Joy and peace in believing. But then our faith must be a resolute reliance, not a mere vague impression that glides upon the surface of the mind; it must be a profound conviction, rooted deeply in our heart, regulating all our thoughts and actions, governing our whole life, and unshakable in any trial whatsoever.

From this firm faith we draw that peace and that joy, which the modern world, devoid of faith, so grievously lacks.

Prayer: To Mary, who in her humble dwelling at Nazareth overflows with peace and joy, while she awaits the fulfillment of what the angel, in the name of the Lord, has announced unto her.

FRIDAY: SECOND WEEK OF ADVENT

JOSEPH, MARY'S SPOUSE

1. St. Joseph is hardly mentioned in the liturgy of Advent. Yet he, more than anyone else except Mary, was involved in the

events that prepared the coming of the Savior. He, better than any other, knew and shared the thoughts and feelings of Mary. What was the daily theme of their holy converse? "Where their treasure was, there was their heart also."

2. *Petition*: That keeping close to Joseph and Mary we may share their thoughts and feelings.

I. The Anguish of Joseph

In the inscrutable designs of Providence, Joseph had been chosen to be the spouse of the Blessed Virgin. The ways of Divine Providence are unfathomable always and our minds can never penetrate them; but the closer a person is involved in "the mystery which hath been hidden from ages and generations" (*Col.* 1, 26), the more inscrutable become the ways of Providence with him. Thus did God for a while hide from Joseph, the virginal spouse of Mary, the great things which He that is mighty had wrought in her.

"Whereupon Joseph, the just man" spent his days haunted by doubt and anguish, whilst Mary, we may be sure, was filled with deep compassion for him . . . until the angel of the Lord appeared to him and dissipated his anxiety.

Why are we astonished, or assailed by doubt, when God intervenes in our lives, or permits things to happen, beyond what we can understand? A providence understandable to our minds would not be a Divine Providence.

Like St. Joseph we should earnestly consider what duty demands of us; we should never act rashly, but wait patiently in the confident conviction that God shapes all things for the greater good of those that love and trust Him.

II. Joy and Peace After Suffering

Now that Joseph knows of the sublime dignity of his spouse, his love and reverence for her have increased immeasurably, and he thoroughly shares her happiness. Joseph too may say, "He that is mighty hath done great things unto me." He is aware of the great responsibility God has placed on him. He is the guardian and witness of Mary's virginal motherhood, the head of the Holy Family, the legal father and foster-father of Mary's Divine Son. Did he also utter a Fiat of complete surrender of himself to God? To him also apply the words, "Blessed art thou that hast believed."

Mary, whose heart is now replete with joy and peace, still more deeply trusts and loves him, whom God has chosen to be her faithful protector, and the supporter of herself and of her Divine Son.

Let us admire and adore Divine Providence in all its decrees, often so incomprehensible to our puny minds. This is the greatest and most pleasing homage we can offer to God.

III. The Advent-Season of Joseph and Mary

Henceforth all the thoughts and sentiments of Joseph and Mary center round the momentous event. Have there ever been holier conversations than between these two chosen souls who were looking forward to the approaching arrival of the long-awaited Messiah, "their Child"? "Where thy treasure is, there is thy heart also," Jesus will say one day. To every father and every mother, their treasure is their child. With what a depth of feeling, then, must Mary and Joseph have cherished the coming Jesus.

We try in imagination to behold Joseph and Mary, as they converse together, or are absorbed in holy thoughts and profoundly recollected; we see them laboring with their hands, Mary busy with her humble household duties, Joseph toiling in his carpenter's shop; above all we see them at prayer, observing the hours prescribed by Jewish custom, "praying always", never losing the sense of God's presence.

Prayer to St. Joseph: Holy Joseph, foster-father of Christ, most chaste spouse of Mary, pray for us. Obtain for us the grace that we may observe this holy season of Advent as thou, together with the Holy Virgin Mary, didst observe the first Advent, in devout recollection and ardent longing for the coming of Him, who is "the expectation of the nations" (*Gen.* 49, 10).

SATURDAY: SECOND WEEK OF ADVENT

"DROP DEW, YE HEAVENS, FROM ABOVE"

1. We have often listened to the hymn "Rorate Coeli" and been profoundly touched by the sacred chant, which so vividly expresses the deepest longings of the human soul. Let it resound now in our ears, that we may feel a sincere yearning for Him that is to come.

2. *Petition*: May our fervent longing obtain the coming of the Savior into our hearts, and into the hearts of all men.

I. "Drop Dew, Ye Heavens, From Above"

"Drop dew, ye heavens, from above and let the clouds rain the Just" (Refrain).

Here the mysterious descent of the Savior from heaven into the womb of the Virgin Mary is compared to the settling down of dew at night. The ancients, in their simplicity, thought that the dew descended silently and mysteriously out of the heavens in the quiet of the night; it was the purest and most virginal water. And it was particularly welcome in those Eastern regions, where showers are few and far between, and the scorched earth thirsts for a few refreshing drops.

A striking and apt symbol at the soul's ardent longing for the Savior, who, through the mysterious intervention of a Virgin Mother comes from on high to refresh and comfort us.

II. Humble Confesion

The first stanza describes the desolation of the Holy City after the exile. "Be not angry with us, O Lord, nor forever mindful of our iniquity. Behold, the holy city is become deserted, Jerusalem is made desolate; and laid waste is the dwelling of Thy sanctifying Righteousness, where our fathers were wont to come and pray Thee."

Sad symbol of a soul whence the spiritual life has departed or where it is waning, a symbol, too, of so many churches where men no longer come to worship, and of a nation that has lapsed into unbelief.

The second stanza is a humble confession of infidelity: "We have sinned and have indeed become unclean; we have all fallen off as dead tree-leaves, and our sins have blown us about as a whirlwind. Thou hast hidden Thy face from us, and hast crushed us by the mass of our iniquity."

May God grant us to arrive at such a salutary acknowledgment of our own infidelity in His service, and make us humbly take our place in the ranks of sinful humanity to confess mankind's common guilt!

III. Trustful Prayer

"Look Thou, O Lord, upon the affliction of Thy people, and send Him whom Thou hast promised to send. Send forth the Lamb, the Lord of the world, from the rocky desert to the mountain of the daughter of Sion, that he may take away the collar of our slavery."

We may cast a glance back on the frightful years of the last World War, and remember the anguish of so many uprooted "refugees", of so many prisoners some of whom to this day still linger in dungeons or concentration camps; remember, too, the bitter discontent and deep anxiety that continue to torture the souls of nations. Christmas is at hand: the Prince of Peace will soon visit us, He who alone can bring harmony among the nations, who has riven once for all the fetters of slavery—of the slavery of sin. But blinded and wilderness-haunting mankind rejects this Liberator. They have no use for Him, so they pretend, and prefer to keep their fetters.

For wandering mankind, then, we pray: "Look Thou, O Lord, upon the affliction of Thy people, and send Him whom Thou hast promised to send."

IV. God's Answer

In the last stanza God, "whose faithfulness endures eternally," reassures His sorrowing people: "Be ye, comforted, be ye comforted, My people; soon will thy salvation come. Wherefore are ye consumed with grief? Wherefore are ye overcome with sorrow? I will save thee: fear not; for I am the Lord thy God, the Holy One of Israel, thy Redeemer."

Thus God spoke of old to His people; thus He speaks to every nation, to every soul, that repents and pleads for assistance. We stand in need of God, the Father who forgives, the Son who redeems, the Holy Spirit who sanctifies.

Prayer: Come, O Lord, and visit us in peace, that, with a perfect heart, we may rejoice before Thee (Antiphon, 1st Vespers of 2nd Sunday of Advent).

CHRISTIAN JOY

1. St. Paul was a prisoner at Rome, and a man of Philippi
    (a city in Macedonia where the Apostle had founded his most
    dearly loved Christian community), had just brought him a
    liberal gift. Paul gives him a letter addressed "to all the saints
    in Jesus Christ who are at Philippi, my dearly beloved brethren
    and most desired, my joy and my crown". We try to behold
    the "prisoner of Jesus Chist" as he calls himself, writing this
    epistle, radiant with happiness, the joy of the Lord filling his
    heart.

2. *Petition*: That we may more deeply understand and express
    in our lives the spiritual joy which, according to Chesterton,
    is "the gigantic secret of the Christian soul".

I. True Joy

The Church so well realizes the lot of man on earth, that
often in her liturgy one perceives the accents of human woe
breaking through. How often she intercedes for her afflicted
children! We are "banished children of Eve, mourning and weeping in this vale of tears"; but we are not like those "who have
no hope in the promise and are without God in this world": her
final word is always a message of hope.

More often still, the liturgy speaks of joy and gladness. This
is the case today, when the Introit of the Mass quotes these words
of St. Paul, culled from one of the letters of the captivity: "Rejoice in the Lord always; again I say rejoice" (*Phil.* 4, 4).

This joy in the Lord is spiritual, pure, lasting. It has nothing
in common with what the world calls enjoyment and generally
is mere pleasure. Pleasure can be bought; it is superficial, short-
lived, and it never wholly satisfies the soul. "A soul that cannot
forego pleasure is incapable of tasting true joy. He that possesses
true joy has no need of pleasure." Look up to this prisoner Paul,
who, in the midst of all his trials, feels overwhelmed with joy.

[Mary, Cause of our joy, pray for us.]

II. The Fountain of Our Joy

From what source did the joy of St. Paul flow? It welled up, in the depths of his soul, from the Lord from whom nothing and nobody could separate him.

It is true that, in one of the Collects, the Church encourages us to pray "that we may be blest with perfect health of soul and body". Health, prosperity, success, which are the Lord's gifts, may become sources of joy in the Lord: we thank Him for these blessings and promise to use them well. But the joy of which St. Paul speaks wells up from a deeper source; nothing can deprive us of it, and it is always within our reach. Its source is the firm conviction that we have a Father who is in heaven, that we are His beloved children; that He has given us His Only-Begotten Son to be our Savior and our Brother, and with this gift all things: peace, pardon for sin, light and life everlasting. This is "the gigantic secret of the Christian".

St. Paul well knew that his recently converted gentiles, who till that day had tasted only pleasure, or endured sadness and despair, would not find it easy to rejoice in the Lord, always, and therefore insisted: "Again I say, rejoice."

III. The Joy of Advent

Today's liturgy points to the particular source of our joy, to which St. Paul appeals in the same passage: "The Lord is near." The expectation of a glad event, which will infallibly occur, and daily draws closer, has the effect of disposing us to patience and contentment; it helps us to overcome every difficulty; we are readily satisfied and make no high demands. Such seems to be the meaning of the Greek word, which is translated into Latin by "modestia", and which in English may be rendered by "contentment" or "leniency, tolerance".

May the feast of Christmas, which draws near, dispose us to contentment. "Let your modesty be known to all men" (*Phil.* 4, 5), especially to those with whom we hold daily intercourse. Mary, who was the first to observe the holy season of Advent, (and with what intense fervor!), will be pleased to let us share her feelings.

Prayer: Holy Virgin, Mother of God, allow us in thought to abide with thee; allow us to share thy ardent longing for the coming of thy Son, our Savior and thine, whom thou art privileged to bear and wilt show to us as the fruit of thy womb.

"THE PEACE THAT SURPASSETH ALL UNDERSTANDING"
(Phil. 4, 7)

1. St. Paul, "a prisoner for Jesus Christ", possesses that joy, about which Jesus said to the Apostles that no one would be able to take it from them. With that joy in his heart, he writes: "The peace of God, which surpasseth all understanding, keep your hearts and minds in Christ Jesus" (*Phil.* 4, 7).

2. *Petition*: The grace to understand the nature of true peace. May He, who alone can give it, bestow that peace on us, and may we faithfully preserve it.

I. Peace

We try to behold in the heart of Paul that peace which illuminates his countenance. His has been a chequered life, and at this moment he awaits the supreme hour of martyrdom. A strong man of sensitive temperament, he feels intensely all that happens to him; but in the midst of manifold tribulations he has always preserved that "peace of the Lord which surpasseth all understanding".

According to the well-known definition of St. Augustin, peace is the *tranquillitas ordinis*: rest and quiet is the result of perfect order. Where all things are in perfect order, say, in a family, or in a community; where each one in his own place does what he ought to do, and does it well, there peace and concord reign. Peace and order may perfectly co-exist with intense activity, nay they are a necessary condition for intense activity. When good order is disturbed, there is an end to peace and quiet and harmony.

Perfect order and undisturbed peace do not belong to this world. They would exist, if God's will were done "on earth *as* it is in heaven". Perfect peace remains a distant "blissful vision". Yet all men and all nations crave for peace. They cry: "Peace, peace. And there was no peace" (*Jer.* 6, 14). How many know the way to true peace, and how many follow it?

If you desire peace in the world, in your family or community, then first establish and preserve in your own heart that peace "which the world cannot give", the peace of God. The more we

conform our will to the Divine Will, the more perfect shall be
our peace; yet we shall never be able to preserve it without
doing battle against our disorderly affections. "Do not think that
I came to send peace upon earth. I came not to send peace, but
the sword," said our Lord (*Matt.* 10, 34). There is a kind of peace
which is false, a sham, a deceit; and that one the Messiah did
not bring, but true peace which is a grace and a victory. He
Himself is our peace and our reconciliation, the Lamb of God
who taketh away the sin of the world (*John* 1, 29).

II. That Peace Is a Grace

No mere human effort can secure the peace "that surpasseth
all understanding". It must come from above and we are expecting it during this season of Advent; it will take human form
in the Babe of Bethlehem, and the angels will greet it with the
words: "Peace to men of good will." It is "the fruit of the Spirit"
(*Gal.* 5, 22).

Though of ourselves we cannot attain this peace, we can yet
prepare our hearts for it. We can with God's grace remove from
our souls what is an obstacle to it, that is sin, disorderly attachments and whatever in our souls goes counter to God's will or
God's inspirations. In this manner we can show our good will,
and peace will descend into our hearts.

III. The Preservation of That Peace

That peace will keep our hearts and our souls steadfast in
Christ Jesus. But we must preserve and defend this peace, which
the Lord will bring us. We must preserve it, for it surpasseth all
feeling and understanding.

Even the severest trials cannot forcibly take it away from us.
During one of his journeys, St. Paul writes about himself: "We
suffered all tribulations, combats without, fears within" (2 *Cor.*
7, 5); but deep down in his soul he retained the peace of the Lord.
On the surface of the soul—where we are most sensitive!—there
storm and stress may rage, but still we can cry out with Paul:
"who then shall separate us from the love of Christ and from his
peace?" (*Rom.* 8, 35.)

The only disturber of the peace is Satan, who first introduced
disorder, that is sin, into the world. Against him we must defend
our peace, for through many wiles he tries to sneak into our souls
and disturb our mind and heart. He managed of old to slip into

paradise, and in the desert he tried his tricks even upon Christ in the hope of unsettling God's plan for our salvation.

"Through Christ our Lord," who comes to expel the prince of this world, we must and can preserve the peace of our hearts. He is "our peace and our reconciliation."

Prayer: To Mary, Queen of Peace and Mother of our Peace; also to the Prince of Peace, who firmly established in the soul of His Mother a "peace that surpasseth all understanding".

TUESDAY: THIRD WEEK OF ADVENT

JESUS, THE UNKNOWN (John 1: 21, 26, 27)

1. In the Gospel of the 3rd Sunday of Advent we hear St. John the Baptist answering the messengers of the Pharisees, who asked whether he was the Messiah. And he said, "I am not ... but there hath stood one in the midst of you, whom you know not: the same is he that shall come after me, who is preferred before me, the latchet of whose shoe I am not worthy to loose" (*John* 1: 21, 26, 27). We greet Jesus, standing there, one of the crowd, unnoticed, unknown.

2. *Petition*: An inward light to discover who Jesus is. He is still always with us, but many fail to recognize Him, and we ourselves only too often overlook Him.

I. Jesus Is Unobtrusive

Everything about Him is remarkably unostentatious: His very entrance into the domain of creatures is effected quietly and obscurely, in Nazareth "from where nothing good can come", with a mother who is a village girl betrothed to a carpenter.... The beginning of His Public Life—far from being spectacular, as Satan proposed to Him—was unassuming under the wing of John, who designates Him in cryptic terms to the multitude and confidentially points Him out to a few of his own disciples as the Lamb of God. Even His miracles are mostly wrought with the least possible publicity if He has His way. "The Almighty seems to be shy of being made a phenomenon."

How superhumanly great He is in His divine unobtrusiveness! And we, how futile in our conceited display! Come, let us go in search of Him and, mingling with the crowd, offer Him our veneration and pray, "O Jesus, meek and humble of heart, make my heart like unto Thine."

II. Jesus, the Unrecognized

They recognized Him not: neither at the start of His Public Life, nor later when He was speaking "as no man has ever spoken before" and working miracles which no man could work except God be with him.

Why did they fail to recognize Him? For one thing, He did not enter upon His work in the manner in which the narrow national pride of the Pharisees had imagined the Messiah would appear; nor had He sought any training at their hands; and He kept aloof from them, though He acknowledged their official standing: they felt outrivalled and resented it. And so, their eyes were blinded.

And as for the people, misled by their natural guides and disappointed in their messianic dreams, they would not accept Him, nay, they would reject Him.

John came "in the spirit and power of Elias" (*Luke* 1, 17) and the people wondered whether he was not the Messiah. The Gospel tells us how indignantly John rejected the surmise when questioned, and he cried: "I am not the Christ." How deeply touching it is to see Jesus and the Precursor vying with each other in humility! Whatever is truly great, whatever truly divine, bears the stamp of humility.

III. Jesus, Unknown Even Today

Even nowadays Jesus remains the great Unobtrusive One, and therefore He is unrecognized: "Behold, in the midst of you (still stands) one whom you know not."

How many are the de-christianized or unchristianized "crowds" amidst which Jesus still stands totally unknown, if not as the butt of contempt or hatred! I grant that He does not, as at the Jordan, stand there in His own Person—unassuming to be sure, yet irreproachable and unblemished: He stands there now in His Mystical Body, the Church, with all the holiness of her sacraments certainly—but also with all the defects and deficiencies of her members. We, Christians of today, especially we priests and religious, should ask ourselves why Jesus is the Unknown: why we do not *make* Him known enough, not bear enough witness unto Him, by the holiness of our lives and, in particular, by the practice of what He called the distinctive mark of His followers, i.e., brotherly love. Wherever this our testimony is missing, there stand around a score of other advocates, eager to announce the coming of a purely earthly bliss—followers, they, of the other unguessed "sovereign of the world", whose kingdom is one of deceit and brute force.

For ourselves, is Jesus to us the uninterruptedly recognized and faithfully followed One? Do we recognize Him in the good dispositions which He evokes in us? in everything that befalls us? He seldom appears in the guise in which we expect Him. Oftentimes He comes into our lives under the appearance of a fortuitous occurrence, of some trial, of some failure, of some grievous bereavement, and we know Him not. Yet it is undoubtedly He Himself, who ever disposes all things to the end of getting nearer to us and drawing us closer to Himself.

At present we are preparing our hearts for the feast of Christmas. He is coming to dwell in our souls, visible and yet unobtrusive. Mary is the Way along which He is coming.

Prayer to Mary: Holy Virgin, Mother of God, help us to recognize the Light that illumines the darkness; ah, make us recognize Him, the fruit of thy womb, Jesus: make His light to shine ever more abundantly in our souls and radiate it brilliantly over the multitudes.

> Break the captive's fetters,
> Light on blindness pour;
> All our ills expelling,
> Every bliss implore—*Ave Maris Stella.*

COOPERATION WITH GRACE (Ps. 23: 3, 4, 7)

1. It is an ancient custom in many countries, on the Wednesday of Ember Week to sing early in the morning the "Golden Mass" in honor of our Lady. Assisting in spirit at this Mass, we listen to the Introit: "Drop down, ye heavens, dew from above, and let the clouds rain the Just. Let the earth be opened and bud forth the Savior." These figures of speech convey to us that to welcome the Savior, heaven and earth, God and man must co-operate. God offers his gift: man must accept it.

2. *Petition*: The grace of throwing our soul wide open to the Savior, by ardent desires, humility and purity of heart.

I. Open the Soul to Grace

Unless rain and dew penetrate the earth, they do not refresh. When the soil is hard the dew evaporates.

Our soul must open itself to grace by a sincere and humble desire to receive it. All that the Lord asks is that we feel our need for Him, that we humbly confess that need, and that with a childlike heart we place our trust in Him. Is that asking too much? Can He require less from a creature which He has made free, on which He will not impose Himself? And yet heedlessness, lack of earnestness, even more than bad will and contempt, keep very many hearts closed to His grace.

The readiness of our soul to receive His gift will be in proportion to the depth of our humility, to the intensity of our desire, to the strength of the confidence we have in God.

Remember the Virgin Mary: when God offered her the most wonderful grace of becoming the Mother of God, her soul wholly opened itself to the divine favor, and she said, "Behold the handmaid of the Lord. Be it done to me according to Thy word." And these sublime words caused the Son of God to become man.

"Mother of the Messiah, Heaven's open Gate, have compassion on us poor sinners."

II. "Lift Up Your Gates"

In the Gradual of the Mass the Church uses another image to express the soul's readiness to receive the Savior that is to come. "Lift up your gates, O ye princes, and be ye lifted up, O eternal gates: and the King of Glory shall enter in" (*Ps.* 23, 7).

These words of the liturgy seem chiefly to point to Mary, "Heaven's open gate" who is also the door opening on to the earth. By that door did the Eternal King leave the seat of His Majesty, and by it He came to us on earth.

We also must lift up the gates of our soul and open them wide; let nothing stand in His way as He comes, neither pride that would refuse Him entry, nor disorderly affections that would raise obstacles on the way; no lack of trust, which would fix limits to His liberality.

The unconditional *Fiat* of Mary is the model of complete surrender.

[Mary, Gate of Heaven, pray for us.]

III. Ascend Into the Mountain

The Gradual of the Mass uses still another image designed to prepare the soul for the coming of Christ. "Who shall ascend into the mountain of the Lord: or who shall stand in His holy places? The innocent in hands, and clean of heart" (*Ps.* 23, 3-4). The mountain of the Lord is Mount Sion, the city of God whereon the Temple is built.

Mountain tops beckon us upwards: on the summits the prospect is pleasing to the eye, the air pure and bracing, the silence undisturbed. Man, escaping from the steaming valley or from the noisy city, longs to climb to the top.

We are ascending to the highest summit of the spiritual world where the Almighty, in a miraculous way, came in touch with His creature, and became the Son of Man, Emmanuel, God with us.

Who may ascend unto the mountain? Only one rose to the very summit to receive the Lord in the name of us all: Mary, the Immaculate Virgin. Under her protection and by her intercession, those too may ascend who are innocent in hands and pure of heart.

May we be drawn to the mountain of the Lord, may we be drawn to Him. In Him we shall find light, life, and peace. Rise up to such a prospect, my soul, in innocence of hands and purity of heart.

Prayer to Mary:

> Mother of Jesus; heaven's open gate,
> Star of the sea, support the fallen state
> Of mortals, thou whose womb thy Maker bore;
> And yet, strange thing, a virgin, as before;
> Who didst from Gabriel's Hail, this news receive,
> Repenting sinners by thy prayers relieve.
> —*Alma Redemptoris Mater*

THURSDAY: THIRD WEEK OF ADVENT

THE GREAT THINGS DONE TO MARY

1. When Mary in the house of Elizabeth sang her Magnificat, she spoke out of the fullness of her heart. Since the moment

of the angel's visit, her whole being was a-thrill with the
consciousness of the great things which the Almighty had done
to her. Behold her, in the little house of Nazareth, keeping
and pondering all these things in her heart.

2. *Petition*: The grace, with her assistance and in her company,
to admire the greatest work of God. We greet her with the
words of the Psalmist: "With thee is the fountain of life"
(*Ps.* 35, 10).

I. Great Things

God "alone doth great wonders" (135, 4), says the Psalmist.
Compared to His works, all man's achievements are puny and
insignificant; the greatest of men saw this very clearly. All they
can accomplish is but second-hand. They merely use what God
has created, and even so they must conform to the laws of
Nature imprinted in her by God's creative hand. To split the
atom is, no doubt, a wonderful accomplishment of 20th century
man (and God grant that it may contribute to man's happiness!).
But what a far greater achievement, and one rich in blessings
at that, is the daily rising of the sun!

Now, the greatest wonder of all, one which has affected in its
very essence the whole spiritual universe, was accomplished by
God in deepest secrecy and most intense stillness, when His Son
was made man in the virginal womb of Mary.

Humbly and truly Mary declares, "He hath done great things
to me." She has not done these things herself; God has done
them to her though not without her consent nor without her
humble, her unique, her sublime cooperation. She is, in Dante's
words, "at once humble and exalted beyond any other creature."

St. Paul's "What hast thou, that thou hast not received?"
(1 *Cor.* 4, 7), Mary has realized in a surpassing degree. Having
been taken nearest to God, she was able to fathom, as none
other could, the nothingness of mere creatures.

II. Done to Her

In her womb God becomes man. She is a mother, yet she remains a virgin; "natura mirante," as we sing in the *Alma Redemptoris Mater*: a favor which fills Nature itself with wonder (no
technical skill can produce that!).

That God becomes man is a miracle, which strikes with astonishment the whole of creation, the angels, the Cherubim and the Seraphim. One of these heavenly spirits is commissioned to solicit her consent; for God ever respects His creature's liberty, most of all the liberty of His most perfect creature, of her that was to be His Mother. The *Fiat* of Mary was not a creative *Fiat*, like the *Fiat Lux* of the Almighty. That was a word of powerful command. Mary's *Fiat* was an expression of humble submission to the Divine Will. But of all words uttered by human lips, Mary's *Fiat* was the most potent: owing to it the Word was made Flesh! We believe, we adore, we thank the Divine Majesty.

III. Great Things That Had Come Before

The liturgy places the following words on the lips of Mary: "When I was little, I was pleasing in God's sight." Did Mary, after the angel's message, receive special illumination about God's dealings with her in the past, about her childhood, her espousal with Joseph, her resolve to preserve her virginity? We do not know. The only thing we know is that she kept all these things in her heart and pondered over them. The Church, guided by the Holy Ghost, has in the course of centuries "pondered" on that fullness of grace, and gradually understood it better. One of the great things done to Mary, as we now know with certainty, was her preservation from original sin.

But all the great things done to her were divinely great; although the Holy Ghost enlightened her in a special manner, and even though she never ceased keeping these things in her heart and pondering over them, Mary, as she once confessed herself, did not fully understand them. We ought not to forget the words of Elizabeth who herself "was filled with the Holy Ghost", and who said to Mary, "Blessed art thou that hast believed."

Prayer to Mary: Alma Redemptoris Mater. To Jesus: O Jesus, living in Mary, come and live in Thy servants,

> in the spirit of Thy holiness,
> in the fullness of Thy power,
> by the solidity of Thy virtues,
> by the perfection of Thy ways,
> by the communication of Thy mysteries.
> Scatter the might of Thine enemies,
> through Thy Spirit, to the glory of the Father. (*Olier*)

HALLOWED SILENCE

1. The season of Advent is an appropriate time to consider the importance of silence in the spiritual life. A modern writer dared maintain that our agitated, noisy modern mode of life is a perpetual conspiracy against all inward life. As a matter of fact, there are not a few who abhor silence, and there may be religious, who fail to appreciate the important part played by silence in the spiritual life. Yet a non-Catholic poet wrote:

> Love thou silence in thy heart,
> Love the silence that inspires:
> Those who dread the hour of silence
> Ne'er discovered their own hearts,
> Never bent their knees in prayer.

Let us go in search of that awesome silence to Nazareth, where our Lady is.

2. *Petition*: The grace to establish silence in our souls and to experience its salutary effects as long as we live.

I. Even Nature Is Silent During Advent

The liturgy uses the world of nature as a magnificent symbol of the spiritual life and utilizes its occurrences to illustrate the sacred mysteries of our salvation: the interplay of light and darkness, rain and dew and the clouds of heaven, winter and summer, all natural phenomena are shown as symbols of the supernatural life, of sin and of grace, of the life and death of the soul, of the Lord's anger and of His good pleasure.

The time of Advent is for Nature a season of silence and concentration. The birds do not sing; no bright and gay colors burst forth; whatever grows and blooms is drawing its life-powers downwards into its hidden roots. Nature is recuperating her youth in a long, silent recollection. Fear not! It is not the silence of death, it is a secret rejuvenation that will result in springtime.

II. Silence in the Soul

The soul too needs recurring periods of silence and recollection. The interior life cannot thrive if we allow ourselves to get completely engrossed in the feverish agitation of outward activities. The rules of all Religious Orders prescribe the observance of external silence as an essential requisite for the gaining of internal stillness in the soul. Not to converse without necessity, to observe the Rule readily and avoid disturbing others, these things are meritorious by themselves; but we seek more than mere outward, material silence: we aim at the possession of a hallowed internal peace and perfect quiet of soul. It is not impossible to abstain outwardly from talking, yet inwardly to lack peace and recollection; for instance, by allowing our eyes to rove pryingly about, or the shifty impulsions of selfishness to agitate our hearts.

The silence of the spiritual life is a sacred, a godly silence, which does not come naturally but is the gift of God, and is nurtured in God's presence. This silence provides a kind of atmosphere that surrounds our prayer, protects it, so to say, and prompts it.

Such were the silence and recollection which hung over Nazareth while Mary and Joseph observed the first, the longest, the most tranquil, and most fervent season of Advent,—not only at prayer-time when the Messianic prophecies in the Psalms filled their grace-illumined minds with awe, but throughout their day's occupations, Joseph's in his carpenter's shop, and Mary's at her household duties.

Humbly, yet perseveringly, we will endeavor, under the eyes and the protection of the great contemplatives, Joseph and Mary, to maintain our soul in that atmosphere of true, inward, dedicated silence.

III. Closer to God

In this hallowed silence we come face to face with God. We *can* live on the surface of our souls; mingling in the bustle and noise, seeking diversions and dulling the sense of God's abiding presence, yea, quite losing sight of Him; and then grudgingly and at great pains enter into our chamber, shut the door and pray to the Father who seeth in secret (*Cf. Matt.* 6, 6).

Priests and religious engaged in the care of souls may be overwhelmed with work; but enlightened by the Spirit and guided by experience, the Church and the Rule ordain that at stated times these busy servants of God should withdraw from their activities. They do need Holy Mass and Holy Communion, the Breviary and common prayer, meditation and other spiritual

exercises. The closer our contact with men is, the more necessary
is our nearness to God.

The season of Advent is the appropriate time for deepening
our spiritual life: in hallowed silence and ardent longing for
His coming our soul ought to draw nearer to God. And how can
this be done better than in the company and under the protection of the Mother of God?

Prayer to Mary: Holy Mother of God, obtain for us that the
hallowed silence which reigned in thy heart and all around thee
at Nazareth may encompass us, too, during this holy season of
Advent. Enable us to abide with thee in spirit, grant us to share
the ardent longings of thy virginal mother's heart.

SATURDAY: EMBER WEEK IN ADVENT

HOLY MASS

1. Already from the 1st Sunday of Advent Holy Church sees
   the Cross looming in the distance. In the 3rd stanza of the
   hymn *Creator alme siderum* (2nd vespers) she sings: "Thou
   who comest to atone for the sins of all, dost—O true Lamb
   without blemish!—come forth from the sanctuary of the Virgin
   Mother on Thy way to the Cross." As matter for this meditation
   we take the Secret of the Mass of the 3rd Sunday of Advent.

2. *Petition*: "May this devout offering of ours, O Lord, be
   proffered to Thee without intermission; that, as we duly carry
   out the rites of this sacred Mystery instituted by Thee, Thy
   saving work may be wonderfully accomplished in us. Through
   our Lord. . . ."

I. Our Devout Offering Proffered Uninterruptedly

To offer sacrifice is the most sacred and most significant
act of religious life. It is the public and joint acknowledgment
of God's absolute dominion over all things. In the Catholic
Church it is at the same time a sacrifice of propitiation, by which
we confess our guilt and acknowledge that we are sinners.

The atoning offering which we present to God is Christ Himself, Son of God and Son of man, who was sacrificed for us on

the Cross. Now, during Advent, we are expecting Him as He will come forth unblemished from the Virgin's womb.

At every hour of the day and of the night this offering is being presented to God. Remember how, throughout the world, as the sun progresses on its course, thousands of Masses are being offered to the Father, offered for the entire Church and for the whole world. Every human being has a share in the fruits of these holy sacrifices, each one according to his own dispositions: only those are excluded who, out of sheer malice, refuse their share. And every Mass is a source of infinite merit, and of solace and confidence as well. "Where sin abounded, grace did more abound," wrote St. Paul to the Romans (5, 20).

> Jesus, to Thee be honor and glory,
> Who wast born from a Virgin;
> Mary, to thee be honor and glory,
> From whom the Lord was born.

II. The Sacred Mystery Is Duly Carried Out

"The mystery instituted by Thee." Holy Mass is not a mere human rite, such as we find in many man-made religions. God Himself has instituted it. The offering was performed once for all on Calvary. Nothing is wanting to it; but Jesus Himself ordained that, as an abiding memorial of His Passion and Death, and for the enduring application and distribution of His merits, "the Holy Mysteries" should be celebrated, in which till the end of time the sacrifice of the Cross shall in an unbloody manner be offered anew to God.

III. "The Saving Work Accomplished in Us"

God's saving work, His pre-eminently divine work: the salvation of the human race, "the mystery which had been hidden from ages and generations, but now is manifested to his saints" (Col. 1, 26). What God effects is really produced. It is the only thing that truly and fully exists; but it is invisible and impenetrable to the mind of man, as He Himself is invisible and His ways are inscrutable.

From every altar whereon Mass is offered, a flood of graces pours down on all the countless multitudes of Christians, nay on the entire human race: graces that unceasingly goad the sinner on to repentance, graces that enlighten those who seek, confirm those who waver, bring comfort to the weary, and spur on the fervent to ever more devoted and more loving service.

So does God accomplish His saving work in our souls. "From the rising of the sun even to the going down, my name is great among the nations, and in every place there is sacrifice and there is offered to My name a clean oblation" (*Mal.* 1, 11). What a marvellous proof of God's prevenient, everlasting, boundless love for man!

That pure oblation is the Body and Blood of the Lamb which is going to come forth unblemished from the Virgin's womb.

Prayer: "We beseech Thee, O Lord our God, that these sublime mysteries, which Thou hast instituted to safeguard our salvation, may be to us a remedy for our present ills and a protection against perils to come. Through our Lord" (Post-communion of today).

DECEMBER 17

O SAPIENTIA

1. On the last seven days before the Vigil of Christmas, special antiphons are sung at Vespers: the "O-antiphons", each of which begins with the exclamation "O", followed by one of our Lord's Messianic titles. They are sung very solemnly before and after the Magnificat, like appropriate settings for the Canticle of love and gratitude of the Virgin who gave us the Messiah.

    Besides an invocation to our Lord under a particular Messianic title each contains a petition prompted by that title.

    We salute Mary, through whom the Divine Wisdom became man.

2. *Petition*: Through Mary's intercession we ask for the grace of becoming possessors of the true Wisdom.

I. O Wisdom

"O Wisdom, that proceedeth from the mouth of the Most High, reaching from end to end and ordering all things with a strong and gentle hand."

Through the Wisdom of God all things have been created.

God's Wisdom is the Word of God. In order to create, God needs neither materials, nor tools, nor effort. His will suffices. The expression of His will is, in human terms, His creative *Fiat*.

God's Wisdom has no limits: it reaches "from end to end" in both time and space. It enfolds the universe in its origin, its development, its completion. Inside the universe it attends to each being, individually and in its relation to the whole; in every being it assists each action in its initiation and its fulfillment. Nothing escapes its eye or its power. "O the depth of the riches of the wisdom and the knowledge of God! How incomprehensible are His judgments! How unsearchable His ways!" (*Rom.* 11, 33).

This Wisdom "ordains all things with a strong and gentle hand": from the heights of heaven it leads all things decisively yet discreetly to their appointed ends. Augustus is not aware that, when from his palace at Rome, he issues a decree, he is only implementing the divine plan. The Messiah is to be born in a stable, and to that purpose the population of the entire Roman world is set moving.

The Wisdom which we invoke, is on the point of manifesting—and concealing!—itself unto the world in that powerless, speechless Babe, born of Mary and laid by her in a manger. Truly, "in whom are hid all the treasures of wisdom and knowledge" (*Col.* 2, 3).

II. Petition

"Come and teach us the way of prudence."

Prudence and Wisdom: not the prudence and wisdom of the world, which are the fruit of effort and study and do make man proud; nor prudence according to the flesh, which is induced by weakness and pusillanimous calculations. Those are not the ways of Wisdom that the Babe of Bethlehem comes to point out to us. The first lesson He teaches us is a pointed and radical one: utter detachment, abysmal humility and obedience unto the end.

This petition, if it comes from the heart, presupposes an ardent longing to learn true "Wisdom" and a sincere love for the Master who is teaching these lessons.

He is coming. Let us not be frightened away, either by the first "School of Christ"—a poor, uncomfortable stable, or by the first of His "Words of Life"—complete renunciation.

Later He will say, "No man can come to Me, except the Father, who hath sent Me, draw him" (*John* 6, 44). The Father

Himself has opened this school, and we know what arrangements He made to open it in a stable. We pray that He may draw us to Christ. He says to us: "This is my beloved Son, hear Him" (*Luke* 9, 35).

We know One whom He has trained in His school, "before he made anything from the beginning", who listened to His word when she uttered her *Fiat*. In her are now hidden "all the treasures of Wisdom and of Knowledge"; she will take Him on her lap and show Him to us and literally be the "Seat of Wisdom".

Prayer to Mary: Seat of Wisdom, holy Mother of God, the Wisdom that proceeds from the mouth of the Most High, shall, as Wisdom made man, be born of thee: be pleased to intercede for us with Him, in whom abide all the treasures of Wisdom, and who dwelleth in thee; obtain us the grace of hearkening to the voice of Him that is the Way, the Truth and the Life.

DECEMBER 18

O ADONAI

1. Adonai is one of the Hebrew names of God; it signifies "the Lord". Here the name is specially applied to the Second Person of the Blessed Trinity, whom we are in the habit of calling "our Lord". In this antiphon we appeal to Him as our powerful Leader.

2. *Petition*: The grace of acknowledging Jesus as our Leader, and of following Him wheresoever He may call. "The Lord ruleth me, and I shall want nothing" (*Ps.* 22, 1).

I. "O Lord and Ruler"

"O Lord and Ruler of the House of Israel, who didst appear to Moses in the fire of the burning bush, and didst give him the Law on Mount Sinai."

Moses is one of the types of the Redeemer. He was appointed by God to deliver Israel, His Chosen People, from the slavery of Egypt. God's strong, chastizing hand compelled the Pharaoh to let the Jews depart. In this exodus Moses was the leader: in the Lord's name he led Israel through the desert into the Promised

Land. In those days, God used to manifest Himself to the Jews
amidst a grand display of terrifying power. He came down on
the top of the mountain and anyone who came near the mountain
—except Moses himself—wouid be struck dead. Amidst thunder
and lightning, He delivered His Law to Moses; He slaked the
people's thirst in the wilderness with water that gushed from
the rock, and fed them with manna from heaven.

The new Leader will adopt quite a different way of approach
—though points of resemblance are not lacking. He becomes Son
of man and draws us to Himself "with the cords of Adam, with
the bands of love" (*Osee* 11, 4). To touch Him is to be healed;
seated on the mountainside surrounded by the multitudes, He
speaks a language of love and proclaims Beatitudes. He is the
good shepherd, who knows His sheep and lays down His life
for them (*John* 10, 14-15).

He is, as St. Ignatius calls Him, "the true Leader to the true
Life;" in great stillness, He descended into a Virgin's womb; from
out of that burning bush yet unburnt (in which the Liturgy sees
a symbol of Mary's untarnished virginity), He shall appear as
"the child that is born to us, the son that is given to us".

O Lord and Ruler, who in the womb of Mary immaculate
didst become man, we long for Thy coming, and we greet Thee
in the womb of her from whom Thou shalt be born.

II. Petition

"Come and redeem us with Thy uplifted arm."

"With uplifted arm": this is the usual figure in Scripture
to express God's power. He commands, He strikes, He protects. . . .

God's Son has been sent, not to chastise, but to deliver us;
and His arm "is not shortened" (*Isa.* 59, 1). He will work greater
wonders than in the days of Moses, not in as spectacular a manner
as under the Old Covenant, but in a manner that manifests
greater power over created beings and an incomprehensibly
merciful love. He will "lift up His arm" not to smite but to heal,
to touch the blind and the leper, to raise up the lame and cure
them of their infirmities, to command the wind and the sea, and
to feed the hungry with bread. And in the end, He will lift both
arms on the Cross in a most powerful gesture, which will put
to rout the "prince of the world" and set us free.

Are not His Sacraments—Baptism, Penance, Holy Communion
'liftings up' of our Blessed Lord's arm to cleanse us through

His priests of all our loathsome diseases and to feed us with the true Manna from heaven?

To be set free, continues to be a great need of man. How often in the liturgical orations do we not beseech God that we may serve Him with a free mind and a free heart, that His healing grace may free us from the snares of our perverse inclinations, i.e., our half-heartedness, our petty selfishness, our worldliness, our lack of trust?

"Stir up Thy power, we beseech Thee, O Lord, and come to our assistance with Thy great power: so that, thanks to Thy merciful eagerness, that may be hastened by the help of Thy grace what our sins are retarding. Who livest...." (Collect, 4th Sunday of Advent.)

And let us pray for the "Church of Silence", where our imprisoned and persecuted brethren, priests, religious and lay people, are longing for deliverance. How meaningful the prayers of Advent sound in their hearts: "Come and deliver us, O Lord; do no longer delay! Set us free with Thy uplifted arm!"

Prayer to Mary: Holy Mother of God, thou didst one day praise God because, "He hath showed might in His arm and scattered the proud in the conceit of their hearts": be pleased to intercede for us with thy divine Son. Hasten to the help of the people that are faltering, but would fain rise up again.

DECEMBER 19

O RADIX JESSE

1. This title belongs to Christ as a descendant of David who was son of Jesse. But the prophets see the Messiah as another David, as an immediate son of Jesse. Of old it was customary to represent the Tree of Jesse over the portals of churches, in their stained-glass windows, or in illuminated missals. At the root stood Jesse; at the top twig, appeared Mary; and from her bloomed the flower Jesus.

2. *Petition*: That we may rally, round the standard which Jesus will raise over the nations, and give Him loyal service.

I. O Offshoot of Jesse

"O Offshoot of Jesse, set up as the standard of the nations, before whom the kings of the earth will not dare to open their mouths, and to whom even the Gentiles will turn in prayer...."

During the ten centuries that lie between Jesse and the Messiah, many branches sprang from the parent root, not all of them hale and sound. The blood of this race, like that of every other race, had suffered contamination. But the last twig that established a relationship between the Messiah and David was an immaculate Virgin, Mary, the Mother of Jesus. St. Jerome was the first to see in the top twig of the tree of Jesse a symbol of Mary, and in the flower that blossomed on this twig a symbol of Jesus. There is in the Divine Office a response dating from the Middle Ages that says, "From the root of Jesse grew a branch, on that branch bloomed a flower, and upon that flower descended the Holy Ghost." God's Virgin Mother is the branch; her Son is the flower, and the Holy Ghost descended upon Him.

There is also an ancient Marian hymn:

A rose twig grew out of a root
(The chronicles say 'tis Jesse's)
and now the twig brought forth a rose
in the winter's depth, at dead of night.

O rose twig, O Mary,
O Virgin without taint,
Thee lauds in song Isaias
and the Bud by thee brought forth;
for, God's design eternal
had chosen thee to bear
the Rosebud of Jesse
to the whole world's avail."

"The standard of the nations." One day that standard will be the Cross, which will be lifted up high above the nations, and from which He shall draw all things to Himself (*John* 12, 32). Furthermore, the prophet foresaw that in the dim future the kings of the earth would not dare to open their mouths before that standard. St. Ignatius beheld, confronting the standard of the Lord, another, that of Lucifer, "the deadly foe of human nature". Both leaders strive to draw men under their banner, Christ by humility and truth, Satan by pride and deceit. Christ intends founding a Kingdom of peace and love, Satan one of

hatred and disorder. For two thousand years, these two kingdoms have been locked in unrelenting warfare; today the conflict is still raging: it is the strife between God's Church and her
enemies. Within our hearts, too, we experience what the Imitation (3; 15, 4) calls the conflicting promptings of nature and
grace.

Christ will not wait to raise aloft His standard until He is
dying on the Cross; that standard will rise above the stable of
Bethlehem and the manger.

We pray that we may be enrolled under His standard and become imbued with His spirit.

II. "Tarry Not, but Come and Deliver Us!"

Once again the same prayer! But can an exile, a captive, a
sorely tried soul change this theme? Jesus Himself, one day, will
keep repeating over and over again the same appeal to His
Father, and each time with greater urgency. "Tarry not: do not
delay." These words imply no lack of reverence or of patience:
they only express a sore distress and an unshakable trust in the
Lord.

It is a great grace to be able to pray thus: for, such a
prayer is a cry of anguish from a soul which in the very depths
of its being feels its need of God—of God's Light, of His Peace,
of His Love.

Prayer: I will trust in Thee, O Lord: my soul will rely on Thy
word. My soul has longed and longed for the Lord, like the
watchman in the night for the dawn. More eagerly than the
watchman for the dawn, we are looking out for the Lord; because
with the Lord there is mercy, with the Lord there is plentiful
deliverance. He comes to free Israel of all its iniquities.

DECEMBER 20

O CLAVIS DAVID

1. The key and scepter are symbols of power and authority.
When a sovereign visits one of his cities, the keys of the gates
are presented to him; when a pastor is inducted into a parish,
the keys of the church are handed to him. In the Apocalypse,

Jesus is called "the Holy One, the True One, he that hath the key of David: he that openeth, and no man shutteth; he shutteth, and no man openeth" (*Apoc.* 3, 7).

We know that though the Messiah has the key of David, the gates of Bethlehem will remain closed to Him and He will have to seek shelter in a cave by the roadside.

2. *Petition*: That we may discover Him in His weakness, believe in His power and open our soul to Him.

I. O Key of David

"O Key of David and Scepter of the House of Israel, who openest so that no man can shut again and shuttest so that none open. . . ." God had commanded King Ezechias to yield his throne to his chief minister: "And I will lay the key of the house of David upon his shoulder; and he shall open, and none shall shut: he shall shut, and none shall open" (*Isa.* 22, 22). We have here a prophetic symbol of the Messiah, the Son of God, who at the hands of His Father receives supreme power over His Father's house and kingdom. He that holds the keys goes in and out as he pleases, admits and excludes whomsoever he chooses, imprisons and releases as he deems fit: he is absolute master and disposes of whatever is in the house.

Thus endowed with full power, Christ comes to deliver us: mankind lay in the power of Satan and could not by its own strength regain its liberty. Out of love and mercy, the Father sent His own Son to throw open the gates of our dungeon. The Evil One will strive hard to prevent Him, and will manage in the end to have Him nailed to the Cross; but the very Cross destroys Satan's rule and sets the captives free. "Christ openeth and no man shutteth."

That power Christ manifested eminently on behalf of one: His Mother. He opened her soul to grace and no one shut it; He shut her soul to the Evil One and none opened it. She was conceived immaculate, she was full of grace.

Although He has the key and is almighty, He will not impose Himself by force on those He has endowed with free will. In the same chapter of the Apocalypse, we hear the Holy One, the True One, He that hath the key of David saying to us, "Behold, I stand at the gate and knock. If any man shall hear my voice and open to me the door, I will come in to him and will sup with him; and he with me" (*Apoc.* 3, 20). His knock is gentle and His call is a soft whisper: they take the forms of mute reproaches

for our acts of cowardice, of unobtrusive invitations to greater
generosity ... all of them manifestations of the omnipotent Love
that treats us with consideration. God grant that we be not
among those who "were His own and received Him not", that
we listen to His voice, open the door to Him and may sup with
Him!

God forbid lest the fate of the foolish virgins overtake us
too! By their thoughtlessness, they forfeited their privilege
and found the doors locked. "He shutteth and no one openeth."

He is also "the scepter of the House of Israel". He not merely
unlocks the gates of the dungeon; He then leads forth those He
has delivered. He is "the good shepherd" who leads us out on
the road to Life and who Himself is "the Way, the Truth and
the Life".

One day we shall hear Him claim, "All power is given to me
in heaven and in earth" (*Matt.* 28, 18); we are now awaiting
our Deliverer and Leader.

II. Come and Deliver From This Prison the Captive That Sitteth in Darkness and the Shadow of Death

This ancient figure of speech, which may have become trite
to us, does express correctly our utter misery. In every man's
heart there burns a fierce desire for freedom, for light, for life—
for the true liberty of the children of God, wherein he was
created but which he lost by his rebellion against God; his will
is fettered, he languishes in a dark dungeon—in the shadow of
death, and he longs for the light of true Life.

How many spiritual captives there are, who are crying for
freedom! How many spiritually blind, who wander in darkness!
But most deserving of compassion are those—and they are millions
—who are not even aware of the deformities of their souls, not
conscious of their extreme spiritual distress and who, consequently, have no desire to be made whole, and do not call out
for a Rescuer! For these last in particular we ought to pray:
for they are our brethren destined, as we are, to eternal bliss.
May God, who "wills all men to be saved", touch their hearts
with His all-penetrating grace, and bestow on them the Light
that sets them free!

And we ourselves as well—let us not overlook it!—we the Lord's
privileged children, are in need of more freedom and more light
on the road to Life and to perfection.

Prayer: Grant, we beseech Thee, Almighty God, that we, who by reason of the old bondage are held down under the yoke of sin, may be delivered by the long-desired advent of Thine only-begotten Son, who with Thee.... (Oration of Saturday in Ember Week.)

O God, whose will it is that all men be saved and come to know Thy truth: send forth, we beseech Thee, laborers into Thy harvest and give them to speak Thy word with all trust, that Thy Gospel may spread and be known, and all nations may recognize Thee, the one true God, and Him whom Thou hast sent, Jesus Christ Thy Son our Lord (Collect, Mass for the Propagation of Faith).

DECEMBER 21

O ORIENS

1. "Oriens," which literally means "he who rises," was the name which five hundred years before Christ, the prophet Zacharias gave to the Messiah: "Behold a man, the Orient is his name" (6, 12). A century later the prophet Malachias calls Him "the Sun of Justice" (4, 2). The most important daily occurrence in the order of Nature, the rising of the sun above the eastern horizon, is thus used as the symbol of the most important event in the work of mankind's salvation, viz. the birth of the Savior, the dawn of the Light that shall shine in the darkness.

   As we look out in expectation to the East where the new day will soon dawn, so we gaze, full of respect, upon Mary, who will give us the Messiah.

2. *Petition*: The grace of an ardent desire for Him who is the Light of the world and who will dispel all darkness.

I. O Dawn

"O Dawning Splendor of eternal Light, O Sun of Justice."
The break of dawn puts an end to the night: it is not yet the splendor of full daylight, it is only a beginning; but a glorious beginning, the joyful expectation of a never-ending day. Here

on earth our eyes cannot endure the full brightness of the Light divine, and therefore "the Word was made Flesh". In the Flesh, the Word is made visible to us, although only through a veil. "For, by the mystery of the Word made Flesh a new ray of Thy Glory has shone upon the eyes of our minds, so that, while we know our God in visible form, we may by Him be drawn to the love of things invisible" (Preface of Christmas).

We also call her the "Dawn" from whom the true Rising Sun will come forth. She is on the horizon, the red glow that fascinates our eyes: it becomes brighter and brighter, illumines the horizon more and more; very soon the Sun Himself will appear. "Who is she that arises as the day-blush?" Holy Church exclaims on the feast of the Immaculate Conception. We greet her with reverence; and with her we long for the rising of the true Sun, with her we pray that "His own may receive Him".

II. Come and Enlighten Them That Sit in Darkness and the Shadow of Death

St. John, who throughout his whole Gospel developed the one theme of the struggle between Light and darkness—"The light shineth in darkness and the darkness did not comprehend it" (1, 5)—points out in his First Epistle a parallel strife between love and hatred. It is there that he gives "Charity" as the very definition of God: "God is charity" (4, 8); and there also he writes, "Darkness is passed and the true light now shineth. He that saith he is in the light and hateth his brother, is in darkness even until now. He that loveth his brother, abideth in the light; and there is no scandal in him. But he that hateth his brother is in darkness, and walketh in darkness, and knoweth not whither he goeth; because the darkness hath blinded his eyes" (2, 8-11).

For twenty centuries now the Light has been radiating; but how deeply has it really penetrated into the minds and the hearts of men? If we were to investigate the effectiveness of the light of faith and the light of fraternal love—for, let us not separate the two!—we would find faith in God, and in Him who was sent by God, languishing in many a region, being persecuted in others, heroically confessed here and there, and everywhere zealously preached . . . and yet darkness still reigning in countless souls.

"Come and enlighten them that are seated in darkness!" And enlighten us, too, who are, in truth, walking in the light of faith, but not in such a way that our lives are transfigured by it and radiate it to the many that are gropingly seeking for it.

"He that loveth his brother abideth in the light; he that hateth his brother is in darkness." If that is so, how black the darkness is that encompasses the world of today! Is it hatred that is arraying our whole earth into two hostile camps? Maybe it is not conscious hatred; but at all events he who stirs up this tumult, and reaps the benefits, is the arch-enemy of God and man, satan who hates us and "was a murderer from the beginning" (*John* 8, 44).

He whose coming we now expect, is God's Love made man, the Brightness of eternal Light and Love everlasting.

Prayer: That Light may shine more brightly, that Love may reign more strongly in the minds and hearts of all men throughout the world; in our family, in our community, in our own heart. "Come, O Dawn, O Sun of Justice: enlighten our minds and enkindle our hearts, for we are sitting in darkness and lovelessness."

DECEMBER 22

O REX GENTIUM

1. The prophets frequently bestow this glorious title on the Messiah. The Angel of the Annunciation, too, spoke to Mary of "the throne of David His father" and of His kingdom "to which there shall be no end". We know in what kind of palace He chose to be born, and to what kind of throne they will raise Him before He leaves the earth. Nevertheless, as He confessed before Pilate, He *is* King, and His Kingdom is the kingdom of Truth; though it is not of this world, His Kingdom must be established in this world, be spread in it, and be restored to the Father when at the end of time it shall be perfect.

2. *Petition*: The grace to receive Him with due honor when He enters into His Kingdom; the grace to establish His reign firmly in our own hearts, and to spread it by prayer and labor in the hearts of others. "Thy Kingdom come!"

1. O King of the Nations, Long-Desired, O Cornerstone That Bindest Together That Which Hath Fallen Apart

The prophet saw in a vision what the Messiah is by right, and what He will be in fact in the remote future. "And all kings of

the earth shall adore him, all nations shall serve him" (*Ps.* 71, 11).
Will this be fulfilled literally one day; or must He who is seated
on the throne first renew all things?

When He walked the earth, His own nation would not have
Him as their king; nor would He Himself accept the kingship of
which Israel was dreaming and which alone they would offer
Him (*John* 6, 15). His Kingdom is a Kingdom of Truth and of
Life, a Kingdom of Holiness and Grace, a Kingdom of Justice,
of Love, of Peace. Truly, such a Kingdom is not, and never shall
be, of this world. And yet He is "the expectation of nations"
(*Gen.* 49, 10).

In our modern world we hear, far and near, shouts that sound
like echoes of those uttered by the Jews before the pretorium of
Pilate; but "do they know what they are doing?" Rooted in the
very nature of every man's soul, there is an indestructible yearning for truth and life, for justice, love and peace, put there by
the Creator. It is by the door of that yearning that the Savior
seeks to enter—not, however, by force of arms—to establish
His own Kingdom in the minds and hearts of men.

"The cornerstone that binds together what has fallen apart."
This figure of speech, first used by the prophets, was taken up
by St. Paul to designate Christ as the One who puts an end to
all human dissensions and lays the foundation of true unity.
He is our peace, who hath made both (i.e., Jews and Gentiles)
one, and hath broken down the middle wall of partition (*Eph.* 2,
14). And to impress upon the minds of his neophytes how deeply
this union of all in Christ affects our being, St. Paul accumulates
the amazing denials, "There is neither Jew nor Greek; there is
neither bond nor free; there is neither male nor female. For you
are all one in Christ Jesus" (*Gal.* 3, 28).

Compared to this, how superficial and petty are the differences
and the causes of conflict that divide men! But, as St. Augustine
says, we are like vessels of clay that get into the way of one
another: where one happens to stand, there is no room for the
others; what one possesses cannot belong to one's neighbor.
This is what happens in a world ruled by greed and jealousy;
"in Christ Jesus" it may not be so: in Him all possess all things.
His own Kingdom that He will establish, in a way that is not
the way of the world. In Him extremes meet: God and man;
in Him "justice and peace have kissed" (*Ps.* 84, 11).

II. Come and Save Man, Whom Thou Didst Mould Out of the Earthly Slime

When we survey the modern world, which has abolished distance, but has erected iron curtains, raised color bars, and is indulging in an armaments race; or when we look into our own souls, we soon realize that man still needs salvation. God molded us out of slime, but to His own image and likeness. Now, what is slime in us binds us to matter: we have base inclinations, we stand in one another's way and collide. God's likeness in us draws us upward and seeks to unite. It is God's own Hand that lifts us unto Himself, but He has to disentangle us from the slime.

Because He loves us with a boundless love, He leaves heaven, as it were, and assumes in the womb of an immaculate Virgin Mother an earthy body like ours, in order to deliver us from all that separates us from Himself and divides us from one another.

In "the body of His humility" He is about to appear among us. Around the manger that will serve Him for a cradle, we shall find His holy Mother, His saintly foster father, some shepherds of Bethlehem and the Wise Men from the East; and, hovering above it, angels of God that announce good tidings of great joy and sing about peace to men of good will.

Prayer: O King of the nations, long desired; O Cornerstone that binds together what has fallen apart, come and deliver man whom Thou hast molded out of the slime to Thy likeness.

DECEMBER 23

O EMMANUEL

1. This title is the one that expresses most perfectly what Christ is to us: "God with us." It was used for the first time by Isaias in the memorable announcement which, according to tradition, foretold the virgin birth of the Messiah: "Behold a virgin shall conceive and bear a son, and his name shall be called Emmanuel (*Isa.* 7, 14).

2. *Petition*: The grace to believe in *the Love*, which is about to manifest Itself as love for man; and the grace to return love for love.

I. O Emmanuel

"O Emmanuel, our King and Law-giver; O long-awaited Savior of the nations of the earth."

No title is more appropriate for the Word of God made man. For ages it had been the boast of Israel that there was "no other nation so great, that hath gods so nigh them, as our God is present to all our petitions" (*Deut.* 4, 7). And yet, how far away from them Jahve was! High above them on the top of Mount Sinai, amidst thunder and lightning! How much closer to us is He whose coming we are now awaiting! His favorite name for Himself will be "the Son of Man". And that is exactly what He is in the mystery laden meaning of the name: that is what He became in the womb of His Virgin Mother, Mary Immaculate (according to Isaias it is the Virgin Mother herself who calls her Son "Emmanuel"). The prophet further says, "For a Child is born to *us*, a Son is given to *us*" (*Isa.* 9, 6). In the *Ave Maris Stella* we express it thus:

> "Show thyself our Mother:
> Offer Him our sighs
> Who, for us incarnate,
> Did not thee despise."

He, who through Mary became "God with us", will remain so forever. During more than thirty years He dwells visibly, audibly, tangibly with us; He associates with everyone; He preaches the glad tidings to all, chooses apostles and trains them, founds His Church. And when His visible sojourn among us comes to an end, He crowns it all by a miraculous prolongation. He institutes the Holy Eucharist as a memorial of His departure in the role of our Victim and at the same time as a divinely contrived means to remain with us till the end of time.

As a result, we still have God with us: in His Church which teaches and guides us; in Holy Mass where He offers Himself to the Father for us and with us; in Holy Communion wherein, as the food of our souls, He becomes "God with us" in the most ineffable way.

"Hail, true Body, born of Mary ever Virgin!"

This last antiphon repeats other titles invoked in previous ones: King, Law-giver, Savior of all,—as if to show that He is going to be all these things not from far away, but close to us as "God with us" still.

II. Come and Save Us, Thou Who Art Our Lord and God

The great mystery of our redemption, "which hath been hidden from ages and generations" (*Col.* 1, 26), is manifested and accomplished by God "in the fullness of time", i.e., at the time and in the manner laid down from all eternity by the Divine Will. The most momentous phases of that mystery are: the incarnation, the life, death and resurrection of our Lord Jesus Christ.

During Advent we look forward, full of hope, to the coming of the Child as the initial step in the realization of the mystery. The incarnation itself is the central point of the mystery; all that went before was a preparation for it; all that comes after it is its further development and its results. The birth of Jesus is the open disclosure of the deepest secret of the mystery; for it evokes already, before the eyes of the Church, the Death on the Cross—so that her Liturgy sings beside the very manger:

> Thou, for the sake of guilty man
> Permitting Thy pure Blood to flow,
> Didst issue from the virgin shrine
> And to the Cross a victim go.

Still more completely does the Church sum up the whole process of the mystery of our redemption in the prayer that concludes the Angelus:

Prayer: Pour forth, we beseech Thee, O Lord, Thy grace into our hearts, that we, to whom the incarnation of Christ Thy Son was made known by the message of an angel, may by His Passion and Cross be brought to the glory of His resurrection; through our Lord.... *end*

VIGIL OF CHRISTMAS

"TOMORROW YOU SHALL WITNESS HIS GLORY"

1. By this time, the sense of expectation has risen to the highest point. During the first two Advent weeks, the liturgy had invited us to "Come ye and adore the King that is coming"; from the third Sunday onwards, that became "The Lord is nigh: come and adore Him"; on December 21 the Lauds' antiphon promised us, "Fear not: four days more and the Lord shall

be with you"; now, on the eve of Christmas the Introit of the Mass gives us the assurance, "This day ye shall know that the Lord will come, and in the morning ye shall see His glory."

2, *Petition*: That in the company of Joseph and Mary, we may spend this day in holy recollection, ardently longing for the Savior, and adoring Him.

I. Glad Expectation

In most towns of the world the eve of Christmas is a day of bustling preparations; but alas! for many, Christ has been taken out of Christmas, which has become a profane festivity. At best there clings to it an atmosphere of homeliness and intimacy, which may remind men of the great event it commemorates.

We ourselves are likely to be busily engaged in material preparations for the external celebrations in the church or the community; but let us endeavor to keep our inner thoughts centered upon the great happenings we want to re-live tomorrow.

When Moses had led the Jews out of Egypt, they had to cross the desert; there they walked in fear lest they should perish of hunger and thirst. Then one day Moses said to them: "In the evening you shall know that the Lord hath brought you forth out of the land of Egypt; and in the morning you shall see the glory of the Lord" (*Exod.* 16, 6-7); and the next morning "a dew lay around about the camp". God had rained down manna from heaven. This is the event recalled in today's Introit, which the liturgy applies to the birth of the Savior.

We too are awaiting salvation: tomorrow will appear the true Savior, the true Manna from Heaven.

II. In Glory and in Poverty

There is a perplexing contrast between the manifestation of the Savior as described by the prophets, and the reality of His appearance among us. In Isaias, e.g., we read about the Child: "The government is upon his shoulder, and his name shall be called Wonderful, Counsellor, God the Mighty, the Father of the world to come, the Prince of Peace" (9, 6). Similarly the Psalmist (see the Offertory of today), "Lift up your gates, O ye princes, and be ye lifted up, O eternal gates; and the King of Glory shall enter in" (*Ps.* 23, 7)—which evokes before our imagination some colossal portals of an Assyrian palace, a triumphal reception. And then we witness the reality: Joseph and Mary trudge their way into Bethlehem; at the close of day, they seek shelter and there is no room for them in the inn; at last they find a dark stable by the roadside and there they put up as best they can.

What a contemptible sight for human eyes! One needs the eyes of faith to discover, beneath the squalor, the invisible glorious splendor. Behold! Far more magnificent than the most monumental gates of an imperial palace, the "blessed gate of Heaven" from which the King of Heaven and earth will step forth. The dark and wretched stable of Bethlehem is in spiritual reality the "Palace of Peace of the Nations", wherein has just been made ready the Charter of true Peace—not a scrap of parchment, but the tiny Body of the Child in whom "dwelleth the fullness of the Godhead", and whose Blood will one day seal the Treaty of Peace between heaven and earth.

We hasten to welcome Mary:

> The Great King's Gate art thou, and bright
> Abode of everlasting Light.
> Ye ransomed nations, hail to heaven
> Our Life's Spring through a Virgin given.
> To God the Father, God the Son
> Of Mary born, be homage done;
> The like to God the Spirit be:
> Eternal Godhead, One in Three.

III. The Other Advent

As at the beginning of Advent, so on the eve of Christmas the Church's liturgy recalls the second coming of Christ too, and duly connects the coming of the Redeemer with the coming of the Judge: "Tomorrow shall the iniquity of the earth be blotted out: and the Savior of the world shall reign over us" (Gradual of today). And in the hymn of Lauds:

> Great Judge of all, in that Last Day
> When friends shall fail and foes combine,
> Be present then with us, we pray,
> To guard us with Thine arm divine,

which shows how concerned Mother Church is that, even when we rejoice at the birth of "the Child that is given to us", we should blend together and foster both a childlike love and a childlike fear.

Prayer: O God, who gladdenest us with the yearly expectation of our salvation, grant that we, who now joyfully welcome Thine only begotten Son as our Redeemer, may also without fear, see Him coming as our Judge, Jesus Christ our Lord Thy Son, who with Thee liveth (Collect of the Mass of today).

CHRISTMAS DAY

1. We kneel by Mary's side. She herself, says Holy Scripture, has "wrapped the Child in swaddling clothes and laid Him in a manger", full of love and respect. Remembering the angel's thrilling message, she now adores the "Son of the Most High", her very own Babe.

2. *Petition*: Impart to us, O Mary, some of thy faith, thy hope and thy love for this Babe, born of thee for our salvation.

I. God Has Become Man

In the inexhaustible subject of the Christmas mystery, we consider first of all the most amazing aspect: the omnipotent, infinite God has become man.

The Blessed Trinity is the "original mystery" inside the very Divinity, that "silence without modes, by whose incomprehensibility all loving souls find themselves overcome" (*Ruusbroeck*). The action of creating makes the Three reach "outside", reach "other beings" in which They are unfathomably present; but outside of the order of creatures, "in Themselves," They have a being that utterly transcends the created universe.

Now, by the incarnation God joins unto His Divinity a human soul and body: "The Word is made flesh" says St. John, the Son of God is now also a man. Henceforth He exists no more apart from His human nature. God can effect nothing more thorough than this in the order of creatures or in the history of mankind. When He was born, He entered the world of creatures. In that weak, speechless little Child, the equal in all things of any human child, "dwelleth all the fullness of the Godhead" (*Col.* 2, 9). Nay, St. Paul uses the adverb "corporeally".

> O Most High, Thou liest there
> In what a homely stable!
> Thou, who mad'st the glowing stars
> Shiver'st with cold in a manger!

> Omnipotence has become weak,
> Immensity is tiny,
> The Deliverer lies in bonds,
> The Eternal One is born.

> He who robes angels in brightness
> Is wrapped in swaddling bands;
> Lo! The Ruler of the heavens
> Is fed at His Mother's breast.

> The refrain: How wonderful are Thy works,
> O Jesus, which Thou didst for man:
> In boundless love for the exile
> Whom sin drove out of Paradise.

II. God Is Love

"God is Love" such is the very definition of God given by St. John, who also writes, "God was made Flesh". Love craves for union, irresistibly; overthrows all obstacles, leaps over all chasms. Infinite Love, "with whom nothing is impossible", unites by the Incarnation, what appeared to be impossible to unite: the Creator and a creature, the All-Holy and "sinful flesh" (*Rom.* 8, 3). The Word of God now joins the ranks of sinful men. We fail to understand: we can only "believe the charity which God hath for us" (1 *John* 4, 16). But if mere human love, not seldom goes beyond the bounds of reason, we should expect God's Love to surpass all understanding. God's Love is not, like man's, a response to the attractions of some object lovable in itself; It is absolutely prevenient: and tenders Its objects worthy of love.

III. Mary Believed in That Love

We are kneeling by the side of our Lady, joining her as she adores the Child. She was the first to believe in God's Love. "Blessed art thou, that hast believed," exclaimed Elizabeth when greeting her. We call her blessed also for having been the first to behold "God made visible" and to believe. He was indeed visible, but at the same time so little, and so weak. All there was in Him, He had drawn from her substance, and He was dependent on her for everything He needed. Yet, as she gazed on Him, there shown from her eyes something more than what sparkles in every new mother's eyes: "You treasure, you are mine." Mary's look was an act of self-surrender "I am all thine!". In "the body of our lowness" (*Phil.* 3, 1), her faith and her love perceived and adored her Creator and her Lord. She loved and adored Him perfectly, on behalf of all of us.

Prayer: May the oblation of this day's festival be pleasing to Thee, O Lord, that by Thy bountiful grace we may, through this sacred intercourse, be found conformed to Him, in whom our substance is united to Thee; and who with Thee liveth.... (Secret, 1st Mass of Christmas.)

> Remember, O Creator Lord,
> That in the Virgin's sacred womb
> Thou wast conceived, and of her flesh
> Didst our mortality assume.
> —*Jesu Redemptor*, Vespers of today

DECEMBER 26

THE VIRGINAL MOTHERHOOD

1. We reverently greet and admire the Virgin Mother, as we see her kneeling in adoration before her Child, who is the Son of the Eternal Father. From heaven, the Father is pleased to look down on her, whom His Power has overshadowed. We may hear Mary, repeating the words of the liturgy: "When I was little, I was pleasing in the sight of the Most High, and my womb has borne Him who is God and man."

2. *Petiton*: The grace to understand the spiritual value of virginal purity; "All men take not this word, but they to whom it is given" (*Matt.* 19, 11). May we generously strive to preserve this purity. "Holy Virgin of virgins, pray for us."

I. Mary Immaculate

Yesterday, we meditated on the mystery that God became man: it is the greatest of all mysteries. From it flow others: that He was born of a Virgin Mother, who herself was conceived without sin.

The Son of God will be the Son of man. His body will be conceived and will grow in a mother's womb, and so He will be a child of Adam.

The genealogies, which we read in the Gospels, show that the Word chose to become a member of our sinful race; for among the ancestors there enumerated, many were guilty of grievous sin, just as is the case with the ancestry of every child of Adam and Eve. "God sent his own son in the likeness of sinful flesh and sin" (*Rom.* 8, 3).

But in His Wisdom, the Almighty had decreed that she, that would be His Mother, should be immune from the stain of original sin. She was indeed a daughter of Adam, in need of salvation, but saved in a most sublime manner. She was preserved from original sin: from the first moment of her existence, she was pleasing in the sight of the Almighty. "He loved her, and adorned her" in the manner God's love alone can love and adorn. How could God's Mother be otherwise than all-beautiful, *Tota Pulchra!*

II. Ever Virgin

Her immaculate conception was a mystery, which even Mary did not fathom. The other great mystery, wrought in Mary, and a great marvel, is her virginal motherhood. "Natura mirante" says the liturgy. Nature understands not these things, nor does man, who thinks he understands nature. It is the work of the Almighty. Nature now obeys God's *Fiat* as readily as when He said *"Fiat Lux"*, "Let light be made!" The Church has always believed, and she confesses in her most ancient creeds that Mary was, and remained virgin before, during and after the birth of Jesus. In the titles bestowed on her in the Litany, we see how in the Middle Ages people were delighted by this mystery: Mother most pure; Mother most chaste; Mother inviolate; Mother undefiled; Mother most amiable; Mother most admirable.

In the second antiphon of Lauds on Christmas Day, the Church sings, "A Mother has given birth to a King whose Name is eternal. She has the joy of motherhood and the honor of virginity; never was such a wonder seen, nor will it ever happen again."

III. The Dignity of Virginity

Through an immaculate virginal Mother, the Word of God became a member of our sinful race. This alone, better than any argument, shows what God thinks about unspotted purity. "All men take not this word," said Jesus, "but they to whom it is given" (*Matt.* 19, 11). And as Jesus clearly states, it is for the Kingdom of Heaven that "they to whom it is given", resolve to preserve virginity; not because they dread the burdens of parenthood, nor because they fear the world. Their purpose is to establish the "Kingdom of God", more firmly in their own souls, and to be at liberty by toil, prayer and penance to establish it throughout the world.

Let us remember the pithy saying of St. Bernard: "Virginity is praiseworthy, but humility is more necessary. We may think that Mary's virginity, if it had not been accompanied by humility, would not have been pleasing to God." And further, St. Bernard writes: "Chastity without love is like a lamp without oil."

Let those, "to whom it has been given to take this word", thank God for the favor they have received. Let them implore the grace always to continue "to take it"; ever generously to correspond to the graces given them, so that they may lead holy lives, and daily become dearer to God and man.

Prayer: O God, who hast given to mankind the price of eternal salvation by means of the fruitful virginity of the Blessed Virgin Mary: grant, we implore Thee, that we may experience the intercession on our behalf of her, through whom we were made worthy to receive the Author of Life, our Lord Jesus Christ, Thy Son, who liveth.... (Collect, Votive Mass of Our Lady).

DECEMBER 27

SAINT JOHN

1. St. John is the disciple "whom Jesus loved", and to whom on the cross He entrusted His holy Mother; "from that hour the disciple took her to his own" (19, 27). We may rightly think that Mary related to St. John all she knew about her Divine Son, "how the Word was made flesh and dwelt among us".

2. *Petition:* Grace to understand better John's lesson of love, and to practice it more thoroughly every day of our life.

I. The Disciple Whom Jesus Loved

John calls himself by that name. We know that he wrote his Gospel when all the other apostles were dead; otherwise, delicacy would have prevented him from claiming this title.

Jesus loved all the disciples with His whole heart; yet among them, there were three to whom He showed special predilection: Peter, James and John. They had accompanied Him to the mountain and seen His glory; they had entered with Him the garden of Gethsemane and had beheld Him lying prostrate on the ground. And among these three, Jesus seems to have shown greater affection for John. At the Last Supper, John was very close to Jesus. "Now there was leaning on Jesus' bosom one of his disciples whom Jesus loved" (*John* 13, 23). To him Jesus revealed who was the man that was to betray Him. John was the only one of the twelve to stand beneath the cross, and Jesus entrusted His Mother to him.

Humbly and reverently, remembering that the Almighty is free to elect whomsoever He pleases, we may ask, Why was John the disciple whom Jesus loved? John was not exempt from petty human failings, no more than the others. He, together with his brother James, had urged their mother to ask that her sons might occupy the first places when the Kingdom would be established; and when, one day they had stood before the closed gates of a town of Samaria, these two sons of Zebedee, whom Jesus Himself had dubbed Boanerges, which means "fanatics", had said to Jesus, "Lord, wilt thou that we command fire to come down from heaven and consume them? And turning, he rebuked them saying, "You know not of what spirit you are" (*Luke* 9, 54-55). Theirs was not yet the spirit of Jesus, who "came not to destroy souls, but to save" (*ibid.* 56). They had yet to learn of Him that He is meek and humble of heart.

There is an ancient tradition that John had preserved his virginity; and for this reason, Jesus bore him special love, and for this reason also, Jesus was pleased to entrust His blessed Mother to him.

God's creative love is free; it is not bound by any law, neither is it subject to caprice. "Is thy eye evil, because I am good?" said the householder to the disgruntled laborers (*Matt.* 20, 15). In all things and at all times, it behooves us to thank God and obey His decrees.

II. Behold Thy Mother!

John himself heard these words from the lips of the dying Savior, and he set it down in his Gospel. "Woman, behold thy son; behold thy mother." Simple but creative words, words which God alone can utter. During many centuries, the Church has pondered over them, ever penetrating deeper into their meaning, and who perhaps is not fully understood.

At the foot of the cross, Mary is given a new mission; she is appointed by Christ to be the mother of all the brothers and sisters of her Son. Together with John, all of us are entrusted to her as her children.

We pray that John, who from that moment "took her to his own", would obtain for us the grace to love and honor the Mother of Jesus as our own Mother, as he did until the day when she was assumed into heaven.

III. The Apostle of Love

The eagle is the symbol of St. John among the Evangelists. What his piercing eye has discovered in God, he has communicated to us in the words "God is Charity, and he that abideth in charity abideth in God, and God in him" (1 John 4, 16). Nor may we fogret those other words: "If any man say: I love God, and hateth his brother, he is a liar" (ibid. 20).

When the Apostle had become very old, his only words to his disciples were, "Little children, love ye one another"; and when they asked him whether he could not teach them any other lesson, he replied, "It is the Lord's own commandment." Our Lord Himself had called brotherly love his own commandment. "This is my commandment, that you love one another, as I have loved you" (John 15, 12). It was not the first commandment, but like unto it, and inseparable from it, and the proof that we truly love God. These words should be remembered by every disciple of Jesus, above all by those who strive to lead a holy life and who would follow Christ closely.

Prayer: Pour into our hearts, O Lord, the spirit of Thy Love, so that all those whom Thou hast fed with the same heavenly Bread, may through Thy fatherly goodness be united in Thee, through Christ our Lord (Postcom. Votive Mass for Concord).

O St. John, who with great love and reverence didst take the Mother of Christ "to thy own", intercede with her for us, and teach us how to abide in the presence of the Mother of God.

DECEMBER 28

THE HOLY INNOCENTS

1. There was dread and consternation in the little town of Bethlehem, as Herod's soldiers were snatching little infants from their mother's arms, and slaying them. Cries of grief resounded everywhere. In profound humility, we bow in adoration before this decree of Providence.

2. *Petition*: May we always and in all things trustfully accept and adore the decrees of Providence, in the government of our souls and of the world at large.

I. The Cruelty of Herod

Only a while ago, the heavens at Bethlehem were filled with the joyful song of the angels, and now the shrieks and groans of stricken mothers fill the air. "A voice in Rama was heard, lamentation and great mourning; Rachel bewailing her children, and would not be comforted, because they are not" (*Matt.* 2, 18).

Herod, a cunning and cruel oriental despot, who out of hatred and jealousy, had murdered many of his own relatives, had decreed to kill the new King, about whom the Wise Men of the East had told him. Then "Herod, perceiving that he was deluded by the Wise Men, was exceeding angry: and sending, killed all the men-children that were in Bethlehem and in all the borders thereof, from two years old and under" (*Matt.* 2, 16). To what monstrous crimes a man can be driven by an unbridled passion! Remorselessly, Herod sacrifices innocent children to his ambition and his jealousy. What had he to fear from the King of Peace?

> *Non eripit mortalia*
> *Qui regna dat celestia.*

> He does not snatch away earthly crowns
> Who bestows a heavenly Kingdom.

Thus the Church sings at Vespers on the eve of the Epiphany. Self-love, when uncontrolled, can drive a man to the utmost limits of stupidity, blindness, and cruelty, where every vestige of justice vanishes. Remember also the cowardice and vacillation of Pilate, who to safeguard his own interests, condemned an innocent Man.

II. God's Ways Are Not Our Ways

In this frightful tragedy, we cannot help asking ourselves: How could God allow it? Are these the ways of Providence? These ways are indeed inscrutable. How often does it seem that supreme Power fails when faced with the powers of Evil. Could not God have saved His Son from the clutches of that tiger, Herod, whose son and heir, Jesus would call "that fox". Why did Divine Justice not strike the brutal tyrant now, as it would chastise him later? Then there would have been no need for Mary to flee with the Child into Egypt, and the innocent babes would not have been slain.

Why did the Divine Justice not stretch out its avenging hand? We humbly confess that the ways of the Lord are inscrutable.

And what did mothers of Bethlehem feel when they were told that their children had perished, whilst the victim sought by Herod, had escaped? Poor desolate Rachel! Her children are the first martyrs to bear testimony to Christ. Their blood will fertilize the earth, and in God's own time a golden harvest of souls will rise.

But it remains true that God's ways are not our ways. We cannot unravel the mystery of His Providence: it is the Providence of a loving Father, of a Father who abideth in heaven, and who sees so much further than our eyes can reach. He is wiser than we are, and more powerful, and infallibly He guides us to the goal He has appointed for us, in His love and mercy: eternal bliss in heaven.

III. Joy and Suffering at the Manger

It has been said that, when Jesus enters the life of a man, He comes with His blessing and His cross. So it was with Mary and Joseph, with the shepherds of Bethlehem, who heard the tidings of great joy: with the mothers of Bethlehem who mourned their little ones.

The life of every man is a succession of blessings and of trials. God Himself has mapped out our course, He spares our weakness, but steadily directs us to the goal He has appointed for us. He does not lay burdens on us that are beyond our strength, and when we fail and falter, He is there to raise us up. Our duty is humbly to trust, to accept, to adore the divine Counsel. "Yea Father, thus it has pleased Thee."

Prayer: O Lord, give light to our minds and strength to our hearts, that we may know and firmly believe that "to them that love God, all things work together unto good", and that nothing "shall be able to separate us from Christ Jesus our Lord" (*Rom.* 8: 28, 39).

DECEMBER 29

THE MASTER'S FIRST PUBLIC LESSON

1. We have considered the most profound mystery of the Incarnation, which bridged the gulf between the creature and its Creator; we have also considered the miraculous birth of the Savior from a Virgin Mother. In the present exercise we shall ponder over another marvel. It is not indeed a miracle, by which God shows that He has made nature's laws and has power over them; but a proof that the Wisdom of the Almighty shapes and fashions natural events in order that, as St. Ignatius Loyola says, "God's Son may be born in the utmost poverty". No, it is not a miracle, but the complete upsetting of our human standards of values.

   Reverently we enter the stable of Bethlehem, our Lord's first audience chamber, whither He has summoned His first disciples, the shepherds. This royal hall is bare and devoid of splendor. All the splendor is within.

2. *Petition*: The grace to learn the first lesson of Him, who in this stable began to do and to teach (*Act.* 1, 1).

I. The Decree of Caesar

During nine months, Mary, remembering the angel's words, dwelt at Nazareth in blessed expectation of the event that would bring great joy to all the people. Everything was now ready. But "it came to pass that in those days there went forth a decree of Caesar Augustus that the whole world should be enrolled". This meant that Mary and Joseph were compelled to make a long journey of four days.

"What are ye doing, ye rulers of this world!—Nothing except co-operating with the divine decrees!" The Roman Emperor's whim sets the whole world in motion in order that the Son of God may be born at Bethlehem, as the prophets had foretold.

Shall we dare ask Mary how she felt when unexpectedly she received this most inconvenient imperial order? Would it be to undervalue her holiness to think that it cost her a great deal at this moment to walk by that faith which Elizabeth had praised, and to read God's will in the imperial command? Shall we not see one day that it cost Jesus Himself a struggle to conform His will to that of the Father?

The Fiat, which she spoke to the angel, when she said, "Be it done to me according to thy word", she has repeated ever since, and she repeats it now, though that *word* is uttered not by an angel, but by a gentile ruler. God's Providence permits Caesar's decree; He uses it to fulfill His own counsel. This is God's way with us and with every other man: He makes everything fit into His own plan.

II. In a Stable

At Bethlehem, the city of their father David, "there was no room for them in the inn". Perhaps they might have found room in the public caravanserai, an enclosure with a thatch-covered gallery all round. In the circumstances, that place was not suitable, and therefore, St. Joseph went in search of a more convenient place, and finally they found shelter in a cave that served as a stable for sheep and cattle. There was a crib, which Mary tried her best to transform into a cradle. In this place is to be born "the Son of the Most High, unto whom the Lord shall give the throne of David his father, and of whose kingdom there shall be no end".

In this stable, Mary became a mother, and "brought forth her first-born Son and wrapped him in swaddling clothes, and laid him in a manger". She herself and she alone does all this. As He comes from His Mother's womb, He is laid on a pallet of straw, in a manger! St. Bernard says, "In heaven there was no poverty, but on earth it abounded. He came to seek this poverty; the straw of the manger was the silk and purple He chose for His raiment."

III. A Lesson in Detachment

That was the first lesson which Christ taught us: He Himself chose the subject; His teaching was eloquent, and it was intended for all times and all generations. "You know the grace of our Lord Jesus Christ, that being rich He became poor, for your sakes; that through His poverty you might be rich" (2 *Cor.* 8, 9).

Had Christ been born in a palace, the Incarnation would still have been an "emptying" of Himself, a renunciation of what is divine; and there was no danger lest He should grow inordinately attached to earthly things. But He is the ideal teacher: "He begins to do and to teach." Of Him it will be true that "the Son of man hath not where to lay his head" (*Matt.* 8, 20).

This lesson is meant for all men, and all need it. There are so many eyes in us and so many hooks around us to get caught on. How shall we, men of our time, surrounded by so much comfort, so many pleasures and amenities, how shall we practice detachment? Material progress and technical inventions are not evil; they are good, they can and must contribute to the establishment of God's Kingdom on earth. Even Mary, though truly poor, was not a pauper, and she had and used many things which prehistoric cave-dwellers did without. Detachment is more an internal freedom of the soul, than an external show of beggarliness.

"Sell what thou hast," said Jesus to the youth who had great possessions, and He added "and follow me." Jesus does not preach detachment for its own sake, but because it frees us from earthly bonds, and enables us to cling to God and serve Him perfectly. These were the feelings of St. Paul, when he wrote: "I know both how to be brought low and I know how to abound: (everywhere and in all things I am instructed), both to be full and to be hungry; both to abound and to suffer need. I can do all things in him who strengtheneth me" (*Phil.* 4; 12-13).

Love makes detachment easy; generous detachment enkindles love.

Prayer: O Jesus,, Thou hast come unto us in a most wonderful manner, but we find it so hard to understand Thy word, when Thou biddest us be detached from the world. Thou hast begun by doing. Grant that we fully understand this Thy first lesson, and that we may have the strength to put it into practice and to follow Thy example.

THE PREFACE OF CHRISTMAS TIME

1. We kneel before the manger, by the side of Mary and Joseph, and with wonder gaze at the "Child that is born to us". Our

faith teaches us that in this frail Infant "dwelleth the fullness of the Godhead".

2. *Petition*: We prayerfully meditate on the Preface for Christmas time. "Truly it is fitting and just, right and conducive to salvation, that we should give thanks to Thee, always and in all places, O Holy Lord, Father Almighty, Eternal God; for by the mystery of the Word made man, the Light of Thy glory has shone anew upon the eyes of our souls: so that, as we gaze upon our God in visible form, through Him we are borne to the love of things unseen."

I. The Mystery That Enlightens

This is surely a strange way of speaking: a mystery, a secret, that brings light. A mystery of our faith must ever remain above our understanding. We may try to express it in human language, adduce comparisons, try to show there is no contradiction. But the tremendous inward reality, however much we try to illustrate it in human language and figures, ever remains incomprehensible, hidden, obscure to the intellect.

Such a mystery is the Incarnation of the Word of God. "And the Word was made flesh." It would be impossible to state the mystery more tersely: the union in one Person of the Most High and the most lowly. But it surpasses our understanding *how* the Godhead can dwell in the Child of Mary, who in all things is like unto us.

Out of that unfathomable mystery, a new light shines before the eyes of our soul: a new light proceeding from a source incomparably above our weak, limited intelligence, from the splendor of God, who "is light and in whom there is no darkness" (1 *John* 1, 5) and that new light "has shone anew upon the eyes of our souls", but not yet in its full brightness. "For we see now through a glass in a dark manner" (1 *Cor.* 13, 12), says St. Paul. Our faith gives us the fullest certainty, but not the relish of understanding. Jesus, who is now lying before us in the manger, will say one day, "I am the light of the world; he that followeth me walketh not in darkness, but shall have the light of life" (*John* 8, 12).

II. Revealed, Yet Through a Veil

God has revealed Himself through His creatures, for these are His handiwork. "The heavens show forth the glory of God, and the firmament declareth the work of his hands" (*Ps.* 18, 1). Created things are the Lord's footprints, or the path by which He has passed. A path, or a trail, reveals something in a deficient manner; it is only a sign of what is not there. And thus, as St. Augustine tells us, God is always most present with us, yet ever hidden.

Man was created in God's image and likeness: in him there is more than a mere sign of God's passage. He is endowed with intelligence and free will, which make him God's image, like to God. An image, indeed, but veiled, bearing a distant likeness to God; a likeness, alas, sometimes disfigured.

In the manger He lies, who is "the image of the invisible God" (*Col.* 1, 15); the perfect Image of the Father, whom no man hath ever seen, so perfect that Jesus one day will say, "He that seeth me seeth the Father also" (*John* 14, 9).

Though He is the perfect image of the Father, it is enough to behold the tiny Babe to realize how thick is the veil. "He emptied Himself", divested Himself of His likeness unto God, and He "took the form of a servant", and in habit—that is, outwardly— He appeared as a mere man (*Phil.* 2, 6-7). Here we gaze at the Word of God become a speechless infant. When later He will manifest Himself, His fellow citizense and His brethren will be astounded and will say, "How came this man by all these things? ... Is not this the carpenter, the son of Mary?" (*Mark* 6, 2-3.)

Indeed He is the son of Mary; we adore Him as the Son of the Most High!

III. "Borne to the Love of Things Unseen"

"With the cords of Adam and the bands of love" (*Osee* 11, 4) He draws us to the love of things unseen, being truly God and truly man in one Person. "That which was from the beginning, which we have heard, which we have seen with our eyes, which we have looked upon, and our hands have handled, of the word of life. For we have seen and do bear witness" (1 *John* 1, 1-2).

"For the grace of God our Savior hath appeared to all men, instructing us, that, denying ungodliness ... we should live godly in this world" (*Titus* 2, 11-12). In the Preface we say, "we gaze upon God in visible form"; our eyes behold the Child of Mary; our spirit, illumined by the new light of faith, is borne to the love of things unseen."

In the son of Mary, "born to us, given to us" our faith sees the Lord, and through Him we discover the only straight and safe road to the Father in heaven. 'Therefore, truly it is fitting and just that we should give thanks to Thee.'

Prayer: Grant, we beseech Thee, O Almighty God, that we who are bathed in the new light of the Word made flesh, may reflect in our works the light which by faith glows in our minds. Through our Lord (Collect, Mass at Dawn, Christmas).

DECEMBER 31

TO PRAISE AND TO THANK GOD

1. The ecclesiastical year and the liturgical cycle begin with the first Sunday of Advent; they pay no heed to the civil calendar. However, it behoves us, before we close the current year, sincerely to thank God for all the graces, known and unknown, which He has showered on us during the last twelve months.

2. *Petition*: May we during this meditation prepare ourselves to offer during Holy Mass, fervent thanksgiving to the Heavenly Father through our Lord.

I. Thanksgiving

Whatever is good comes from God, and whatever comes from God is good. Every good thought, every salutary desire of the heart, every good action, has its origin and beginning in God, is His work and has Him as ultimate object. If, as consecrated minister of Christ, it has been our privilege to pass one more year in His service, we should thankfully exclaim with the Psalmist: "Better is one day in thy courts above thousands" (*Ps.* 83, 11).

Whatever comes from God is good: prosperity and adversity, joy and grief, success and failure, trials, blessings, above all trials nobly borne. The Lord uses all these things to sanctify us, to detach us from the world, to free us from chains, to draw us unto Himself. "Everything," said Therese of Lisieux, "is a grace from God." She was asked whether she would gladly die a holy death and answered, "Yes, but if God permits that I depart without the Last Sacraments, then I shall be just as happy; for everything is a grace from God." "Truly it is fitting and just, right and conducive to salvation, for us at all times and in all places, to give thanks to Thee, O Holy Lord."

II. Pardon

When we remember what an abundance of graces God has lavished on us throughout the year, then it seems also fitting and just, right and conducive to salvation, to set against these graces our many acts of cowardice and infidelity in His service, our want of reverence in prayer, our lack of trust in Him, and our remissness in serving our neighbor.

The remembrance of our countless sins and backslidings will not dishearten us; it will rather spur us on to more ardent effort and to renewed generosity. We shall not forget the Lord's mercy, which is ready to forgive till seventy times seven times. We doubt not His goodness and we know that He is patient in our regard. "In his sight we shall persuade our hearts, for if our heart reprehend us, God is greater than our heart, and knoweth all things" (1 *John* 3, 19-20).

"The mercies of the Lord, I will sing forever" (*Ps.* 88, 2).

III. Trust in God

The best way of showing our gratitude to God for past favors, is to give Him our full confidence in regard to the future. No man knows what the new year will bring to each of us individually, and to the world at large. And it is better so. For this uncertainty allows us to pay to God the homage which is most agreeable to Him, and which best fits our condition of frail creatures and of children of the Heavenly Father: childlike trust. "The Lord ruleth me and I shall want nothing . . . for though I should walk in the midst of the shadow of death, I will fear no evil; for thou art with me" (*Ps.* 22: 1, 4). If David could pray thus even before the coming of the Savior, how much more are we entitled to have confidence now, we to whom "the goodness and kindness of God our Savior appeared" (*Tit.* 3, 4).

Truly the world is passing through a severe crisis and there is distress upon the earth, more than at any time in the past; and we tremble with fear and anxiety on the threshold of the new year, when we think of the terrible calamities that threaten us, the Church, the whole of mankind. But we hear Jesus say, "Let not your heart be troubled: you believe in God, believe in Me. Peace I leave with you, my peace I give unto you, not as the world giveth do I give unto you. Let not your heart be troubled nor let it be afraid. . . . Remember the word that I said to you: the servant is not greater than his master; if they have persecuted

me, they will also persecute you. ... These things I have spoken
to you that in me you may have peace. In the world you shall
have distress: but have confidence, I have overcome the world"
(*John*, chap. 14-16).

These were the Savior's last words, when before the Passion,
He bade farewell to the disciples; may they be deeply engraven
on our hearts, then we shall confidently face the future.

Prayer: "O God, whose mercies are without number, and the
treasure of whose goodness is infinite: we render thanks to Thy
Most Gracious Majesty for the gifts Thou hast bestowed upon
us, evermore beseeching Thy clemency; that as Thou dost grant
the petitions of them that ask Thee, so, never forsaking them,
Thou wilt prepare them for the rewards to come. Through our
Lord (*Oremus* of the *Te Deum*).

JANUARY 1

OCTAVE OF THE NATIVITY OF OUR LORD

1. According to the custom of Israel, the Child Jesus was circumcised on the eighth day after birth. Generally this rite was
performed in the house of the parents and, as the Gospels are
silent about the matter, we may suppose that, after a while,
St. Joseph had secured a humble dwelling. He, the "Child
that is born to us," begins to suffer for us.

2. *Petition*: We pray that the year, which begins today, may be
to us really a "year of the Lord", a year entirely spent in His
grace and His service. "One thing I have asked of the Lord;
this will I seek after, that I may dwell in the house of the Lord,
all the days of my life" (*Ps.* 26, 4).

I. Obedience to the Law

Mary and Joseph were devout Jews, and on this occasion,
we see them dutifully fulfilling a precept of the Law. The Child
had been conceived and was born in a wonderful manner, not
foreseen by the Law, *natura mirante*. But for the moment these
things were to remain hidden. "God sent his Son, made of a
woman, made under the law"(*Gal.* 4, 4). "The Holy which was

born of Mary", God had sent "in the likeness of sinful flesh and
of sin" (*Rom.* 8, 3).

As thirty years later Jesus would inaugurate His public ministry
by receiving John's baptism of penance, as if He Himself stood
in need of penance, so now, as a new-born Child, He consents
to be enlisted in the religious and civil society of Israel through
the rite of Circumcision. Mary and Joseph saw no reason why
they should exempt themselves and their Son from this precept
of the Law. Even now they were led by the spirit of Jesus, and
that is a spirit of obedience, submission, modesty, humility.

Mary and Joseph here give us a salutary example. We easily
make pretexts to exempt ourselves from keeping the rules or the
orders of Superiors. We are profoundly convinced that humility
is the foundation of all solid virtue, but we are prone to forget
that genuine humility consists in the practice of ready and
complete obedience.

This is what Mary and Joseph teach us by their example; this
is the lesson given us by Jesus, whose whole life, from the manger
to the cross was one continual act of obedience to His Father.

II. The First Drops of Blood of the Lamb

In her hymn of the Advent Vespers the Church sings:

> *E virginis sacrario*
> *Intacta prodis victima*

> Thou didst issue from the Virgin's shrine
> And to the cross a victim go.

On this occasion our Savior sheds the first drops of that saving
Blood, the last of which will flow from His Heart pierced by the
lance. "In the likeness of sinful flesh and of sin," He was sent
by the Father to redeem us. He took our sins upon Himself that
He might destroy them. "Without shedding of blood there is no
remission" (*Heb.* 9, 22). We remember these words of St. Paul
when we see His Blood flowing. We are saved "pio cruore" says
the Church in her Easter liturgy, "by His Sacred Blood", or
rather "by His Blood that was shed out of great love". In the
same liturgy the Church utters this cry of wonder: "O admirable
lavishing of Thy goodness to us! O untold excess of love, that
to redeem a slave Thou hast delivered Thy Son."

III. Circumcision of the Spirit

The rite of Circumcision, still practiced by the Jews, was abolished in the new Covenant and replaced by Baptism. Baptism is no mere outward rite, but a Sacrament ordained by Christ; an outward sign indeed, accompanied by divinely ordained words, which, in virtue of Christ's institution, cleanses the soul and bestows on it a new and supernatural life. This Sacrament imprints its seal or mark on the soul making us "a chosen generation, a kingly priesthood, a holy nation, a purchased people" (1 *Peter* 2, 9). These privileges are bestowed on us not because of our common race or origin; they flow from our incorporation into the Mystical Body of Him, who purchased us and redeemed us in His Blood.

The seal of Baptism is so deeply impressed in the soul that nothing can efface it; it is at the same time a principle of life, which, through faith and love, must spur us on to lead in all things a Christlike life.

About the Old Covenant St. Paul said, "For ... he is not a Jew who is so outwardly ... but he is a Jew that is one inwardly; and the circumcision is that of the heart, in the spirit, not in the letter" (*Rom.* 2, 28-29). With greater reason may we say that he alone is a true Christian, who has been "inwardly" baptized, who with Christ is dead to sin, and who with Christ has risen unto holiness.

In the Epistle of the Mass of this day we read what the circumcision of the heart consists in. We must "deny ungodliness and worldly desires; we should live soberly and justly, and godly in this world" (*Titus* 2, 12).

If by God's grace we are in the religious state, then let us apply the Apostle's words to our vocation: he is not a religious that lives in a monastery. The true religious is he whose heart is in his calling; who is a religious according to the spirit and not according to the letter, who is faithful to that spiritual circumcision which consists in the faithful observance of the vows. If we live thus, we shall find joy and peace in Christ, and the new year will be happy and salutary.

Prayer: "We who have been admitted to Thy holy Banquet, O Lord, have joyfully drunk from their source the waters of our Savior: grant, we pray, that His Blood may be for us a spring of water gushing forth to eternal life. Who liveth and reigneth ... (Postcommunion, Mass of the Precious Blood).

THE HOLY NAME OF JESUS (Luke 2, 21)

1. All the titles by which the prophets had called the Messiah have fallen into disuse; and now we generally call Him "Jesus", a name not given Him by man but by God Himself, through the mouth of an angel. "And thou shalt call his name Jesus."

   During His public ministry they called Him "Jesus of Nazareth" or "Jesus, the Son of Mary". "And Pilate wrote a title also and he put it upon the cross, and the writing was: Jesus of Nazareth, the King of the Jews."

2. *Petition*: The grace always to pronounce the sweet Name of Jesus with due reverence; the grace to die with that Name on our lips, "for there is no other name under heaven . . . whereby we must be saved" (*Act.* 4, 12).

I. Given by God Himself

The sweet Name of Jesus was given by the Father to His Son made man, even before He had been conceived. For St. Luke writes: "And after eight days were accomplished, that the child should be circumcised, his name was called Jesus, which was called by the angel, before he was conceived in the womb"(2, 21). Mary had been the first to hear this Name from the lips of the angel. The next to hear it was St. Joseph, when the angel said to him, "And thou shalt call his name Jesus; for he shall save his people from their sins" (*Matt.* 1, 21). St. Joseph, being the head of the Holy Family, had the privilege to give the Child its name.

When St. John the Baptist was circumcised, wonderful things had happened with regard to the imposition of a name. "And all they that heard them laid them up in their heart, saying: What a one, think ye, shall this child be?" (*Luke* 1, 66).

This very question must have struck Mary and Joseph with regard to Jesus, their Son. The angel had said, "He shall be great, and shall be called the Son of the Most High, and the Lord God shall give unto him the throne of David his father" (*Luke* 1, 32). And to Mary and Joseph, "He shall save his people from their sins." How all this was to happen had not been revealed to them as yet. "But Mary kept all these words, pondering them in her heart" (*Luke* 2, 19). Mary believed and her trust was in God.

II. Meaning of the Holy Name

The Name Jesus literally means "the Lord saves" and is a reminder of God's love. In the Old Covenant, God had chosen the mysterious name of Jahve, which signifies "He that is", and which the Jews dared not even pronounce. But "God in these days hath spoken to us by his Son" (*Heb.* 1, 2), giving him the name Jesus, that is, Savior.

A name, given by God Himself, is not a mere symbol or a shadow; it reveals a reality that never fails: He shall deliver us from sin, He shall be our Savior! "For God so loved the world, as to give his only-begotten Son; that whosoever believeth in Him may not perish, but may have life everlasting" (*John* 3, 16).

The power of that Name: Many a time Jesus said to His disciples: "If you ask the Father anything in My name, He will give it you" (*John* 16, 23). In the name of Jesus, Peter wrought his first great miracle at the Beautiful Gate of the temple, when he said, "Silver and gold I have none; but what I have, I give thee. In the name of Jesus Christ of Nazareth, arise, and walk. And taking him by the right hand, he lifted him up, and forthwith his feet and soles received strength" (*Act.* 3, 6-7).

St. Paul wrote to the Philippians: "For which cause, God also hath exalted him, and hath given him a name, which is above all names; that in the name of Jesus every knee should bow, of those that are in heaven, on earth, and under the earth; and that every tongue should confess that the Lord Jesus Christ is in the glory of God the Father" (2, 9-11).

III. Reverence and Love

In the East, more than elsewhere, a person's name symbolizes the person himself. It seems natural to us to transfer to a person's name the affection and the reverence we have for the person; and it happens not seldom that the people's love and admiration results in strange alterations of names.

During the Middle Ages, when people loved to express their devotion in feeling words, the Name of Jesus became the "Sweet Name of Jesus". Thus they manifested their tender love for Christ, who was "their Beloved Lord". He is our Savior and we know what it has cost Him to deliver us. To utter His Sacred Name again and again, fills a grateful and loving heart with transporst of delight. "His Name", said St. Bernard, "is honey to our lips, music to our ears and purest joy to our hearts."

It is meet that we utter with reverence that mighty Name, which puts Satan to flight; when in choir or at the altar the priest pronounces this name he reverently bows his head.

"For there is no other name under heaven given to man, whereby we must be saved" (*Act.* 4, 12). The last words in the Sacred Scriptures are: "Come, Lord Jesus." May they be the last words we speak on earth!

Prayer: Fill us, O Lord, with a lasting love as well as fear of Thy Holy Name, for we shall never be deprived of Thy guidance, if Thou hast thoroughly trained us in Thy love. Through our Lord (Collect, 2nd Sunday after Pentecost).

JANUARY 3

"DO ALL IN THE NAME OF THE LORD" (Col. 3, 17)

1. Writing to the Colossians from his Roman prison, St. Paul urges them to lead holy lives in Christ. "All whatsoever you do in word or in work, do all in the name of the Lord Jesus Christ, giving thanks to God and to the Father by him" (*Col.* 3, 17).

2. *Petition*: That we may feel the joy of living in the Lord, and of doing all things in the name of Jesus, for His glory.

I. In the Name of Jesus

Compare these words with those of St. Paul "in Christ", which occur 164 times in the Epistles of the Apostle of the Gentiles. He lives in Christ, ever intent on pleasing Him, offering all things to Him, loving Him in all things and in all men; feeling continually united with Him, he acts and speaks in the spirit of Christ, by the grace of Christ, fulfilling the will of Christ, in the Name of Christ.

To men and women, parents and children, slaves and masters, St. Paul commands: "Whatsoever you do, do it from the heart, as to the Lord, and not to men" (*Col.* 3 23).

A Christian must live and sanctify his whole life in the Name of Jesus. Would to God that this ideal were ever present before our mind. All things, sin excepted, have a meaning in Christ and

can be sanctified in His Name. "Therefore whether you eat or
drink, or whatsoever else you do, do all to the glory of God"
(1 *Cor.* 10, 31). He alone understands the meaning of a true Christian life, who regards it as a continual renovation from within;
not merely as the performance of precepts imposed from without.
"Whatsoever you do, do it with your whole heart, do it in the
Name of Jesus, to the glory of God."

II. "Gathered Together in His Name"

Where there are two or three gathered together in my name,
there am I in the midst of them" (*Matt.* 18, 20). We have been
gathered, united in Him with one another, through Baptism,
which to us was a new birth and made us members of Christ's
Mystical Body; we have been gathered together through Holy
Communion, where we are all seated at the same table, and partake of the same Bread. At the Holy Table our union in Him and
in His Flesh finds its clearest manifestation, and its daily food.

If we are religious, then we are in a very special manner
gathered in His Name: "And every one that hath left house, or
brethren, or sisters, or father, or mother, or wife, or children,
or lands, for my name's sake, shall receive a hundredfold, and
shall possess life everlasting" (*Matt.* 19, 29). Surely here those
other words of our Lord may be applied: "Where there are two
or three gathered together in my name, there am I in the midst
of them" (*Matt.* 18, 20). In a religious community the spirit of
Christ should live in every member and should govern all things,
for "the love of Christ hath made us one".

III. To Work and to Suffer in the Name of Jesus

All work—above all a work of mercy—must be done in the
name of Jesus. "And taking a child he set him in the midst of
them; whom when he had embraced he saith to them, Whosoever shall receive one such child as this in my name receiveth
me. And whosoever shall receive me, receiveth not me but him
that sent me" (*Mark* 9, 35-36). "And whosoever shall give to
drink to one of these little ones a cup of cold water only in the
name of a disciple, amen, I say to you, he shall not lose his reward" (*Matt.* 10, 42).

Performing miracles and driving out devils are also done in the
Name of Jesus. But Jesus loved to point to small things, which

in the eyes of the world are of little account, and which therefore are done in His Name with a purer intention, as for instance, when He praised the poor widow that had cast two mites in the treasury (*Mark* 12, 42).

Let this bring comfort to the hearts of so many dedicated men and women who, filled with the true spirit of Jesus, consecrate their lives to the service of the poor, the humble, the little ones, "the least of His brethren".

But whether it be God's will that our light be put under a bushel, or that it be rather put on a candlestick; whether our labors be known to men and approved by them or hidden from the eyes of the many, let us do all things in the Name of Jesus and for God's glory.

It is the lot of some to glorify Jesus' name by toil and labor, while others serve Him by patient suffering. "And you shall be hated by all men for my name's sake" (*Matt.* 10, 22), said the Lord. When after the resurrection the Twelve began to preach the Name of Jesus, they were summoned before the Council, and the High Priests, after they had scourged them, charged them that they should not speak at all in the Name of Jesus. "And they indeed went from the presence of the council, rejoicing that they were accounted worthy to suffer reproach for the name of Jesus" (*Act.* 5, 41).

If ever it happens that, for the Name of Christ, we have to bear insult or contempt let us rejoice at these little trials. It is exhilarating to suffer for Him! Let us remember the thousands of steadfast disciples of Jesus, who at this moment endure false accusations, imprisonment, torture, every sort of indignity, because they are loyal to Jesus. We pray that He may console and strengthen them, whose bitter Passion they share, and for whose Name they are ready to suffer and to die.

Prayer: O Jesus, Thy holy Name is all glory and grace, all love and strength. O sweetest of Names, Thou art the refuge of the penitent, the standard that leads us in the spiritual struggle, the strength of our souls. Thou art healing balm to the sufferer, comfort to the believer, light to the preacher, reward to the laborer, help of the sick. Thou art the object of our devotion, the answer to our petitions, the sweetness of our prayer; Thou, O Holy Name of Jesus, art the glory of the Saints forever and ever (St. Bernardine of Siena).

JANUARY 4

TO PRAY IN THE NAME OF JESUS

(John 14: 13, 14; 15:7; 16:24)

We can do all things in the Name of Jesus, above all we can pray in His Name.

1. In His moving farewell discourse after the Last Supper, Jesus again and again exhorts the disciples to pray to the Father in His Name. He assures them that, whatever they ask the Father in His Name, the Father will give them. During Holy Mass nearly every prayer ends with the words: Through our Lord.

2. *Petition*: The grace to understand better the role of our Lord in the mystery of our redemption and to place our whole trust in Him as our sole Mediator.

I. "Ask the Father in My Name"

It is significant that Jesus does not urge the disciples to address their petitions to Himself; they must ask the Father: "Amen, amen I say to you; if you ask the Father anything in my name, he will give it you. Hitherto, you have not asked anything in my name. Ask and you shall receive; that your joy may be full" (*John* 16, 23-24).

It is equally significant that prayer, addressed to the Father in His Name, is heard by Him, as much as by the Father, for "I and the Father are one" (*John* 10, 30). "I go to the Father; and whatever you shall ask the Father in my name, that will I do: that the Father may be glorified in the Son" (*John* 14, 13).

Asking the Father in His name does not mean primarily that we trust in the merits of Christ Our Lord, and appeal to them; it means specially that we are His disciples and "abide in Him," filled with His spirit continuing His redemptive work, and that we ask what is pleasing to Him. How could we dare ask in His name something that is not pleasing to Jesus? Whenever we ask a favor from the Father in the Name of Jesus, there is always this condition, explicit or implied, "if this be the good pleasure of our Lord". What pleases Him is best!

II. So Prays Holy Church

The Church lives by His spirit, "abiding in Jesus, and Jesus in her". She is the Bride, He the Bridegroom, and Mediator with the Father. She concludes all her liturgical prayers with, Through our Lord Jesus Christ, Thy Son. This consecrated formula is really an abbreviation, which should be completed thus: This we ask from Thee, O Father, through our Lord Jesus Christ, Thy Son. For Christ hath an everlasting priesthood, whereby He is able also to save forever them that come to God by Him, always living to make intercession for us" (*Heb.* 7, 24-25).

As Intercessor, or Mediator, He is very close both to the Father and to us. He is our Lord and we are His entirely, redeemed by Him, that is, bought with His Blood; He is Jesus, that is, our Savior; He is Christ, that is, our anointed High Priest before the Father; He is the Son of the Father.

Whatever the Church asks the Father for her children, be it bodily or spiritual health, peace, protection, progress in virtue, good weather—the petition is always through Christ our Lord. Whenever she offers solemn thanks to "the Lord, to the Father on High, to the Almighty Eternal Creator", still it is "through Christ our Lord".

In her Eucharistic prayer and sacrifice the Church feels most united with Christ; she speaks and acts in His Name, and offers Him together with herself a pure oblation to the Eternal Father. At this moment above all, the Church implores and thanks the Father in the Name of Jesus for all men and for all things.

III. That We Might Pray in That Manner

The closer we come to Jesus, the more truly we live by His spirit, the more we "ask in His Name"—so much more will our prayer be an act of pure worship of God, so much more ardently will it plead for the spread of the Kingdom and the salvation of souls. The prayer which is easiest to pray in His Name is the Lord's Prayer, His own prayer, which He Himself taught us. The first part comprises what Jesus Himself asks from the Father. Hallowed be Thy Name, Thy Kingdom come, Thy Will be done on earth as it is in heaven! These are His own petitions, which, in His Name, we address to the Father.

The second part asks the Father for things, that Christ has no need of, but of which we sorely are in want: when we ask them from the Father, we ask in His Name, according to His spirit, in the very words He placed on our lips. We beg that our temporal needs may be provided for, that our sins may be pardoned, and that we may be delivered from all evil. Since St. Paul tells us that "We know not what we should pray for as we ought" (*Rom.* 8, 26), let us try and pray as Jesus prayed; let us make the Lord's prayer our own. It contains abundant treasures of spiritual joy and grace for the soul that has learnt to pray in the Name of Jesus.

Prayer: Our Father, who art in heaven. . . .

JANUARY 5

BETHLEHEM, THE PALACE OF PEACE

1. We kneel before the Child Jesus, whom Mary holds on her lap. We adore the Prince of Peace, and greet Mary, the Queen of Peace.

2. *Petition*: The grace to enjoy true peace in our hearts, and to spread it around us.

I. The Palace of Peace

God Himself has chosen it, and here peace between heaven and earth has been sealed. It is not a palace built by man: in such a palace Herod keeps his court in Jerusalem. Heaven has carefully prepared all the circumstances that will attend the inauguration of this peace: a stable, a manger, an Infant wrapped in swaddling clothes, a humble carpenter and his wife, so poor that there was no room for them in the inn; there is also a small group of shepherds . . . and the cave is all dark and damp.

God is wonderful in His works; but here we fail to comprehend His ways; everything here goes counter to our human standards. We are in admiration.

We adore the Prince of Peace.

II. Peace Between Heaven and Earth

A peace treaty is inscribed on a parchment, or engraved on bronze or granite. Sheets of parchment, bronze plates and granite tablets are perishable material. Of shorter duration still is the peace engraved on them.

Very different is the peace bestowed on us at Bethlehem: this peace is a pure gift of God, who, at His own initiative, grants it to us out of infinite love and mercy. His own Son, made man, is the living tablet on which this peace is engraved, or rather our peace and reconciliation are made tangible in His Son, in the Lamb of God that taketh away the sins of the world. One day the most precious Blood of the Lamb will seal our peace.

> Thou, for the sake of guilty men,
> Permitting Thy pure Blood to flow
> Didst issue from Thy Virgin shrine
> And to the cross a victim go. *Creator Alme Siderum*

III. The Authors of Our Peace

The three Persons of the Blessed Trinity are the Authors of our peace: The Father sends His Son; the Son says, "Behold I come . . . that I should do thy will, O my God" (*Ps.* 39, 8-9); the Holy Ghost who came upon Mary and in her womb fashions the Body of the Word of God. Mary's role in establishing this peace is subordinate, but profoundly real. After her consent the Son of God descends on earth saying, "Sacrifice and oblation thou wouldst not; but a body thou hast fitted me" (*Heb.* 10, 5).

We greet Mary:

> O Gate, through which hath passed the King,
> O Hall, whence Light shone through the gloom;
> The ransomed nations praise and sing
> Life given from the Virgin womb. *O Gloriosa, Lauds*

IV. The Heralds of Our Peace

God's angels were the first heralds of our peace. They announced it to the shepherds (*Luke* 2, 9-14). Heaven and earth are reconciled; the chasm that yawned between God and man has been bridged. "Today true peace has come down to us from Heaven; this day Heaven overflows with honey over the whole world" (Responsory of Christmas).

Peace on earth to men of good will! God is the giver of peace and He offers it to all men, on one condition: that we be of good will; that humbly and gratefully we accept the peace that is offered us. If we do that, we give glory to God in the highest, and possess in our hearts "that peace which the world can neither give nor snatch away".

Prayer: I will hear what the Lord God will speak to me, for he will speak peace . . . and unto his saints, and unto them that are converted to the heart. Surely his salvation is near to them that fear him: that glory may dwell in our land. Mercy and truth have met each other; justice and peace have kissed. Truth is sprung out of the earth; and justice hath looked down from heaven. For the Lord will give goodness; and our earth shall yield her fruit. Justice shall walk before him; and shall set his steps in the way (*Ps.* 84, 9-14).

JANUARY 6

THE EPIPHANY OF OUR LORD—I (Matt. 2, 1-12)

1. The Greek word "Epiphany" means manifestation or revelation. The birth of Christ, which we commemorate on the 25th of December, is the manifestation of the Lord to His own people; this day we remember His revelation to the Gentiles, whom the Wise Men from the East represent. . . . In today's canonical office two other manifestations of Jesus are alluded to: His Baptism in the Jordan, with which Jesus inaugurated His public ministry, and the miracle at Cana, of which the Gospel says, "This beginning of miracles did Jesus in Cana of Galilee and manifested his glory" (*John* 2, 11).
Christian art has revelled in the representation of the adoration by the Wise Men. It may be better for us to see the event in a simpler setting: no royal train but a poor man's dwelling, the Child on Mary's lap, the Wise Men adoring Him.

2. *Petition*: That enlightened by faith and filled with love, we may, with the Wise Men, discover beneath the lowliness, the sublimity of the mystery.

I. The Call of the Wise Men

"He lies in a manger, while He shines in the heavens" says the liturgy about the new-born Savior. The shepherds had been summoned by angels to go and adore Him; a star had appeared in the heavens to lead the Wise Men of the East to His cradle. They may have been learned men from Arabia or Persia, where star-gazing was greatly practiced. Tradition says they were three, but the only reason seems to be that the Gospel mentions three kinds of gifts presented by them. They had seen the apparition of a new star in the firmament, and to these devout souls this was a token that, far away in the land of the Jews, a King had been born. According to the custom prevailing in the East, they felt a strong desire to go and pay homage to this Prince.

These are mere surmises, for the whole event is shrouded in mystery. God is greater than our hearts and our minds.

The Lord has many means to enter our lives and to manifest Himself unto us. He is often pleased to employ those means that are specially suited to a person's character and occupations. Mostly, God's inspirations and the prompting of His grace are not accompanied by noise and bustle, and it depends greatly on our personal dispositions whether we notice them and obey them. When our soul is free from carnal attachments, when we truly desire to know and follow God's will, we shall readily heed His inspirations and the calls of His grace. "Speak, Lord, for thy servant heareth" (1 *Kings* 3, 9).

II. The Journey of the Wise Men

They leave their homes without knowing whither the star beckons them nor how long the journey will last, nor what awaits them in the end. The star was their guide and they firmly hoped that they would not be disappointed; they followed its course, through the dreary sands of the desert, into Judea, till Jerusalem. And then the star disappeared.

Quite naturally they thought that here they would find the newly born King, obviously in the royal palace. But Herod, the jealous old tyrant, "was troubled and all Jerusalem with him", and "assembling together all the chief priests and the scribes of the people, he inquired of them where Christ should be born. But they said to him, In Bethlehem of Juda.... Then Herod, privately calling the wise men, learned diligently of them the time of the star which appeared to them; and sending them into Bethlehem said, Go and diligently inquire after the child, and when you have found him, bring me word again that I also may come and adore him" (*Matt.* 2, 4-8).

We may find here much matter for devout meditation: how vain are all the wiles and precautions of Herod; how blind, notwithstanding all their learning, are the scribes and chief priests; how God bends them all to be His instruments in assisting the Wise Men and leading them to their goal!

III. The Reward of the Wise Men

Their faith did not falter when the star vanished and when no one in Jerusalem seemed to have heard about the new King, whom they had come to seek. Even now, when extraordinary help failed them, they did whatever was in their power to reach their destination. Their reward came quickly: "Behold, the star which they had seen in the East went before them, until it came and stood over where the child was. And seeing the star they rejoiced with exceeding great joy. And entering into the house, they found the child with Mary his mother. And falling down they adored him" (*Matt.* 2, 9-11).

The Lord had led them in a most wonderful manner. With them we adore the King.

Prayer: O God who, having guided them by a star, on this day didst manifest Thine only-begotten Son to the Gentiles; mercifully grant that we, who by faith already have knowledge of Thee, may be brought also to the full vision of Thy beauteous Majesty. Through our Lord (Collect, Mass of Epiphany).

JANUARY 7

THE EPIPHANY OF OUR LORD—II

1. On Christmas Day the Church commemorates our Lord's manifestation in the poverty and silence of the stable, with a small band of humble shepherds kneeling before the manger. On this 6th of January we remember another manifestation, when the Wise Men came from the distant regions of the Gentiles, to pay homage to the new-born King and to adore Him. The humble cottage above which the star stood still was not a palace, and whatever they saw bespoke poverty and humility; but beneath these lowly externals their faith beheld the divine reality. In the same way today's liturgy looks beyond what is humble and lowly, and proclaims the world-wide effects of this "Manifestation". Every text in the Mass speaks of power and glory.

2. *Petition*: That our faith may pierce the surface of things, and see the Lord's hand in the humdrum happenings of our own

lives, as well as in the great events that shake the world. May we see God in all things.

I. The Lord and Ruler Is Coming

The very first words of the Introit of the Mass strike a lofty note: "See the Lord and Ruler, He is coming armed with royal power and dominion." He has proved that He is truly the Lord and the Ruler, whom heaven and earth obey: angels have heralded His birth, and a star has summoned to His cradle Wise Men of the East and guided them to Bethlehem; the Roman Emperor has set in motion the mighty machine of world-dominion, that the prophecy might be fulfilled, which announced that the Messiah was to be born in Bethlehem. Does the entire universe revolve round this child?

"Keeping this most holy day when Thy sole-begotten Son, co-eternal with Thee in the same glory, hath visibly appeared, clothed with our mortal flesh" (*Communicantes*) together with the Wise Men we pay Thee homage and adore Thee.

II. Peoples and Kings Pay Homage

In the Epistle of the Mass we read about the glorious vision of the prophet Isaias: with transports of joy Isaias sees the return of Israel after the Babylonian captivity, and he consoles the deserted city of Jerusalem, "Arise, be enlightened, O Jerusalem: for thy light is come, and the glory of the Lord is risen upon thee ... And the Gentiles shall walk in thy light, and kings in the brightness of thy rising. Lift up thy eyes round about and see: all these are gathered together, they are come to thee. . . ." (*Isa.* 60, 1-4.)

Further still the prophet beholds the triumph of the true Jerusalem, of the Church, of the Kingdom of God, which this Child will establish. The Wise Men are the first among the Gentiles to see the Light shining in the darkness, and they have hurried to Jerusalem, they are the vanguard of the nations, and the first kings that, throughout the centuries, have come to adore the Savior.

III. The Prince of This World at Work

While the Wise Men adore the Child, and offer their symbolic gifts, an unscrupulous potentate entertains murderous designs against this supposed rival. The Scribes are aware that the Messiah is to be born in Bethlehem, but what they hear from the Wise Men leaves them indifferent: they will not go to Bethlehem. Years later they will obstinately refuse to acknowledge Him, and treat Him as an enemy, demand that He suffer the penalty of the cross. But He will rise and conquer them and the world. "The prince of the world shall be cast out" (*John* 12, 31), Jesus will say, before He Himself was cast out—forever they imagined— by the minions of the prince of the world. But He, if He be lifted up from the earth (on the cross) will draw all things unto Himself (*John* 12, 32).

In our own days we behold this same battle being fought fiercely on the one side between the prince of the world, whom Jesus has cast out but whom his evil angels ever try to bring in again, and on the other, the Ruler "whose Kingdom is not of this world", but is to be established and propagated through struggle and suffering.

What the prophet saw in vision has come true in the course of the centuries. "The gentiles shall walk in thy light and kings in the brightness of thy rising" (*Isa.* 60, 3).

How in ages still to come the prophet's vision will be further realized is a secret, not known to us, but known by the little Child on Mary's lap: He is the Lord and Ruler, the King of kings, "the Kingdom is in His hand, and power and dominion". Our eyes behold a little Child, our faith sees Him who shall reign in the house of Jacob forever. Why should we fear or doubt? "Whatever is born of God overcometh the world. And this is the victory, which overcometh the world, our faith" (1 *John* 5, 4).

Prayer: Grant, we beseech Thee, Almighty God, that the manifestation which we have celebrated in solemn festival, may be realized also within our souls, purified from sin. Through our Lord (Postcommunion).

JANUARY 8

VIRTUES PRACTICED BY THE WISE MEN

1. For a long while the Wise Men remain prostrate before the King and His Mother, their hearts full of joy and gratitude. We admire the wonderful manner in which God has led them

to Bethlehem. They have followed the divine guidance, and co-operated with God's grace.

2. *Petition*: May we too, following their example, allow ourselves to be led by God's grace. May we faithfully tread the path of virtue, even if for a while the star disappears.

I. In the Beginning

We ought to remember two things: these Wise Men were godly men, and, God had given them a sign.

We know very little about them, just what is related in the Gospel: suddenly they emerge from the darkness, they hold the center of the stage for a moment, and then they vanish, never to appear again. For centuries there were in the East learned men who were given to the observation of the heavenly bodies; from the movements of the stars they hoped to learn about future events. We may rightly suppose that this new bright star had been noticed by others, but only these men read in it a sign from heaven, and an intimation that the great King had been born. God alone knows why they, and they alone, were privileged to understand this. Possibly the reason was that they were godly men, "men of good will", righteous, intent on serving God according to their lights, ready to follow the divine guidance.

To them this star was a heavenly sign that in the land of the Jews a new King had been born, not an ordinary prince, but the anointed of the Lord. Led by the star, they will go and adore Him.

God is with us always, discreetly guiding us with His grace, but we must be ready to heed His promptings. A vocation, natural or supernatural, generally has its beginnings in a gentle whisper in the soul. If silence and recollection reign in that soul, and if the heart is ready to accept God's grace when offered, the whisper will be heeded, and God may speak again and bestow further graces. Our disposition should ever be that of little Samuel, when he said, "Speak, Lord, for thy servant heareth" (1 *Kings* 3, 9).

II. With and Without the Star

As long as the star pointed the way, they felt secure, even though they did not know whither it would lead them; every morning they set out with new courage, further away from home, but closer to God. The Gospel does not tell us when and where the star disappeared, though we may surmise that this happened when they were close to Jerusalem. If they thought that they had reached the goal, and that the new King had been born in the capital, they must have been amazed when they found that no one had heard about the birth of a prince in the house of King Herod. The star had vanished, but their faith remained unshaken; therefore, in the absence of extraordinary help from above, they had recourse to the human means that were at their disposal, and made inquiries where they hoped to find further information. They made honest efforts, and were not discouraged when they discovered that Herod was troubled and all the city with him. The scribes appeared to have some information, but were not interested, and definitely determined to stay at home. At last, when they had gathered what information they could they departed; but no sooner had they left Jerusalem than the star appeared again; and "they rejoiced with exceeding great joy" (*Matt.* 2, 10). Though they had never yielded to doubt, the disappearance of the star had been a severe trial; but now the star shone again, and they knew that they had acted rightly when the Lord tried them, and that the goal of their long and weary journey was in sight. They "rejoiced with exceeding great joy".

Here we receive salutary lessons, useful to all those who, in the midst of perils and temptations, seek the way to God; those above all to whom the Lord has shown the star of a religious or priestly vocation, can learn from the Wise Men that God may try them, but will never forsake them. They should be grateful for the light God is pleased to give them here and now; even if they fail to see "the distant scene", that is, what God may ask in future. Let us pray as Cardinal Newman prayed, when the surrounding gloom seemed to hide the path from his view:

> Lead kindly Light, lead Thou me on,
> Keep Thou my feet; I do not ask to see
> The distant scene; one step enough for me.

Even without a star, that is, without extraordinary light and special consolation, which God frequently vouchsafes to beginners, we must persevere, and ever struggle forward towards the goal that beckons us on. At such times it is good to seek counsel from those whose office it is to guide us; and let us pray with greater fervor, especially to Mary, Star of the Sea.

> Hail, Queen of Heav'n, the Ocean Star,
> Guide of the wanderer here below.

III. Till They Find Jesus

The star did not vanish again but stood "over where the child was". Then they knew they had reached the end of their journey, "and entering the house, they found the child with Mary his mother".

They "had seen his star in the East" and now they behold Him in person. Their faith does not falter. This little Child, so frail and so lowly, has summoned them, has guided their steps, has shown them a sign in the heavens, and has endowed them with unshakable faith. They behold Him, and "falling down they adored him". Mary showed them Jesus, the Fruit of her womb.

O Holy Mother, when our star comes to a standstill in the heavens, be pleased to show us too the Fruit of thy womb.

Prayer: O God who, having guided them by a star, on this day didst manifest Thine only-begotten Son to the Gentiles: mercifully grant that we, who by faith already have knowledge of Thee, may be brought also to the full vision of Thy beauteous Majesty. Through our Lord (Collect, Mass of Epiphany).

JANUARY 9

"THEY OFFERED HIM GIFTS"

1. After they had adored Him, they offered Him their gifts. This scene is one of those most dearly loved by Christian painters, attracted more by royal state, and pomp, and splendor than by hidden intimacy. In reality things must have happened simply enough: it is probable that Mary, who held her Son on her lap, was a little perturbed when the Wise Men entered her modest little house.

    The visitors bring forward their gifts, precious objects for which their country is famed, and which caravans go to seek in their land: gold, frankincense and myrrh. They offer them to Mary, and through her to Jesus. (St. Joseph, who is never absent from the pictures, is not mentioned in the Gospel.)

2. *Petition*: The grace to admire and understand the ways of divine Providence. Show us, O Lord, what gifts we shall offer Thee together with the sacrifice of the cross.

I. Gold Offered to the King

Gold is the most precious metal, and the symbol of the highest virtue, love. No gift is too precious if it is to be offered to the King. But gold, and love, must be absolutely genuine; we will offer neither alloy, nor mere outward gilding.

Gold and love differ in this: gold is not within reach of every man and only the rich have it; whilst love, above all divine love, is given to every man. We have not to earn it, for we have received it from God's bounty in Baptism. "The charity of God is poured forth in our hearts, by the Holy Ghost, who is given to us" (*Rom.* 5, 5). And, "in this is charity, not as though we had loved God, but because he hath first loved us". Let us therefore love God, because God hath first loved us" (1 *John* 4: 10, 19). God will always have the better of us, for our love can never be anything else but a return of love, our gifts no more than the offering of what we have received from Him.

Let the gold of our love be absolutely pure, free from all alloy of self-love. We must generously and patiently pass it through the crucible, or better still, God Himself will cast it into the crucible of trial and suffering, to refine it until it is absolutely pure.

There is another difference between gold and love: for centuries men sought for the philosophers' stone, that would turn all metals into gold; they never found it. But love does transform what is mean and of little value into pure gold. The two mites of the widow were worth more than all the gold in the pharisee's purse. "These people honor me with the gold of their purses, but their hearts are far from me!"

II. Frankincense Offered to God

Among most nations incense is the symbol of worship, a "sacrifice of agreeable odor" offered to the deity alone. In the early centuries legions of Christians preferred to shed their blood rather than offer incense to idols.

Incense, cast on the fire burns and fills the entire church with its fragrant aroma. "Let my prayer be directed as incense in thy sight", sings the Psalmist (140), and the priest at High Mass repeats these words as he incenses the altar. Without fire the grains of incense remain hard and emit no fragrance; in the same way, without love, in our hearts our noblest aspirations are cold and earthly, and neither honor God nor warm the soul. If we want to learn how to pray, then let us say "Come, Holy Ghost, fill the hearts of Thy faithful, and kindle in them the fire of Thy Love" (Sequence, Mass of Pentecost).

III. Myrrh Offered to the Humanity of Christ

Myrrh, an aromatic substance, was used among other things, for the embalming of dead bodies. Many Fathers of the Church and mystic writers are of opinion that this gift of the Wise Men alluded to the Passion and Death of the Savior. We read in the Gospel: "And Nicodemus also came ... bringing a mixture of myrrh and aloes. . . . They took therefore the body of Jesus, and bound it in linen clothes, with the spices, as the manner of the Jews is to bury" (*John* 19, 39-40). It is immaterial whether the Wise Men had been enlightened about the tragic death that was in store for the King they had come to adore: the Church, and we too, her faithful children, see all things in the light of the cross. Nothing will enkindle love in our hearts so readily as the remembrance of the sufferings this Child will endure for love for us; and nothing will give us greater courage to have a share in His redemptive passion.

Myrrh, frankincense, gold, are three precious substances, the symbols of three closely connected gifts of God: love, prayer and suffering.

Prayer: We implore Thee, O Lord, to look with favor on the gifts of Thy Church, which are no longer gold, frankincense and myrrh; for He, whom these gifts symbolized, is now offered in sacrifice and received in Communion, Jesus Christ, Thy Son our Lord (Secret of today's Mass).

JANUARY 10

THE ADORATION OF THE MAGI—MARY'S PLACE

(Matt. 2, 11)

1. The Gospel is always concise, and it refers all things to Jesus; it says nothing about the thoughts and feelings of Mary, when she received this wonderful, and wholly unexpected visit of the Wise Men of the East. We may try to understand these feelings, which she pondered in her heart.

2. *Petition*: Greater love and reverence for the Mother of God, and deeper trust in her powerful intercession.

I. "They Found the Child With Mary, His Mother"

When the shepherds came to adore the Savior in the manger, the presence of St. Joseph is explicitly mentioned by St. Luke. When the Wise Men adore Christ, St. Matthew simply says, "They found the Child with Mary, His mother." It was not necessary to mention Joseph, but Mary's name could not be omitted. Without His Mother this Child would not be thinkable, and without her we would not be able to find Him!

When the Wise Men entered the house, "they found the Child with Mary," they saluted His Mother, and praised her, "and falling down they adored him". Mary, holding Jesus in her lap, gazed with wonder at these distinguished pilgrims, absorbed in prayer at the feet of her Child, and she praised God for the great things He had done to her. After the Wise Men had adored the King, and offered Him their gifts, they entered into conversation with Mary, and told her about their journey and about the star. St. Luke, who is always anxious to tell us all he knows about the Blessed Virgin, says that, on the occasion of the adoration of the shepherds, "all that heard wondered; and at those things that were told them by the shepherds. But Mary kept all these words, pondering them in her heart" (2, 18-19). On this occasion Mary does the same.

Perhaps our childish curiosity would fain know how she used the gifts of the Wise Men: that hardly matters. But the story of the call of the Wise Men, and the mystical meaning of their oblations, "these things she kept pondering in her heart."

II. Mary's Thoughts and Feelings

Did Mary see a connection between the prophecy of the Angel Gabriel on the day of the Annunciation, and the royal gifts, which the Wise Men had brought to the new-born King? Did Mary now remember the prophetic words of aged Simeon, the "just and devout man," on the occasion of the Presentation in the Temple (which must have preceded the visit of the Wise Men): "My eyes have seen the salvation, which thou hast prepared before the face of all peoples, a light to the revelation of the Gentiles, and the glory of thy people Israel"? (*Luke* 2, 30-31.) Were these men, who had come from so far, the first Gentiles to whom it was given to see this Light? Still these other words of Simeon:

"Behold this child is set for the fall and for the resurrection of many in Israel, and for a sign which shall be contradicted. And thy soul a sword shall pierce" (*Luke* 2, 34-35). Did Mary recollect these words when the myrrh was offered her, and when so soon after, she received the command to flee in order to preserve the life of the Child? We can presume that Mary was privileged gradually to fathom the mystery of our salvation through suffering, death and resurrection; and as the veil was slowly lifted, she accepted it all, and again uttered a loving and unconditional *Fiat*: God's Will be done!

It is by trying to understand better the thoughts and feelings of Mary, that we shall grow familiar with the thoughts and feelings of her divine Son: for Mary's Heart was ever most like unto the Heart of Jesus.

We admire her greatness and her lowliness; we gaze on her as on a living "monstrance", offering the Child on her lap for the adoration of the Wise Men, and of all of us, and she herself was all the while the most humble and most loving worshipper of all.

III. "Show Unto Us the Blessed Fruit of Thy Womb"

This had been Mary's privilege at Bethlehem with the shepherds, and here again with the Wise Men. When they arrived, this was their prayer: "Show us the Fruit of thy womb."

Are not we also, travelling on a long journey, weary and footsore, seeking Him, who by the star of our faith has called us "out of darkness into his marvellous light"? (1 *Peter* 2, 9.) We shall find Him only with Mary, His Mother. She will show Him to us, for He is her Son: and she conceived and bore Him, that we might be saved:

> "Who for us incarnate
> Did not thee despise.
> *Qui pro nobis natus*
> *Tulit esse tuus.*"

Thus the Church sings in her *Ave Maris Stella*. One day Mary's greatest joy will be to show us, after we have been released from this exile, "the Blessed Fruit of her womb".

Prayer: *Alma Redemptoris Mater*:
> Mother of Jesus, heaven's open gate
> Star of the sea, support the fallen state
> Of mortals, thou whose womb thy Maker bore;

> And yet, strange thing, a virgin as before;
> Who didst from Gabriel's Hail this news receive,
> Repenting sinners by thy prayers relieve.

And show us the Fruit of Thy womb, our Savior and our everlasting bliss.

JANUARY 11

THE FLIGHT INTO EGYPT AND THE RETURN

(Matt. 2: 13-15; 19-23)

1. In order that the Savior might escape the rage of Herod, the angel had commanded Joseph to take the Child and His Mother and to flee into Egypt. It was a journey of at least three days. And the angel had added: "And be there until I shall tell thee." The Gospel does not tell us how long the exile lasted; but in the light of contemporary events we can easily grasp how bitter is the lot of exiles, or of "displaced persons". Let us follow the Holy Family on its lonesome journey, mostly through the desert; we see them in exile, not knowing when the call to return may come. We try to feel with Mary and Joseph.

2. *Petition*: The grace to follow their example: prompt obedience to God's will and trust in Providence.

I. The Command of the Angel

It is noteworthy that, when God gives a command to the Holy Family, He does so through Joseph. Only once was an angel despatched to Mary. This was at the time of the Annunciation; and the reason is obvious: there was question of something that concerned Mary most personally, and God saw to it that she had the most absolute freedom in giving her consent. But after that, God communicates His will concerning her and the Child, through St. Joseph. Four times an angel appeared to him in a dream in order to announce God's will; and then Joseph is commissioned to trasmit the command to Mary.

Perhaps the petty, but very human, question occurs to us: Was Mary not far superior in virtue and dignity to Joseph? And is it becoming that she should learn the will of God from one so far below her? A very human query indeed! We are so easily hurt, or piqued, if we are overlooked or not treated according to what we consider to be our deserts. Let us take to heart the salutary lesson which Mary here teaches us. In her there is no trace of susceptibility or petulance, and she deems it right that God's message be addressed not to her, but to Joseph, the head of the family, her support and her protector. She ever remains the humble "handmaid of the Lord", not only with the angel, but with all those whom the Lord has placed over her.

II. They Obey

It is striking that, both when they are commanded to flee and when they are ordered to return, the very same words are used to express the command and to state the execution of it. "Arise and take the child and his mother and go into the land of Israel. For they are dead that sought the life of the child. Who arose, and took the child and his mother, and came into the land of Israel" (*Matt.* 2, 20-21). This does not seem to be merely a matter of scriptural style; it appears intentional on the part of the author, and is meant to express how promptly Joseph obeyed the Lord's command.

When the command to return came, the angel indicated why it was safe to go back: "They are dead that sought the life of the child." The Gospel does not tell us, but we know from history, that the tyrant had died from a very cruel disease, in the midst of terrible torture. The Evangelist evidently knew these facts, but may have thought it inappropriate to mention them here: we admire his discretion. The divine decrees to us are unfathomable.

III. The Prudence of St. Joseph

The angel had commanded St. Joseph to proceed to the land of Israel, which may be Judea as well as Galilee. St. Joseph himself had to make up his mind to what province he should go: and the Gospel narrative leaves us with the impression that, at first, he felt inclined to choose Judea in preference to Nazareth. Perhaps he preferred Bethlehem, where, before their flight into Egypt, the Holy Family seems to have found suitable shelter. "But hearing that Archelaus reigned in Judea in the room of Herod his father, he was afraid to go thither; and being warned in sleep retired into the quarters of Galilee" (*Matt.* 2, 22). Joseph may have had difficulty in making up his mind, even after talking it over with Mary, and asking advice of others; finally guidance came from on high.

Even divine intervention does not dispense man from co-operating with God's grace, and it is God's will that we should use our natural powers, which are God's gifts to us. Such was the course adopted by the Wise Men when the star disappeared, and such was the course St. Joseph followed. And, if we are unable to solve a difficulty, God is always able and ready to help. He knows a multitude of ways to shape events according to His will, and to guide men invisibly but infallibly to the end He has in view.

It is our duty to do God's will, employing all the means which God has placed at our disposal to implement the commands of our Superiors, and to place the most implicit confidence in His loving Providence.

Prayer: O Saint Joseph, faithful servant of God, and loving protector of Jesus and Mary, thou hast shown us a bright example of prompt and humble obedience to God's commands, and of trust in the divine guidance: obtain for us the grace of faithfully and lovingly serving Jesus and His holy Mother.

JANUARY 12

CONCLUDING MEDITATION ON THE MYSTERY OF CHRISTMAS

1. The coming of Jesus on earth is the mystery of Light shining in the darkness. On the very first page of Holy Writ, we read: "Be light made, and light was made." With the incarnation and the birth of the Word of God, supernatural light breaks through the spiritual darkness that had descended on mankind after the sin of Adam. On that night at Bethlehem "the brightness of God shone round about" the shepherds, and an angel brought them good tidings of great joy, that a Savior had been born to them. A star appeared in the East, and led the Wise Men to the cradle of "him that was born King of the Jews." This Light in our darkness is the Child now on the lap of Mary, whose *Fiat* brought Him on earth.

2. *Petition*: May the light of faith shine brightly in our soul, illuminate our every action, and cast its brightness around us.

I. Light and Mystery

We are aware immediately that the Christmas mystery transcends the domain of mere natural science. Science may throw light on many natural mysteries and partly solve them. Much remains wrapped in darkness. True men of science know and confess this.

The Christmas liturgy frequently speaks of Light shining in the darkness; of the invisible becoming visible; of the veil (the flesh) which reveals the Word. "We gaze upon God in visible form" says the Preface of the Christmas Mass; but that sight must enkindle in our hearts the love of things invisible. He "who inhabiteth light inaccessible, whom no man hath seen, nor can see" (1 *Tim* 6, 16), has come down to us, divested of His glory and majesty, "taking the form of a servant, being made in the likeness of man" (*Phil.* 2, 7). "We have seen with our eyes . . . our hands have handled" the Word of Life made man (1 *John* 1, 1).

A new Light shines on us, yet through a veil; a new knowledge is given us, yet partial and incomplete; though only partial knowledge, still it is absolute, certain knowledge of the Highest Truth, of the Truth that saves. Partial knowledge of the highest, of the Infinite Truth is far more precious than full knowledge of things earthly.

We offer thanks to the Father, who has called us to behold the most wonderful Light of Life; we intercede for those to whom it has not yet been given to see that Light; we beseech God to have mercy on those who have closed their eyes to the true Light in order to pursue shadows and phantoms.

II. Wonderful Exchange of Gifts

O Admirabile Commercium!

The Liturgy often calls the mystery of the Incarnation an "exchange": God assuming our nature, and in exchange rendering us partakers of the divine nature (1 *Peter* 1, 4). The exchange took place in Mary's womb. In the first antiphon of Lauds, on the feast of the Circumcision, the Church sings, "O wonderful exchange, the Creator of the human race assumed a living body, and deigned to be born of a virgin; and having been born of a virgin mother, He bestowed on us His Divinity." God, the source and author of all good, takes the initiative, Mary utters her *Fiat*, and through Mary the ineffable "exchange" is accomplished. The Son of God has become the Son of man; and "to as many as received him, he gave the power to be made the sons of God" (*John* 1, 12). His Body, through which He has become like us, is the instrument through which the exchange has been accomplished, and through which He makes us like unto Himself and partakers of His divine nature.

A like exchange, intimately connected with the Incarnation, is accomplished in the sacrifice of the Mass and in Holy Communion: we offer our gifts of bread and wine; God changes them into the Body and Blood of His Son, and gives them back to us to be the food and life of our souls.

These are the sacred mysteries, which we celebrate daily, and which nourish our supernatural life.

III. Light and Food by Which We Live

In the liturgy of Christmas we are frequently reminded that through the birth of Christ in the flesh we have been redeemed, saved, purified. This redemption is a divine work, far above anything that man could achieve. And yet the Church often reminds us that our salvation is not a work in which we have no share, or in which we remain simply passive. In the Collect of the second Mass on Christmas Day, we pray thus, "Grant, we beseech Thee, O Almighty God, that we, who are bathed in the new light of the Word made flesh, may reflect in our works the light which by faith glows in our minds. Through the same Jesus Christ. . . ." The new light of the Word is made to shine on us that we may live by it: it waxes, wanes and fades, it glows and shines brightly, according to the lesser or greater intensity of our fervor.

Prayer: We beseech Thee, O Lord, in Thy Divine pity to accede to the prayers of Thy people who cry to Thee; that they may know their obligations and have the strength to fulfill them. Through our Lord (Collect, 1st Sunday after Epiphany).[1] *end*

---

1 Here might follow the 5 meditations on the Hidden Life of our Lord (see further: January 16—January 20). But on January 13, the Church keeps the feast of the Commemoration of our Lord's Baptism, and the feast of the Holy Family on the 1st Sunday after the Epiphany, a day which will vary from year to year. (see meditation: January 16). So also will vary the date of the 2nd Sunday after the Epiphany, (see meditations January 14 and January 15).

THE BAPTISM OF OUR LORD

(Matt. 3: 13-17; John 1: 29-36)

1. On this day (which used to be the Octave of the Epiphany), we commemorate the Baptism of our Lord. From the earliest times the Church, in her liturgy, was wont to establish a connection between the three manifestations of Jesus: His manifestation to the Gentiles, represented by the three Wise Men from the East; the manifestation of His Divinity, when John baptized Him in the Jordan; the manifestation of Jesus as a worker of signs and miracles at Cana, where He performed His first miracle. Today we consider the Baptism of our Lord by John. We have often seen the event depicted in our churches and above our altars.

2. *Petition*: Jesus begins His public ministry with an act of the profoundest humility, followed by a heavenly testimony to His Divinity. May we penetrate deeper into these mysteries.

I. The Baptist Points Out the Messiah

St. John the Baptist was the last of the Prophets of Israel, who had announced the Messiah as "He That was to come". On the banks of the Jordan he points to Him standing in their midst: He has come!

In the hallowed silence of the house of Nazareth the Son of God had become the Son of man by the *Fiat* of a lowly maiden. On the banks of the Jordan the Precursor solemnly and publicly presents Him to Israel. It was befitting that His Mother should shine with the splendor of virginal purity; befitting too was it that the Precursor be a man who sought God alone and spoke in His name. He gives his solemn testimony to the Messiah, and then withdraws into obscurity. Mary and John, both very closely connected with the Messiah, teach us that He must increase and that man must decrease.

When John had baptized Jesus, he saw "the Spirit of God descending as a dove and coming upon Him", and John testified: "And I saw; and gave testimony that this is the Son of God" (*John* 1, 34). "The next day again John stood and two of his disciples, and beholding Jesus walking he said, Behold the Lamb of God" (*Ibid* 1, 35-36). And before this, when he had seen Jesus coming towards him, he had said, "Behold the Lamb of God. Behold him who taketh away the sin of the world. This is he of whom I said, After me there cometh a man, who is preferred before me, because he was before me" (*John* 1, 29-30).

It is good to fix our gaze on the Baptist, at the moment when Israel hails him as the great Prophet—perhaps the Messiah—before the whole nation and in the presence of his own disciples declining the honor that is offered him, and bearing testimony to another who is the true Messiah. He has testified; now he may pass into the night of obscurity.

II.   The Father and the Holy Ghost Manifest Jesus

"And Jesus, being baptized, forthwith came out of the water; and lo, the heavens were opened to him, and he saw the Spirit of God descending as a dove and coming upon him. And, behold, a voice from heaven, saying: This is my beloved Son, in whom I am well pleased" (*Matt.* 3, 16-17).

When the Word was made flesh and came to dwell among us, the Three Divine Persons were present and wrought the wonderful mystery; so also, when the Son of man enters upon His office as Messenger of the Father, the Three Persons cooperate: we hear the voice of the Father, whom no man hath ever seen, proclaiming His love for His only-begotten Son; the Holy Ghost appears in the form of a dove, a symbol of love and of meekness. Jesus, the Son of man, at His Baptism assumes the form of a sinner, "for which cause also God hath exalted him" (*Phil.* 2, 9).

At that moment, on the banks of the Jordan, the veil is partly removed from the most unfathomable of divine mysteries; and we are allowed to cast a glance into the abyss of the Deity. We rejoice at this solemn testimony of the Father's love for His Son, Jesus Christ. May we understand something of the feelings of the Heart of Jesus. "Sacrifice and oblation thou wouldst not; but a body thou hast fitted to me.... Then said I, Behold, I come to do thy will, O God" (*Heb.* 10: 5, 9).

III.   The Inauguration of the Public Ministry

In the presence of the Jews watching from the banks of the Jordan, Jesus, humble and meek, enters into the water and, as if He were a sinner, receives the baptism of penance.

Jesus begins His own ministry by paying homage to John; He begins His labors very close to the spot where John was preaching; His first disciples were sent to Him by John, not that

He had enticed them from their first allegiance, but because John himself had sent them to Jesus. It is good to reflect on the humility and the courtesy of Jesus, tactfully blending the old and the new.

Jesus adopted a new method: John's manner had been that of the ancient Prophets "and there went out to him all the country of Judea and all they of Jerusalem, and were baptized by him . . . confessing their sins" (*Mark* 1, 5). And they hearkened to his stern message.

John's mission is a spectacular success, and the whole nation is aroused; but Jesus, the Messiah sponsored by John, enters upon the scene most discreetly, apparently attracting scant attention. The Jews fail to understand the message of Jesus, and the day is at hand when they will obstinately refuse to listen. They will oppose Christ, and finally reject Him. Both the inauguration and the conclusion of the Lord's ministry are marked by two contrasts: the humiliating Baptism of Penance, followed by the solemn testimony of the Father from heaven; and at the end, Christ's ignominious death on the cross, which heralds His entry into the glory of His Father.

Such was the divine plan of our salvation; and in the Heart of Jesus there was at all times the most perfect acceptance of the Father's decrees: "Be it so, Father, because it is pleasing in thy sight." We admire, we praise, we give thanks.

Prayer: O Lord Jesus, whose ways are not our ways; our minds are too small and too carnal to grasp the meaning of Thy words and of Thy actions; Thou hast said to Thy disciples, "My meat is to do the will of him that sent me, that I may perfect his work" (*John* 4, 34), and again "I came down from heaven, not to do my own will but the will of him that sent me" (*Ibid.* 6, 38). May we learn from Thee to be humble and to seek only God's will. "Jesus, meek and humble of heart, make our hearts like unto Thine."

JANUARY 14

THE MARRIAGE AT CANA—I (John 2, 1-11)

1. "This beginning of miracles did Jesus in Cana of Galilee and manifested his glory, and his disciples believed in him" *John*

21, 11). "And the Mother of Jesus was there," most probably as an invited relative of the bride or bridegroom. Jesus also had been invited, and His disciples with Him, probably the first five, Andrew, Peter, John, Philip, Nathanael. On such occasions people practiced proverbial oriental hospitality and every one was welcome.

2. *Petition*: The grace to understand this miracle, so rich in symbolical meaning; also the grace to understand Mary's role as Mediatrix, and to trust in her intercession.

I. "Jesus Also Was Invited"

The Son of Man had not, like the Baptist, grown up in the desert, but had lived, and sanctified, a normal family life. Therefore it is natural that He should have accepted an invitation to the marriage of two young people, whom He knew. Surely, there too He was "about His Father's business". If Jesus could find His Father in the lilies of the field, which are today and tomorrow are cast into the oven, all the more did He find Him in these two children of Israel, whom God had united, and who, with heaven's blessing on them, had promised to serve the Lord together until death did them part.

Paul rejoiced with those that rejoice, and wept with those that weep. Jesus did the same in a manner worthy of His human and of His divine natures; for in all things He was like unto us, even in our joys, and always conscious of being about His Father's business.

We do not know whether on this occasion Jesus raised matrimony, which from the beginning had the divine sanction, to the status of a sacrament that confers grace and supernatural life. We may be sure that His presence was a blessing to all the guests, and chiefly to the bride and bridegroom, who were privileged to receive His best wishes.

II. "They Have No Wine"

The charitable eye of Mary, good and careful housewife that she was, soon noticed that something was going wrong: the supply of wine—which in any case depended on what the guests brought along themselves—was running short. Did Mary ask for a miracle? She certainly asked Jesus to help, and she knew that He could and would help.

"They have no wine": these words clearly imply a request,

however discreetly it may be expressed. Jesus answered, "Woman, what is that to me and to thee? My hour is not yet come" ·(*John* 2, 4).

How strange this answer sounds! Is not the Son speaking to his Mother? Does Jesus perhaps want His Mother to understand that, since He has started His public life, His relations with His Mother are totally different? What does He mean when He says, "My hour is not yet come"? Do these words imply a refusal? We fail to understand this mysterious manner of speaking.

However, the entire context proves that Jesus did not refuse, still less did He refuse peremptorily, to comply with His Mother's implied request; for Mary evidently was convinced that Jesus would hear her prayer, even at the cost of a miracle. "His mother saith to the waiters, Whatsoever he shall say to you, do ye" (*John* 2, 5). These words show how Mary had understood the words of her Son.

III. The Miracle

The waiters were only too ready to do what Mary told them. "Jesus saith to them, Fill the water-pots with water. And they filled them up to the brim. And Jesus saith to them, Draw out now and carry to the chief steward of the feast, and they carried it. And when the chief steward had tasted the water made wine, he calleth the bridegroom, and saith to him: Every man at first setteth forth good wine . . . but thou hast kept the good wine until now" (*John* 2, 7-10). Had Jesus changed His mind? Humanly speaking we may say He did. Why did He act thus? Due to His Mother's prayer. It had been a humble and very discreet request, for Mary was aware of His Divinity; and yet she did not think it presumptuous reverently to use with her Son her motherly power on behalf of humble folk who were in distress. These things are indeed wonderful and mysterious.

"This beginning of miracles did Jesus in Cana of Galilee, and manifested his glory. And his disciples believed in him" (*John* 2, 11). The Messianic ministry had been inaugurated, Jesus had shown His glory, that is, His power, and the first disciples believed. At the same time Mary's power of intercession with her Son had also been manifested. May our confidence in her ever grow, and may she be our advocate with Jesus!

We humbly pray that we may understand the relation that exists, has existed and always will exist between Mary and the Son of God made man. The more we meditate on these matters, the more we shall realize that we must place our trust in her whom Jesus on the cross made the Mother of all His disciples.

Prayer: O Lord Jesus Christ, our Mediator with the Father, who hast appointed the most blessed Virgin, Thy Mother, to be our mother also, and our mediatrix before Thee: grant that whosoever draweth nigh to Thee to beseech any benefit, may receive all things through her and rejoice. Who livest.... (Collect, Mass of the Feast of Mary Mediatrix.)

JANUARY 15

THE MARRIAGE AT CANA—II

1. All the words and actions of Jesus are words and actions of a Divine Person; they may be simple and commonplace and yet in some way they are divine; their meaning is unfathomable, as is the Person who revealed Himself in these words and actions. St. John, the disciple whom Jesus loved, the seer of Patmos, and the last survivor of the twelve Apostles, understood best the teachings of Jesus, and penetrated deeper than others into the feelings of the Heart of the Lord. An ancient author says about the Gospel of St. John, "No one can grasp its meaning unless his head has reclined on the Heart of the Savior, unless he has received Mary from Jesus as his Mother.... Only one who lives by that spirit can taste the spiritual meaning that is hidden in the human words."

2. *Petition*: May we, through the intercession of Mary, "Mother of Divine grace", penetrate into the mysteries that are manifested in this miracle: the Lord's glory, and Mary's power with her son.

I. Jesus "Manifested His Glory"

St. John is the only evangelist consistently to call the miracles of Jesus "signs", things that point to other things; they are related to the supernatural order, they are proofs that Christ is God, they "manifest His glory". God never works a wonder merely to astound, or to satisfy people's frivolous curiosity.

The disciples who, on John's advice, had left the Baptist in order to adhere to the new Prophet of Nazareth, knew that

Jesus was "He that was to come", the One who had to increase while John must decrease. They had never seen John working a miracle, and at Cana for the first time their eyes beheld a most marvellous thing, utterly unexpected; not a sign in the heavens, but a simple thing connected with the everyday life of the people, and yet a true miracle, performed to help humble folk that were in trouble.

On St. John, who is the only evangelist to relate this miracle, and who was present and saw everything with his own eyes, the event made a profound impression. "This beginning of miracles did Jesus in Cana of Galilee; and manifested his glory. And his disciples believed in him" (2, 11). He manifested His glory, that is, His divine power. Some of the ancient prophets had wrought miracles, never to manifest their own glory or power, but to prove that the Lord rules the world. Jesus manifests His own glory and power, which ultimately are the glory and power of the Father. Jesus said, "I honor my Father . . . I seek not my own glory" (*John* 8, 49-50). The closer we go to Jesus, the better we shall understand His feelings, and the more we shall realize that He and His Father are One, and that His food is to do the will of His Father.

II. The Meaning of the Miracle

Jesus changed water into wine. That is the historical fact. He did it to assist humble people in response to His Mother's prayer. We may profitably ponder over these things.

The Fathers of the Church, well versed in the Scriptures and acquainted with St. John's symbolism, regard the wine as the symbol of Messianic blessings, whereas the water represents the Old Covenant. They praise God for the wonderful liberality with which He fulfilled the promises He had made; they see Jesus inaugurating the New Covenant with the help of the Old.

Other Fathers see in the changing of the water into wine, a type of what Jesus will do for us on the eve of His Passion, when He changed the wine into His own Blood. Did Jesus think of this at Cana of Galilee? Did St. John insinuate a connection between Cana and the Cenacle? The whole life of Jesus had been planned by God, and He knew "that he came from God and goeth to God" (13, 3), He also knew the manner of His going. We may lovingly and reverently endeavor to enter into the Master's feelings at the moment when He manifested His glory by changing water into wine, as well as later on, when He manifested His glory by changing water into wine, as well as later on, when He manifests the immensity of His love by changing the wine into His Blood, that It may be the sustenance of our souls.

III. Mary's Power

St. John always calls Mary "the Mother of Jesus", and he sees himself only in his relation to Jesus, as "the disciple whom Jesus loved". It is at the intercession of Mary that Jesus worked His first miracle, by which "he manifested his glory" and because of which "his disciples believed in him". Indirectly it was Mary that enabled the disciples to understand that their Master was the Christ, the Son of God.

On the cross, whence Jesus also addressed her by the title "woman", that is "Lady", Jesus will solemnly appoint her Mother of all His disciples, saying to John, "Behold thy Mother."

At Cana we see Mary in her role of Mediatrix between us and her Son. Who would dare say that it was by mere accident that Jesus wrought His first miracle, not only in His Mother's presence, but also at her intercession, and even before His hour was come? How powerful will be that intercession once the hour has come; when by His death and resurrection He has completed His work and has become our High Priest with the Father. Mary's role in the New Testament is a motherly role, unique, universal, utterly dependent on and subordinate to Christ, yet indispensable.

Prayer: As in the previous meditation.

JANUARY 16

THE HOLY FAMILY

1. The wonderful happenings at the time of the birth of Jesus had aroused a certain amount of public interest at Bethlehem. "And all that heard wondered; and at those things that were told them by the shepherds" (*Luke* 2, 18). At Nazareth, whither the Holy Family returned after the flight into Egypt, these things were unknown: Joseph was "the carpenter" and Mary a hard-working housewife, and their Child, who advanced in wisdom and age and grace with God and men, was obedient to them (*Luke* 2, 52).

2. *Petition*: The grace to understand better, and to admire, the hidden greatness of their humble family life: the Son of God, His Mother, His Foster-Father, glorifying God by doing His Will in small things. Such should be the life of all Christians.

I. The "Wonderful Virtues of Family Life"

The Collect of the Mass of the feast mentions the wonderful virtues, practiced by the Holy Family. Would to God that these virtues flourished in every Christian home in our days. With us everything tends to disrupt the family, and to keep its members apart. Not only work, but also relaxation and pleasure are being sought outside the home, in the busy world, where everything is hustle and bustle. There are those to whom the peace and quiet of the home have become boring and tedious. Perhaps even our cloisters are in danger of being invaded by the spirit of the world, and there may be religious who prefer the world's hustle and bustle to recollection and silence.

We therefore stand in sore need of the lessons which are taught us at Nazareth; the virtues practiced there are the very foundation of the Christian life, nay of all truly human life.

"O Lord Jesus, make us ever imitate the examples of Thy Holy Family" (Post-communion, Feast of Holy Family).

II. The Common Life Nobly Lived

"Common" may mean "lived in common", as well as "ordinary". The life of Jesus, Mary and Joseph at Nazareth is very ordinary: they are a working man's family; Joseph is the village carpenter and the bread-winner; Mary is assiduous at her daily chores and keeps her house in order; Jesus is growing into a young man, and shares the labor of Joseph in the carpenter's shop. Theirs is a peaceful, monotonous, laborious life. Besides the annual pilgrimage to Jerusalem, absolutely nothing happens at Nazareth. Pope Pius XI, speaking about Blessed Brother Benilde who all his life had been a teacher in a primary school, mentioned "those terrible daily occupations" of the ordinary man. We may think that the Holy Family was far less affected by those terrible daily occupations than we are, who rush about in our noisy and mechanized world. But the "Son of Man" deliberately chose *that* village, "whence no good could come," and *that* humdrum life of a poor toiler, to show us by His example that even *that* life can be nobly lived, and is not beneath the dignity of the Son of God.

About the community life at Nazareth the Gospel says, He

"was subject unto them ... and advanced in wisdom and age
and grace with God and men" (*Luke* 2, 51-52). It may be that
here St. Luke reproduces the very words used by Mary, who
had been the happy witness of this unique growth in wisdom,
age and grace, and who had kept all these words in her heart.

It is easy to imagine what spirit reigned in the holy house:
mutual esteem, sincere love, exquisite kindness. Never had there
been such a family anywhere, and yet everything was ordinary,
so that neither relatives nor neighbors were aware that God had
visited them in a special manner. When some years later Jesus,
coming into his own country, taught them in their synagogues,
they wondered and said, how came this man by this wisdom and
miracles? Is not this the carpenter's son? Is not his mother Mary?
(*Matt.* 13, 54-55.) They knew all His relations, all humble folk.
How did He come by this wisdom? Indeed "He emptied Himself",
and His infinite Divinity was hidden within the narrow limits
of a human "form".

Even the religious life of the Holy Family appeared ordinary,
at least to the outward eye. Mary taught her Son to pray, and
later they would recite together the Psalms, which all the Jews
knew by heart. Even on the cross Jesus will intone a Psalm,
"O God, my God, ... why hast thou forsaken me?" (*Ps.* 21, 1.)

To live and to labor in God's presence, elsewhere invisible,
but here visible and palpable, is the unique privilege of Mary
and Joseph, and an intense source of happiness. Jesus Himself,
in whom "dwelleth all the fullness of the Godhead corporeally"
(*Col.* 2, 9) whether He prays, or works, or speaks, or remains
silent, "is never alone, but with him always is the Father" (*John*
8, 16).

III. The Christian Family

The whole of family life must be lived "in the Lord": these
words are used by St. Paul whenever he speaks of the Christian
family. "Children, obey your parents in the Lord. . . . You fathers,
bring up your children in the discipline and correction of the
Lord. . . . Servants, be obedient to them that are your lords according to the flesh, as to Christ, as the servants of Christ. . . . You
masters, know that the Lord both of you and of them is in
heaven. . . . Wives, be subject to your husbands as it behoveth
in the Lord" (*Eph.* 6: 1-9; *Col.* 3: 18-25; 4: 1).

Above all, those who are united with Jesus, and among themselves by the bond of a higher calling, must live their lives in the

Lord. Religious have a special right to say, "The charity of Christ
has brought us together." But this imposes on them a grave responsibility. Let them pray that the spirit of Nazareth may ever
prevail in their communities.

Prayer: We offer Thee this victim to appease Thine anger,
O Lord, and beg and implore Thee, through the intercession of
the Virgin Mother of God and blessed Joseph, solidly to establish
our families in Thy grace and peace. Through our Lord (Secret
of today's Mass).

JANUARY 17

THE HIDDEN LIFE AT NAZARETH (Luke 2, 51)

1. Everything in our Savior's life is a mystery, not least the
    fact that thirty years of His life on earth were spent in obscurity,
    whilst He was advancing in grace with God and man. How
    can we comprehend the decree of Providence, which keeps
    the Savior hidden away during all that time? And yet does it
    not teach us the salutary lesson, which we so often forget, that
    it is not unrestrained activity, but prolonged reflection and
    seclusion which is the secret of all greatness?
        Let us behold Jesus in His daily life, He is now a grown-up
    man. We see Him planning and chiselling at the carpenter's
    bench.

2. *Petition*: The grace to understand the greatness of this hidden
    life. "Come, let us adore the Son of God, obedient to Mary and
    Joseph" working like a humble wage-earner! (Invitat., Feast
    of the Holy Family.)

I. Obedient

To most people it is hard—to few it comes easy—to be subordinate and to obey. Not to be one's own master, never to do
a thing according to one's own will, to execute what another
commands, and to execute it as this other wants it to be done:
to a man who is in possession of all his faculties and who is
ready to do and dare, all that appears unworthy of our manhood,
fit only for children, weaklings, or misfits. Let this kind of people
remain the thralls of others all their born days!
    And it is true that there may be cases where, humanly speaking,

dependence on others may damp one's energy, destroy the spirit of initiative, and interfere with the orderly development of the human personality.

But the obedience of Jesus at Nazareth was, in its very essence, the loving adherence of His Will to the Father's Will, which was interpreted to Him by Mary and Joseph. Even if, personally, they were perfect interpreters of the divine Will, yet their authority had its source not in their virtues, but in their appointment by God as parents of Jesus. Once only would the Savior withdraw from their authority, when He remained in Jerusalem: and the reason was that God wanted Him to be "about His Father's business". And that business must always come first. Did He not say, "My meat is to do the will of him that sent me, that I may perfect his work"? (*John* 4, 34.)

It is a fact that about Christ's first thirty years on earth the Scriptures tell us nothing except that "he was subject to them". With this example before our eyes, let us examine how we obey our Superiors, — gladly, promptly, blindly? . . . that is, making abstraction of personal views and not permitting them to interfere with the execution of orders received, but always "in the Lord".

II. Hidden

In Him dwelt the fullness of the Godhead (*Col.* 2, 9); but It *was* hidden, and in habit (that is outwardly) He was just a man; so that no one, Mary and Joseph excepted, had the faintest suspicion that this Child, this Youth, this Young Man, this Son of the carpenter, carried within Himself the most ineffable mystery.

Did Mary, who kept and pondered in her heart the words of the angel and of Simeon, ask herself when at last "the salvation which God had prepared before the face of all peoples, a light to the revelation of the Gentiles, and the glory of His people Israel" would be manifested to the world? Mary's faith never faltered. But to think that her faith too was tried and through trial waxed stronger, is no irreverence to Mary, and it makes her salutary example more compelling. "Blessed art thou that hast believed": these inspired words of Elizabeth were as true in the end as at the beginning.

We know the excess of spiritual and temporal misery, which afflicted Israel during these thirty years: the blind were legion, and the lame, the lepers, the sinners; the Heart of Jesus yearned for the flock that lay without a shepherd, for those that longed for the consolation of Israel. Jesus knew and saw, and He had compassion: and yet He stayed at Nazareth and labored with His hands. To our short-sighted impatience this seems an incomprehensible mystery. "My time is not come; but your time is always ready" Jesus would say one day (*John* 7, 6).

III. "The Father's Business"

But every action of this hidden life had infinite value and did contribute to our salvation, and during all this time Jesus was "about His Father's business", yea, even when He performed the most humdrum tasks at Nazareth. A modern writer erred grievously when he said, "Jesus, a man longing to be up and doing, must have found the hidden life at Nazareth exceedingly hard." Did Jesus not say, "My meat is to do the will of him that sent me, that I may perfect his work"? (*John* 4, 34.) Jesus was perfectly aware that His every action had an infinite value for our salvation, not only His public ministry, and His death on the cross, but also His hidden life, so wonderfully begun in the stable at Bethlehem.

It matters little where we may live or what work we do, as long as we live in the place where God wants us, and do the work He imposes on us, that is, as long as we are "about our Father's business". He bears his share in the great redemptive work of Christ, who serves in the kitchen, as well as he that ascends the pulpit of a cathedral, as long as both can say, "Yea, Father; for so hath it seemed good in thy sight" (*Matt.* 11 26).

Prayer: Almighty and eternal God, make our will be ever devoted to Thee, and our hearts pure in the service of Thy Majesty (Collect, Sunday after Ascension).

JANUARY 18

THE PROGRESS OF JESUS (Luke 2, 40-52)

1. Jesus, like unto us in all things, sin excepted, was like any other child; as His body grew, so did His mental faculties. It was a case of normal and healthy growth, not impeded by any sickness or ailment. Of all this, Mary and Joseph were the delighted witnesses. With awe and reverence we behold this gradual development of the divine Child.

2. *Petition*: That we may believe and trust "in the grace that rests upon us", through which we can grow "in grace with God and men."

I. Gradual Development

"And the child grew and waxed strong, full of wisdom, and the grace of God was in him" (*Luke* 2, 40). After writing these words St. Luke proceeds to relate the unexpected and mysterious unveiling of the Divinity in the ordinary life of Jesus who, at the age of twelve, unknown to His parents, remained in Jerusalem. And then the evangelist continues, "And he went down with them, and came to Nazareth, and was subject to them. And his mother kept all these words in her heart. And Jesus advanced in wisdom and age, and grace with God and men" (*Luke* 2, 51-52).

Whatever was human in Jesus was subject to natural growth: *as man* He learnt to speak, even to pray, learning from His holy Mother to recite the Psalms; He acquired *human* knowledge as other children acquire it; St. Joseph taught Him the work of a carpenter.

Nay more: Mary had her share in the molding of the God-man's heart, just as other mothers have a share in the molding of their children's hearts. Therefore it was befitting that the Mother of Jesus be immaculate in her conception, full of grace, exempt of even the shadow of sin. She who was to train this divine Infant had to be a paragon of perfection.

These thoughts should increase our admiration and our reverence for Mary. Holy Mother of God, pray for us; Virgin of virgins, pray for us.

II. Grace With God and Men

As the human faculties of the Child Jesus reached their normal development, He, *as man*, came to know His Father better, who is in heaven, to praise and love Him more perfectly. In the one Person of Jesus the human and the divine natures were united, with the result that never had human nature given to God such perfect praise, love and service. Christ's humanity was God's ideal instrument, indissolubly united to the Divinity, and giving perfect service to God. Several times the Father will bear this solemn testimony to Christ, "This is my beloved Son, in whom I am well pleased."

The Gospel says that Jesus also grew more pleasing to men. The chief witness of this was Mary, His Mother. It had to be so: for the time being the Divinity was hidden in the shape of a perfect man, "the most beautiful of the children of men". Of Him the Prophet had said, "He shall not cry ... neither shall his voice be heard abroad.... The bruised reed he shall not break, and smoking flax he shall not quench" (*Isa.* 42, 2-3). At Nazareth He was meek and humble of heart, as He would be later, when along the highways of Galilee he "went about doing good and healing all that were oppressed" (*Act.* 10, 38).

The day would come when His own would cast Him out, but at this time He had as yet offended no susceptibilities; and His fellow villagers saw in Him only the Son of Mary, whom they all knew.

With awe and wonder we contemplate this splendid example.

III. Divine Example

Every day we can and must grow in perfection. Remember that such growth does not consist in external practices, or mere feeling. Real progress and spiritual growth take place within the soul, and produce purer intentions, more self-forgetting love, deeper humility. "We faint not," says St. Paul, "but though our outward man is corrupted, the inward man is renewed day by day" (2 *Cor.* 4, 16). This inward renewal must be a never ending process.

"He advanced in grace with God and men," loving God and being loved by Him, loving men and deserving their love. To love God is the first and greatest commandment, but the second is like unto the first. Whosoever pretends to love God, and cares not for his brother, is a liar (1 *John* 4, 20). Let all who strive after perfection never forget that strong expression.

May we "henceforth be no more children tossed to and fro, and carried about by every wind of doctrine, by the wickedness of men, by cunning craftiness, by which they lie in wait to deceive" (*Eph.* 4, 14). St. Paul wants us to be manly and steadfast in God's service, and not like children, who yield to passing moods and impressions. Then we shall be spiritually grown up, "unto a perfect man, unto the measure of the age of the fullness of Christ" (*Eph.* 4, 13).

Prayer: Lord Jesus, true God and true Man, in whom our human nature grew into a perfect instrument in the Father's service, we beseech Thee, help us "to do the truth in charity, so that in all things we may grow up in Thee, who art the head."

JANUARY 19

JESUS FOUND IN THE TEMPLE (Luke 2, 41-50)

1. Only one event in the hidden life, and one word spoken by Jesus, are recorded in the Gospel. But these made such a profound impression on His Mother that, more than thirty years later, she was still able to repeat the words which on that occasion she had spoken to Jesus, and the answer Christ gave her. Most probably St. Luke, had his information from our Lady herself. Even then Mary confessed that she and Joseph "understood not the word that he spoke unto them" (*Luke* 2, 50).

We accompany Mary and Joseph during their sorrowful return journey to Jerusalem, until they find Him in the temple, sitting in the midst of the doctors, hearing them and asking questions.

2. *Petition*: May we take to heart the lessons which Jesus teaches us: that everything must yield before God's interests; that, even if we fail to understand them, we must abide by the divine decrees.

I. Jesus Stays in Jerusalem

In order to teach us a lesson, Jesus, then a Child of twelve, deliberately stays in Jerusalem, without informing His parents, and knowing well what grief He is causing to His holy Mother and to His Foster-Father. It may appear strange that Mary and Joseph left the city without making sure in whose company, the Child was. "And thinking that he was in the company, they came a day's journey, and sought him among their kinsfolk and acquaintance; and not finding him, they returned to Jerusalem, seeking him" (*Luke* 2, 44-45).

Whilst His parents, above all His holy Mother, are filled with anxiety and seek Him, Jesus is peacefully sitting in one of the halls of the temple, in the midst of the doctors, listening to their teaching and asking questions.

The Divinity, which from the beginning has been dwelling in this Child, but which was absolutely hidden, now suddenly breaks through: the veil is lifted. There is a terrible pang in Mary's heart: being the Mother of the Redeemer, she is given a share in the great work of redemption. "And thy own soul a sword shall pierce," said the venerable old Simeon.

II. Jesus Found in the Temple

What were Mary's feelings when she beheld Him seated in the midst of the doctors of the Law? "And seeing him, they wondered," says St. Luke, who reports what he has heard from Mary. Well might they be struck with wonder when they saw Him there, demurely seated among the learned of Israel, as if He were perfectly at home in their midst and as if He had completely forgotten His parents. Did Mary, always so humble and discreet, tarry a brief while, till she could approach her Son without attracting too much notice? The words she utters are a cry straight from her Mother's heart, almost a reproach, "Son, why hast thou done so to us?" And with exquisite courtesy to St. Joseph she adds, "Behold, thy father and I have sought thee sorrowing."

They failed to understand why Jesus had acted thus, and the Child's answer was a question, which they could not understand any better, "How is it that you sought me?" These words, as we read them in the Gospel, might sound harsh, especially as they follow His Mother's impassioned appeal; but we may believe that the tone in which they were spoken, and the countenance of the Child, softened the apparent harshness. Jesus added, "Did you not know that I must be about my Father's business?" (Another translation is: in my Father's house.)

We may note that Mary used the word father: "Thy father and I have sought thee sorrowing." Jesus repeats the word, but in order to designate His Father in heaven.

This answer deeply impressed Mary, and reminded her of the mysterious origin of her own Child.

"My Father's business." God's demands must ever come first, and He may call for great sacrifices both from parents and from children, which may break the most sacred ties. But when God breaks, He also mends, perhaps not at that very moment, nor in a palpable manner, but sooner or later, and truly: provided we trust in Him and obey His holy Will. For, the little we give, He returns a hundredfold.

III. "They Understood Not the Word That He Spoke Unto Them"

Mary, full of grace, enlightened from above more than any other human being, did not understand! God's ways are not those of man, nay not even those of the Mother He had chosen for Himself. Mary did not understand but "she kept all these words in her heart", humbly accepting the trial and awaiting the hour when light would be vouchsafed to make it all clear.

We all need to take this lesson to heart, whenever it pleases God to intervene in our lives and we fail to understand His decrees. Why should we be astonished if the ways of Providence are inscuhtable to us, when even the Mother of the Lord "understood not the word that he spoke unto them"? In these circumstances we ought to follow Mary's example. She kept all these things in her heart, devoutly pondered over them, humbly accepting the divine Will. She was aware God knows best, that His Wisdom and infinite Goodness rule the world for our good and His glory. One day His light will reveal it all to us, and we shall praise God forever and ever.

Prayer: Holy Mother of God, teach us to accept our trials as thou didst accept thine. When we suffer and fail to understand God's ways, have compassion on us and teach us to keep those things in our hearts until God is pleased to give us light. Until the hour when thou didst stand at the foot of the cross, thou hast lived by the *Fiat* which was spoken at Nazareth, "Be id done to me according to thy word." How similar these words were to those of Jesus, "Yea, Father, for so hath it seemed good to Thee" (*Matt.* 11, 26). Mother Most Amiable, pray for us; Mother Most Admirable, pray for us; Mother of Good Counsel, pray for us.

JANUARY 20

JESUS LEAVES NAZARETH

1. "In those days, Jesus came from Nazareth of Galilee and was baptized by John" (*Mark* 1, 9). This terse statement is characteristic of St. Mark, who seems intent chiefly on enlightening us about our Lord's public ministry. With due reverence we may try to fill in the details, and see the events as they must have taken place, though they are not related in the Gospel.

One day Jesus, who, according to St. Luke, was then about thirty years of age, bade farewell to His holy Mother, departed from Nazareth, and alone took the road to the Jordan, where John was preaching and baptizing.

2. *Petition*: The grace to understand the sacrifice, offered for our salvation, by Jesus and by Mary. May we follow their example whenever God calls for self-denial.

I. The Hour Has Come

Rather often our Lord speaks about the "hour that has come, or has not come"; also of "the times and the moments, which the Father hath put in his own power" (*Act.* 1, 7). God Almighty, in His infinite Wisdom and Goodness, has determined the time and the hour, when He will accomplish the mysterious work of our salvation. For thirty years Jesus has lived, hidden at Nazareth, being commonly regarded as the son of a poor laboring man; after St. Joseph's death they call Him the Son of Mary, or simply "the village carpenter". Mary alone knew His divine origin.

For Mary these years at Nazareth were a time of the most perfect inward happiness, even though the words of Simeon were ever ringing in her ears, "Behold, this child is set for . . . a sign that shall be contradicted, and thy own soul a sword shall pierce" (*Luke* 2, 34-35). We do not know whether Jesus gradually enlightened His Mother about the nature of His mission, about the coming events of His public ministry, about her own share in His passion and in the work of redemption. When the hour came at last, Jesus told His Mother that He had to leave her in order to be entirely about His Father's business.

II. The Farewell

Mary is the valiant woman of the Scriptures, but also the Mother of Fair Love, and the Mother of the Most Beautiful of the children of men. From the moment she had assented to the angel's proposal, she had been the handmaid of the Lord, and such she will remain until she stands by the cross on Calvary. Truly, He is her Son; but His Father is in heaven. He was "born to us, given to us": Mary knows all that, she has known it from the outset; and because her heart is like unto the Heart of her Son, she is ever ready to offer to God any sacrifice He may demand. But she does possess a motherly heart that feels and suffers.

Jesus, in all things like unto us, sin excepted, tenderly loves

His Mother. Do we not read in the Gospel that He was "moved with mercy" towards the widow of Naim and that "he gave him to his mother"? (*Luke* 7: 13, 15). When the hour of parting came Jesus consoled and comforted His Mother. Yet one day He will say, "He that loveth father and mother more than me is not worthy of me" (*Matt.* 10, 37).

On this occasion too, Jesus began to do and teach.

III.   After the Parting

Mary sees her Son going His way and, entering her little house, she prays. Her heart is with Him, and follows Him all these years, as He treads the dusty roads of Judea and Galilee; more than ever she now lives for Jesus and for the work He must accomplish. The prayer of Jesus, "Yea, Father, for so it hath seemed good in thy sight" (*Luke* 10, 21) is Mary's own prayer. Or we may hear her repeat, "Behold the handmaid of the Lord! Be it done to me according to thy word." On a few occasions she will meet Jesus again, sometimes in distressing circumstances; but never again as before at Nazareth. Her Mother's heart feels this change, and accepts it, thus bearing her share in the work of the redemption.

Jesus pursues His lonely course: He has carefully determined, or rather, the Father has determined for Him, how He shall inaugurate His public ministry. All beginnings have great importance: He will receive the Baptism of penance at the hands of the Precursor, who had prepared His way and made the paths straight. In doing so He pays tribute to the Old Covenant and takes His place in the line of the Prophets; He humbles Himself before the people—an extraordinary beginning for One who stands forth as the Messiah of Israel!

One day Jesus will say, "I am come to cast fire on the earth, and what will I but that it be kindled? And I have a baptism wherewith I am to be baptized: and how am I straitened until it be accomplished!" (*Luke* 12, 49-50.) These words pointed to the passion. At present we behold Him on His way to the Jordan, that He may be baptized by John, "knowing all things that should come upon him" (*John* 18, 4). We may suppose that at this moment also, as would happen later, His "soul was troubled"; but now He does not cry: "Father save me from this hour. . . . For this cause I came unto this hour." (*John* 12, 27).

We endeavor to fathom the thoughts and the feelings of Him,

who one day will say "Learn of me because I am meek and humble of heart" (*Matt.* 11, 29).

Prayer: Holy Mother of Jesus, we praise and thank thee, because for us thou hast offered up Him, who, born for us, deigned to be thy Son. Thou hast given Him to us when, for our sake, He left thee solitary in the little house of Nazareth. Be pleased to console and comfort all those mothers who have seen their sons and daughters leave them, so that they might follow Jesus.

O Lord Jesus, Thou hast left Thy holy Mother in order to be wholly about Thy Father's business, announcing the glad tidings and saving that which was lost. We beseech Thee, be pleased to give strength and courage to all those that are called to drink the chalice which Thou hast drained.

JANUARY 21

THE CHRISTIAN IDEAL OF LIFE—I (Rom. 12)

We have meditated on the manner of life of the Holy Family at Nazareth. Leading ordinary lives in the company of Jesus, Mary and Joseph reached the highest degree of holiness.

Now we shall consider what ought to be the ideal of all Christians, of "God's family", or of "God's holy people", as the Canon of the Mass calls us. We shall study the twelfth chapter of St. Paul's letter to the Romans, which we read in the Epistles of the first three Sundays after the Epiphany.

1. The Romans to whom St. Paul wrote were a small group of disciples, mostly Gentiles, and recently converted. They met regularly in order to pray together and to encourage one another. It was indeed a "little flock", lost in that huge city of Rome, where Nero ruled and the heathen gods claimed worship. A few years later Nero would furiously persecute them, tie them to wooden posts and burn them as living torches to illuminate the revelries of the populace in his gardens.

2. *Petition*: The grace which Jesus, on the eve of His passion, asked for His disciples, "Holy Father, I pray not that thou shouldst take them out of the world, but that thou shouldst keep them from evil. They are not of the world, as I also am not of the world" (*John* 17, 15-16).

I. "Be Not Conformed to This World (Rom. 12, 2)

Thus St. Paul wrote to the Romans. In the first chapter of that letter Paul had drawn a gruesome picture of the corruption that was rampant in the heathen world. Vice runs riot wherever, and whenever, man turns away from God. Under the influence of the Prince of the world, as St. Ignatius calls him, the enemy of human nature, present everywhere yet hiding his hand, evil triumphs everywhere, vice runs riot and crime abounds.

Be not conformed to this world, even when it abstains from frontal attacks but tries to insinuate itself gradually and to draw us away from Christ by slow degrees. Jesus found traces of the wordly spirit even among His Apostles. When first He spoke to them about His future passion, "Peter, taking him aside, began to rebuke him. Who turning about and seeing his disciples, threatened Peter, saying, Go behind me, Satan, because thou savorest not the things that are of God" (*Mark* 8, 32-33). On another occasion our Lord rebuked James and John, who wanted to call down fire from heaven to destroy a city that had refused to receive Him, "You know not of what spirit you are" (*Luke* 9, 55).

Fear of suffering, severity prompted by personal resentment: he who yields to these feelings is led by the spirit of the world. Peter will purify himself and fight against Satan's influence, and Judas will not, even though Jesus had prayed for him also. Greed would blind the man, till Satan entered into him.

II. "Be Reformed in the Newness of Your Mind"

A Christian life does not consist merely in a series of outward observances, nor in simply avoiding certain things. Religion springs from the deepest recesses of a man's being; a man lives it and lives by it; it molds his exterior actions and his conduct towards the neighbor. The value of external acts depends on a man's intentions and on the spirit that inspires them. This holds good even of the religious life and of the observance of the vows.

A Christian is a "new creature", says St. Paul; and a creature is a thing which God alone can bring into being: God alone can produce the transformation which occurs in the soul at the moment of Baptism. In God's sight, and therefore really and truly, a baptized person has become a new man, absolutely different from what he was before, a new creature. It is hard to express in human words the change that has taken place. St. Paul says, "For you are all the children of God by faith in Christ

Jesus. For as many of you as have been baptized, have put on Christ. You are all one in Christ Jesus" (*Gal.* 3, 26-28).

"You have put on Christ" says Paul, which may signify that the change has been wrought not by our own strength, but through God's grace. And furthermore St. Paul says, "We are members of his body, of his flesh, and of his bones" (*Eph.* 5, 30); "Buried with him in Baptism, in whom also we are risen again by the faith" (*Col.* 2, 12). How intimate is our union with Christ!

If a Christian truly lives by Christ, then he is reformed in the newness of his mind: all his judgments, feelings, words and actions are according to the spirit of Christ. "Then this mind will be in us which was also in Christ Jesus" (*Phil.* 2, 5). "Be reformed", says St. Paul, urging us to make a personal effort. Yet, he is deeply convinced that it is God's work with which we co-operate, gently urged on by His grace.

III. "That You May Prove What Is the Will of God"

"That you may prove what is the good and the acceptable and the perfect will of God" (*Rom.* 12, 2).

In order to discover God's holy Will amidst the changing conditions of life, and in the midst of the passions and desires that agitate the soul, we need "newness of mind", that is the Light of Life, the light that illumines and warms the soul and enables us to lead holy lives. And in its turn, this light is fed and trimmed by holiness of life. "Jesus spoke to them saying, I am the light of the world; he that followeth me walketh not in darkness but shall have the light of life" (*John* 8, 12). He that has that light sees what is good, and acceptable and perfect before God.

Prayer: We beseech Thee, O Lord, in Thy Divine pity to accede to the prayers of Thy people, who cry to Thee; that they may know their obligations and have the strength to fulfill them. Through our Lord (Collect, 1st Sunday after Epiphany).

JANUARY 22

THE CHRISTIAN IDEAL OF LIFE—II (Rom. 12)

1. At Nazareth this ideal was realized in all its perfection, and in the most ordinary conditions of life. At Nazareth we behold

the smallest, the holiest community, that ever lived: theirs
was life in Christ, through Christ, with Christ, a most perfect
example to all those whose calling it is "to live in the Lord",
"having but one heart and one soul" (*Act.* 4, 32).

2.   *Petition*: The grace to live together, to work together, in the
spirit of the Lord, in perfect fraternal charity.

I. The Common Life in Christ Jesus

The great brotherhood of those that have been baptized in
Christ Jesus, is no longer the "little flock" of the Roman believers
to whom St. Paul wrote his letter. Those men were few, they
lived their faith with the fervor of recent converts, and they had
been compelled to break completely with the past, and therefore
they strongly felt their brotherhood in Christ.

Today the Church has hundreds of millions of members,
scattered over the face of the earth. We have countless brothers
and Sisters, men and women whom we have never seen. What
binds us to them is far deeper and far more sacred than the bonds
of blood, of race, of language. Christ is the bond, and we are
the mystical, or mysterious, body of Christ, a living body, made
one by Christ, its Head. And this unity is manifested, and nourished, in Holy Communion which is the Body and Blood of
Christ. An ancient writer said, "I am a man, and therefore whatever concerns man, concerns me." How much more truly should
a Christian say and not only say, but prove it by his actions,
"I am a Christian, and whatever concerns any human being is
my concern", for Christ has made us all brothers.

Now more than ever, when the earth has grown so small and
distances no longer exist, we have opportunities of practicing
Christian charity towards our brothers and sisters in Christ who
suffer and die for their faith in Christ. Do we remember them
in our prayers? Do we sympathize with them in their trials?

And each of us is also a member of a smaller community, for
instance, a parish, a religious house.... Such groups ought
never to become self-centered, exclusive associations. To the
members of those smaller groups we owe our first duty: love, service, forbearance extended to them every day. Genuine, pure love
of the neighbor, must be practiced first of all towards our actual
neighbors, the people with whom we have daily intercourse,
whom we see every day, but who perhaps may get into our way.
Let us meditate on what St Paul writes to the Ephesians, "I, therefore, a prisoner of the Lord, beseech you that you walk worthy of

the vocation in which you are called; with all humility and mildness, with patience, supporting one another in charity" (*Eph.* 4, 1-2).

II. "Different Gifts. Loving With the Charity of Brotherhood"

Just as in the Church, Christ's great community, so also in all smaller societies there are various offices and activities. St. Paul says: "And having different gifts, according to the grace that is given us . . . to be used according to the rule of faith." Each one, therefore, ought as best he can to fulfill the office entrusted to him, in the spirit of Christ and for the welfare of the entire community. Among brothers and sisters of the same household there may be diversities of character and talent, yet there should be neither envy nor jealousy; they should not thwart one another, but rather each must aid and support the other. "Love one another with the charity of brotherhood, with honor preventing one another" (*Rom.* 12, 10).

Where men are united not by ties of blood but by the bonds of Christ, not by a relationship of feeling but of faith, the Holy Ghost must pour charity into hearts, increase and preserve it.

Even in the small community of Christ's chosen Twelve there arose ambition and rivalry. They wanted to know who among them would hold the first places in the Kingdom that was coming, and more than once our Lord had to rebuke them. At the Last Supper He gave them a supreme lesson, saying, "If then I, being Lord and Master, have washed your feet, you also ought to wash one another's feet" (*John* 13, 14).

"Love one another, with honor preventing one another," that is, esteeming others above self (*Rom.* 12, 10). St. Paul called himself the least of the Apostles. At times we wonder how the Saints could think so despicably of themselves, whilst esteeming others highly. St. Ignatius regarded himself as the least fit to govern the Order he had founded, and the great Xavier wrote to Ignatius, on bended knee and signed, "the least of your sons."

We have cause to blush at our petty ambition. Jesus, meek and humble of Heart, make our hearts like unto Thine.

III. "Have Peace With All Men"

"If it be possible, as much as is in you, have peace with all men." And it is St. Paul, the restless champion of Christ, who bids us be at peace! To Timothy he wrote, "Labor, (that is, fight) as a good soldier of Christ Jesus" that thou mayest please thy Commander (2 *Tim.* 2, 3). This Commander is the Prince of Peace, who never shed blood except His own. In this manner St. Paul himself labored, and fought, "by the armor of justice, on the right hand and on the left", but as far as it depended on him he would have peace with all, striving to be all things to all men so that he might gain them all for the Kingdom of Christ, which is the Kingdom of peace.

"With all men!" above all with our immediate neighbors. On Maundy Thursday, during the Mandatum or washing of the feet, the choir sings the following hymn, Let us then, wherever we live together—Beware lest we be divided in spirit—Put an end to strife and division—Then Christ our God will abide with us.

"With all men", not a single exception; with strangers and all those that think differently from us, nay with our very enemies!

Prayer: Grant, we beseech Thee, O Lord, that this Holy Communion, which signifies the union of all the faithful in Thee, may earn for Thy Church the grace of oneness. Through our Lord (Postcommunion, Mass to remove Schism).

JANUARY 23

THE CHRISTIAN IDEAL OF LIFE—III (Rom. 12)

1. St. Paul writes further, "in carefulness, not slothful; in spirit fervent, serving the Lord." Another rendering reads thus, "I would see you unwearied in activity, aglow with the spirit, waiting like slaves upon the Lord" (*Rom.* 12, 11). These burning words issue straight from the heart of St. Paul, which was aglow with burning zeal for Christ. Later, from his Roman prison he was to write to the Philippians, "Not as though I had already attained, or were already perfect; but I follow after, if I may by any means apprehend, wherein I am also apprehended by Christ Jesus" (3, 12).

2. *Petition*: That our hearts may be aglow with that fire which Jesus came to cast upon the earth, the fire of divine love, "which he willed that it be kindled" (*Luke* 12, 49).

I. "Not Slothful"

We are weak and inconstant; we set out, brimful of zeal and overflowing with courage, but gradually we grow weary, get into the rut of routine, and our strength appears to be exhausted. When that happens, we must pray for perseverance and for courage, and be resolved not to yield to sloth.

It may happen that various trials overtake us, that we feel disappointed in God's service, think ourselves misunderstood, have to face opposition, are the object of censure and criticism, perhaps bitter criticism. We think that our life is a failure; our prayer is empty and brings neither light to the mind nor warmth to the heart.

St. Paul, a man of strong feelings, had his dark hours. To the Corinthians he wrote, "We would not have you ignorant, brethren, of our tribulation, which came to us in Asia; that we were pressed out of measure, above our strength, so that we were weary even of life. But we had in ourselves the answer ... that we should not trust in ourselves, but in God ... who hath delivered us, in whom we trust that he will yet also deliver us" (2 *Cor.* 1, 8-10).

One of the greatest dangers is the gradual weakening of the spiritual life, due to neglect of prayer, to conscious lukewarmness and to deliberate infidelities in God's service. Let us take to heart St. Paul's exhortation, "In spirit fervent, serving the Lord." He is a good and gracious Lord, who knows and has borne the weaknesses of our nature. He said: "Come to me, all you that labor and are burdened, and I will refresh you" (*Matt.* 11, 28). If at prayer and after Holy Communion we try to hear His voice, He will speak to us, and our hearts will burn within us, as when the men of Emmaus listened to Him in the way.

II. "In Spirit Fervent"

Here St. Paul speaks of that fervor and enthusiasm in the service of Christ which are the opposite of laxity and lukewarmness. He alludes to that lively zeal which is the effect not of a natural and unreasonable craving for action, but is kindled by pure and self-forgetting love of God and of one's neighbor. St. Paul's heart was aglow with this inward fire, which devoured his soul. To the Christians of Corinth, where some had expressed doubts about his disinterestedness and his authority, he wrote, "I most gladly will spend myself and be spent, for your souls" (2 *Cor.* 12, 15).

"Be ye in spirit fervent": thus we can, and must all be, each one according to his gifts, his office, and according to the demands of God's grace, which is given to all.

"Serving the Lord." We serve Him who said, "I am come to cast fire on earth, and what will I but that it be kindled?" (*Luke* 12, 49.) He Himself was consumed by the fire of love, and on the cross He gave Himself to us.

"On the cross, with outstretched arms, despoiled of everything, I have freely offered Myself to the Father, so that nothing in Me was left which had not been sacrificed as a holocaust for thy sins; in the same manner it behoves thee wholly to sacrifice thyself, with all thy faculties and desires, as a spotless victim in the sight of the Lord" (*Imit.* 4, 1).

In His plaint to St. Margaret Mary, Jesus said, "Behold this Heart that has loved men so much and has spared nothing, but has exhausted itself in order to prove its love to men. And in return from most of them I receive only coldness and ingratitude. And what grieves Me most is that I am treated thus by persons consecrated to Me." Jesus promised that all who would practice devotion to the Sacred Heart would receive the grace of fervor in God's service.

Prayer: O Lord Jesus, may Thy sacraments inspire in us such heavenly fervor that our experience of the sweetness of Thy most tender Heart may lead us to despise what is earthly, and to love what is heavenly. Who livest and reignest . . . (Postcommunion, Feast of the Sacred Heart).

JANUARY 24

THE CHRISTIAN IDEAL OF LIFE—IV (Rom. 12)
PERSEVERANCE IN PRAYER

1. "Be instant in prayer." Jesus said, "we ought always to pray and not to faint" (*Luke* 18, 1). And our Lord gave us a most compelling example of continual prayer. He was always "about his father's business", always most intimately united and conversing with the Father, whether He passed the night in prayer on the mountain, or labored with His hands at Nazareth, or sat at table at Cana.

2. *Petition*: The grace generously, patiently, confidently to strive for the attainment of those dispositions which prepare

the soul for the gift of continual prayer. May I abide in Thee, O Lord, and Thou in me.

I. Persevering Prayer of Supplication

"Be instant in prayer." St. Paul speaks of the prayer of impetration, mostly vocal prayer, the pleading of the beggar. Jesus often mentions that kind of prayer. "And he spoke also a parable to them, that we ought always to pray and not to faint." There was a judge, who feared not God, nor any man. When a poor widow besought him to do her justice, he refused to listen. But as she kept insisting, he finally did her justice, merely to be rid of her importunity. If the unrighteous judge acted thus, will not God do justice to His elect who cry to Him night and day? (*Luke* 18, 1-6.)

Our spiritual needs are many, and so are our temporal needs. Blessed are those, who so live that the eye of their soul can discern the greatest need of their soul: that need is closer and more intimate union with God. This longing for God made the Psalmist cry out, "As the hart panteth after the fountains of water, so my soul panteth after Thee, O God" (41, 1). And when he was in distress he cried, "My eyes are ever towards the Lord, for he shall pluck my feet out of the snare" (24, 15).

We have beheld Mary at Cana insistent in prayer, reverently and discreetly indeed, as was becoming, yet perseveringly. Out of a deeply felt desire of the soul flows continual prayer that never faints. St. Augustine writes, "Our very desire is a prayer; if our desire does not faint, neither does our prayer; from fervor of our love springs the cry of the heart."

II. Persevering Inward Prayer

When the soul draws closer to God and seeks to be united with Him alone; when it purifies itself and allows God to purify it of all stains and spots, then prayer of petition and prayer of inward adoration come closer to each other and become one. Then the soul feels only one need and one desire: to serve God perfectly here on earth; to seek and find and love Him in every action, in every event. Periods of formal prayer then become moments of more fervent intercourse and more conscious converse with God. In between the soul walks in the presence of the Lord, with the eyes of faith fixed upon Him. "Whether you eat or drink, or whatsoever else you do, do all to the glory of God" (1 *Cor.* 10, 31). We may believe that the Corinthians, who were not such holy people, understood Paul's exhortation in the proper light. And that was the manner in which the Saints acted and lived. They always beheld God close to them, within themselves. Even when they were engaged in the most distracting occupations, they lovingly clung to God, and did what they did, for Him, aware that they lived for Him, and loved Him. That is the secret of the Saints.

To love, said a mystic writer, is to mind! The more intensely we love, the more our heart minds the beloved. He that truly loves never allows the eye of his mind to stray from the beloved. He that loves God intensely, abides in God's presence, lives with God, and in God.

If we want to persevere on the road of inward prayer, we must detach ourselves more and more from whatever is not God, and we must allow God to break the bonds that bind us to creatures. When the soul is cleansed of all earthly dross, it can seek God alone; and when we seek God alone and love Him above all, then our work, done for His glory, is a prayer and unites us with Him.

All that is; first and foremost a gift of God. Every good thing, above all that which is best, is God's bountiful gift, coming from His Heart—a free and gratuitous gift, though He wills that, by courageous, patient, humble, persevering and relentless effort, we cooperate with His grace.

Prayer: Almighty and most merciful God, cast Thy gracious eyes upon us; enkindle in our hearts an ardent desire to possess Thee; deliver us from whatever would estrange us from Thee, draw our hearts unto Thee, in whom alone we can find peace, partly here on earth, perfectly with Thee in heaven.

JANUARY 25

THE CHRISTIAN IDEAL OF LIFE—V (Rom. 12)

SYMPATHY

1. The heart of St. Paul was like unto the Heart of Christ, above all in this: the Apostle possessed in a remarkable degree the gift of sympathy. To the Romans he writes, "Rejoice with them that rejoice, weep with them that weep" (12, 15).

In the Gospel we behold Jesus "moved with mercy" before the bier of the widow's only son at Naim; before the sepulchre of Lazarus He sheds tears with Martha and Mary. At the marriage feast of Cana, and at the table of Zacheus, He rejoices with them that rejoice. In this manner "the goodness and kindness of God our Savior appeared" (*Titus* 3, 4).

2. *Petition*: The grace to follow our Savior's example in loving our neighbor; that we may love all men with true christian charity.

I. Sympathy

Our self-love shuts us up within ourselves. At times it may be hard to look beyond the narrow circle we have drawn around ourselves, hard so far to forget ourselves and our personal feelings as to be able sincerely to share the feelings of others, to rejoice with them that rejoice, and to mourn with them that mourn.

Don't we at times feel that our congratulations, and our condolences too, are sheer formality, empty words not expressive of feelings of our hearts. Christian charity should enlarge our hearts and make them tender. St. Paul told the Corinthians that we are all one body, members of Christ, "and if one member suffer anything, all the members suffer with it: or if one member glory, all the members glory with it" (1 *Cor.* 12: 12, 26). Let us strive to keep in mind that ideal of life, which exalts and ennobles the soul; whereas selfishness deadens the heart and debases the soul.

Heart of Jesus, full of goodness and of love, make our hearts like unto Thine.

II. "In Deed and in Truth"

"My little children, let us not love in word, nor in tongue, but in deed and in truth" (1 *John* 3, 18). God has loved us "in deed and in truth", when He became man for our sake, in all things like unto us, sin excepted; when He suffered for us, and out of love and compassion for us died on the cross.

St. Paul showed his charity by becoming all things to all men. "For whereas I was free as to all, I made myself the servant of all.... And I became to the Jews a Jew ... to the non-Jews a non-Jew. To the weak I became weak" (1 *Cor.* 9, 19-22). Christian charity made him forget himself to such a degree that he was able to identify himself with the neighbor. St. Paul was entitled to utter those proud, yet humble, words, "Be ye followers of me, as I also am of Christ" (1 *Cor.* 11, 1). With these examples before our eyes, we are compelled to blush at our own selfishness, at our love of comfort, which prevent us from practicing the virtue of fraternal charity in our daily life. We want to have things our own way; the other man must always give in and humor us. To be all things to all men, we must utterly forget self. That is what St. Paul did. Was he the loser by it?

III. "That I Might Gain Them All to Christ"

Paul's charity was absolutely free from all self-seeking. For him, self did not exist. "For me to live is Christ" (*Phil.* 1, 21) he cried, and his burning zeal and restless toil all pointed to Christ. "And I do all things for the Gospel's sake", that is, in order to announce the good tidings and to preach Christ. And in all humility he adds, "that I may be made partaker thereof (of the Gospel)" (1 *Cor.* 9, 23). The best means to gain men to Christ is to practice the charity of Christ—love of Christ, which is at the same time love of the neighbor, active love. All, even the humblest, can understand that kind of preaching; and all of us can preach in that manner. The charity of Christ presseth us" (2 *Cor.* 5, 14) to forget ourselves, to become all things to all men, and thus to gain them all to Christ, first of all those of our own household.

Prayer: O God, who givest peace and lovest charity, grant that we Thy servants, may, according to Thy will, abide in true concord, so that we may be delivered from all the dangers that beset us. Through our Lord (Collect, votive Mass for concord).

JANUARY 26

THE CHRISTIAN IDEAL OF LIFE—VI (Rom. 12)

HUMILITY

1. The twelfth chapter of the Epistle to the Romans, part of which we have meditated on, abounds with salutary counsels, breathing the purest spirit of Christ's Gospel. St. Paul lays

down several precepts, ultimately coming to this, "be not proud, but humble". We behold the Master, saying to us, "Learn of me, because I am meek and humble of heart" (*Matt.* 11, 29).

2. *Petition:* The grace that "this mind be in us, which was also in Christ Jesus" (*Phil.* 2, 5), that is, that we may learn to be humble according to the example of Christ, who humbled Himself even unto the death of the cross (*Phil.* 2, 8).

I. "Do Not Mind High Things" (12, 16)

Do not seek your own glory. The Christian should not seek what the world esteems and longs for, honor and power. He should not be vainglorious. The natural man, with every fibre of his being, longs and labors to rise in the world and to shine before his fellows, and to lord it over them. As long as He was with them, Jesus by word and example cautioned the Twelve against ambition and lust for power. "He that will be first among you, he shall be (let him be) your servant" (*Matt.* 20, 27). "When thou art invited ... sit not down in the first place. ... Go and sit down in the lowest place" (*Luke* 14: 8, 10).

We have a craving for honor and want to hold the center of the stage, we want to supplant others! "Let that mood be in you, which was in Christ Jesus."

II. "Consent to the Humble" (12, 16)

Another translation is: "fall in with the opinions of the common folk," that is, be readily satisfied and love all that is poor and humble. That is the pure spirit of the Gospel, heroically put into practice by St. Francis of Assisi. He was the *poverello,* the small poor man! Charles de Foucauld was, in our times, another little poor man. And that was the lesson inculcated by Jesus from the manger to the cross. He was born, grew up, worked for thirty years, in a working man's family; He chose His Apostles, not from the elite of Israel, not from among the scribes and the pharisees, but from the humble ranks of society. Once a young man who had great possessions knelt before Him, and asked to become His disciple. Jesus did not turn him away; He "loved him", says the Gospel and invited him to become His follower. But the youth lacked the courage and went away sad (*Mark* 10: 17, 22).

Jesus felt and showed special affection for children, and the Apostles failed to understand and murmured, and Jesus told them, "Amen, I say to you, whosoever shall not receive the kingdom of God as a little child, shall not enter into it" (*Mark* 10, 15).

There have been Saints who frequented the great and the powerful of this world. (Did not Jesus accept the Pharisee's invitation; and don't we see Him seated at table with rich publicans?) But their aim was to gain men to Christ, and to establish and spread the Kingdom of Christ. St. Vincent de Paul was a frequent visitor at the Court in Paris, when he sent noble ladies to serve the sick in the public hospitals, or abandoned children rescued from the streets. St. Ignatius did not refuse the assistance of great Roman matrons in the foundation of a refuge for fallen women.

Indeed, there are different fields of labor, but the Christian spirit is, and will always be, to go down to the humble.

III.   High-Minded Humility

Christian humility is by no means timidity, or lack of courage or want of initiative. It is not an inferiority complex, nay it is utterly inconsistent with such a frame of mind. Christian humility is ambitious, ambitious for God's glory.

"He hath put the mighty from their seat, and hath exalted the humble", thus sang Mary, the humblest of women. A philosopher once praised God for seeking out the humble and transforming them into a new race of heaven-inspired men. Men of that breed aim at, and achieve what is highest, best and noblest—not indeed according to the judgment of this world, whose judgments are warped; but things great and noble in the sight of God. These men have no great opinion of themselves, and they love obscurity: the Lord, whom they serve "must increase" and must rule; their desire is to decrease and be forgotten.

Let us try and delve deep into our hearts, to discover whether this mood is in us which "was also in Christ Jesus". Do we love the poor? Oh, that the Lord would make our hearts like unto His, humble, and yet ambitious, and insatiably so.

Prayer: O Lord Jesus Christ, pattern and reward of true humility, who through contempt of earthly honors hast made the Saints Thy glorious followers, grant, we beseech Thee, that on earth we may imitate their humility, so that in heaven we may partake of their reward. Who livest and reignest.

CHRIST CLEANSES THE LEPER (Matt. 8, 2-4)

1. The Gospels often mention leprosy as a dread disease, which even today is widespread in the East. Till recently the sickness was regarded as extremely contagious and as incurable. Often it disfigures its victims terribly and inflicts much suffering on them. The Law of Moses ordained that lepers should be excluded from the community; these unfortunate people were wont to find shelter close to the city gates and, keeping at a distance, they would cry for alms. Whosoever touched them was legally unclean and excluded from the temple.

   "And behold a leper came and adored him, saying, Lord, if thou wilt, thou canst make me clean. And Jesus, stretching forth his hand, touched him saying, I will. Be thou made clean. And forthwith his leprosy was cleansed. And Jesus saith to him, See thou tell no man; but go, show thyself to the priest, and offer the gift which Moses commanded for a testimony unto them" (*Matt.* 8, 2-4).

2. *Petition*: That, seeing how our own soul is covered with leprosy, we may with confidence approach Christ, and be cured by His touch in Holy Communion. "Lord, if thou wilt, thou canst make me clean."

I. The Leper

St. Luke, who was a physician, describes the poor man as "full of leprosy". It is probable that this poor man had heard about the new Prophet that had arisen in Israel, and that healed every disease. He believed, and he hoped! Oh, if the Prophet would have compassion on him and cleanse him of the dread disease. And he prayed with his whole heart. It is quite possible that the unfortunate man was out of bounds, and had broken the rule that forbade lepers to come close to other people. We see him coming closer and closer to Christ, who does not repel him, as most people would have done. And in the Heart of Jesus there is immense compassion, and the leper reads it in His very eyes and "he adored him", says the Gospel. We see him prostrate before Jesus, and we hear his cry, Lord, if thou wilt, thou canst make me clean!

He firmly believes that Jesus has this power, and Jesus is pleased

to hear him profess his faith. Less strong was the faith of the
father of the boy with the dumb spirit. His prayer was, "If thou
canst do anything, help us, having compassion on us. And Jesus
saith to him: if thou canst believe, all things are possible to him
that believeth" (*Mark* 9, 21-22). With God all depends on the
divine Will; with man, it depends on faith. And when man believes, God wills. Let that distraught father's prayer be ours,
"I do believe, Lord; help Thou my unbelief."

II. Jesus Cleanses the Leper

Jesus was moved with compassion as He saw the poor leper,
covered with sores, bowing down before Him. The sick man's
profession of faith, which was at the same time a cry for help,
touched the Heart of Christ. "And Jesus stretched forth his hand,
saying, I will, be thou made clean."

Jesus could as well heal from a distance, as He did in the case
of the centurion's servant (*Matt.* 8, 13). Here the Gospel says
explicitly, "Jesus, stretching forth his hand."

What could have been our Lord's purpose? Did He do so to
show us that His divine power is exercised through His sacred
Humanity? or would He intimate that He is above the Law,
and beyond all spiritual or material defilement? Surely it was
an act of the most exquisite kindness towards one whom society
had cast out, and treated as an "untouchable".

Heart of Jesus, fountain of life and holiness, have mercy on us!

III. Our Lord's Prudence

"And Jesus saith to him, See thou tell no man, but go show thyself to the priest, and offer the gift which Moses commanded
for a testimony unto them." It is possible that the Apostles were the
only witnesses of the miracle. The happy man is bidden by Jesus
to reveal to no one that Jesus of Nazareth has cleansed him, not
even to the priest, whose office it is to bear testimony to the
man's cure, and to receive the offering prescribed by the Law.
This discretion on the part of Christ might astonish us. He works
miracles to prove that He is the Messiah; and at the same time
He sees to it that they are not bruited about throughout the land.
The reason may be that, in those days, the Jews and their leaders
entertained strange notions concerning the Messiah who was to
come. Jesus had no wish to become the tool of their national
ambitions, nor would He flatter their hopes of earthly greatness.
Everywhere we see Jesus shunning what we desire so keenly,

show, pomp and popularity. His divine greatness was infinitely above those vain things.

Prayer: Almighty and eternal God, in Thy mercy consider our weakness; and protect us under the right hand of Thy Majesty. Through our Lord (Collect of today's Mass).

MONDAY: THIRD SUNDAY AFTER EPIPHANY

CHRIST CURES THE CENTURION'S SERVANT (Matt. 8, 5-13)

1. A Roman officer, stationed at Capharnaum, had heard about the miracles of Jesus and, when his servant lay grievously ill, he went to Jesus and asked Him to heal the man. "And Jesus saith to him, I will come and heal him. And the centurion, making answer, said, Lord, I am not worthy that thou shouldst come under my roof; but only say the word, and my servant shall be healed" (*Matt.* 8: 7, 8).

2. *Petition*: Grant us, O Lord, the faith and the confidence of this Gentile centurion, whose words are so often placed on our lips by Holy Church.

I. A Noble Character

He was a Gentile, an officer in the Roman army, a representative of the occupying power, the greatest political power on earth. Most of the Romans, conscious of being the conquering race, despised the Jews, as we see in the case of Pilate. But this man was well disposed towards the conquered people. St. Luke says, "He loveth our nation; and he hath built us a synagogue" (8, 5). Another pleasing feature in his character is that he loved his servant, who must have been a slave. When he heard that the great wonder-worker of Nazareth was in the city, he at first sent some distinguished Jews, and next some of his own friends to plead with Jesus. His messengers tell him that Jesus is on his way to the house, and immediately he goes to meet the Master and addresses Him in words expressive of such profound humility, fervent faith and utter sincerity, that we can never admire them enough, "Lord, I am not worthy...."

We have before us a truly righteous man, a noble character, free from petty prejudices. A Roman officer pays homage to a

Jew, and pleads in favor of a slave: such a man is ready to follow God's grace from whatever source it comes.

And it is remarkable that Jews of standing were ready to beg for favors on behalf of a Gentile. Did they believe in, or were their eyes closed to, the "Light to the revelation of the Gentiles and the glory of His people Israel"? (*Luke* 2, 32.) We are face to face with the unfathomable decrees of Divine Providence, as well as with the unpredictable decisions of man's free will.

Lesson: Righteousness is more precious than privilege.

II. The Centurion Meets Jesus

Out of humility, and in a spirit of courtesy, the Roman wants to spare Jesus the trouble of a visit to his house. "Lord, I am not worthy that thou shouldst enter under my roof." Any other man would have been proud to welcome the Prophet in his house, but the Centurion sees things differently. With the utmost simplicity, in terms befitting a soldier, he makes a wonderful profession of faith, "Only say the word and my servant shall be healed. For I also am a man subject to authority, having under me soldiers; and I say to this, Go, and he goeth, and to another, Come, and he cometh, and to my servant, Do this and he doeth it."

This soldier understands the power of a command. His faith sees in Jesus the Lord and Master whom all things obey: He need only command and the sickness will depart. Blessed are the single-minded, blessed the righteous; without being aware of it they accomplish great things; rather, through them God accomplishes great things, because in them there is neither self-seeking nor vainglory. St. Therese of Lisieux never suspected what a luminous message she was delivering to the world in her "Little Way". St. Francis Xavier dying in sight of the coast of China had no idea that he had achieved great things for God.

III. "Jesus Marvelled"

"And Jesus, hearing this, marvelled.... I have not found so great faith in Israel.... Go, and as thou hast believed, so be it done to thee" (*Matt.* 8, 10-13). At that very moment the servant was healed. It is noteworthy that the Gospel mentions only two occasions where Christ showed astonishment: here, where He marvels at the faith of the Gentile soldier; and on the day of His first visit to Nazareth, His home town, when He preached in their synagogue, and they were scandalized in His regard; "and He wondered because of their unbelief" (*Mark* 6, 6).

Jesus is man, like unto us in all things, sin excepted; and therefore, as a man He is susceptible to human feelings like joy and grief, wonder and disappointment. And this is not make-believe. As man, He truly wonders, though as God—on another plane—He knew the centurion's faith and had aroused it by His grace. Let us remember that what our Lord values and requires from us is trustful faith. That is the homage that pleases Him.

Prayer: I do believe, Lord; help thou my unbelief (*Mark* 9, 23).

<hr>

TUESDAY: THIRD SUNDAY AFTER EPIPHANY

"LORD I AM NOT WORTHY"

1. These noble words, which aroused the wonder and admiration of Christ Himself, will, till the end of time, be on the lips of the priest and the layman before they receive the Body of Christ. The sense of unworthiness is with us from the very beginning of the celebration of the sacred mysteries; and that sense we express in the centurion's words at the moment when, in the most ineffable manner, we are about to be united with Christ.

2. *Petition*: May we truly have the dispositions expressed in those words, so that in all sincerity we may say, Lord, I am not worthy.

I. "Lord, I Am Not Worthy"

Who is the Lord, to whom we speak? At this moment, Christ in His glory, in "whose name every knee should bow of those that are in heaven, on earth and under the earth" (*Phil.* 2, 10). "The Lamb that was slain is worthy to receive power, and divinity, and wisdom, and strength and honor (*Apoc.* 5, 12): these words St. John in his vision heard from the mouth of thousands and thousands. The centurion felt unworthy to receive under his roof the mortal Christ, when He was still with us in the form of our poor human nature; and *we* dare receive His glorified Body within ourselves. In order to realize our unworthiness we may read chapter 7 of Book IV of the Imitation of Christ: "Sigh and grieve that

thou art still so carnal and worldly; so much inclined to exterior
things, so negligent to the interior; so prone to judge, so severe
in reprehending."

II. Not Worthy, Yet Confident

Throughout the Holy Sacrifice the priest has an abiding sense
of his unworthiness, and yet he has confidence and, without fear
or anxiety, offers the Sacred Mysteries. He and the faithful three
times strike their breast, confess their unworthiness, and then
receive the Lord's Body and Blood. "For," says the Imitation,
"there is no oblation more worthy, nor satisfaction greater, for
the washing away of sins, than to offer thyself purely and entirely
to God, together with the oblation of the Body of Christ, in the
Mass and Communion" (4 *Imit. of Christ* 7, 4).

We read in the Spiritual Diary of St. Ignatius that, one day,
he had clearly understood this, "Humility, reverence, awe must
be accompanied not by fear but by love. I felt this so deeply in
my soul that I prayed incessantly, Give me, O Lord, loving humility, loving reverence, loving awe."

With these feelings we should celebrate the Sacred Mysteries
which are mysteries of love, mysteries of most loving intercourse
between the soul and the most Holy God.

III. "And My Soul Shall Be Healed"

The glorified Christ is the divine Physician of our souls; the
divine medicine is His Sacred Body, sacramentally present and
working within us. Our Lord said, "My flesh is meat indeed, and
my blood is drink indeed. He that eateth my flesh and drinketh
my blood, hath everlasting life ... abideth in me and I in him"
(*John* 6: 55, 57). Nor is this Body only good for our souls, it also
heals and cleanses; it extinguishes the fires of concupiscence,
effaces traces and scars left by repented sin, and renders us fit to
receive God's grace. Such fruits of the sacrament are not shared
by all in equal measure, nor does the soul remain absolutely
passive. The working of God's grace, to a large extent, is conditioned by our dispositions, our faith, our confidence, the ardor
of our desires, our fervor. May the humble, and yet trustful,
words of the Centurion arouse in us the right dispositions.

Prayer: We implore Thee, O Lord, that the Sacrament we have
received may afford us assistance towards salvation both in soul
and body: that thus we may attain to the enjoyment in Heaven

of the fullness of the Redemption. Through our Lord (Post-communion, 11th Sunday after Pentecost).

WEDNESDAY: THIRD SUNDAY AFTER EPIPHANY

"GOD'S EYE AND GOD'S HAND"

1. Holy Writ, especially the Old Testament, frequently mentions God's eyes, casting a benevolent look on man, or which are turned away in anger. It also speaks of the Lord's right hand, stretched out to protect or to chastise. These are figures of speech, intended to make us grasp something of the Majesty of God, whom no man hath ever seen. Jahve was the God of the Jews, their own God, who with a mighty hand had delivered them from Egypt, but who also severely chastised them whenever they forsook His Law. He was the God of the nation, the God of every son of Israel as well.

What the Old Testament said figuratively about the eye and the right hand of God has become reality in the New Testament. Through Jesus of Nazareth God's eye looks down on mankind, and through Him the Almighty's right hand touches the sick and heals their ailments. Did not Jesus stretch forth His hand and cleanse the leper, or raise the dead youth at Naim?

2. *Petition*: The grace prayed for in last Sunday's Collect, "Almighty and eternal God, mercifully look upon our weakness; and for our protection stretch forth the right hand of Thy Majesty. Through our Lord."

I. The Lord's Gracious Eye

From the manner a person looks at us we know and feel what are his dispositions towards us. All understand the meaning of a scowl.

When the Psalmist feels desolate, he cries to the Lord, "How long, O Lord, wilt thou forget me unto the end? How long dost thou turn away thy face from me?" (12, 1.)

"The Lord hath looked from heaven: he hath beheld all the sons of men. . . . Behold the eyes of the Lord are on them that fear him, on them that hope in his mercy" (*Ps.* 32: 13, 18). "For the Lord is high and looketh on the low: and the high he knoweth afar off" (*Ps.* 137, 6). Mary's soul rejoiced in God her Savior, because "he hath regarded the humility of his handmaid".

With boundless delight the Father's eyes beheld the Son made man. We may feel certain that more than once Christ cast a look of reproach at the proud and faithless Pharisees, as He rebuked them. But on most occasions His look was one of tender love and deep compassion, as He beheld the crowds that surged around Him. In the Collect of the Mass of last Sunday the Almighty and eternal God, in His mercy, is asked to cast a glance on our weakness: the humble and sincere confession of our misery, and the avowal of our sins, are the most potent means of drawing God's gracious glance on ourselves.

II. God's Protecting Hand

The "hand" and the "finger" of God are the symbols of His power. In the plagues that overtook Egypt, Pharao's sorcerers saw "the finger of God"; and "God's mighty hand" delivering the Jews from the yoke of their Egyptian slavery, and leading them into the promised land. The just man has a right to trust in God's protecting hand. "If I shall walk in the midst of tribulation, thou wilt quicken me; and thou hast stretched forth thy hand against the wrath of my enemies, and thy right hand hath saved me" (*Ps.* 137, 7).

We see the right hand of God's Majesty, working through the hands of Christ Jesus. Jesus said to the Apostles, "Philip, he that seeth me, seeth the Father also" (*John* 14, 9). Jesus stretched out His hand and touched the leper, and the fell disease was healed. He touched the eyes of the blind and they saw; He took the dead child of Jairus by the hand and "her spirit returned; and she arose immediately" (*Luke* 8, 55). He laid His protecting hand on the heads of the little children, brought by their mothers; He touched the ear of Malchus, and he was healed (*Luke* 22, 51).

We shall not forget that "it is a fearful thing to fall into the hands of the living God" (*Heb.* 10, 31). But "now, O Lord, thou art our father, and we are clay, and thou art our maker, and we all are the works of thy hand" (*Isa.* 64, 8). One day, with childlike confidence, we shall pray, as Jesus Himself prayed, "Father, into thy hands, I commend my spirit," into the saving hands of His divine Majesty.

Prayer: O God, the protector of all that trust in Thee, without whom nothing is strong, nothing is holy, multiply Thy mercies upon us; that having Thee for our Ruler and Guide, we may so pass through things temporal, that we may not finally lose those which are eternal. Through our Lord (Collect, 3rd Sunday after Pentecost).

THURSDAY: THIRD SUNDAY AFTER EPIPHANY

"BE NOT OVERCOME BY EVIL" (Rom. 12, 21)

1. The last words of Sunday's Epistle propose a splendid ideal, "Be not overcome by evil, but overcome evil by good" (*Rom.* 12, 21). Such is the divine program, which we should act upon every day. When He was about to overcome the greatest evil by the greatest good, Jesus concluded His last discourse to the disciples with the following words, "Have confidence; I have overcome the world" (*John* 16, 33).

2. *Petition*: That Christ's program may always be our program.

I. Be Not Overcome by Evil

The Romans, to whom St. Paul addressed his Epistle, were a small group of converts, lost among the multitudes of that huge Babylon, which Rome was in those days. That fact we should carefully bear in mind, if we want to understand the full bearing of Paul's advice.

In the context of the Epistle the first meaning is, "Do not yield to the spirit of revenge, bless them that persecute you, bless, and curse not; to no man render evil for evil. Revenge not yourselves, my dearly beloved" (12, 14-19).

If, when a person has wronged us, or slighted or offended us, we do the same to him, we allow ourselves to be overcome by evil. That, of course, is not the opinion of the worldly, who must have the last word, and long to teach the other fellow a lesson. When they have managed to do so, they fancy they have won a victory. But St. Paul has given us the true doctrine of Jesus, who said, "You have heard that it hath been said, an eye for an eye, and a tooth for a tooth; but I say to you not to resist evil; but if one strike thee on thy right cheek, turn to him also the other" (*Matt.* 5, 38-39).

We may be overcome by evil in many ways: whenever within ourselves, in our brethren, around us, or in the world at large, we see *only* that which is evil or *especially* that which is evil; whenever we magnify the evil that does exist, or are more prone to believe evil than good, we are overcome by evil. Such a disposition is most deplorable and, with God's grace, we must get rid of it and rise above it, remembering our Lord's words, "Have confidence, I have overcome the world."

II. Overcome Evil by Good

"Bless them that persecute you; bless, and curse not.... But if thy enemy be hungry, give him to eat; if he thirst, give him to drink. For, doing this thou shalt heap coals of fire on his head" (*Rom.* 12: 14, 20). Perhaps the meaning of the Apostle is: If you do a kind deed to one that bears you ill will, if you render him a service, then there is hope that he may be converted, and that he may listen to the reproaches of his own conscience: in that case you have evercome evil by good.

To seek what is good, to make others see it and believe in it, to encourage it; and then boldly, patiently and confidently to struggle against what is evil in ourselves and in others, and to feel assured of final victory of good over evil, that is Christian optimism. "Have confidence, I have overcome the world" (*John* 16, 33), these are the words of Jesus: and we know that "heaven and earth shall pass, but His words shall not pass" (*Matt.* 24, 35). Nor should we forget the solemn testimony of St. Paul, "Where sin abounded, grace did more abound" (*Rom.* 5, 20.)

The noblest and most godlike manner of overcoming evil is to forgive from the heart, and to be determined never again to remember the offence. We all have a great deal to forgive one another: that is the unavoidable result of living at all, still more of living in the company of other men. Therefore we daily repeat, Forgive us our trespasses, as we forgive them that trespass against us.

Prayer: Almighty and merciful God, who showest Thy power over evil chiefly by pardoning sin and sparing the sinner, grant us, we beseech Thee, light and strength: so that, following Thy example, with the help of Thy grace, we may overcome evil by good. Through our Lord.

GOD HAS OVERCOME EVIL

1. God uses His power, His wisdom, His love, His patience, to oppose and to overcome evil. In our Lord, Jesus Christ His Son, who liveth and reigneth with Him world without end, He has overcome evil.

2. *Petition*: The grace to admire God's struggle against evil; the grace to have a share in it. May we have strong faith in the triumph of good over evil.

I. God Allows Evil to Abound

Evil does not come from God, who is the source of all good, and only of what is good. Evil entered the world against the divine will, as a result of the freedom of rational creatures. The Scriptures tell us that the first to bring evil into God's creation was a pure spirit: God had made him to be "Lucifer", that is "Bearer of Light"; but pride and self-complacency transformed him into the spirit of darkness. It also was brought into the world by man, who is a creature consisting of matter and spirit, weaker than the angels; he allowed himself to be deceived by Satan into breaking the Lord's command. God had endowed man with reason, and consequently with free will, a wonderful and yet an awful privilege, and God would never interfere with that freedom. He demands that man's homage and service be given freely, and He will not use coercion. Our free will is capable of giving, and of refusing, that homage and that service.

Herein lies the "mystery of evil", which has its roots in man's liberty, as well as in his weakness, and in God's decree rather to permit evil than to deprive man of his free will.

With hearts filled with awe and reverence we praise and adore the ineffable decrees of God, infinitely powerful, infinitely wise, infinitely good, infinitely holy.

II. God Has Overcome Evil

God may permit evil, but ultimately He must have the victory. He will not take revenge, but He must restore the right order. The fallen angels persist in their sin, and so does the impenitent sinner, who departs from this life in the state of mortal sin, re-jecting till the end God's proffered pardon. In those cases we see the consummation of evil, and God punishes it, or rather, that soul merits its own damnation by despising God's mercy and love till the bitter end.

Even when He has to punish, because the sinner so wills it, God does overcome evil. But God's original plan to overcome evil in man was to triumph, not by meting out retribution, but by granting pardon, or by forgetting evil. And that He might be able to do so, He delivered His only-begotten Son, permitted that He suffer and die on the cross and rise again. And thus evil was overcome in a manner divine, by Him who is the infinite Good. If the mystery of evil makes us tremble, by its side we behold the mystery of divine love for man, that compels us to return love for love.

God always triumphs—by chastisement, if He must; by for-giving, if we so will it.

III.　God Still Overcomes

During the Easter Vigil the liturgy sings about the glory of that night, which "drives away crimes, cleanses faults, restores innocence to sinners". The prince of the world has been cast forth, and through Christ God Almighty has won the victory. Satan, sin, death, evil in its source and in its final consequences, have been overcome.

But within ourselves the victory has not yet been completely won. Yet "he who hath begun a good work in us will perfect it unto the day of Christ Jesus (*Phil.* 1, 6). Within us the Father continues the struggle against evil, through the fruits of Christ's death and resurrection, that is, through the Sacraments which are administered to us by our Mother the Church, Christ's Bride. And this the Father does with infinite patience, with burning zeal, with loving compassion.

Prayer: O holy, almighty and merciful God, who with infinite patience and ardent zeal never ceasest to struggle against the evil that is on earth, grant us, we beseech Thee, the grace to resist evil within and without ourselves. Pour into our hearts the firm confidence that good shall overcome evil, and that where sin abounded, grace will more abound. Through our Lord.

SATURDAY: THIRD SUNDAY AFTER EPIPHANY

MARY HAS OVERCOME EVIL

1. At the end of time, when the battle between good and evil will have been fought to a finish, and won, when the Son of man shall hand over the Kingdom, glorious and perfect, into the hands of His Father, our eyes shall behold in all its splendor God's victory over evil. In Christ Jesus Himself, the Alpha and Omega, the First and the Last, the Source and the Crown of the work of our salvation, the triumph of good over evil will be complete. Christ has permitted His holy Mother to share in, and to co-operate with, this great victory. Therefore Mary is represented as crushing under her foot the serpent's head, symbol of evil.

2. *Petition*: May we, together with our Lady, praise and thank God for this wonderful triumph; may we, under her protection, continue the struggle against all evil, whether it be within us or around us.

I. The Triumph Foretold

With the sin of our first parents evil entered into this world. God drove them out of Paradise, and said to the serpent, "I will put enmities between thee and the woman, thy seed and her seed; she shall crush thy head, and thou shalt lie in wait for her heel" (*Gen.* 3, 15). Another translation says, "it (the Messiah) shall crush thy head." In whatever way we may translate the passage (which is often called the proto-evangel, the first good tidings) it remains that an important role in the struggle against evil is assigned to a woman: through her Son she will vanquish the serpent. The evil one, who lies in wait for her, that he may wound her, will have his head crushed under her foot. She becomes the New Eve, close to the New Adam, the Mother of all the living. Her task, though in complete subordination to Christ, is essential in God's scheme: with and through her Son, she overcomes evil.

Thus from the beginning of time, she appears by the side of her Son, inseparably united with Him who is the Messiah, the Redeemer, the Destroyer of evil. Hail Mary, full of grace, thou, who hast crushed the head of the serpent, turn then, most gracious

Advocate, thine eyes of mercy towards us, banished children of Eve. To thy protection we fly for safety.

II. The Beginning of the Triumph

Mary's victory began with the first moment of her existence, when through the merits of Christ she was completely preserved from the dominion of the evil one. She was conceived without original sin; her soul was full of grace; she was "a garden enclosed and a fountain sealed up" (*Cant.* 4, 12), a paradise of delights, where the evil one failed to gain entrance, overshadowed by the Most High.

She became Mother of the Savior, who was to cast forth the Prince of the world. When God's hour had struck, Life and Death were locked in a fierce duel; and the Lord of Life was slain, but rose from the grave living and reigning. When on Calvary the battle was being fought,

> By the cross her station keeping
> Stood the mournful Mother weeping,
> Close to Jesus to the last.

It is as if He had summoned her, that at this supreme moment He might associate her with Himself in the great mystery of Redemption.

When from the cross Jesus beheld her, and spoke to her those mysterious words, "Woman, behold thy son", Mary, we may believe, was enlightened by the Holy Ghost and understood that her Son's creative word had forged a new bond between her and the beloved disciple, who at that moment represented all those that would believe in Christ. And there by the cross, Mary spoke her last *Fiat*, and became—this time in pain and sorrow—Mother of all the living.

III. The Triumph Completed

In Mary, the first of those that are saved and the Mother of all, the triumph of good over evil was accomplished in a glorious manner. Through her Son, Mary overcame death and the last consequences of sin. St. Paul writes, "And when this mortal hath put on immortality, then shall come to pass the saying that is written, Death is swallowed up in victory. O death, where is thy victory? O death, where is thy sting?" (1 *Cor.* 15, 54-55.) Our

Mother Mary even now enjoys this glorious victory, which shall be ours only after the resurrection of the dead.

As Queen of heaven she shares in the glory of her Son. From her heavenly throne she ever intercedes for us, and keeps her merciful eyes on us, who are still struggling against evil; her powerful prayer obtains for us grace and forgiveness of sin.

During the centuries the Church has greeted her thus, "Rejoice, O Virgin Mary; thou alone hast destroyed heresy throughout the world." Mary's share in the work of our salvation is so important that, if we fail to grasp it, we fail to understand the entire divine economy.

Prayer: Grant, O Lord that, assisted by the prayers of Thy Mother and our co-Redemptrix, we may through Thy grace and by our participation in these Sacred Mysteries, advance on the road to eternal salvation. Who livest and reignest (Postcommunion, Mass of the Feast of Mary Mediatrix).

Tota Pulchra es O Maria:

Thou art all-beautiful, O Mary;
In thee there is no stain of original sin;
Thou art the glory of Jerusalem,
The joy of Israel,
The honor of our people,
Thou prayest for the sinners,
O Mary, Virgin most prudent,
Mother of divine grace,
Intercede for us with our Lord Jesus Christ.

FOURTH SUNDAY AFTER EPIPHANY

CHRIST STILLS THE TEMPEST (Mark 4, 35-40)

1. We behold the God-man , overcome with fatigue, asleep, in the midst of a violent storm. This is the only occasion when the Gospel mentions that Jesus slept. The frightened disciples awaken Him, and "rising, he rebuked the wind and said to the sea, Be still, and the wind ceased" (*Mark* 4; 37, 40).

2. *Petition*: That neither trials nor temptations may ever weaken

our trust, or cause our faith to falter. "If God be for us, who is against us?" (*Rom.* 8, 31.)

I. The Circumstances

The miracle is related by the three Synoptics nearly in the same words; only St. Mark differs from the others, in that he first says that Jesus stilled the storm, and then that the Lord rebuked the frightened disciples for their lack of faith. This order appears more natural.

"And he saith to them, when evening was come, let us pass over to the other side" (*Mark* 4, 35). Was it not rash to risk the passage at night on these inland waters, where sudden squalls were frequent? And what hurry was there? However, the disciples obey.

We often compare life to a voyage across dangerous and stormy seas to the "opposite shore" of life. Two considerations should fill us with confidence: if we are obeying the orders of our Superiors, we are safe; and, if we are in the state of grace, God is with us. Even if He appears to be asleep, we cannot perish.

If we have acted rashly, and have done our own sweet will; or, what is more grievous, if through disobedience we have got ourselves into trouble, even then humble prayer, and trust in God, can save us. God is almighty, and to His mercy there is no limit.

II. The Miracle

"And behold, a great tempest arose in the sea, so that the boat was covered with waves; but he was asleep. And they came to him, and awaked him, saying, Lord, save us, we perish. And Jesus saith to them, Why are you fearful, O ye of little faith? Then rising up, he commanded the winds and the sea, and there came a great calm" (*Matt.* 8, 24-26).

We easily understand the terror of the disciples, though, if the Master had been awake, they would have felt safe. But now He lay asleep, apparently unaware of the danger. Could He save them even in His sleep? At last they awaken Him, crying, "Lord, save us, we perish." In the midst of these frightened men, we see Jesus calm and majestic and confident: "He rebuked the winds and said to the sea: Peace, be still, and the wind ceased and there was made a great calm" (*Mark* 4, 39). A sign from His hand,

and a word of command, as startling and as amazing as the command He will later utter before the tomb of the dead man, "Lazarus, come forth", and the elements obey.

In the beginning, God's creative word "*Fiat Lux,* Let light be", was still more powerful, but no man was there to hear it and wonder; no man could have heard it. But this word spoken to the wind and the sea, "Peace, be still", proceeded from the lips of a man, and "the wind ceased and there was made a great calm" (*Mark* 4, 39). In the hearts of the Apostles too, there was a great calm. "Blessed be the Lord, the God of Israel, who alone doth wonderful things" (*Ps.* 71, 18).

III. After the Miracle

Jesus rebuked the Apostles, "Why are you fearful, O ye of little faith?" Did you not know that I cannot perish at sea? How often do we hear that same complaint from the lips of Jesus, "little faith"? To believe, that is the most difficult thing God asks from us. To believe is to have won the victory: "And this is the victory which overcometh the world, our faith" (1 *John* 5, 4); "*the world,*" that is whatever the natural man can allege against the faith.

Don't we often deserve that same rebuke, and is there any need of violent storms to make our faith falter? A humiliation seems enough, or a disappointment, opposition where we expected sympathy, even lesser things disturb our peace and discourage us. "Why are you fearful, O ye of little faith?" And yet He has said to us, "Behold I am with you all days, even to the consummation of the world" (*Matt.* 28, 20).

When those storms arise, let us pray, "I believe, Lord, help thou my unbelief." Even when He seems to be asleep, even when He does not come to our rescue in the visible manner He used on the Lake of Genesareth, yet at all times He is with us, and His Providence turns all things to our greater good. His ways are not those of man; they are mysterious, and often we fail to comprehend them; yet they are the best.

Prayer: O Lord Jesus Christ, behold us men of little faith; we beseech Thee to help our unbelief. Give us the grace never to doubt Thy infinite goodness and power, never to distrust Thy Fatherly Providence. Pour into our hearts the comforting assurance, which knows that Thou permittest us to be tried so that we may turn to Thee, and be united more closely with Thee.

THE CHURCH IN THE STORM

1.   It is customary to see in the storm-tossed boat of the Apostles
a symbol of the Church of Christ. She steers her course across
tempestuous seas, faced by countless dangers, threatened by
hostile winds. But her Captain, Christ, is always on board,
the Master of the winds and the waves, steering her to the port
of perfect calm and of eternal peace.

2.   *Petition*: That, with confidence in the guidance of the Church,
we may manfully maintain the struggle in our appointed place
and office.

I. The Church in the Tempest

The bark of Peter never knew a quiet passage under clear
skies and over unruffled waters. She is the Church Militant; hated
by the world: "In the world you shall have distress" (*John* 16, 33),
said Jesus, that is persecution, sometimes more, sometimes less
violent. In our own days we witness tremendous strains and con-
vulsions, which dislocate the entire social structure, and create
insoluble problems: these are the result of social and economic
maladjustments, of amazing technical progress, of an unheard of
increase of the means of pleasure.

Opposed to God and to His Church we behold atheistic Com-
munism: on the one side God's Kingdom, that must be established
in the world, but the spirit and purpose of which are not of this
world; on the other side the kingdom of the world, of which
Satan is king, and where he rules by force and fraud. And there
is another danger, perhaps more insidious even than Commun-
ism, threatening the Church, viz., the spread of religious indifference in all strata of society, men caring not at all about things
spiritual, and utterly forgetful of their immortal souls.

We must have the courage to face these things, though it may
be difficult to form a correct estimate of the situation: for our
eyes see neither deep enough nor far enough into the surrounding
gloom. We do not know the divine plan, nor when His almighty
hand will be stretched forth to overcome evil by good. But this
we know: the Church is built on the rock; against it the waves
may hurl themselves, but the gates of hell shall not prevail.
"Have confidence, I have overcome the world" (*John* 16, 33).

II. Our Duty

What did the Apostles do when "the waves beat into the ship", while Jesus was "asleep upon a pillow"? They were seasoned fishermen, acquainted with the whims and moods of the lake, and experience had taught them how to fight the storm and withstand the wind and the waves. Each man at his own post did his duty, until they felt over-powered and then they awakened the Master, who, by a gesture and a word saved them.

We too must have confidence, because Christ is with us, and will never forsake His ship. Yet, though He be with us, darkness and heavy seas may assail us: at that time it is each man's duty to struggle with all his might, and to stay at the post that was assigned to him, whether it be his duty to issue commands, or to hold the helm, or to trim the sails. In that manner each contributes to the safety of all.

"Do your best, and leave the rest to God" that is true of our personal spiritual life, as well as of our share in the work of God's Church. We shall say with the Psalmist, "The Lord is my light and my salvation, whom shall I fear? The Lord is the protector of my life; of whom shall I be afraid? . . . If armies in camp should rise up against me, my heart shall not fear. If a battle should rise up against me, in this will I be confident" (*Ps.* 26: 1, 3).

III. The Gates of Hell

Jesus said, "Thou art Peter, and upon this rock I will build my church; and the gates of hell shall not prevail against it" (*Matt.* 16, 18). Whether by the gates of hell we understand all the forces that stand arrayed against Christ's Church, or simply "time", the destroyer of all earthly things, here we have the Lord's promise to His Church that she shall never be destroyed. God's Kingdom on earth may suffer violence; it shall never know destruction.

It behoves us, children of the Kingdom, to feel absolutely safe; but we, who are within, have a grave duty to our fellow-men who in our own country or in distant lands grope in darkness, or despair of seeing the light, or have strayed beyond the gates, or have never yet heard the good tidings. Nor may we forget our fellow believers, in the countries where at this moment "the kingdom of heaven suffereth violence" (*Matt.* 11, 12), the suffering members of the "Church of Silence", which God's enemies endeavor to strangle in secret.

Let us, this day, earnestly ponder over these things, that we may understand that a personal responsibility lies on us. Whosoever we are, and wheresoever we be, it depends on the intensity of our personal christian life whether, through us, God's light will shine in the darkness. It depends on our own apostolic zeal and on the fervor of our prayers, whether our persecuted brothers shall be firm in the faith and loyal to Christ. These great intentions ought to goad us into greater fidelity in the service of God, and more assiduous prayer for those that endure persecution.

Prayer: O God, who knowest the greatness of the dangers that envelop us, and the inability of our weak nature to withstand them; keep us safe in soul and body, that, with Thy assistance, we may overcome the sufferings, which are inflicted on us for our sins. Through our Lord (Collect of the 4th Sunday after Epiphany).

TUESDAY: FOURTH SUNDAY AFTER EPIPHANY

THE WHOLE LAW (Rom. 13: 8, 10)

1. In last Sunday's Epistle we read, "He that loveth his neighbor hath fulfilled the law.... Love therefore is the fulfilling of the law" (*Rom.* 13: 8, 10). These words, if hyperbolical, certainly contain the marrow of Christ's doctrine, and deserve our consideration.

2. *Petition*: That our whole life and struggle for perfection be inspired by the above principle.

I. The Greatest Commandment

"And a doctor of the law asked him, tempting him, Master, which is the greatest commandment in the law? Jesus said to him, Thou shalt love the Lord thy God, with thy whole heart, and with thy whole soul, and with thy whole mind. This is the greatest and the first commandment. And the second is like to this, Thou shalt love thy neighbor as thyself" (*Matt.* 22, 35-39).

The scribe must have been amazed when he heard Jesus thus linking together the second with the first commandment. Jesus refuses to separate love of God from love of neighbor. No one had ever before attributed such importance to brotherly love.

St. John, the disciple whom Jesus loved, very clearly expresses the connection between the two precepts: "If any man say, I love God, and hateth his brother, he is a liar. . . . This commandment we have from God, that he who loveth God, love also his brother" (1 *John* 4, 20-21). The more we love God, the more we love our neighbor. For those who profess to follow Christ more closely, love of the neighbor is the touchstone which proves that their love of God is genuine. Jesus Himself said, "This is my commandment, that you love one another, as I have loved you" (*John* 15, 12).

II. To Love Our Neighbor Is to Love God

For the Christian, fraternal charity is a theological virtue, inseparable from love of God. "Two precepts, but one love" says St. Augustine. In Baptism the Holy Ghost infuses this virtue into our soul. "For whosoever are led by the spirit of God, they are the sons of God. For you have not received the spirit of bondage again in fear; but you have received the spirit of adoption of sons, whereby we cry, Abba (Father)" (*Rom.* 8, 14-15). In that spirit we call one another brothers, children of the same Father, brothers of the same Lord Jesus Christ. It is a supernatural virtue: yet it is true, sincere, human love; broader, purer, more effective, more unselfish than mere natural philanthropy. "Behold how they love one another" said the Gentiles concerning the first Christians, whilst an ancient heathen philosopher said, "Every man to his fellow man is a wolf." After nearly twenty centuries of Christianity we have not yet fully tamed the wild beast that is in every man, not in our relations with our neighbor, and still less where relations between different nations are concerned.

"Come, Holy Ghost, enkindle in our hearts the fire of Thy love, whence shall spring love of the neighbor."

III. If We Love Our Brethren, We Love God

St. John says: "He that loveth not his brother whom he seeth, how can he love God whom he seeth not?" (1 *John* 4, 20.) How shall we ascertain whether we truly love God? There are those who, in this matter, grievously delude themselves: those for instance that shun contact with others because they despise them; those that go up to the temple, like the Pharisee, to thank God because they are not like the rest of men. It is still more abominable in God's sight to fancy that one loves God because one does not care for men.

We can love God, whom we do not see, only in men, whom we
see, and whom God calls "His own". When we treat as brothers
those whom God calls "the least of my own", when we assist
them in their needs, solace them in their sorrows, and serve them
without seeking personal advantage, then we shall have a proof
that we truly love God!

If we love Him, we shall keep His commandments, above all
the second, which is like unto the first and can never be separated
from it, "Love thy neighbor as thyself", or as Jesus Himself said:
"Love ye one another as I have loved you."

Prayer: O God, who turnest all manner of things to the profit
of those that love Thee; establish unshakably in our hearts the
spirit of Thy love, so that our desires may spring from Thy inspiration, and remain unshaken by temptation. Through our Lord
(Collect to beg for the grace of the love of God).

WEDNESDAY: FOURTH SUNDAY AFTER EPIPHANY

JESUS PREACHES AT NAZARETH (Luke 4, 16-27)

1. "And he came to Nazareth, where he was brought up: and
   he went into the synagogue . . . and rose up to read . . . and all
   gave testimony to him, and wondered at the words of grace
   that proceeded from his mouth." That was the first impression.
   Later they would be filled with anger and threaten violence.
   It is easy to imagine the whole scene. Our Lady most probably
   was present.

2. *Petition*: The grace to understand the feelings of Jesus and
   of Mary, now that in His own city He has become a sign that
   is contradicted. Grant, O Lord, that we may never be scandalized in Thee, in Thy Mystical Body, Holy Church.

I. Jesus Preaches in the Synagogue

St. Luke gives us the most circumstantial account of this extraordinary occurrence during the public ministry of Jesus (*Luke* 4,
16-27). Probably he had the facts from Mary herself, who had
kept these things in her heart and had pondered over them.

"And he came to Nazareth, where he was brought up, and he

went into the synagogue according to his custom, on the sabbath day." To pay Him honor the minister handed Him the scroll of Holy Writ, and requested Him to read the sacred text and to comment on it. "And he rose up to read. And the book of Isaias the prophet was delivered to him, and as he unfolded the book he found the place where it was written, The spirit of the Lord is upon me; wherefore he hath anointed me to preach the gospel to the poor, he hath sent me to heal the contrite of heart: to preach deliverance to the captives, and sight to the blind, to set at liberty them that are bruised, to preach the acceptable year of the Lord, and the day of reward" (*Luke* 4, 17-19).

Then He folded the book, returned it to the minister and sat down, and the eyes of all in the synagogue were on Him. He said, "This day is fulfilled this Scripture in your ears."

The words He had read were most pertinent. He Himself is "the Lord's anointed", He is the One "who is to come", He is the Messiah. "The fame of him had gone forth through the whole country" (*Luke* 4, 14). And the glad tidings are being announced by Him to the poor, the contrite of heart, the captives, to them that are bruised.

When the Baptist, from his prison, sent men to ask, Art thou He that art to come, or look we for another? Jesus appeals to the same tokens as a guarantee of His mission: the blind see, the lame walk, to the poor the gospel is preached (*Luke* 7, 22-23). Love of the humble and of the poor ever was, and still is, the hallmark of the true spirit of Christ: that is a point which no Christian, least of all those in high position, should ever forget.

We may be struck by the straightforwardness and the assurance of our Lord's claim: "This day is fulfilled this Scripture in your ears!" Never yet had a man spoken thus. Later it would be said of Him: "He was teaching them as one having power, and not as the scribes and the Pharisees" (*Matt.* 7, 29).

All those men, whose eyes were on Him, had long known Him; He had grown up in their midst, and there was nothing about Him which they did not know; but the manner in which at this moment He stood forth and in which He addressed them, that indeed was a revelation.

II. The Impression Produced

At first they were charmed by His fascinating personality. "And all gave testimony to him. And they wondered at the words of grace, that proceeded from his mouth" (*Luke* 4, 22). But the impression was superficial, as with the people about whom Jesus spoke in the parable of the Sower, "they who, when they hear, receive the word with joy, and have no roots" (*Luke* 8, 13). Soon doubts arose, petty surmises, and mean cavilling.

"Is not this the son of Joseph . . . the carpenter's son? Is not his mother called Mary? Don't we know the whole family? How came this man by all that wisdom?" Jealousy, envy, mean and petty feelings closed their minds and their hearts to the words of grace which He spoke. Others said, "And what are those miracles with which he is credited? Why will He perform them at Capharnaum, and not here before his own people, in his own city?" Their pride felt slighted because others seemed to have been preferred to them. The attitude of the men of Nazareth seems rather despicable, yet how human! How frequently will Jesus have to endure the same things during the public ministry . . . and in our own days! Grant us light, O Lord, that we may see how often Thou meetest in our souls mean and selfish sentiments and dispositions.

Prayer: O Lord, searcher of hearts and reins, who seekest not to condemn or to chastise, but whose will it is to heal and to show mercy, look down on us with compassion; pardon us and cleanse our hearts from whatever is petty and mean and from those things that close the soul to divine grace. Heart of Jesus, full of goodness and love, have mercy on us.

THURSDAY: FOURTH SUNDAY AFTER EPIPHANY

THE PEOPLE OF NAZARETH ARE SCANDALIZED

1. "And they were scandalized in regard of him," says St. Mark. All those present in the synagogue knew Him quite well, and some were related to Him. Even though the Gospel does not mention Mary, she must have been there. If so, she was a witness of the absurd anger of the crowd, and was deeply hurt by their conduct.

2. *Petition*: May we never be scandalized with regard to Christ's Mystical Body, the Church, neither by ordinary nor by extraordinary occurrences.

I. Scandal Not Justified

The Baptist had told the Jews, "There hath stood one in the midst of you, whom you know not, the same is he that shall come after me" (*John* 1, 26-27). Jesus, after receiving John's baptism, had begun to announce the Kingdom, in a very unspectacular manner.

On this occasion He stands up for the first time as teacher in his own village of Nazareth, among people that have known Him for a long time, among men who, perhaps, have approached Him too closely; yet who would say that Jesus can be approached too closely? He, of all men, was not like those heroes who are not heroes to their valets. In Him everything is great; and the closer we come to Him, the more vividly do we realize His greatness.

But to the villagers of Nazareth there never had been anything extraordinary about Jesus, even though under their eyes He had advanced in age, and wisdom and grace with God and with men. They could see in Him no more than the Son of Mary and of the village carpenter. We can understand that all these years they had failed to discern the Divinity hidden under the trappings of human nature. The Divinity was hidden. But now It manifested Itself and not only did words of grace come from His lips, but He had performed signs that bespoke supernatural power. Willful blindness sealed their eyes, so that they refused to see in Him anything more than the carpenter's son. And when He stands forth as the Prophet, they are scandalized in regard of Him.

"Like unto us in all things, sin excepted": that is how the Son of Man appeared on earth. As Head of His Mystical Body, the Church, the glorified Christ is all-holy, and the source of all holiness; but the members of that Mystical Body, the highest as well as the lowest, are all human, weak sinners. They all have the grace to strive after higher and nobler things but the glorious Church, not having spot or wrinkle (*Eph.* 5, 27) is not yet. Too often we see only the human failings; at other times we behold the glory that is hers and her evident divinity.

If we lack faith we may take scandal at the spots and the failings, and even at what is plainly supernatural: the spots and wrinkles may make us blind to the glory; and what is supernatural may frighten, may be hard to understand, may arouse doubt. May the Holy Spirit open our eyes. Mary, Seat of Wisdom, pray for us.

II. Faith and Knowledge in Mary

No one knew Jesus more intimately than Mary. She had seen
Him grow daily; her influence had molded His soul; before her
eyes He had advanced in wisdom and grace with God and men.
But except for one incident, when He had stayed with the Doctors in the temple, everything in their life at Nazareth had been
commonplace. The Holy Family was certainly a model family,
and a happy family; but not different from other devout families
in the village of Nazareth. The Divinity lay hid under the most
ordinary appearances.

One day Jesus bade farewell to His Mither, abandoned the
workshop, and began to announce the coming of the Kingdom.
Once His mother met Him at Cana, and prevailed on Him to
work His first miracle.

And now Mary sees Him in the synagogue, at the ambo or
reading desk; "and the eyes of all in the synagogue were fixed on
Him", certainly the eyes of His Mother. Better than the others,
Mary understood "the words of grace that came from His lips".
Perhaps at this hour it dawns on her that the Holy One, that was
born of her, was less her own than He had been heretofore; that
He grew ever greater, in a way beyond her mother's love; and
her mother's heart gave her consent to it all. She had borne Him
and fed Him at her breast; she had known Him and carried Him
as a helpless infant; and now He was moving beyond her reach,
and her love could bear that; her faith remained unshaken, for
she accepted the fact that it had to be so, that such was God's
will in her regard. Her faith gave her the courage to see her own
Son ever growing in spiritual stature, ascending into those mysterious regions where the human eye cannot reach; and Mary repeated her *Fiat.* Therein consisted the greatness of Mary (Guardini).

Mary believed, and often did not understand; never did she
entertain a doubt; faithfully she kept all these things in her heart,
and pondered over them. Blessed are we if we follow her example.

III. Mary's Suffering

It hurt her mother's heart to hear vulgar minds indulging in
petty criticism, and envious carping against the Son she loved,
"Is he not the son of Mary?" or "a mere carpenter!" Simeon had

foretold it: "Behold this child is set for a sign which shall be contradicted." She feels this contradiction the more as it comes from the very persons that ought to have known Him so well, perhaps from close relations. And some remarks were so bitter and so mean: it was hard for His Mother to bear that.

One day Jesus will say, "Do not think that I came to send peace upon earth. I came not to send peace, but the sword. For I came to set man at variance against his father, and the daughter against her mother, and the daughter-in-law against the mother-in-law. And a man's enemies shall be they of his own household" (*Matt.* 10, 34-36). These words have their application in extraordinary cases; yet Jesus and His Mother experience these things: "He came unto his own, and his own received him not" (*John* 1, 11). Within ourselves and all round us we experience how difficult it is to see God's hand at work in the world.

Prayer: Holy Mother of Christ, Seat of Wisdom, who wert wont to keep these words in thy heart, and to ponder over them: strengthen our faith, confirm our confidence, teach us to pray for those that are scandalized in regard to thy Son, and who reject Him.

Lord Jesus, Thou excludest no man from Thy mercy, but strivest to save all: grant us, we beseech Thee, light and strength, so that, endowed with Thy spirit and following Thy example, we may with love and courage preach Thy Name to all men.

FRIDAY: FOURTH SUNDAY AFTER EPIPHANY

CHRIST'S FAILURE AT NAZARETH (Luke 4, 28-30)

1. There was some tumult in the synagogue; "and all they in the synagogue, hearing these things were filled with anger. And they rose up and thrust him out of the city, and they brought him to the brow of the hill whereon their city was built, that they might cast him down headlong. But he, passing through the midst of them, went his way" (*Luke* 4, 28-30). The visit to the town where He was brought up, turned out a bitter disappointment; they laid hands on Him, ready to take His life.

2. *Petition*: To share the feelings of Jesus at this hour. Learn from Him to bear failure and disappointment.

I. The Failure

Our Lord had not begun His public ministry at Nazareth, but at Capharnaum, an important town some 24 miles away. There He had found faith in the hearts of many and had wrought miracles, the fame of which soon reached Nazareth. His fellow villagers, therefore, were aware of the fact that Jesus was preaching the Kingdom: but the words of grace, which they heard from His mouth, may have charmed them a while, but failed to dissipate their narrow prejudices. When Jesus had shown them with examples from the Scriptures that no Prophet is acceptable in his own country, they were filled with fury, and would have killed Him. Jesus seems to have allowed them to lay hands on Him and to have suffered them to drag Him to the brow of the hill. It is probable that along the way, or at the end, there was some quarrel among the rioters, so that Jesus, "passing through the midst of them, went his way." "His hour was not yet come"—the hour appointed by the Father—and Jesus knew it—and therefore their violence and their fury were powerless against Him.

But His Heart yearned for these misguided folk, and He "*wondered* because of their unbelief", says St. Mark (6, 6). As man our Lord felt astounded: we know that, as man, Jesus did feel wonder, and disappointment and all other human emotions. We read that on other occasions, Jesus "*grieved* for the blindness of their hearts" (*Mark* 3, 5). Jesus *loved* His own people: "I was not sent but to the sheep that are lost of the house of Israel" (*Matt.* 15, 24). We shall see Him shedding tears over the fate of His beloved Jerusalem, which had rejected Him and which was to experience the divine wrath.

"And he could not do any miracles there" (*Mark* 6, 5), says the Evangelist. Not that He did not have the divine power, but because He would not use compulsion with free human beings. When man deliberately closes his soul to grace, or refuses to co-operate, God respects his freedom and does not use His power against his will.

We co-operate by faith and trust, and these are offered us by God; if we accept them, we shall be saved by God. We can also will our own damnation. Terrible responsibility! In the struggle for perfection we are able to accept, and able to reject, God's grace.

II. A Lesson for the Apostles

Jesus had taken His Apostles with Him to Nazareth. He had chosen them that "they be with Him", that from day to day they might share His lot. They should see not only His miracles, but also His failures; witness His power and His impotence; and behold how He bore Himself in the midst of trials and tribulations. One day He will say unto them, "The servant is not greater than his master; if they have persecuted me, they will also persecute you" (*John* 15, 20). When they had seen how Jesus did not find faith among His own people, who finally would put Him to death, then, how could they wonder, or feel discouraged, when their own message was rejected, or when they had to counter opposition. "As the Father hath sent me, I also send you" (*John* 20, 21), "for a sign which shall be contradicted, that out of many hearts thoughts may be revealed" (*Luke* 2, 34-35).

Let all the followers of Christ, above all such as are called to spread the ·Kingdom, take to heart this salutary lesson. They must meet with opposition or, what may be worse, with indifference; often the sense of failure will invade their soul; they will think that their labors, their zeal, their sufferings and humiliations are all in vain. Throughout the years of His public ministry, Jesus met with scant success and much failure; His labors often seemed fruitless, and He had little solace from men. He found His joy and His peace in doing His Father's will, and in that alone.

And yet in the end He gained the victory; and His last words to the disciples, before He sent them to conquer the world, were, "Have confidence, I have overcome the world" (*John* 16, 33).

Prayer: Lord Jesus, grant us the grace ever to live and labor for Thee alone, with a pure intention; not to wonder nor to be disheartened when we suffer opposition and fail in our efforts. Whisper into our ears those words of Thine: "Have confidence, I have overcome the world."

SATURDAY: FOURTH SUNDAY AFTER EPIPHANY

THE PRAYER OF ST. NICHOLAS VON FLUE

1. St. Nicholas von Flue was born in Switzerland in 1417. He was of peasant stock, had been a soldier, and later held a civil

office in his Canton. He was the father of ten children. When he was fifty years old, he felt a call to the solitary life, left home and wife and children, to lead a life of prayer and penance in a hermitage. On several occasions, when strife had broken out in the Cantons, he emerged from his solitude to act as arbiter and peace-maker between the contending parties. He died in the odor of sanctity in 1487, and was canonized by Pius XII in 1947. He summed up the whole of the spiritual life in a touching prayer, which he often repeated in his hermitage, and which will form the subject matter of this meditation.

2. *Petition*: O Lord God, take from me whatever keeps me from Thee; O Lord God, give me whatever brings me closer to Thee; O Lord God, take me from myself and give me to Thyself.

I. What Keeps Me From Thee

First of all,—sin! Mortal sin, by which man deliberately turns away from God; venial sin, which weakens his union with God; then, all more or less deliberate resistance to what man knows to be God's good pleasure. Ultimately what separates man from God is self-love, in so far as it runs counter to love of God. Its most dangerous form is PRIDE, which erects a barrier between God and the soul.

We experience every day how deeply self-love is rooted in our nature, how it affects our whole being, and our every action, how it prevents us from drawing closer to God; and we do feel so powerless to shake off its shackles!

Therefore the holy Hermit prayed, "O Lord God, take from me what keeps me from Thee." God alone can do it. We must patiently wait till He is pleased to deliver us, and always trust His healing hand. He has many means to take away what separates us from Him: for instance He can deprive us of a thing to which we are inordinately attached; He may try us by sending us failure and humiliation: in these things His purpose is to take from us what prevented us from coming closer to Him.

Through the Sacraments, Penance, Holy Mass, Holy Communion, He continues in us His work of purification, and frees us from fetters that bind us.

O God, may Thy Sacraments heal the wounds of our souls, and bring us to the reward of eternal salvation! (Postcommunion, 17th Sunday after Pentecost.)

II. What Brings Me Closer to God

The entire creation, and whatever comes from God, is a way leading to God. When the soul has been cleansed completely, it will seek God, approach Him and find Him in every creature, in every event, except in sin. In all these things God comes closer to us, as St. Paul told the wise men of Athens, "that they should seek God, in the hope that they may feel after him and find him, although he be not far from any one of us" (*Act.* 17, 27).

Two things that lead us closer to God are: strong faith and ardent love. The Father has given us His Son and, through Him, He has not only drawn us closer to Himself, but even made us His own children. And the Son, through His sacred Body, unites us with Himself: "He that eateth my flesh and drinketh my blood abideth in me and I in him" (*John* 6, 57).

Of course, over all this remains spread the veil of faith; but one day this veil, which still separates us from God will be withdrawn. What can death be to us, except meeting the Lord and seeing Him face to face?

III. Give Me Wholly to Thyself

Take me from myself, and give me to Thyself: the final deliverance from all that is petty, from all that limits; the final and thorough burning out of self-love, through which we surrender our whole being to God, or rather, by which He gives us entirely to Himself. The final and absolute oblation of ourselves to the Lord will be offered at the hour of our death. At that moment the priest will thus address us, "Dear brother (or sister) I commend thee to God Almighty, and I entrust thee into the Hands of Him that created thee, so that after thou hast paid through death the debt of our humanity, thou mayest return to thy Maker, who hath fashioned thee out of the slime of the earth" (Prayers for the agonizing).

At that moment occurs what Ruusbdoeck describes at the end of the Spiritual Marriage: "There we shall rest eternally in a beatific embrace of loving surrender, lost in that boundless Being, the desire of all fervent souls. This is the dark solitude in which all true lovers are plunged. That we may then understand God's essential oneness and contemplate this oneness in the Trinity: may He that never said nay to a beggar bestow on us that supreme favor."

Prayer: Bring us, we beg Thee, O Lord, to the eternal possession and enjoyment of Thy Divinity, which is prefigured by our
reception in time of Thy precious Body and Blood. Who livest
and reignest.... (Postcommunion, Feast of the Blessed Sacrament.) ⟶ end

FIFTH SUNDAY AFTER EPIPHANY

THE PARABLE OF THE COCKLE

(Matt. 13: 24-30; 37-40)

1. In the parable of the cockle among the wheat, Jesus gave the
   country folk of Galilee an answer to the old problem why God,
   who is the source of all good, permits so much evil in the world.
   A husbandman had sowed good seed in his field, but at
   night his enemy came and oversowed cockle among the wheat.
   When the servants informed the good man of the house, he
   said, "An enemy hath done this". The servants desired to uproot the weeds, but the good man said, No, lest you uproot the
   wheat with the cockle, wait till harvest time, and then you
   will burn the cockle and carry the wheat to my barn.
   Jesus Himself explained the parable to the Twelve: "He that
   soweth the good seed is the Son of Man, and the field is the
   world, and the good seed are the children of the kingdom.
   And the cockle are the children of the wicked one. And the
   enemy, that sowed them, is the devil. But the harvest is the
   end of the world." The wicked shall be cast into the furnace of
   fire, and the just shall shine as the sun in the kingdom of their
   Father. "He that hath ears to hear, let him hear" (*Matt.* 13,
   37-43).
   We try to hear this explanation from the lips of Jesus: He
   knows, and every day during His public ministry He experiences more vividly, that the Prince of the world is secretly
   sowing cockle in the field of Galilee and Judea. And down the
   centuries He sees that titanic battle between good and evil,
   between truth and error, that is being fought at all times, and
   in all places and which will cease only when He shall have won
   the final victory. And from His mouth we hear the mysterious
   warning, "He that hath ears, let him hear!"

2. *Petition*: That we may have ears to hear. Show us, O Lord, how to hate sin while loving the sinner. Grant us the assurance that, in Thy own appointed time, good shall overcome evil.

I. The Good Seed

Jesus loved, and frequently used the symbol of the seed, the tiny grain endowed with a mysterious principle of life. It is sowed and disappears under the ground, where it dies, to rise and live again and to produce a plentiful harvest. His own death and burial whence He rose, not only having, but also giving life, He compared to the grain, which dies, is buried in the earth, that it may bring forth new life in abundance.

Whatsoever proceeds from God is good, and the Father is the author and giver of all that is good. His own Son is His most precious gift to us, the Divine Seed, sowed in our human nature. He, as Son of man, in His turn scatters the good seed. He is the Word of the Father, that gives life and light to all such as have ears to hear, and eyes to see. It was only after His death and resurrection that the seed could grow, and that the harvest could be gathered.

The good seed bears within itself the mysterious power to sprout and to grow: and the seed springs and grows up, and the sower knows not how. For the earth of itself bringeth forth fruit, first the blade, then the ear, afterwards the full corn in the ear (*Mark* 4, 27). These words were spoken by Jesus on another occasion.

Here our Lord stresses an important truth, viz. that the establishment of the Kingdom within ourselves, and throughout the world, is, first of all and above all, God's own work. To know this will not cause our zeal to flag; but it will spare us much anxiety and soften the pangs of disappointment in times of failure. Ours is the duty to sow, to plant, to water, but God alone can give the increase as St. Paul proclaimed long ago. Yet Paul added, "We are God's coadjutors" (1 *Cor.* 3, 6-9).

Let these be our habitual dispositions, and we shall toil with God, like God, in peace and with zeal.

II. The Enemy

The husbandman's enemy, filled with wrath and envy, came by stealth and when the men were asleep, oversowed cockle among the wheat, and went his way. No one had seen him, but after a while both the wheat and the cockle sprang up. "The enemy, that sowed the cockle, is the devil", man's bitterest enemy, said Jesus. The first evil thought that ever defiled a mind, was born in Satan's mind: pride which lifts self above God. And Satan sowed that evil seed in the souls of Adam and Eve, where until that day original justice, the good seed sowed by the Creator, had grown and prospered.

Ever since that day, "the enemy" has been busy oversowing cockle among the wheat, laboring to foil God's plan for the salvation of mankind, in our own souls, throughout the wide world, at night and by stealth. He strives to damp our fervor to stifle our good resolutions, to discourage us and to make us tepid in the service of God.

Lust for wealth and lust for power are his favorite weapons to conquer the great ones of the earth, who, at times unknown to themselves, more often with open eyes, and deliberate intent, follow his lead. "While his men were asleep the enemy oversowed cockle among the wheat and went away."

Prayer: Assist Thy people, we beg Thee, O God, to avoid all contact with the devil and with pure minds, to seek Thee, the only true God. Through our Lord (Collect, 17th Sunday after Pentecost).

MONDAY: FIFTH SUNDAY AFTER EPIPHANY

GOD'S POLICY

1. In the parable of the cockle among the wheat, the servants, fearing lest the weed should choke the good grain, propose the immediate uprooting of the tares. The master will not let them do so, because his plan is to let good grain and weeds grow together, and to make the separation at harvest time. Such is God's policy with regard to evil in the world: He is holy and omnipotent, and at the same time infinitely patient.

2. *Petition*: The grace to understand the Lord's patience, inspired by His love and His wisdom. May we follow His example.

I. The Lord's Patience

The enemy is Satan! God knows him, abhors him, has cast him out of heaven forever, and will not tolerate him within His sight. Once Satan was Lucifer, the bearer of light: but now he is the prince of darkness, utterly wicked in himself and the source of all evil. With him God can have neither patience nor mercy.

But with sin on earth, with the sinner, God is infinitely patient and infinitely merciful. We ourselves have been and are the objects of this patience and this mercy, for which we return most humble thanks to His Divine Majesty. And all around us we behold this patience and this mercy and we wonder ... and at times are ready to take scandal. We see evil overcome good: evil is powerful, and good is weak. We tremble with fear and we doubt and we ask why God does not stretch forth His mighty hand to destroy evil.

Such is not the divine policy: He permits the simultaneous growth of good and evil, for His eye sees the distant future and He knows the ultimate result. At times we are abashed at the spectacle of good and evil being inextricably intertwined even in the same soul. God sees this too and He knows how and when to disentangle it all. Strife on earth between good and evil may have salutary results, "that out of many hearts thoughts may be revealed" (*Luke* 2, 35). Evil may cause virtue to flourish; the cowardice of one may give an opportunity to the other to be heroic. God can afford to wait, for eternity belongs to Him: He waits till harvest time, and "the harvest is the end of the world". We, short-sighted men, born yesterday, cannot see beyond our little horizon, and we grow impatient.

God grant us a firm trust in His love and His wisdom; may we imitate His patience and His mercy towards sinners.

II. The Victory

"Now shall the prince of this world be cast out" (*John* 12, 31), said Jesus before the Last Supper. And a while before He had said, "Amen, amen, I say to you (Jesus uses these words to preface a solemn declaration), unless the grain of wheat falling into the ground die, itself remaineth alone, but if it die it bringeth forth much fruit" (*John* 12, 24-25).

"Death and life were locked in a fierce duel; the Prince of life was slain, but arose from the dead and won the victory." He alone achieved the victory, but He permitted His Mother to have a share in it.

The battle between good and evil is still being fought in His Mystical Body: in each of us within our soul; in the whole Church. The eternal enemy of God and of man, Satan, with truly "satanic" fury, though with less power than of old, ceaselessly fights against Christ's Kingdom on earth.

Of the final victory there never was any doubt: "Even as cockle therefore is gathered up, and burnt with fire, so shall it be at the end of the world. The Son of man shall send his angels, and they shall gather out of His Kingdom all scandals, and them that work iniquity. And shall cast them into the furnace of fire; there shall be weeping and gnashing of teeth. Then shall the just shine as the sun in the Kingdom of the Father. He that hath ears to hear, let him hear" (*Matt.* 13, 40-43).

Nor have we to await the Last Judgment and the end of time to witness God's triumph over evil. On that day the victory will be complete and will put an end to strife forever and ever. Now on earth the battle between good and evil sways backwards and forwards; there are brilliant victories, grievous defeats, set-backs, sombre moments and dark hours. At times virtue shines out in all its brightness, at others it pales and sin is in the ascendant. Let us never forget the last word Jesus spoke to the Apostles before the Passion, "In the world you shall have distress: but have confidence, I have overcome the world" (*John* 16, 33). And again what He said just before He ascended into heaven, "I am with you all days, even to the consummation of the world" (*Matt.* 28, 20).

Through His abiding presence in each of us, and in the whole Church, through His grace and His sacraments, Jesus bestows strength and power on those that strive for the victory of good over evil; even while He strenuously opposes evil, He patiently endures it; with infinite mercy He forgives it when He can, and He makes use of it to make better what is good.

God, being Holiness Itself cannot but hate evil; but the evil-doer He loves so much that, to save him, He has delivered His only-begotten Son. When tares and weeds have invaded the field, He does discern the good seed which He Himself has sowed: by means of the refreshing showers and the warm sunshine of His grace, He prepares the soil and enables the wheat to grow and mature. "The tremendous mystery of the Christian soul" is rooted in the firm conviction that "where sin abounded, grace did more abound" (*Rom.* 5, 20).

Prayer: We implore Thee, O Lord, ever to watch over Thy children with loving care; that they who place all their hopes in heavenly favor, may always be secure under Thy protection. Through our Lord (Collect, 5th Sunday after Pentecost).

TUESDAY: FIFTII SUNDAY AFTER EPIPHANY

REMEMBER THY LAST END (Eccl. 7, 40)

1. In the parable of the cockle and the wheat there is mention of the harvest, that is the end of time: "But the harvest is the end of the world", when the wheat and the cockle, the good and the wicked, shall hear their doom from Him, who alone can "separate" them, and who can afford to wait for the day of "separation".

"Remember thy last end, and thou shalt not sin," is an ancient and a salutary proverb, to which we may add, "and you'll find it very profitable". Let us not be exclusively preoccupied with the present, so as to grow inordinately attached to things, or so as to be scandalized by them. St. Paul says, "The fashion of this world passeth away" (1 *Cor*. 7, 31). One day, as our Lord "was going out of the Temple, one of the disciples said to him, Master, behold, what manner of stones (i.e. of huge size), and what buildings are here! And Jesus answering saith to him, Seest thou all these great buildings? There shall not be left a stone upon a stone, that shall not be thrown down" *Mark* 13, 1-2).

2. *Petition*: That undisturbed by things of earth, even by the fierce battle between good and evil, we may firmly believe in the ultimate triumph of God. This faith will be a source of comfort and a fountain of strength.

I. The Coming of the King and Judge

The coming of the Judge is described in Psalm 96, parts of which were read in the Introit of last Sunday's Mass. In his description the sacred writer uses images drawn from the most stupendous phenomena of nature. A frightful tempest has burst forth over the face of the earth. Thick clouds and the blackest darkness (a symbol of God's hidden presence) envelop the whole world, and then fearful shafts of lightning and tongues of fire leap forth to destroy the wicked. The heavens are in turmoil, the earth trembles and is saken to its foundations; a deluge of water streams down the mountains, which melt like wax...

These are inadequate symbols to describe the awful things that one day will happen, when God, One in Three, shall be revealed in might and majesty: the Father, who created heaven and earth; the Son, our Redeemer and the supreme Judge of the whole race; the Holy Spirit, who is the "First Love". Time has ceased, eternity has begun, the eternal lot of every man has been sealed.

"But of that day and that hour no one knoweth, not the angels of heaven, but the Father alone" (*Matt.* 24, 36).That day is drawing closer and closer, inexorably, pitilessly. We fancy it is still far away: in truth it is here, on us, for "one day with the Lord is as a thousand years, and a thousand years as one day" (2 *Peter* 3, 8). On that one day—which is the span of our life—the whole of our eternity depends. "Time flies fast. Do not waste it!"

II. The Punishment

The Psalmist thus describes the lot of the wicked (*Ps.* 96)

A fire shall go before him,
And shall burn his enemies round about;
Let them all be confounded that adore graven things
And that glory in their idols,
Adore him, all ye angels.

The godless of our day may not worship graven things: nevertheless they worship other idols, and they furiously hate God and His Church. The state is their idol, the most coldly cruel of all monsters, and to it they sacrifice what is most precious to man, his human dignity and his personal freedom. It fills the soul with grief to behold on earth the temporary triumph of brute force, force that knows no law. But be comforted and take courage, and strive boldly: for inevitably the day will come when evil shall utterly perish.

No, we do not imagine that God tastes the "sweetness of revenge"; He is not vengeful; in Him there can be no hankering after vengeance, nor does He take pleasure in the suffering even of the guilty creature. But He is just, and therefore must avenge! "Justice and judgment are the establishment of his throne" (*Ps.* 96, 2). The impenitent sinner rejects God's mercy till the end, and

God must do justice, and punish evil; or rather, the sinner willfully casts himself into the abyss, and damns his own soul.

Psalm 96 thus praises the divine judgments:—

> The heavens declared his justice,
> And all people saw his glory,
> And the daughters of Juda rejoiced
> Because of thy judgments, O Lord;
> For thou art the most High Lord over all the earth;
> Thou art exalted exceedingly above all gods.

III. The Reward

"Then shall the just shine as the sun, in the kingdom of their Father. He that hath ears to hear, let him hear" (*Matt.* 13, 43). We ought to keep these words in our hearts and ponder over them. Let us pray for the millions of Christians, our brothers and sisters in Christ, who endure cruel persecution on account of their loyalty to Christ, who are cast into prison and cruelly tortured—tortured in body and soul. We beseech Thee, O Lord, make them taste how sweet it is to suffer for Thee. "Blessed are they that suffer persecution for the sake of justice, for theirs is the kingdom of heaven, Blessed are ye when they shall revile you, and persecute you, and speak all that is evil against you, untruly, for my sake. Be glad and rejoice, for your reward is very great in heaven" (*Matt.* 5, 10-12).

Psalm 96 concludes thus:—

> You that love the Lord, hate evil;
> The Lord preserveth the souls of his saints,
> He will deliver them out of the hand of the sinner
> Light is risen to the just
> And joy to the right of heart.
> Rejoice ye in the Lord,
>
> And give praise to the remembrance of his holiness.

Prayer: Almighty and eternal God, who to the last art patient and merciful, grant to our fainting hearts firm confidence and constant courage: so that, after having persevered in the struggle against evil, we may hear from Thy lips these blessed words, "Forever and ever enter ye into the joy of the Lord." Through our Lord.

THANKING GOD THROUGH CHRIST OUR LORD

(Col. 3: 15, 17)

1. In the Epistle of the Mass of last Sunday, St. Paul urges on
the Colossians the practice of a great many virtues, notably
thankfulness. "Be ye thankful," he says, "do all (things) in the
Lord Jesus Christ, giving thanks to God and the Father by
him" (3: 15, 17).

We may behold Christ our Lord, as the Evangelists frequently represent Him, in the humble attitude of prayer. Oh
that we were able to pray thus, worshipping God with our
whole being and rendering worthy thanks!

2. *Petition*: The grace to feel "what was in Christ Jesus" and to
realize how "truly it is fitting and just, right and conducive to
salvation, that we should give thanks to Thee, always and in
all places, O holy Lord, Father almighty, eternal God".

I. Gratitude the Godly Man's First Duty

Many a time Jesus spoke to the Twelve thus, "Ask and you
shall receive. Hitherto you have not asked the Father anything
in my name" (*John* 16, 23-24). Jesus knows our human nature:
we are inveterate beggars, and God is an ... inveterate giver.

Our first and highest duty as creatures is to thank God. God is
always ahead of us in conferring benefits, even before we ask
for them. When we were not, He gave us, out of His bounty, life
and being.

By nature we are needy creatures, nor are we ever satisfied.
We keep our gaze fixed on our destitution; we crave after all
sorts of satisfactions; and if ever we look up to God, it is not to
render thanks for favors received, but rather to plead for further
gifts. Gratitude is a noble sentiment, but man's narrow selfishness finds it hard to rise so high.

The ideal godly man is the God-man, Jesus Christ. In the
Gospel we read that He prayed for the Apostles, for Peter, for
all those that in ages to come would believe in Him. Only once
did He pray for Himself, when during His bitter agony, after
having sweated blood, He besought the Father to take away the
chalice ... if it is possible!

Nearly always His prayer is a prayer of thanksgiving to the

Father, or a hymn of praise and worship. Such was His continual prayer, His soul's very breath.

Lord, teach us to pray; teach us the excellence of the prayer of thanksgiving.

II. Humble Gratitude

Gratitude is not genuine if it is not humble. Not genuine, nay abhorrent to God, was the proud Pharisee's thanksgiving. That man gave thanks to God because he was not like the rest of men, nor like that publican down there in the back corner (*Luke* 18, 11). He fasted twice a week and gave tithes of all he possessed. Surely he imagined that God lay under obligation to him, because he had done so much for the Almighty! A grateful man gladly confesses that he is, and remains, under an obligation: the proud man, if he happens to have manners, will think that he has done enough when he has uttered the customary formula, and then he promptly forgets the favor he has received.

With regard to God how can our gratitude be other than profoundly humble? He has made us out of sheer love, and whatever we are and have is the gift of His hand. We have absolutely nothing that is not His gracious gift. We can claim no merit. And if we dare reflect on the use we have made of God's gifts, then shame and confusion should make us still more humble: we have shown so little appreciation of His gifts, we have been so unresponsive, we have been positively ungrateful. And around me there are so many that would have used those gifts far better. These were the dispositions of the Saints; the more graces they had received, the greater was their gratitude and the deeper their humility.

III. Through Jesus Christ Our Lord

Our gratitude goes to the Father "through our Lord, Jesus Christ". The Father is the giver of all good gifts; He has given us His only-begotten Son, "and how hath he not also with him given us all things?" (*Rom.* 8, 32.)

"With Him": together with Jesus the Father gave us the means to offer to Him a fitting, and just, and all-sufficient prayer and thanks-offering, the hallowed "eucharistic", that is thanksgiving, prayer, viz. Holy Mass. In the beginning of the Preface, which introduces the most sacred part of the Mass, the priest admonishes the faithful, "Sursum corda: lift up your hearts on high!" The faithful answer, We have them lifted up to the Lord!

The priest: Let us give thanks to the Lord!
The faithful: It is right and just.

Immediately before the Consecration the liturgy places before us Christ Himself, "Who the day before He suffered, took bread into His holy and venerable hands and, raising eyes heavenward to Thee, Almighty God, His Father, He gave thanks, blessed and broke.... So also after they had supped He took this glorious chalice into His holy and venerable hands, again giving thanks to Thee, He blessed it.... Whenever you repeat these things, it shall be in memory of me."

And the great encharistic prayer ends with these solemn words of praise, "Through Christ our Lord: through whom, O Lord, Thou dost create all these things which are good, dost sanctify them, make them life-giving, consecrate them, and give them to us: through Him, in Him, with Him, there is rendered to Thee, God the Father Almighty, in the unity of the Holy Ghost, all honor and glory. World without end."

And after the celebrant has taken the Body of Christ, he cries out, "What return shall I make to the Lord for all that He has given to me?" Indeed, what return can he make? "I will take the chalice of salvation." It is an extraordinary way of making a return to God, and yet what else could he do? He adds, "I will call upon the name of the Lord."

In this manner the sacrifice of the Mass unites us with Him, who alone, in His own name and in ours, can render worthy thanks to the Father Almighty.

Prayer: O God, whose mercies are without number, and the treasure of whose goodness is infinite: we render thanks to Thy most gracious Majesty for the gifts Thou hast bestowed upon us; evermore beseeching Thy clemency that, as Thou dost grant the petitions of them that ask Thee, so, never forsaking them, Thou wilt prepare them for the rewards to come. Through our Lord (After the *Te Deum*).

THURSDAY: FIFTH SUNDAY AFTER EPIPHANY

CHRISTIAN BEHAVIOR

1. In his letters St. Paul deals with various aspects of the mystery of salvation; but to the main topic he often adds very

practical directions concerning the daily life of his converts. He has the art of ennobling small things and actions by grafting them on to the Mystical Body of Christ. Said a wise man, "The habit of performing un-important duties with a great purpose will teach us always to do all things in a great manner." Such is the privilege and the duty of every Christian.

The Christian soul which has died with Christ to the world, and has risen with Him to a heavenly life, must put off the old man and put on the new one: "Put ye on therefore, as the elect of God, holy and beloved, the bowels of mercy, benignity, humility, modesty, patience: bearing with one another, and forgiving one another if anyone have a complaint against another: even as the Lord hath forgiven you, so do you also. But above all these things have charity, which is the bond of perfection (or: the most perfect bond); and let the peace of Christ, wherein also you are called in one body," rejoice in your hearts (*Col.* 3, 12-15). And Christ tells us "Learn of me, because I am meek and humble of heart" (*Matt.* 11, 29).

2. *Petition*: The grace to understand how in daily life we can practice the highest virtues.

I. The Elect of God, Holy and Beloved (Col. 3, 12)

The Colossians, to whom St. Paul is writing, were new converts, who only recently had renounced the vices, then rampant in pagan society, "fornication, uncleanness, lust, evil concupiscence and covetousness . . . in which you also walked some time, when you lived in them" (*Col.* 3, 5-7). Out of all that misery God had called them; they were the object of God's election; they had listened to God's voice calling them. Baptism, which they had received in the proper dispositions, had cleansed them from sin, and "sanctified" them; and so they were now "saints", "new creatures", "temples of the Holy Ghost, brothers and sisters in Christ." Human language is inadequate to express the invisible, yet very real and very wonderful, change that has taken place in their souls. St. Paul loves to call Christians "saints", not as we speak of canonized saints, but men sanctified by baptismal grace, saints, because they are cleansed of sin and dedicated to God.

Therefore they are the "beloved of God"; they have been "incorporated" into the Church, which Christ loves. "He delivered himself up for it (the Church), that he might sanctify it, cleansing it by the laver of water in the word of life; that he might pre-

sent it to himself, a glorious church, not having spot or wrinkle
or any such thing, but that it should be holy and without blemish"
(*Eph.* 5, 25-27).

She is not yet without spot or blemish, but Christ is fashioning
her into holiness: and therefore it behoves us "to put on Christ",
that is, to make ours the feelings of Christ.

As reborn in Baptism, as Christians, and—if God has deigned
to call us to the priesthood or to the religious life—as specially
dedicated to Christ, we are God's elect, holy and beloved. As
St. Paul tells his neophytes, we do have cause to be grateful to
God. Let us take to heart the precepts which the Apostle gives
to the "elect".

II. Put Ye on the Bowels of Mercy (Col. 3, 12)

It seems strange that as the "elect of God, holy and beloved"
we are admonished, not to render love for love to God, but to
love the brethren. "Put ye on, therefore, the bowels of mercy,
benignity, humility, modesty, patience, bearing with one another
and forgiving one another. Even as the Lord hath forgiven you,
so do you also" (*Col.* 3, 12-13). These virtues, which the ancients
called the minor virtues (to distinguish them from the major virtues—courage, daring, stoic forbearance) are the distinguishing
marks of the Christian. And that does not mean that Christians
lack those "major" virtues: we have only to think of the martyrs,
who surely were heroic: but whilst they displayed their heroism,
they were meek and prayed for their executioners. Christ had
given them the example.

"Be ye therefore merciful," Jesus had said, "as your Father also
is merciful" (*Luke* 6, 36), and "learn of me, because I am meek
and humble of heart" (*Matt.* 11, 29). There is nothing spectacular
about meekness and mercy and humility: the world despises
them, calls them weakness, which demean man, rather than
elevate him. Yet these are the virtues Jesus wants in His disciples.

Another point demands our attention: those towards whom
St. Paul wants his converts to practice mercy and benignity ...
are precisely the "elect of God, holy and beloved." So these needed
mercy! Indeed wherever human beings live and work together,
even holy men, there the practice of these virtues will be called
for. "Everything on earth is imperfect; God has willed it so, in
order that the principle of man's judgment should be mercy, and
the principle of his action should be effort." Thus spoke a wise
man.

Such an attitude towards whatever is weak and imperfect is noble, truly Christian, nay, divine. We must always hope and trust that God will have mercy on us, and no less do we hope and pray that our neighbor may treat us with mercy. Therefore it behoves us in turn, to have mercy on our neighbor.

Prayer: Almighty and merciful Father, bestow on us, Thy children, the spirit of mercy; so that we may be truly called Thy children.

Jesus, Good Master, allow us to penetrate deeper into Thy Heart, that of Thee we may learn to be meek and humble of heart.

Holy Ghost, who art "Forgiveness of sin", enkindle in our hearts the fire of Thy love, which is peace and meekness.

OUR WAVERING WILLS

1. Last Sunday, in the Secret of the Mass, we prayed God to guide "our wavering wills". Our will, indeed, is inconstant and readily wavers. Jesus permitted that Peter, the rock on which He was to build His Church, should experience how a very little thing could shake even a rock. Peter wavered and faltered before a servant-maid.

   But the Lord had prayed that his faith might not fail and that, being once converted, he should confirm his brethren (*Luke* 22, 32).

2. *Petition*: May Jesus, "always living to make intercession for us" (*Heb.* 7, 25), guide and confirm our wavering wills.

I. Our Wavering Wills

Man's heart is fickle. It may be ready to receive the good seed, perhaps it "receives the word with joy"; for a time the seed grows, "but there are no roots". Perseverance is so terribly hard; it is so difficult to keep one's faith and trust from wavering, when one stands face to face with stern reality. Perhaps we meet obstinate or violent opposition, or bitter disappointment, and frustration strikes us with paralysis. To be fervent is easy in the beginning, and for a short while: but it costs so much to hold on to the end. An ancient mystic compares the soul to a hazelnut shrub. It blossoms in early spring, and then there is a very long period before the fruit appears: it reaches maturity in late autumn. We find it difficult to remain faithful all these months.

Perhaps we have built on the sand; "and the rain fell and the floods came, and the winds blew, and they beat upon that house, and it fell, and great was the fall thereof" (*Matt.* 7, 27).

God forbid that we should come to such an extremity; but it is salutary for us to know and feel our weakness. Therefore we pray in the Secret of Holy Mass, "We offer Thee, O Lord, this sacrifice of propitiation to beg of Thy mercy pardon of our sins and guidance for our wavering wills. Through our Lord. . . ."

II. Unwavering Through Christ's Peace and Christ's Word

In last Sunday's Epistle St. Paul tells us where our wavering hearts can find constancy: "Let the peace of Christ rejoice (that is, reign) in your hearts . . . let the word of Christ dwell in you abundantly" (*Col.* 3, 15-16).

Why do our hearts waver and why are they inconstant? Because the peace of Christ does not reign there, the peace that filled the Heart of Jesus and was the result of His loving obedience to the will of the Father: "for I do always the things that please him" (*John* 8, 29). Once the Heart of Jesus suffered a terrific onslaught, in the garden of Gethsemane just before the Passion; but It did not waver: "Not my will, but thine be done" (*Luke* 22, 42). And "after the storm there was made a great calm", and He went forth to Calvary, without heeding the cries and the blasphemies of His enemies.

St. Paul also had to fight many battles: "combats without, fears within" (2 *Cor.* 7, 5), but deep down within his soul he possessed "the peace of God, which surpasseth all understanding, and which keeps your hearts and minds in Christ Jesus" (*Phil.* 4, 7).

May the peace of Christ extend its influence over all those things that cause our wills to waver: our cowardice, our lack of faith, and all the temptations that arise from our self-love.

St. Paul mentions another source of strength: "Let the word of Christ dwell in you abundantly." The word of Christ is Christ Himself, His doctrine which we profess and by which we live; His precepts which we observe. And thus He dwells in us, and we in Him, "abundantly", that is not superficially (as it were on the outer surface of the soul) where there is continual change and wavering, caused by the varying impressions of daily life; not superficially, but deep down in ourselves where "we are strengthened by the spirit, with might unto the inward man, that Christ may dwell by faith in our hearts, that we be rooted and founded in charity" (*Eph.* 3, 16-17).

In order to strengthen us, He gives us His peace, His word, even His Body. There we find the remedy that cures our weakness, and the food that restores our strength: *Bella premunt hostilia.* . . .

> Our foes press on from every side
> Thine aid supply, Thy strength bestow.

III. Confirm Thy Brethren

When the peace and the word of Christ reign in our hearts, we shall in turn be able to help and to strengthen others, to teach and admonish them fraternally, to enlighten and comfort them. But this is done more by example than by precept. When "the God of hope fills you with all joy and peace in believing" (*Rom.* 15, 13), then your whole life and personality are radiant with an awe-inspiring force, which the heathens used to admire in the early disciples of Christ and in the martyrs, and by which they were fascinated.

Prayer: O God, who knowest the greatness of the dangers that envelop us and the inability of our weak nature to withstand them; keep us safe in soul and body: that, with Thy assistance, we may overcome the sufferings which are inflicted on us for our sins. Through our Lord (Collect, 4th Sunday after Epiphany).

THE UNWAVERING HEART OF MARY

1. The Heart of Jesus never wavered, being obedient unto death. The heart of Mary, more than any other human heart, was steadfast in its fidelity and unwavering in its faith. All of us have received from the fullness of the Heart of Jesus, but none received as much as His holy Mother. She is the Virgin most faithful, the Mother of Good Counsel, the "virtuous

woman". By the cross she stands, her soul pierced by the sword, yet never wavering.

2. *Petition*: That, through Mary's intercession with her Son, we may have grace to persevere in faith and love, in the service of God and in the struggle for perfection.

I. Mary's Faith and Love Never Wavered

It is a universally accepted tradition that, from even her earliest years, Mary had resolved to keep her virginity. She is the "Virgin of virgins". When from the lips of the Archangel she heard that she was "to conceive in her womb and bring forth a son, and that she should call his name Jesus", she was troubled and appealed to the resolution she had taken: "How shall this be done, because I know not man?" The throne of David, and the rule in the house of Jacob forever, and the other glorious vistas into the distant future opened by the angel, did not cause her will to waver. Firmly she adhered to the promise she had made to God, humbly, wisely, steadfastly.

Virgin most faithful, Seat of wisdom, Virgin most prudent, pray for us.

The angel's message surpassed Mary's understanding, and she felt stunned by Gabriel's explanation; but enlightened by the Spirit, she believed with her whole heart and said, "Behold the handmaid of the Lord; be it done to me according to thy word." Henceforth nothing can make her faith and her love waver, neither the stable and the manger, nor the long years of the hidden life at Nazareth, nor the fearful tragedy of the Passion, the cross and Calvary, nor even the shadows of the grave; throughout it all she believed and loved. There was much she failed to understand: humbly and patiently she kept those things in her heart, and pondered over them.

Peter, on whom Jesus was building His Church, woefully wavered and fell, but being once converted he *confirmed* his brethren. Mary's relationship towards the Church is not that of Peter, but is, in a manner, of a more intimate nature. She is the Mother of Jesus, who trod the roads of Galilee. By our Lord's will, she is also the Mother of Jesus, who still lives in the Church. Mary was present when on Pentecost day the Holy Ghost came down from heaven to hallow the Mystical Body, that is, the Church which that day was born. It was not Mary's mission to preach or to work miracles: but the Mother of Jesus, who had never stood in need of conversion, was destined to *confirm*, as she was the visible, unwavering witness to them of that "which was from the beginning, which they had heard, which they had seen with their eyes, which they had looked upon, which their hands had handled of the word of life" (1 *John* 1, 1).

Mary gives us a splendid example of simple, constant, unwavering fidelity. With the most absolute self-surrender, inspired by faith and love, she has all these years lived the *Fiat* which she had uttered at Nazareth. As we say in the *Salve Regina*, Mary turns her eyes of mercy towards us, her poor banished children, whose wills so often waver, now that she, the Lord's humble handmaid, has entered into the joy of her Lord and her Son.

II. Mary Ever Faithful to Her Children

Throughout her life Mary was heroically faithful to the Father, to the Son, and to the Holy Ghost. Now her Son has glorified her, the Father has crowned her and, seated on her throne as Queen of Heaven, she shares the glory of her Son. St. Paul says that Christ is "always living to make intercession for us" (*Heb.* 7, 25). Jesus has willed that Mary also should intercede for us. When dying on the cross, Jesus indicating John, said to His Mother, "Behold thy son," and at that moment once again Mary repeated the *Fiat* of Nazareth and accepted to be the Mother of all those that would believe in Jesus. Through the mouth of Osee the prophet, God had said, "I will draw them with the cords of Adam, with the bands of love" (*Osee* 11, 4). God has done this by sending us His own Son, like unto us in all things, sin excepted. Is the Mother of Jesus not one of those "cords of Adam," which bind us to Jesus and, through Jesus, to the Father in heaven?

Mary is unwaveringly faithful to her office of Mother of all believers: for she is also the Lord's handmaid and the dispenser of God's mysteries; and "from dispensers it is required that a man be found faithful" (*Cor.* 4, 1-2). Mary, as dispenser of the divine treasures, is faithful to Jesus, the source and fountain of all good things, and to the brothers of Jesus who are her children.

"Let us therefore, go with confidence to the throne of grace; that we may obtain mercy, and find grace in seasonable aid" (*Heb.* 4, 16) (Introit, Mass Mary Mediatrix).

Prayer: Memorare, Remember, O most gracious Virgin Mary, that never was it known that any one who fled to thy protection, implored thy help, or sought thy intercession, was left unaided. Inspired with this confidence, I fly unto thee, O Virgin of virgins, my Mother; to thee do I come, before thee I stand, sinful and sorrowful; O Mother of the Word Incarnate, despise not my petitions, but in thy mercy hear and answer me. Amen—(St. Bernard).

(For the 6th Sunday after Epiphany see next volume, before the last Sunday after Pentecost.)

SEPTUAGESIMA SUNDAY

"PRE-LENTEN DISPOSITIONS"

1. The Introit of the Mass strikes a note of mourning. "The sorrows of death surrounded me; and the torrents of iniquity troubled me. The sorrows of hell encompassed me; and the snares of death prevented me. In my affliction I called upon the Lord, and I cried to my God, and he heard my voice from his holy temple" (*Ps.* 17, 5-7).

"And David spoke to the Lord the words of this canticle, in the day that the Lord delivered him out of the hand of all his enemies, and out of the hand of Saul. And he said, the Lord is my rock, and my strength and my savior" (2 *Kgs.* 22, 1-2).

In the Tract of the Mass the soul in need utters the same cry of distress: "Out of the depths I have cried to thee O Lord: Lord, hear my voice" (*Ps.* 129, 1-2).

2. *Petition*: The grace to acquire gradually the dispositions that will enable us to commemorate devoutly the sufferings, death and resurrection of our Lord.

I. The Fitting Dispositions

The Christmas cycle with its joyous hymns is closed. Septuagesima (the 70th day before Easter—really the 63rd) inaugurates the Easter cycle. The season of Advent was a preparation for Christmas, a period of happy expectation. "A child is born to us, a son is given to us;" Mary laid the Child in the manger, the yet unscathed victim: the day will come when they will nail Him to the cross.

Henceforth our eyes are directed towards Calvary: at Holy Mass white vestments are replaced by violet ones; the Gloria and the Alleluia are omitted; and our attention is being drawn to the Lord's bitter sufferings. And all the while we are profoundly conscious of the cause of Christ's passion, our own sins! Slowly silence grips the soul, and an earnest desire to do penance: these two make worldlings shiver with fear.

Such are the feelings which the Church, through the liturgy, would arouse in the souls of the faithful. At least priests and religious, who live so close to the altar, ought to make an effort to feel like the Church, and with the Church, during this penitential season. Let them aim at greater recollection and at more intimate union with God.

How shall I deepen my spiritual life? Ought I to do more penance?

II. We Rightly Suffer for Our Sins

In the Collect of today's Mass we implore God's mercy and confess that we rightly suffer for our sins. Are we not members of the Church of sinners? The Church, holy in her Head, in her doctrine, in her sacraments, is profoundly aware of the sinfulness of her children, more than they are themselves; nor is she slow in acknowledging it, but humbly and with utter sincerity she confesses her guilt before God. Through her lips the true children of the Church acknowledge that they are deservedly tried and chastised; nor do they complain, for they know that here below God's chastisements are meant to heal rather than to punish.

In this spirit we ought to pray when the cross is laid on our shoulders; in this spirit also we should pray all together, remembering that we are brothers and sharers in each one's weal and woe. We are the people of God, gathered together in the name of Jesus crying to the Father of mercy, each for all and all for each.

III. Mercifully Delivered

After our humble confession of guilt, we ask God to "add glory to His name by mercifully delivering us from the evils we rightfully suffer for our sins".

We are unable to save and deliver ourselves, nor are we able to merit salvation. The only way out, therefore, is and ever shall be, that God, out of sheer love, should have mercy on us. He has had mercy and always will be merciful: that is His privilege and glory, as Lord and Master. He could not show His almighty power better than by having mercy. "That Thou mayest add to the glory of Thy Name," says the Church, when she implores that her wayward children may receive deliverance.

At the present moment she is not yet the Bride "not having spot or wrinkle" (*Eph.* 5, 27); but she pleads for us with the Bridegroom, while she urges us to prepare our soul for the great internal renewal of Easter, which is the passing through suffering and death unto the resurrection. During the weeks ahead we will try to be humble, contrite of heart, and deeply conscious that we are sinners. Yet never shall we entertain a doubt about God's mercy and love. Such are the sentiments appropriate to the time.

Prayer: Graciously hear the prayers of Thy people, we beseech Thee, O Lord, and add glory to Thy name by mercifully delivering us from the evils we rightly suffer for our sins. Through our Lord (Collect of today's Mass).

MONDAY AFTER SEPTUAGESIMA SUNDAY

THE LABORERS' HIRE (Matt. 20, 1-16)

1. In the parable of the laborers in the vineyard our Lord alludes to scenes that are still familiar in our day: unemployed workmen standing idle in the market place, or men approaching the counter to draw their salary (*Matt.* 20, 1-16).

2. *Petition*: O Lord, teach us the lesson of this parable. God admits us to His service, allots us a task, gives us a reward that is just. In all His dealings He is not only just but also kind and indulgent. Yet He always remains the Master, who has not to account to anyone. Let our eye not be evil because He is good.

I. Always and Everywhere God Takes the First Step

In the natural as well as in the supernatural order, the initiative always lies with God. The householder goes out to hire laborers into his vineyard; according to the customs of the country and of the period, he goes early at 6 o'clock; then at 9, 12, 3, and lastly at 5 o'clock—the 11th hour according to the reckoning of those days. He addresses every man, whom he finds loitering in the market place, and he hires them all "into his vineyard".

He pays them the salary they have earned, and patiently answers their remonstrances. He is at the source of everything; but he uses compulsion towards no man, because they are free laborers and not slaves: all are given their opportunity, and are free to use it.

Thus God deals with us. He always takes the initiative: He created what was not, and He saved what had perished. The prophet Isaias said, "They have sought me that before asked not for me; they have found me that sought me not; I said, Behold me, behold me, to a nation that did not call upon my name" (65, 1): the meaning is that the Lord offers mercy, even though they seek it not.

St. John writes, "In this is charity: not as though we had loved God, but because he hath first loved us. . . . Let us therefore love God, because God first hath loved us" (1 *John* 4: 10, 19).

We praise God and thank Him, who loved us even before He had made us, who recalled us when we had wandered away from Him, whose love at every moment beckons us to come to Him. Always and in all things God takes the first step.

II. God Is Just

God is infinite in all perfections, also in His justice. But we are unable to fathom the divine decrees. When early in the morning the householder hires "laborers into his vineyard", he makes a clear agreement with them, that they shall receive "a penny a day", which was the current wage. And when later, at the 3rd, the 6th . . . hour, he sends other groups to the vineyard, he explicitly tells them that he "will give them what shall be just"; it looks as if deliberately he did not fix the wage. When the day's toil was over, they were all summoned to his presence to receive the reward of their work. The first to come were those that had been recruited at the 11th hour, those that had come last of all: lo and behold, they received a full day's wage, though they had worked for only one hour. Naturally enough, though certainly not because justice would have it so, the others concluded that they would receive more. And when they received the current wage, and only that, they murmured. "Had they not borne the burden of the day, and the heat, had they not toiled the livelong day, whereas the late comers had just done a spot of work, and that too in the coolness of the evening!" "And thou hast made them equal unto us!"

We can understand their disappointment. According to our human calculations the householder's way of acting is surely unusual, to say the least. On the other hand, we must admit that they had no real ground for complaining and that no injustice was being done: for they received the wage that was customary, and that had been explicitly agreed upon. They chose to compare their work and their reward to the work and the reward of the late arrivals. That may have been natural enough, and quite in accordance with human standards. But God's standards are not ours, and His judgments differ from ours—does He not see things which we do not see, does He not take into account facts that are hidden from us? We may pity those poor men, for not understanding: but they ought not have fallen a prey to thoughts of envy.

When we stand face to face with God, the Giver of all grace and the Rewarder of all good, we have no right to compare ourselves to others. He is the Master and we are nothing, and know nothing! And He is just.

III. God's Will Is Law

To one of those who murmured the householder, without anger, said, "Friend, I do thee no wrong; didst thou not agree with me for a penny? Take what is thine and go thy way. Is it not lawful for me to do what I will? Is thy eye evil, because I am good?" (*Matt.* 20, 13-15.)

God is just. He is infinite Justice. Can our mind understand God, can it understand His justice, can we measure His justice by our standards? Our standards even when right and just, are human, apply to things human; but fall short of, and are insufficient to measure divine Justice. It cannot be measured by us, it is beyond our intelligence: just as God's Being and God's Wisdom are incomprehensible.

Our mind and our eye behold and judge only the surface of things but "the searcher of hearts and reins is God" (*Ps.* 7, 10), and therefore God sees and takes into account the very marrow of things: His Wisdom knows what we know not, foresees what we cannot see, weighs and discerns motives of which we are ignorant; and His judgments are always just.

He is not swayed by humor or caprice, and yet no one can set bounds to His power; He does what He judges right, sanctions what His holy will chooses: that is justice, or better, that is love! "Or is thy eye evil because I am good?"

Let us humbly adore God's unbounded freedom; now and always we pay homage to the Father's unlimited power. This absolute freedom of God "to do what he wills" is for us an inexhaustible source of divine blessings. God's absolute freedom co-operates with His infinite love. He was the first to love us, when freely He made us; and freely He has loved us unto the end, unto death. "May our eye be good" as His eye is good!

Prayer: O Lord, how great are thy works!
Thy thoughts are exceeding deep.
The senseless man shall not know,
Nor will the fool understand these things.
The just shall flourish like the palm-tree:
He shall grow up like the cedar of Libanus.
They that are planted in the house of the Lord
Shall flourish in the courts of the house of our God.
They shall still increase in a fruitful old age,
And shall be well treated,
That they may show, that the Lord our God
    is righteous,
And there is no iniquitly in him (Ps. 91, 6-16).

TUESDAY AFTER SEPTUAGESIMA SUNDAY

GOD'S INFINITE GOODNESS

1. "The eyes of the Lord are towards them that fear him, and he knoweth all the works of man" (Eccl. 15, 20). Thus spoke the Wise Man. The eyes of the Son of Man were full of kindness and love.

2. Petition: The grace to tear out from our hearts whatever may make our eye evil. Jesus, meek and humble of heart, make our hearts like unto Thine.

I. Is Thy Eye Evil Because Mine Is Good?

One of the evil things, of which Jesus says that they proceed from the heart (Mark 7, 22), is envy. Envy is a mean and despicable passion, the source of immense evil on earth. "By the envy of the devil, death came into the world," says the Book of Wisdom (2, 24). Satan envied man's happiness and succeeded in destroying it. Because God was pleased with Abel's sacrifice (the heart of Abel being pure), "Cain was exceedingly angry, and his countenance fell. And the Lord said to him, Why art thou angry? and why is thy countenance fallen? If thou do well, shalt thou not receive? but if ill, shall not sin forthwith be present at the door?" (*Gen.* 4, 5-7). The sin that lurked before the door of Cain's heart, was envy. It gained an entrance, and Cain slew his brother.

Holy Writ tells us about the anger of Saul, and that "he did not look with a good eye" on David, after the maidens of Israel had sung in chorus, "Saul slew his thousands, and David his ten thousands" (1 *Kings* 18, 7). Jesus Himself fell a victim to the envy of the Pharisees: "For (Pilate) knew that for envy they had delivered him" (*Matt.* 27, 18).

II. "Because I Am Good"

The Lord is just; but "His mercy endureth forever". Ours would be a sad fate, if His mercy did not temper His justice. Our relations with God are not based on a bargain or a contract, but He deals with us in accordance with His infinite goodness and love. In the parable of the laborers, there enters the notion of a proportion between the service and the reward. But the reward which God will bestow on us is infinitely beyond the value of the service rendered. In Genesis (15, 1) God already said, "I am thy reward exceeding great." And on the last day the Judge will say to His faithful servant, "Well done, good and faithful servant, because thou hast been faithful over a few things, I will place thee over many things; enter thou into the joy of thy Lord" (*Matt.* 25, 23).

In those "few things", as Jesus calls them, there are great differences. St. Paul says that we all have different gifts according to the grace of God given to us, natural gifts and supernatural ones. In His goodness and in His wisdom God has willed it so, for His own glory and for our happiness. It is a mistake, and a misfortune, to allow ourselves to be blinded by petty self-love and to stand aside from the body of which God has made us members, and then to gaze at ourselves and compare ourselves with those around us. Instead of looking up to heaven, and thanking God for His many mercies, we look to the right and to the left; we foster either an inferiority or a superiority complex. "Why dost thou compare thyself with others? Is it not enough for thee that thou art God's child?" We have indeed cause to be ashamed, without being discouraged, when we realize that such petty sentiments are "present at the door" of our heart, and want to enter. Unless we walk warily, and struggle manfully, they will force an entrance.

Let us pray: Jesus, meek and humble of heart, never permit that our eye "grow evil because Thou art good".

III. "Charity Envieth Not"

Once again we think of that laborer who felt mortified and complained, not because an injustice had been done to him, but because his fellow laborer, who had worked less, received as much as he himself.

It would have been fine, and the proof of a noble disposition, perhaps it would have been superhuman, if his heart had swelled with joy, because the householder was generous and because his neighbor felt happy. Had he felt thus, it would have shown that in his soul selfishness had given place to true love. Such is the bliss of the Saints in heaven, who feel happy because of the happiness of all the other blessed; for in heaven God is all in all.

The great destroyer of happiness in our world is self-love, which is interested only in self and is made miserable by the happiness of others. The murmuring laborer felt no joy when he received the wage he had earned, perhaps spite urged him to fling it away, and the "penny" which the late comers received is to him a thorn in the flesh.

O Lord, do grant us an increase of true Christian charity. The Mystical Body of Christ is one, and yet has many members. "If one member suffer anything, all the members suffer with it; or, if one member glory, all the members rejoice with it" (1 Cor. 12, 26). Thus our eye will grow better because God is good and because our brethren, through God's grace, grow in goodness.

Prayer: Fill us, O Lord, with the spirit of Thy love, that, by Thy mercy, we, who have all partaken of one heavenly Bread, may also be of one mind. Through our Lord (Postcommunion, Mass for Concord).

"NOT I, BUT THE GRACE OF GOD WITH ME"
(1 Cor. 15, 10)

1. In the Gospel of last Sunday's Mass, stress is laid on the fact
    that in all things, most of all in the work of our salvation, God
    is the first and principal agent. The Epistle, however, reminds
    us that we must cooperate with God. St. Paul compares us to
    competitors in a race, where everything depends on the effort
    put forth.

    We behold the Son of Man, seated on the throne of His
    Majesty, and to those that are on His right hand we hear Him
    say, "Come ye blessed of my Father, possess the kingdom pre-
    pared for you from the foundation of the world" (*Matt.* 25, 34).

2. *Petition*: That we may understand that it is worth while to
    strive manfully to gain an eternal reward. Grant, O Lord, that
    we may persevere unto the end.

I. Our Cooperation

From the parable of the laborers in the vineyard some might
feel tempted to conclude that the measure of our reward will
depend neither on the duration of our service, nor on the efforts
we have made. This would be an unwarranted conclusion. In
his first Epistle to the Christians of Corinth, where every second
year the Pan-Hellenic Games were held, St. Paul looks at things
from another angle. "Know you not that they, that run in the race,
all run indeed; but one receiveth the prize. So run that you may
obtain" (1 *Cor.* 9, 24).

These two manners of viewing the work of our salvation are
by no means contradictory, but they express that mysterious
interplay of God's grace and man's free will. It is a matter of
faith that in the work of our salvation God takes the first step,
and that all along we completely depend on His grace, till the
very end. But "God is faithful".

It is quite certain that this work requires not only our free consent, but also our free and continual cooperation; and we are
liable to falter. For we are weak and have the free choice between
good and evil. If we so will, we can loyally and generously play
our part and cooperate with divine grace; we can also close our
hearts to grace, we can yield to sloth and cowardice, we can

obstinately refuse to do what God demands from us. Concerning his own co-operation with grace St. Paul wrote, "By the grace of God, I am what I am; and his grace in me hath not been void; but I have labored more abundantly than all they; yet not I, but the grace of God with me" (1 *Cor.* 15, 10).

God Almighty could coerce our will, but He does us the honor of giving us a share in the work of our salvation. It is His work, and yet He is pleased to fit our free will and our efforts into His scheme, and thus He permits us to share in the great work.

Let our cooperation with God be humble and trustful, generous and joyful, fervent and calm. What does God demand of me today?

II. The Effort

The athlete wants to gain the prize, and every detail of his daily life is regulated with a view to preparing himself for the great contest. He shuns whatever might impair his physical fitness, he recoils neither from fatigue nor from effort which may improve his chances. We may admire his tenacity, his power of endurance, his courage. Such courage is a fine feature of our human nature: and yet it springs from a far less noble motive than does the courage that we need in the contest to which St. Paul invites us. In this contest the prize is not a crown of perishable laurels, but one that never perishes; and the motive is a supernatural one, love of Christ, whom I would apprehend, as I also am apprehended by him (*Phil.* 3, 12). The motive is also love for the neighbor, for whom we are prepared to sacrifice ourselves.

This indeed is a powerful motive, and for noble souls there is none more powerful. We feel humbled, and ashamed, but not disheartened, at the thought that this exalted ideal has so little fascination for us. O God, that our eyes may see!

Perhaps the day when we chose the priestly or the religious life—or rather not we, but God's grace in us—we did have the courage to sacrifice something for the sake of the kingdom of heaven. May that same grace strengthen and assist us in our daily life to be worthy disciples of Christ. Then with St. Paul we shall say, "I can do all things in him who strengtheneth me" (*Phil.* 4, 13), at the altar, in prayer, in Holy Communion.

III. The Reward

"And they indeed that they may receive a corruptible crown, but we an incorruptible one" (1 *Cor.* 9, 25). It is true that this corruptible crown is placed on their head here and now, and the crowds cheer, and the press spreads their fame. Human nature greedily savors all these things, and popularity is so sweet; who could resist the fascination of this vain display and the splendor of short-lived glory? The crown which we strive for is indeed imperishable, but at present it is invisible and it is generally won in silence and humility, not amidst the glamor of popular acclaim and noisy publicity. "This is the victory, which overcometh the world; our faith" (1 *John* 5, 4). Our treasure is in heaven, our names are recorded in the Book of Life, not headlined in the daily papers, to be forgotten tomorrow. "He that shall overcome, shall thus be clothed in white garments, and I will not blot out his name out of the book of life, and I will confess his name before my Father, and before his angels (*Apoc.* 3, 5).

Prayer: Bring us, we beg Thee, O Lord, to the eternal possession and enjoyment of Thy Divinity, which is prefigured by our reception in time of Thy Precious Body and Blood. Who livest and reignest (Postcommunion, Feast of the Blessed Sacrament).

THURSDAY AFTER SEPTUAGESIMA SUNDAY

NO UNEMPLOYMENT IN THE KINGDOM OF GOD

1. In the parable of the laborers in the vineyard every man is offered work in the vineyard. "Why stand you here all the day idle? (*Matt.* 20, 6), said the householder to the men of the 11th hour. And they answered, "Because no man has hired us." In God's Kingdom there is no unemployment problem.

2. *Petition*: To understand to what a glorious task all men are invited, and how every man ought to acquit himself of his honorable task. "For the perfecting of the saints, for the work of the ministry, for the edifying of the body of Christ: until we all meet into the unity of faith, and of the knowledge of the Son of God, unto a perfect man, unto the measure of the age of the fullness of Christ" (*Eph.* 4, 12-13).

I. All Are Called to Work

Our modern social and economic system experiences periodical ups and downs, booms and slumps. One day there is a shortage of labor, and the next there is excess. Often only a skilled laborer, preferably if he is young and strong, will find employment; while for the unskilled worker, or for him that is advanced in years, there are "no vacancies". A sick man, or one who has become invalid by an accident, may go on the dole, or receive state support, but he is doomed to stay "unemployed".

In God's Kingdom things are otherwise: here there are no unemployed, though, alas, there may be those that have gone on strike, or that simply refuse to work. God will have no forced labor, no slaves. He does call all men into the vineyard; if they heed the call, they do so freely. And there is plenty of work, and for every one, for the old, and the young, for the weak, and the strong, for the skilled and the unskilled: all are "called", "hired", "sent", offered some task or other. "Go you also into my vineyard", said the householder.

This is a source of great comfort to all of us. At any time God can use the services of any man. What a solace to poor bedridden invalids, who had dreamt of strenuous years of toil for God's glory and for the salvation of souls; what a solace to them, who after rendering faithful service "are retired", compelled to rest! They know that their present lives are not useless, their sufferings are not wasted. In God's Kingdom the most deserving laborers are not those that do the toiling, but those that pray and suffer!

Their merit is great; they earn an imperishable crown for themselves, and showers of graces on the Church. "For none of us liveth to himself", nor labors, nor suffers, "nor dies to himself" (*Rom.* 14, 7).

Our lot is cast in a tormented world: never did the Kingdom of God have so many, and such ferocious enemies. Now less than at any other time may a Christian idly stand aside and refuse to take part in the fray. "Good Master, what good shall I do," what shall I suffer, "that I may have life everlasting?" (*Matt.* 19, 16.) NOW, at this moment.

II. "Great Diversities"

"Now there are diversities of graces, but the same Spirit; and there are diversities of ministries, but the same Lord; and there are diversities of operations, but the same God, who worketh all in all" (1 *Cor.* 12, 4-6). Whether you be priest or layman, whether you dwell in the cloister or in the city, whether you are a cleric or a lay brother, whether you are engaged in the ministry or employed in the meanest services, whether you are a choir nun or a simple lay sister, whether you teach a class or handle saucepans, whether you enjoy a great reputation or are utterly unknown, as long as you are about "your Father's business", doing the work He has given you and doing it for His glory, you are serving the Lord; and it is "the same God who worketh all in all".

"Although one hath received more, another less, yet all are Thine, and without Thee even the least cannot be had. He who hath received greater things cannot glory of his own merit, or extol himself above others, nor insult even the lesser; because he is indeed greater and better, who attributeth less to himself, and is more humble and devout in returning thanks. . . . He who hath received less ought not to be saddened, nor take it ill, nor envy him that is more enriched: but attend rather to Thee, and very much praise Thy goodness; for Thou bestowest Thy gifts so plentifully, so freely and willingly, without respect of persons. . . . Thou knowest what is expedient to be given to each; and why this one hath less and the other more, is not ours to decide, but Thine by whom are determined the merits of each" (*Imit.* 3, 22).

III. The Punishment of One Who Refused to Work

In the parable of the talents (*Matt.* 25, 14-26) the faithful servants are rewarded according to their labor. The first had been trusted with five talents and had earned another five; the second had received two talents and he returned four talents to his master. What had been entrusted to them the master calls "a few things" and as a reward he places them over "many things", that is, they are bidden to "enter into the joy of their lord".

The third, who had received only one talent, "going his way digged into the earth, and hid his lord's money". Did he perhaps act out of spite, because he had received the least? That may be so: in any case, he will not bestir himself, and hides the talent in the ground and when the master comes back, he returns it with very ill humor, using contumelious language. The master said, "Wicked and slothful servant . . . cast ye (him) out into the exterior darkness" (*Matt.* 25, 26-30).

To each of us God has given, and gives "talents", and these we must use to serve Him; we may not, out of sloth or out of coward-ice, let them lie idle. If the third servant, like him that had received five talents or the other that had received two, had taken the trouble to make his talent bear fruit, he too would have heard from the master's lips, "Well done, good and faithful servant; because thou hast been faithful over a few things, I will place thee over many things; enter thou into the joy of thy lord."

Whatever we do, however hard we labor, however much we may shine, it is only "a few things", and is utterly out of proportion with what God gives—"entering into the joy of the lord!" This is, according to St. Bernardine of Siena, a mysterious expression; "this joy is not only within us; it grips us and permeates us; we are plunged in it as in an abyss."

O God, grant that, out of gratitude to Thee, we may labor for Thy glory, spend ourselves and be spent for Thee, using every "talent" we have received in the task which Thou art pleased to entrust to us, for Thy greater glory and for the salvation of souls.

Prayer: O God, who preparest rewards that are not seen for them that love Thee: instill in our hearts such affection and love for Thee, that our love for Thee in all things and above all things may bring us to the enjoyment of Thy promises, which surpass all our longings. Through our Lord (Collect, 5th Sunday after Pentecost).

FRIDAY AFTER SEPTUAGESIMA SUNDAY

A PRAYER OF ST. THOMAS AQUINAS

1. The prayer of St. Thomas which we take as subject matter for this meditation bears the seal of this great genius, a man of intense prayer. It is tersely expressed and pregnant with meaning. Often the Saint repeated it in his cell at the beginning of his long hours of study.

2. *Petition*: "O Merciful God, grant me what is pleasing to Thee; may I ardently desire it, prudently consider it, clearly see it, perfectly execute it, to the praise and glory of Thy name."

I. "What Is Pleasing to Thee"

Evidently there is no question here of God's commandments, but of God's will and desire concerning things that are left to our own free decision. We turn to our merciful Lord, the source of all graces. What is pleasing to Him is the supreme rule of all holiness. That was the rule which Jesus always had before His eyes: "I do always the things that please my Father. . . ", "I do nothing, of myself, but as the Father hath taught me, these things I speak" (*John* 8, 28-29). Jesus did not need to ask what was the Father's will. "I and the Father are one", He said (*John* 10, 30). We must pray to know God's will, through Christ, our Lord, who has revealed to us the Father, and who will show us what is pleasing to the Father.

II. "Ardently Desire It"

An ardent desire is the first thing that is required from us. Of course, even the desire is God's gift, and yet it is our first step in co-operating with grace: a sincere, personal, ardent desire. Our heart's desires stir all our faculties into activity. Possibly we shall not fulfill every one of our desires, but that which we do not desire is altogether beyond our reach. The more ardent our desire is, the wider does our soul open itself to grace.

What do I desire, really, truly, from the heart? That is a question we ought to ask ourselves in all simplicity and sincerity.

God's holy will is the most desirable thing in heaven and on earth. Jesus taught us to pray, "Thy will be done on earth as it is in heaven." We repeat those hallowed words so often: would to God they came from the bottom of our hearts! With St. Thomas we say, Grant me, O merciful God, ardently to desire what is pleasing to Thee.

"Prudently to Consider It"

Experience shows that even the most ardent desires may lead us astray. St. Paul said: "Extinguish not the spirit . . . but *prove* all things, hold fast that which is good" (1 *Thes.* 5: 19, 21). To do this we need what St. Ignatius calls "discretion of spirits", by which we gain insight into the secret working in the soul of the good and of the evil spirits, so that we may know whether we are moved by grace, which beckons us heavenward, or by nature which seek self-satisfaction. This is the true wisdom, which we so often beg the Holy Ghost to pour into our hearts. When Jesus was tempted by Satan, He immediately discerned the devil's deceit. He had no need of asking for light, but we have such need, and therefore we humbly pray, O merciful Lord, grant that we may prudently consider what is pleasing to Thee.

"Clearly to See It"

In order to see clearly our eye must be single, and our heart detached from earthly things. Any disorderly attachment to creatures, or any prejudice, will make us blind; so that we fail to see what God wants of us. We grow deaf to God's whispering voice in the soul, or misunderstand its message, or, to suit our own desires, pervert its meaning. O merciful Lord, grant us clearly to see what is pleasing to Thee.

"Perfectly to Execute It"

All that has preceded is a preparation for this last grace. From the first desire, deep down in our hearts, till the last act of virtue and the supreme grace of final perseverance, everything is the work of God's grace. "For it is God who worketh in you, both to will and to accomplish, according to his good will" (*Phil.* 2, 13).

But from the first moment to the last, God requires our co-operation. Experience has taught us how much courage, patience, constancy, we need in order to execute perfectly God's good pleasure, to know which we have prayed so ardently. Jesus has trod the way before us and given us an example, even at the cost of sweating blood in the garden of Gethsemane. He remained steadfast till the end, when on the cross He said, *Consummatum est*: it is accomplished.

III. "To the Praise and Glory of Thy Name"

This is the final goal. Our happiness and our peace on earth and in heaven consist in fulfilling God's will. But first and above all, our happiness and our peace are a hymn to the praise and glory of God, as Dante sang in his *Paradiso* (27, 1-9).

> To the Father, to the Son, to the Holy Ghost
> Honor and glory: thus sang the voice of the Blessed,
> And their sweet melodies threw me into a trance.
> What I beheld appeared to me a smile
> Of the universe, so that the ecstasy
> Gripped me through eyes and ears.
> O joy, O delight ineffable,
> O life, perfect in love and peace,
> O riches securely possessed, and all desire satiated.

Prayer: A prayer for fulfilling the will of God (3 *Imit.* 15, 3). Grant me Thy grace, most merciful Jesus.... Grant me always

to will and desire that which is most acceptable to Thee, and
what pleaseth Thee best. Let Thy will be mine, and let my will
always follow Thine, and agree perfectly with it. Let me always
will, or not will, the same with Thee; and let me not be able to
will, or not to will, otherwise than as Thou willest or willest not.

SATURDAY AFTER SEPTUAGESIMA SUNDAY

"ROOT OF JESSE, GATE OF MORN, WHENCE THE WORLD'S TRUE LIGHT WAS BORN"

1. From the 2nd February Mary is commemorated in the divine
    office in the anthem "Ave Regina Coelorum", whence the above
    words are taken. (Salve radix, salve porta; Ex qua mundo lux
    est orta.)
       In the most ancient liturgies it was already customary to
    apply to Mary the words used by the Canticle of Canticles to
    describe the beauty of the Bride, "Who is she that cometh
    forth as the morning rising?" (*Cant.* 6, 9.) She is indeed the
    bright ray on the eastern horizon, that heralds the rising of the
    Sun. She is the bringer of light.

2. *Petition*: May the eyes of our soul be ever intent on the Light
    which Mary brought us. May that Light so shine in us and
    through us, that we may be able to lead unto Christ those that
    grope in darkness.

I. Our Need of Light

Man will always stand in need of the Light of life. Those that
do not have the faith truly grope in the dark, while doubts and
uncertainty torment their souls. Modern science has made marvellous progress in the discovery and the practical use of the forces
of nature, that is, of the material world. And yet its knowledge
is incomplete, for it fails to discern the beginning and the end.
How did matter, with all its dynamic contents, come into being,
and why did God make it? Only faith, that is God Himself, Alpha
and Omega, the Creator, can reveal those things to us, and He
came unto us through Mary.

"The unknown man", when not illumined by faith, has so little certain knowledge about "whence he cometh and whither he goeth", about the sense, the value, of life on earth. We, to whom the Light of life has been given, and who have not had to grope for it, ought to feel the deepest sympathy and compassion for the millions all around us, and in distant lands, who walk in darkness, seeking the Light, and not seldom straying into devious paths. We must pray for them, for they are our fellow travellers towards eternity. *Profer lumen coecis,* vouchsafe light to the blind, so prays the Church in the *Ave Maris Stella.*

We, the children of Light, as St. Paul called his Christians, we too are in need of more Light, so that faith may illumine our soul more brightly, that we may judge more fairly and speak more wisely, and truly "walk in the Light"; the Light of faith will make us live of our faith; and the life of faith will produce an increase of Light.

II. Mary the Bearer of Light

The Gospel says of St. John the Baptist, "He was not the light, but he was to give testimony of the light" (*John* 1, 8). Of Mary we may say, She was not the Light, but she was to give us the Light, nay to bear it for us. "The true light, that enlighteneth every man that cometh into the world," and it came through Mary. The "great sign appeared in heaven, a woman, clothed with the sun" (*Apoc.* 12, 1) may be understood as pointing to the Church; but the liturgy generally sees in it a symbol of Mary, the Mother of Jesus, and also the mother of all believers. She conceived in her womb "the splendor of eternal Light", the Son, "Light of Light". Within herself she has the source of Light. In the *O Gloriosa Virginum* the Church sings of her,

> The Great King's Gate art thou, and bright
> Abode of everlasting Light.

She is the shining mirror that receives the Light and faithfully reflects and spreads it.

She is the Ocean Star: *Ave Maris Stella* Hail Star of the Sea. Before the invention of the mariner's compass, by night the pole star guided sailors across the oceans. As long as we keep our gaze fixed on Mary, we shall be safe and may defy the winds and the waves; if we bring our skiff to land close to where Mary is, Jesus cannot be far, and she will lead us to Him.

In the Litany of Loreto the Church calls Mary "Morning Star", that is, the Venus of the astronomers, which always appears close to the sun. It is a planet and, like the moon, has no light of its own. It is illumined by the sun, and shines brighter than the other stars; in the morning we see it in the east, and towards evening it appears in the west. None comes closer to the "Sun of Justice" than the Immaculate Virgin Mother of Jesus; but even her brightness springs from the Source of all Light.

What shall we ask her now? That to all those who grope in darkness and stray from the road of salvation, she may be a beacon and that she may guide them safely into the harbor of truth.

> Ave Maria! thou portal of Heaven,
> Harbor of refuge, to thee we flee;
> Lost in the darkness, by stormy winds driven,
> Shine on our pathway, fair Star of the Sea!

O Mary, thou art "clothed with the sun", thou hast received the fullness of Light in order that thou mightest enlighten our darkness, be pleased to illumine our souls, make us true children of Light, and obtain for us the grace to be, in turn, bearers of light to those that walk in darkness.

Prayer: Mary, thou art the star, shining with the light of Jesus, fair as the moon, and bright as the sun, the star of the heavens which it is good to look upon, the star of the sea which is welcome to the tempest-tossed; at whose smile the evil spirit flies, the passions are hushed, and peace is poured upon the soul (*Newman*).

SEXAGESIMA SUNDAY

THE PARABLE OF THE SOWER—I

(Matt. 13, 3; Mark 4, 1; Luke 8, 4)

1. Let us join the "great multitudes that were gathered unto him" anxious to hear the Prophet of Nazareth. He spoke as no other had ever spoken before: it went straight to their hearts, stirring them and raising them up to heaven. In simple words, with images drawn from their daily experience, He

announced a message which went to the very depths of their souls.

2. *Petition*: The grace to "have ears to hear", according to our Lord's own expression; that "in a good and perfect heart", we may hear the word and keep it, "and bring forth fruit in patience" (*Luke* 8, 15).

I. The Seed

Our Lord seems to have a predilection for the image of "the seed", when He speaks of the Kingdom of God. The multitudes, gathered around Him, were mostly country folk, and appreciated the value of seed grain, on which their livelihood depended. The tiny grain had to be hidden in the earth, where it silently died, then germinated, and in a mysterious manner pierced through the hard surface of the soil. Warmed by the fostering rays of the sun, refreshed by the dew and the rain from heaven, it grew up, increased and produced the swelling ears, filled with golden grain.

This is a simple, concrete image, easily understood by simple folk. It illustrates the mystery of life and death, of burial and resurrection, of nature's wonderful fertility: one small grain, growing into several well-filled ears, producing a hundredfold. And the entire process takes place silently, it lasts a long while, and the final result depends on a multitude of secondary causes. "O Lord, our Lord, how admirable is Thy name in the whole earth!" (*Ps.* 8, 2) and in the tiny seed! And how touchingly Jesus, Thy Word, has made use of it to reveal to us the process of our salvation!

II. The Word of God

Jesus Himself explains the parable: "The seed is the word of God." Through His Word God expresses His Being, and makes men partakers of the divine nature (2 *Peter* 1, 4), giving us salvation, supernatural life, sanctifying grace, which is offered to all men. In the votive Mass for the Propagation of the Faith, we pray, "O God, whose will it is that all men should be saved and come to know the truth. ..." Every grace is a seed. Such is the gift of faith, received in Baptism; so is every inspiration of the Holy Ghost and every salutary desire. Deep down in our heart, where God speaks to us, every salutary movement is a "seed", small indeed, but pregnant with great possibilities.

The "Word of God" is He Himself, who speaks to us. Shortly before His death Jesus solemnly declared, "Amen, amen, I say to you, unless the grain of wheat, falling into the ground, die, itself remaineth alone; but, if it die, it bringeth forth much fruit (*John* 12, 24-25). But whether this *Seed*, which is about to be buried in order to rise again, will bear much fruit, must depend on the soil in which it falls.

III. Differences of Soil

God sows nothing but the best seed: as it comes from the Sower's hand it has in itself the power to yield a hundred-fold. But it must fall on good ground, not by the wayside, where it is trodden under foot and devoured by the fowls of the air; nor on stony ground, where there is neither earth nor moisture; not even on good ground, that is overrun by thorns and thistles, and where the grain may germinate only to be choked by the thorns.

Unfit for the seed is the soul which is immersed in worldliness and frivolity; nor can it thrive in a heart which for a moment accepts God's grace, but is enslaved by passions and possessed by disorderly affections. In such souls the seed can neither germinate, nor shoot up, nor grow to maturity, nor produce a plentiful harvest. So much good seed, so many inspirations and urgings of God's grace, so many invitations to do good and shun evil, fail to bear fruit!

We know that God is ready to forgive and infinitely patient: it is not His way to sow seed only once. Throughout the centuries that follow one another, His almighty hand scatters the seed bountifully. He waits, sows again, waits, and continues having mercy on wayward man. Never does He abandon a soul in distress.

Such is God's policy with all souls, whether He wants to draw them out of the abyss of sin, or urges them to bear more abundant fruit, or endeavors to raise them to greaer holiness.

Let us pray that "the word of God may run and may be glorified", (2 *Thes.* 3, 1), that the hard and stony soil of man's free will may be softened to receive the seed, that our own hearts may open the gates wide to the reception of God's grace.

Prayer: Let Thy grace, we beseech Thee, O Lord, both always precede and follow us, and may it make us ever devoted to good works. Through our Lord (Collect, 16th Sunday after Pentecost).

THE PARABLE OF THE SOWER—II

1. We join the small group of the Twelve. After He had proposed the parable, Jesus took them aside, and said to them: "To you it is given to know the mysteries of the kingdom of heaven." "You", that means especially all those that have left everything in order to follow Christ. It is their privilege, and their responsibility, to penetrate deeper into God's mysteries, so that they may bring forth more abundant fruit.

2. *Petition*: The grace to cast out from our hearts—or rather, to allow Jesus to cast out—whatever stands in the way of a more abundant harvest.

I. The Seed by the Wayside

"And they by the wayside are they that hear; then the devil cometh and taketh the word out of their heart, lest believing they should be saved" (*Luke* 8, 12). It would seem that the devil, the mortal enemy of the Sower and of man, has free access to those souls in which he rules as lord and master. No good thought finds entrance there, because every avenue is closed; worldliness has utterly dulled their sense of the supernatural. Perhaps we know not a few men and women, who are not hostile to religion but who have not the faintest interest in religion; they are absolutely indifferent to the things of God; they enjoy the present, and have no care about eternity.

And yet, even those unfortunates have an immortal soul, whose eternal fate depends on the manner in which they live now; they are God's children, our brothers and sisters, redeemed by Christ. Till the end Jesus will endeavor to save them from the devil's snares; and we, in the name of the Communion of Saints, are called upon to cooperate with Christ, that those people too may be saved.

II. The Seed on the Rock

"Now they upon the rock are they who, when they hear, receive the word with joy; and these have no roots; for they believe for a while, and in time of temptation they fall away" (*Luke* 8, 13).

They are what we might call "good people", kindly, excitable,

sensitive natures. "They receive the word with joy", a thing which
Jesus said of no other class; but it makes on them merely a brief
and superficial impression; it neither sinks deep nor takes root;
it fails to produce a profound, personal conviction and to move
the will. And therefore that soul is unable to face the slightest
trial, to make the slightest sacrifice.

The wealthy young man who ran up to our Lord, knelt before
Him in the best dispositions. But when Jesus spoke of renuncia-
tion and demanded a heavy sacrifice, the seed fell on the rock of
the man's disorderly attachment to his "great possessions". The
Lord had looked on him with love, and yet "he went away sad"
(*Matt.* 19, 22).

Is this not the daily experience of our weakness and cowardice?
Let us pray fervently for grace to understand, and at the proper
moment to remember, that trials well borne are most precious
graces. "Because thou wast acceptable to God, it was necessary
that temptation should prove thee" (*Tob.* 12, 13). "Power is
made perfect in infirmity" (2 *Cor.* 12, 9).

III. The Seed Among the Thorns

"And that which fell among thorns, are they who have heard
and, going their way, are choked with the cares and riches and
pleasures of this life, and yield no fruit" (*Luke* 8, 14).

The ground is excellent, but weeds abound, and the "enemy
has oversowed cockle". In the parable of the sower and the
cockle, the husbandman allowed the tares to grow up with the
good grain. There will always be wicked people on earth, and
God will not cast them out as long as life lasts.

In this parable our Lord speaks of those things which, in every
soul, threaten to choke what is good, "the cares, and riches and
pleasures of this life". St. Gregory asks, "How can you call riches
and pleasures thorns?" He answers, "Thorns prick and give pain;
riches and pleasures caress and are sweet. And yet they *are* thorns.
Earthly cares and worries are like thorns that wound the soul;
if they lead to sin, they inflict bleeding wounds." Let us beware
lest, "while we are going our way", our striving after perfection
—which is the good seed sowed by God—wax gradually weaker
and weaker. It is sad to reflect how many graces are offered us,
that never bear fruit. The modern comforts of life, which technical
progress supplies with increasing abundance, are not evil in themselves. When does use become abuse? When inordinate attachment to those things makes us their slaves, extinguishes what is

noblest in our souls (that is the seed, sown by God), and prevents us from leading holy lives.

Let us pray that the sensual man, who perceiveth not the things that are of God, and calls them foolishness, may not gain in our hearts the upperhand over the spiritual man, who judges what is of the spirit (cf. 1 *Cor.* 2, 14).

Prayer: Show favor to Thy people, we beseech Thee O Lord, that they may reject what is displeasing to Thee and rather find pleasure in fulfilling Thy commandments, Through our Lord (Thursday after Passion Sunday, Prayer over the people).

TUESDAY AFTER SEXAGESIMA SUNDAY

THE PARABLE OF THE SOWER—III

1. Jesus "the Master" never sat solemnly on the seat of the Pharisees. The Galileans had seen Him sitting on the grass, when He taught on the slope of the mountain; now He sits on a small bench, in a fisherman's boat, close to the shore. "And again he began to teach by the seaside; and a great multitude was gathered together unto Him, so that he went up to a ship, and sat in the sea; and all the multitude was upon the land by the sea-side" (*Mark* 4, 1).

2. *Petition*: The grace to hear the words of Jesus and to keep them "in a good and perfect heart".

I. The Seed on the Good Ground

"But that on the good ground are they, who in a good and perfect heart, hearing the word, keep it and bring forth fruit in patience" (*Luke* 8, 15), that is by persevering.

"A good and perfect heart": the literal sense of the Greek words is "beautiful and good", and the expression conveys the idea of a noble, and excellent heart. Perhaps we have the impression that God requires, as a previous condition, a disposition which is not within the reach of every man. There seems to be question here of a special grace, which is the sequel to other graces which were duly accepted and faithfully made use of, rather than of a previous condition.

For in this matter too, it is a fact that God always takes the

first step, and that He is absolutely free in the distribution of His
graces. In that nobility and excellence of hearts there are countless
degrees. At first this excellence may have been no more than a
tiny germ, or perhaps a readiness to let the germ be implanted
in the heart; or a fundamental uprightness of soul, and ardent
desire to receive and to cooperate, an unconditional surrender.
"Sursum corda!" Hearts on high, upwards to God, because nothing
binds them to earth nor drags them down. With such a good and
perfect heart young Samuel had hearkened to God's voice, when
he said, "Speak Lord, for thy servant heareth" (1 *Kgs.* 3, 9). The
heart of the youth with great possessions was not so good and
perfect, for it shut itself to the voice of Jesus, and the man went
away sad.

II. We Must "Keep" the Word

We must "keep" the word: neither lose it, nor let it be taken
away, nor cease to heed it. Within and without ourselves there
are many things against which we have to protect and to defend
the word. Only a good and perfect heart can, with God's help,
firmly adhere to, and never forsake the word of God, that is,
the faith of Christ, the life of grace, the struggle for perfection,
the promptings of the Holy Spirit, the good resolutions taken
under God's guidance.

We must never allow our trust in God's grace to abate one
whit, nor let go our reliance on what is best in us; to these things
we cling with humility, with firm confidence, with intense joy,
because we serve a good Master. "I know whom I have believed,
and I am certain that he is able to keep that which I have committed unto him" (2 *Tim.* 1, 12).

III. To Bear Fruit

The sower scatters the seed in order that he may reap the harvest; but it takes a long time before the wheat is ripe for the
sickle. Our time is short, our powers are limited, and we readily
grow impatient; we want to see results, to make progress, to
measure how far we have advanced, to compare our performance
with that of others. The Kingdom of God comes not in that manner, neither in the soul nor in the world.

Napoleon is supposed to have said, "One must have the patience
of the night," which never hurries. If he needed such patience to
change the world (and how superficial was that change!) what

patience is called for to renew spiritually the entire world? Divine patience, the patience of Him who is almighty and eternal. Many Saints did have a share in that patience: their restless zeal and their insatiable ambition for God's glory never impaired their long-suffering patience. The mystic writers of the Middle Ages loved to use the hazelnut shrub as a symbol of the divine patience: it is the first to blossom in early spring, and the last to yield ripe fruit in late autumn. God's love is patient and can afford to wait.

We must keep the seed, which God sows in our soul; we must never falter, but always trust and persevere, and finally bear fruit. The same is true of the seed which, in the name of the Lord, we sow in the souls of men. We must possess the patience of the night, must have faith in the slow, hidden workings of grace; we must not expect immediate and tangible results; we must have confidence, and be content that others reap where we have sowed. But in God's own good time the grain will rise, and the harvest will be gathered.

God alone scans the depths of our hearts; He sees how courageously and how joyfully we strive to be constant. And His eye also peers into the secrets of other men's souls where, with His blessing, the seed scattered by our hand will one day grow, and bear fruit a hundredfold, if it be pleasing to His Divine Majesty.

Prayer: Almighty and eternal God, make our wills be ever devoted to Thee, and our hearts pure in the service of Thy Majesty. Through our Lord (Collect, Sunday after the Ascension).

WEDNESDAY AFTER SEXAGESIMA SUNDAY

PRIVILEGED KNOWLEDGE (Luke 8, 10)

1. The parables of Christ had a double purpose: Those that were well disposed, that "had ears to hear", understood them, but those that "had ears not to hear", and merely came to heckle and haggle, failed to understand them and found themselves in a quandary.

The privileged ones are the Apostles, to whom Jesus explains what was taught in the parable in a veiled manner. Jesus "knows what is in man", and He grants His full confidence to them that have faithfully followed Him. "And his disciples asked him what this parable might be. To whom he said, To

you it is given to know the mystery of the kingdom of God"
(*Luke* 8, 9-10).

2. *Petition*: That we, who as priests and religious have been
called to live in intimate intercourse with God, may humbly
hear, gratefully accept, and wisely employ the "privileged
knowledge", which He may be pleased to grant us.

I. The Apostles Are Privileged

Every Christian has received a personal call from God, and
as they said of old, is one of the "elect". Till this day countless
millions have never yet heard the Glad Tidings of salvation. We
know that God could reach them all, and save them all through
His Son Jesus Christ, who died for all men: but it is God's express
will that the Gospel be preached by men until the farthest limits
of the earth.

Even among Christians there are many that have received
privileged treatment from God, for instance such as were born
of pious parents, and received a thoroughly Christian education.
Most privileged of all are those to whom God vouchsafed a special
call to dedicate themselves to the service of the Lord.

More than other men they, like the Apostles, have the opportunity of holding intimate intercourse with Jesus: they must
speak to Him, listen to His voice, gain a deeper insight into His
doctrine; they have a right, nay a duty, humbly to ask for explanations, as did the Apostles. Such is the purpose of the regular
spiritual exercises, of the daily period of mental prayer, of Holy
Mass and of Holy Communion. Holy Communion is a personal
interview between the soul and Jesus, in which two loving hearts
commune with each other. "He that eateth my flesh and drinketh
my blood abideth in me; and I in him" (*John* 6, 57). Never omit
your thanksgiving after Holy Mass or Holy Communion: this is
the most appropriate occasion to commune with the Lord of our
soul.

II. "To You It Is Given"

It is *given* to them, says Jesus. They did not earn the privilege.
"What hast thou that thou hast not received?" (1 *Cor.* 4, 7.)
It is a sheer grace, God's bountiful gift, utterly undeserved. Such
is above all the very personal invitation, which is implied in a
priestly or a religious vocation. "By the grace of God I am what
I am" (1 *Cor.* 15, 10), says St. Paul; and he adds "and his grace

in me has not been void, but I have labored more abundantly than all they; yet not I, but the grace of God with me".

Those gifts are bestowed on us by God that we make them bear fruit, that like Paul we may "labor" for God. The Apostle is speaking chiefly of his apostolic labors; but he also used God's gifts in the work of his own sanctification. He fears "lest perhaps, when I have preached to others, I myself should become a cast-away" (1 Cor. 9, 27).

God's gifts are given that all may benefit by them: this is true of spiritual as well as of earthly goods; they must be distributed: selfish spiritual hoarding, or stark capitalism, is opposed to the spirit of the Gospel. Even hermits of old, in the solitude of the desert, prayed and did penance for the world whence they had fled.

In the Apostles, whom He initiates into the secrets of the Kingdom, Jesus beholds His first co-operators in the work of establishing the Kingdom of the Father. St. Paul cried out, "A necessity lieth upon me; for woe is unto me if I preach not the Gospel" (1 Cor. 9, 16). This is our task: our entire life, even more than our preaching, and our apostolic prayer, must co-operate in the establishment of the Kingdom.

III. "To Know the Mystery of the Kingdom of God"

There is no question here of the mysteries that are the object of the investigation and research of men of learning, but of the things of which Jesus speaks in His prayer to the Father, "I confess to thee, O Father, Lord of heaven and earth, because thou hast hid those things from the wise and prudent, and hast revealed them to little ones. Yea Father, for so hath it seemed good in thy sight" (Matt. 11, 25-26).

"Those things", "the dispensation of the mystery which hath been hidden from eternity, in God who created all things (Eph. 3, 9), are now being revealed by the Father, through His Son. Jesus, who speaks to the Apostles, fathoms all the secrets of the Kingdom; for He and the Father are one, and he, who sees Jesus, sees the Father. To know the mysteries of the Kingdom is to know Jesus; and to learn to know Jesus, through daily and familiar intercourse, that was the privilege of the Apostles.

The same privilege is granted to those whom Jesus has called to "abide with Him", to learn from Him the secrets of the Kingdom, to gain an intimate knowledge of Him, God and man, and of His silent work in the Church and in the souls of men.

Such knowledge is not vain, but is the source of love of God and of the neighbor; it feeds our prayer, it strengthens us in our labors, and comforts us in our sufferings.

Prayer: Lord Jesus, who revealest Thyself and the secrets of Thy Father's Kingdom to the little ones, grant that, through our familiar intercourse with Thee, we may become like unto those little ones. Grant us a share in the treasures of wisdom and knowledge of Thy Sacred Heart; so that our souls may be enriched by them, and that we may help others to have a share in them.

THURSDAY AFTER SEXAGESIMA SUNDAY

SAINT PAUL ON THE DEFENSIVE

1. In last Sunday's Epistle we see how St. Paul defends himself, or rather, how he defends the work he has done in Christ's name; perhaps we should say, how he defends Christ. The Apostle makes a strong plea in his own defence, without seeking for any personal ends. Paul, "a servant (literally, a slave) of Jesus Christ, called to be an apostle" (thus he describes himself in the beginning of the letter to the Romans), never dreamt of seeking his own interests: that is a lesson we may well take to heart.

2. *Petition*: The grace to follow Paul's example; to forget our own petty desires and ambitions, in order to serve only the interests of Christ.

I. Compelled to Defend Himself

Opponents of St. Paul had calumniated him at Corinth: possibly they were Christians of Jewish origin, who were bent on preserving the prescriptions of the Old Law that were now obsolete. They represented St. Paul as a second class Apostle, or even less; they had tried to bring his person into contempt, in order to discredit his doctrine, the burden of which was that Christ and His disciples had definitely broken with Judaism. It was clear to St. Paul that here he had to face an attack on the doctrine which he had received from Jesus, as well as on his apostolic ministry among the Gentiles.

The Christians of Corinth ought to have stood up in his defence, but they had failed to do so. He tells them, "I become foolish, you have compelled me; for I ought to have been commended by you" (2 *Cor.* 12, 11). (If it looks foolish to defend oneself, then you have compelled me to do it.)

From the whole context it is plain that Paul is pleading, not to defend his own reputation, nor to maintain his personal authority, nor even to save his personal work; but to uphold the cause of Christ. If one or other at times fails to act with an absolutely pure intention, what matters it provided by all means, "whether by occasion or by truth, Christ be preached?" (*Phil.* 1, 18.)

Here we touch, as it were, the greatness of Paul's heart; and cannot but sincerely admire the ardent, and absolutely disinterested zeal of the Apostle. Shall we not blush at our own pettiness? When we have to take up our own defence, how much self-love enters into it all. Our feelings have been hurt, we have been personally aggrieved; we defend not "Authority" but our own authority and our prestige, not God's work but our own paltry performance. The heart of St. Paul was like unto the Heart of Jesus. "Christ did not please himself" (*Rom.* 15, 3), that is, He did not seek His personal advantage; neither did Paul, "the servant of Jesus Christ and His apostle".

II. The Manner of His Defence

"If I must glory": he cannot help it, but he will do it in the Lord, who has blest his labors. Again and again he apologizes for that "glorying", and he says "it is not expedient", that is, in ordinary circumstances it would not be. "The others glory according to the flesh. . . . I will glory also. . . . Whatever they dare, I dare also. . . . They are Hebrews, so am I. . . . They are ministers of Christ (I speak as one less wise) I am more so. . . . The God and Father of our Lord Jesus Christ, who is blessed forever, knoweth that I lie not." Next he gives a brief summary of all he has endured in the service of Christ, and of the extraordinary graces, visions and revelations which God has granted him. "And lest the greatness of the revelations should exalt me, there was given me a sting of my flesh, an angel of Satan to buffet me" (2 Cor. 12, 7). It seems likely that St. Paul is alluding to a painful ailment, which often was to him a cause of humiliation before men.

In this defence we may admire three things: (1) the extreme reticence and tact of the Apostle when he has to testify in his own favor; (2) his transparent sincerity, so that he can call God to witness; (3) his promptitude in confessing what may humiliate him. He concludes thus, "Think you that we excuse ourselves to you? We speak before God in Christ: but all things, my dearly beloved, for your edification" (2 *Cor.* 12, 19). Whatever he has said, was said with the purest intention, in the presence of God, for their salvation.

Here we have a precious lesson to learn. It will happen that our merits are ignored or denied, that our work is belittled, that our authority meets with resistance. What are our reactions in those circumstances? We may have a right—possibly, a duty— to defend ourselves, especially when our intention is pure and we are not yielding to personal resentment. If, on such occasions, we state the truth, the whole truth and no more than the truth, as we honestly and humbly see it, if we seek not a personal triumph but desire solely the glory of God and the salvation of souls, then we speak as Paul did, "before God, in Christ, for the salvation of your souls".

Prayer: O Lord Jesus Christ, Thou hast chosen Paul to be Thy Apostle, and hast made him Thy chosen instrument to preach Thy Name to nations and rulers; Thou hast cleansed his heart and made it holy and perfect before Thee: be pleased to cast a look of mercy and compassion on our pettiness and our selfishness; give us strength to conquer that selfishness, to seek nothing in Thy service except Thy glory and the salvation of souls.

FRIDAY AFTER SEXAGESIMA SUNDAY

SAINT PAUL WEAK AND YET STRONG

1. While writing in his own defence, St. Paul mentions his weakness, which he will not hide; in a way, he glories in the weakness; Christ is strong in him, because he is weak.

2. *Petition*: That we may obtain a clear understanding of Paul's weakness, which is strength in Christ: humble, yet undaunted, courage in the Lord's service.

I. St. Paul Is Weak

St. Paul felt rather humbly about himself, when he compared himself with the Greeks whose wise men and artists in those days led the world. And this feeling may have become stronger, after the learned men of the Areopagus at Athens had politely, yet none the less peremptorily, dismissed him after he had dared to speak to them about the resurrection. It is generally admitted that the Apostle's stature and outward appearance were neither impressive nor attractive. Some one is supposed once to have called him "an ugly little Jew". He certainly was eloquent, though he cared little for the graces of rhetoric. In his first letter to the Corinthians he says, "When I came to you (that was after his failure at Athens), I came not in the loftiness of speech or of wisdom, declaring unto you the testimony of Christ. For I judged not myself to know anything among you, but Jesus Christ, and Him crucified. And I was with you in weakness, and in fear, and in much trembling. And my speech and preaching was not in the persuasive words of human wisdom, but in showing of the Spirit and power; that your faith might not stand on the wisdom of men, but on the power of God" (1 *Cor.* 2, 1-5). His enemies said that "his bodily presence (that is, his personal appearance) was weak, and his speech contemptible" (2 *Cor.* 10, 10).

Paul was perfectly aware of his weakness and of whatever might bring him into contempt with men. And still more vividly did he realize his absolute unworthiness and impotence before God. But in vain would we try to find in him what we call an inferiority complex, which is the result of a sorry lack of true humility. Paul's soul is too great to succumb to such feelings. "By the grace of God I am what I am", he says (1 *Cor.* 15, 10), and he knows clearly that by himself he is absolutely powerless; whereas with the grace of God, that strengthens him, he can do all things.

II. St. Paul Is Not a Weakling

He certainly is sensitive, and feels strongly, and quickly passes from one emotion to another. When he thinks of the enemies of the cross of Jesus, he writes with tears flowing from his eyes; and opposition at times causes him profound depression. "But God, who comforteth the humble" quickly comforts him (2 *Cor.* 7, 6).

At Athens he dares face an assembly of the wisest and most

famed men of the time: he fails to impress them, and suffers under the failure; but he is not at all discouraged. When summoned before a tribunal by the raving Jews, he rejects the authority of the judges and, invoking the right of his Roman citizenship, makes appeal to Caesar; he is ready to appear before the Emperor at Rome. From his prison cell at Rome he writes to the brethren to rejoice in the Lord; he was beheaded and died a martyr.

That man, who was to God "a vessel of election", was anything but a weakling. Though he was what we would call a strong character, he was intimately aware of his human weakness, to which he gladly confessed before his fellow workers and his converts. But when he is face to face with Jesus, who has laid hold of him on the road to Damascus, then, though by himself powerless, he can do all things in the name of Him who has laid hold of him.

Paul's richly endowed and strong personality, purified of all self-seeking, dedicated to Christ, and yet still with his own nature, devotes itself to the service of the Lord Jesus.

III. Champion and Martyr

When on the road to Damascus Saul had been struck down, he exclaimed, "What shall I do, Lord?" And Jesus answered, "Arise and go to Damascus, and there it shall be told thee of all things that thou must do" (*Act.* 22, 10). And when in the city of Damascus Christ appeared to Ananias, and commanded him to cure Saul who had been struck blind, He added, "I will show him how great things he must suffer for my name's sake" (*Act.* 9, 16).

What he must do, what he must suffer, these two can never be separated. He is "a good soldier of Christ", armed with the armor of light: "in chastity, in knowledge, in long-suffering, in sweetness, in the Holy Ghost, in charity unfeigned, by the armor of justice on the right hand and on the left" (2 *Cor.* 6, 6-7).

For the name of Jesus he "labors even unto bands, as an evildoer" (2 *Tim.* 2, 9), and he dies as a faithful witness to Christ. "But in all these things we overcome, because of Him that hath loved us" (*Rom.* 8, 37).

What must we do? What must we suffer? God will let us know; and the choice will not be ours, nor will the measure. We shall be good soldiers of Christ Jesus, if we are loyal and zealous in His service; we shall be faithful witnesses, if we suffer patiently and joyfully. Then we may rest assured "that neither death, nor life, nor angels, nor principalities, nor powers, nor things present, nor things to come, nor might, nor height, nor depth, nor any other creature shall be able to separate us from the love of God, which is in Christ Jesus our Lord" (*Rom.* 8, 38-39).

Prayer: Thou knowest, O God, that we place no trust in our own powers; mercifully grant, therefore, that we may be protected and defended from all adversity by the Doctor of the Gentiles. Through our Lord (Collect, Mass of Sexagesima Sunday).

SATURDAY AFTER SEXAGESIMA SUNDAY

THE WORD OF GOD IN THE MOST PURE HEART OF MARY

1. In the parable of the Sower some of the grain fell on good ground: that is, the word of God, received and kept in a good and perfect heart, which bringeth forth fruit in patience (cf. *Luke* 8, 15). This was most perfectly realized in our Blessed Lady: she received and kept the word of God in her most pure and most perfect heart. "Drop down dew, ye heavens, from above: and let the clouds rain the just. Let the earth be opened and bud forth a savior; and let justice spring up together. I, the Lord, have created him (*Isa.* 45, 8).

2. *Petition:* The grace, through Mary's intercession and under her protection, to keep the word of God in our hearts, and to make it bear fruit in patience, that is, through perseverance.

I. Mary's Privilege

"To you it is given to know the mystery of the kingdom of heaven." If Jesus spoke these words to the Twelve, are we not entitled to apply them, in a loftier sense, to Mary? The Mother of Christ was not commissioned, as were the Apostles, to establish the Church. She did not preach, nor was she one of Christ's appointed witnesses to the world. Yet in the economy of salvation Mary played a most important role, that of Mother. She was the first to whom the most startling mystery of the Kingdom was revealed, viz., the Incarnation, in which her role was essential. When she uttered her *Fiat* to the angel, she conceived the Word of God in her virginal womb. And it is more than probable that, during her long years of daily intimate intercourse with Jesus at Nazareth, her Son made her penetrate deep into many of the mysteries of the Kingdom. Wasn't hers a good and perfect heart? more perfect than any other human heart, always open to God's grace, most pure and ever ready to do the will of God: "Be it done to me according to thy word."

With awe and reverence we look up to the Mother of Jesus; we praise and congratulate her, and we thank God, because He has willed that she, more than any other, should know the mysteries of the Kingdom of God.

II. Mary Kept These Things in Her Heart

Twice we read in St. Luke that Mary kept these things in her heart. "Mary kept all these words, pondering them in her heart", and "His mother kept all these words in her heart" (*Luke* 2: 19, 51). It would seem that in each case there is reference to events or sayings which at the moment she did not fully understand. The same must have occurred on other occasions, not only when her Son was lost at Jerusalem; but also during the long years at Nazareth, when absolutely nothing happened; and later during the years of the public ministry of our Lord. Though her soul had received more light from God than had been vouchsafed to any human being, yet many a time she had to "keep and ponder" many a word, until God gave her more light. Mary was discreet, and her faith was strong enough to wait till the day when the divine plan would be fully unfolded to her.

Mary was human, and we do not dishonor her, if we think that there were times when it cost her to keep all these things and to wait. If Jesus Himself, as man, had to struggle to be able to accept the chalice, why should not His holy Mother have known struggle? And this very struggle brings her so much closer to us, and makes her example so much more compelling. Keeping her example before us, let us be "no more children, tossed to and fro and carried about by every wind of doctrine . . . but do the truth in charity, and in all things grow up in him, who is the head, even Christ" (*Eph.* 4, 14-15).

Who can assist us more efficaciously than Mary to grow in Christ by doing the truth in charity? With her help we shall be no more children, tossed to and fro, and disheartened, who "believe for a while, but in time of temptation fall away" (*Luke* 8, 13).

III. Mary Brought Forth Fruit

She brought forth *the* fruit of her womb, the Savior: and in Him she gave us all things. She brought forth fruit "in patience", that is by perseverance. She never retracted her *Fiat* in the midst of the severest trials, and more than any other, she had a share in the redemptive sufferings of her Son. Of Him St. Paul says, "Whereas indeed he was the Son of God, he learned obedience by the things which he suffered; and being consummated he became, to all that obey him, the cause of eternal salvation" (*Heb.* 5, 8-9).

Mary also, although she was Christ's Mother, learnt to believe and to be firm in her faith, until on Calvary she stood by the cross. At that tragic hour her soul may have been shrouded in darkness, but her faith in the angel's message, which all these years she had kept in her heart, was never shaken. "He shall be great and shall be called the Son of the Most High. And the Lord God shall give unto him the throne of David his father; and he shall reign in the house of Jacob forever" (*Luke* 2, 32).

At that solemn moment, her Son with His dying lips said unto her, "Woman, behold thy son." These words appointed her Mother of all those that were to believe in Jesus, and made us her children.

Such is the precious fruit, which Mary produced, and still produces "in patience".

Prayer: O God, who hast given to mankind the prize of eternal salvation by means of the fruitful virginity of the Blessed Virgin Mary; grant, we implore Thee, that we may experience the intercession on our behalf of her, through whom we were made worthy to receive the Author of Life, our Lord Jesus Christ, Thy Son (Collect, votive Mass of our Lady, Christmas to Purification).

QUINQUAGESIMA SUNDAY

WORTHLESS PERFORMANCES (1 Cor. 13)

1. When the disciple whom Jesus loved, had grown very old, he was wont to speak only of one thing: fraternal charity; and when the brethren complained, he would reply, "This is the Lord's commandment." What St. John inculcated so insistently

became under the pen of St. Paul an inspired hymn in praise
of charity, the sublime chapter 13 of the first Epistle to the
Corinthians. This is the Epistle of the Mass of this Sunday.

2. *Petition*: The grace always to be mindful of the "Lord's commandment". Unless we observe it strictly, we shall not make
progress in virtue.

I. Those Volatile Corinthians

The Corinthians were converts of yesterday, and they were
extremely anxious to witness extraordinary and striking manifestations of the Spirit. In the first years of the Church, for the general
welfare of the community, God not seldom granted such favors,
spectacular gifts which did not necessarily imply that the recipient
possessed greater holiness. The Corinthians were young in faith,
and human vanity made them set too much store by things that
surprise and astound; St. Paul therefore thought fit to give a
serious, though altogether kindly, admonition: "You desire what
is highest and best? God be praised, but remember that what is
highest and best above all is within, as I shall show you."

This is a lesson which men need at all times: we are very inclined to see nothing but what appears to the eye; we crave for
esteem and consideration, and are very anxious to please; because
we forget that man seeth those things that appear, but the Lord
beholdeth the heart.

II. Worthless Performances

St. Paul enumerates some of those extraordinary manifestations
of the Spirit, for which the Corinthians craved so ardently even
in their most excellent form, and he concludes that in themselves
these things have no value. "If I speak with the tongues of men
and of angels, and have not charity, I am become as sounding
brass, or a tinkling cymbal." Perhaps men may stare at me in
stupefaction, but that makes me no better. "And if I should have
prophecy and should know all mysteries and all knowledge, and
if I should have all faith, so that I could remove mountains, and
have not charity, I am nothing." Woe to all learning that does not
lead to charity; even faith without charity avails nothing! And
lest they misunderstand him, Paul adduces a last argument:
"And if I should distribute all my goods to feed the poor, and if
I should deliver my body to be burned, and have not charity, it

profiteth me nothing." If a man should do these things, excellent in themselves, not out of love but to earn esteem or popularity, his liberality is worthless in God's eye.

In God's eye, that is, in very truth, the value of our actions depends on our intention. Striking deeds, crowned with success, even in the field of apostolic labors, may earn human applause, nay, they may even contribute to the salvation of souls: but their value before the Lord, and the credit they will earn for me, in heaven, depend on my intention.

Do I always "seek first the Kingdom of God and his justice"? Out of love for God and for men? Possibly much self-seeking impairs the purity of my motives.

III. Without Charity

From the whole context it is evident that St. Paul, in the beginning of the chapter, deals explicitly with fraternal charity. Besides, love of God and love of the neighbor can never be separated: "two precepts, but one love" said St. Thomas. The second commandment is like unto the first, and Jesus called it "My own commandment", and the sign by which men would know that we are His disciples.

We do not know for certain what induced that quaint Greek philosopher Diogenes to live in absolute poverty and to take up his abode in a tub. One of his friends said that his sole motive was proud contempt for what the common herd pursue. In a manner it was a heroic act, yet hardly more than vain ostentation.

Utterly different was the motive of Anthony, the young wealthy orphan of Alexandria in Egypt, who sold all his possessions and distributed the price to the poor, in order to withdraw into the desert. He acted out of love and hoped that, detached from all earthly things, he might cling to God alone. The absolute purity of his love was demonstrated later, when the city folk flocked to the desert to seek out the anchoret, who by then had become famous, and whose efficacious prayer healed all ailments of body and soul.

St. Paul clearly told his simple, and somewhat light-headed, Corinthians where they ought not to seek what is truly great and good, viz. in vain display, extraordinary manifestations and things that cause a stir. Perhaps we might take that lesson to heart: possibly we need it. Let us pray that we may not forget it.

Prayer: O Lord Jesus, Thou hast said unto us, Learn from me because I am meek and humble of heart; be pleased to teach us what is truly great and good. Thou hast shown to the Saints where to find true greatness. Thou art "the more excellent way", mentioned by St. Paul: love unto the end of Thy Father, who is in heaven; and of Thine own that are in the world.

MONDAY AFTER QUINQUAGESIMA SUNDAY

"A MORE EXCELLENT WAY" (1 Cor. 13)

1. Those good Corinthians were a little too fond of extraordinary manifestations of the Spirit, which are not vouchsafed to everyone. St. Paul reminds them that there is "a more excellent way" (1 *Cor.* 12, 31), open to all, and which all can tread every day, the way of fraternal charity.

2. *Petition*: The grace to travel by that way, which is the ordinary way and yet the royal road: the road of charity, that never falleth away.

I. Charity Towards What Is Weak

"Charity is patient." It is striking that St. Paul so frequently mentions these two virtues in the same breath: charity, the noblest of all virtues, and patience the virtue that has to be most commonly practiced. Where there is love, there is patience. Think of a mother's love and her unwearied patience with her child. "God is love," said St. John (1 *John* 4, 8), and long ago the Psalmist cried out, "The Lord is gracious and merciful, patient, and plenteous in mercy" (*Ps.* 144, 8), towards His chosen people in the old Covenant: so is Jesus towards His disciples, His executioners, towards each one of us. Indeed "God is patience", just as He is love.

Further, St. Paul says, "Charity seeketh not her own, is not provoked to anger, thinketh no evil, . . . beareth all things." Such are the dispositions of genuine charity towards all which is sorely lacking in this world.

Patience is the virtue for daily practice, the common virtue that hardly shines and rarely brings renown; and yet it is the virtue of the strong. "Heart of Jesus, patient and full of mercy; make our hearts like unto Thine."

II. Charity Towards What Is Good

"Charity envieth not . . . rejoiceth with the truth, believeth all things, hopeth all things." Charity is kind, merciful, believes in the goodness of others. St. Teresa of Avila wrote, "Those that truly love God love whatever is good, seek whatever is good, always take sides with the just, favor them and stand up in their defence, because they love truth alone and all that deserves love."

From this charity springs the optimism of the Christian, which is by no means the optimism of simpletons. Thus, in order that he may be perfect as his Father in heaven is perfect, in order that he may be conformed to Christ his Savior and his Brother, the Christian believes in goodness, puts his trust in God's grace, hopes against hope. If God Himself sees so much good in man, if He deems that man is able to do so much good, why should we despair of our brother's goodness? "Charity believeth all things", not lightly and unthinkingly, which would bring immediate disappointment and discouragement. The Christian's optimism is like the optimism of God.

III. Charity Towards Self

"Charity is not puffed up . . . is not ambitious . . . seeketh not her own." Here we are face to face with the fundamental disposition, whence flow all other good dispositions: true charity excludes that love of self, which seeks its own interests first. Selfishness makes self the center of all things, and judges all things from the standpoint of personal interests. Often consciously, at times unconsciously, it seeks personal advantage; it strives to raise itself and to cast others down. In everything it is the opposite of true charity, which never seeks self, which is discreet, simple, single-minded, humble.

It happens that the world tolerates the humble and the discreet, because they do not stand in its way: but it will hardly grant them its esteem; for it has no undertsanding of true nobility of soul, and still less of Christian charity.

In all these things our model is Christ, from whom we shall learn how charity deals with the weak and the imperfect, that is with divine patience; what its attitude is towards what is good in man, viz., an attitude of divine optimism; how it treats self, viz., with divine self-forgetfulness.

St. Paul sings in this lyrical chapter, above all, about fraternal charity: true human love, more genuine and deeper than mere philanthropy: the latter has "neither the depth, nor the height, nor the length, nor the breadth, of brotherly love in Christ our Lord."

(N.B. Chap. 5 of Bk. 3 of the Imitation of Christ is also a hymn in praise of fraternal charity.)

Prayer: Fill us, O Lord, with the spirit of Thy love: that by Thy mercy, we who have all partaken of the Heavenly Bread may also be of one mind and heart. Through our Lord (Postcommunion, Mass for Concord).

TUESDAY AFTER QUINQUAGESIMA SUNDAY

"CHARITY NEVER FALLETH AWAY" (1 Cor. 13)

1. St. Paul's hymn in praise of charity deals first with fraternal charity, but ends on a more sublime note, divine charity.

2. *Petition*: We ask what St. Ignatius directs the exercitant to pray for, as the fruit of the Exercises: "Give me, O Lord, Thy love and Thy grace: that is enough for me."

I. All Other Gifts Pass Away

"Prophecies shall be made void, tongues shall cease, knowledge shall be destroyed." Those extraordinary charismata, marvellous things on which the Corinthians were so intent, have no enduring value. They are signs, pale manifestations of the power of God, but they do not render the soul more pleasing to the Lord; they lack finality. "For we know in part, and prophecy in part; but when that which is perfect is come, that which is in part shall be done away."

Why do you attach such importance to what is merely transitory? Aren't you like children that hanker after marvels? "When I was a child, I spoke as a child; I understood as a child, I thought as a child. But when I became a man, I put away the things of a child."

In things connected with religion, or with the spiritual life, not a few of us are like children, or like very immature people. We allow ourselves to be fascinated by externals, and are filled with wonder and admiration before spectacular feats, and showy achievements. These things are no more than "the fashion of this world, which passeth away" (1 Cor. 7, 31). "The brightness within", which is lit by charity, endureth forever.

II. Even Faith and Hope Will Not Last Forever

Faith is a gift; it is also knowledge. This gift was bestowed on us in Baptism, through the outpouring of the Holy Ghost into our soul. Faith is also knowledge, but indirect and imperfect, which gives certitude; but not "sight". "We now see in a glass, in a dark manner" says St. Paul, that is as in a mirror. The picture in the mirror is God's universe, the whole creation, which indeed proclaims His power and His majesty; yet the image is not perfect. The awesome vastness of the ocean, the boundless expanse of the starry heavens, the marvellous working of the powers of nature, tell us of an omnipotent Artificer, of the Creator ... if we have ears to hear. Hope is also a gift of God by which we expect that God will give us eternal bliss with Him in heaven; but hope is not possession. "We are saved by hope. But hope that is seen is not hope. For what a man seeth, why doth he hope for? But if we hope for that which we see not, we wait for it with patience" (Rom. 8, 24-25). Faith one day will yield to sight, and hope to possession.

III. "The Greatest of These Is Charity"

"And now there remain faith, hope and charity, these three: but the greatest of them is charity." The greatest on earth and in heaven: the greatest on earth, because faith and hope derive their value from charity which is their crown; the greatest in heaven, because of the three theological virtues charity alone will survive in heaven, where it will achieve its full perfection. In heaven faith ceases, because our eyes *see* the Light Eternal. "We shall see face to face ... we shall know as we are known." Nor can there be hope in heaven, because we *possess* the Eternal Bliss that was promised.

Nor is charity on earth of a different nature from the charity that will endure in heaven: for it is sanctifying grace, which in heaven makes everyone happy forever and ever. On earth grace made us truly partakers of the divine life; but we could neither taste, nor feel, nor enjoy it. In heaven we shall taste and feel it, and forever we shall relish the consciousness of our intimate union with God.

"O God, our Lord, may Thy divine Love, which never yet sent away a beggar empty-handed, grant us to see and taste the sweetness of Thy Divine Majesty." Thus prayed the ancient mystics.

Prayer: O God, who preparest rewards that are not seen, for them that love Thee: instill in our hearts such love and affection for Thee, that our love for Thee in all things and above all things may bring us to the enjoyment of Thy promises, which surpass all our longings. Through our Lord (Collect, 5th Sunday after Pentecost).

ASH WEDNESDAY

DUST AND ASHES—LIFE ETERNAL

1. Let us assist at the imposition of the ashes, and hear "Remember, man, that thou art dust and unto dust shalt thou return." Later, when the priest distributes Holy Communion, he thus addresses us, "May the Body of our Lord Jesus Christ preserve thy soul unto eternal life."

2. *Petition*: Humbly remembering that we are dust, yet comforted by the knowledge that the Body of Christ will preserve us unto eternal life, we ask the grace to begin this solemn and venerable period of fasting with due piety, and calmly and devoutly to complete it (Collect, today's Mass).

I. "Thou Art Dust"

Lent is in the nature of an annual retreat for the whole Christian people. During this time the Church calls on her weak and sinful children to make earnest reflections, to repent for sin and to do penance, so that our hearts may be prepared for the great internal renewal that is to take place on the solemn feast of Easter.

The first step on this road is that we duly realize our own nothingness and our sinfulness. *Memento homo....* Remember, O man, that thou are dust, and unto dust thou shalt return. It is good for thee, proud son of Adam, who dost boast of so many achievements, to be told the truth bluntly: dust thou art, and unto dust thou shalt return. A while hence, what will be left of thee? A handful of dust! And whilst God's minister thus admonishes us, he signs us with the cross, and applies ashes to our forehead.

Fire is the great destroyer, which spares nothing, and reduces all things to ashes. When a moment ago the priest blessed the ashes, he asked God, "whose will it is that sinners should repent and not die . . . in His great Goodness graciously to bless those ashes, which we propose to place on our heads, as a token of our humility and to render ourselves worthy of forgiveness". We acknowledge that we are but ashes, and as a punishment of our wickedness must return to dust.

After impressing on us that we are nothing of ourselves, the Church reminds us of the fact that we are guilty of sin, and that the wages of sin is death. When Adam had rebelled against God in Paradise, God spoke to him thus, "In the sweat of thy face shalt thou eat bread, till thou return to the earth, out of which thou wast taken" (*Gen.* 3, 19).

But no Christian can ever despair, for he does not face the bottomless pit of annihilation. The Church prays that God "may sanctify those ashes, that they may profit to salvation all those who humbly call upon Thy Holy Name, and who, knowing their guilt, confess their sins. Grant, by the invocation of Thy Holy Name, that all who are sprinkled with these ashes for the remission of their sins, may enjoy also health of body and security of soul. Through Christ our Lord. . . ."

II. Preparation for Easter

The regulations for the observance of Lent used to be called "the exercises of Christian warfare". They have been greatly mitigated by the Church, and rigorists at times ask with some bitterness what is still left of those regulations. For many and excellent reasons the Church has thought fit to reduce greatly the number of obligatory fasts, and of other penitential practices that were formerly obligatory during this holy season. Nevertheless the Church solemnly reminds us that penance and mortification are an essential element of the Christian life. Even today she still *imposes* a minimum of penitential observances, whilst she urges us all, freely and generously to determine what penances and mortifications we shall practice during Lent. This she expects especially from those who are more deeply imbued with the Christian spirit, and desire to join her in offering reparation for the sins of the world. In our modern world there are many who scarcely pay heed to these exercises of the Christian warfare. So many seek only pleasure, and always more pleasure.

What shall we do during Lent? What exercises of Christian warfare shall we adopt? Possibly we have more occasion for mortification than people had of old; we certainly have more occasions to seek our ease and to enjoy ourselves. Have we not also more reasons to labor for the conversion of sinners by penance and mortification, to try and obtain the return of those that have strayed from the fold? In that manner we shall be preparing the great paschal renewal in the Mystical Body of Christ.

III. "Unto Life Everlasting"

The imposition of the ashes before Mass reminded us of the fact that we are mere dust, nay sinners. In this humble and penitential mood we assist at the Holy Sacrifice, and then, with the cross still marking our forehead, we approach the Holy Table. The same sacred minister, who had gravely reminded us of our lowly estate—dust and sin—now offers us the Lord's Body, the true Body, but One that did not, and will not, return into dust, the glorified Body of Jesus, and he addresses us thus, "May the Body of our Lord Jesus Christ preserve thy soul unto life everlasting." After the salutary humiliation comes the glorious rehabilitation, and it comes through the Body of Christ, who died, but dying conquered death. "He that eateth my flesh and drinketh my blood hath everlasting life: and I will raise him up in the last day" (*John* 6, 55).

Thus the Church speaks to us on this day: she is in real earnest and first utters words of solemn warning; but she, the true Bride, in the name of the Bridegroom concludes with "words of eternal life" (*John* 6, 69).

Prayer: (Prayer over the People) Look graciously on us, O Lord, as we prostrate ourselves before Thy Majesty: that, having been refreshed by this Divine gift, we may ever be comforted by heavenly assistance. Through our Lord.

THURSDAY AFTER ASH WEDNESDAY

"THY FATHER, WHO SEETH IN SECRET" (Matt. 6: 1-8; 16-21)

1. In the beginning of Lent the Church would have us remember that, though she imposes on us certain external practices, the value of these depends wholly on our internal dispositions. In the Gospel of Ash Wednesday (*Matt.* 6, 16-21) Jesus, Lover of whatever is true and sincere, warns us against hypocrisy and simulation, the leaven of the Pharisees and Sadducees.

2. *Petition*: The grace to perform the exercises of "Christian Warfare", in the presence of the Father, who seeth in secret.

I. Good Works

"Good works", external practices, the open performance of virtuous acts, are indispensable. In the Sermon on the Mount, where our Lord wanted "not to destroy the Law but to fulfill it", Jesus did not condemn good works; but He told us clearly in what their goodness consists. "Take heed that you do not your justice before men, to be seen by them; otherwise you shall not have reward of your Father, who is in heaven" (*Matt.* 6, 1). Then Jesus mentions three kinds of virtuous acts: almsdeeds, prayer, fasting. Do these things in secret, and the Father, who seeth in secret, will reward you. "And when you fast, be not as the hypocrites sad, for they disfigure their faces that they may appear unto men to fast. But thou, when thou fastest, anoint thy head, and wash thy face, that thou appear not to men to fast, but to thy Father, who is in secret. And thy Father, who seeth in secret, will repay thee" (*Matt.* 6, 16-18).

Jesus knows what is in man (*John* 2, 25), and how difficult it is to keep our intention absolutely pure. Even in the "doing of justice" man may seek himself, his earthly profit and interests. To hope for a reward is by no means wrong, but it is wrong to expect it from men, to pursue vain glory or earthly gain. "Expect your reward from your heavenly Father, and from Him alone; and therefore take heed lest you do your justice before men. Do it before your Father, who seeth in secret, and He will repay you."

II. Woe to Hypocrites

Jesus is Uprightness itself. He loathes deceit under any form, above all He abominates hypocrisy in matters spiritual. Many

a time He severely censured the leaven of the Pharisees and the
Sadducees. "This people honoreth me with their lips; but their
heart is far from me" (*Matt.* 15, 8).

But we should draw a sharp distinction between trying to
appear better than we are and trying to *become* better. The hypo-
crite does not care a whit for what he actually is; he does not
strive to be virtuous, but he wants to appear virtuous for the sake
of his own vain glory. He both simulates and dissimulates.

Not so the man that sincerely wishes to become better than
he is, who with effort practices a virtue which he wants to acquire.

To deny that principle is to assert that only what is spontaneous
can be sincere, and it is to erect an impassable barrier on the
road to self-improvement and perfection. Mere pretence is despicable; but to strive, against odds, towards a distant goal is
laudable.

III. The Light of Good Works

Our Lord exhorted His disciples to perform good works in
secret, "let thy left hand not know what thy right hand doeth",
and "when you fast anoint your head, that you appear not to
men to fast". And yet in the very same Sermon on the Mount our
Lord declared, "You are the light of the world. . . . Let your light
shine before men, that they may see your good works, and glorify
your Father who is in heaven" (*Matt.* 5: 14, 16).

These last words take away whatever apparent contradiction
there might have been. We neither can be permitted nor are
permitted, to do all our good works in secret. We must bear witness; our light must shine to all who are in the house, that is to
all men around us, "that they may see our good works" and,
looking higher, "that they may glorify their Father who is in
heaven." And the purer our intention is, the further removed
from self-seeking, all the more brightly will our light shine, and
all the more efficaciously shall we glorify the Father who is in
heaven.

Jesus gave us an example. "I am the light of the world. He that
followeth me, walketh not in darkness, but shall have the light
of life" (*John* 8, 12). But He honors His Father and seeks not His
own glory (*John* 8, 49-50). Whether He works miracles, or carries
His cross, or dies on it, He is in our place the true adorer, who
adores the Father in spirit and in truth" (*John* 4, 23).

Prayer: O God, to whom every heart is open, and every will speaks: purify the thoughts of our hearts by the infusion of the Holy Spirit, that we may love Thee perfectly, and praise Thee worthily. Through our Lord (Collect to ask the grace of the Holy Ghost).

FRIDAY AFTER ASH WEDNESDAY

THE PREFACE OF LENT

1. On the occasion of the imposition of ashes and the administration of Holy Communion, we have seen how the Church can humble man without belittling him, and how she can raise him up without making him proud. In another manner she does the same in the Preface for Lent.

2. *Petition*: That we may ever entertain more firmly those dispositions which are the foundation of the spiritual life.

I. The Text of the Preface

The Preface of the Mass is the introduction to the great "prayer of thanksgiving", which is the celebration of the Eucharist. In the Lenten Preface we thank "our Holy Lord, Father Almighty, Eternal God, who by bodily fasting crushes our vices, raises up our souls, bestows on us virtue and its reward, through Christ our Lord...." Here as everywhere the liturgy speaks of the Father as working within us: He casts down and raises up, He bestows strength and rewards.

We must remember that the work of our salvation, in the first instance, is not our work nor the result of our efforts: it is the work of the Almighty Father. But He will not perform that work all alone: He works "by bodily fasting", the fasting of *our* bodies. That is our contribution, and it derives its value from our Lord Jesus Christ. When our sacrifice, however paltry it may be, is united with the sacrifice of Christ, it becomes well-pleasing in the eyes of the Father.

II. "To Crush Our Vices"

The reference is to the lowest passion of our nature, the lust of the flesh. Faith teaches us, and our experience has convinced us, that in these matters our nature is not in a healthy condition. It is in these things that most men feel their utter weakness. During the season of Lent the Church sings, "Behold, now is the acceptable time, now is the day of salvation" (2 *Cor.* 6, 2). Fasting is a remedy against concupiscence, and bids fair to crush it.

Even worldlings at times understand the value of privations which are imposed by the circumstances of life, or by duty to the community and to the nation, or which one imposes on oneself to help a fellow man. But they rebel against the notion of mortification. Why should one not enjoy a lawful pleasure that is within one's reach? Why inflict pain on one's own body? Penance and mortification simply do not make sense to our materialistic age, which knows nothing better than pleasure, and which does not even suspect the existence of spiritual values.

And yet, Jesus did fast forty days in the desert and, "having joy set before him, he endured the cross, despising shame" (*Heb.* 12, 2). And St. Paul preached Christ crucified . . . "unto the Gentiles, foolishness" (1 *Cor.* 1, 23). In every age the Saints have understood that foolishness. Their penance is love, love of Christ suffering, and love of men whose sins they would expiate.

There are other vices that have to be crushed during Lent. But let us not forget that the best penance is interior penance. The most important renunciation imposed on us during this season is renouncing sin, as the liturgy often tells us. He, who during Lent strives to overcome his pride, his vanity, his impatience, his violent temper, his lack of sympathy for others, has creditably performed exercises of the "Christian Warfare".

III.   "To Raise Up Our Souls"

If we crush the vices, that is, if we gain the mastery over whatever is low and mean in our nature, we shall at the same time be raising up what is best in us. But this "gaining of the mastery" is not merely a temporary silencing, or a half-hearted control of our passions, while we remain more or less aware that we do not want to pull them out root and branch. Whatever is low and mean must be utterly destroyed, so that our soul is hampered by nothing in its upward flight. "He that shall lose his life for me shall find it" (*Matt.* 10, 39).

We renounce life "according to the flesh", which is bent on enjoying earthly pleasure; not because we despise pleasure, but because we love Jesus, whom we strive to find and to follow.

"To raise up our souls": we raise them to God in prayer: penance and mortification always go together with prayer and contemplation, such was the experience of the Saints of all ages: and very often the liturgy mentions them in the same breath. *The Imitation of Christ*, Bk. I, chap. 11, says, "If we were perfectly dead to ourselves, and in no way entangled with earthly pursuits, then might we taste the savor of divine things, and experience something of heavenly contemplation. The whole hindrance, and a very great one, is that we are not free from passions and lusts, and strive not to walk in the perfect way of the Saints."

Finally, in today's Preface we return thanks to the Father Almighty "because He bestows on us virtue and its rewards": virtue, that is, strength for our will to crush our vices; and rewards for our souls, that they may behold Him and be one with Him.

Prayer: O God, by whose gracious gift Thy Blessed Confessor Peter was distinguished for his wonderful spirit of penance and lofty contemplation, grant, we pray, that aided by his merits we may, by mortifying our flesh, have a readier understanding of heavenly matters. Through our Lord (Collect, Mass of St. Peter Alcantara, October 19).

SATURDAY AFTER ASH WEDNESDAY

FASTING: TRUE AND FALSE (Isa. 58, 1-10)

1. In the Epistle of the Mass today and yesterday we hear Jahve sternly declaring unto Israel what is the "fast that He has chosen" and what sort of fast He condemns. Most appropriately the Church has embodied that message in her liturgy in the beginning of Lent, as a serious warning addressed to all her children.

2. *Petition*: The grace to take that warning to heart and to understand how we may profit by it in our daily life.

I. A Permanent Danger

Though we ought to be "true adorers, in spirit and in truth" (*John* 4, 23), we are not pure spirits; but are composed of body and soul. It is impossible to live our religion without external rites and practices.

Because our human nature readily clings to what is material and visible, and quickly forgets what is spiritual and invisible, there is always danger lest external rites and observances should be regarded as having value in themselves, and lest they should be kept up for their own sake. It may happen that the rite has become just an empty ceremony, the meaning of which has been long forgotten, mere formalism: and those that observe it do not even feel that its rigidity has stifled the soul, which once was in it. Outwardly there is scrupulous observance, inwardly there is no trace of righteousness. "Then came to him from Jerusalem Scribes and Pharisees, saying, Why do thy disciples transgress the traditions of the ancients? for they wash not their hands when they eat bread. But he answering, said to them, Why do you also transgress the commandments of God for your tradition?" (*Matt.* 15, 1-3.)

We must loyally observe our Rules, and we ought faithfully to keep certain religious practices and pious customs. But above all we must live by the spirit of which rules, practices, and customs are the embodiment. On this spirit depends the value of our observance. Let us remember what Jesus said to the Pharisees, "These things you ought to have done, and not to leave those undone" (*Matt.* 23, 23.)

II. False Fasting

The Prophet Isaias lived about the year 700 B.C. in Judea, during a period of profound religious and moral decay. The children of Israel rigidly observed certain external practices, like fasting; and for this they gave themselves so much credit that in the face of the Lord they dared to boast of their fidelity. Then God sent them the Prophet Isaias. "Cry, cease not, lift up thy voice like a trumpet", and God reproached them "for their wicked doings". "Behold, you fast, and all the while you seek your profit, and you extort the last farthing from your debtors. Behold, you fast, and you quarrel and fight, and strike with the fist wickedly. . . . As long as you fast in that manner your cry shall not be heard on high. Do you imagine that this is a fast that pleaseth me? That a man should humble himself just one day, and make his bed in ashes and sackcloth, is that what you call fasting? Do you call that a day acceptable to the Lord?" (*Isa.* 58, 1-5.)

Fasting does not please God, when it is accompanied by injustice, scandalous selfishness, oppression of one's neighbor. Humble and contrite outward behavior, to which corresponds no internal disposition, is sheer hypocrisy, loathed by God and despised by men. Indeed, external observances are indispensable; far more indispensable is the service of God "in spirit and in truth".

III. True Fasting

The Prophet proclaims that true fasting consists in doing the works of mercy and loving one's neighbor. "Is not this rather the fast that I have chosen? Loose the bands of wickedness, undo the bundles that oppress; let them that are broken go free; and break asunder every burden." Here the Prophet stigmatizes one abuse that was common in Israel—inhuman treatment of debtors, who were unable to pay the usurious interest claimed by money-lenders.

"Deal thy bread to the hungry and bring the needy and the harborless into thy house; when thou shalt see one naked, cover him and despise not thy own flesh." Further the Prophet says, "If thou wilt banish from thy midst oppression, and the finger pointed scornfully, and the plotting of harm; if thou wilt spend thyself giving food to the hungry, relieving the afflicted, then shall light spring up for thee in the darkness" (*Isa.* 58, 6-10).

If, in order to deal mercifully with your brother, you forget your greed, your impatience, your anger; if, in order to help another, you deprive yourself of something, or take trouble, or renounce your own ease and advantage, then you are truly fasting. That means that the season of Lent must first of all help us to practice fraternal charity more assiduously.

When Charles de Foucauld was still a Trappist, he wrote to one of his nieces how he deplored that Leo XIII had granted to the Trappists a dispensation of the rule, so that they might henceforth use oil and butter. "So there is an end to our water and salt diet. You understand how I regret the concession; a little less mortification means that we give a little less to God; a little more expense means that we give a little less to the poor."

Such is true fasting, "the fast that I have chosen" says Jahve to His people (*Isa.* 58, 6). Our Lord did not come to destroy the Law, but to fulfill it, most of all with regard to the precept of brotherly love, the second commandment, which Jesus called His own commandment. If we want to observe the fast "that he hath chosen", let us observe fraternal charity. "Then shalt thou call, and the Lord shall hear; thou shalt cry, and he shall say,

Here I am" (*Isa.* 58, 9). "Because the Lord, thy God, is a merciful God" (*Deut.* 4, 31).

Prayer: Accompany us with Thy gracious assistance, we beseech Thee, O Lord, in the fast we have undertaken; that, as we thus submit our bodies to Thee, in like manner we may worship Thee with pure hearts. Through our Lord (Collect, Friday after Ash Wednesday). ⟶ end

FIRST SUNDAY IN LENT

THE FAST OF OUR LORD (Matt. 4, 1-11)

1. Immediately after He had received John's baptism, "Jesus was led by the spirit into the desert", where He fasted and prayed forty days and forty nights. We crave for the privilege to behold Him in solitude, absorbed in prayer; our hearts are full of awe and reverence.

2. *Petition*: The grace to penetrate a little deeper into the aweful mystery of the God-man, and to grasp the lessons which He teaches us while in the desert.

I. "Led by the Spirit"

"Then Jesus was led by the spirit into the desert, to be tempted by the devil" (*Matt.* 4, 1).

The Son of man, like unto us in all things, sin excepted, is shown here as being influenced by the good Spirit and by the evil one. He allows the former to lead Him; the other He drives away.

The Spirit of God, "whom Jesus saw descending as a dove, and coming upon him", has always led Him, and shown Him how He must be about His Father's business. Now that He is about to begin His public ministry, He listens even more carefully to His inspirations, and faithfully follows them.

II. Into the Desert

The Baptist had withdrawn into solitude in early youth, to be initiated into the "spirituality of the desert"; Jesus had not acted in the same way, and His "spirituality" would be different, completely new, more perfect, and more humane.

However our Lord followed the example of Moses, Israel's great law-giver, and of Elias, the great Prophet: during forty days and forty nights He dwelt in the solitude of the desert, fasting and praying. After that He was tempted by the devil.

It would seem that such has always been the program of all spiritual athletes: all religious leaders, all reformers and prophets. After his vision on the road to Damascus and his conversion, Paul withdrew to "Arabia",—probably a solitary place—there in prayer and silence to ponder over his marvellous meeting with Jesus, to re-read the Scriptures, and to prepare himself prayerfully for the work that lay ahead.

Jesus, Son of God but also Son of man, when following this plan which human psychology deems very wise, may have intended to teach us a lesson: without solitude, without silence, there can be neither intense spiritual life, nor intimate intercourse with God, nor fruitful spiritual ministry, nor complete conformity with God's holy will, nor absolute fidelity in carrying out His designs with regard to our soul. We must allow ourselves to be led by the Spirit, who led Jesus into the desert. Every day He leads priests and religious, and all those that have received God's call, to the solitude of prayer. Woe to them, woe to God's Church, when they can no longer cultivate silence and solitude and fly back to the noise and bustle of the world. "Thou wilt find in thy cell what thou wilt too often lose abroad. The cell continually dwelt in groweth sweet, but ill guarded it begetteth weariness" (1 *Imit. of Christ,* 20, 5).

III. Fasting and Praying

Jesus "fasted forty days and forty nights". Why should our Lord have fasted? His human nature was free from the taint of original sin; it had no lower passions to control in order that the spirit might take its flight on high. Jesus certainly had no need of fasting, but we had need of His example: and we are grateful for His goodness and His love. Out of love, for the weak he became weak, that he might gain the weak (1 *Cor.* 9, 22). In this matter also, although He had no need of it Himself, "He began to do and to teach" (*Act.* 1, 1).

It is not explicitly stated in the Gospel that Jesus spent those forty days and forty nights in prayer. There was no need of saying it: prayer was to Jesus the breath of His soul, as natural and as necessary as physical breathing was to His body. No earthly care or preoccupation could in the least disturb His continual and intimate intercourse with the Father. And yet we read in the Gospel that Jesus went into retirement to pray, and that many a time He passed the whole night in prayer. Now, before setting out on His public ministry, He spent forty days and forty nights in uninterrupted prayer. And this prayer was an unconditional and loving act of acceptance of the plan of our salvation, as the Father had mapped it out for Him. "Christ had to suffer, and so enter into his glory" (*Luke* 24, 26). "Yea, Father, for so it hath seemed good in thy sight" (*Luke* 10, 21).

Whenever obedience assigns us a new task, whenever we are face to face with a future that seems dark and full of trials, we ought to follow the example of Jesus, and draw closer to the Source of all strength; then, with childlike confidence and absolute self-surrender into God's hands, we shall be strong to face whatever may come. "He will over-shadow thee with his shoulders, and under his wings thou shalt trust. His truth shall compass thee with a shield" (*Ps.* 90, 4-5).

Prayer: May we be renewed by the holy offering of Thy Sacrament, O Lord: that purified of our old faults, we may be introduced to fellowship in the mystery of eternal salvation. Through our Lord (Postcommunion of today's Mass).

MONDAY: FIRST SUNDAY IN LENT

OUR LORD IS TEMPTED (Matt. 4, 1-11)

1. We return to the desert, where Jesus "was with beasts" (*Mark* 1, 13) and where Satan came to tempt Him. (Had the devil heard the voice from heaven, and was he eager to find out who this well-beloved Son of God was?) Jesus permitted the evil one to come close to him. Had the Spirit not led Him in to the desert "to be tempted by the devil"? We assist at this mysterious encounter between Him who is "the Light of the world", and the prince of darkness.

2. *Petition*: The grace to follow the example of Jesus in resisting temptation calmly, resolutely, "strong in faith".

I.   Meaning and Purpose of the Temptations

St. Paul wrote to the Hebrews (4, 15), "We have not a high priest who cannot have compassion on our infirmities; but one tempted in all things like as we are, without sin." The Word of God assumed our human nature so truly, that it was possible for Satan to approach Him and subject Him to the test of temptation.

Though the temptations came from without, yet they were for Jesus, at the moment when He began His public ministry, an occasion to uphold against Satan's wiles the plan laid down by His Father. "He that hath not been tried, what manner of things doth he know?" (*Ecclus.* 34, 11.) Jesus wanted to pass through the crucible of temptation as we must pass through it, that He might show us the absolute conformity of His will with that of the Father.

The manner in which Jesus repelled Satan's assaults also affords us a lesson. He clearly sees the devil's snares; and His answer is calm, to the point, peremptory.

II.   The Temptations

Satan sought to attack the Prophet in his weakest point. Jesus is hungry. "If thou be the Son of God, command that these stones be made bread" (*Matt.* 4, 8). Was there anything more reasonable than that He should use His power to provide for His bodily needs? But this was precisely what Jesus would not do. He would work miracles to feed others, not to provide for His own well-being. It was beneath His dignity to call on His Messianic powers for such a purpose. Jesus replied, "It is written: Not in bread alone doth man live, but in every word that proceedeth from the mouth of God." Jesus lives on other food: "My meat is to do the will of him that sent me, that I may perfect his work" (*John* 4, 34).

Here we may learn two lessons: "Seek you therefore first the Kingdom of God and its justice" (*Matt.* 6, 33), and then, remembering the primacy of the supernatural at all times, seek those things that are necessary for the body. Without bread man cannot live; but he shall not procure it by means that are wrong. And that is why Jesus peremptorily said 'No' to the devil.

Secondly, to employ for one's own temporal advantage spiritual powers which were given for the salvation of souls, is an abominable abuse. It is true that Jesus did say to the Apostles, "The laborer is worthy of his hire" (*Luke* 10, 7), that is, he has a right to be rewarded for work done and effort made; but not to be paid for what belongs to the spiritual order. We may admire our Lord's complete forgetfulness of self, even in His great need; for the Scripture says: "He was hungry." He will use His Messianic prerogatives for the good of others, not to satisfy His own needs.

"Then the devil took him up into the Holy City, and set him upon the pinnacle of the temple, and said to him, If thou be the Son of God, cast thyself down, for it is written: that he hath given his angels charge over thee, and in their hands shall they bear thee up, lest perhaps thou dash thy foot against a stone" (*Matt.* 4, 5-6).

In this second attack the devil had recourse to a passage from Psalm 90; he urged Christ to commit a rash deed, or to make a spectacular display of power, that might bring immediate success. Such was not part of the Father's plan, and Jesus silenced the tempter with another quotation from Scripture, "It is written, thou shalt not tempt the Lord thy God." Later Jesus will one day say to the Pharisees, "The kingdom of God cometh not with observation" (*Luke* 17, 20).

Do we not attach excessive importance to outward display, and to success? If so, we forget that it was in God's plan that only "when he had been lifted up from the earth (on the cross) Jesus should draw all things to himself". Nothing could induce Christ to depart ever so little from the path which the Father had drawn for Him.

In the last attack Satan casts off all disguise and is seen in all his ugliness. "The devil took him up into a very high mountain, and showed him all the kingdoms of the world, and the glory of them, and said to him, 'All these will I give to thee, if, falling down, thou wilt adore me." Ambition and lust for power are two fierce passions, especially of the great ones of this earth. The prince of the world tries this weapon with the mysterious "Great One", whom he has not yet recognized. But Jesus, who came to cast out the prince of this world, will no longer suffer his presence and chases him away: "Begone, Satan, for it is written: The Lord thy God shalt thou adore, and him only shalt thou serve."

Jesus has won the victory. The purpose of the temptations was to induce the Messiah, even before He began His ministry, to swerve ever so little from God's plan, in order to serve His personal interests. Jesus defeated Satan by firmly upholding the purely spiritual nature of our salvation, which He was to accomplish through His own passion, death and resurrection.

Our Lord here teaches a precious lesson to all who would spread or maintain God's Kingdom on earth against the devil's attacks. The prince of this world has indeed been cast out by Jesus and we are no longer in his power; but he is not powerless. In every soul and everywhere in the world, sometimes by deceit and stratagem, sometimes by brute force, he makes ferocious attempts to wreck God's plans for our salvation, and to hurl men into the abyss of eternal woe.

III. The Reward

"Then the devil left him, and behold angels came and ministered to him." After the fierce battle there is peace and rest and comfort.

We thank Jesus for the example He has been pleased to give us, and for having deigned to reveal to His Apostles the things He did and suffered in the solitude of the desert.

Prayer: Assist Thy people, we beg Thee, O God, to avoid all contact with the devil: and, pure of soul, to seek Thee, the only true God. Through our Lord (Collect, 17th Sunday after Pentecost).

TUESDAY: FIRST SUNDAY IN LENT

THE SEPARATION OF THE SHEEP FROM THE GOATS

(Matt. 25, 31-46)

1. The impressive picture of the Last Judgment, which was given us in yesterday's Gospel, reminds us of the contents of the Epistles of the previous Friday and Saturday. The lesson to be learnt from them is the paramount importance of fraternal charity.

2. *Petition*: The grace so to think, act and live, that on the Last Day the Judge may be able to say to us, Come ye blessed of my Father, possess you the Kingdom.

I. Jesus the Supreme Judge

On the last day, the solemn event that will close the history of our race will be the appearance in the heavens of Jesus, who will judge the living and the dead. "And when the Son of man shall come in his majesty, and all the angels with him, then shall He sit upon the seat of his majesty. And all nations shall be gathered before him" (*Matt.* 25, 31-32). Now is fulfilled what Jesus had foretold, "Neither doth the Father judge any man, but hath given all judgment to the Son, that all men may honor the Son, as they honor the Father" (*John* 5, 22-23). When Jesus stood arraigned before Caiphas He spoke thus to the high priest, "You shall see the Son of man sitting on the right hand of the power of God, and coming in the clouds of heaven" (*Matt.* 26, 64).

This is the solemn homage, which the Father has reserved for His Son. So long He has been the Good Shepherd (whom the Prophet Ezechiel had announced in the words which yesterday we read in the Epistle of Holy Mass); now He is the Supreme Judge.

The expectation of this triumphant apparition of Jesus however far away it may be in time, fills our hearts with gladness. In the *TE DEUM* we proclaim our joy in the following words, "Thou art the King of glory, O Christ. . . . Thou sittest at the right hand of God in the glory of the Father. . . . We believe that Thou wilt come to be our Judge."

II. The Good Separated From the Wicked

There is something that strikes us with wonder, whenever we read this page of the Gospel: when the good are separated from the wicked, the only standard by which their lot is determined is the practice of fraternal charity. And those concerned are no less surprised. The good never seem to have suspected that their service of their neighbor was such a wonderful thing. "Lord, when did we see thee hungry and feed thee?"—"And the king answering shall say to them, Amen, I say to you, as long as you did it to one of these my least brethren, you did it to me" (*Matt.* 25, 40). And to those who did not show kindness, "Amen, I say to you, as long as you did it not to one of these least, neither did you do it to me."

Whether we are conscious of it or not, all our actions, all our omissions, have this meaning and this bearing: they are done to Christ, or not done to Christ; to Christ in all his brethren, above all, in the poor and the lowly.

It is useful to ponder over these things, and to draw our own conclusions.

III. But Who Are the Best?

Those that consecrate themselves entirely to the service of the neighbor. The Gospel mentions only the corporal works of mercy, and these are done mostly to "the least of His brethren"; not alone by the "best of His brethren", but by these they are done with a degree of self-sacrifice, generosity and devotion, characteristic of the true followers of Christ. This should bring solace and comfort to the hearts of so many of our religious brothers and sisters, who lead dedicated lives in the service of "the least of the Lord's brethren".

God grant that love may shine forth from their eyes, that the touch of their hands may be soft, that their hearts may overflow with tenderness, while they minister to Him in His suffering members.

Still, any work undertaken out of brotherly love is a work of mercy, a service, a ministry: to study, to preach, to teach, to hear confessions, to be employed in administration or in the humblest domestic services, all that is being about our Father's business, is serving Jesus and His brethren. And to them who served in that manner the King will say, "Come, ye blessed of my Father, possess you the kingdom prepared for you from the foundation of the world."

"Possess you": as long as we dwell here on earth we lack the blissful and secure possession; but as a sure guarantee of the glory and splendor to come, we have Holy Communion, and His promise, "I am thy reward, exceeding great" (*Gen.* 15, 1).

It is striking, and it reveals the relation between Christ and the Father, that Jesus says, "Come ye blessed of my Father"; He is the Judge, but the Father gives the reward. To the damned He says, "Depart from me ye cursed"; He drives them from His presence, but He does not say that they are cursed by the Father or by Himself; for they have damned and cursed their own selves.

Prayer: O Lord Jesus, my Judge on the Last Day, and my Savior, graciously imprint in my heart the law of Thy love; enlighten my eyes so that I may recognize Thee and serve Thee in Thine own, most of all, O Lord, in the least of Thy brethren.

SAFE IN GOD'S HANDS (Ps. 90)

1. "Safe in God's hands" is the summing up of Psalm 90, which the Church has inserted in the Introit and other parts of the Mass of last Sunday. The reason for this may be that from this Psalm were taken the words, which Satan quoted to our Lord, "He hath given his angels charge over thee to keep thee in thy ways. In their hands they shall bear thee up, lest thou dash thy foot against a stone." This Psalm is the touching prayer of a soul that commits itself wholly to almighty God.

2. Petition: Always and in every circumstance to give to God that homage which honors Him most: full trust; this gives the soul unalterable peace and inexhaustible strength.

I. We Live Dangerously

Not seldom does one hear these words from men in the world; for not a few keenly feel how many dangers threaten our spiritual and temporal life at every moment. Nor is it only the individual that feels the threat of imminent disaster; the entire human race is tortured with fear and anxiety, and entertains terrible forebodings: the Western world, Christian civilization, the Church . . . what will happen next?

We have no insight into the divine plans, nor do we know how God will reach the goal He has Himself set: but He rules the world, as He rules every single individual, and nothing happens on earth without His permission. From heaven His eye pierces all heights and fathoms all depths, and nothing is hidden from His sight. He is almighty and infinitely wise, and His power reaches from end to end, in time and space; and His Providence, with a mighty, yet gentle hand, leads all men and things to their everlasting bliss for which He has created them, though man, endowed with free will, has the power to resist and thwart the divine plan. During Lent we ought to pray, and do penance, for the conversion of sinners.

All of us live dangerously; "with fear and trembling work out your salvation," said St. Paul to the Philippians (2, 12). There is no reason why we should allow ourselves to be tortured by fear and doubt; but we must be wary, and determined to do our duty, and ever to listen to the promptings of divine grace.

II. Childlike Trust

To live dangerously is the lot of every man, to foster childlike trust is his duty. These two are frequently the theme of the Psalmist's outpourings; and the last word of Jesus to the Apostles was, "In the world you shall have distress, but have confidence; I have overcome the world" (*John* 16, 33).

This feeling is expressed in lofty terms and striking images in Psalm 90:

> He that dwelleth in the aid of the Most High
> Shall abide under the protection of the God of heaven.
> He shall say to the Lord, Thou art my protector and
>   my refuge:
> My God, in him I will trust.
> For he hath delivered me from the snare of the hunters,
> And from the sharp sword.
> He will overshadow thee with his shoulders,
> And under his wings thou shalt trust,

Further we read:—
> But thou shalt consider with thy eyes
> And shalt see the reward of the wicked.
> There shall no evil come to thee.
> Nor shall the scourge come near thy dwelling.

When we read these last lines we cannot help saying to ourselves that they hardly describe the facts as they occur. Do the wicked always meet with retribution here on earth, and are the good always rewarded and protected against evil by God? No, such is not the case; and that sort of trust in Providence could quickly be disillusioned. The childlike trust, which God requires from us, reaches deeper and further, beyond time, as St. Paul eloquently expressed it, "If God be for us, who is against us? ... Who then shall separate us from the love of Christ? Shall tribulation? Or distress? Or famine? Or nakedness? Or danger? Or persecution? Or the sword? .... Nothing shall be able to separate us from the love of God, which is in Christ Jesus, our Lord" (*Rom.* 8, 31-39).

Whatever may happen in the wide world, or to each of us individually, "if God is with us," and we are with Him, we shall have the protection of His power, and need entertain no fear.

III. A Beautiful Night Prayer

Psalm 90 is part of the Office of Compline on Sunday. The Christian goes to rest "in the aid of the Most High, under the protection of the God of heaven", "He will overshadow him with his shoulders, and under his wing man shall trust", "he shall not be afraid of the terror of the night, nor of the arrow that flieth in the day", "for he has given his angels charge over thee, to keep thee in all thy ways".

Thus the liturgy would have us commend ourselves into the hands of Almighty God every evening before sleep, during which we drift unconscious and helpless into the night's darkness. God grant that this prayer be the supreme expression of our childlike trust in God, when the call shall come for us to pass unto Him.

Prayer: As the apple of Thy eye protect us, O Lord; shelter us under Thy wings; guard us when we are awake, and watch over us when we sleep: that we may watch with Christ and rest in peace. (The antiphon of the *Nunc Dimittis at* Compline.)

THURSDAY: FIRST SUNDAY IN LENT

THE WOMAN OF CANAAN (Matt. 15, 21-28)

1. A mother in distress has pushed her way through the multitude, and beseeches Jesus to cure her daughter. Jesus refuses, but she continues to plead for help, and is heard, because "great was her faith".
2. *Petition*: The grace to fathom the Heart of Jesus, on which

    the faith of this Gentile woman had such power. "I do believe, Lord, help my unbelief" (*Mark* 9, 23).

I. The Mother's Prayer

Jesus, wishing to find a little rest, and hoping to escape the attacks of His enemies, had departed from Capharnaum, and proceeded to the very borders of Syria, where the Gentiles were in the majority. The renown of the Prophet, who worked so many miracles, had spread even to those parts, and a woman of Canaan, a descendant of the original inhabitants of Palestine who had remained idolaters, had heard about Him, had learned that he was in the neighborhood. Her daughter lay seriously ill, and she would go to Him for help. When she had come close to Him, she cried out, "O Lord, thou Son of David, my daughter is grievously troubled by a devil." She greeted Him with a Messianic title, "Son of David". Perhaps we may think that a mother's distress drove her to it; but ought we not to take into account the inscrutable workings of God's grace in that soul? God alone can read man's heart, and why should we be more exacting than He was? Often it is through the door of grave need that God finds entrance into a heart. Extreme need seeks for comfort, often last of all, where we are most sure of finding it—with God.

II. The Refusal

Though we ought to think that this woman had been drawn to Christ by His grace, yet in the beginning the great Prophet refused to listen to her. "He answered her not a word." At this we feel astonished, and so did the Apostles. The distraught mother next addressed herself to the disciples. Would they not plead for her with their Master? "And the disciples came and besought him saying, Send her away for she crieth after us. And he, answering said, I was not sent but to the sheep that are lost of the house of Israel." Some time before Jesus had imposed the restriction on the Apostles, "Go ye not into the ways of the Gentiles" (*Matt.* 10, 5). The hour of the Gentiles had not yet struck.

St. Jerome suggests the following explanation to this restriction: "lest the Jews might say, We have rejected the Messiah that had been promised to us, because He sent His Apostles to the Gentiles and to the Samaritans, and not to us." Whatever be the reason, the answer of our Lord was a definite refusal.

However, the poor woman was not discouraged. "But she came and adored him saying, Lord, help me." And now Jesus did give her an answer, but it was not the answer she desired. "Who, answering said, It is not good to take the bread of the children and to cast it to the dogs." God's words are not our words. A cold, nearly a biting expression on the lips "whence proceeded "words of grace" (*Luke* 4, 22). The poor woman displays no hurt feelings, and her reply is wonderfully to the point: "Yea Lord, for the whelps also eat of the crumbs that fall from the table of their masters." So much more discreet and reverent was the request of Mary at Cana, "They have no wine; . . . whatsoever he shall say to you, do ye" (*John* 2: 3, 5). But Mary well knew who Jesus was while this woman had only just begun to believe. But "great was her faith".

III. Jesus Grants the Request

"O woman, great is thy faith; be it done to thee as thou wilt." And in St. Mark we read (7, 29-30): "And he said to her, For this saying, go thy way. The devil is gone out of thy daughter. And when she was come into her house, she found the girl lying upon the bed, and that the devil was gone out." Her faith, expressed in such a terse and forcible manner, has conquered the Heart of Jesus. Her great faith has performed a feat far more wonderful than the removal of a mountain: humanly speaking, it has persuaded Christ to "change His mind".

Why did Jesus refuse in the first instance? Perhaps that He might give her the occasion, as well as the grace, to increase her faith. That faith, which had its origin in God's grace more than in her maternal love, increased under the influence of further grace, until it was a power which God Himself could not resist.

Every day we have occasions to grow in faith and in confidence: whenever we are in need, and approach Christ for help. Perhaps our prayer is not heard at once, and we have to persevere in prayer even longer than the poor woman of Canaan. But he that perseveres always wins, if not with man, who is not always able to grant what he is asked; most certainly with God, with whom nothing is impossible.

Prayer: Most Sacred Heart of Jesus, I believe that Thou dost listen to my prayer;

Most Sacred Heart of Jesus, I am confident that Thou wilt answer my prayer beyond my highest expectations;

Most Sacred Heart of Jesus, I leave it to Thy good pleasure to hear me in the manner and at the time it may please Thee.

FRIDAY OF THE EMBER WEEK IN LENT

BEFORE THE FACE OF THE LORD

1. Often Holy Writ speaks of "the face of the Lord", "His countenance", "His eyes". When God commanded Abraham to go out of his country, He said, "I am the Almighty God; walk

before me and be perfect" (*Gen.* 17, 1). "The eyes of the Lord are upon them that fear him" (*Ecclus.* 34, 19).

2 *Petition*: The grace always to walk before His face, so that His eyes may look on us with love.

I. Before the Face of the Lord

To the children of Israel, Jahve was by no means an abstract Deity nor an impersonal primeval power that acts blindly and cares not for man. They knew that God was a Person between whom and themselves there existed personal relations. He was a spirit, invisible, and could not be represented in a tangible manner; wherefore He had severely forbidden His people to make any graven images of Him. Our limited human mind cannot represent to itself this person otherwise than in a human likeness.

And this invisible God sees all things; He is Holy, the Just One, the True One. "For his eyes are upon the ways of men; and he considereth all their steps. There is no darkness, and there is no shadow of death, where they may be hid who work iniquity." (*Job.* 34, 21.)

Our eyes are the windows of our soul: they reflect what passes in our heart. Thus the Jews read on the Lord's countenance what they were to expect from His hand. When they did evil in His sight, He turned His eyes away from them. For "the countenance of the Lord is against them that do evil things" (*Ps.* 33, 17). "Let my judgment come forth from thy countenance: let thy eyes behold the things that are equitable." (*Ps.* 16, 2).

The godly Israelite was wont to lead the whole of his life before the face of the Lord, as the Scripture says, "God set his eye upon their hearts" (*Ecclus.* 7, 7). God's eye in our hearts is our conscience.

To live in the presence of God is the most solid foundation, and also the aim, of the spiritual life: on earth He is present to us through the light of faith; hereafter the veil will be torn away and we shall see Him face to face.

II. The Lord's Eyes Are on Us

In the Psalms and in many of the liturgical prayers we frequently cry to God, that He may be pleased to cast a glance on us, or that His eyes may mercifully rest on us.

The sorely tried soul ardently prays, "How long, O Lord, dost thou turn away thy face from me, how long wilt thou forget me unto the end?" (*Ps.* 12, 1.)

When Solomon had built a temple in His honor, God said to him, "I have heard thy prayer and thy supplication, which thou hast made before me. I have sanctified this house, which thou hast built to put my name there forever: and my eyes and my heart shall be there always. And if thou wilt walk before me, as thy father walked, in simplicity of heart and uprightness, I will establish the throne of thy kingdom" (3 *Kgs.* 9, 3-5).

"The Lord hath looked from heaven: he hath beheld all the sons of men. From his habitation, which he hath prepared, he hath looked upon all that dwell on earth. He who hath made the hearts of every one of them, who understandeth all their works. . . . Behold the eyes of the Lord are on them that fear him, and that hope in his mercy. To deliver their souls from death and feed them in famine" (*Ps.* 32, 13-19).

God's eyes, mercifully resting upon us, are a source of light, peace and happiness. When eyes that see so far watch over us, we are safe: a single glance into those eyes, which are filled with love and mercy, gives the most perfect peace.

III. Keep Your Eyes Fixed on Him

When we are wont to walk before the face of the Lord, what is more natural than that we gaze aloft at Him, whose eyes rest on us with a Father's love? "My eyes are ever towards the Lord" (*Ps.* 24, 15), not only to find help and salvation at His hands; but also "as the eyes of servants are on the hands of their masters, as the eyes of the handmaid are on the hands of her mistress" (*Ps.* 122, 2), to know their commands and promptly to obey them.

We also keep our eyes fixed on Him to seek and find Him in all the works of His hands, most of all in our fellow men, whom He has made to His own image and likeness.

In our own work our eyes are directed towards God, and not towards men, "as it were pleasing men, but as the servants of Christ, doing the will of God from the heart" (*Eph.* 6, 6).

In this manner we walk before the face of the Lord, keep our eyes fixed on Him, and strive to serve Him perfectly.

Prayer: Direct, we beseech Thee, O Lord, our actions by Thy holy inspiration, and carry them on by Thy gracious assistance; that every prayer and work of ours may always begin from Thee, and through Thee be happily ended (Prayer after the Litany of All Saints).

"WHO IS MY MOTHER?"

(Matt. 12: 46-50; Matt. 3: 31-35; Luke 8: 19-21)

1. All the words of Jesus are human words, addressed to men, but spoken by One who is God and man. They arise from depths which we cannot fathom, and not seldom they surprise us, and compel us to ponder over them. One of these words, which we read in the Gospel of last Wednesday, is "Who is my mother?" (*Matt.* 12, 48) and He pointed to his disciples.

2. *Petition*: The grace to grasp the meaning of these mysterious words, and to draw profit from them.

I. The Circumstances

The public ministry of Jesus had lasted for some time and He had performed a goodly number of miracles. He spoke as no man had ever spoken before (*John* 7, 46). The goings on of this man, who was the Son of Mary, and for so many years had been their fellow villager, aroused a good deal of interest among the people of Nazareth. They had no faith in His miracles; and even His relations "were scandalized in Him". They pretended to feel some anxiety as to His mental condition, and wanted to bring Him home, perhaps with the use of a little force.

Mary knew all that, and even in her own family circle old Simeon's words were being verified, "Behold this child is set for a sign that shall be contradicted. . . . Thus out of many hearts thoughts shall be revealed, and thine own heart a sword shall pierce." Mary allowed herself to be persuaded to accompany her relatives to Capharnaum, though she certainly did not share their feelings, and still less their intentions. It is easy for us to realize what a painful journey this must have been for Mary: to hear around her that continual carping at the conduct of Jesus, the shrugging of shoulders, the absurd attributing of motives. . . . She knew who He was, and that He had to be about His Father's business.

When they reached Capharnaum, Jesus happened to be preaching; He and His disciples had retired into a house, and a group of men was crowding round the door and blocking the entrance. Some one, therefore, sent a message to Jesus to say that His

Mother and brothers (relatives) were waiting without, and wished to see Him.

II.   The Declaration of Jesus

This indiscreet intervention was a piece of unwarranted interference. In the desert Jesus had given a sharp and peremptory reply to the tempter, who tried to make Him turn aside from His God-appointed task; this time too His answer is curt and decisive: "Stretching forth his hand towards his disciples, he said, Behold my mother and my brethren. For whosoever shall do the will of my Father that is in heaven, he is my brother, and sister, and mother" (*Matt.* 12, 49-50). St. Mark (who is St. Peter's interpreter, and often more concrete and more graphic than the other Evangelists) says that "He looked round about on them who sat about him" (*Mark* 3, 34). Had Jesus seen His Mother standing without? Did Mary hear those words?

If she did, then her thoughts must have gone back to what had happened years before at Jerusalem, and to the words Jesus had spoken then. On that occasion Mary had "not understood the words that he spoke to them". Ever since she had pondered over them, and all these years she has lived in loving intimacy with her divine Son: we may suppose that gradually the meaning has been revealed to her. And as she fathomed the meaning, she also understood what sacrifice they implied for her, and her heart ached. But now again she gave her consent, and surrendered her whole self to God.

III.   Jesus, the Founder of a New Family

With these unexpected and surprising words Jesus does not abolish the ties of blood. The Law says, "Thou shalt honor thy father and thy mother"; and Jesus has come, not to destroy the Law but to fulfill it and to raise its observance to a higher plane. But He uses this opportunity to teach us, by word and by deed, an important lesson. Natural kinship, ordained by God and hallowed by Him, has its own rights; but in the spiritual order these rights yield to more sacred claims; at times, even at the cost of much pain, they must be sacrificed unto God's glory.

Jesus is the author of a new relationship; He is the new Adam; all those who believe in Him are born again, and receive a new life. "All those that believe in him", or as Jesus says on this occasion, "whosoever shall do the will of my Father." That will we know: He reveals it to us. "This is my beloved Son. Hear ye Him" (*Matt.* 17, 5).

In this new family Mary holds a unique place. For no one fulfilled the Father's will more perfectly than Mary? No word ever spoken was so like unto the "Yea Father" of Jesus, as was Mary's *fiat*. On the present occasion Jesus does not think of Mary as His Mother according to the flesh. There was question of higher things; but from the cross He speaks to her as to His Mother according to the flesh and, with all the love of a devoted Son, He entrusts her to the beloved disciple; at the supreme hour, when His death is about to put the seal on the work of our salvation, He appoints her our spiritual mother and gives her unto us.

All those who believe in Jesus and have been reborn through Baptism are members of the new family, who have left brother and sister, father and mother, in order to dedicate themselves to the service of God. Let there be no rapine in their holocaust and, when their Father's business and the salvation of souls require it, let them say: "Those that need me so that they may learn to know and to observe the Father's will, *they* are my brothers and sisters, father and mother."

Prayer: Holy Mary, Mother of Jesus and my Mother, who wert always wise and prudent in all thy actions, generous and heroic in thy sacrifice, teach us prudence and loving surrender to God's holy will.

Heart of Jesus, formed by the Holy Ghost in the womb of the Virgin Mary, abyss of every virtue, in whom the Father is well pleased, have mercy on us.

SECOND SUNDAY IN LENT

THE TRANSFIGURATION OF OUR LORD—I
(Matt. 17, 1; Mark 9, 1; Luke 9, 28)

1. Only a few days before, Jesus had praised Peter highly, "because flesh and blood had not revealed to him, but the Father, who is in heaven, that Jesus is Christ, the Son of the living God". Shortly after, the Master was compelled to rebuke him severely, because flesh and blood—or rather Satan, as our Lord said—had induced the Apostle to take scandal, when Jesus for the first time foretold His passion and death. On the present

occasion Jesus invites Peter, together with James and John, to witness His transfiguration on the mountain.

2. *Petition*: The grace firmly to believe the great mystery that "Christ ought to suffer and so to enter into His glory".

I. The Three Privileged Disciples

Peter, James and John are the three chief Apostles. Our Lord never acts out of mere caprice, nor is He fickle or unreasonable in showing favor. True, He is the Supreme Master, and He chooses whomsoever He pleases; but when doing so His choice is the result of infinite Wisdom and infinite Goodness. These three Apostles are now to behold a ray of His glory, as they will witness His utter humiliation in the garden of Gethsemane.

We know not the way God will lead us: but now and always we completely surrender ourselves into His hands, and with child-like trust in His goodness we allow Him to dispose of our entire self.

"Lord, Thou knowest what is best; do this or that as Thou wilt. Give what Thou wilt, and as much as Thou wilt, and when Thou wilt. Do with me what Thou knowest to be best, what pleases Thee most, and is most to Thy glory" (3 *Imit. of Christ*, 15, 2).

II. The Transfiguration

"And whilst he prayed," says St. Luke, "his countenance was altered." His face shone with the brightness of the sun, "and his garments became shining and exceeding white as snow, so as no fuller upon earth can make white" (*Mark* 9, 2). On this one occasion Jesus permitted that His divine nature should for a moment illumine His humanity with its splendor. He had freely assumed the "body of our lowliness", which veiled His glory; now "the body of his glory" shines through the veil, and His Majesty is manifested.

Thus far He has hidden under the cloak of His humanity the divine splendor, that is His birthright, and that ought to make us marvel much more than does this brief manifestation of His glory.

O Jesus, whether Thou art hidden or glorified, whether Thou shinest as the brightest rays of the sun, or liest prostrate in the garden of Gethsemane, we adore Thee, true God and true Man.

And now we see the vision growing more impressive and its message becoming more awe-inspiring. Moses the law-giver of the

Hebrews, and Elias the greatest of the ancient Prophets, representing the Old Covenant and incarnating the entire history of the chosen people, appear "in majesty" by the side of Christ. They pay homage to the Messiah, whose coming they have announced. "And they spoke with him of his decease, that he should accomplish in Jerusalem." Here once again, and at the very moment when Jesus grants them a glimpse of His glory, we are reminded of the unbreakable link between humiliation and glory.

And Peter said to Jesus, "Lord, it is good for us to be here. If thou wilt, let us make here three tabernacles, one for thee, one for Moses, and one for Elias" (*Matt.* 17, 4). And St. Mark adds, "For he knew not what he said, for they were struck with fear" (9, 5).

Indeed, when Moses and Elias have just conversed with Jesus about His "decease" in Jerusalem, that is, about the great tragedy of the cross, the comfortable suggestion of Peter appears singularly out of place. Jesus does not reply to the poor Apostle, who has still so much to learn about the mystery of our redemption. How patient, Thou art, O Lord, with these carnal men, who are nevertheless full of good will! We know that Thou treatest us with the same love and forbearance, provided we also have good will.

III. "It Is Good For Us to Be Here"

We might translate the Gospel text thus: "What a blessing to be here!" These words ought to express our feelings, in whatever circumstances we may find ourselves, more so if we are priests or religious, that is, specially called always to "abide with Him". Let us tell Him of our joy "to be here", not only when He reveals to us a ray of His glory, but also when His power remains hidden from our sight, and when we feel lonely and grope in the dark. "Lord, it is good for us to be here" with Thee. Can we utter words that please Him more? can we pay Him homage that gives Him greater honor? "They who love Jesus for Himself, and not for any consolation they hope to draw from Him, bless Him as much among every kind of trial and anguish of heart, as when they enjoy the greatest delight" (2 *Imit. of Christ* 11, 2).

Prayer: "O Lord, grant only that my will may remain true and firm towards Thee, and for the rest, do with me just what pleases Thee. For nothing that Thou dost with me can be anything but good. If Thou wishest me to be in darkness, be Thou blessed; and if Thou wishest me to be in light, again be Thou blessed. If Thou art pleased to comfort me, be Thou blessed; and if it be Thy will to try me, still be Thou blessed for ever" (*Imit. of Christ* 17, 2).

MONDAY: SECOND SUNDAY IN LENT

THE TRANSFIGURATION OF OUR LORD—II

1. "And as Peter was yet speaking, behold a bright cloud overshadowed them. And lo, a voice out of the cloud, saying, This is my beloved Son, in whom I am well pleased. Hear ye him. And the disciples hearing fell upon their face and were very much afraid" (*Matt.* 17, 5-6).

2. *Petition*: The grace to hearken to the Father's behest, and always to "hear His beloved Son", whenever He speaks to us —be it through the voice of His Church, or through our Superiors, or through the promptings of the Holy Ghost in our hearts.

I. The Father Speaks

"No man hath ever seen God" the Father "at any time" (*John* 1, 18). In this mystery the Father intervenes, as He was wont to do in the Old Testament, as "a voice out of the cloud". It was "a bright cloud", says St. Matthew. This bright cloud, and the voice that issues from it, strike the Apostles with terror: man trembles before any direct manifestation of the divine power.

"This is my beloved Son, in whom I am well pleased: hear ye him." In the Gospel we often hear Christ speaking to His Father; but when the Father deigns to speak, He never addresses Himself to His Son, but to us, men, to teach us that the Son of man is His only-begotten Son, and to reveal to us that His Son is invested with His own power. Such was the meaning of the words that came from heaven at the time of the baptism in the Jordan, and which were addressed to John and his disciples; such is their meaning on this occasion, and the Father commands the Apostles: "Hear ye him".

Does this precept not allude to the great mystery about which Moses and Elias had conversed with Jesus, viz. that "Christ ought to suffer these things and thus enter into his glory". That was a thing which the Apostles simply could not grasp: only shortly before the Transfiguration, when Jesus had for the first time told them about His coming passion and death, Peter had protested: but Jesus turning about threatened Peter, saying, Go behind me, Satan, because thou savorest not the things that are of God but that are of men (*Mark* 8, 33). And now the Father Himself solemnly adjures them, "Hear ye him." One day they shall hear, but now they are "foolish of heart and slow to believe", and blinded by their dreams of national power and greatness; they will be able to hear only after they have seen Him risen from the dead, and after the Holy Ghost has taught them all things, and brought all things to their mind, whatever He had said to them (*John* 14, 26).

Meanwhile Jesus patiently strives to enlighten their petty understanding, teaching them till the very last hour. With them the Lord was divinely patient; and so He still is with us. "Learn from me, because I am meek and humble of heart."

II. After the Vision

"And Jesus came and touched them, and said to them, Arise and fear not. And they, lifting up their eyes saw no one but only Jesus." Once more He is to them the Master, with whom they have lived in such wonderful intimacy; all the glory and splendor has vanished, and they see Jesus of Nazareth, like unto us in all things, sin excepted. "All the fullness of the Godhead, that dwelleth in him" (*Col.* 2, 9), and of which they have seen a ray illumining His countenance and His garments, has again hidden itself under the ordinary appearance of His human nature and of His grey habit.

But they have beheld Him in His glory, and that vision will never be effaced from their memory. Twenty years later Peter will write, "For he received from God the Father honor and glory, this voice coming down to him from the excellent glory: This is my beloved Son, in whom I am well pleased; hear ye Him. And this voice we heard, brought from heaven, when we were with him in the holy mount." (2 *Peter* 1, 17-18.)

O Jesus, there have been days and hours, when we too were privileged to behold Thee, and to catch a glimpse of Thy glory through the bright cloud of faith. We pray that we may recognize Thee in the humble garb in which Thou art with us all days, under the species of bread and wine on the altar; we beg that we may recognize Thee when in silence Thy grace solicits our souls to rise unto Thee. Above all, may we be ever mindful of the Father's command to hear His beloved Son, when His voice calls us to sacrifice.

III. "Tell the Vision to no Man"

"And as they came down from the mountain, Jesus charged them, saying, tell the vision to no man, till the Son of man be risen from the dead." After the resurrection all the Apostles shall see Him in His glory; then there will be no further danger of mere human interpretations, because by that time all will have understood that Christ ought to suffer these things and so to enter into His glory.

Let us praise and admire the wisdom and the discretion of Jesus: the Father has glorified Him and called Him His beloved Son; and as they descend from the mountain Jesus calls Himself the Son of man: in this appears the incomparable greatness, divine and human, of our Lord.

Prayer: O God, who in the glorious transfiguration of Thine only-begotten Son didst confirm the mysteries of the faith by the testimony of the fathers, and who by Thy voice from the shining cloud, didst in wondrous manner foreshow the perfect adoption of sons; make us, in Thy loving kindness, we beseech Thee, as co-heirs with Him, who is the King of glory, and in that very glory call us in the end to share. Through the same our Lord (Collect, Mass of the Transfiguration).

TUESDAY: SECOND SUNDAY IN LENT

JESUS AND THE PHARISEES

1. Jesus could not ignore the Scribes and the Pharisees, who were the official leaders of the Jewish people. "The scribes and the Pharisees have sitten on the chair of Moses" (*Matt.* 23, 2). What attitude was our Lord to adopt in their regard? In virtue of their office they interpreted the law, which Jesus had come not to destroy but to fulfill. From the moment Jesus began to preach the Kingdom, they have set their face against this fulfillment; though they flaunt their fidelity to the Law before the people, they do not observe it, but seek their own gain and

glory. Jesus is the Righteous One. They said, "Master, we know that thou art a true speaker, and teachest the way of God in truth. Neither carest thou for any man, for thou dost not regard the person of men" (*Matt.* 22, 16). Again and again our Lord has tried to open their eyes; but each time it was in vain. If we find the reprimand severe, which Jesus administers to them, then let us try to fathom the feelings of His Heart. He has compassion on the multitude, that lie without a shepherd and are being deceived by their leaders. St. Mark (3, 5) says that He was "grieved for the blindness of their hearts". He sees in them the allies of Satan, and yet His last word concerning them was, "Father, forgive them, for they know not what they do" (*Luke* 23, 34).

2. *Petition*: The grace to take to heart the warnings which Jesus addresses to the people and to the Apostles.

I. Jesus Reprimands the Pharisees

"Then Jesus spoke to the multitudes and to the disciples, saying, the Scribes and the Pharisees have sitten on the chair of Moses. All things therefore whatsoever they shall say to you, observe and do; but according to their works do ye not. For they say and do not" (*Matt.* 23, 1-3). Next, Jesus condemns their scandalous conduct: they seek only their own comfort, their own profit, their own honor.

Jesus had always acknowledged the official position of the Pharisees; but they kept spying on Him, trying to trap Him in His words, attempting to bring Him into discredit with the people. Jesus appealed to His miracles, and quoted the Scriptures to show them that the Father had sent Him. But they refused to listen. Then at last Jesus tore the mask from their face, castigated their hypocrisy, and warned the people and the Disciples against "the leaven of the Pharisees."

All those that are invested with authority have to walk warily lest they should become guilty of the faults censured by Christ. It may happen that they use their authority for their own personal advantage. It is possible that they teach others their duties whilst they fail to perform their own.

"For they say and do not." May these words resound in the ears of all those that have been chosen to preach the Gospel, either by word of mouth or by their office or their religious habit. There will always be a gap between the perfect message they deliver and the imperfect manner in which they put it into practice themselves; and this should preserve them in a humble frame of mind. But let them remember that they are bound ever to make that gap narrower and narrower.

II. "Jesus Began to Do and to Teach"

With Jesus there was no gap between doctrine and practice. What He said to the Apostles at the Last Supper, after the washing of the feet, that was true of His entire life: "You call me Master and Lord; and you say well, for so I am. If then I, being your Lord and Master, have washed your feet, you also ought to wash one another's feet. For I have given you an example, that as I have done to you, so you do also" (*John* 13, 13-15). Such was the Lord's way from the beginning. "He began to do and to teach" (*Act.* 1, 1). When He imposes a precept on His Apostles, saying, Do this or do that, He always adds, "as I have done". "Love one another as I have loved you.... If you keep my commandments, you shall abide in my love, as I also have kept my Father's commandments and do abide in his love" (*John* 15; 10, 12).

If it was said truly that no one ever had spoken like Him and with so much authority, then it was because no man had ever acted as He did. In all simplicity he could say, "I am the way, the truth and the life" (*John* 14, 6).

III. Jesus Warns the Disciples

The Pharisees covet titles, and first places, and salutations in the market place. "Be not you called rabbi, for one is your Master, and you all are brethren" (*Matt.* 23, 8). Many a time did Jesus repeat this warning, but the Twelve were slow to understand that lesson. Even at the Last Supper there was strife among them as to "which of them should be greater" (*Luke* 9, 46).

Jesus knew "what was in man", and what will be in man as long as he remains man—ambition, envy, susceptibility. To all, especially to such as wield authority in His name, He has said, "Learn of me, your Master, because I am meek and humble of heart", "Amen, amen, I say to you: the servant is not greater than his lord, neither is the apostle greater than he that sent him. If you know these things you shall be blessed if you do them" (*John* 13, 16-17).

Prayer: Almighty and everlasting God, by whose Spirit the whole body of the Church is sanctified and governed, hear our prayers for all orders, that, by the gift of Thy grace, all in their different degrees may faithfully serve Thee. Through our Lord (Collect for the whole hierarchy of the Church).

WEDNESDAY: SECOND SUNDAY IN LENT

TRUE PENANCE

1. When the Church ordains that during Lent we abstain from certain kinds of food, her main purpose is not that we should mortify the flesh, but that we should put into practice the words of Jahve to Israel, "Be converted to me with all your heart in fasting, and in weeping and in mourning; and rend your hearts and not your garments, and turn to the Lord, your God" (*Joel* 2, 12-13). We shall "rend our hearts" only if we are deeply conscious that we are sinners.

2. *Petition*: O Lord, grant us the precious grace to see our sinfulness so that we may acquire the true spirit of penance. "That Thou wouldst bring us to true penance, we beseech Thee, hear us."

I. We Are Sinners Before God

The closer a man draws to God, the more he feels awed by the sense of the Divine Majesty and Holiness, and the more he stands aghast at his own nothingness and above all at his own sinfulness. When Peter beheld the miraculous draught of fishes, it dawned on him in a flash that he was face to face with the All-Holy One; and "he fell down at Jesus' knees, saying, Depart from me, for I am a sinful man, O Lord" (*Luke* 5, 8). Peter was not thinking of this or that offence which he had committed; but he shuddered at his absolute unworthiness in the presence of Him that is supremely holy. And yet fear does not drive him to flight; he merely says, "Depart from me, O Lord." He himself did not depart; still less did Jesus, whose Heart loved Peter. Therefore let us pray with St. Augustine, "O Lord, that I might know myself as a sinner; that I might know Thee as the All-Holy."

Together with that knowledge will grow in us truth, humility, reverence, love.

The further a man departs from God, the readier he becomes to believe in his own importance; where heaven's light has ceased to shine, dark shadows and foul blots multiply. "And they healed the breach of the daughter of my people disgracefully, saying, Peace, peace. And there was no peace" (*Jer.* 6, 14).

II. True Penance

From sincere awareness of sin arises penance. The Greek word, which the Latins translated by *Paenitentia,* literally meant "change of mind", or an internal reversal, "conversion". In the presence of God, and in the light of God's grace, man grows more and more aware that he has wandered away from God, gone against His will, ignored His desires; and that worldliness has invaded his soul.

True penance does not consist first and foremost in the practice of external austerities; it consists in this that we turn away from all things that separate us from God, that we renounce all disorderly affections, and that with our whole soul we turn to God. "Let them turn round", St. Augustine cries to sinners, "and seek Thee, O Lord; for they have forsaken Thee, their Creator; Thou hast not forsaken them. They must return to Thee, and cast themselves into Thy embrace. They must shed tears upon Thy breast. And Thou, who art gracious and merciful, dost dry their tears; and still they will shed more tears, but these are tears of joy. For Thou, O Lord, art not a fragile human being of flesh and blood; but Thou hast made them, and Thou healest their infirmities, and fillest them with solace" (*Confessions* V, 2).

III. Sorrowing Love

True penance is unthinkable without sincere contrition, and sincere contrition is sorrowing love. Let us have a clear understanding of the difference between remorse and contrition, so that we may be spared the former and open our hearts to the latter. Remorse is self-accusation, a consciousness of sin that warps the soul, because it turns its eyes away from God's mercy; it paves the way to despair; it tortures the soul and smothers its life. May heaven preserve us from that kind of remorse and anxiety, which involves a woeful denial of God's mercy and love. Peter was profoundly conscious of his unworthiness when he exclaimed, "Depart from me, for I am a sinful man, O Lord."

When, after the multiplication of the loaves and the promise of the Eucharist, "some said, this saying is hard, . . . and went back, and walked no more with him", Jesus asked, "Will you also go away?" Then this same Peter gave the noble answer, "Lord, to whom shall we go? Thou hast the words of eternal life; and we have believed and have known that Thou art the Christ, the Son of God" (*John* 6, 67-69).

One day Peter will deny His Master, and he will "weep bitterly". "Simon, son of John, lovest thou me?" Peter will answer, "Lord, thou knowest all things, thou knowest that I love thee" (*John* 21, 17). His was sorrowing love, love which burnt all the more ardently because of the pardon that had been granted. "In this we know that we are of the truth: and in his sight we shall persuade our hearts. For, if our hearts reprehend us, God is greater than our heart, and knoweth all things" (1 *John* 3, 19-20).

Blessed are we if we are inspired by these feelings in our penitential practices during Lent, in our struggle to serve the Lord more perfectly, and in our efforts to forget ourselves in order to help our neighbor.

Prayer: O Lord, repay us not according to the sins we have committed, nor according to our iniquities. O Lord, remember not our former iniquities, let Thy mercy speedily prevent us, for we are become exceeding poor. Help us, O God, our Savior; and for the glory of Thy name, O Lord, deliver us, and forgive us our sins for Thy name's sake (Tract of the Mass, Ash Wednesday).

THURSDAY: SECOND SUNDAY IN LENT

GOD'S MERCY

1. When we confess our sinfulness before the throne of our Holy God, we never forget that He is infinitely merciful. This mercy was revealed to us by Jesus Himself in the parable of the Prodigal Son, where our heavenly Father appears as the Father of Mercy. Surely Jesus did know His Father, for He said, "Neither doth any one know the Father but the Son, and he to whom it shall please the Son to reveal him" (*Matt.* 11, 27).

2. *Petition*: The grace that firm trust in the Lord's mercy may enkindle sorrowful love in our hearts.

I. God Is Merciful

The whole story of our race might be summed up thus: "Man rebels against God, and God pardons the rebel . . . world without end", till seventy times seven times. Adam recklessly disobeys God's solemn command: God's Holiness could not but punish the offence; but at that very moment His Mercy promised salvation to the sinner. The chosen race behaved outrageously towards Jahve, their Deliverer, and clung to other gods, offering them sacrifices: the Lord chastised His people until it humbly confessed its guilt and did penance. "My heart is turned within me, my repentance is stirred up. I will not execute the fierceness of my wrath. I will not return to destroy Ephraim: because I am God, and not man; the holy one in the midst of thee, and I will not enter into the city" (*Osee* 11, 8-9).

By sending us His only-begotten Son, God has proved that He loves man unto the end, and that unto the end He is prepared to pardon. The Son appeared amongst us, commissioned by the Father "to seek and to save that which was lost". "In order to save the servant, He delivered His own Son."

And let us cast a backward glance on our own past: what has our life been but an endless series of offences and pardons?

II. The Mystery of God's Mercy

In God everything is mystery. Why did He love us even before we had been made? Why has His love no limit, neither in time nor in intensity? "I am the holy one in the midst of thee" He said to his people, and He says to us.

God is also almighty, and that is why He can be patient and merciful. St. Thomas Aquinas says that mercy is an attribute of the master, not of the subject. Mercy stoops down towards the lowly and raises them up. And therefore, God, the Supreme Being, can be merciful more than any other, merciful towards all, and happy when He has an opportunity to exercise mercy and to forgive, as we read in the parable of the Prodigal.

A noted scholar wrote the following: "Philosophy tells us that God suffers no emotions, and is stirred neither by feelings of joy, nor by pangs of grief. As a philosophical formula, let that be correct. But it is just as certain, and most comforting to our hearts, that among the divine attributes there is one which is like unto human love and solicitude; nay, not merely like, but infinitely more tender and more loving. And it is because he knows this that the sinner dares to love God. It is precisely this divine attribute of His Father, which Jesus wanted to impress upon us in the parable of the Prodigal Son."

Other considerations may throw a ray of light on the divine mercy: God "is Father, as no other father is father".

"For according to the height of the heaven above the earth, he hath strengthened his mercy towards them that fear him. As far as the east is from the west, so far hath he removed our iniquities from us. As a father hath compassion on his children, so hath the Lord compassion on them that fear him: for he knoweth our frame. He remembereth that we are dust" (*Ps.* 102, 11-14).

He made us to His image and likeness. However much man may desecrate and disfigure that image, as long as we live it is never disfigured beyond repair. God still sees the resemblance, and with divine patience He strives to restore it to its pristine beauty.

And indeed it is worthy of God and a glory to Him that He should have compassion on erring man. It is true that every sin implies guilt, greater or smaller, according to the degree of deliberation with which the sinner has committed the offence. But man's will and intelligence are no longer what God made them: the will has been weakened and the intellect has been clouded as a result of original sin. As far as a man is guilty he *deserves* not compassion but punishment. But in so far as every man, even when he sins, suffers the consequences of the sin of Adam, there is room for mercy.

"Mercy is a gift, it is not imposed on us."

God's justice and holiness are infinite. So is His mercy; and therefore remorse and consciousness of sin readily pass into contrition; therefore anxiety, that tortures the soul, is changed into sorrowful love, which spurs us on to generosity.

During Lent, in many of the liturgical prayers we ask God to have mercy on us, sinners. Let us, during this holy season, join our brethren, and our holy Mother the Church, in praying for the conversion of her sinful children.

Prayer: O God, the restorer and lover of innocence, direct to Thyself the hearts of Thy servants; that fervent in Thy spirit, they may be found both steadfast in faith and zealous in good works. Through our Lord (Prayer over the People of last Wednesday).

JESUS, "A FRIEND OF PUBLICANS AND SINNERS"

1.   Before relating the parables of the lost sheep, the lost groat,
and the prodigal son, St. Luke shows us Jesus surrounded by
repentant sinners, and by proud and supercilious Pharisees.
"Now the publicans and the sinners drew near unto him to
hear him. And the Pharisees and the scribes murmured, saying,
This man receiveth sinners and eateth with them" (15, 1-2).

2.   *Petition*: The grace of penetrating deep into the feelings of
the Heart of Jesus, of trusting in His mercy, and of sharing
His love for sinners.

I. The Facts

In the Gospel we behold Jesus associating with sinners; at
least the Pharisees called them sinners, and made it a point of
religion to shun contact with them. They were publicans, that
is tax-gatherers for the Romans, "collaborators" with the occupying power, traders, men that seemed careless in the observance
of the minute regulations imposed by the scribes; and therefore
dubbed by them "unclean".

Seated at the table of Simon, the Pharisee, Jesus allowed "a
woman that was in the city, a sinner", to touch Him as she bewailed her sins at His feet, and He pleaded her cause with the
Pharisees, and "said to her, thy sins are forgiven thee". At the well
He enters into conversation with the Samaritan woman and brings
her to the repentance of her sins. He accepts the invitation of
Zachaeus, the publican, of Jericho and partakes of his hospitality.
He truly goes in search of sinners. "They that are well have no
need of a physician, but they that are sick. For I came not to call
the just, but sinners" (*Mark* 2, 17). The Son of an Immaculate
Mother, "the brightness of eternal light" (*Wis.* 7, 26), is not particular about conforming with pharisaical etiquette and decorum.
He delivers the woman taken in adultery from the clutches of her
merciless judges, not because He regards sin as a trifle just to be
glossed over: He abominates sin, as only infinite Holiness can
abominate it. But with the weak sinner He has compassion; and,
if in the sinner's heart He discerns sincere contrition, then, He
forgives the sin, and dismisses the sinner in peace: "Go, and now
sin no more" (*John* 8, 11).

II. The Mystery

We admire, though we comprehend not, "what is the breadth, and length, and height, and depth of the charity of Christ, which surpasseth all knowledge" (*Eph.* 3, 18-19).

Sinners sorely need Him, and He seeks them out and calls them unto repentance. To Him they are His own Father's children, who have strayed from the Father's house, have suffered grievous misery in a foreign land, and by themselves are unable to return to the Father. And then the Son, "the first-born among many brethren" (*Rom.* 8, 29), is sent by the Father to take them by the hand and lead them home. Surely He cannot but feel intense compassion for His younger brothers; for in each of them He beholds, and He loves, His Father's image, sadly disfigured and besmirched indeed, yet the true image.

As man, Jesus experiences in Himself, in a human and in a divine manner, for what infinite happiness every soul has been created. He feels the utter misery of the sinner, who squanders his life on trifles; He knows the immense void that desolates the sinner's soul.

And He also knows His Father, and His Father's will to save that which was lost; He has told us what joy there shall be in heaven upon one sinner that doth penance. Let the Pharisees reproach Jesus because He receiveth sinners and eateth with them, and is a friend of publicans and sinners: He loves them because He loves His Father, and all the children of His Father.

III. The Pharisees Take Scandal

These proud men thought that they had no need of Christ; for they thanked God because they were not like the rest of men, sinners, as also that publican (*Luke* 18, 11).

Nay, Jesus was very much in their way: He worked miracles, wonderful signs, but not signs in the sky as they demanded. And He dared "work" miracles on the sabbath, disregarding their vain observances. A single word from His mouth struck them dumb. He even dared to tear the mask off their faces, "Woe to you, scribes and Pharisees, hypocrites, because you are like to whited sepulchres, which outwardly appear to men beautiful, but within are full of dead men's bones and of all filthiness" (*Matt.* 23, 27).

"Take heed and beware of the leaven of the Pharisees" (*Matt.* 16, 6). We readily perceive why Jesus so sharply warned us against hypocrisy, a vice which He, who is Uprightness itself, loathed with His whole heart.

Under the cloak of religion, and of strict adherence to the Law, they sought personal gain and earthly profit. In their self-complacency and their pride they looked down on "the rest of men", themselves incapable of practicing true virtue, and blind when they saw it practiced by others.

We admire the dispositions of our Lord's Heart: He was always about His Father's business, nor "did Christ ever please himself" (*Rom.* 15, 3), that is, He never sought personal gain. He came, not "to be ministered to but to minister" (*Matt.* 20, 28), not to judge but to save. Jesus never despised any man, nay, not even the Pharisees, whose willful blindness saddened Him; least of all sinners whom He sought out, and "who drew near to Him".

On this point all the Saints have followed the Lord's example: thus the Cure d'Ars, St. John Vianney, was wont to speak of "my beloved sinners"; and therefore they drew near unto him, even from far countries. Let us pray for all sinners; and pray also that Christ's representatives on earth may ever be the friends of publicans and sinners.

Prayer: O Lord Jesus, Friend of publicans and sinners, whose Heart is a burning furnace of charity, a vessel of justice and love whence flow torrents of mercy and grace, make our hearts like unto Thine. Fill the hearts of Thy ministers with zeal, gentleness and patience; and following Thy example, may they always be friends of publicans and of sinners.

SATURDAY: SECOND SUNDAY IN LENT

THE PRODIGAL SON (Luke 15, 11-32)

1. This is the third of three touching parables, a sort of trilogy, in which Jesus strives to make us grasp how happy our heavenly Father is when a sinner returns to Him: they are the parables of the lost sheep, of the lost groat, and of the prodigal son. This is one of the most sublime and most touching pages in the Gospel. Nowhere else do we feel, as we feel here, how "God has drawn unto himself man, with the cords of Adam, with the bands of love" (*Osee* 11, 4).

2. *Petition*: May this parable of Jesus make us know the deepest feelings of our heavenly Father's heart. "Neither doth any one know the Father, but the Son" (*Matt.* 11, 27).

I. The Prodigal's Departure

A groat is a mere lifeless thing, a sheep is a living being but not endowed with reason; the subject of the third parable is a man, endowed with reason and with free will. He himself makes up his mind to leave his father. He is the younger of two brothers, and he says to his father, "Give me the portion of substance that falleth to me. And he divided unto them his substance." And the father allowed the rash youth to go his way.

Perhaps we wonder why our Lord represents the father as yielding so readily to the foolish boy's wishes. But this indulgent parent represents our heavenly Father, who has endowed man with free will, and who leaves man really free to act as he pleases. We have the power to use our liberty wrongly, and thus to make an evil use of all the gifts with which our Maker has loaded us. From creatures that have free will God asks free service: He will not use compulsion in their regard.

Healthy and strong, attired in clothes of the latest fashion, carrying a well-filled purse, the reckless youth blithely leaves home. He goes abroad into a far country, where no one knows him, and where neither consideration for family ties, nor fear of public opinion, will prevent him from giving free rein to all his passions. "There he wasted his substance, living riotously", says Jesus. Note that our Lord expresses things rather mildly, whereas the elder brother later will use much harsher words.

II. The Father Waits Patiently

At this point there is a striking difference between the first two parables and this one: the woman seeks diligently until she finds the lost groat; the shepherd goes after the sheep that was lost, he takes great trouble until he finds it, and then lifts the footsore creature on to his shoulders and lovingly carries it to the fold.

In this parable the father stays at home, though from the context it is evident that his heart anxiously longs for the wanderer's return, and that he frequently scans the horizon in the direction whence the sinner is expected to return. That is all the parable tells us.

In reality our heavenly Father treats His erring children

otherwise: He sends down His only-begotten Son, (this very Son, who proposes the parable to us), in order "to seek and to save what was lost" (*Luke* 19, 10).

In the parable the son is a reasonable creature: freely he has resolved to forsake his father; freely he can resolve to return. The things which, God's grace helping, finally make him resolve to go home are—first, his utter misery, for he is reduced to the most absolute destitution; next, the thought that in his father's house even the servants enjoy abundance; also regret for having treated his father so outrageously; and lastly, his conscience, "God's eye upon our hearts" as Ecclesiasticus calls our reason and our conscience (*Ecclus.* 17, 7). No, God does not abandon the sinner to his lot. "Behold, I stand at the gate and knock" (*Apoc.* 3, 20); and with divine patience He waits until the gate opens under the powerful, yet gentle, pressure of the Lover of our souls.

III. The Reception

"And when he was yet a great way off, his father saw him, and was moved with compassion, and running to him fell upon his neck, and kissed him." It is worth-while carefully to weigh every word used by Jesus. The aim of the parable is not to show to what depths a soul can descend, nor in what dispositions it returns to its Father, nor how henceforth it will behave towards Him who has forgiven everything. The aim is to show us how glad God is to welcome the repentant sinner.

The father did not give his son time to complete the confession which he had pondered in his heart. But "the father said to his servants, Bring forth quickly the first robe and put it on him, and put a ring on his hand and shoes on his feet. And bring here the fatted calf, and kill it, and let us eat and make merry: because this my son was dead and is come to life again, was lost and is found." The sinner is immediately, completely, and publicly restored to his former estate; all traces of the past must be obliterated: and they will celebrate his safe return with feasting, dancing and music. Never could we have dared to believe that God is indeed the Father of Mercy, if Christ Himself, "who knoweth the Father" had not so plainly revealed it to us. Perhaps we may regard the feast that is celebrated on the return of the prodigal as a symbol of Holy Communion, after the sinner has recovered the spotless garment which is the state of sanctifying grace.

What the parable narrates of the resentment of the elder brother is intended to make us see better, by contrast, the tenderness of the father's heart.

And we know that there is no difference between the feelings of our Father in heaven, and those of His well-beloved Son on earth. For Jesus said, "I and the Father are one" (*John* 10, 30).

Prayer: Watch over Thy family with unfailing affection, O Lord, and since its only hope lies in assistance from heaven, may it ever enjoy the protection of Thy Divine Power. Through our Lord (Prayer over the people).

THIRD SUNDAY IN LENT

CHILDREN OF THE LIGHT (Eph. 5, 1-9)

1. The Epistle of today's Mass is taken from St. Paul's letter to the Ephesians, chap. 5, 1-9. To those recent converts from paganism, living in a city that was notorious for its loose morals, the Apostle proposes an ideal that is in sharp contrast with the mode of life that had been theirs till then. Hence we see how strong Paul's trust was in the power of divine grace. It needed courage to call those men "children of God, saints, children of light. . . ."

2. *Petition*: The grace to have implicit trust in the Father, "who hath delivered us from the power of darkness, and hath translated us into the kingdom of the Son of his love: in whom we have redemption through his blood, the remission of sins" (*Colos.* 1, 13-14).

I. "Followers of God"

"Be ye therefore followers of God, as most dear children, and walk in love as Christ also hath loved us, and hath delivered himself for us, an oblation and a sacrifice to God, for an odor of sweetness."

If God is love, as St. John teaches us, the only way of following Him, and of becoming His most dear children, is to live in charity with our neighbor. Jesus, the "first-born among many brethren" (*Rom.* 8, 29), has taught us by word and example. "Love one another as I have loved you" (*John* 15, 12), and He added, "This is my commandment." "He hath delivered himself as an oblation and a sacrifice to God for an odor of sweetness."

We shall be followers of God and true disciples and brothers of Christ exactly to that extent to which we surrender ourselves as an oblation and a sacrifice. "To walk in love" means that in our daily intercourse with our neighbor we forget ourselves to serve our neighbor with entire devotion. We shall be followers of God if we zealously toil and pray for the conversion of sinners, whether they be close to us or in distant lands; if we gladly unite our little gifts and sacrifices with the great sacrifice of Christ in Holy Mass "for an odor of sweetness".

II. "Children of the Light"

"For you were heretofore darkness, but now light in the Lord. Walk then as children of the light." St. Paul had just mentioned the works of darkness—fornication, covetousness, of which formerly they were guilty, but "which now should not so much as be mentioned among them, as becometh saints". The greatest contrast on earth is that existing between darkness and light: these in Holy Writ and in the liturgy symbolize the kingdom of sin and the kingdom of grace, the realm of the prince of darkness and the realm of Him who is the Light of the world.

If we are children of God, then we also are children of the light. "God is light, and in him there is no darkness" (1 John 1, 5). And St. John, who taught us that God is love and that God is light, also tells us who is in the light and who is not: "He that saith he is in the light, and hateth his brother, is in darkness even until now. He that loveth his brother, abideth in the light. . . . But he that hateth his brother is in darkness and walketh in darkness and knoweth not whither he goeth, because the darkness hath blinded his eyes" (1 John 2, 9-11).

That we are children of God and children of light will be shown by the love we bear to our neighbor. And then we shall, in turn, through Him who is light within us, become sources of light, so that our light may shine before men, that they may see our good works, and glorify our Father who is in heaven (Matt. 5, 16).

III. "The Fruit of the Light"

"The fruit of the light is in all goodness and justice and truth." In these natural virtues, purified and perfected by grace, Christian perfection consists.

"All goodness": whatever is good, that is upright, whatever is genuine and true in word and deed, and in every detail of our daily life: these things are the fruits of the light. Let those who, within or without the cloister, strive after Christian perfection, not reduce that perfection to mere routine practices, nor make it consist in external observances and devout exercises: these things have their value, nay, they are indispensable as fruits of the light, and as far as they make us advance "in all goodness, and justice and truth".

"Prove (that is, approve or pursue) what is well pleasing to God." In this search we must "be guided by true wisdom." In the actual circumstances and events of our daily lives, the Holy Ghost will make us feel and "taste" what is well-pleasing to God.

Prayer: Grant, we beseech Thee, Almighty God, that we, upon whom is poured the new light of Thy Word made flesh, may show forth in our actions that which by faith shineth in our minds. Through our Lord (Collect, Mass at Dawn, Christmas).

MONDAY: THIRD SUNDAY IN LENT

"BLESSED ARE THEY THAT DWELL IN THY HOUSE" (Ps. 83, 5)

1. Let us think of our parish church, or our domestic chapel: it is the house of the Lord, where we gather in the name of the Lord, to pray and to offer sacrifice to God; where we are seated together at the Lord's Table. The versicles, sung after Communion at Mass yesterday were taken from Psalm 83, 4-5. "For the sparrow hath found herself a house, and the turtle a nest for herself, where she may lay her young ones: Thy altars, O Lord of hosts: my King and my God. Blessed are they that dwell in Thy house, O Lord: they shall praise thee forever and ever."

2. *Petition*: "One thing I have asked of the Lord, this will I seek after, that I may dwell in the house of the Lord, all the days of my life. That I may see the delight of the Lord, that I may visit his temple" (*Ps. 26, 4-5*).

I. The House of the Lord

To the Jews the Temple of Jerusalem was the House of the Lord where every year the three great festivals of Israel were solemnly observed. On those occasions countless pilgrims came, mostly in large groups, from the whole of Palestine; and also from the far-flung diaspora, the distant lands where Israelites had settled down. While they trod the dusty and winding paths, they prayed aloud, or sang hymns and extracts from the Psalms. "How lovely are thy tabernacles, O Lord of hosts. My soul longeth and fainteth for the courts of the Lord. My heart and my flesh have rejoiced in the living God. . . . For better is one day in thy courts above thousands. I have chosen to be an abject in the house of my God, rather than to dwell in the tabernacles of sinners" (83: 2, 3, 11).

If the children of Israel took such delight in coming from distant lands in order to behold the temple, to worship in its courts, to prostrate themselves before the Holy of Holies, where God did not abide but where the Ark of the Covenant and the tablets of the Law were preserved, what ought to be our feelings, since we possess the Lord Himself in our churches! Nor is Christ really present in one Temple only, for the benefit of the entire Christian people; but He dwells bodily in the church in every Christian village, in every ward of our cities; and in thousands of religious houses. There we can every day celebrate the sacred mysteries, offer Him to God as our sacrifice, partake of His Flesh and Blood; there we may visit Him and adore Him whenever we wish. "If this most holy Sacrament could be celebrated only by one priest and in one place in the world, with what desire would not men be drawn to that place, and to such a priest of God, to see the divine mysteries celebrated" (4 *Imit. of Christ* 1, 13).

Our daily lives are spent, and all our labor is performed, so close to Him; and yet we are so unmindful of His presence. Increase our faith, O Lord, enkindle our love, augment our gratitude, so that we may in all truth abide with Thee.

II. They That Dwell in the House of the Lord

"Blessed are they that dwell in the house of the Lord; they shall praise thee forever and ever." Thus chanted the pilgrims on their way to the city of Sion, and they had in mind the few privileged ones that "never departed from the Temple". That is the very privilege which Christ has bestowed on those whom He has chosen to abide with Him, to be dedicated to His service—His priests and His religious. Especially the latter, for they "are gathered in his name", and have been adopted into His family. Among them, above all, His spirit should prevail. "That they may be one as I and the Father also are one" (*John* 17, 22), thus Jesus prayed for all those that were to believe in Him, for His great family which is Holy Church. All those who profess loyally to follow the teachings of Jesus ought to strive with heart and soul to fulfill this wish of Christ: that they may be one.

"Blessed are they that dwell in thy house, O Lord", and that are glad to dwell there, because the spirit of Christ reigns there; and who labor to foster and preserve that spirit in their midst. Jesus Himself told us through the mouth of St. Paul, "If there be therefore any consolation in Christ, if any comfort of charity, if any society of the spirit, if any bowels of commiseration, fulfill ye my joy, that you be of one mind, having the same charity, being of one accord, agreeing in sentiment. Let nothing be done through contention, neither by vain glory: but in humility, let each esteem others better than himself. Each one not considering the things that are his own, but those that are other men's" (*Phil.* 2, 1-4).

III. Grateful Perseverance

"For better is one day in thy courts above thousands. I have chosen to be an abject in the house of my God, rather than to dwell in the tabernacles of sinners." God be praised, those homes, where Christian parents are willing to give their children to God when He calls them, are not tabernacles of sinners. But if God deigns to invite us to come and dwell in His house, then both for our parents and for ourselves it is good that we go there, remain there, work there. Even if we are admitted only to the "courts", that is the portals, to be "an abject", or, as another translation says, to stand on the threshold; that is, if we are not granted that exhilarating sense of His abiding presence, with which He often fills the souls of those that love Him, still it is far better to be with Him. St. Therese of Lisieux once wrote, "Our Lord leaves me alone; He does not even look at me, which proves that I belong to the family." The cloister is in very truth the portal, or the threshold, of heaven: throughout eternity we shall praise and thank God for having allowed us to live there.

Prayer: O Lord God, grant that union and peace prevail in Thy Church, above all among those that are especially dedicated to Thee; confirm them in the spirit of Thy Son, in whose name they are gathered; preserve them against all strife and discord, so that they may serve Thee in joy and gladness, and bear witness to the world that blessed are they that dwell in Thy house. Through the same Christ.

"IF THY BROTHER SHALL OFFEND"

(Matt. 18: 15-17; Luke 17: 3-4)

1. We behold our Lord in familiar intercourse with His disciples; they happen to be discussing among themselves what relations ought to prevail among the brethren; and while we listen to Him, we pray that we may fathom the feelings of His Sacred Heart "full of goodness and of love".

2. *Petition*: The grace to let our hearts to be gradually made like unto His Heart, through the faithful observance of *His* commandment—brotherly love.

I. Fraternal Correction

"But if thy brother shall offend against thee, go and rebuke him between thee and him alone. If he shall hear thee, thou shalt gain thy brother. And if he will not hear thee: take with thee one or two more, that in the mouth of two or three witnesses every word may stand. And if he will not hear them: tell the church. And if he will not hear the church: let him be to thee as the heathen and publican" (*Matt.* 18, 15-17).

If in the first line we omit the words "against thee", as many manuscripts do, then there is question here not about forgiveness of offences, but about fraternal correction. This is always an extremely delicate task, which no one should assume lightly, but which in certain circumstances we cannot escape, either because our office or fraternal charity imposes it on us.

The aim is, in the words of Jesus, "to gain a brother"; and therefore we must spare his feelings as much as possible, we must not put him to shame before others, nor hurt his feelings. We must choose a suitable occasion, and carefully choose the appropriate expression. Brotherly love must inspire and direct the whole process. To be gentle, zeal must be absolutely pure and disinterested.

Such correction may at times be a sacred duty, when it would be sinful to say, as Cain said to God, "Am I my brother's keeper?"

Let us remember our Lord's supreme effort to "gain" Judas, at the very moment of the betrayal, "Friend, whereto art thou come?"

And, if a correction is administered to ourselves, let us submit to it with humility and gratitude, as the Psalmist says, "The just man shall correct me in mercy and shall reprove me" (Ps. 111, 5).

Then let us take note of the order to be followed: first a remonstrance or an observation, without any witnesses—if that is beseeming; secondly a clear statement of the facts, with convinc-beseeming; secondly a clear statement of the facts, with convincing proofs; lastly putting the case before the Superior, if that be necessary. And let the only aim be all along to "gain thy brother".

St. Thomas says, "In that manner the Lord teaches His disciples the perfect manner of brotherly concern, and fraternal correction."

II. To Forgive

"Then came Peter unto him and said, Lord, how often shall my brother offend against me, and I forgive him? Till seven times? Jesus saith to him, I say not to thee seven times; but till seventy times seven times" (Matt. 18, 21-22).

The answer of Jesus strikes us as being final, and as coming straight from the depths of His Heart. Peter fancied that he was wonderfully generous, when he proposed to forgive as often as seven times. Jesus says, "Till seventy times seven times", that is as often as the sinner stands in need of pardon.

St. Luke reports our Lord's words in a slightly different manner. "If thy brother sin against thee, reprove him; and if he do penance, forgive him. And if he sin against thee seven times in a day, and seven times in a day be converted unto thee, saying, I repent; forgive him" (17, 3-4).

It is not so very difficult to forgive when the offender expresses regret and craves pardon; but, if he refuses to repent, what are we to do? That question was answered by Jesus on another occasion, "If one strike thee on thy right cheek, turn to him also the other. And if a man will contend with thee in judgment, and take away thy coat, let go thy cloak also to him. And whosoever will force thee one mile, go with him other two.... Love your enemies, do good to them that hate you, and pray for them that persecute you and calumniate you" (Matt. 5, 39-44).

But those are not the ways of man: such conduct is superhuman; God's grace alone can raise man to those heights. And therefore Jesus added the following words, "That you may be the children of your Father who is in heaven, who maketh his sun to rise upon the good and upon the bad, and raineth upon the just and the unjust" (*Matt.* 5, 45). For God's forgiveness and mercy know no limits.

Wherever men, even the best of them, live and work together, there arise differences of opinion, misunderstandings and all kinds of friction. "Whence comes the trouble?" asks St. Augustine, and he answers, "Because we are human, mortal beings, frail and weak; earthen vessels, that get in one another's way. The selfishness of one squeezes out that of another; brotherly love creates room for all and provides freedom of movement for all."

Man has two essential needs—to eat and to forgive. Therefore we say in the Lord's Prayer, Give us this day our daily bread, and forgive us our trespasses as we forgive them that trespass against us.

Prayer: Fill us, O Lord, with the spirit of Thy love, that by Thy mercy, we, who have all partaken of one Heavenly Bread, may also be one of mind and heart. Through our Lord (Postcommunion, for concord Mass).

WEDNESDAY: THIRD SUNDAY IN LENT

HONOR THY FATHER AND THY MOTHER
(Exod. 20, 12; Matt. 15, 4)

1. In the Gospel of today's Mass we once again see the sharp contrast that exists between the spirit of Christ and that of the Pharisees. The latter are proud of their exterior observances; Jesus wants religion to be something that lives in the soul. "Why do thy disciples transgress the tradition of the ancients? For they wash not their hands when they eat bread. But he, answering, said to them, "Why do you also transgress the commandment of God for your tradition?" (*Matt.* 15, 2-3.) And then He showed them by an example how, on the pretext of religious observance, they manage to evade observing God's most sacred commandment.

2. *Petition:* The grace always, everywhere, and in all things to observe faithfully God's commandment, "Honor thy father and thy mother."

I. God's Commandment

"Honor thy father and thy mother, that thou mayest be long-lived upon the land, which the Lord thy God will give thee" (*Exod.* 20, 12). "He that curseth his father, or mother, shall die the death" (*Exod.* 21, 17).

The first of these texts is one of the Ten Commandments which God delivered to Moses on Mount Sinai. Of these Commandments the first three express our obligations to God Himself. Among the seven others, which regulate man's behavior with regard to other men, the first is, "Honor thy father and thy mother." In this manner Jahve consecrated and solemnly sanctioned the Natural Law, which is His own law, and the very foundation of human society.

The close connection between religion and parental love is shown by the Latin word *pietas*, and the English word *piety*: both words express the sense of love and reverence not only of men towards God, but also of children towards their parents, and of parents towards their children.

Sometimes it is said that nowadays filial love and reverence are on the decline. If that were true, it would be a sign that our modern civilization is degenerating. Both parents and children should strive to observe and hold sacred the law which God Himself has ordained, and which is the foundation of human society.

Quite in the spirit of the Old Covenant an earthly reward is promised to those that observe the law: long life on earth for such as fulfill the precept; death for such as deliberately break it. Jesus came to fulfill the Law, and also to increase the reward: God's blessing rests on children that honor their parents, often visibly here below, always in very truth, and through the peace which God pours into the soul.

II. Jesus Takes Up the Defence For Parental Rights

And He told them, You have quite defeated God's commandment, to establish your own tradition instead. Moses said, Honor thy father and thy mother.... But you say, Let a man tell his father or his mother, All the money out of which you might get help from me is now Corban (that is, an offering to God), and then you will not let him do any more for father or mother. With this, and many like observances, you are making God's law ineffectual through the traditions you have handed down (cf. *Mark* 7, 9-13).

In these words Jesus lashed out against the most loathsome

pharisaical hypocrisy. Their tradition held that, if one pronounced the word Corban (offering) over any material object, the thing was thereby consecrated to the temple: henceforth the object itself and all it could produce belonged to the Temple. Unnatural children, who refused to support their parents, would thus devote their goods to the Temple: hence parents could not receive part of the income. But in fact the dedication was mere fiction, and the property remained in the hands of the owners.

Such dishonest quibbling naturally aroused our Lord's indignation: for He is righteous, and for Him brotherly love, the second commandment, is sacred, like unto the first. "If therefore thou offer thy gift at the altar, and there thou remember that thy brother hath anything against thee; leave there thy offering before the altar, and go first to be reconciled to thy brother, and then coming thou shalt offer thy gift" (*Matt.* 5, 23-24).

If such is the law where "thy brother", that is any neighbor, is concerned, how much more do we owe to our parents!

Let us be honest and sincere with God, with ourselves, with our fellow men; let us never debase religion or virtue by appealing to it as an excuse for neglecting the practice of fraternal charity. The Lord preserve us from the hypocrisy for which He castigated the Pharisees, viz: the violation of God's commandment—His own commandment, He called it—in the name of outworn traditions.

III. Jesus Takes Up the Defence of God's Supreme Rights

More than once Jesus lays stress on the supreme rights of God, but He by no means brushes aside the rights of parents over their children. In the providential order there can be no clash between God's rights and the rights of parents. When Jesus says: "He that loveth father or mother more than me is not worthy of me" (*Matt.* 10, 37), He does not abolish the precept, "Honor thy father and mother." Those who, in order to follow Christ, leave all things, honor their father and their mother not less, but more. The sacrifice offered both by the child and by the parent purifies, ennobles, elevates their natural love. At times certain words of our Lord in the Gospel may seem to sound harsh: they are not harsh, though the sacrifice they call for may cause grievous pain. But parents and children, that have left each other for the sake of God's Kingdom, are aware of a more sacred, and a more intimate, union which they enjoy in the Lord.

May they never claim back part of the holocaust they have offered to Christ.

*Prayer:*Lord Jesus, who against pharisaical hypocrisy didst assert the rights of parents, and at the same time didst consecrate and perfect those rights by elevating them to the hallowed sphere of Thy Father's business: mercifully grant to parents and children, on whom Thou art pleased to bestow a special call, that right intention and generous courage which will make them find peace and joy in the fulfillment of Thy holy will.

THURSDAY: THIRD SUNDAY IN LENT

JESUS AND THE SICK (Luke 4, 40)

1. On that Sabbath day, in the synagogue of Capharnaum, Jesus had cast out an unclean spirit; later He had cured Simon's wife's mother. "And when the sun was down, all they that had any sick with diverse diseases brought them to him. But he laying hands on every one of them, healed them" (*Luke* 4, 40).

   In the same manner, even now, our Lord goes about, for instance, at Lourdes, when the priest raises the Sacred Host over each of the many sufferers that have been brought to that hallowed spot. He alone knows how many invisible miracles are being wrought in the souls of those many patients.

2. *Petition:* The grace to fathom the feelings of our Lord's Heart, as He passes by His suffering brothers, healing their bodies and their souls.

I. Jesus and the Sick

The sick and the sinners have always been numerous among the children of Adam. Jesus came down unto us that He might heal them; and we need not wonder that the sick, even more than sinners, sought to approach Him. Certainly Jesus did not wonder at this, for "He knew what was in man" (*John* 2, 25). Whenever His coming was announced anywhere, the people brought their sick unto Him. How differently people act when kings or great men visit their cities or villages: on such occasions let there be no unpleasant sights along the road. But when Jesus trod the ways of Galilee, all people with all sorts of miseries flocked to the roadside, the blind, the lame, the deaf, the dumb, even the dreaded

lepers came. "For virtue went out of him and healed all," says
St. Luke (6, 19), whether He touched them, as we read in today's
Gospel, or whether they touched Him, were it only the hem of
His garment. At times He makes use of material objects: spittle
from His mouth, clay from the earth. Also from a distance He
heals, but even then it is through word of His mouth.

When in S. J. Bach's "Passion of Matthew", Pilate asks the
people, "What evil has He done?", the soloist replies,

> To all of us He has done good;
> To the blind He restored their sight;
> The lame He made to walk;
> Into our souls He poured His Father's word;
> The demons He has cast out;
> The sorrowing He raised up;
> To the sinner He was mild;
> Nought else has He ever done!

To whom else could we go? His word heals, His contact heals,
and His message bestows life everlasting.

II. The Feelings of Christ

His Heart overflows with tender compassion, when He beholds
all that human misery, when so many sufferers hopefully look up
to Him, or from afar cry out to Him. How well He knows what
they desire: healing of their bodily ailments, even more than
pardon for their sins. And He also knows, and that grieves Him,
that all will not be grateful. But He rewards their faith, howso-
ever imperfect it may be, and their trust, even if it is not disinterested.

The miracles, which He works so lavishly, have an object be
yond the mere cure of bodily diseases: they are signs, intended
to show to the Jewish people that He is the Messiah, the One
that is sent by the Father.

When the Baptist, who had been cast into prison by Herod,
sent Him two of his disciples to ask, "Art thou he that is to come,
or look we for another? Jesus answering said to them, Go and
relate to John what you have heard and seen: the blind see, the
lame walk, the lepers are made clean...." (*Luke* 7, 18-22). At
Jerusalem the Jews say to Him, "How long dost thou hold our
souls in suspense? If thou be the Christ, tell us plainly. Jesus
answered them, I speak to you and you believe not; the works

that I do in the name of my Father, they give testimony of me" (*John* 10, 24-25).

These "works" are His miracles: indeed, they are not the spectacular portents in the heavens which the Jews demanded; they are works of healing that relieve human pain, and He performs them without the slightest ostentation. The "works" of Jesus, as they are related in the Gospels, avoid all pomp and show; their aim is manifestly spiritual. They avoid all vain display, and are in most perfect harmony with the life and doctrine of the humble Prophet of Nazareth. He is about His Father's business, He fulfills the mission entrusted to Him by the Father, He never seeks His personal glory.

Heart of Jesus, full of goodness and love, have mercy on us.

Jesus, meek and humble of Heart, make our hearts like unto Thine.

III. The Spiritual Background

Often we hear Jesus saying to those that have been healed, "Thy faith hath made thee whole." At times He requires, He even imposes a previous condition: "If thou canst believe, all things are possible to him that believeth." At Nazareth He could not work any miracles because of their unbelief (*Matt.* 13, 58; *Mark* 6, 5). The healing power that went out from Him did not cure the body, as long as the mind remained closed to the light. He is the Light.

It is hardly probable that Christ's wonderful power confined itself to relieving bodily ailments, and did not heal the infirmities of the soul.

When four men brought Him a man sick of the palsy, Jesus first forgave him his sins, and the sudden cure came after, as proof that "the Son of man hath power on earth to forgive sins" (*Mark* 2, 1-12).

Our Lord is sublime in all His words and in all His actions. Let us devoutly contemplate Him, and strive to understand His feelings, so that we may trust Him more confidently and serve Him more generously.

Prayer: Almighty and eternal God, in Thy mercy consider our weakness; and for our protection stretch forth the right hand of Thy majesty. Through our Lord (Collect, 3rd Sunday after Epiphany).

JESUS AND THE SAMARITAN WOMAN (John 4, 6-26)

1. St. John's account of this incident is one of the most graphic in the whole Gospel; it is picturesque, dramatic, and pregnant with most precious spiritual lessons.

Whilst returning from Jerusalem to Galilee, Jesus had to pass through Samaria; the way was long and steep, and the sun stood high in the heavens, so that Jesus and the Apostles were tired, and glad to halt close to the old well of Jacob at Sichar. Whilst the Disciples went into the village to secure provisions, "Jesus sat thus on the well", when a Samaritan woman came at midday to draw water. Sheer accident, we might say; to Jesus it was the occasion to preach the Kingdom and to offer grace to a sinner.

2. *Petitions* May we admire the ardent zeal of our Lord, and grasp the doctrine which He teaches.

I. The Conversation

To the Jews the Samaritans were infidels, whose contact rendered unclean. Ignoring those prejudices, Jesus spoke to the Samaritan woman, and very soon the conversation grew into an earnest effort on the part of Jesus to gain the soul of a poor creature that had gone astray. The woman was on the defensive, but Jesus gently led her on to reveal to Him the most intimate secrets of her sinful life. At first she appeared somewhat flippant but, under the influence of God's grace she grew repentant, and even wanted to be an apostle. She returned to the village saying, "Come and see a man, who has told me all things whatsoever I have done. Is not he the Christ?" (*John* 4, 29.)

We lovingly contemplate the Good Shepherd, as He rescues the straying sheep from the thorns and the briars. How His Heart yearns for the soul of that sinner! Without uttering one harsh word, He speaks the whole truth; and delves deep into the sinner's soul, till He reaches the hidden source of goodness that was there. Now again it can flow freely, for the erring woman does not offer resistance to grace. She confesses her weakness, she receives the pardon of her sins, and she proclaims her faith in the Messiah.

II. "If Thou Didst Know the Gift of God"

The words spoken by Jesus to this woman proceed from the very depths of His being: they are replete with mystery and bear the profoundest spiritual meaning.

The woman is astounded that a Jew should ask her, a Samaritan, for a drink of water. "Jesus answered and said to her, If thou didst know the gift of God, and who he is that saith to thee, Give me to drink; thou perhaps wouldst have asked of him, and he would have given thee living water.... He that shall drink of the water that I will give him, shall not thirst forever. But the water that I will give him shall become in him a fountain of water, springing up into life everlasting" (*John* 4: 10, 13, 14).

"The gift of God" that is the faith, the life of grace, the partaking of the divine life, was bestowed on us in the Sacrament of Baptism. This is the source of living water within us, inexhaustible, ever flowing more copiously, refreshing and comforting, "springing up into life everlasting". As long as we are on earth this fountain is hidden, its flow is limited; but the day will come when its stream will overflow all limits, and guide us into the arms of God and into bliss everlasting.

If we but knew the gift of God, how immensely grateful we would be, how we would cherish it and cling to it, and live by it every minute; how our heart would burn with the desire to share it with those many millions who have not received it yet!

III. "To Adore the Father in Spirit and in Truth"

Here our Lord refers to an ancient dispute that existed between the Jews and the Samaritans: Where was Jahve to be adored? At Jerusalem, or on Mount Garizim in Samaria? "Jesus saith to her, Woman, believe me that the hour cometh when you shall neither on this mountain, nor in Jerusalem, adore the Father.... The hour cometh and now is, when the true adorers shall adore the Father in spirit and in truth. For the Father also seeketh such to adore him. God is a spirit; and they that adore him must adore him in spirit and in truth" (*John* 4, 21-24).

These are words that have influenced man's destiny, and have determined the future religious history of the world. "Heaven and earth shall pass away, but *this* word shall not pass away."

True religion is not confined by time or place, still less by rank or race. Already at Bethlehem the Glad Tidings had been announced to all men of good will. Jesus Himself, the Son of Man, is the first perfect adorer of the Father in spirit and in truth. He came not to destroy the Law, but to fulfill it. He fulfilled it by lifting it above material things and spiritualizing it, by abolishing its limitations and making it universal. He founded a Church, a visible society, with its hierarchy, its sacraments, its rites and external modes of worship. But this Church knows no boundaries, no distinctions of race or color; it is Catholic, that is, universal. In every land it builds temples, ordains priests of every race. Wherever they may be, God knows and loves those that adore the Father in spirit and in truth. But it is the Father's will, revealed to us by His Son, that we adore Him in spirit and in truth *with* and *through* Jesus Christ, whom He has sent, and *in* the Church, which the Son has founded.

And yet, the sublime words of Jesus retain their full force. "God is spirit, and those that adore him must adore him in spirit and in truth." Let all Christians remember them, above all those who are specially consecrated to God. It is their privilege to adore and serve God, more than others, and with more external obligations, yet ever "in spirit and in truth".

Prayer: Almighty God, whom it behoves us to serve and to adore in spirit and in truth, grant, we beseech Thee, that we may always with a devout will be obedient unto Thee, and that we may ever with a sincere heart serve Thy Divine Majesty. Through Christ our Lord. . . .

SATURDAY: THIRD SUNDAY IN LENT

CHRIST AND THE WOMAN TAKEN IN ADULTERY
(John 8, 3-11)

1. Early in the morning Jesus had entered the Temple, and "all the people came to him: and sitting down, he taught them" (*John* 8, 2). A group of scribes and Pharisees noisily interrupted Him, bringing along a woman who just then had been taken in adultery. What were they to do with her? Ought they to stone her, as Moses had prescribed? . . .

2. *Petition*: The grace to understand the feelings of our Lord's Heart. May we admire the wisdom, the serenity and the mercy, which He displays in dealing with this ticklish question.

I. The Pharisees

They, and the scribes, who had brought the guilty woman to Him, were the custodians of the Law; and it was their duty to pronounce judgment. But they thought they had discovered a means, not only of ridding themselves of an unpleasant obligation, but also of trapping Jesus, whom they called the friend of sinners. They wanted Him to pronounce judgment: if He let her go, they would be able to discredit Him with the people as a despiser of the Law; (Moses indeed had ordained that an adulterer should be stoned, but that law had long been in disuse); if he decided that she should be stoned, they would have branded Him as a cruel bigot.

The motive of the Pharisees was by no means zeal for the Law; it was envy of Him, whom they hypocritically addressed as Master. Even towards that poor sinful woman, they behaved in an outrageous manner: that she should "repent and live" was the least of their cares; they just made use of her to further their own evil designs.

It is dangerous, and utterly mean, severely to censure in others the faults we commit ourselves, readily condone in our own case. "Why seest thou the mote that is in thy brother's eye; and seest not the beam that is in thy own eye?" (*Matt.* 7, 3.) "All things therefore whatsoever you would that men should do to you, do you also to them" (*Ibid.* 7, 12).

Such was not the way of the Pharisees.

II. Jesus Faces the Pharisees

Jesus refuses to act as judge. "For God sent not his Son into the world to judge the world; but that the world might be saved by him" (*John* 3, 17). To show them that He does not want to meddle with this judicial matter, "Jesus, bowing himself down, (probably He was seated on a low stool whilst teaching) wrote with his finger on the ground" most probably only a few straight lines. "When, therefore, they continued asking him, he lifted up himself and said to them, He that is without sin among you, let him first cast a stone at her. And again stooping down, he wrote on the ground" (*John* 8, 7-8).

Now it was they themselves that had fallen in the trap. Perhaps they felt the keen eye of Jesus penetrating into the innermost recesses of their guilty souls? "But they, hearing this, went out one by one, beginning at the eldest." When standing face to face with an invisible God in the Temple, the Pharisee dared pray and thank God that he was not like the rest of men, extortioners, adulterers. But here, under the sharp eye of the dreaded Prophet of Nazareth, who might tear the mask off their face, they had more discretion; and shamefacedly they sneaked out, one by one, leaving their victim "standing in the midst".

It is good here to behold the wonderful greatness and wisdom of Jesus; we shall love and admire Him all the more, when the hour comes freely and meekly to deliver Himself into the hands of the powers of darkness, for our salvation, and out of love for us.

III. Jesus and the Sinful Woman

He, who is without sin, is left alone with the poor sinner. St. Augustine describes the scene most graphically, as *misera* face to face with *misericordia*, the pitiable face to face with infinite Pity. "Then Jesus, lifting up himself said to her, Woman, where are they that accused thee? Hath no man condemned thee? Who said: No man, Lord. And Jesus said, Neither will I condemn thee. Go, now sin no more." On the present occasion Jesus does not say: "Go, thy sins are forgiven thee", as He did under other circumstances. These words would not have been appropriate here.

From the gravity with which He addresses her, it is evident how earnestly He disapproves of her conduct. But in this woman's soul terror has gradually yielded place to humility and repentance; and Jesus is happy because He has been able to save a straying sheep from the claws of bloodthirsty wolves. And it has all been done without display, even without the uttering of a loud word.

The Lord is moderate even in His castigation of the Pharisees, and merciful without weakness in His dealings with the sinner. Indeed, "never did man speak like this man" (*John* 7, 46).

Prayer: O God, whose nature it is ever to have mercy and to spare, receive our petition; that we and all Thy servants, who are chained by the fetters of sin, may be mercifully absolved by Thy loving kindness. Through Christ our Lord (Oration after the Litany of All Saints).

THE SECOND MULTIPLICATION OF THE LOAVES
(John 6, 1-15)

1. A great multitude had followed Jesus and all day they had
not tasted food. Jesus sat down on the grass on the mountain
slope in the midst of His disciples. "When therefore he had
lifted up his eyes and seen a very great multitude," He resolved
to give them food before dismissing them (*John* 6, 1-15).

2. *Petition*: The grace to understand our Lord's actions on this
occasion: also the grace to know what at the present hour He
demands from us.

I. Jesus Tries the Apostles

"Jesus Himself knew what he would do;" but He did not reveal
it to the Apostles as yet, because He desired to try them. He therefore said to Philip, "Whence shall we buy bread that these may
eat?" The anxiety of the Apostle is patent in his reply: "Two hundred pennyworth of bread is not sufficient for them, that every
one may take a little." Where could they find such an enormous
amount of bread, and whence was the money to come? The thing
was impossible.

Perhaps Andrew went among the people to ask whether any
provisions were available: for he informed Jesus that "there is
a boy here that hath five barley loaves and two fishes. But what
are these among so many?" Jesus does not pay any heed to these
expostulations, but simply orders that the multitude be made to
sit down and the Apostles, who are utterly bewildered, do as the
Master tells them. They go among the crowd and make them sit
on the grass in orderly groups.

On this occasion Jesus demands blind obedience. The same
He requires from us whenever our Superiors give us a command
of which we fail to understand the reason, or impose on us a task
that appears to be beyond our strength. We are entitled, on such
occasions, with due respect to raise objections, as Philip does in
the present case. But, if our reasons are not deemed valid, then
we ought like Philip simply to comply with the command.

II. The Miracle

"And Jesus took the loaves, (the other Evangelists add: and looking up to heaven) and when He had given thanks, He distributed to them that were set down." For "giving thanks" St. John uses the word *eucharistia*: we may piously believe that Jesus, who well "knew what he would do" one day, was thinking even now of that other "living Bread", His own sacred Body, which, as food of our souls, He would multiply for all generations to come until the end of time.

In performing this miracle Jesus makes use of the paltry contribution which men offer Him: five loaves and two fishes. There ie not the slightest proportion between that contribution and the ultimate effect, and Jesus could have fed the multitude just as well without using those five loaves. He will, however, not do so; but prefers to use the human means that are at hand.

This teaches us a salutary lesson. Not seldom do we allow ourselves to be troubled by anxious questionings such as "What relation can there be between what I can do, what I propose to do, or what I actually do, and the achievement of the lofty ideal that beckons me on? A small victory over my slothfulness so that I may render service to a brother; a little act of self-denial; a more reverent attitude at prayer; the ready assumption of a painful task that could be shirked; greater cordiality towards one with whom I am out of sympathy; the more perfect fulfillment of my daily chores, etc. How can these things show my love for God and for souls, obtain the conversion of sinners, make me become perfect as our Father in heaven is perfect?"

Let us never forget that our utterly inadequate performances, are grafted on, and a thousandfold multiplied, by Christ's own great sacrifice: and thereby made capable of achieving our supernatural ideal. As Pascal was wont to say, We must perform small things as if they were great on account of Christ's Majesty, who performs them in us whilst He lives in us; and perform mighty things as if they were light and small because His almighty power aids us.

Jesus makes use of the services of the Apostles. What they are by themselves and what their personal virtues are, is of no importance: they simply are His intermediaries, keeping in touch with Him. Jesus is in the midst of the multitude and to Him alone do they look up. Nowadays things are different: Jesus is no longer visibly present, though through His Sacraments He is still active in the Church and working wonders of grace in the souls of men.

The minister of the Sacraments must by his intention keep in touch with Christ in His Church, but his personal worthiness or unworthiness is irrelevant to their efficacy. Still, the priest is not merely the minister of Christ's Sacraments, he is also the representative of Jesus among men: and often men's estimate of the Church, of the sacred Person and doctrine of Christ, depends on how these are made known to them in the personal conduct of the priest.

The same holds true of all religious and of men dedicated to God, whose very habit marks them as Christ's own. Theirs is a heavy responsibility, heavier even than that of the Apostles as long as Jesus dwelt visibly in their midst. It behoves us ever to remember whom we represent; and let this remembrance spur us on to greater trust in Him, and to greater generosity towards Him, who said, "Behold, I am with you all days, even to the consummation of the world" (*Matt.* 28, 20).

III. After the Miracle

"Jesus, therefore, when he knew that they would come to take him by force, and make him king, fled again into the mountain himself alone." We admire the superhuman greatness of Christ: He fled from "the concerns of man", that He might be about His Father's business. Neither earthly success, nor earthly failure, influences Him.

Prayer: Lord Jesus, grant us to unite our prayer to Thine: "Father, hallowed be Thy name, Thy kingdom come, Thy will be done on earth as it is in heaven." "Yea, Father, for so it hath seemed good in thy sight" (*Luke* 10, 21).

MONDAY: FOURTH SUNDAY IN LENT

JESUS CASTS THE SELLERS OUT OF THE TEMPLE

(John 2, 13-25)

1. Jesus had come to Jerusalem to celebrate the Pasch and, when He entered the Temple, He saw that it had been invaded by "them that sold oxen, and sheep and doves", animals that were needed for the daily sacrifices. There were money-changers too. Jesus was roused to holy anger by this desecration of God's

house; He made as it were a scourge of little cords, and drove
out the traffickers (*John* 2, 13-25).

2. *Petition*: The grace to understand our Lord's zeal for His
Father's house and to be mindful of that zeal, lest we should
ever permit filthy lucre to defile the sanctuary.

I. Our Lord's Zeal

We might feel surprised at our Lord's severity. What those
people offered for sale—oxen, sheep, doves—were things required
for the sacrifices; and, as on solemn feasts pilgrims came from
every country, it was necessary to enable them to exchange foreign money against Jewish currency. Jesus was aware of all that;
but, what aroused His indignation was the fact that these traders
had invaded the sacred precincts of the Temple, and had transformed His Father's house into a public market.

Jesus held in abomination the profanation of what is dedicated
to God. "No man can serve two masters. . . . You cannot serve God
and mammon" (*Matt.* 6, 24). No man can do that, least of all
those that are consecrated to the service of the altar, or who,
leaving all earthly possessions have devoted themselves entirely
to God's service. St. Paul (1 *Cor.* 9, 13-14) affirms that they who
serve the altar, and preach the Gospel, are entitled to live by the
altar, and by the Gospel; yet it is imperative that they should
shun all appearance of covetousness. St. Paul prides himself on
the fact that he personally refused to benefit by that right,
so that he might preach the Gospel only for the sake of Christ.
Such disinterestedness is not always possible: the great St. Teresa
herself had her financial troubles, and she learnt that she needed
money to establish her convents.

But Jesus demands from those who follow in His footsteps,
that they should be absolutely detached from earthly possessions,
that they should be immune from every trace of avarice, that
they should use temporal goods exclusively "about their Father's
business".

II. The Lord's Zeal Is Wise and Prudent

It is noteworthy that Jesus does not treat all those traffickers
in the same manner. The sellers of oxen and sheep, men that
made big profits, He drives out with a scourge; "The money he
poured out, the tables he overthrew"; let them pick up their coins
and set up their counters outside the sacred place. "To them

that sold doves, he said, Take these things hence." He does not throw open their cages, because He does not wish to cause them any loss. It looks as if those humbler folk received milder treatment at His hands, though to them also He addressed the words, "Make not the house of my Father a house of traffic."

"And his disciples remembered that it was written, The zeal of thy house hath eaten me up."

We behold with awe that ardent zeal. Notwithstanding his utter indignation Jesus remains master of Himself, moderate and tactful. Here all those that are invested with authority may learn a salutary lesson. Let them model themselves on Christ, when they are obliged to take strong measures against certain abuses. They must remember that Jesus said later on, "Learn of me, because I am meek and humble of heart."

III. Our Lord's Mysterious Answer

The rulers of the Temple had been present at the occurrence: they refrained from interfering, because they were awed by the boldness and the majestic bearing of the great Prophet. At last some of them spoke out, "What sign dost thou show unto us, seeing thou dost these things? Jesus answered and said to them, Destroy this temple and in three days I will raise it up. The Jews then said, Six and forty years was this temple in building, and wilt thou raise it up in three days?"

At that moment, neither the Jews nor the disciples were able to understand those words. Later, before the tribunal of Caiphas they will be alleged against Christ, as implying a sacrilege against the Temple. "But he spoke of the temple of his body. When therefore he was risen again from the dead, his disciples remembered that he had said this, and they believed the Scripture and the word that Jesus had said."

"What sign dost thou show unto us?" On the part of the Jews this question was a piece of insolence. God alone is competent to choose the signs which He deigns to give unto men. No one is entitled to lay down the law to Him. We have no right to interrogate Him, nor to demand a sign from Him. "My ways are not your ways," He tells us through the prophet. In the same manner, "my signs are not your signs". It is our duty to trust Him, and to believe "the Scripture, and the word that Jesus had said" (*John* 2, 22); we must pray humbly that we may recognize His signs; whether He gives them through the guidance of our Superiors, or through the events which His Providence permits, or through the inspirations of His grace. And, if here and now we fail to understand the sign which God gives us, then we ought to treasure it in our hearts. "Thou knowest not now", Jesus said to Peter at the washing of the feet, "but thou shalt know hereafter" (*John* 13, 7).

Prayer: Lord Jesus, who wert zealous, prudent and righteous in the pursuit of the interests of Thy Father, who didst not permit Thy Father's house to be anything but a house of prayer: be pleased to deliver us from all disorderly attachments, so that we may always serve Thee with a sincere heart.

TUESDAY: FOURTH SUNDAY IN LENT

"MY DOCTRINE IS NOT MINE" (John 7, 16)

1. Jesus had come to Jerusalem for the feast of the Tabernacles. Only three months separated Him from His passion; but even now events were moving fast and the Pharisees had resolved to put Him to death. Jesus knew it; nevertheless He entered the Temple and taught publicly. "And there was much murmuring among the multitude concerning him. For some said, He is a good man. And others said, No, but he seduceth the people" (*John* 7, 12).

2. *Petition*: We ask the grace ever to enter deeper into the feelings of the Heart of Jesus, and to profit by the lessons which He teaches us.

I. The Modesty of Our Lord

Whenever the Pharisees hear Jesus speaking, they wonder at His knowledge of the Scriptures. "How does this man know letters (that is, the Scriptures), for he has never learnt?" they enviously objected. At Nazareth every one knew, and the rumor had spread to Jerusalem, that the great Prophet had never attended the schools of the rabbis. That alone sufficed to render Him suspect in the eyes of the scribes and the ruling clique. He had once said that He had not come to destroy the Law, but to fulfill it; but that fulfillment was hardly to their liking; it was revolutionary, an invention of His.

Jesus answered them, "My doctrine is not mine, but His that

sent me." These words bear a very profound meaning and they are proof of a genuine modesty. He does not preach a doctrine which He has invented Himself: "He speaketh not of himself, nor seeketh His own glory." The doctrine He preaches is not His own; it is the doctrine "of Him that sent me".

It is a striking feature, especially of St. John's Gospel, that Jesus frequently seems to be anxious to divert the attention of the people from Himself, in order to direct it to the Father whose ambassador He is. In the same manner the Baptist had said of Jesus, "He must increase, but I must decrease" (3, 30). To the rich young man, who had addressed Him as "good Master", Jesus said, "Why callest thou me good? None is good but One, that is God" (*Mark* 10, 18). Absolute and fundamental dependence on the Father seems to be the most essential characteristic of Christ's being. "Amen, amen, I say unto you, the Son cannot do anything of himself, but what he seeth the Father doing; for what things soever he doth, these the Son also doth in like manner" (*John* 5, 19). "That which my Father hath given me is greater than all; and no one can snatch them out of the hand of my Father. I and the Father are one" (*John* 10, 29-30).

Let us try reverently to penetrate into the profound depths of the soul of Jesus and abide there for a while. There we shall learn that loving adherence to the Father, which excludes all thought of self, is the hallmark of those who possess the true spirit of Christ.

II. Truth and Righteousness

"If any man will do the will of Him (the Father), he shall know of the doctrine, whether it be of God or whether I speak of myself." By these words Jesus points to the importance of interior dispositions and of a virtuous life, if a man wants to gain a correct understanding of both His Person and His doctrine. "He that doth truth cometh to the light.... Everyone that doth evil hateth the light and cometh not to the light" (*John* 3, 20-21). By that light He means the "Light of life", the Light that enables us to walk in the truth. It is also the Light of life in the sense that it springs and derives its brightness from a virtuous life. The more our eye—God's eye in us—is single, the more our whole body, our whole life, shall be lightsome, and the more clearly we shall discern the course we must follow. When we are truly ready to obey God's will, then we are able clearly and readily to see what is that will in our regard.

III. Judging Fairly

Jesus had healed a man on the sabbath (*John* 5, 1-18), and this man had, as Jesus had commanded him, taken up his bed and carried it home. In the eyes of the bigots this was a violation of the sabbatical rest. The striking miracle, that had bestowed health on a man who had suffered during eight and thirty years, was censured because of the transgression of a minor prescription.

Appealing to the custom which sanctioned the bestowing of circumcision on the sabbath, Jesus asks them, Why "are you angry at me because I have healed the whole man on the sabbath day? Judge not according to the appearance, but judge just judgment" (*John* 7, 23-24).

How often do we judge the words and actions of our brothers "according to the appearance", or in accordance with our private sympathies or antipathies? When we act thus, we tread in the footsteps of those narrow-minded and envious Pharisees. They closed their eyes to the "sign", the great miracle that manifested the kindness of the heart of Jesus; they saw only breach of one of their petty regulations, and this infuriated them. What a sacrilege!

"Judge not, that you may not be judged" (*Matt.* 7, 1). Our Lord's command is quite general: judge not, for it is exceedingly difficult to judge fairly and justly. When we judge at all, we so often offend against the most elementary virtues of truth, justice, mercy.

Prayer: We implore Thee, O Lord, that the fasts of this holy season may obtain for us an increase of piety, and Thy constant assistance and mercy. Through our Lord (Collect of today's Mass).

WEDNESDAY: FOURTH SUNDAY IN LENT

JESUS GIVES SIGHT TO THE MAN BORN BLIND (John 9)

1. In the early Church it was the custom to begin today the preparation of the catechumens who were to be baptized, i.e. "illumined", during the Easter Vigil. For this reason we read at Holy Mass the cure of the man who had been born blind and other texts of the liturgy that refer to washing, cleansing, and enlightening.

The man to whom Jesus had given sight had not yet seen

his Benefactor, when after a couple of days he met Him and Jesus said to him, "Dost thou believe in the Son of God? He answered and said, Who is he, Lord, that I may believe in him? And Jesus said to him, Thou hast both seen him; and it is he that talketh with thee. And he said, I believe, Lord. And falling down, he adored him" (*John* 9, 35-38).

We fall down with the man born blind and adore Jesus.

2.   *Petition*: That we may be grateful for our Baptism, by which we have been 'enlightened', and may always faithfully observe our baptismal vows.

I. The Miracle

No other miracle has been narrated by St. John with such a wealth of detail. In itself, the giving of sight to a man born blind is a remarkable cure; the enquiry that immediately followed places the facts beyond all doubt. For St. John, to whom Jesus is the Light that shineth in darkness, it bears a symbolical meaning, which is conveyed in the whole of the Gospel of St. John.

Jesus and the Apostles knew this blind man, who was wont to beg for alms at one of the gates of the Temple, and it was well known that he was born blind. The blind beggar had heard about Christ, "that man that is called Jesus", as he said. Unasked Jesus approached him to cure him. "He spat on the ground and made clay of the spittle, and spread the clay upon his eyes. And said to him, Go, wash in the pool of Siloe, which is interpreted Sent."

What a strange way of giving sight to a blind man! We might feel, "This is going to increase the blindness!" But we have herein a symbol of the sacramental anointing which precedes Baptism. From the time the Word became flesh, God uses matter as the bearer, or the transmitter, of spiritual graces. In all the Sacraments, especially in Baptism and in the Holy Eucharist, we believe that God operates in a way which is most mysterious, and yet perfectly adapted to our human nature.

When Jesus had anointed the man's eyes with clay, He bade him to "go and wash in the pool of Siloe", "which is interpreted Sent," says St. John. The waters of Siloe, through the will of Him, "whom the Father has sent," that is, Jesus Himself, possess the power to give sight to the blind: this is a figure of Christian Baptism.

The man "went and washed and he came seeing". He did not come to Jesus, to cast himself at the feet of his Benefactor and to give Him thanks, as we might have expected. He is hardly a model of gratitude; also, his faith needs further strengthening. Jesus is aware of all that, but His grace is at work. Surely the good man displayed wonderful confidence, when with the clay on his eyelids, he sought his way to the pool of Siloe; and when he believed that the common water of the pond would wash away the blindness together with the clay. He obeyed blindly and trustfully whatever Jesus had commanded him and, having received his sight, he returned home.

"I believe whatever the Son of God has told;
What the truth hath spoken that for truth I hold."

II. The Willful Blindness of the Pharisees

It is sad to behold the dispositions of those men, sad to realize how an ill-disposed person can deliberately close his eyes to the light, how he can resist the irrefutable truth, and shamefully get entangled in his own fallacies, thus "sinning against the light". From such a calamity may the Lord preserve us! "For we can do nothing against the truth" (2 *Cor.* 13, 8). Let us remember the words of Christ, "I confess to thee, O Father, Lord of heaven and earth, because thou hast hidden these things from the wise and prudent, and hast revealed them to little ones" (*Matt.* 11, 25).

III. The Faith of the Man Born Blind

In the beginning the man hardly distinguished himself by the nobility of his sentiments; but he was fearless, ready to accept the truth and to receive God's grace. After his cure he boldly gave testimony before the Pharisees. "We know Moses, but as to this man, we know not from whence he is." The man replied, "Why, herein is a wonderful thing that you know not from whence he is. . . . We know that God doth not hear sinners. . . . Unless this man were of God, he could do nothing. . . ." And they cast him out.

This was a sort of excommunication, with all its unpleasant consequences. When we stand up for our faith, when we suffer for it, we grow in faith, and we become fit to receive more light.

"Jesus heard that they had cast him out. And when he had found him, he said to him, Dost thou believe in the Son of God? He answered and said, Who is he, Lord, that I may believe in him? And Jesus said to him, Thou hast both seen him; and it is he that talketh with thee. And he said, I believe, Lord, and falling down he adored him" (*John* 9, 35-38).

Prayer: Lord Jesus, Light of the world, who through Baptism hast made us children of light, grant to those that have been cast out, and that suffer for having borne testimony to Thee, the strength to persevere unto the end; give to all of us the courage faithfully to observe our baptismal vows, which we renew during the night vigil of Thy resurrection and of our illumination.

THURSDAY: FOURTH SUNDAY IN LENT

TWO RESURRECTIONS FROM THE DEAD

(Luke 7, 11. 4 Kgs. 4, 8)

1. One day Jesus and His disciples were going to the little town of Naim; at the gate they came across a funeral procession. Jesus went close to the mother of the deceased, a widow, and said to her, "Weep not" and there, "before a great multitude of the city", He touched the bier, and bade the carriers stand still. "And he said, Young man, I say to thee, arise. And he that was dead sat up, and began to speak. And he gave him to his mother."

    We prayerfully behold this touching scene.

2. *Petition*: The grace of faith and trust in Him who said, "I am the resurrection and the life", and who by this miracle proved that He is the Lord of life and death.

I. Death and Resurrection

As we gradually draw closer to the commemoration of the great Passover—the passing of our Lord through death to His resurrection—the liturgy calls from the Old and the New Testaments passages and scenes that prepare our souls for the great mystery. God is the Giver of life; of death, the wages of sin, God is not the Giver, He is its Conqueror.

Death and life are going to be locked in a fierce combat; the Lord of life will die, but He will rise again and thus triumph over death. Certainly, whenever Jesus came face to face with death along the roads of Galilee, He must have thought of His own death; and whenever He raised a dead person to life, He must have wanted to prefigure His own resurrection. Even when for a brief while He manifested His glory on Thabor, He conversed with Moses and Elias about "his decease that he should accomplish in Jerusalem" (*Luke* 9, 31).

Let us, during these days, give more thoughtful consideration to the great mystery of our salvation: thoughtfulness bespeaks love.

II.   Two Different Procedures in Raising the Dead

The Epistle of today's Mass relates how Eliseus raised to life the son of the Sunamite woman. The manner of Eliseus differs greatly from the manner of Jesus at Naim (4 *Kgs.* 4, 25-28).

The Prophet Eliseus had often received hospitality from a devout matron and her husband at Sunam; and, through his prayers, she that had been barren for many years had obtained a son from the Almighty. After some years the child, having followed his father to the field, suffered a sunstroke, and died in his mother's arms. The distracted mother hurried to the retreat of the prophet and, bathed in tears, implored his help. Eliseus, out of gratitude for all the kindnesses he had received from this family, prayed to God; and sent Giezi, his servant, with his staff which he was to lay on the child's body. But the staff worked no miracle. Then the prophet entered the child's room, closed the door, stretched himself out over the dead body, eye to eye, mouth to mouth, and pleaded with God . . . until at last life returned into the dead body. Then he arose, and told the mother, "Take up thy son."

Such was the way of "the man of God". By himself he was utterly powerless: he prayed; he made a first attempt and failed; he made greater efforts, persevered, and finally obtained a miracle.

How different is the manner of Jesus! First of all He acts out of sheer kindness and compassion. He did not lie under any obligation to the widow of Naim. He has no need of praying to obtain the resurrection. By the grave of Lazarus we hear Jesus praying to the Father, but it is only to thank the Father and "because of the people who stood about". He Himself is the Lord of life and of death, and His voice gives commands. He has no need of making attempts, has not to redouble His efforts nor to wait "till life returns". He orders the carriers to halt. "He touched the bier, and said, Young man, I say to thee, arise. And he that was dead sat up, and began to speak. And he gave him to his mother."

Still another difference: Eliseus performs the miracle behind closed doors; Jesus raised the dead man in public, by the gate of the city, before a great multitude in the presence of the dead man's mother.

"And there came a fear on them all: and they glorified God, saying, A great prophet is risen up among us, and God hath visited his people."

It is meet that man should experience fear, when he comes suddenly face to face with a manifestation of God's omnipotence; and it is right that he should glorify God and thank Him for revealing His loving kindness. Such was the reaction of the men of Naim when they beheld this stupendous miracle. They pay homage to Him that had wrought the miracle: "a great prophet is risen up among us"; and yet they see beyond the Prophet, for they "glorify God, who hath visited his people". That is exactly how Jesus would have it, He who seeketh not His own glory, but the glory of Him that sent Him. And for this Jesus thanked the Father.

Prayer: Grant, we beseech Thee, almighty God, that we, who are chastised by the fast we have undertaken, may rejoice with holy devotion: that, our earthly affections being weakened, we may more easily grasp heavenly things. Through our Lord (Collect, today's Mass).

FRIDAY: FOURTH SUNDAY IN LENT

THE RAISING OF LAZARUS (John 11, 1-46)

1. Our Lord chose to give this miracle a special sort of solemnity and to perform it before the eyes of many. Lazarus had been buried for three days and decomposition had already set in. The raising of the dead man occurred close to the gates of Jerusalem, shortly before the solemn feast of the Passover, in the presence of numerous witnesses, some of whom were favorably disposed, while others were hostile. In the hearing of all, He calls upon His Father before the miracle He is about to perform, and which is to be a clear proof of His messianic mission.

2. *Petition*: The grace firmly to believe in Him, who is the resurrection and the life. He said, "He that believeth in me, although he be dead, shall live."

I. Jesus Is Truly Man

On no other occasion do we face so squarely the fact that Jesus is at one and the same time true God and true man. At Naim, His heart was moved by the grief of the widow, who was a perfect stranger to Him; here things happen to a family where Jesus and His Apostles when visiting Jerusalem had frequently received generous hospitality. Jesus is the God-man, that is, not less man but more man, and a better man, than we are. Whatever belongs to our nature is found in Him, only more so, and in a more perfect manner, than in any other human being. "In all things like as we are, without sin", says St. Paul (*Heb.* 4, 15), and this sinlessness perfected and ennobled all the emotions of His eminently human nature.

When Jesus arrived at Bethany, and saw and heard how grievously Martha and Mary suffered under their great bereavement, He experienced a profound shock. "When he saw her weeping, he groaned in the spirit and troubled himself.... And Jesus wept." At His request, they lead Him to the sepulchre, and here again, as the Evangelist notes, "Jesus was groaning in himself". With love He thinks of His friend. Soon He will solemnly, in the hearing of all the bystanders, command the dead man to come forth from the grave.

On the occasion of other miracles, even when he raised the dead to life, we have always seen the Master calm and serene; here He is visibly moved; and He is well aware that His present attitude will put an end to the last hesitations of His enemies: they will now resolve that He must die.

We humbly try to fathom the sentiments of our Lord and Savior, of the Son of man, as He is wont to call Himself; and we pray: Heart of Jesus, substantially united with the Word of God, have mercy on us; Heart of Jesus, full of goodness and love, have mercy on us.

II. Jesus Is Truly God

While Jesus shows Himself perfectly and fully man, we behold Him at the same time truly God, speaking and acting as God alone can speak and act. When He received the message of the two sisters, that their brother Lazarus, "whom He loved", was sick, He replied, "This sickness is not unto death, but for the glory of God that the Son of God may be glorified." These words are full of mystery and the Master's way of acting is still more incomprehensible. "When he had heard therefore that he was sick, he still remained in the same place two days." After that He resolve to go to Bethany: He said to the Apostles, "Lazarus our friend sleepeth, but I go that I may awake him out of sleep." And then, to the astounded disciples, He clarified His meaning, "Lazarus is dead. And I am glad for your sakes that I was not there, that you may believe." These words clearly indicate the special purpose of this miracle.

On meeting the grief-stricken Martha, Jesus says to her, "Thy brother shall rise again.... I am the resurrection and the life." And when they have reached the sepulchre, He orders, "Take away the stone." Martha, under the impression that it was the Master's desire to behold His friend once more, ventures a gentle remonstrance, "Lord, by this time he stinketh, for he is now of four days." Quite different, however, as His answer to Martha intimates, "Did not I say to thee that, if thou believe, thou shalt see the glory of God?" Then the heavy stone was rolled back. How solemn the moment was is evidenced by the attitude of Jesus, and by His prayer of thanksgiving to the Father. "And Jesus lifting up his eyes said, Father, I give thee thanks that thou hast heard me. And I knew that thou hearest me always, but because of the people who stand about have I said it, that they may believe that thou hast sent me."

"When he had said these things, he cried out with a loud voice, Lazarus, come forth. And presently he that had been dead came forth, bound feet and hands with winding bands, and his face was bound about with a napkin. Jesus said to them, Loose him, and let him go."

Here Jesus is truly God: it is He that leads the events. He, who even in the performance of His miracles remains always so humble and so modest, has seen to it that this miracle has witnesses. With set purpose He waits until Lazarus has been in the grave for three days; a large group of people is present, some friendly, others clearly ill-disposed; all hear Him pray and call upon the Father to bear witness that He has sent Him; all have heard the loud command re-echoing from the dark tomb; all have seen Lazarus emerging alive from the sepulchre.

We offer to Jesus our adoration and our love, as we gaze up

at Him, so close to us and yet so infinitely above us. He wept before His friend's grave: then He was truly man. But before that grave He did not, like other children of men, stand powerless. To Martha He had said, "I am the resurrection and the life", and at His command Lazarus comes forth from the grave. This is a visible, though a feeble prelude to His own glorious resurrection, in an immortal and glorified Body. Jesus must have been thinking of that great event, which was so near. So do we, full of faith and gratitude.

Prayer: Lord Jesus, true God and true man, graciously teach us to be perfectly human, as thou wert, with a large, tender, and stout heart; grant us an unshakable faith in Thee, who art the Resurrection and the Life, until the day when we shall forever abide with Thee.

SATURDAY: FOURTH SUNDAY IN LENT

THE SOLICITATIONS OF GOD'S GRACE

1. The "annual retreat" of the entire Christian people proceeds; the lessons and prayers of the Mass of this day are a final appeal to the catechumens, who are preparing to receive Baptism during the Easter Vigil. In the Introit, we read, "All ye that thirst, come to the waters, come and drink with joy" (*Isa.* 55, 1). Besides, there are others, baptized souls but sinners, whom God's grace solicits to return to Him. "Behold the Lord stands at the gate and knocketh" (*Apoc.* 3, 21). For them also, and for ourselves, we must pray with our Holy Mother the Church.

2. *Petition*: "Lord, draw our hearts to Thee in spite of our waywardness" (Secret of today's Mass).

I. Our Free Will

Man does not serve God under compulsion: that is his most precious privilege, as well as a terrible responsibility. Man is able to say "No" to God. God alone "searcheth the reins and hearts"; He alone knows what is in man, and He alone judges when man acts through weakness, through ignorance or through sheer wickedness. In hell resistance to God is sheer wickedness, and there it implies damnation.

Our free will is God's most precious gift to us: the best use we can make of it is freely to render it conformable to God's holy will. To bend our puny, weak, fickle will, so as to make it agree with the "most holy will of the Divine Majesty", does not mean the destruction of our free will; it means that we perfect it, even when, nay, above all when we feel that we make a sacrifice. Our Lord once said to St. Catherine of Siena, "Nothing in man is so much opposed to me as his free will. I will continue importuning him until he surrenders it; when he has surrendered it, and I have accepted the offering, then I will begin to fashion him as I please." The first thing which St. Ignatius in his famous oblation offers to God is his freedom: "Take, O Lord, and accept my liberty."

II. God's Gracious Importunity

In the Secret of the Mass we plead that God may compel our rebellious wills, or draw to Himself our hearts in spite of their waywardness. Such is the mysterious and ineffable method of our Creator, to draw us to Himself while respecting our freedom. The more God asks, the more freely we ought to offer it to Him. "Do not imagine," says St. Augustine, "that you are being drawn against your will. Love makes the soul respond like iron to a magnet. Anyone that has love in his heart understands my words; but he that is cold cannot even guess what I am talking about."

God's gracious importunity gradually wears down the resistance of our will, and disentangles us from what weakens and cripples it. Often in the Postcommunion, at the end of the Mass, we pray for this disentanglement, purifying, healing, strengthening. . . .

III. God's Patience

God's love is infinite; therefore His patience is without limit. In the Epistle of the Mass, today, Israel complains to God saying, "The Lord hath forsaken me, and the Lord hath forgotten me." (Too often the chosen people had deserved such chastisement by its infidelity.) God answers them, "Can a woman forget her infant, so as not to have pity on the son of her womb? And if she should forget, yet will not I forget thee" (*Isa.* 49, 14-15).

God is patient with all sinners. In today's prayer over the people, we say that it is His good pleasure to be merciful rather than angry. To the Church of Laodicea, which had fallen into lukewarmness, Jesus sent this message, "Be zealous and do penance. Behold, I stand at the gate, and knock" (*Apoc.* 3, 19-20). During this holy season of Lent Jesus does stand at the door of so many, knocking and trying the lock. How He longs to enter! We pray that they may heed the voice of their conscience and open the door to the Lord of their souls. "Then I will come in to him, and will sup with him and he with me" (*Apoc.* 3, 20).

And how patient He is with such as are consecrated to Him, but heed not His invitation to greater fidelity, to more generosity in His service. During ten years St. Teresa of Avila had been deaf to our Lord's voice which called on her to sacrifice long and useless conversations in the convent parlor. Perhaps for a long while Jesus has stood knocking at one or other of the inner doors of my soul, begging to be allowed to enter further and deeper into it? With the priest, who at the altar offers our oblation to God we pray,

Prayer: Accept and be appeased by our offering, we implore Thee, O Lord, and mercifully subdue our rebellious wills unto Thy service. Through our Lord. (Secret of today's Mass).

PASSION SUNDAY

THE ONE, GREAT SACRIFICE

1. Today all crucifixes and statues in the church are veiled; at Vespers we sing the solemn strains of the "Vexilla Regis":

   The royal banners forward go
   the cross shines forth in mystic glow.

   In the responses of the breviary office the "Gloria Patri" is omitted. Let us share in the mourning of Mother Church.

2. *Petition*: May God grant us an increase of love for our Redeemer, and a deep understanding of the great mystery of the death and resurrection of Christ. "Passion of Christ, strengthen me."

I. Jesus Suffers Freely

Jesus is not a tragic hero crushed by blind fate. Again and again, and most emphatically, the Gospels declare that He delivered Himself freely to the powers of darkness. My life "no man taketh it away from me, but I lay it down of myself, and I have power to lay it down, and I have power to take it up again. This commandment have I received from my Father" (*John* 10, 18). He will surrender His life, not when His enemies so decide, but when He Himself wills it. Six months before the Passion, when He had revealed to them His divine origin, "they sought to apprehend him, and no man laid hands on him, because his hour was not yet come" (*John* 7, 30). When they were on the point of apprehending Him at Gethsemane He said to the soldiers and their leaders, "Are ye come out as it were against a thief, with swords and clubs? When I was daily with you in the temple, you did not stretch forth your hands against me; but this is your hour and the power of darkness" (*Luke* 22, 52-53). Freely! and yet "Christ ought to have suffered and so to enter into his glory." Such was the unfathomable decree of the Father and by the Father's will the Son would abide, even at the cost of an agonizing struggle: "Not my will, but thine be done" (*Luke* 22, 42). Jesus suffered freely and "he learned obedience by the things which he suffered", says St. Paul (*Heb.* 5, 8), and Paul adds, "whereas indeed he was the Son of God".

And we, what are we doing? During this Passiontide we shall unite our tiny sufferings and sacrifices with the great sufferings, which even now Jesus endures in His Mystical Body, and offers to the Father.

II. Out of Love For the Father and For Us

The whole life of Christ can be summed up thus: loving adherence to the will of the Father, and self-sacrificing love for us. He was sent to make the Father known to man: this mission He could not fulfill without revealing that He Himself is the Son of the Father, and that the Father and He are One. This testimony, solemnly delivered before the High Priest of Israel, will seal his condemnation to death. Jesus is *the* Martyr, *the* Witness. In the sacrifice which He then offered all martyrdom finds its beginning (Secret, Thursday of 3rd week in Lent).

"Self-oblivious love for us." "He loved me and delivered himself for me," says St. Paul (*Gal.* 2, 20). "Jesus possessed nothing that was His own; He wholly belonged to us: His Body and His Soul, His Mother and His Apostles, His robe and His cloak.... For our sake He ate and drank, for our sake He lived and died" (*Ruysbroeck*). This thought profoundly impressed Blessed Angela di Foligno, when from the mouth of Jesus she heard these words, "My love for thee was no joke; My service of thee was no mere pretence; it was not at arm's length that I touched thee."

May God grant us the grace to make generous return to Him, who has loved us first.

III. The Fruits of His Sacrifice

In the Epistle of the Mass St. Paul draws a contrast between the blood of the sacrificial victims in the Old Covenant, and the divine Blood, shed by Jesus on Calvary. In the Old Testament everything was type and symbol: in the perishable Temple of Jerusalem countless oblations, every year to be repeated were offered to cleanse from legal impurities. In the New Covenant the High Priest pours out His own Blood, the "precious Blood of the innocent Lamb". "By his own blood he entered once (that is, once for all) into the Holies, having obtained eternal redemption" (*Heb.* 9, 12). This sacrifice of infinite value "cleanses our conscience from dead works (sin) to serve the living God".

"Once for all." To that sacrifice nothing is wanting; it needs no renewal, as if the sacrifice of the Cross had not been all-sufficient. In Holy Mass it is the same sacrifice of the Cross that is offered to the Father by the same High Priest (in whose name the celebrant acts and speaks); and then the infinite fruits of the great Sacrifice of the Cross are distributed to the faithful. All those who assist at Mass share the priest's office of "offering", as the celebrant reminds us when he turns to the people and says, "Pray, brethren, that my sacrifice and yours may prove acceptable to God the Father Almighty."

If we desire during Passiontide to share more intimately in the great Sacrifice, then let us unite all our sufferings, whatever they may be, with the sufferings of the Mystical Body of Christ, and join it all to the oblation, which Christ, through the hands of the priest, offers to His Father.

Prayer: We beseech Thee, O Lord, that these offerings may free us from the bonds of sin, and win for us the treasures of Thy mercy. Through our Lord (Secret of today's Mass).

MONDAY AFTER PASSION SUNDAY

JESUS, SOURCE OF LIVING WATER (John 7, 37-39)

1. It happened on the last, and the most solemn day of the feast of Tabernacles. On that day libations, drawn from the spring of Siloe, were poured out in the Temple, amidst a great concourse of pilgrims, and the joyful singing of Alleluias. Jesus was present in the Temple. When He is teaching the people, He is seated, as was the rabbinical custom. But on this occasion, as St. John states, "Jesus stood and cried, saying, If any man thirst, let him come to me and drink" (*John* 7, 37). These words are pregnant with mystery and with symbolism.

2. *Petition*: The grace to be numbered among those that thirst, and whom Jesus is addressing. May we drink from this source of living water, which is Christ.

I. "If Any Man Thirst"

We know how thirst can torment the body: water is one of the elementary necessities of the human body. Jesus used the figure of thirst in one of the Eight Beatitudes, "Blessed are they that hunger and thirst after justice (that is, after the accomplishment of God's will, or perfection), for they shall have their fill" (*Matt.* 5, 6).

That hunger and thirst consumed the Heart of Jesus. "I am come to cast fire on the earth; and what will I but that it be kindled? And I have a baptism wherewith I am to be baptized: and how I am straitened until it be accomplished!" To the Apostles who, after His conversation with the Samaritan woman, pressed Him to take food He said, "I have meat to eat, which you know not. . . . My meat is to do the will of him that sent me, that I may perfect his work" (*John* 4, 32-34).

"To hunger and thirst after justice," that is a thing which the world fails to understand. An ancient Roman poet speaks of the "accursed thirst for gold"; this thirst is still torturing the human race. Holy Church says in praise of her Saints, "Who is he that hath not gone after gold, nor put his trust in money? Who is he, and we shall praise him? For he hath done wonderful things in his life" (*Ecclus.* 31, 8-9).

"If any man thirst, let him come to me and drink." All those that thirst after righteousness, after salvation, more light, true life, after peace and joy, are invited to approach the fountain of salvation and of true happiness.

"Let him come to me." The invitation is addressed to all, at all times; but they must desire to drink, and desire ardently, and they must go to the fountain. It is not enough to desire half-heartedly, nor to stop at desiring; they must go to Christ, kneel close to the source, and drink full draughts. This we do in Holy Communion.

II. Rivers of Living Water

"If a man believes in me," as the Scripture says, "fountains of living water shall flow from his bosom" (*John* 7, 38, Knox' translation). Jesus is the Spring, whence flow living waters that cleanse, refresh and give strength. He, who through faith and the Sacraments, draws from that spring, will receive from its fullness, and share with others what he has received. "From his bosom": out of his own personal, interior life flows forth this abundant stream, bringing vigor and refreshment to all whom it reaches.

Here a salutary lesson is given to all those that would be apostles, that is, to all Christians in the world, laymen and priests, and in the cloisters, contemplative and active religious. The "living water" is not theirs by nature but Christ is the source. And it flows best if they themselves have drunk deep draughts of it. Modern man, so inclined to spend himself completely in external activities should ever remember the saying of St. Bernard, "In Holy Church there are many channels, but few cisterns", channels of grace wherein no grace flows.

III. Outpouring of the Holy Ghost

"Fountains of living water shall flow from his bosom"; and St. John continues, "Now this Jesus said of the Spirit, which they should receive who believed in him; for as yet the Spirit was not given, because Jesus was not yet glorified" (*John* 7, 39).

Water is a symbol of the Holy Ghost. In eastern lands, notably in Palestine, which borders on the desert, ever threatened by drought, water was far more than with us an obvious symbol of fertility and life. It is the Holy Ghost who pours into the soul spiritual life and spiritual fertility; and the full outpouring of them was to be granted only after Christ had entered into His glory. Therefore Jesus said to his disciples, "It is expedient to you that I go; for if I go not, the Paraclete will not come to you;

but if I go, I will send him to you" (*John* 16, 7). On Pentecost day the Mystical Body of Christ came into being through the abundant outpouring of the Spirit: henceforth it possesses a soul, and is fully equipped. The great work of salvation, initiated by the Father, accomplished by the Son, perfected by the Holy Ghost, continues in the Church till the end of time.

Prayer: Blest Trinity, we praises sing
      To Thee, from whom all graces spring;
      Celestial crowns on those bestow,
      Who conquer by the Cross below.

                                  Vexilla Regis

TUESDAY AFTER PASSION SUNDAY

THE AGONY AT GETHSEMANE

The "Bitter Passion" or the "Blessed Passion" of Jesus (as in certain countries the pious folk are wont to call it) is an inexhaustible fountain of contemplation; and it spurs us on to generosity in the service of God. It is a "hidden treasure", from which strong and spiritually grown up souls may draw. If, to our shame, we have to confess that the grievous sufferings of our Savior leave us cold and unmoved, we are like those little children that can neither understand nor share the boundless grief of their mother who has lost her husband.

      Holy Mother pierce me through,
      In my heart each wound renew
      Of my Savior crucified.

1. In the gloom of night, we behold Jesus, overwhelmed with grief, restlessly seeking assistance from his Father, from his apostles, and finding relief from none. "And being in an agony, he prayed the longer" (*Luke* 22, 43).

2. *Petition*: The grace to watch and pray with Jesus, so that His example may make us strong.

I. The Agony

All these years Jesus had been longing for this hour, and now, when it has struck, He appears distressed. Only a few days before

He had spoken about the grain of wheat that must die in order to bear fruit; on that occasion too his soul was troubled, "Now my soul is troubled, and what shall I say? Father, save me from this hour." But immediately He adds, Nay, "but for this cause I came unto this hour. Father, glorify thy name" (*John* 12, 27-28).

In the garden of Olives, He experiences, as deeply as possible, our human weakness; a collapse, one might call it in all reverence, which implies neither sin nor even any moral imperfection. He is overwhelmed by the imminence of the terrible catastrophe; the stress and tension, caused by the latest events, have utterly exhausted his strength. "For we have not a high priest who cannot have compassion on our infirmities, but one tempted in all things like as we are" (*Heb.* 4, 15). Even this supreme trial Jesus would bear and sanctify.

Fear, anguish, loathing seem to crush Him down; he breaks into cold sweat of agony; He trembles in every member, and in the extremity of His anguish "his sweat became as drops of blood trickling down upon the ground" (*Luke* 22, 44).

His disciples are near by, the three most beloved that have beheld a ray of His glory on Thabor; He had asked them to watch and pray with Him. Lo, they are asleep! His Father in heaven is unresponsive; all alone He has to fight this inward struggle, grappling with something in His Humanity that rebels against pain and suffering.

Here we are face to face with a profound mystery: we may believe that it points to His love for His Father, with whom He is one, and to His love for us, like unto whom He is in all things, sin excepted.

II. The Prayer of Jesus

What else could Jesus do, but what He had always done? He prayed; but now His prayer was a cry of distress, repeated over and over again. Many nights He had spent alone in prayer, on the mountains of Galilee; those were hallowed moments when His "Yea, Father" expressed that close union of wills between Him and the Father. But now, "with a strong cry and tears, in the days of his flesh, he offers up prayers and supplications "to him that is able to save him from death" (*Heb.* 5, 7).

"Father, if thou wilt, remove this chalice from me; but yet not my will be done but thine" (*Luke* 22, 42). It still remains "Yea, Father", but at the cost of a fearful struggle.

The medieval mystic Ruysbroeck writes, "When Jesus came close to His passion, He repeated the same word (not my will, but thine be done), with humility unto complete destruction of His self. To Him, this was the most satisfying, the most loyal word He had ever spoken; to us it was the most profitable, to the Father the most lovable, and to Satan the most confounding."

St. Teresa loved to abide in spirit with Jesus at Gethsemane: "There I could keep Him company, so I thought to myself; there He was so lonely and so forsaken, so overwhelmed with grief and distress, that He surely would permit me to stay close to Him."

God grant that, in times of darkness, and spiritual aridity, we may be mindful of His agony, or when we feel crushed under the weight of a severe trial; that in such moments we may be able to pray the prayer of Jesus, a cry of distress to Him who can save us; that on such occasions we may persevere in prayer, ready to abide by His holy will and trusting in Him. That would bring us closer to God than the sweetest transports of spiritual consolation.

III. The Prayer of Jesus Is Heard

Not quite after the *manner* He had asked, "for by the things he suffered he had to learn obedience," says St. Paul (*Heb.* 5, 8). The chalice is not removed. Even the Father, whose voice He had heard from heaven at the Jordan and on Thabor, now remains silent, and will remain so until Jesus expires on the cross. An angel descended from heaven and comforted Him.

On one occasion before He began His public ministry, Jesus had met an attack of Satan, and had upheld the Father's plan of salvation against the wiles of the devil. And when the evil spirit was defeated, he departed from Him, and "behold angels came and ministered to him". In the Garden Jesus had to fight a fiercer battle, entirely an interior one. Here Satan is not mentioned, but the Scripture tells us of the angel that came to strengthen Him.

And in the end we hear Jesus say, "Arise, let us go", and we behold Him taking the road to Calvary firm, calm, unshakable till the end.

Prayer: Lord Jesus Christ, who in the Garden by word and example hast taught us to pray that we might not enter into temptation, grant us the grace always to be assiduous in prayer, and ever to taste its abundant fruits.

JESUS IS APPREHENDED

1. Bravely Jesus goes forth to meet His captors. Every detail we know about this event shows how completely our Lord dominates the situation. It would seem that the Divinity, which, as St. Ignatius says, is veiled during the Passion, wanted to illumine this dark hour with at least one flash of its brightness before He surrendered Himself.

2. *Petition*: The grace of a deeper understanding of St. Paul's words, "He loved me, and delivered himself for me" (*Gal.* 2, 20).

I. Cruel Humiliation

When Jesus saw the band of soldiers and temple retainers before Him, He said, "You are come out as it were to a robber, with swords and clubs to apprehend me. I sat daily with you, teaching in the temple, and you laid no hands on me" (*Matt.* 26, 55). The noble and delicate soul of Jesus feels keenly hurt by the ignoble manner in which He is being treated. Is He a robber, whom they must surprise in His lair, and arrest while it is dark? And one of His own is acting as leader of this motley crowd; he has brought them to the spot; to make doubly sure, he has given them a sign: the Son of man shall be betrayed with a kiss! "O innocent Lamb," cries St. Anselm, "what hast Thou in common with that wolf?"

And all His disciples leave Him in the lurch. Not long before they had declared, "Let us go and die with him" (*John* 11, 16), a thing which every leader is entitled to expect from his followers. But when put to the test, all flee: truly, the greatest humiliation that can befall a leader. Alas, how often will this humiliation be inflicted on Christ in the course of the centuries!

II. The Divinity Manifests Itself

St. John, whose keen and loving eye has penetrated most deeply into the mystery of His beloved Master, writes, "Jesus therefore, knowing all things that should come upon him, went forth and said to them, Whom seek ye? They answered him, Jesus of Nazareth. Jesus saith to them, I am he.... As soon therefore as he had said to them, I am he, they went backward and fell to the ground."

In the sharpest contrast with this is the divine meekness with which Jesus answers Judas, "Friend, whereto art thou come?", a remonstrance full of love without a trace of hurt feelings.

There follow more signs to show that Jesus dominates the situation. "If ye seek me," He says, "let these go their way." The Shepherd gives His life, but secures that of His Sheep. "Put up thy sword again into its place," He orders Peter, thus safeguarding the purely spiritual character of His mission.

He heals the ear of Malchus: His last miracle, wrought in favor of an enemy.

Once again the Divinity has shown Itself, in order to save not Himself, but others for whom He will freely lay down His life.

III. Jesus Delivers Himself Up to the Soldiers

More than once the Apostles had seen how their Master, at the very last moment, escaped from the hands of those that sought to kill Him. But now the hour had come, the enemy's "hour and the power of darkness" (*Luke* 22, 53).

Meekly He allows them to bind and manacle Him and to lead Him away, "like a lamb among wolves", or "like a sheep that is led to the slaughter".

Henceforth He will tread the path of suffering all alone, surrounded by brutal soldiers who treat Him cruelly; by gloating Pharisees, grimly exulting that at least they have Him in their power; by the rabble of Jerusalem that jeer at Him as an imposter.

Jesus has experienced in the highest degree what the *Imitation of Christ* calls 'the interior banishment' when He cried out on the cross, "My God, my God, why hast Thou forsaken Me?" It is much, and very much, to be able to do without any consolation, human or divine, and to bear patiently this interior banishment, for God's honor' (2 *Imit. of Christ* 9, 1).

Reverently, lovingly, we strive to share the dispositions of Christ's human and divine Heart: in all things He sees the hand of His Father, with whose adorable Will His own will is in the most perfect conformity. Did we not, anon, admire the filial confidence with which he bade Peter sheathe his sword? "Thinkest thou that I cannot ask my Father, and he will give me presently more than twelve legions of angels? How then shall the Scriptures be fulfilled that so it must be done?" (*Matt.* 26, 53-54.)

Let the Father's will prevail; let the Scriptures be fulfilled: thus the powers of darkness be cast out, and thus good shall overcome evil.

Prayer: Lord Jesus, bound and forsaken by all, we behold Thee disappearing in the darkness of the night, betrayed by one who had sat at thy table, abandoned by all Thine own, delivered to the powers of darkness, and "knowing all things that should come upon Thee" (*John* 18, 4). Thou art the Lamb of God, led to the slaughter, whose Blood will cleanse our souls and redeem us. Grant us the grace reverently and lovingly to commemorate Thy Sacred Passion, and in it to find the strength generously to bear our share in Thy sufferings.

THURSDAY AFTER PASSION SUNDAY

JESUS PUBLICLY HUMILIATED

We intend contemplating the Passion of our Lord, not in the order of time, nor episode by episode; each day we will consider a special aspect of the Passion as a whole. This should enable us to penetrate more deeply into the intimate dispositions of our Lord's Heart. Let every one, as St. Ignatius suggests, ask himself the following questions—"What has Christ, my Creator, done for me, a sinner? What have I done for Christ? What ought I to do for Him?"

Jesus so ordains events that His failure may be evident to the whole world.

1. We follow Jesus as they drag Him up and down the crowded streets of Jerusalem. He is utterly exhausted after the frightful night throughout which He was the play-thing of the brutal soldiery.

2. *Petition*: The grace to follow Jesus on His long way of suffering. I beg to offer my humble and loving homage to Him, who is "despised and the most abject of men" (*Isa.* 53, 3).

I. Christ's Wonderful Departure From This World

> "Then he closed in solemn order
> Wondrously His life of woe."

So we sing in the Pange Lingua. In every man's life the beginning and the end are of supreme importance; yet man is master neither of the one nor of the other. For the Son of God made man, such was not the case. The Father (and the Son is one with Him) has, with divine wisdom and love, pre-ordained every detail. The prophets have foretold it centuries before. At least thrice Jesus warned His Apostles of what lay ahead, "Behold, we go up to Jerusalem, and the Son of man shall be betrayed to the chief priests and the scribes, and they shall condemn him to death; and shall deliver him to the Gentiles, to be mocked and scourged and crucified, and the third day he shall rise again" (*Matt.* 20, 18-19).

Everything in the life of the God-man has divine dimensions, a divine meaning, a divine value. An ordinary mortal, if he is given the opportunity, carefully plans what he will say and do during his last hours: that is precisely what Jesus did, with divine omnipotence, and absolute freedom. Let us, therefore, reverently and lovingly contemplate His departure from this life: every detail of which was well planned.

II. Crushing Public Humiliation

The Son of man had chosen to enter this world without any pomp or circumstance: His immaculate Virgin Mother was a humble maiden of the village of Nazareth. After having spent many years in utter obscurity in a Galilean hamlet, He began His public ministry: He had to establish by miracles His claim as the Messiah; but He never courted fame, and deliberately shunned the exuberant manifestations of popular enthusiasm. His kinsmen did not comprehend how one that did such things should not manifest himself to the world (*John* 7, 3-4). He forbids his three favored disciples, to whom he had shown a glimpse of His glory on Thabor, to mention the vision until He shall have risen from the dead, (and until they will have seen Him lying prostrate in agony in the Garden).

But now that failure has overtaken Him, Jesus so directs events that it may not be hidden from any man. He deliberately leaves the obscurity of Galilee, that He may be crucified at Jerusalem. He comes to celebrate the Pasch, whereat He, who is the true Paschal Lamb, is to be slain. For the feast of the Passover, thousands of devout Jews from every corner of the world have come as pilgrims to the Holy City; and they will all be witnesses of the crucifixion and of all that went before. Jesus is apprehended, arrayed before three tribunals: first before the highest religious tribunal of the nation, the Sanhedrin, which condemns Him as a blasphemer; next before the highest political tribunal, before

Pilate, who incarnates the *Majestas Romana*, the might of the greatest world-power, which in a cowardly manner abandons Him to His enemies; lastly before the sensual puppet king Herod, who treats Him like a fool.

Every man and woman in Jerusalem has seen Him stumble through the crowded streets of the city, at first bound and man-acled, later carrying the infamous cross to the hill of Calvary. And there, in full view of the city, He expired nailed to a cross, between two malefactors, bearing above His head the derisive inscription, written by Pilate in three languages, Latin, Greek and Hebrew, This is Jesus, the King of the Jews!

All through the proceedings not one word was uttered in His defence, not one testimony was borne in His favor. His disciples, those men that would go and die with Him, had all vanished during the tragic night, and were in hiding "for fear of the Jews"; their leader, who had had an opportunity of standing up in his Master's defence before Caiphas, had, instead, sworn that "he knew not the man".

Such is the extraordinary manner in which Jesus went forth to His death. It would appear that Providence had minutely or-dained every detail so that the Son of man might, before the whole nation, be humiliated, dishonored and derided as a blasphemer, an impostor, a revolutionary, a false prophet.

Prayer: Jesus, meek and humble of heart, make our hearts like unto thine. Heart of Jesus, saturated with revilings, have mercy on us.

FRIDAY AFTER PASSION SUNDAY

OUR LADY OF DOLORS

Although the feast of our Lady of Dolors, which used to be kept on this Friday, has been suppressed, yet we deem it fit to meditate on this subject, because Mary, more than any one else had a share in the bitter and saving Passion of her Son. Jesus willed that His Mother should be in a very special manner connected with the work of our salvation, even, in a way, associ-ated with it.

1. Mary stands near the cross and hears Jesus saying to her, "Woman, behold thy son! . . . and to the disciple, Behold thy mother" (*John* 19, 26-27).

2. *Petition*: The grace to be given a share in the sufferings of Mary, the grace to understand better her motherhood of men.

I. Mary's Via Dolorosa

By her unconditional *Fiat* at the time of the visit of the Angel, Mary had accepted whatever was implied in being the Mother of the Redeemer. This would be gradually revealed to her and experienced by her.

Gabriel had said that her Son "would be great, the Son of the Most High, seated on the throne of David. . . ." But much had happened to her since that moment: Old Simeon had told her that her Child, who was to reign in the house of Jacob forever, "was set for the fall and the resurrection of many in Israel, and for a sign which shall be contradicted" and "thy own soul a sword shall pierce. . . ." Her destiny will therefore be closely linked with that of her Son, which will be a tragic one. These forebodings she surely has kept in her heart, pondering over them.

During the years of the public ministry Mary remains in the background. That He is "a sign which is contradicted", she learns soon enough, in her neighborhood and from her own kith and kin. Again and again she hears reports of the hostility of the Pharisees; she is aware of the violence of their hatred; she knows they are plotting to take her Sons life. Mary accepts it all, maintaining her *Fiat*, though the sword ever enters deeper into her heart.

These things are not mentioned in the Gospel; nor was there any need to mention them. "The Evangelists supposed that we have common sense," is St. Ignatius' annotation in connection with the meagre details found in the Scriptures concerning Mary. All the more precious, then, to us are the details which St. John supplies in his account of the Passion.

During those days before the Passover Mary was at Jerusalem, and she would thus be a witness of the great tragedy. Did she, after the arrest of our Lord, follow from a distance all the proceedings? Did she hear the mad yells of the mob, "Not this man, but Barrabas". . . "Crucify him!"? They must then have been so many torturing thrusts of the sword penetrating ever more deeply into her soul. Did Jesus meet His Mother along the Via Dolorosa? . . . These are devout surmises to supplement the incomplete Gospel account.

But one thing is absolutely certain: Mary, in the company of John, of Mary Cleophas and of Mary Magdalen, went up to Mount Calvary and stood by the cross of her dying Son. It has all the appearance of a summons from God Himself: When the Word was made Flesh to dwell among us, she had by her *Fiat* called Him down and welcomed Him. The sacrifice whereof that was the beginning is now about to be consummated: she ought, therefore, to be present at its completion too, and by her ultimate *Fiat* to be associated with its final oblation.

II. Christ's Creative Words

"When Jesus therefore had seen His Mother and the disciple standing whom He loved, He said to His Mother, Woman, behold thy son. After that He said to His disciple, Behold thy Mother. And from that hour the disciple took her to his own" (*John* 19, 26-27). Words most painful to hear, but how "blessed" too!

St. Bernard has pointed out to us in burning accents how soul-torturing they must have been for Mary. "What an exchange! In the place of Jesus thou receivest John, the servant instead of the Lord, the disciple in place of the Master, the son of Zebedee to take the place of the Son of God, a mere man in exchange for the true God. How is it possible that at the hearing of those words thy soul should not have been pierced through, since the mere remembrance of them breaks our hearts of stone and steel?"

Painful words to Mary, but how full of solace to us; nay creative words, according to the opinion of many theologians and exegetes. By these simple words, quietly spoken, now that "His hour is come", Jesus in the fullness of His power solemnly appoints Mary Mother of all those who, like John, will believe in Him. Thus in sorrow and pain Mary becomes the Mother of all the living. And so she is forever associated in a unique manner with her Son in the work of redemption, becoming the Mediatrix of all graces.

Just as, "from that moment, the disciple took her to his own", i.e., took her into his house as the Mother of Jesus and his own Mother, so will we give to Mary in our lives the place that is her due as the Mother of Jesus and our own Mother.

III. Mary Unites Her Sacrifice With That of Her Son

At no other moment did Mary feel, live, and suffer so closely in union with her divine Son as when He, utterly surrendering

Himself to the Father, consummated His work of salvation. By a most sublime *Fiat* she associated herself with, and acceded to, the Sacrifice which achieved our and her own redemption. "As Jesus, with arms stretched out on the cross, and His Body naked, offered Himself to the Father a willing victim for our sins, so that nothing remained in Him which was not entirely offered in sacrifice" (*4 Imit. of Christ* 8, 1), so also Mary, standing by the cross, offered herself to the Father, together with her Son and through Him, with all her powers and desires, a pure and holy sacrifice. *Consummatum est.* It is consummated.

Prayer: O God, at whose Passion, as Simeon had prophesied, the most gentle soul of Mary, Thy Virgin Mother, was pierced with a sword of sorrow; mercifully grant through the glorious merits and intercession of all the Saints who loyally stood round Thy Cross, that we, who devoutly recall to mind her transfixion and sorrows, may attain to the happiness won for us by Thy Passion; who livest and reignest. . . . (Collect of today's Mass).

SATURDAY AFTER PASSION SUNDAY

JESUS, THOUGH INNOCENT, SUFFERS PATIENTLY

1. We behold in spirit Jesus during that terrible night. After a preliminary hearing before Caiphas, He is delivered into the hands of cruel and vile underlings. We shudder to think of what befell the Lamb of God.

2. *Petition*: The grace to fathom the feelings of the Heart of Jesus, "patient and rich in mercy". May we, following His example, bear with patience all sufferings of body and soul.

I. Jesus, the Innocent Lamb, Suffers

In Himself, He is "the brightness of eternal light, the unspotted mirror of God's Majesty, and the image of his goodness" (*Wis.* 7, 26). Of Him the Father bore witness, "This is my beloved Son, in whom I am well pleased" (*Matt.* 3, 17). He is the Son of an immaculate Virgin Mother. To His enemies, who reproach Him with being a friend of sinners, He could say, "Which of you shall convince me of sin?" (*John* 8, 46.) The words "He went about doing good" (*Act* 2, 38), sum up His whole life.

When John the Baptist saw Jesus coming to him, he said to the bystanders, "Behold the Lamb of God, behold him who taketh away the sin of the world" (*John* 1, 29). Among all nations the lamb is the symbol of innocence; but here it is in a mysterious manner linked with the name of God and with the sins of the world.

The innocent Lamb of God carries the burden of the sins of mankind. Thus did the Prophet Isaias behold Him, "He hath borne our infirmities and carried our sorrows.... He was wounded for our iniquities, he was bruised for our sins. The chastisement of our peace was upon him and by his bruises we are healed.... The Lord hath laid upon him the iniquity of us all. He was offered because it was his own will, and he opened not his mouth. He shall be led as a sheep to the slaughter, and shall be dumb as a lamb before his shearer.... And the Lord was pleased to bruise him in infirmity.... And he hath borne the sins of many and hath prayed for the transgressors" (53).

St. Paul writes, "Him, who knew no sin, he hath made sin for us" (2 *Cor.* 5, 21). How justice and love were reconciled here, that is Heaven's inscrutable secret. God demands chastisement, and He grants pardon. One in the name of all suffers the penalty of death; and through His death and resurrection we obtain life everlasting.

II. Jesus Suffers With the Patience of the Lamb

"Innocent and meek, as the lamb that is led to the slaughter." The Lamb was to redeem all the sheep. Let us recall to mind some of the events of the Passion: the gentle answer to the treacherous kiss of Judas; the calm and serene question to the cowardly lackey of Caiphas, who had struck Him a blow in the face while He stood bound before the tribunal (*John* 18, 23); the brutality of the soldiery during the long night in the barrack-room; the scourging at the pillar; the crowning with thorns and the cruel mock-homage.... Never a word of reproof nor complaint; always that awesome and perplexing silence. Isaias puts the following words in the mouth of the servant of Jahve, the Messiah, "the man of sorrows acquainted with infirmity": "I have given my body to the strikers, and my cheeks to them that plucked them; I have not turned away my face from them that rebuked me, and spit upon me" (*Isa.* 50, 6).

He allows the powers of darkness, whose hour it now is, to make Him their plaything. He knows they "would not have any power against him, unless it were given to them from above" (*John* 19, 11). We shall esteem this patience more highly when we remember how often a mere glance of His eye, a word from His mouth, have struck terror into His enemies. But then He was the "great Prophet, mighty in word and deed"; now He is the Patient Sufferer, the "one struck by God and afflicted" (*Isa.* 53, 4).

Now He is truly "about His Father's business", and that business is our redemption through His suffering, death and resurrection. That thought filled His mind throughout those dreadful hours. He thought of His Apostles, of us all; He prayed for His executioners, "Father, forgive them, for they know not what they do."

Jesus, the Innocent Victim, was patient in His sufferings; how innocent and how patient! and yet how great were His sufferings!

We, who are guilty, are impatient under suffering! O, how guilty and how impatient! and how little are our sufferings!

Jesus expiated the sins of all. Let us not forget that our sufferings, if united with those of Jesus, possess power to save.

Prayer: Almighty and eternal God, who, in order that all mankind might have His example of humility for their imitation, didst cause our Savior to become man and to suffer on the cross; mercifully grant that we may both keep in mind the lessons of His patience and be made partakers of His resurrection. Who with Thee.... (Collect, Palm Sunday).

PALM SUNDAY

THE TRIUMPHAL ENTRY OF JESUS INTO JERUSALEM
(Matt. 21, 1-9)

1. Today, for a short while, the liturgy lets us turn our eyes away from the sufferings of our Lord. The blessing of palms, the procession, the singing of triumphal hymns, are a symbolic representation of the solemn entry of Jesus into the city of David, and of His victory over death.

   Jesus, seated on the foal of an ass and surrounded by His disciples, rides down the slope of Mount Olivet towards the holy city. As the group advances, a multitude of people joins the procession; they carry palm-branches and cheer the Savior, "Hosanna to the Son of David."

2. *Petition*: We pray that we may understand what is mystically meant by that event, when on this day the crowd, inspired by knowledge from heaven, went forth to meet their Redeemer, and strewed those boughs of palm and olive trees before His feet: The palms signify His triumph over the Prince of Death; and the sprigs of the olive-tree in a manner proclaim the advent of the spiritual unction. (From the Former Blessing of the Palms)

I. Jesus Takes the Initiative

On previous occasions Jesus had always nipped in the bud every attempt of the people to pay Him public homage, lest He encourage the national aspirations of Israel and exacerbate the Pharisees. But now that they have resolved to kill Him, He will before their eyes and in the sight of the whole nation, fulfill the Messianic prophecy, "Tell ye the daughter of Sion, Behold thy King cometh to thee, meek and sitting upon an ass, and a colt, the foal of her that is used to the yoke" (*Matt.* 21, 5).

Jesus takes the initiative by sending two of the disciples to the next village to fetch "a colt, tied, upon which no man yet hath sat"; He allows the disciples to spread their mantles on the animal and He takes His seat upon it. He has resolved to ride triumphantly into the city. So He wills and so it shall be.

II. Homage Paid to the Messiah

The homage, if improvised, is spontaneous, solemn enthusiastic. "And a very great multitude spread their garments in the way; and others cut boughs from the trees and strewed them in the way. And they that went before and they that followed cried 'Hosanna to the son of David: blessed is he that cometh in the name of the Lord: Hosanna in the highest' (*Matt.* 21, 8-9).

Truly a triumphal procession! And Jesus Himself, how modest, how peaceful! As he will say to Pilate, "My kingdom is not of this

Truly a triumphal entry! And Jesus Himself, how modest, how world"; nor is this triumphal entry the cortege of a victorious conqueror. No soldiers line the road, nor are the spoils of war carried before Him; instead of glittering swords we behold boughs of palm trees. Surely it was a feat on the part of Jesus, to have communicated His own spirit to this jubilant multitude, and to have made them, for the moment, assent to the purely spiritual character of his Kingdom, "a Kingdom of truth and life, a Kingdom of holiness and grace, a Kingdom of justice, love and peace!' (Preface, Mass of Christ the King).

Shall we try and fathom the feelings of His Heart during these wonderful hours? He is too great, and He knows too well what is in man, to be carried away by this brief moment of triumph. He is about His Father's business. "Jesu, Rex admirabilis, Et Triumphator nobilis: O Jesus, Thou King so wonderful, How nobly dost Thou triumph!" Teach us, O Lord, to bear for Thy sake both success and failure with equanimity and selflessness.

III. Jesus Weeps Over Jerusalem

"And when he drew near, seeing the city, he wept over it, saying, If thou also hadst known, and that in this thy day, the things that are to thy peace; but now they are hidden from thy eyes. For the days shall come upon thee; and thy enemies shall cast a trench about thee, and compass thee round, and straiten thee on every side; and beat thee flat to the ground, and thy children who are in thee; and they shall not leave in thee a stone upon a stone: because thou hast not known the time of thy visitation" (*Luke* 19, 41-44).

As He rides down the slope of Mount Olivet, the city of Jerusalem comes into full view: the white marble turrets and golden domes of the Temple a-glitter in the rays of the sun. So little is He carried away by the enthusiasm of the cheering multitude, that the sight of the city which five days hence will scornfully reject Him, and which fifty years later will be razed to the ground by the Roman legions, stirs Him to the deepest compassion. Hear the lament from the spurned heart: "If thou hadst known, and that in this thy day." For, the Son of man did love His nation, the chosen people, His country and the holy city of David.

May this sad plaint uttered by Jesus help us to penetrate deeper into His Sacred Heart, a Heart both human and divine, full of goodness and love, patient and rich in mercy, saturated with revilings, crushed for our iniquities.

Prayer: O God, who for our salvation didst send into this world Thy Son, our Lord Jesus Christ, ... grant, we beseech Thee, that for Him we may prepare the way of faith; from which the stone of offence and the rock of scandal being removed, our actions may flourish before Thee with the branches of justice: that we may deserve to follow His footsteps, who with Thee liveth.... (Oration, Former Blessing of the Palms).

JESUS SUFFERS WITH HUMILITY AND DIGNITY

1. We contemplate the Passion of Jesus as a whole, fixing our special attention on those scenes, where we see Him most deeply humiliated, yet commanding our most profound reverence.

2. *Petition*: The grace "that this mind may be in us, which was also in Christ Jesus", that we may acquire it and carefully preserve it.

I. The Lord's Humility

While we strive to keep close to our Savior, as He treads the winepress, we ponder over the words of St. Paul, which reveal unto us the very essence of Christ's whole Being: "Let this mind be in you, which was also in Christ Jesus. Who, being in the form of God, thought it not robbery to be equal with God: but emptied himself, taking the form of a servant, being made in the likeness of men, and in habit found as a man. He humbled himself, becoming obedient unto death, even to the death of the cross" (*Phil.* 2, 5-8).

This is the humility of Christ: the Creator stooping down to serve us, His worthless, sinful creatures, with an incomprehensible, prevenient, unlimited love. That He might raise it up unto Himself, He stooped down, "emptied" Himself, renounced as it were "the form of God", and made Himeslf totally the servant of sinful man. Says a modern writer, "The attitude of the small man who bows before his superior is not humility, it is sheer honesty: humility is the attitude of the great man who bows before the small one. In the eyes of the truly humble what is little has a mysterious dignity. To discern this dignity, to esteem it and bow before it, that is humility" (*Guardini*).

Whether we behold Jesus kneeling before his disciples to wash their feet—He, their Lord and Master; or offering them at table His Body and Blood with the words, Eat, this is my Body; drink, this is my Blood: I give them to you; or allowing Himself to be mocked, spat upon, scourged, crowned with thorns, nailed to the cross—"a worm and no man, the reproach of men and the outcast of the people" (*Ps.* 21, 7) ... in all these things He is serving us. Therein lies the boundless humility of the Word of God made Flesh.

II. With Infinite Dignity

Will it cause astonishment that such a divine humility should be accompanied by a superhuman majesty? At no moment do we gather the impression that the divine Victim outwardly a worm and no man, is inwardly upset or crushed: He never hesitates, never falters, never shows a sign of mental anxiety or uncertainty; but ever serene and deliberate He pursues His steady course through the bustle of petty intrigues that encompass Him on all sides.

Whether He speaks or keeps silent; gives an answer or puts a question of His own; is standing before Caiphas, Pilate, Herod, the mean lackey that slaps Him in the face, the soldiers that scourge Him and crown Him with thorns or the howling mob that clamors for His death; whether He addresses one of the two robbers between whom He hangs on the cross or His Blessed Mother and the beloved disciple who are standing near ... in every case He is fully master of Himself and of the situation, takes all circumstances into consideration, gives the appropriate answer, asks the relevant questions; always we behold Him equally tranquil, unperturbed, dignified.

The Roman Governor, on his judgment seat, looks with awe on the man they have brought before him: outwardly He is a woeful wreck of a man; yet Pilate, an unprejudiced and shrewd judge of human nature, is deeply impressed by His supreme moral greatness, and for a moment shudders before this accused who is so calm and so serene. Never had he understood so well the truth of the saying of Seneca, his contemporary: "Res sacra, miser: a being worthy of pity is a sacred thing".... But the woe of *this* pitiable man had a divine halo about it.

On the other hand, we do not detect in Jesus the faintest trace of "offended dignity", of contemptuous pride, such as might come naturally enough to a man who is unjustly condemned by judges of whose meanness and hypocrisy he is fully aware.

Compare his behavior with that of Socrates: conscious of his moral superiority and of his innocence, the philosopher irritated and defied his judges. Jesus too is innocent, He is the embodiment of Innocence but He is also conscious of being the Lamb of God who bears the burden of our sins; therefore it behooved Him to remain humble and meek till the very end. Those eyes that on certain other occasions had blazed with indignation were now downcast or kept closed; if He happened to raise them, nothing else could His judges or His executioners have read in them than sadness and compassion, "Father, forgive them, for they know not what they do."

St. Ignatius bids us consider how, "in the mysteries of the Passion the Divinity veils itself, i.e., how It could destroy Its enemies but will not do so, and how It lets the most sacred Humanity of Christ endure the most cruel tortures". But that very veil now and then lets through a refulgence that can come only from the hidden Divinity. No man has ever suffered in the manner the God-man suffered—with such boundless meekness and such incomparable dignity. Says Pascal, "Great is the pomp and marvellous the splendor wherewith He appears to the eyes of the heart, which can discern Supreme Wisdom."

Prayer: Jesus, meek and humble of heart, make our hearts like unto Thine. Teach us to suffer meekly and with dignity.

TUESDAY IN HOLY WEEK

JESUS TREADS THE WINEPRESS ALONE, YET HE WAS IN TOUCH WITH ALL MANKIND

1. The loneliness of Jesus began when His disciples abandoned Him in the Garden, to the vengeance of His enemies and it reached its highest point on the Cross, when it tore from His Heart the cry of distress, "My God, my God, why hast Thou forsaken me? (*Mark* 15, 34.)

2. *Petition*: That, full of reverence and compassion, we may remain close to Jesus in this "interior banishment", and find in it the strength to bear with fortitude the trial of loneliness if God sends it to us for our chastisement.

I. One For the Sake of All

Caiphas, the high-priest of that year, had arrived at the conclusion that Jesus must be done away with: from the stand-point
of religion as well as of politics He had made Himself intolerable.
On the one hand He was undermining the authority of the rulers
with the people; on the other, He had gained so powerful an
influence on the masses that at any moment He could start a rebellion against the Romans.

"If we let Him alone," the chief priests and the pharisees said,
"all will believe in Him; and the Romans will come and take
away our place and nation. . . . But one of them, named Caiphas,
being the high-priest of that year, said to them, You know nothing;
neither do you consider that it is expedient for you that one man
should die for the people and that the whole nation perish not.
(And this he spoke not of himself: but being the high-priest of
that year, he prophesied that Jesus should die for the nation.
And not only for the nation, but to gather together in one the
children of God that were dispersed") (*John* 11, 47-52).

How very true those words have proved to be, "One shall die
for the sake of all"! Though the high-priest was not aware of it,
his words, dictated by mere politics and evil intention, took on a
spiritual and world-wide meaning: they did but promulgate the
eternal divine decree which was about to receive its glorious
fulfillment.

Puny and short-sighted man frames his own wicked plans:
"Why have the Gentiles raged and the people devised vain things?
The kings of the earth stood up, and the princes met together,
against the Lord and against His Christ. . . . He that dwelleth in
heaven shall laugh at them, and the Lord shall deride them"
(*Ps.* 2: 1, 2, 4). No man can elude the almighty grasp of the
infinitely wise, infinitely good, infinitely merciful God: "To them
that love Him, He makes all things work together unto good"
(*Rom.* 8, 28).

II. Jesus Bears His Sufferings Alone

Of necessity, Jesus was lonely all His life. "He dwelt amongst
us", but to understand Him was not possible to anyone, not even
to His Apostles, nay nor to His holy Mother. In starker loneliness
He suffered, in utter loneliness He died.

During His Agony He had no one to watch with Him. From His
arrest onward He beheld around Him only faces distorted with

hatred and envy. The Liturgy of Matins makes Him say, "I have trodden the winepress alone ... and I have looked for one that would grieve with me: but there was no one" (*Ps.* 68, 21). On the way to Calvary one man was found, or rather 'compelled', to help Him carry the cross: and the Gospel further mentions "women who bewailed and lamented Him" as He passed carrying His cross. Besides that, Christian piety beholds Veronica boldly making her way through the crowd and wiping the blood, sweat and dirt off His sacred countenance, and an ancient tradition permits us to believe that His Mother met Him while He carried His cross. But in His innermost heart, where no one—not even His Mother—could penetrate, He ever remained totally alone.

Then shortly before He expired on the Cross, this abysmal loneliness reached its greatest depths. Before the Passion He had said to His apostles, "Behold, the hour comes that you shall leave me alone, and yet I am not alone; the Father is with me" (*John* 16, 32). But now the hour has struck when even the Father seems to abandon Him: We hear Him crying with a loud voice, "My God, my God, why hast Thou forsaken me?" This is indeed an awful mystery. How close to the brink of eternal banishment did the Father in fact lead His beloved Son, who was "to redeem us from the curse by being made a curse for us"? (*Gal.* 3, 13.)

III. Jesus in His Sufferings Was Reaching Out to All Men

His sufferings benefited all men. Everything in Jesus was 'given in partnership' to all men. All He was, all He had, all He did was given to be imparted to us—without any consideration for Himself; everything without reserve ... up to the very last drop of His Blood; His whole human nature, and through His human nature His divine nature too. . . .

Ruysbroeck calls Him "the lover of each and every man". "Consider now," he writes, "how Christ gave Himself to all by complete surrender. His ardent Sacerdotal Prayer was addressed to the Father in favor of all that should be saved. He reached out to the universality of men in His love, His teaching, His rebukes; in solacing gently, in giving liberally, in pardoning mercifully and compassionately. His soul and body, His life and death, His labors and toil were, and are still being passed on to all. Whenever He as much as partook of food or drink to sustain His Body, He intended thereby to bring blessings to the universality of those that would live, until the end of the world. He considered nothing as His exclusive possession, but whatever was His, He made it ours too: His body and soul, His Mother and disciples, His garments and cloak. He ate and drank for our sake, He lived and died for our sake. . . . His sorrows and sufferings alone, and His destitution, did He claim for Himself; but all the advantage and the benefit that accrued from them He bestows on us, and the glory of His merits shall be shared by all forever and ever."

Prayer: Grant, Almighty and everlasting God, that we may so celebrate the mysteries of the Passion of our Lord as to deserve to obtain the remission of our sins. Through the same. . . . (Collect, today's Mass.)

WEDNESDAY IN HOLY WEEK

JESUS OBEDIENT UNTO DEATH

1. We keep close to Jesus throughout all His sufferings; we enter into the sentiments of His Sacred Heart, which all along remains faithful to His "Yea, Father", until He declares, "It is consummated."

2. *Petition*: The grace to fathom better the mystery of the great work of salvation, which is being accomplished before our eyes; and to see how obedience is the hall-mark of Christ-like actions.

I. Yea, Father. . . !

This is the "saving word" that has been on the lips and in the Heart of Jesus throughout His life. When He enters this world, the Prophet makes Him say, "sacrifice and oblation thou wouldst not; but a body thou hast fitted to me. Holocausts for sin did not please thee. Then I said, Behold, I come: in the head of the book it is written of me that I should do thy will, O God" (*Ps.* 39; *Heb.* 10, 5-7).

The world into which Jesus enters is a sinful world, which has been estranged from God through disobedience. The holocausts of the Old Covenant are powerless to effect a reconciliation; and so, Jesus comes to replace and complete them. He is "the Lamb of God that takes away the sins of the world" once and forever, through His death on the cross and His rising from the grave. The entire life of Christ, then, from the cradle to the cross, will be one continuous exercise of the virtue of obedience: the Will of the Father, "to be about His Father's business", will be His only concern. "My meat is to do the will of him that sent me" (*John* 4, 34), "Yea, Father, for so it hath seemed good in thy sight" (*Matt.* 11, 26). This absolute conformity of will with the Father is the root from which grow all His actions and endeavors.

II. "He Learned Obedience"

The expression is St. Paul's: "Who in the days of his flesh, with a strong cry and tears, offering up prayers and supplications to him that was able to save him from death, was heard for his reverence. And whereas indeed he was the Son of God, he learned obedience by the things he suffered" (*Heb.* 5, 7-8).

All the days of His life, He never lost sight of Calvary and of the cross. His voice sounded grave, and hinted at dark forebodings, when He asked the sons of Zebedee, "Can you drink the chalice that I shall drink?" (*Matt.* 20, 22.) On another occasion He saw the chalice as a baptism, "I have a baptism, wherewith I am to be baptized; and how am I straitened until it be accomplished" (*Luke* 12, 50).

As the fatal day draws closer, we get the impression that His human nature recoils from suffering. A couple of days before the final catastrophe (possibly under the impression of what He beholds as imminent), Jesus speaks of the grain of wheat that must fall into the earth and die, in order to bear fruit: suddenly He interrupts Himself and remarks, "Now is my soul troubled, and what shall I say? Father, save me from this hour. . . . But for this cause I came unto this hour. Father, glorify thy name" (*John* 12, 24-28).

What at that time He would not do, He will indeed do during the dreadful night at Gethsemane, "with a strong cry and tears" "Father, if it be possible, let this chalice pass from me. Nevertheless, not as I will, but as thou wilt" (*Matt.* 26, 39). This is still "Yea, Father", but not quite spontaneously; here He is indeed "like unto us" as far as He can be, "sin excepted". He does hold fast onto the will of His Father, but it is at a frightful cost. "He learnt obedience," says St. Paul: and at which other school could He learn it than at fallen man's school of suffering? O Lord Jesus, we love Thee all the more, because for our salvation and to leave us an example, Thou hast deigned to learn at that school.

III. Obedient Unto Death

After the agony, where He has experienced the weakness of the flesh, He rises, comforted in spirit: and goes to meet His death, unerringly obedient to the will of the Father. He could still ask the Father to send Him twelve legions of angels; but He refrains from that. How then should the Scriptures be fulfilled that it must be so? (*Matt* 26, 54.)

"It must be so." Thus has the mysterious and unfathomable decree of His Father ordained. And this decree the Son, in the fullness of His freedom, unalterably obeys, through the most atrocious torments and the most crushing humiliations, holding on to His "Yea, Father", even in those moments of darkest void that wrested from His Heart the loud cry, "My God, my God, why hast thou forsaken me!"

Having been obedient unto death, even to the death of the cross, He can bear witness to Himself, "Consummatum est, It is consummated." Then, trustfully turning to His Father, He adds, "Father, into thy hands I commend my spirit." "And bowing his head, he gave up the ghost" (*John* 19, 30).

Prayer: Look down, we beseech Thee, O Lord, upon this Thy family, for which our Lord Jesus Christ was willing to be delivered into the hands of the wicked, and to undergo the torment of the Cross; He, who with Thee liveth.... (Prayer over the people on this day).

MAUNDY THURSDAY

THE INSTITUTION OF THE BLESSED SACRAMENT

1. "Sui moras incolatus, Miro clausit ordine: Then He closed in solemn order, Wondrously His life of woe". Wondrously, i.e., by the institution of the new Pasch, the Holy Eucharist.

   Jesus has gathered the Twelve around Himself, to eat the Pasch with them before He suffers. This is the "Last Supper", and the very first distribution of Holy Communion. We are present in the large upper room, the "Cenacle", lent by a friend of the Lord; an atmosphere of sadness seems to fill the place.

2. *Petition*: To fathom with reverence and faith the "Sacra Mysteria", the holy mystery of the most intense love that ever consumed a heart.

I. The Last Lesson

As the fatal hour draws closer, every word, and every action of Jesus seems pregnant with a more profound meaning. As the Twelve were going to recline at the supper table there had been among them some contention as to who should occupy the places of honor. Jesus, who more than once had rebuked them for their petty ambitions, resolved to give them a last practical lesson. And when the hour was come, "knowing that the Father had given him all things into his hands, and that he came from God, and goeth to God, he riseth from supper, and layeth aside his garments, and having taken a towel, girded himself. After that, he putteth water into a basin, and began to wash the feet of the disciples, and to wipe them with the towel, with which he was girded" (*John* 13, 2-5). To wash a guest's feet on arrival was the task of a slave.

The Twelve, Judas included, now behold their Master, "in the form of a servant", kneeling before each of them and washing their feet. A modern writer observes: "This He did, not to renounce His dignity, but to reveal unto them the divine mystery of humility" (Guardini).

This touching incident is narrated in the Gospel of today's Mass. From ancient times the liturgy ordained that the "Washing of the feet" be performed in church on Holy Thursday during the night office. This ceremony was called "the Mandatum, the Lord's command". "Then, after he had washed their feet and taken his garments, he sat down again and said to them, Know you what I have done to you? . . . If I being your Lord and Master, have washed your feet, you also ought to wash one another's feet. . . . If you know these things, you shall be blessed if you do them" (*John* 13, 12-17). Here for the last time, Jesus proclaims blessed all those who, out of love for Him and for His brethren, dedicate their lives to the humble service of the neighbor.

II. The Institution of the Holy Eucharist

The circumstances: The Canon of the Mass on this day expresses the connection between the Passion and the institution of the Holy Eucharist, in the following terms: "Gathered together in spiritual fellowship, we commemorate this most holy day, on which our Lord Jesus Christ was delivered up for us . . . Who, on the day before He suffered on behalf of us and all mankind, that is on this day, took bread into His holy and venerable hands. . . ."

Jesus fulfills the terms of His mission: "I am not come to destroy, but to fulfill" (*Matt.* 5, 17). The new Pasch wonderfully completes the old. He Himself is the true Paschal Lamb, that shall be slain to deliver us from the bondage of sin.

The institution bears the unmistakable stamp of the divine mode of acting: outwardly, i.e., for what the senses perceive, everything is most simple; no idle display; nothing sensational. The words uttered by Jesus, the materials He uses, His gestures, His whole behavior and attitude, it is all simple and commonplace. But what actually occurs is awe-inspiring and bewildering. What was bread is now the Body of Christ; what was wine is now His Blood. Under the species of bread and wine the Apostles truly eat their Master's Flesh and drink His Blood. "Mysterium fidei, a mystery of faith": these words—an exclamation of wonder and a profession of faith—were inserted by Holy Church in the formula of consecration at Holy Mass.

God alone can operate in a manner at once so simple and so omnipotent. The Creator alone can in such a quiet way alter so profoundly the very substance of material things. We believe, O Lord, and we adore.

How humble in its origin was the sacrificial rite which Holy Church, Christ's Mystical Body, was to evolve so magnificently in the course of the centuries!

III. The Meaning

Every word and every action of Jesus has a divine and therefore an inscrutable meaning; but these last words and actions at the Supper, what an inexhaustible subject they offer for devout consideration. They are "Sacra Mysteria, Holy mysteries", which the Church celebrates every day.

After uttering the mysterious words of consecration, Jesus had added, "Do this for a commemoration of me" (*Luke* 22, 19), a commemoration of Himself, of His sufferings and His love. The bread had become the body "which shall be delivered", the wine was now the Blood "which shall be shed": and thus the Eucharist and the death on the cross become one and the same sacrifice.

"Greater love than this no man hath, that a man lay down his life for his friends" (*John* 15, 13). That excess of love Jesus showed towards us. Love craves for union: When He was departing from this world, our Lord devised a means to abide with us and in us, and we in Him; each one of us united to Him, and all of us united together in Him.

In the solemn evening Mass of this day we shall celebrate those "Sacred Mysteries" and, as He commanded us, we shall remember Him, Him and His toil and travail, Him and His love "unto the end".

Prayer: O Holy Lord, Father Almighty, Everlasting God, we pray that our Sacrifice may be rendered acceptable to Thee by Jesus Christ Himself, Thy Son, our Lord, who on this day directed His disciples to offer It for a remembrance of Him: Who liveth and reigneth.... (Secret of today's Mass).

GOOD FRIDAY

VEXILLA REGIS PRODEUNT, FULGET CRUCIS MYSTERIUM

BEHOLD, THE ROYAL ENSIGNS FLY,
BEARING THE CROSS'S MYSTERY

1. Today's liturgical color is black; yet during the adoration of the cross the Church sings, "By this wood has joy come to the whole world." While with the entire congregation we pay homage to the cross, we meditate with wonder and gratitude on "the mystery of the cross".

2. *Petition*: We pray for the grace to draw light, strength and confidence from the cross of our Lord Jesus Christ.

I. The Mystery of the Cross

This mystery has "the breadth and length, and height, and depth of the charity of Christ, which surpasseth all knowledge" (*Eph.* 3, 18-19). There is superabundant matter for meditation, wonder and grateful praise in the thought that here Good conquered evil through love.

The mystery of the cross is a mystery of weakness, of impotence, of consummate failure: Jesus is betrayed, denied, condemned as a blasphemer and sedition-monger, mocked as a fool.

A mystery of God's power: "And I, if I be lifted up from the earth, will draw all things to myself" (*John* 12, 32). By His death on the cross He overcomes powers which till then had ruled supreme: the prince of the world, sin and death.

A mystery of foolishness: To the Gentiles, who search for wisdom, a crucified God is foolishness; more so His resurrection, which is sheer absurdity.

A mystery of divine Wisdom: "It is written, I will destroy the wisdom of the wise; and the prudence of the prudent I will reject" (1 *Cor.* 1, 19). The wisdom of the Greeks has only scorn for Christian wisdom; yet the day comes when the latter will illumine the former.

A mystery of wickedness: Was it possible that men could treat so ignominiously Him, who not only was absolutely guiltless, but also infinitely good? How could they prefer Barabbas to Him? These were not the deeds of human beings, but the works of the prince of darkness, of Satan himself.

A mystery of righteousness: Man, who had rebelled against God, owed his Creator a debt, which he could not pay. Jesus assumed the burden and paid our debt on the cross. "He blotted out the handwriting of the decree that was against us, which was contrary to us. And he hath taken the same out of the way, fastening it to the cross" (*Col.* 2, 14).

It is a mystery of deadly hatred and of life-giving love.

II. Until the End of Time

Still in our own day the cross is to the world a stumbling block, and utter foolishness (1 *Cor.* 1, 24). To worldlings Christ and His Cross are the enemies of life, the destroyers of earthly enjoyment. Even in many a Christian land the Crucifix is ordered to be removed from schools, judgment halls and hospital wards. In his epistle to the Philippians St. Paul mourned over those Christians who behaved "as enemies of the cross of Christ... whose god is their belly" (*Phil.* 2, 18-19).

On Good Friday the solemn adoration of the cross is held in all the churches: the whole congregation, the entire family, offer public homage to the cross, which has been just unveiled by the celebrant and is displayed for the veneration of all.

During this moving ceremony we should ponder over the place we give to the cross in our personal life: how eagerly we embrace it, when in the shape of trials, it is offered to us, how patiently we carry it, whether we truly tread the "Royal Road of the Holy Cross", of which *The Imitation of Christ* speaks with such unction.

"If any man will come after me, let him deny himself and take up his cross daily and follow me" (*Luke* 9, 23). "He has gone before you, carrying His cross, and died for you upon the cross, that you too might have strength to carry your cross, and be willing to die upon the cross. . . . In the cross is salvation, in the cross is life, in the cross is sure protection from enemies, in the cross is an abundance of heavenly delight, in the cross is courage, in the cross is gladness of heart, in the cross is height of virtue, in the cross is perfection of sanctity." (2 *Imit. of Christ* 12, 2.)

The cross is the symbol of love, of suffering and salvation: "Then shall appear the sign of the Son of Man in heaven. . . . Then shall all the tribes of the earth see the Son of Man coming in the clouds of heaven with much power and majesty" (*Matt.* 24, 30). . . . In what measure "the tribes of the earth" and each individual human being shall have paid homage to, or rejected, Christ and His cross, in that measure they will, on that day and throughout eternity, rejoice or lament.

"The Cross stands; the world moves on." Such is the trustful and triumphal motto of the Carthusian Order.

Prayer: Hail, Cross; our hope, on thee we call,
Who keep this mournful festival.
Grant to the just increase of grace,
And every sinner's crimes efface.
Blest Trinity! we praises sing
To Thee, from whom all graces spring;
Celestial crowns on those bestow,
Who conquer by the Cross below. (*Vexilla Regis*)

HOLY SATURDAY

WITH MARY, THE MOTHER OF THE LORD

1. Since the memorable restoration of the Easter Vigil, Holy Saturday is the most silent day of the liturgical year. In his

thirty days' "Spiritual Exercises" St. Ignatius makes his exercitant devote a whole day to the consideration of the loneliness of our Lady, after she had come down from Calvary and retired to a house in Jerusalem. We shall endeavor to spend this day in Mary's company, to suffer with her because of the death of her Son, and also to feel comforted with her because man's redemption has been accomplished and the resurrection is close at hand.

2. *Petition*: We ask through Mary's intercession for the abovementioned graces.

I. Mary's Grief

When, forty days after His birth, Mary was bringing her Child to the Temple of Jerusalem to offer Him to God, the aged Simeon had said to her in prophecy, "And thy own soul a sword shall pierce" (*Luke* 2, 35). These words Mary kept in her heart; and many a time, during the hidden life and still more, during the years of the public ministry, she must have felt the thrust of the sword entering deeper into her soul. On Calvary the tragic death of her Son brought the ultimate fulfillment of the ominous prophecy.

Before her very eyes the dead Body was taken down from the cross, and for the last time laid on her lap, before "they bound it in linen clothes with the spices", and that very night carried it to the "new sepulchre wherein no man yet had been laid". The funeral procession consisted of two men, who carried the sacred Burden, and two women, who wanted to see where they laid the Body. So far the Gospel narrative.

Our thoughts may go back to that large procession which Jesus met one day at the gates of Naim; and help us to realize how pitiable *this* burial was.

St. Bernard objects, "But, did Mary not know that Jesus was to die?"; and he answers, "Indeed she did know. Did she not believe that He would rise again? She firmly believed, and her faith was strong as the rock. And did she nevertheless mourn for His death on the cross? She mourned, more than any other mother had ever mourned. But who art thou, my learned brother, and whence hast thou drawn thy wisdom, which wonders at Mary's compassion and not at the sufferings of her Son?"

"Great as the sea is thy destruction. Who shall heal thee?" (*Lam.* 2, 13.) Such are the words of the prophet Jeremias, wherewith Holy Church addresses the Mother of Sorrows. But Mary does not grieve "as others who have no hope" (1 *Thess.* 4, 13).

II. Mary's Faith

In those far away days, when Mary had gone into the mountain-country to visit her cousin, Elizabeth had proclaimed her blessed because she had believed the prodigious message of the angel, that "She was to bear a Son and yet would remain a virgin. Her Son would be called the Son of the Most High; and the Lord would give unto Him the throne of his father David, and he was to reign in the house of Jacob for ever. And of his kingdom there shall be no end" (*Luke* 1, 31-33).

How all this would be realized she did not understand. Indeed, keeping all these words faithfully in her heart, and pondering over them, she had shared the whole life of Jesus, failing on many occasions to understand, notably when Jesus remained in the Temple.

How, then, could she have witnessed His tragic end, and His ignominious death on the cross, without undergoing her own inward agony—a deadly struggle to preserve her faith unimpaired through such grievous trial? May we not think and say that she too was like unto us in all things, sin excepted? And that she too, like Her Son, "learnt by the things she suffered to obey and to believe"? (*Heb.* 5, 8.) Blessed is she who has believed unto the end!

III. The Apostles Around Mary

Comforted by the reflection that her Son's death on the cross had accomplished the salvation of mankind, and supported by her certitude that on the third day He would rise again, Mary wended her way back to the City, where John "took her into his own". Around her (so we are entitled to think) the scattered sheep of the stricken Shepherd soon came together again. For, where could Peter, for instance, have gone for comfort and encouragement except to John his bosom-friend, and to the Mother of his Master? And so must the other apostles have done. The Gospels are silent about all this; but there were so many reasons why the Apostles should have been anxious to seek out Mary: They must have longed to condole with her; and besides, bewildered as they were, they must have been drawn irresistibly to the side of her who had known the Master so much better and so much longer than any of them. Could she, perhaps throw some light on their problem?

In truth, Mary did know Jesus more intimately than they did, and her faith was incomparably stronger. Moreover, now that, by the last will and disposition of her dying Son, she had been appointed mother not of John only but of all those that would believe in Him, it was her office and her privilege to impart to them her firm faith and her unshakable confidence; to comfort and prepare them for the hour of triumph that was imminent.

Prayer: Pour forth, we beseech Thee, O Lord, Thy grace into our hearts: that we, to whom the Incarnation of Christ Thy Son was made known by the message of an angel, may by His Passion and Cross be brought to the glory of His resurrection; through the same Christ our Lord. Amen. (Prayer after the *Angelus*.)

THE RESURRECTION OF OUR LORD

1. The Easter Vigil, so replete with mystery and sacred symbolism, has given us an insight into the drama of our salvation. We have celebrated the 'novum Pascha', the new Passover: the passing from darkness into light, from sin to grace, from death to life, which has been triumphantly accomplished in the risen and immortal Christ, our Lord and our Brother through His humanity; but this is still to be fulfilled in us.

2. *Petition*: Grant, O Lord, to us and all Christians that the renovation which we have celebrated may henceforth inspire every thought and action of our daily life.

I. The Resurrection: The Fact

The event bears the hallmark of the all-powerful intervention of God's omnipotence. The resurrection itself took place in profound stillness, in deepest secrecy; how else could it have been effected? "O truly blessed night, which alone didst deserve to know the time and the hour when Christ arose from the dead!" thus sings Holy Church in a transport of spiritual joy. Behind the heavy seal-secured stone and the sleeping guards, the Soul of Christ was re-united with His Body; and the glorified Savior passed quietly out of our matter-bound world, just as He had entered it quietly at the Virgin's *Fiat*. At His coming Mary had perforce to be present; at His resurrection no one is present: no one is needed.

The earthquake, the stone being rolled back, the terror-stricken guards, the angels standing near the empty tomb, these are mere adventitious happenings to give indications that the wonder has taken place. "God's ways are unsearchable" always, but above all in His manner of geing born from a virgin and of rising from the grave. We believe, and humbly adore.

We are not able to form in our minds a correct picture of the risen Savior: His sacred Body is a truly human body, now more intimately animated by His Soul and His Divinity than "in the days of his flesh", rid of the shackles of matter, immortal, spiritualized. The Man-Christ has now entered the glory of His Father. Christ ought to suffer and so to enter his glory (*Luke* 24, 26). In a human way of speaking, Jesus is now more than ever "the beloved Son, in whom the Father is well pleased".

We intensely rejoice with Christ, and congratulate Him on the ineffable bliss which now overwhelms His humanity: "Thou alone art holy; Thou alone art the Lord; Thou alone art most high, O Jesus Christ; together with the Holy Ghost in the glory of the Father. Amen."

II. The Implications of the Resurrection

Jesus always gave the resurrection as the conclusive proof that the Father had sent Him and that His doctrine was true. Whenever He foretold His Passion and death, the conclusion would be, "and on the third day I shall rise from the dead". To the fact of the resurrection the Apostles bear testimony and it constitutes the corner-stone of their teaching: "If Christ be not risen again, then is our preaching vain, and your faith is also vain" (1 *Cor.* 15, 8). God does not prove by arguments which the worldly-wise understand; He proves by facts: a Christ that was crucified. died, was buried, and rose back to life. When Paul preached this doctrine at Athens, the wise men of Greece shrugged their shoulders at what they deemed nonsense, and summarily dismissed the Apostle.

But "unto them that are called" the resurrection of Christ "is

the power of God and the wisdom of God" (1 *Cor.* 1, 24). Christ
has vanquished His enemies: sin, death and Satan.

As we sang during the Easter Vigil, "He has destroyed sin. . . .
He has broken the chains of sin." And today the Sequence of the
Mass exults, "For the sheep the Lamb has bled, sinless, in the
sinners' stead. Christ, the Victim undefiled, Man to God hath
reconciled."

Death has been vanquished: "Then in strange and awful strife
Met together Death and Life. He that life to sinners gives, After
dying rose and lives." When they beheld Him in agony on the
cross, the chief priests had challenged Him, "Let him come
down from the cross and we will believe him" (*Matt.* 27, 42);
He does infinitely more, but not in the spectacular manner they
demanded: He breaks the fetters of death, He rises alive from
the tomb.

And the arch-enemy who had brought sin and death into the
world, Satan, the prince of this world, who for a brief while
seemed to have won the victory, is now "shamefully cast out",
and his kingdom is destroyed.

In the risen Christ the victory is complete and final. St. Paul
says, "Christ is risen from the dead, the first-fruit of men that
sleep" (1 *Cor.* 15, 20); in Christ everything is for us, for our
profit an example to us and a sacred pledge. "By baptism" says
St. Paul, "we are buried together with Christ, we die to sin, are
raised up with Christ, that we may walk in newness of life." That
is why, during the early centuries of the Church, catechumens
used to receive Baptism during the Easter Vigil; for the same
reason, the new Paschal ritual ordains that during the Easter
Vigil the entire congregation shall renew their baptismal vows.

In our souls the victory is more than begun, since the triumph
is assured if we abide in Christ through lively faith and loyal
love: victory over sin; and one day, when the Lord shall come,
victory over death, our last enemy, "when the enemy, death,
shall be destroyed" (1 *Cor.* 15, 26).

All these things we commemorate on Easter Day, the Solemnity of Solemnities. "This is the day, which the Lord hath made;
let us be glad and rejoice therein" (*Ps.* 117, 24).

Prayer: O God, who on this day, through Thine only-begotten
Son, didst overcome death, and open to us the gates of everlasting
life: as by Thy preventing grace Thou dost breathe good desires

into our hearts, so also by Thy gracious help bring them to good effect. Through our Lord (Collect of today's Mass).

APPARITION TO THE DISCIPLES OF EMMAUS (Luke 24, 13-35)

1. Some time in the afternoon of Easter day two disciples, who had loved Jesus dearly, were returning to their village, called Emmaus, about two hours' walk from Jerusalem. They were sorely disappointed, and naturally they could speak only of the thing that was uppermost in their heart. After a while a stranger overtook them, and gradually took part in the conversation.

2. *Petition*: The grace to allow Jesus, who often is our fellow-traveller on our way to heaven, to operate in our souls, so that He may relieve us of what depresses us and that He may impart His own joy and peace to us.

I. Doubt and Darkness

From what they tell the stranger it is clear that they were profoundly attached to Jesus, "who was a prophet mighty in word and work before God and all the people". They were, however, still more attached to their erroneous prejudices concerning the Messiah: "We hoped that it was He that should have redeemed Israel." And now He had died and been buried: it had all been a vain dream. True, this morning the tomb had been found empty; but He Himself had not been seen.

In two words St. Gregory sketches the feelings of these disappointed men, "amabant, dubitabant: they loved, but they doubted". They could not possibly cease thinking of Him, and they did not see how any man could have aught else on his mind; but neither could they rid themselves of their narrow Messianic notions and keep their minds open to different possible interpretations of the events. Against the very dawning of the healing truth, their eyes were completely shut.

Deeply discouraged then, they were returning to their village and to the drab realities of everyday life, somewhat like the rich young man who lacked the courage to accept the Lord's invitation and walked away sad.

II. Gradual Enlightenment

The two disciples owe their rescue to the Good Shepherd, who went in search of the straying sheep and brought them back to the fold. Yet they provided Him with a means of contact: their conversation was all about Him; they gladly admit Him into their company and let Him join in the conversation; they readily answer His questions.

He allows them fully to unburden themselves, but anon He bluntly gives them a piece of His own mind, "O foolish, and slow of heart in believing all the things which the prophets have spoken! Ought not Christ to have suffered these things, and so to enter into His glory?" (*Luke* 24, 25-26.) Rather stern words . . . but the disciples were not hurt, for they were at once impressed by the earnestness of the Stranger. "And beginning at Moses and all the prophets, He expounded to them in all the scriptures the things that were concerning Him." And while He thus walked along by their side, and unveiled to them the great mystery to which hitherto their hearts and their minds had remained closed, their eyes gradually perceived the light and their hearts grew warm within them, as they later on confessed. The risen Savior, through the grace which He pours into their hearts, now began to come back to life in their souls too. "He cleansed them thoroughly from every taint of their old nature and fitted them to receive a holy newness" (Prayer over the People, Tuesday of Holy Week).

Even in our own days our Lord operates in our souls in the same manner: Again and again He assists us to grope our way through the profound mystery that comforts us in the life of His Church and in our own individual lives, through the mystery of suffering and humiliation to victory. Let us be attentive and listen to His voice when, under some disguise or other, He teaches us along the road: then our hearts also will burn within us, if we readily and confidently open them to His working.

III. The Final Revelation

They have listened with rapt attention to the stranger's explanations. Meanwhile they have reached Emmaus, and Jesus "made as if he would go further". This provides them with the opportunity to show their excellent dispositions and to perform an act of kindness. "They constrained him saying, Stay with us, because it is towards evening and the day is now far spent. And he went in with them."

St. Gregory has a bit of advice for us at this stage: "Do you wish to understand (more fully) what you have heard? Then hasten to put into practice as much as you have understood." Such practical applications are themselves a source of light: do not demand to receive by anticipation the light that can only come from action.

The final revelation was vouchsafed them while they were at table with their Guest. "He took bread, and blessed, and broke, and gave to them. And their eyes were opened and they knew Him; and he vanished out of their sight. . . . And rising up the same hour, they went back to Jerusalem, and they found the eleven gathered together, and those that were with them, saying, The Lord is risen indeed, and hath appeared to Simon. And they told what things were done in the way, and how they knew him in the breaking of the bread."

During the short journey their minds had received so much light, and their hearts had grown so full of love, that the merest incident or gesture—we know not which—opened their eyes to the full truth. It is quite possible that Jesus renewed for them the miracle of the last Supper; what is certain is that He poured into their hearts His own joy and His own strength.

And rising from table they returned at that late hour all the way to Jerusalem to announce the glad tidings to their brethren. Instances of similar overwhelming illumination are experienced by all those that serve the Master devotedly. They should take note of St. Augustine's remark, "The purpose of such favors is not that they should be relished in idle quietude, but that they should spur us on to zealous action."

Prayer: When once Thou visitest the heart
   Then Truth begins to shine,
   Then earthly vanities depart,
   Then kindles love divine.

EASTER TUESDAY

APPARITION TO PETER

1. Jesus favored Peter with a personal apparition. So say the Apostles to the returned men of Emmaus. They seem to attach

very great importance to this particular apparition. When, where, in what circumstances, did it take place? We do not know: Peter alone could have told us, and that he did not do. However, we can well imagine what happened at that meeting. Peter, now grown wiser through experience, must have fallen on his knees before Jesus, exclaiming with even greater humility than after the miraculous draught of fishes, "Depart from me, O Lord, for I am a sinful man." Jesus, like the father of the prodigal son, raises him up, and then confirms him in his function of leader.

2. *Petition*: Grant, O Lord, that after every fall we may find Thee raising us up, and thenceforth with Thee we may "walk in newness of life" (*Rom.* 6, 4).

I. The Dispositions of Peter

Abysmal shame. On the occasion of the Master's explicit warning he had been the first to protest and the loudest, "Yea, though I should die with Thee, I will not deny Thee" (*Matt.* 26, 35). And alas, it had happened: He, the leader of the Twelve, the rock on which Jesus had promised to build His Church, had denied his Master; the dauntless hero had been worsted by a servant maid.

Contrite love of the most intense and most pure kind. Jesus while passing by, cast a glance at Peter ... and he had gone out to weep bitterly. In the process his love had increased and deepened; but he had had no opportunity of saying one word to the Master.... Had the Lord disowned him?

But Peter had not broken away from the brethren. They all knew of his fall, but they must have tried to soothe and comfort him—most of all, his friend John.

The words of the women who that morning had gone to the grave had brought him relief and hope. They had found the tomb empty, but angels had spoken to them, and charged them with a message: "Go, tell the disciples and Peter...." He had been mentioned by name!

II. The Apparition

Upon hearing the women's message, Peter and John run to the tomb: it is empty. The winding-sheet and the linen cloths, folded and laid aside in an orderly manner, are proof that the Body has not been snatched away. John had let Peter enter first and now followed him. John says of himself, "and he saw and believed"

(20, 8); he needed no further proof. "Peter went away wondering in himself at that which was come to pass" (*Luke* 24, 12).

It is possible that Jesus appeared to Peter on his way back from the tomb. We would love to know what Jesus said to the repentant Apostle. Did He say: Peace be to thee, Peter. Thou art fully forgiven; thou art still the leader of thy brethren...? Peace, joy and ardent love flooded Peter's heart as he knelt before his Master, and he rose "a more prudent, a more humble, a more dedicated man." Jesus had foretold it all: had He not said to Peter: "Simon, Satan hath desired to have thee, that he may sift thee as wheat; but I have prayed for thee that thy faith fail not; and thou, being once converted, confirm thy brethren" (*Luke* 22, 31-32).

That is what Peter is going to do—humbly, gently, mercifully. In Jesus we have "a high priest who can have compassion on our infirmities, one tempted in all things like as we are, without sin" (*Heb.* 4, 15): in Peter, Christ's Vicar, we have the same, sin included. Jesus had permitted it all to happen, and now Peter has "learned the lesson"; and, owing to Christ's special prayer for His Vicar on earth, Peter is forever the solid rock on which the Church will be built.

III. Peter Confirms His Brethren

Having been irrevocably confirmed in his supreme office, Peter returned to the Cenacle. The Apostles were anxiously debating about the reports they had received: Mary Magdalen had affirmed that she had seen the Lord and had spoken to Him; John had confirmed the testimony of the women: the tomb was in fact empty. And now Peter arrived and related how the Master appeared to him. Here was the testimony of a man, and that man Peter, whose leadership all acknowledge and whom the Lord had now clearly confirmed in his office! When, then, in the night the men from Emmaus entered the Cenacle, they were greeted with the joyful tidings, "The Lord is risen indeed, and hath appeared to Simon" (*Luke* 24, 34).

We admire Peter, who without any false shame speaks and acts with the authority which is his; we admire the Apostles, who are jubilant over their Master's resurrection and rejoice at Peter's confirmation; we admire, above all, Jesus for the tact and the wisdom wherewith He handles His own. To "the disciple whom He loved" He does not appear: John had seen and believed; he needed no personal vision . . . and he had remained steadfast throughout. But to Peter, deeply repentant and tormented by anxiety, and the leader of the group,—He does appear. Into this troubled soul Jesus came to pour light, peace, pardon and assurance.

Prayer: O God, who dost brighten this most sacred night with the glory of the Lord's Resurrection: preserve in the new offspring of Thy family the spirit of adoption which Thou hast given; that, renewed in mind and in body, they may render to Thee unsullied service. Through our Lord (Collect, Easter Vigil).

EASTER WEDNESDAY

APPARITION BY THE SEA OF TIBERIAS (John 21, 1-23)

1. Jesus had commanded the apostles to return to Galilee, where they would see Him and receive further instructions. They seem to have in the meantime reverted to their former occupation as fishermen. On one occasion seven of them, Peter and John being of the company, had labored a whole night without making any catch; at early dawn someone called out to them from the shore to cast their net on the right side of the ship. "They cast the net, and now they were not able to draw it for the multitude of fishes."

John was the first to recognize Jesus. They pulled ashore, breakfasted with our Lord; and then took place the solemn appointment of Peter as supreme pastor. We try to behold these scenes.

2. *Petition*: The grace to understand the words of Christ and that we may love Him as Peter loved Him.

I. They Recognize the Lord

The first to recognize Jesus from afar was "the disciple whom Jesus loved"; the first to take any action was Peter. "Simon Peter, when he heard that it was the Lord, girt his coat about him (for he was naked) and cast himself into the sea." Two kinds of love: the contemplative, keen of eye; and the active, prompt to act. Each of these has its own part to play, and they complement each other where several cooperate to achieve a common task.

From the entire Gospel, and especially from the latter portion of the present incident, it is apparent that Peter and John were intimate friends. Jesus had revealed something to Peter about what the future had in store for him; and now he would very much have liked to learn something about the lot that was reserved for his friend John. Jesus saith to him: "So I will have him remain till I come," He said, "what is that to thee? Follow thou me." Peter's digression, dictated by curiosity as well as by friendship, earned him a gentle reproof. We must keep our gaze fixed on Jesus alone: Follow thou me!

Jesus demands that He should be the sole object of all our thoughts and actions, of all our inquiries and efforts. Daily, humbly, steadfastly, we must strive after this absolute purity of intention.

II. Peter Is Appointed Supreme Pastor

The frugal meal by the shore of the familiar Lake of Genesareth, with Jesus in their midst, filled their herats with the comforting assurance that Jesus was still the same as before, the same and yet how different: for, at any moment He could be by their side and again not be there. It was another kind of presence; yet there was no question of doubting it; He was alive and in His intercourse with them He was as He had always been; and so were they with Him. His doctrine, His commands, His mandates, everything was the same.

And then suddenly came the thrice-repeated, and solemnly-worded, question, "Simon, son of John, lovest thou me more than these?" Peter answers in the affirmative, discreetly omitting the comparison, "Yea, Lord, thou knowest that I love thee:" Jesus said, "Feed my lambs." A second time Jesus asks the same question and Peter gives the same answer: and again Jesus said, "Feed my lambs." But when Jesus puts the same question a third time, Peter's answer betrays profound emotion, "Lord, thou knowest all things. Thou knowest that I love thee." And this time Jesus said, "Feed my sheep."

The first requisite for the exercise of authority in God's Church, and in the Lord's name over Christ's flock, is—love of Jesus.

And the moving metaphorical representation, chosen and immortalized by Christ Himself, for those who wield such authority is—the shepherd, who exercises his powers in the most gentle way and with utter personal dedication. On another, and no less solemn occasion, Jesus had called Peter by a different name, "Thou art Peter and upon this rock I will build my church, and the gates of hell shall not prevail against it" (*Matt.* 16, 18). He is both rock and shepherd. Firm as granite when the Lord's doctrine is at stake, but a tender of sheep in his ways with men; immovable and infallible in his office of teacher, gentle and merciful as a ruler of souls. That is the way any authority in the Church of Christ must be exercised, "fortiter et suaviter, with a hand that is at once firm and gentle".

III. The Fate of Peter

In a veiled manner Jesus thereupon foretells the martyrdom of Peter, "Amen, amen, I say to thee, when thou wast younger thou didst gird thyself and didst walk where thou wouldst; but when thou shalt be old, thou shalt stretch forth thy hands and another shall gird thee, and lead thee whither thou wouldst not." Mysterious words at the time when they were spoken; but how clear they had become to John when, after Peter's death on the cross, he set them down in writing.

Once, for fear of death, Peter had denied his Master, but Jesus had offered a special prayer for him, Peter had "learned" in the school of experience, and he had—besides—received the Holy Ghost. As supreme pastor he would lay down his life for his flock for love of the Lord who had been the first to love "unto the end".

Prayer: We beseech Thee, O Lord, that, being purified from our old nature, the solemn reception of Thy Sacrament may transform us into a new creature. Who livest... (Postcommunion of this day).

EASTER THURSDAY

APPARITION TO MARY MAGDALEN (John 20, 11-17)

1. Early that morning Mary Magdalen, with Mary, the mother of James and Salome, had gone to the sepulcher. They found the stone rolled aside and the tomb empty. At once she hastened back to inform the apostles. Peter and John ran to the tomb, found that her statement was correct, and went away. Mary Magdalen came back to the sepulchre after they had left... and

lingered there, filled with anxiety, and weeping bitterly. Then
Jesus appeared to her.

2. *Petition*: The grace to understand what Jesus wished to
reward in Magdalen and what He wants to find in our own
hearts.

I. Mary Magdalen's Ardent Love

After her conversion she had wholly dedicated herself to the
service of the Lord; she had followed Him to Calvary; she had
stood near the cross with His Virgin Mother and the beloved
disciple; she had seen Him expire; and she had assisted at His
burial. And now the taking away of His dead Body made her
lose Him a second time: nothing at all was left of Him.... The
thought that He had perhaps risen from the dead does not seem
to have occurred to her for an instant, no more than to the
other women, or to the Apostles. What distresses her most
profoundly is that His dead Body has been removed and she
does not know whither.

St. Augustine rightly remarks, "Whereas the men return home,
the weaker sex, because of a stronger love, lingers on about the
place. Mary's eyes, which have sought Jesus without finding
Him, fill and overflow with tears. That He should have been removed from the tomb causes her greater grief than that He had
died on the cross. Alas! Of the dear Master, whom she would
never behold alive any more, there were now left no sacred remains whatever!"

How wonderful the workings of God's grace and God's love
can be in a human heart! "I am still weak in love, and very
wanting in holiness.... O Lord, make me inwardly sound, worthy
to love Thee, brave to suffer, steadfast to persevere" (3 *Imit. of
Christ* 5, 2).

II. Magdalen's Perseverance Is Rewarded

"But Mary stood at the sepulchre without, weeping. Now as
she was weeping, she stooped down and looked into the sepulchre.
And she saw two angels in white, sitting one at the head and one
at the feet, where the body of Jesus had been laid. They say to
her, Woman, why weepest thou? She saith to them, Because they
have taken away my Lord and I know not where they laid him."
Once more she looks into the tomb; she hardly notices the angels

and probably is not conscious of having been questioned and having answered: one object only preys on her mind—Where, Oh where is He?

"When she had thus said, she turned herself back and saw Jesus standing; and she knew not that it was Jesus. Jesus saith to her, Woman, why weepest thou? Whom seekest thou?" And saying this, He comes a little closer, to draw her attention.

"She, thinking that it was the gardener, saith to him, Sir, if thou hast taken him hence, tell me where thou hast laid him, and I will take him away. Jesus saith to her, Mary. She, turning, saith to Him, Rabboni (which is to say Master). Jesus saith to her, Do not thus cling to me, for I am not yet ascended to my Father." These last words are obscure; the rest is clear: Mary hears her name, the affectionate voice, the Master. She casts herself at His feet and from her heart comes the cry, one word only: Rabboni, a word that expresses all her love and adoration.

Thus was Mary rewarded "because she had loved much". According to St. Mark, Mary was the first to whom Jesus appeared; and he adds "out of whom He had cast seven devils". God is wonderful in His saints.

III. The Message Entrusted to Magdalen

Mary Magdalen was privileged to enjoy the presence of her Lord just a little longer than the disciples of Emmaus, out of whose sight He vanished as soon as they knew Him. But only a little. "Do not cling to me thus," said Jesus, "but go to my brethren and say to them, I ascend to my Father and your Father, to my God and your God." How honorable a mission He commits to her! She is to go and announce the glad news to the apostles, "my brethren".

"My brethren!" These words reveal to us the sentiments of the risen Savior. When He was still with them, "in the days of his flesh," He once had said to them, "I will not now call you servants, for the servant knoweth not what his lord doth; but I have called you friends, because all things whatsoever I have heard from my Father, I have made known to you" (*John* 15, 15). Now, when He was entered into His glory, He no longer calls them friends, but brothers. He and they have the same Father: He, as the Only-Begotten Son, by nature equal unto God; they, as adopted sons, brothers by the grace of the Son. "I ascend to my Father and your Father, to my God and your God." How is it that we can be so intimately united with Him, and yet so utterly different from Him? Here we discover "the charity of Christ, which surpasseth all knowledge" (*Eph.* 3, 19).

Mary arose and announced to the disciples, "I have seen the Lord, and those things he said to me."

Prayer: O Lord Jesus, who hast so wonderfully rewarded the love of Mary Magdalen, when with tears she searched for Thee; be pleased to pour Thy love into our hearts, a love which in all things seeks Thee alone humbly and confidently, a love that is ready to assume every task and to make every sacrifice in order to preach Thy holy Name.

EASTER FRIDAY

APPARITION TO THE APOSTLES (Luke 24, 36; John 20, 19)

1. On the evening of that memorable Easter day all the Apostles, except Thomas, are together in the Cenacle. While they are eagerly discussing the wonderful events of the day, suddenly Jesus stands in their midst, and greets them with the familiar words, "Peace be to you." When they have recovered from the sudden shock, they gaze at Him in utter surprise. Jesus gives them tangible proof that it is He Himself, and entrusts them with a special mission.

2. *Petition:* The grace to understand and to admire the kindness and the condescension of Jesus, so that the Lord may deliver us from our faint-heartedness and grant us a share in His joy and His peace.

I. That Day's Last Apparition

Human reason fails to grasp how a spiritual and mysterious event like the resurrection of our Lord Jesus Christ could manifest itself in our material world, which is so conditioned by sense perception. God can do infinitely more than what our mind can grasp. We firmly believe, and humbly adore.

As to the sequence in the series of apparitions on that day, we are left to guess. Our Lord did show Himself to those who stood in greatest need of His help—the pilgrims to Emmaus, who without His intervention would have been lost; Peter, the leader of the Apostles, whose ardent soul was being tried beyond endurance; but also to those who would be most ready to accept the miracle—the holy women and Mary Magdalen.

The tidings about those repeated apparitions has prepared the group of apostles to believe; the latest news has just now been communicated by the two men from Emmaus. Still there are those among them that could not believe, as St. Mark tells us (16, 13) "out of sheer joy", says St. Luke (24, 41).

II. The Apparition

And while they were discussing it all "behind closed doors" suddenly Jesus stood in their midst. The previous apparitions of the day had taken place out of doors, but on this occasion Jesus enters "the doors being shut": His Body is no longer subject to the laws of matter. "But they, being troubled and frightened, supposed that they saw a spirit. And he said to them: why are you troubled, and why do thoughts arise in your hearts?"

They had seen Lazarus coming forth from the grave, but this apparition of Himself was altogether another thing. Jesus (adapting Himself in an unintelligible manner to the weakness of their perceptive powers) will make it evident to them that He is not a spirit, but that He has a true Body, though a subtle and spiritualized one. "See my hands and my feet, that it is myself," He said. Those limbs, bearing the scars of the wounds, should even more than His features convince them that He is the Man who was nailed to the cross. "And when he had said this, he showed them his hands and feet. But while they yet believed not, and wondered for joy, he said, have you here anything to eat? And they offered him a piece of broiled fish and a honeycomb. And he ate before them."

Let no "thoughts arise in our hearts", except to believe humbly that God's power surpasses our understanding and to admire, with loving gratitude, how He was pleased to preserve the marks of the sacred wounds in His glorified Body.

III. The Mission of the Apostles

According to the Gospel of St. John it was during this apparition that Jesus formally commissioned His Apostles. "He said therefore to them again, Peace be to you. As the Father hath sent me, I also send you. When he had said this, he breathed on them, and He said to them, Receive ye the Holy Ghost. Whose sins you shall forgive, they are forgiven them; and whose sins you shall retain, they are retained" (*John* 20, 21-23).

In His sacerdotal prayer after the Last Supper, Jesus had said, "As thou hast sent me into the world, I also have sent them into the world" (*John* 17, 18); and now He acts as a mediator between the Father and the Apostles: He, whom the Father has sent, sends them; the power, which the Father has bestowed on Him, He bestows on them. O marvellous confidence of the Son of God in men whose weakness He well knew! And for those men themselves, what a tremendous responsibility is laid on them! Therefore did Christ pray to the Father that, as He and the Father are one, so these also may be one with Him. "I in them, and thou in me; that they may be made perfect in one: and the world may know that thou hast sent me and hast loved them, as thou hast also loved me" (*John* 17, 23).

This is a most solemn moment. The Holy Ghost also, who has not yet descended on them, is made an accessary to this Ordination. As, in the beginning, "the Lord God breathed into Adam's face the breath of life", so here too "Jesus breathed on them", and bestowed on them a new life. "When he had said this he breathed on them, and he said to them, Receive ye the Holy Ghost. . . ." Now that Jesus by His death and resurrection has destroyed sin, they also, through the power of the Spirit, who is equally the Spirit of the Son, will have power to remit sin.

Glory be to the Father, and to the Son, and to the Holy Ghost, that "gave such power to men" (*Matt.* 9, 8).

Prayer: Almighty and eternal God, who in the covenant of man's reconciliation, hast bestowed the Paschal Mystery, grant that we may show forth in our lives what we profess outwardly in our faith. Through our Lord (Collect, Mass of today).

EASTER SATURDAY

JESUS APPEARS TO HIS HOLY MOTHER

1. The Gospel mentions no apparition of Jesus to His Holy Mother. Mary could hardly act as an official witness; for she belongs to another sphere since her role is uniquely an intimate one, entirely centered round the interior life. Yet for many centuries, if not from the earliest days of the Church,

Christian piety has taken it for granted that in the early dawn of Easter Jesus appeared first of all to His Mother.

2. *Petition*: The grace to share the exultation of Mary to whom was given the fullness of the Easter joy. "Mary, cause of our joy, pray for us."

I. Mary Waits For the Apparition

The Gospel says nowhere that our Lady went to the sepulchre in the company of the pious women who had stood by the cross. To her, at any rate, the grave could not have been the last word. The angel had said to her, "of his kingdom there shall be no end", which words Mary had always kept in her heart. Nor was she heedless of the prophecy of Jesus, well known to her, that on the third day He would rise again. Mary believed.

Just as at Nazareth she had waited nine months, till He would appear in the "weakness of our flesh" from her virginal womb, so now she waits and longs for the dawn of that third day, when she will see Him anew in His glorified Body.

We may surmise that, at this moment, whilst with every fiber of her whole being, she adheres to her *Fiat* the wonderful events of these last years are passing before her mind: Nazareth, Bethlehem, Egypt, the hallowed years in the carpenter's cottage, the troubled period of her Son's ministry, the tragedy of the Passion and Calvary. She has not understood it all, but the hour approaches when she will understand fully.

II. The Apparition

On Easter morning, then, while Mary Magdalen and the other Mary hastened to the sepulcher to complete the provisional embalming of Friday night, Mary stayed at home. Suddenly Jesus is standing before her, in all His glory! At the departure of her children from this world Holy Church prays, "May the gentle and radiant countenance of Christ Jesus appear to thee"; this wish was fulfilled for Mary in an inexpressible way, when she beheld her risen Son. . . .

"The more smarting the wound, the more delightful the cure," cries the ancient mystic Hadewych. Old Simeon had prophesied, "Thy own soul a sword shall pierce"; now that she gazes upon the resplendent marks of the wounds in the glorified Body of her Son, the wound in her heart is changed into a fount of heavenly bliss. . . . Thus did Jesus and Mary, in the words of a devout medieval writer, celebrate that first Easter in delight and jubilation, "Regina coeli, laetare alleluia; O Queen of Heaven, thrill with joy!"

> "And e'en as from His manger bed
> He gave Her His first smile;
> So now, while seraphs wait,
> He talks with Her a while." (*Keble*)

III. Jesus Entrusts a Task to His Mother

It is highly probable that our Lord now enlightened His blessed Mother about the office He had entrusted to her when with His dying breath He said to her, "Woman, behold thy son." Among the Apostles and in the infant Church, which is her Son's Mystical Body, she had an important task to fulfill, a mother's task, delicate and unobtrusive yet universal and permanent in its influence, through subordinate but indispensable co-operation with Himself.

Jesus filled her soul with light and strength for the fulfillment of that task. When He shall have ascended into heaven, His Mother will be the most precious keepsake left by Him to the apostles. When they assemble, she is in their midst; around her they persevere in prayer; and she is with them when, on the day of Pentecost, the Holy Ghost comes to infuse life into the newborn Mystical Body of Christ, His Church.

For many years Mary still remained on earth: those were years of great solitude and blessed expectation when, even more ardently than St. Paul, she "desired to be dissolved and to be with Christ" (*Phil.* 1, 23). May we not piously presume that, on this hallowed Easter morning, Jesus revealed to Mary how, without being 'dissolved', she would soon and forever be with Him. And surely, the sight of His glorified Body gave her a glimpse of the bliss that was to come. She would be the first, and that immediately at the close of her earthly life, to reap the full fruit of redemption: she was to be assumed into heaven, to be enthroned by the side of her Son; till the end of time she would distribute to us the graces that flow from Christ, the source of all grace.

Prayer: O God, who by the resurrection of Thy Son, our Lord Jesus Christ, didst deign to give joy to the world: grant, we beseech Thee, that through His Mother, the Virgin Mary, we may obtain the joys of everlasting life. Through the same Jesus Christ, our Lord (Prayer after the *Regina Coeli*).

APPARITION TO THOMAS AND THE OTHER APOSTLES
(John 20: 24-29)

1. On the eighth day after Easter, the Apostles once again were gathered together in the Cenacle, and this time Thomas was with them. Notwithstanding the unanimous testimony of his brethren he stubbornly refused to believe in the Resurrection. Suddenly Jesus stood in their midst, and straightaway addressed Thomas.

2. *Petition*: The grace to be, and ever to remain, one of those whom Jesus called blessed because they have not seen and have believed.

I. The Obstinacy of Thomas

We do not know why, but Thomas was not with the other Apostles when, on the evening of Easter day, Jesus appeared to them in the Cenacle. On his return to the group the others told him, "We have seen the Lord! but he said to them, Except I shall see in his hands the print of the nails, and put my finger into the place of the nails and my hand into his side, I will not believe."

These challenging words were prompted by the disappointment of a headstrong man. Thomas lacked neither generosity nor courage. When Lazarus lay sick, and Jesus spoke of returning to Judea, where their lives were in danger, it was he who had said to the others, "Let us also go, that we may die with Him" (*John* 11, 16). And now he is the only one who has not seen the risen Master, and this arouses his resentment. There might have been lamentable consequences if Jesus had not intervened.

Don't we all know of such occasions, when we have made a mistake and, though in our heart of hearts we know better, we take shelter behind pretexts and sophistry; we are discontented, we know we are wrong, but we are too proud to confess that we have erred? The sooner we plead guilty, in such cases, the better it will be for us.

II. Jesus Rescues Thomas

Just as in the case of the disciples of Emmaus, so here our Lord acts as the Good Shepherd who goes in search of the straying sheep and carries it back to the fold.

"And after eight days again his disciples were within, and Thomas with them. Jesus cometh, the doors being shut, and stood in the midst and said, Peace be to you. Then he said to Thomas, put in thy finger hither, and see my hands; and bring hither thy hand and put it into my side; and be not faithless but believing. Thomas answered and said to him, My Lord and my God."

No sooner had Thomas beheld Jesus looking at him with infinite love than his obstinacy vanished. The Master's invitation to "lay his finger into the place of the nails" made him feel profoundly humble; he cast himself at the feet of Jesus and from the depths of his contrite heart uttered the most sublime profession of faith found in the Gospel, "My Lord and my God."

Admire our Lord's way: how, knowing Thomas thoroughly, He reached out, through the apostle's flimsy armor of resentment, to his true nature so fundamentally generous and faithful.

II. The Last Beatitude

"Jesus saith to him, Because thou hast seen me, Thomas, thou hast believed; blessed are they that have not seen, and have believed."

Thomas ought to have believed on the testimony of his companions without laying down any conditions. Far more meritorious had been the faith of John who, seeing the sepulchre empty and the linen cloths laid aside in an orderly manner, "saw and believed" that Jesus was risen.

"Because thou hast seen me, Thomas, thou hast believed." On those words St. Augustine comments, "What he saw and what he touched was the man; what he acknowledged was the Divinity, which he did not see and touch. But what he saw and touched destroyed his doubts, and made him believe in the Divinity."

Therefore Jesus said, "Blessed are they that have not seen, and have believed." We and all the generations that were not privileged to see Jesus when He was on earth, are grateful to Him for those words. Thirty years after those events St. Peter, writing to the Christian communities of Asia Minor, all converted Gentiles, said, "Rejoice ... that the trial of your faith (much more precious than gold which is tried by fire) will bring you praise and glory and honor at the appearing of Jesus Christ: whom having not seen, you love; in whom also now, though you see him not, you believe: and believing shall rejoice with joy unspeakable and glorified; receiving the end of your faith, even the salvation of your souls" (1 *Peter* 1, 6-9).

And St. Paul to the Romans, "May the God of hope fill you with all joy and peace in believing" (15, 13).

Here below our happiness consists in loving Him, whom we have not seen.

Prayer: Thy wounds, as Thomas saw, I do not see;
Yet Thee confess my Lord and God to be.
Make me believe Thee ever more and more;
In Thee my hope, in Thee my love to store.

MONDAY AFTER LOW SUNDAY

PRESERVING THE EASTER GRACES

1. In His farewell discourse after the Last Supper, Jesus repeatedly said to the Apostles, "Abide in me, and I in you. . . . He that abideth in me and I in him, the same beareth much fruit. . . . If you abide in me and my words abide in you, you shall ask whatever you will, and it shall be done unto you" (*John* 15, 4-7). Now that Easter week has passed, let us try to hear Jesus saying to us, "Abide in me, and I in you."

2. *Petition*: "Grant, we beseech Thee, Almighty God, that we who have been celebrating the Paschal festivities may, through Thy bounty, ever retain their effect both in our life and in our actions" (Collect, Low Sunday).

I. Low Sunday

"White Sunday", as this day was also called after the Latin "Dominica in Albis", was the day on which the newly-baptized laid aside their white garments. During eight days they had worn their spotless robes, and had daily participated in the Sacred Mysteries, kneeling as a group close to the altar. Today they have donned their ordinary clothes and taken their place among the ranks of the faithful. In a sermon preached on this occasion St. Augustine says, "Today's celebration closes the Paschal solemnities. Therefore on this day the newly-baptized lay aside their white garments, yet intending to keep forever in their hearts the brightness of the garments which they lay aside."

Our souls, in union with the entire Church, have experienced their annual 'renewal'; our risen Savior, through His victory over sin and death, has chastened and strengthened our hearts. In the Gospel we read that from the mortal Body of Jesus a power went out that healed all ailments; in His glorified Body that power is not lessened nay it is enhanced. Through Holy Communion we are in the most intimate contact with that Body, the source of all holiness; there He cleanses our hearts of every remnant of the old leaven—despair, faint-heartedness, sadness—and makes us susceptible of a holy renewal of life. He pours into our souls the strong, meek, gentle, manly Easter joy—"that gigantic secret of the Christians", and the Easter peace, which He wished to His Apostles and which no man can take away from us. "These things I have spoken to you, that my joy may be with you" (*John* 15, 11). We must jealously preserve these gifts.

II. To Preserve and to Maintain

It is from God's almighty Hand that we must receive the continuance of the effects of the Easter graces, as Holy Church asks for her children in the Collect of the Low Sunday Mass. "But the God of all grace, who hath called us into his eternal glory, in Christ Jesus . . . will himself perfect you, and confirm you, and establish you. To him be glory and empire forever and ever. Amen" (*Peter* 5, 10-11).

As long as we are on earth, we shall be harassed by weakness and fickleness, but "this is the victory, which overcometh the world, our faith" (*John* 5, 4). Through this faith He dwells in our hearts "who is mightier than he that is in the world" (1 *John* 4, 4). This faith places on our lips the humble and trustful prayer of the Church, "Grant us, we beseech Thee O God Almighty, the grace faithfully to preserve in ourselves the Paschal mysteries." These Paschal mysteries, this Paschal joy, this Paschal peace we must preserve in "our life and actions". A truth that is meant to influence a man's whole life and conduct can be preserved only if one lives by it. This is true above all of the dogmas of our faith and of our faith itself. Unless we make our faith influence our actions, we cannot preserve it. Just as for lack of oxygen the flame of a candle must grow faint and die out, so does the light of faith need to be fed by action or else it fizzles out.

"If you abide in me, and my words abide in you. . . . Abide in my love. If you keep my commandments, you shall abide in my love; as I also have kept my Father's commandments, and do abide in his love. . . . This is my commandment that you love one another as I have loved you" (*John* 15, 7-12). If we wish to preserve in us the Paschal mysteries, we must live by them, abide in Him by letting Him influence all our actions; abide in Him through the observance of His commandments, above all of this His own commandment, "that we love one another as he has loved us".

Three times—in the Postcommunions of the Easter Vigil, of Easter Sunday and Easter Monday, we pray for this grace of brotherly love and union which is to be the best means of preserving the Paschal mysteries in our life and actions.

Prayer: Pour forth upon us, O Lord, the Spirit of Thy love; that by thy loving-kindness Thou mayest make those to be of one mind, whom Thou hast fed with the Paschal Sacraments. Through our Lord. . . . (Postcommunion, Easter).

TUESDAY AFTER LOW SUNDAY

OUR FAITH OVERCOMETH THE WORLD
(1 John 5, 4)

1. In his Panegyric on Martyrdom St. Cyprian says, "One day I saw an executioner torture a Christian, and heard one of the bystanders observe: think of it that this man has a wife and children; yet the thought of his dear ones does not make him give way. There is something awe-inspiring in those Christians."

2. *Petition*: The grace to learn the value of what is awe-inspiring in our faith, and always to live up to it.

I. The World

The Epistle of the Mass of Low Sunday is taken from the first letter of St. John to the Christians of Asia Minor: They formed small communities in the midst of the heathen masses of those frivolous maritime cities. In those circumstances it required heroic courage to profess the Christian faith and to live by its precepts, and St. John desires to encourage them: "for whatsoever is born of God overcometh the world, and this is the victory, which overcometh the world, our faith" (1 *John* 5, 4).

By "the world" is not meant here the material universe, which is the handiwork of the Almighty; still less is there question of the marvellous inventions of man, whose genius discovers and harnesses the latent forces of God's creation; though at times man uses his technical skill to thwart God's plan. All the forces of nature can, and must, contribute to man's eternal salvation. For we know "that the creature also itself shall be delivered from the servitude of corruption, into the liberty of the glory of the children of God" (*Rom.* 8, 21).

Neither is there question of the world which "God so loved as to give his only-begotten Son" (*John* 3, 16).

There is question of the world "for which Jesus does not pray", the world of which Satan is the prince, and about which St. John writes, "Love not the world, nor the things that are in the world. If any man love the world, the charity of the Father is not in him. For all that is in the world is the concupiscence of the flesh, and the concupiscence of the eyes, and the pride of life, which is not of the Father, but is of the world. And the world passeth away, and the concupiscence thereof" (1 *John* 2, 15-17).

And that world is powerful; it offers man immediate tangible enjoyment; it stimulates his ambition, his thirst for power. Once Satan tried to make use of these three allurements against Jesus Himself, but he was ignominiously defeated. Now the fight continues in the world around us, and in the heart of every man.

II. "This Is the Victory, Our Faith"

Our Lord Jesus Christ is the One who has overcome the world and cast out the prince of the world: in Himself actually, completely, finally; in us, through our faith, not yet completely nor finally.

"Whatever is born of God, overcometh the world," says St. John, that is, he stands on the side of the victorious Christ. "To be born of God", to "be of God", is to believe that Jesus is the Christ, the Son of God, that He has taught us the truth, has revealed unto us the Name and the Will of His Father.

Through Baptism we are born of God, not indeed as the Son "before the world was" (*Ecclus.* 24, 14), but on the day when through the word and water we became new creatures, so that in Jesus "we should be called, and should be, the sons of God" (1 *John* 3, 1). Through our faith and our Baptism we partake in the victory which Christ has won for us over the world; in Him and from Him we have the strength to maintain and to complete that victory in our soul, "looking on Jesus, the author and finisher of faith. For think diligently upon him . . . that you be not wearied, fainting in your minds" (*Heb.* 12, 2-3).

III. Living Faith

"In the world you shall have distress; but have confidence, I have overcome the world" (*John* 16, 33).

Distress! in the case of the Apostles and of legions of other believers from the first century until this day, this implied the shedding of their blood. Blandina, a small slave girl of Lyons, who suffered martyrdom in the year 177, endured the most frightful tortures. The chronicler, an eyewitness, relates, "The Saint, like every other martyr, drew renewed strength from the confession of her faith. When the other champions of Christ saw her hanging at the stake, and heard her praising God aloud, her example filled them with new courage. In the midst of their own sufferings they recognized in Blandina, with the eyes of the body, Him who was crucified for them that He might make all those that suffer for the honor of Christ live forever with the living God."

We live at a time when thousands, in many countries, suffer dire distress for their faith, unto death! Let us pray for them, that through their faith they may persevere till the victory is won.

All of us have to struggle manfully against the world: in our own hearts, where the passions still smoulder; and around us, where the powers of darkness fiercely assail the kingdom of Light.

Prayer: Grant, we beseech Thee, Almighty God, that we who have been celebrating the Paschal festivities, may through Thy bounty ever retain their effect, both in life and in action. Through our Lord (Collect, Low Sunday).

WEDNESDAY AFTER LOW SUNDAY

EASTER JOY (John 15, 11)

1. "These things I have spoken to you, that my joy may be in you, and your joy may be filled" (*John* 15, 11). These words, spoken by Jesus in His farewell address after the Last Supper,

are even more appropriate on the lips of the risen Savior. In every apparition He made the Apostles partakers of the fullness of His joy. These same words He addresses to us too.

2. *Petition*: The grace that our soul may ever be open to that joy; that always we may "draw waters with joy out of the savior's fountains" (*Isa.* 12, 3).

I. Easter Joy

There are circumstances—and consequently prayers—wherein we, "banished children of Eve, mourning and weeping in this vale of tears", cry to heaven, in which we implore, "to be delivered from the present evils". In the same farewell discourse Jesus said, "Amen, amen, I say to you that you shall lament and weep, but the world shall rejoice" (*John* 16, 20).

Yet the dominating feeling in the heart of a Christian is joy: "Your sorrow shall be turned into joy," said Jesus. (The world's rejoicing, on the contrary, very often turns into sorrow.) The Christian does not despise the sources of natural pleasure: nay he asks them from God as a favor, "that through the intercession of the Blessed Virgin Mary, we may rejoice in the blessing of continued health of body and mind." But he is ready, whenever it may please God, to forego this continued health, and any other earthly favors.

The sources of our Easter joy lie deeper: we have been saved from perdition, we are children of our Father in heaven, brothers and sisters of our Lord Jesus Christ; "the charity of God is poured forth in our hearts, by the Holy Ghost, who is given to us" (*Rom.* 5, 5). "And our joy no man shall take away from us" (*John* 16, 22).

A pious writer said, "To me Easter is the most cherished feast of all; I believe this is a truly Catholic sentiment. The early Christians lived in the continual remembrance of the resurrection. If God grants us the same grace, let us accept it with our whole heart; it will help us rise above the petty troubles and miseries that afflict us every day."

II. Let Us Preserve It

Chesterton once said that joy, which was an imperceptible ripple on the surface of the ancient heathen's life, is the gigantic secret of the Christian. We must preserve our Easter joy, and safeguard it against whatever would mar it. The only destroyer of joy and peace of heart is sin, unrepented sin; repentance, inspired by love, said an ancient spiritual writer, in a certain sense is joyful; since it gives us the assurance that we are forgiven and spurs us on to generosity.

One enemy against whom we have to safeguard the strong, profound, noble Easter joy, is that depression of spirits which is caused by injured self-love. Inevitably we shall meet with trials, perhaps severe trials, suffer painful bereavements. St. Paul shed tears, when he thought of the enemies of the cross of Christ (*Phil.* 3, 18), but the source of true joy never ceased flowing deep down in his heart: "Rejoice in the Lord. Again I say, rejoice. . . . And the peace of God, which surpasseth all understanding, shall keep your hearts and minds in Christ Jesus" (*Phil.* 4, 7).

St. Francis of Sales never wearied of telling his nuns that they should serve the Lord joyfully: "Live joyfully amidst the thorns of the Lord's crown; and like the nightingale in his coppice, let your song be: long live Jesus."

III. The Fullness of Joy

"These things I have spoken to you that my joy may be in you, and your joy may be filled" (*John* 15, 11). Full, undisturbed, never-ending joy does not belong to this world. It is true that, deep down in our souls, we do possess "the fruit of the spirit, which is charity, joy, peace" (*Gal.* 5, 22); but on the surface we are subject to all the ups and downs of life. Darkness may envelop us, and within our soul violent storms may blow, but our "sorrow shall be turned into joy" (*John* 16, 20). "They shall no more hunger nor thirst; neither shall the sun fall on them, nor any heat. For the Lamb, which is in the midst of the throne shall rule them, and shall lead them to the fountains of the waters of life and God shall wipe away all tears from their eyes" (*Apoc.* 7, 16-17).

> O Jesu, from the death of sin
> Keep us, we pray: so shalt Thou be
> The everlasting Paschal joy
> Of all the souls new-born in Thee.

Prayer: Grant, we beseech Thee, O Almighty God, that we, who have reverently kept the Paschal festivities, may by them be made worthy to attain the heavenly joys. Through our Lord (Collect, Easter Saturday).

THE VOWS OF RELIGION, SOURCES OF JOY

1.   Against the background of the Paschal joy, let us consider how the vows of religion are inexhaustible fountains of joy. They are inspired by virile faith, which gains a resounding victory over the world. Love of God and love of the neighbor prompted the offering of those sacrifices, which fill the heart with the noblest and the purest joy.

Jesus Himself invited us to make these considerations, when he whispered into our ears, "These things I have spoken to you that my joy may be in you" (*John* 15, 11).

2.   *Petition*: The grace to grasp better this true aspect of our religious vows.

I. Poverty, Source of Joy

In direct contradiction to the worldly conviction of all times Christ asserted in His first Beatitude, "Blessed are the poor in spirit, for theirs is the kingdom of heaven" (*Matt.* 5, 3). Our Lord has in mind first of all the humble and lowly, and therefore the poor, that is, those that patiently bear poverty or freely embrace it. Whosoever vows poverty in religion does so freely, and out of love. Religious poverty calls for complete detachment from earthly things, even more than for privation of them. Neither the happiness, nor the good or ill humor of a religious depends on whether he has anything or nothing, little or much. "I know both how to be brought low and I know how to abound; I am instructed both to be full and to be hungry; both to abound and to suffer need" (*Phil.* 4, 12); thus spoke St. Paul about himself.

This complete detachment fills the soul with an exilarating sense of freedom: even pagan philosophers had experienced this. About Christian poverty there is a halo of gentleness, kindliness, humility; for, it is embraced out of love, which seeks conformity with Christ, which gladly shares the lot of the poor, and strives through voluntary privation to alleviate the sufferings of the indigent. The story of St. Francis, the poor man of Assisi, has proved to the world what a source of the purest joy poverty can be: was he not the poorest and yet the most cheerful man that ever lived?

Voluntary poverty will be to us a cause of pure joy, provided we understand and observe it, not merely according to the rule, but conformably to the spirit of the Gospel—out of love for Jesus, who was poor.

II. Chastity, a Source of Joy

Of perfect chastity Jesus Himself said, "He that can take, let him take it" (*Matt.* 19, 12): only those can grasp and observe it who are called to it by the Father. Virginal purity, gentle and serene, embraced absolutely and uncompromisingly out of love for Jesus and for souls, is a fountain of purest spiritual delight. It is the result of a holocaust, which sacrifices to God one of the deepest and strongest cravings of man's nature, which it would be rash to offer without a special grace of God.

And the joy is all the greater because the sacrifice is made whole-heartedly, unreservedly. "Blessed are the clean of heart, for they shall see God" (*Matt.* 5, 8).

The clean of heart, in the context, are those that have a clear conscience, that strive to serve God with a sincere heart: but it is perfectly correct to apply this Beatitude to those who profess to keep their heart virginally inviolate: those who have consecrated their heart to God alone "shall see God." When Jesus appeared to the Apostles on the shore of the lake of Tiberias, it was John, the virgin Apostle and beloved disciple, who first recognized the Lord. "By two wings a man is lifted up from earthly things, namely by simplicity and purity. There must be simplicity in the intention, purity in the affections. By simplicity we seek God and God alone, by purity we gain Him and enjoy Him. . . . If there be any joy in the world at all, surely it is the man of pure heart that enjoys it" (2 *Imit. of Christ* 4, 1-2).

If we want our ministry to bear abundant fruit without endangering our own salvation, then unspotted virginal love must keep us closely united with Jesus.

III. Obedience, a Source of Joy

Just like the two other vows, so the vow of obedience too becomes to the religious a source of joy, in the measure in which he strives after the perfection of obedience. There can be neither joy nor peace in the heart of him who outwardly complies with his Superior's command but fails to make the Superior's will his own, and therefore does not do gladly what he is commanded. He ought even, as far as possible, to conform his opinion to that of his Superior. He is entitled, with respect and courtesy, to express his opinion to him that commands: but the last word must ever remain with the one in authority. By that last word the inferior must, and can safely, abide, though it comes from a man liable to err. Thus he will be "of one mind" in his heart, and will preserve peace and joy.

"Yea, Father, for so hath it seemed good in thy sight" (*Matt. 11, 26*) was our Lord's rule of life. And that "Yea Father", the religious can make his own, though the Superior who stands between him and Jesus be a fallible man. Such conduct has the blessing of our Lord, and He Himself bears the responsibility of the consequences, which anyway are controlled by His wisdom and His omnipotence.

"A man who can listen is a trustworthy witness", or as we read in the Vulgate translation, "an obedient man shall speak victory" (*Prov. 21, 28*). Of one thing we may be quite certain: perfect obedience brings peace and joy to the heart.

Prayer: O Lord Jesus, who hast called us to follow Thee in the observance of voluntary poverty, virginal purity and perfect obedience, and thereby hast opened unto us abundant sources of joy, strengthen in us the spirit of faith and love, that we may faithfully fulfill our obligations and serve Thee in the gladness of our hearts, Thee, who livest and reignest. . . .

FRIDAY AFTER LOW SUNDAY

THE RELIGIOUS LIFE, A SOURCE OF HAPPINESS

1. On Thabor Peter cried out, "Master it is good for us to be here" (*Matt.* 9, 33). We should be able to repeat the same exclamation, under all circumstances, to Jesus who dwells in our midst concealed in His tabernacle.

2. *Petition*: The grace always to promote in our community the union of all in Christ and to realize what a fountain of peace and joy this union provides.

I. Gathered in The Name of Jesus

"Where there are two or three gathered in my name, there am I in the midst of them" (*Matt.* 18, 20). Through Baptism all Christians are not only united in the name of Christ, but have been made one Body. "Now you are the Body of Christ, and members of member" (1 *Cor.* 12, 27), that is, organs of it depending upon one another. Holy Communion, where we all partake of one bread, and are all one in Him, symbolizes and effects that oneness.

In a most special manner are those "gathered in his name" who were invited by Him to "come and see" where He dwells, and who were permitted to stay with Him. One by one, they have been recruited by Him from different surroundings; He led them by different paths that He might gather them into one family.

They do indeed form a family, the members of which are bound to one another not by ties of flesh and blood, but by the spirit of Jesus, the divine Recruiter and Founder of the new fellowship. And that spirit is the spirit of love: "Abide in me and I in you. . . . This is my commandment that you love one another as I have loved you" (*John* 15: 4, 12), gathering you together and fashioning you into one family, that by your united efforts you may joyfully cooperate to the founding and extending of my Kingdom.

II. We Must Preserve the Spirit of Jesus

The happiness of fraternal union of hearts is described in Psalm 132: "Behold how good and how pleasant it is for brethren to live together in unity." The Psalmist compares this unity to the soothing property of oil, to the freshness of heaven's dew, which bestow strength and fertility.

But wherever men live and labor together, even men dedicated to God and animated by the best of intentions, there is need for patience, tolerance, benevolence—attitudes that come easy to no one.

Dom Marmion wrote, "God be praised for all things and in all things, especially because He knows how to enlist the help of His elect in the work of sanctifying one by the other. He uses one diamond to polish another." If God Himself cherishes each of us so dearly, who knows us so thoroughly, if He is so patient and so merciful, how dare we be stern, exacting or impatient with our brethren?

With all His followers, most of all with those who are called to be His disciples of predilection, our Lord has laid stress on the first and last lesson which He chose to give us: "Learn of me because I am meek and humble of heart." Remembering that lesson and ever keeping in sight His divine example, let us strive to make His spirit prevail within us and around us. That will be the best proof that we do abide in Him, and He in us. "Where there is love and friendship, (according to the older reading: where love is genuine), there is God" as we sing in the Hymn on Fraternal Charity.

Let this be our chief care: to preserve and radiate in our communities the spirit of Jesus, the Master of us all and the Founder of our Brotherhood.

III. The Religious Life, Faithful and Joyful

Every form of Christian life has a full, an eternal value. We give to our life the fullest value, when we live it in the manner which God has ordained for each of us in particular. Comparisons with others are unprofitable: for these are too often vitiated by vanity and spiritual pride. If it has pleased God to call us to dedicate ourselves entirely to Him, to spend our whole life in His service and, for love of Him, in the service of our neighbor, then our attitude should be one of humble gratitude: gratitude, because the grace to live so close to Him, and so wholly for Him, is not granted to all; humble gratitude, because this call is in no way due to any merit of ours, and because we have been so often remiss in the service of our Lord, and of immortal souls.

But all that does by no means destroy the consoling certainty that our lives, however hidden and insignificant they may be in the eyes of men, have the highest value that a human life can have, viz, true service of God where God was pleased to place us. This is, here on earth a source of the purest joy; and one day, as true and faithful servants, we shall "enter into the joy of the Lord" (*Matt.* 25, 21).

Prayer: O Lord Jesus,, who, out of sheer goodness, hast deigned to call me to abide with Thee, to live and labor in union with others who likewise were called and formed by Thee: pour forth into our hearts the spirit of Thy love, so that we may experience ourselves, and show to the world, how happy those are who serve Thee.

How lovely are thy tabernacles, O Lord of hosts!
My soul longeth and fainteth for the courts of the Lord.
Blessed are they that dwell in thy house, O Lord,

They shall praise thee forever and ever.
Blessed is the man whose help is from thee.
In his heart he has disposed to ascend by steps.
They shall go from virtue to virtue;
The God of gods shall be seen in Sion.
For better is one day in thy courts
Above thousands.
I have chosen to be an abject in the house of my God,
Rather than to dwell in the tabernacles of sinners (*Ps.* 83).

MARY—"CAUSE OF OUR JOY"

1. More than any other human being Mary has participated in her Son's resurrection: she alone enjoys the full fruits of the redemption: she has entered body and soul into the joy of the Lord. Applied to her, the words which Jesus spoke to the Apostles must be taken unreservedly, "These things I have spoken to you, that my joy may be in you, and your joy may be filled" (*John* 15, 11). Of this fullness, poured into her soul by her divine Son, we have all received. Behold her enthroned in the resplendent glory and joy of her Son.

2. *Petition:* The grace to turn in all our troubles and trials with childlike confidence to Mary "cause of our joy", that she may lead us to the prime source of all joy and delight, Jesus.

I. Mary's Beauty, Cause of Our Joy

All beauty, being an irradiation of God's Beauty, engenders joy. Mary is the "All-Beautiful", unspotted even in the sight of God; immaculate and full of grace. How could she not be wholly well-pleasing in the eyes of the Lord? The liturgy makes her cry out, "All ye that love the Lord, rejoice with me; for when I was little I was pleasing to the Most High." As Dante sings, "With a single glance of her eyes she, who is loved and revered by God, obtains for us all graces."

We, children of Adam, conscious of our sinfulness, gaze in wonder at this marvel of spotless beauty; we congratulate her, and we exult in the Lord, because one of our race has been endowed with so much grace that she was deemed worthy to be the Mother of God. Enraptured we sing with the Church, Thou art all-beautiful, O Mary; thou art the glory of Jerusalem, the joy of Israel, the honor of our people. Thou art the Advocate of sinners, O Mary, Virgin most prudent, Mother of Love; pray for us, and intercede for us with our Lord, Jesus Christ.

II. Mary Our Mother, Cause of Our Joy

To every man his mother is a sacred source of noble and unalloyed joy. In the supernatural order, too, God has given us a Mother. So has the Church understood the words, which at the hour of His death Jesus addressed to Mary, "Woman, behold thy son"; and to John, "Behold thy mother." These were simple, solemn, divine, creative words.

In the beginning God said, "Be light made, and light was made" (*Gen.* 1, 3). On the cross God said, "Behold thy mother", and she was made our Mother; "Behold thy son", and he was made her son. At that moment Mary became the Mother of all those that would believe in Jesus and through Baptism would be incorporated into Him.

When she was about to become the Mother of Jesus, Mary by her *Fiat* gave her full consent to whatever that motherhood would imply; here there was no need of renewing that consent. She was the Mother of God's Son, and as such she became the Mother of all those who, in Christ, have been made children of God.

Can aught be closer to Mary's heart than this last charge committed to her by her dying Son? And to us, what a cause of joy it is, to know that we have received from Jesus Himself His own Mother as our Mother too. When such a son commends us to such a Mother, how safe we feel and how happy! "To thy protection we fly, O Holy Mother!"

III. Mary's Divine Motherhood, a Cause of Our Joy

Mary was the first to hear "the good tidings"; and "the great joy that shall be to all the people", which the angel announced to the shepherds, filled first the heart of Mary when "the Holy" was born as her child.

Through Mary the Father gave us His Son, and with Him all things. When the Holy Ghost "came upon her", she conceived in her womb the Prime Fountain of all bliss and all grace, of all

joy and all peace, on earth and in heaven. Rightly do we greet
Mary as the "Cause of our joy"; for she has borne, nourished, and
given birth to Him who was to say, "I am the way and the truth
and the life" (*John* 14, 6).

She is the Alma Redemptoris Mater, the fostering Mother of
the Redeemer, though only a creature, the "handmaid of the Lord",
herself redeemed, but sublimely redeemed. In her first of all was
poured the fullness of salvation and of joy; then of that over-
fullness we all have received. From her we have received Him
as our Brother in manhood; from Him we have received her, as
our Mother in the divine scheme of redemption. And one day she
will "show us the fruit of her womb" and introduce us into the
eternal joy of her Son our Lord.

Prayer: O Mother blest, whom God bestows
On sinners and on just
What joy, what hope thou givest those
Who in thy mercy trust!
O Mother blest, for me obtain,
Ungrateful though I be,
To love that God, who first could deign
To show such love to me.

$\longrightarrow$ end

SECOND SUNDAY AFTER EASTER

THE GOOD SHEPHERD (John 10: 11-16)

1. The oldest representation of Christ, found in the Catacombs,
    represents Jesus as a shepherd, carrying a sheep on His shoul-
    ders. Even now He is often thus represented on the doors of
    our tabernacles. Jesus gave Himself that name, "I am the good
    shepherd."

2. *Petition:* The grace to understand His predilection for that
    emblem, to put our trust in Him, and to follow His lead.

I. The Shepherd's Rule, Gentle and Strong

This is a primeval and a biblical emblem, referring us to the
nomad era in the history of man, when kings were called "the
shepherds of the nations". Jahve was the Shepherd of Israel,

and the chosen race was His flock, which He led forth to pasture and protected. In the days of Christ the shepherd and his flock were integral parts of the Palestinean landscape. And even in our industrialized Western countries he has not yet wholly vanished; for here and there one may meet a forlorn shepherd, leading his sheep through all weathers over fallow fields and by-lanes, lone and gentle, watching attentively over his flock.

Jesus chose this symbol to describe Himself and the kind of rule He exercises, the most complete power in its gentlest form.

The shepherd is one, set over many; in dignity, since he is a man, he stands far above his flock, and yet keeps ever so close to his sheep, living in their midst, leading them, watching over them, guarding them against all danger, ready to lay down his life in their defence.

II. Jesus Is the Good Shepherd

All the good qualities of the shepherd are found in Jesus in the highest degree. He is One, set over many, yea over all. "And there shall be one fold and one shepherd" (*John* 10, 16). Being God, He is infinitely superior to man; as the God-Man, "he dwelt among us", like unto us in all things, sin excepted. He is "come that they may have life, and may have it more abundantly" (*John* 10, 10).

He lays down His life for His sheep. That a shepherd should die for his sheep, a man endowed with reason for an irrational animal, seems outrageous; but how much more unjustifiable it seems that the Father should have let His only-begotten Son die for us, His rebellious creatures! Such love indeed surpasses our comprehension. However, man was created in God's image and likeness, and for an eternal destiny. "God so loved the world" (*John* 3, 16).

But mark how unbelievably the reality transcends the symbol drawn from pastoral life: "The Good Shepherd giveth his life for His sheep" and after He has died and risen again He gives Himself as food to them till the end of time. As the *Lauda Sion* has it,

> Jesus Shepherd, Bread indeed,
> Thou take pity on our need:
> Thou Thy flock in safety feed:
> Thou protect us, Thou us lead!

III. Pastoral Authority in the Church

All authority, exercised in Christ's name in the Church, must be exercised in a pastoral spirit. At the head of the whole Church Jesus has placed a supreme Pastor; and at the head of every parish there is a pastor. Authority is exercised in a pastoral spirit, when it is wielded with selfless, loving devotion to the flock. Peter, the first Supreme Pastor, appointed by Jesus Himself, addressed the following solemn admonition to those that are vested with authority, "The ancients therefore that are among you, I beseech, who am myself also an ancient, and a witness of the sufferings of Christ: as also a partaker of that glory which is to be revealed in time to come: feed the flock of God, which is among you, taking care of it, not by constraint but willingly, according to God: not for filthy lucre's sake, but voluntarily; neither as lording it over the clergy, but being made a pattern of the flock from the heart" (1 Peter 5, 1-3).

Let these words ring constantly in the ears of all those who wield authority in the name of Christ, and who ought to be imbued with the spirit of Christ. Theirs is a grave responsibility, "which no man doth take unto himself, but he that is called by God" (Heb. 5, 4). St. Paul addressed these last words to priests, but they are applicable to all who exercise authority in the Church.

To these grave duties of Superiors correspond grave obligations laid on inferiors, viz. confidence and loyalty, inspired not by flesh and blood but by the spirit of faith and filial love. Before Jesus appointed Peter Supreme Pastor He asked the Apostle, "Simon, son of John, lovest thou me?", and Peter answered, "Yea Lord, thou knowest that I love thee." Thereupon only was the flock entrusted to Peter. Jesus asks us the same question, "Lovest thou Me?", and when we have answered "Yea Lord, Thou knowest that I love Thee," Jesus would say, "Then hear those whom I have placed over thee"; for "he that heareth them heareth Him" (Luke 10, 16).

To command and to obey, to lead and to follow, these describe in God's Church the relations between Superiors and subjects based on and consecrated by—love of Jesus.

Prayer: We beseech Thee, O Lord, be pleased, in Thy infinite goodness, to appoint pastors over Thy Church who by their loving devotion to their flock will be well-pleasing in Thy sight; and grant us the grace to lovingly and loyally follow their lead.

"I KNOW MY SHEEP" (John 10: 11-16)

1. In the days of our Lord several flocks of sheep used to be sheltered during the night in large common folds. Early in the morning every shepherd would come to fetch his own sheep. Each one knew his own, and called them and they recognized their shepherd's voice and gathered around him. The shepherd went ahead, and the sheep followed for the day's pasture. The parable of the Good Shepherd recalls these details.

2. *Petition*: The grace always to trust Him who has called me, and faithfully to follow whithersoever He leads.

I. Jesus Knows His Own

All men are His own by right: He has created them, and therefore they are His. Moreover the Father has given to His Son made Man, all things and all men. "All things are delivered to me by my Father" (*Matt.* 11, 27). By His death He has redeemed them all.

But Jesus calls "His own" in a very special manner those who believe in Him, who have freely dedicated themselves to Him, who are firmly resolved to belong to Him. By Baptism they have been incorporated into Him, and form one Body of which He is the Head.

In a more intimate way still He calls the Apostels "His Own", "whom the Father has given Him out of the world (*John* 17, 16). He Himself called them, but the Father gave them to Him.

The knowledge, which Jesus has of His own, is the knowledge of love, of divine love, which is all-wise, almighty, and full of mercy. Jesus tells us that He knows them, as the Father knows Him, and as He knows the Father. "I know mine and mine know me, as the Father knoweth me, and I know the Father" (*John* 10, 14-15). Here again, to our utter amazement, we hear Jesus placing on the same level our relation to Him and His relation to the Father: both are ineffably intimate, though in a different way.

There are also some whom He knows not: those who refuse to know Him and to believe in Him, like the Pharisees, or the foolish virgins who, through their own fault, arrived late for the wedding feast.

II. Jesus Knows Me

He knows me as the Creator knows His creature. "Lord, thou hast proved me and known me; thou hast known my sitting down and my rising up; thou hast understood my thoughts afar off. ... Thou hast formed me and laid thy hand upon me" (*Ps.* 138, 1-5).

In Baptism I became one of His own, and by my Baptismal vows, so solemnly renewed during the Easter Vigil, I dedicated my whole self to Him.

Again, in a special manner I became one of His own, when He called me "out of the world", that I might freely consecrate myself to Him. He knew me, far better than I knew myself, with all my frailties and all my faults; but His knowledge was loving knowledge, laden with grace: a divine knowledge that "searcheth the reins and the heart". "He needed not that any should give testimony of man, for he knew what was in man" (*John* 2, 25). And as He was first to know me, so He was first to love me, with a creative love. Knowing me thus, and loving me thus, He called me; in that knowledge and in that love I place my fullest trust.

III. He Has Trusted Me

No, not me left to my own strength; He knows me too well for that. But he has trusted Himself, who operates in me. He knows what He can expect from me, provided I can believe and accept the grace He offers. One day God charged Jeremias with a mission that struck terror into the prophet. Jahve said to him, "Say not, I am a child; for thou shalt go to all that I shall send thee. ... For I am with thee to deliver thee" (*Jer.* 1, 7-8). And St. Paul exclaimed "I can do all things in him who strengtheneth me" (*Phil.* 4, 13).

What we all lack is trust in Him, who has called us. We keep our eyes fixed on ourselves, are blinded by our weakness and yield to doubt. Why? Because we fancy that it is we ourselves that must fulfill the task, which is beyond our strength. Why cannot we forget our own selves, stop computing what we can and cannot accomplish; and cling to Him, in whom we can do all things? So often we deserve the rebuke, which Jesus many a time addressed to His own—during the days of Galilee and throughout the ages—"Why have you doubted, O ye of little faith?" Let us therefore have confidence in ourselves as He has confidence in us; not because we are strong, but because "greater is he that dwells in us, than he that is in the world" (1 *John* 4, 4).

Prayer: O Lord Jesus, before whom every heart lies bare and every will is an open book, and to whom no secret is hidden; in Thy ineffable goodness Thou hast called me, knowing all about me when Thou didst invite me to become Thine in a special manner: continue in Thy mercy to recognize me as one of Thine own; grant me the grace every day to cling more closely to Thee, that I may faithfully follow wherever Thou deignest to lead me.

TUESDAY: SECOND SUNDAY AFTER EASTER

"AND MINE KNOW ME" (John 10, 14)

1. As soon as the shepherd's call sounded at the door of the common fold, his own sheep recognized his voice and flocked to him. They followed him, feeling safe under his protection; they understood the slightest sign of his hand, the slightest modulation of his voice: and followed.

2. *Petition*: The grace to understand ever more thoroughly "the shepherd and the bishop of our souls" (1 *Peter* 2, 25) and to follow Him with complete trust.

I. "Mine Know Me"

We have become "His own", first of all because it has pleased Him to call us; yet also, because, aided by His grace, we have willed it. "No one knoweth the Son, but the Father" (*Matt.* 11, 27); "No man can come to me, except the Father, who hath sent me, draw him" (*John* 6, 44). And therefore Jesus declared that the Father has given him His own. Everything comes from the Father, everything happens out of pure love.

"You were as sheep going astray; but you are now converted to the shepherd and bishop of your souls" (1 *Peter* 2, 25). "Converted" because the Father drew us. "As one tries to allure a sheep with a verdant twig, thus God has used His Son to call us unto Himself" says St. Augustine.

In Baptism, we were made His own before we were capable of knowing Him. One of the first things we remember is how at our mother's knee we began to know Him; later that knowledge grew and waxed strong in prayer and through the reception of the Sacraments. Often He spoke to our soul in gentle whispers, inviting us to know Him more intimately and to follow Him more faithfully. And since the day when we surrendered ourselves entirely to Him, we have experienced how good He is, how long-suffering, how merciful: He is always ready to forgive and to comfort.

With St. Paul, we may exclaim, "I know in whom I have believed" (*Phil.* 1, 12). We do know Him, but our knowledge of Him must grow and increase.

II. Imperfect Knowledge

Even after three years of familiar intercourse with the Master and after so much counsel and direction imparted to each one personally, the Apostles knew Him not: Jesus had spoken to them about the Father, "If you had known me, you would without doubt have known my Father also: and from henceforth you shall know him, and you have seen him. Philip said to him, Lord, show us the Father, and it is enough for us. Jesus said to him, Have I been so long a time with you, and have you not known me? Philip, he that seeth me seeth the Father also" (*John* 14, 7-9). That the Father has, as far as that is possible, become visible in the Son was a revelation; but of a truth not fully grasped: they knew with perfect certitude, but the fullness of light was still lacking.

At times we know Jesus and recognize Him in the profound peace which He pours into our souls, or in the joy which is His and of which He makes us partakers.

Do we know Him, too, and recognize Him when He tries us, or demands increasing sacrifices from us? He never asks more than what with His aid we can bear; one thing at a time: He can wait so patiently. Do we know Him when He gives us hints through the events of every day, ordinary or unexpected, pleasant and above all unpleasant? Do we recognize our divine Pastor's voice in the commands of our Superiors, which sometimes sound strange to us?

Our knowledge is but imperfect. "We see now through a glass," says St. Paul (1 *Cor.* 13, 12). That glass is misty, and our sight is clouded. Strong faith alone pierces the mist.

III. Trust

Psalm 22 sings the praises of trust in the Shepherd:
"The Lord ruleth me: and I shall want nothing.
He hath set me in a place of pasture.

He hath brought me up on the water of refreshment;
He hath converted my soul.
He hath led me on the paths of Justice for his own
    name's sake.
For though I should walk in the midst of the shadow
    of death,
I will fear no evils, for thou art with me.
Thy rod and thy staff, they have comforted me....
And thy mercy will follow me all the days of my life.
And that I may dwell in the house of the Lord unto
    length of days."
    Soon the veil will be removed. "Then we shall see face to face
... then we shall know even as we are known" (1 *Cor.* 13, 12).

Prayer: Creator of all things, alas
            that here below
       I see Thee but as in a glass,
            as a faint glow;
       The glass is all too often dimmed
            by earthly dust,
       The emblems haplessly are rimmed
            with matter's crust!
       But one day, in Thy glory's light
            I shall behold
       unveiled Thy Count'nance bright
            'mid bliss untold:
       a drop afloat in the vast Sea
            of consciousness
       of the all-beauteous Deity....
            in timelessness!   *G. Gezelle Pr.* (*translated*)

<h3 style="text-align:center">WEDNESDAY: SECOND SUNDAY AFTER EASTER</h3>

INTRUDERS, HIRELINGS, OR PASTORS (John 10: 1, 10-13)

1.   The true shepherd, who seeks the well-being of his sheep,
is simple and straightforward in all his dealings; he need not
use violence or ruse to gain access to the flock; he simply enters
by the door of the sheepfold. "He that entereth not by the
door into the sheepfold, but climbeth up another way, the
same is a thief and a robber.... The thief cometh not but

that is not the shepherd, whose own the sheep are not, seeth the wolf coming, and leaveth the sheep and flieth ... because he is a hireling and hath no care for the sheep" (*John* 10: 1, 10-13).

2. *Petition*: If in any way we are responsible for others (and are we not all our brothers' and sisters' keepers?), may God give us the grace to be good shepherds after the pattern of Jesus and to divest ourselves of every vestige of the hireling's mentality.

I. "He That Is Not the Shepherd"

Whether he be a thief who by deceit or violence gains access to the sheep in order to steal them and slay them, or a mere hireling, his sole care is his personal profit; not the welfare of the sheep. The robber sells them; the hireling "looketh for the end of his work" (*Job* 7, 2), and for his wages: as soon as danger threatens, his sole thought is his own safety and he betakes himself to flight.

Through the mouth of the prophet Ezechiel God upbraided the bad shepherds, "Woe to the shepherds of Israel that fed themselves! Should not the flocks be fed by the shepherds? ... The weak you have not strengthened, and that which was sick you have not healed; that which was broken you have not bound up, and that which was driven away you have not brought again, neither have you sought that which was lost; but you ruled over them with rigor and with a high hand.... I will require my flock at your hand ... and the shepherds shall feed themselves no longer" (*Ezech.* 34: 2, 4, 10).

We shudder at beholding that picture of loathsome degradation: let us humbly and sincerely examine whether selfishness and self-interest have not crept into *our* service of the Lord and of our neighbor. Blessed are those who are awake to such failings, who wholeheartedly repent, and with God's grace strive quickly and zealously to become true shepherds, not mere hirelings. Blessed Claude de la Colombiere knew by experience the severity of this strife but he wrote, "It does not disturb me nor make me lose patience. How would that help me? I beseech our Lord to enlighten me as to what I can do for His service and how I can chasten my zeal. But I am firmly resolved to patiently bide the time He will deign to work that miracle. I know that He alone can accomplish it."

III The True Shepherd

The Gospel enumerates eight characteristics of the true shepherd. He enters by the door and that door is Christ, as He Himself says. (This reminds us of the question which Jesus put to the first Supreme Pastor, "Simon, son of John, lovest thou me?": he that does not love Jesus is not allowed near the sheep); the porter opens the door to him; the sheep recognize his voice and come to him; he calls his own sheep by name; he leads them out; he goes before them; the sheep follow him; he gives his life for his sheep.

Let us ponder on the fourth trait: he calls each of his own sheep by name, He Himself has given that name which shows that He knows it and loves that sheep; it is not a mere number, one in a crowd. He knows them all individually, each with its character and qualities, and addresses them appropriately. That is the way Jesus is the ideal Pastor: He knows us and speaks to us personally.

Towards those over whom He places us we shall not be good pastors unless we approach and know each one personally, unless we know them with a knowledge that is love and sincere personal interest.

III. The Sheep Know the Shepherd

The sheep know and follow the shepherd; for they have experienced how much he cares for them and how devotedly he toils for their welfare. "But a stranger they follow not, but fly from him, because they know not his voice."

It is soon manifest whether a shepherd seeks himself, his glory, his advantage, his ease. Assuredly we are all human beings and we have all to battle against our intemperate and inveterate self-love. St. Francis of Sales, a keen observer of human nature, is credited with the saying that "a man's self-love dies only a quarter of an hour after he has expired".

When Jesus said, "Learn of me, because I am meek and humble of heart," He undoubtedly spoke as the Good Shepherd seeking to pattern others on His own heart.

Prayer: O Lord Jesus, who truly art our Good Shepherd and dost long to form good shepherds, deign to uproot from our souls all self-love and self-seeking, and make our hearts like unto Thine.

"I AM THE DOOR" (John 10, 7-9)

1. When speaking of the sheepfold, Jesus mentions the door by which the flock is led out to pasture. Then He applies the word metaphorically to Himself, "Amen, amen I say to you, I am the door of the sheep . . . I am the door. By me if any man enter in, he shall be saved: and he shall go in and go out, and shall find pastures" (*John* 10, 7-9).

2. *Petition*: The grace to find, through Jesus, a safe road to the true life, to the Father, to men's souls "through our Lord Jesus Christ, Thy Son, Who liveth and reigneth with Thee and with the Holy Ghost, world without end".

I. The Door to True Life

A door supposes an enclosed place, to which it lends or forbids entrance, according as it stands open or is closed. Now, in the nature of things an entrance is narrow, and so Jesus warns us, "Enter ye in at the narrow gate; for wide is the gate and broad is the way that leadeth to destruction, and many there are who go in thereat. How narrow is the gate and strait is the way that leadeth to life; and few there are that find it" (*Matt.* 7, 13-14). We shall understand these words better, if we remember the parable of the Good Shepherd. Jesus Himself is that narrow gate, just as He is the strait way. He calls every man, to every man He shows the way, and He goes before us all. "I am the way, and the truth, and the life" (*John* 14, 6). He leads us "out of darkness into his marvellous light" (1 *Peter* 2, 6), out of death into life, out of sin into holiness, out of the kingdom of Satan, "into the kingdom of the Son of his love, in whom we have redemption through his blood, the remission of sins" (*Col.* 1, 13-14).

We ask every grace "through our Lord, Jesus Christ, Thy Son": He, as God made Man, as our Lord, as Son of God, is our Mediator: the Door by which He has made it possible to gain access to God, to whom we had no possible approach.

II. Access to the Father and to the Holy Ghost

By assuming our human nature unto His divine Person, He has made it possible for us to rise to the knowledge of the

Blessed Trinity. "No one knoweth the Father but the Son, and he to whom it shall please the Son to reveal him" (*Matt.* 11, 27); "No man cometh to the Father but by me. If you had known me, you would without doubt have known my Father also: and from henceforth you shall know him, and you have seen him. . . . He that seeth me, seeth the Father also" (*John* 14, 6-9).

And Jesus also revealed unto us the Holy Ghost: "the Paraclete, whom I will send from the Father, the Spirit of truth, who proceedeth from the Father, he shall give testimony of me" (*John* 15, 26).

This mystery surpasses indeed all understanding; but the Father has revealed it to us through His Son, who became man. "Him the Apostles have seen with their eyes, they have looked upon Him, their hands have handled Him, they have heard Him" (1 *John* 1 1).

Through Jesus we know that the Blessed Trinity is the fountain of salvation—"Te, fons salutis, Trinitas." In all our prayers, most of all in our solemn Eucharistic prayer, we confess this ineffable mystery. When we are about to leave this world the Church will pray at our bedside, "He may have sinned, but never has he denied the Father, and the Son, and the Holy Ghost. He has always confessed the Trinity."

III. Access to the Souls of Men

"By me if any man enter in, he shall be saved; and he shall go in, and go out, and shall find pastures" (*John* 10, 9). These words do not refer to the sheep but to the shepherds. They inculcate the salutary lesson, which Jesus will repeat in His farewell address after the Last Supper, "I am the true vine and my Father is the husbandman. . . . I am the vine; you the branches; he that abideth in me, and I in him, the same beareth much fruit" (*John* 15: 1, 5).

If he that has been constituted shepherd by Jesus remains united with Christ, speaks and acts in the name and in the spirit of Christ, then he enters through Christ; he will be safe in this world and he will lead his sheep to wholesome pasture. "As the branch cannot bear fruit of itself, unless it abide in the vine, so neither can you, unless you abide in me" (*John* 15, 4).

Jesus is the Door: unless we pass through that Door, we cannot go to the Father; and no way to the souls of men is safe, unless Christ be that Way. Whatsoever we need, we ask and obtain through Him.

Prayer: O Lord Jesus, who art the Door, the Way, the Truth, the Life, we beseech Thee, keep our feet on the strait road; grant that we may devoutly and safely go in and out through Thee to Thine and our Father, and to men, Thy brothers and our brothers.

"ONE FOLD AND ONE SHEPHERD" (John 10, 16)

1. When Jesus uttered those words, He had only a little flock around Him; but He would send forth that handful of men to the whole earth. He would be with them, and through them He would establish the Catholic, universal Church. He foresaw how, notwithstanding His most ardent wish, and His most fervent prayer, this flock, through the fault of his own followers, would be rent asunder into sects and schisms.

2. *Petition*: The grace to understand better that ardent wish of the Heart of Jesus; the grace to contribute through fraternal charity and fervent prayer to the reunion of all the sheep of Christ under one shepherd.

I. "Other Sheep"

"And other sheep I have, that are not of this fold" (*John* 10, 16). By "this fold" Jesus meant the people of Israel. Yet He Himself one day had said, "I was not sent but to the sheep that are lost of the house of Israel" (*Matt.* 15, 24). This limitation, merely a temporary one, was part of God's unfathomable designs.

The "other sheep" are all the non-Jewish nations. Before ascending to heaven, Jesus gave to the Apostles this solemn command, "All power is given to me in heaven and in earth. Going, therefore, teach ye all nations" (*Matt.* 28, 18-19). Henceforth all barriers between people of different races, different tongues, different social conditions, are removed. "There is neither Jew nor Greek; there is neither bond nor free; there is neither male nor female. For you are all one in Christ Jesus" (*Gal.* 3, 28). The Father has given Him all men; His Blood has redeemed them all from slavery; all men belong to Him.

II. "Them Also I Must Bring"

"And I, if I be lifted up from the earth," said Jesus, "will draw all things to myself" (*John* 12, 32). He Himself draws them, and by His gentle inspirations He leads them along paths unsearchable. He draws them, and leads them, making use of "His own", and of all those whom He has appointed to be leaders and shepherds over the flock; seeking the help of those whom He has drawn closer to Himself, and who are entirely dedicated to His service. These, by word and example, by the holiness of their lives, bear witness to Him; by prayer and penance they assist the wanderers in finding the straight way; they help the weak and the weary to persevere and to enter by the Door.

But the only true Leader is Jesus Himself, "the Way, the Truth and the Life". He deigns to accept the assistance of His own, of all His own, of the pastors appointed by Him, and with these of all the members of the Church. Through their Christian lives, through the supreme hallmark of the Christian, fraternal charity, they bear witness to Jesus, and help Him to draw, and lead, and "bring" those other sheep that still wander in the wilderness, or grope in the darkness of night. Our example and our intercession draw them to the Good Shepherd. All of us must help in bringing stray sheep to the fold.

III. "One Fold and One Shepherd"

"And they shall hear my voice, and there shall be one fold and one shepherd" (*John* 10, 16). In these words our Lord gave utterance to the deepest and most ardent desire of His Heart. To Him, as to us all, it is profoundly saddening to behold the divisions that have arisen in the flock. It is sad that all His own, those who believe in Him and strive to love Him, have not remained as one fold; sad and saddening that a large portion of the flock has deserted the one fold, and without guide wanders in the desert. Nothing can be more pleasing to the Master's Heart than the zeal and the efforts of those who labor to bring all Christians closer together in Christ, to make them understand one another and love one another; and thus to make His Church more one, more holy, more universal. Was not this our Lord's last prayer to His Father: "And not for them only do I pray, but for them also who through their word shall believe in me; that they all may be one, as thou, Father, in me, and I in thee, that they also may be one in us; that the world may believe that thou hast sent me" (*John* 17, 20-21).

This longing for unity and reconciliation is a profoundly Christian, and truly Catholic, sentiment. All who love Jesus feel deeply afflicted by the spectacle of the divisions that rend the Church of Christ. To pray for union will make our hearts like unto the Heart of Jesus; it will broaden our outlook, and raise us above petty conceits and narrow prejudices.

Prayer: O Lord Jesus Christ, who saidst to Thine Apostles, Peace I leave you, my peace I give you: look not upon my sins, but upon the faith of Thy Church; and vouchfsafe to it that peace and unity which is agreeable to Thy will: Who livest and reignest God world without end. Amen (Prayer from the Mass, before Communion).

SATURDAY: SECOND SUNDAY AFTER EASTER

"THE GOOD ODOR OF CHRIST (2 Cor. 2: 14, 15, 17)

1. Some years ago the so-called Untouchables of India were in a state of ferment. They were seeking to shake off the cruel yoke imposed upon them by the Hindus, and determined to improve their social and economic position. As they were deliberating whether they would abjure Hinduism and embrace the religion of Christ, some Christian missionaries, Catholics as well as Protestants, are said to have tried to influence them by showing them that the embracing of Christianity would bring them not only spiritual, but also temporal advantages. There was nothing wrong in this; yet Gandhi used this opportunity to teach the missionaries a salutary lesson. "You came here," he wrote, "as agents of the Gospel. The Gospel needs no agents, no more than does a sweet-scented rose. The blind cannot see the rose, but they do smell it. The sweet scent of the rose, that is its glad tidings. The glad tidings of Christ spread a sweeter, a more subtle, a stronger aroma than does the rose. See to it that your personal lives are redolent with the sweet odor of the Gospel; and, please, spread it in the land in which you were born."

But for the last sentence the Hindu sage points here to the best, the most fruitful, method of practicing "Catholic Action". That method is within the reach of all. Possibly Gandhi did not know that very long ago St. Paul had made use of the same metaphor to describe his own apostolate. In his second epistle to the Corinthians St. Paul relates how God has blest his apostolic labors in Macedonia: "Thanks be to God, who always maketh us to triumph in Christ Jesus, and manifesteth the odor of his knowledge by us in every place. For we are *the good odor of Christ* unto God. . . . For we are not as many, adulterating the word of God" (2: 14, 15, 17).

2. *Petition*: While we meditate on the words of St. Paul, we beg for the grace that our lives may spread the good odor of Christ.

I. The "Action" of the Rose

Its influence is quiet, but strong, gentle, but irresistible; it spreads continuously and penetrates everywhere; indeed, it needs no agents; its presence alone is sufficient. Its perfume is its "action"; it spreads that perfume inevitably, without any pretence of doing so; most effectually in its immediate surroundings, and gradually further away.

Occasionally it is said that in our times many are tainted with the "heresy of action". That metaphor ought to remind us of what constitutes the sum and substance of the Christian apostolate. Of course, preaching is necessary, and the message must be delivered. "Faith then cometh by hearing and hearing by the word of Christ," says St. Paul (*Rom.* 10, 17) and the same Apostle admonishes Timothy "to labor as a good soldier of Christ Jesus" (2 *Tim.* 2, 3). The latter metaphor does appeal more to Paul than that of the rose. Yet the weapons which the good soldier of Christ wields are not those "of the flesh", but the weapons of light, and truth and love, . . . finally the perfume of the rose.

II. "The Good Odor of Christ"

The good odor of Christ, "of his knowledge", "manifested by Paul" is love: love of God, proved authentic by genuine love of one's neighbor. "This is my commandment, that you love one another, as I have loved you. Greater love than this no man hath, that a man lay down his life for his friends" (*John* 15, 12-13).

This is Christ's own commandment. On another occasion Jesus said that charity was to be the distinguishing mark of those who were His disciples. "By this shall all men know that you are my disciples, if you have love one for another" (*John* 13, 35). The Gentiles of Greece and Rome were astounded at the brotherly love of the Christians and cried out, "Lo, how they love each other!" That was the perfume and the "essence" of the Gospel, which first aroused the interest of the Gentiles.

"He that loveth his neighbor, hath fulfilled the law" (*Rom.* 13, 8). That is a strong expression, and it was used by St. Paul. Who on earth can resist the attraction of Love, as St. Paul described it in 1 *Cor.* 13: "Charity is patient, is kind; charity envieth not, dealeth not perversely, is not puffed up; is not ambitious, seeketh not her own, is not provoked to anger, thinketh no evil; rejoiceth not in iniquity, but rejoiceth with truth; beareth all things, believeth all things, hopeth all things, endureth all things."

"Let your personal lives spread the good odor of Christ": this, the most effective method of the Christian apostolate, lies within the reach of all. There is nothing spectacular about it, but "thy Father, who seeth in secret, will repay thee" (*Matt.* 6, 4), and bless thee. Our neighbors, especially those with whom we have daily intercourse, will reap the benefit: the nearer the rose is to us, the stronger will be the perfume.

And that perfume will be pure and strong in the measure in which we "abide in Christ and He in us".

III.   Different Ways

The rose gives out its perfume in our gardens and displays its beauty in full sunshine; the tiny violet hides under the grass, but nevertheless it diffuses its fragrance; smaller still are myriads of little flowers, tiny, invisible, innumerable, that fill the woods with their aroma. There are herbs that must be crushed, so that they be able to emit their invigorating scent. Mary, the sister of Lazarus, broke the alabaster box "of ointment of right spikenard, and all the house was filled with the odor of the ointment" (*John* 12, 3). "The Message to Mary", Violaine, after becoming a leper, says: "Now that I am broken and crushed I can spread the good odor." Whether we shall spread around Christ's good odor by occupying a prominent position, or by living a life hidden from the world; whether we shall serve Christ blithely passing through life, basking in God's sunshine; or shall be weighed down by a heavy cross: generally that does not depend on our choice. A Christian poet said, "We are where God chose us to be and nought else have we to do but be God's flower and spread His fragrance." The greatest proof of love a man can give is to lay down his life. As in the past so in our own days, it is the blood of martyrs that most powerfully, and most widely, spreads the good odor of Christ.

Jesus was most lovable, and drew all men to Himself, less on Thabor than on Calvary. The nails, the thorns, the wounds, the blood shed for us, will, as long as the world lasts and human beings carry a heart in their breast, draw souls to Jesus by their supernatural fragrance.

Prayer: O Mary, Mother of Fair Love, Mystical Rose, who in the silence of Nazareth, and at the foot of the cross, hast flowered and spread thy fragrance, make us partakers of the fullness of thy grace, so that every day of our lives we may spread the good odor of Christ Thy Son.

THIRD SUNDAY AFTER EASTER

"A LITTLE WHILE AND YOU SHALL SEE ME" (John 16, 16-22)

1. In the Gospel of this day's Mass, we hear our Lord telling His Apostles that He is going away, but that He will return. They shall have joy and also distress, until they enter into His own joy, "which no man shall take away from them".

2. *Petition*: The grace, in the midst of trials and temptations, to place our trust in Him, who is the Way, the Truth and the Life, and who said to us, "Surely, I come quickly" (*Apoc.* 22, 20).

I. Alternation of Joy and Distress

"A little while, and now you shall not see me; and again a little while and you shall see me.... Amen, amen, I say to you that you shall lament and weep, but the world shall rejoice: and you shall be made sorrowful, but your sorrow shall be turned into joy. A woman, when she is in labor, hath sorrow, because her hour is come; but when she hath brought forth the child, she remembereth no more the anguish, for joy that a man is born into the world" (*John* 16, 16-22).

Jesus is alluding to His passion and death, over which "the world would rejoice", and His apostles "lament and weep". Jesus does not say what that joy of the world is worth, nor how long it lasts. Wordly joy is never of long duration, and it leaves a bitter aftertaste. "You shall be made sorrowful, but your sorrow shall be turned into joy" (*John* 16, 20). Not only does the sorrow pass away; but out of the very sorrow shall spring joy, and such joy as those only can taste who have born the sorrow. "Ought not Christ to have suffered those things, and so to enter into his glory?" All the Saints have known bright days and gloomy ones, just like all other children of Adam; nay, even more, because they live more intensely. St. Paul passed through dark hours and through tribulations, he was "weary even of life" (1 *Cor.* 2, 8). Before attaining everlasting bliss, the soul must drain the dregs of the chalice. With the most implicit confidence we may leave it to God to determine how joy and grief will alternate in our lives. "All is grace", said little Therese of Lisieux, and she peacefully pursued her "little way".

II. Joy in the Midst of Trial

"Your sorrow shall be turned into joy." Not only will sorrow cease and be followed by joy, as in the case of the mother who has borne a child, "and no more thinketh of her anguish"; but sorrow itself will become joy.

When the Apostles had been scourged by order of the Sanhedrin because they had preached the name of Jesus, "they went from the presence of the council, rejoicing that they were accounted worthy to suffer reproach for the name of Jesus" (*Act.* 5, 41). We know that suffering has a meaning; that our sufferings, patiently borne, and united with the sufferings of the mystical Body of Christ, have power to save and to sanctify, even more than our actions. This conviction helps us to bear tribulation courageously and gladly. St. Teresa of Avila wrote: "What then is this life of ours, but a slight burden borne not without internal relish?"

St. Francis of Sales, in his own peculiar manner, urged his nuns "to live cheerfully amidst the thorns of the cross of Christ, and like the nightingale in his coppice to sing: Long live Jesus!"

III. Perfect Joy

The joy which no man shall take away from us is one of the fruits of the Holy Ghost. No earthly event can disturb the hallowed source whence this joy wells up; earthly happenings may, perhaps, cause a feeble ripple on the surface of the soul; but they cannot lessen the conformity of our will with the will of God. From this fundamental oneness of wills spring our joy and our peace. Yet in this world our joy can never be perfect. "A little while, and you shall see me." On those words St. Augustine comments as follows: "Time is short and our own fleeting hour is part of it. A little while still, and we shall see Him, where we shall no longer have to beg for favors, nor ask questions, where no desire shall remain unsatisfied, where we shall lack nothing." The same Saint concludes his great book, "The City of God", with these ecstatic words: "There we shall rest and see, see and love, love and praise. That will be world without end!"

"Amen, come Lord Jesus": these are the very last words of our Holy Books.

"My child, when you feel a desire for everlasting bliss poured into your soul from above, and you long to go forth from the prison of the body, that you may behold My brightness without shadow of change, enlarge your heart and receive this holy inspiration with all the fervor of your soul" (3 *Imit. of Christ*, 49, 1).

Prayer: May our earthly passions be subdued by these mysteries, O Lord, and our love for things heavenly increased. Through our Lord. . . . (Secret of the Mass).

MONDAY: THIRD SUNDAY AFTER EASTER

"IT IS EXPEDIENT TO YOU THAT I GO" (John 16, 7)

1. We hear Jesus telling His Apostles about His impending departure from them, and we see sadness clouding their countenances. Jesus says, "But because I have spoken these things to you, sorrow hath filled your heart. But I tell you the truth: it is expedient to you that I go: for if I go not, the Paraclete will not come to you; but if I go, I will send him to you" (*John* 16, 6-7).

.2 *Petition:* The grace to maintain firm trust, even when, for a while, we do not *feel* His presence. He knows best what is salutary for our soul.

I. Their Love Must Be Tried and Purified

He had called them, and they had given themselves unreservedly to Him. Their love was sincere, yet it had to grow more sincere, more pure, more spiritual. His visible presence in their midst made it impossible to them to penetrate to the very depth of His divine Personality.

"Out of sight, out of mind", is a true enough saying, where there is question of purely human affections. But from them Jesus demanded more than merely human love. He is God and man, and must be loved as God and as man. His visible presence, the charm of the words that flowed from His lips, "words of life" as no man had ever yet spoken: that is, His human personality had fascinated them and attached them to Him. Later St. John will proclaim: "That which was from the beginning, which we have heard, which we have seen with our eyes, which we have looked upon, and our hands have handled of the word of life" (*John* 1, 1). But in order that they might realize that He was the Word of Life, it was necessary that Jesus should go away for a while. To the eye of the flesh He had to be invisible, so that He might become invisibly present and active in their minds now grown more enlightened and their hearts more purified.

And in this way He is truly present not merely with a few fishermen of Galilee who had been privileged to deal familiarly with Him during two or three years, but with all men of all times, who believe in Him and partake of His Body as their food.

It may happen that we cease, perhaps for a time, *to feel* His mysterious spiritual presence. Whenever this is not a chastisement due to our negligence and our lukewarmness, we should find solace in recalling the words of Jesus, "it is expedient to you that I go." Meanwhile we patiently bear the trial, by which God purifies our soul.

II. "If I Go, the Paraclete Will Come"

"For if I go not, the Paraclete will not come to you; but if I go I will send him to you" (*John* 16, 7).

The Apostles did not understand why the Paraclete would not come to them unless Jesus went away. On this occasion Jesus reveals to us something of the most ineffable mystery of our faith: the internal relations of the Three Divine Persons, and their joint co-ordinated action.

The Father Himself does not come, except in the Son, whom He sends. The Son has come from the Father, He has revealed the Father to us, and returns to the Father. And then the Third Person of the Blessed Trinity can come; He is sent by the Father and the Son. "But when the Paraclete cometh, whom I will send you from the Father, the Spirit of truth, who proceedeth from the Father, he shall give testimony of me" (*John* 15, 26).

These are human concepts and human words, used by the Incarnate Word of God to speak to us about the stupendous and ineffable mystery of the Blessed Trinity. At least this much it is given us to understand: all the Three Persons have cooperated in the work of our redemption, all Three together, and Each according to His own Personality. With humility and gratitude we listen to Jesus, "who hath made known to us all things whatsoever he hath heard from the Father" (*John* 15, 15).

III. "He Will Teach You All Truth" (John 16, 13)

When Jesus will have ascended to heaven, His "image" will be complete. Then the Apostles can reflect upon the whole image and ponder over it in their hearts. This divine image is stamped as a seal on their souls and the Holy Ghost, whom Jesus will send to them, will illumine it brightly. They will reaize all that He was to them, they will understand what He has taught them. "These things have I spoken to you, abiding with you. But the Paraclete, the Holy Ghost, whom the Father will send in my name, he will teach you all things, and bring all things to your mind whatsoever I shall have said to you" (*John* 14, 25-26).

Don't we experience something of the sort even in the purely natural order? We realize best what our parents were to us, when the image has been completed and we can contemplate their life as one whole: then each detail completes the whole, and the whole illumines each detail and gives it its proper meaning.

Henceforth, under the never-failing guidance of the Holy Ghost, the Apostles will remember their Master and grasp the full bearing of His message. "But when he, the Spirit of truth is come, he will teach you all truth. For he shall not speak of himself, but what things soever he shall hear" (*John* 16, 13).

The Paraclete, sent by the Father, will come down on them, never to depart again. With the Apostles He will close the divine revelation, and through the Church He will preserve the sacred deposit.

Prayer: May our souls be enlightened, we pray Thee O Lord, by the Paraclete, who proceedeth from Thee: and may He fulfill

the promise of Thy Son, by guiding them to all truth. Who liveth
and reigneth. . . . (Collect, Pentecost Ember week).

TUESDAY: THIRD SUNDAY AFTER EASTER

"I GO TO THE FATHER" (John 16, 16)

1. We hear our Lord, stating in human language, His inexpress-
    ibly intimate relationship with the Father. No man knows the
    Father but the Son, and he to whom it shall please the Son
    to reveal him (*Matt.* 11, 27).

2. *Petition:* The grace to be enlightened by the Holy Ghost,
    and to be introduced by Him into a deeper knowledge of the
    Father and the Son.

I.   "I Go to the Father"

Thus Jesus spoke in His farewell discourse after the Last
Supper. He was returning to His Father, but in a "form" different
from that in which He came from the Father. Then He was "in
the form of God, equal with God". "But he emptied Himself,
taking the form of a servant, being made in the likeness of men"
(*Phil.* 2, 7). Now He goes back to the Father as God made man,
with His glorified Human Nature, which is indissolubly united
with the Divinity.

After His glorious resurrection, He said to Mary Magdalen,
"I am not yet ascended to my Father. But go to my brethren and
say to them, I ascend to my Father and to your Father, to my
God and your God" (*John* 20, 17). Because of His Human Nature,
He is our Brother; and as our Brother, He returns to His Father,
who now is our Father also. Our human nature has been associ-
ated with, assumed unto, the very being of the Godhead. "Thou,
who sittest at the right hand of the Father, have mercy on us.
For Thou alone art holy, Thou alone art the Lord, Thou alone,
O Jesus Christ, art most high."

II.   "The Father Is Greater Than I"

"If you loved me, you would indeed be glad because I go to
the Father; for the Father is greater than I" (*John* 14, 28).
True love consists in this, that we wish the greatest possible

happiness to the person we love. Now, the greatest happiness that could befall the Son of man, after He had fulfilled His mission, was to enter with His Human Nature into the glory of His Father. If we love Christ, our Brother, it behoves us to be intensely glad, because He now enjoys the glory of the Father.

"For the Father is greater than He!" He is the "One that is sent by the Father, entrusted with a mission by the Father. That is why Jesus so frequently stresses His complete dependence on the Father. St. John the Baptist assumed the same attitude towards Jesus. Just as the Baptist strove to draw men towards Jesus, that the Christ might increase while he himself decreased: so Christ endeavored to make us see the Father, while He Himself withdrew into the background.

"His doctrine is not His own, nor are His works, nor His life. The Father tells Him what He shall speak and what He shall do. With His eyes continually fixed on this supremely noble and dearly loved rule of life, He speaks, He acts, He dies. And whilst He, the Son, professes this absolute dependence on the Father, there is between them a boundless and most intimate love. Just as the Father, with infinite love, communicates Himself to the Son, so it is the Son's highest joy to receive from the Father and to be dependent on Him. Here we penetrate to the very depths of the soul of Christ. The more we enter into the mystery of His life, the better we shall understand and relish those expressions of humble dependence by which Christ invited His Apostles to discern the Fountain of all life, of all goodness, of all light, God the Father" (*Lebreton*).

Let this mind be in us, which was also in Christ Jesus (*Phil.* 2, 9), and which He Himself recommended to us: "Learn from me, because I am meek and humble of heart."

III. "I Go to Prepare a Place For You"

This is another reason why the Apostles should rejoice at His departure: He goes to prepare a place for them. "In my Father's house there are many mansions. If not, I would have told you: because I go to prepare a place for you" (*John* 14, 2). And in a prayer addressed to His Father, being fully conscious of the power which the Father had given Him, He said, "Father, I will that where I am, they also whom thou hast given me may be with me: that they may see my glory, which thou hast given me because thou hast loved me before the creation of the world" (*John* 17, 24). The joy of Jesus will be theirs, and it will be perfect.

But even before He brings them into His Father's Kingdom, He and the Father will come to them. "If any one love me, he will keep my word, and my Father will love him, and we will come to him, and make our abode with him" (*John* 14, 23).

This will be fulfilled in the day of the final revelation, when every veil is torn away; we have a foretaste of it during brief periods of spiritual joy, when God grants special light and solace to His own; it is a reality in the silent, unfelt, yet true indwelling and loving presence of the Father, and the Son, and the Holy Ghost in every soul that is in the state of sanctifying grace.

Prayer: O Lord Jesus Christ, who wert sent to us to reveal unto us the Name of Thy Father, and to show us the way that leads to Him; who hast returned to the Father, that Thou mayest prepare a place for us; who hast prayed and still prayest that where Thou art, there also we may be; we heartily rejoice with Thee because Thou hast entered the glory of Thy Father; we trust in Thy promise, and in Thy power to save us, who come to God by Thee, who art "always living to make intercession for us" (*Heb.* 7, 25.)

WEDNESDAY: THIRD SUNDAY AFTER EASTER

"MY PEACE I GIVE UNTO YOU" (John 14, 27)

1. In His farewell address Jesus again and again refers to His going away from them, and His coming back; and His promises to send them the Paraclete, who will remain with them. He also speaks of the joy and peace that will be theirs. "These things I have spoken to you that my joy may be in you" (*John* 15, 11). He concludes thus: "These things I have spoken to you that in me you may have peace" (*John* 16, 33). Let those words sink deep into our hearts: they come from the depths of the Sacred Heart of Jesus.

2. *Petition*: The grace that, however much we may be tried, we may always preserve the peace Jesus gives us.

I. "My Peace I Give Unto You"

Just as the joy, which Jesus gives, differs from the joy of the world; so does the peace of Christ differ from what the world calls peace. "Peace I leave with you, my peace I give unto you; not as the world giveth do I give unto you" (*John* 14, 27). History tells us, and perhaps we have learnt by the grim experience of long years of war and foreign occupation, how the world gives peace in so-called peace treaties. What is the value of such peace? Of late it has earned the name of "cold war".

When Jesus was born, the angels sang, "Glory to God in the highest, and peace on earth to men of good will." How can there be peace in the hearts of men, and among nations, when men are not of good will, when they wage war against God, or simply ignore Him?

The peace, which Jesus gives, "His peace" is the profound peace of the soul: "the tranquillity of order," as St. Augustine describes it, perfect order, which never reigned in any heart so completely as in the Heart of the God-Man. Its best description is in the words "Yea Father, for so hath it seemed good in thy sight" (*Matt.* 11, 26). It is the perfect and loving conformity of the human will with the most holy will of the Father.

Every day we pray for peace, before the Communion of the Mass, "Lamb of God, who takest away the sins of the world, give us peace." He can give us peace, for He is "our Peace and Reconciliation", reconciliation with God and with our fellow men on earth. The "Pax," that is the kiss of peace at High Mass, is the symbol of what must be our dispositions when we receive Holy Communion: reconciliation and peace with all men through Christ.

II. "Not Peace, But the Sword"

"Do not think that I came to send peace upon earth; I came not to send peace but the sword" (*Matt.* 10, 34). Do these words, which also were spoken by Christ, contradict what He said on other occasions? The words of our Lord are living words, always true, never involving the faintest contradiction, provided we will remember the circumstances under which they were uttered.

Jesus did come to bring peace to the world, but the "world knew him not ... and his own received him not; but as many as received him, he gave them power to be made sons of God" (*John* 1: 10, 12). Simeon, the old man, said to Mary, "Behold, this child is set for the fall and for the resurrection of many in

Israel, and for a sign that shall be contradicted, that out of many hearts thoughts may be revealed" (*Luke* 2, 34-35).

Every man has to take his stand, either for or against Christ; either for or against His doctrine, either for or against His commandments. And therefore Jesus could say truly, "I came to set a man at variance against his father, and the daughter against the mother, and the daughter-in-law against the mother-in-law. And a man's enemies shall be they of his own household. He that loveth father or mother more than me, is not worthy of me; and he that loveth son or daughter more than me, is not worthy of me" (*Matt.* 10: 35, 37).

There shall always be strife on earth: but the author of it is not the Prince of Peace; the prince of this world is the disturber of the peace. The sword, which Jesus brought into the world, is not wielded by Him for the destruction of men. By it He Himself was slain, and by His death on the cross He earned peace for all men of good will.

Heart of Jesus, our peace and our reconciliation, have mercy on us; have mercy on all those who reject Thee, not knowing what they do.

III. "Let Not Your Heart Be Troubled Nor Let It Be Afraid"

Jesus said, "Peace I leave with you, my peace I give unto you; not as the world giveth, do I give unto you. Let not your heart be troubled nor let it be afraid" (*John* 14, 27).

We know how He has overcome the world: by suffering and death He entered upon His glory. We have a High Priest who knows our infirmities, and has compassion on them; His Heart also was troubled and He was afraid in the hour of His agony, but He offered up prayers and supplications and was heard for his reverence (*Heb.* 5, 7), and so He overcame. Until the end of time Christ will suffer affliction in His Church, but against her the gates of hell shall not prevail: they may persecute her, close or "dis-affect" her sacred edifices, torture her children (and this we have seen happening in our own day on a vaster scale than ever before), but never shall they destroy her.

Whether they refer to the struggle between the "Two Cities" which is raging throughout the world, or to the fierce duel between good and evil which is being fought within our own soul, these words of Jesus must always comfort us: "Have confidence, I have overcome the world" (*John* 16, 33). "Abide in me, and I in you" (*Ibid.* 15, 4).

Prayer: O God, who art the author and lover of peace, to know whom is to live, and to serve whom is to rule; guard from every attack those who beseech Thee, that we who place our confidence in Thy protection, may not fear the weapons of the enemy. Through our Lord (Postcommunion, Mass for Peace).

THURSDAY: THIRD SUNDAY AFTER EASTER

"A NEW COMMANDMENT I GIVE UNTO YOU" (John 13, 34)

1. At least five times Jesus refers to the precept of charity in His farewell discourse: love of God, love of the neighbor, "two commandments, one love". Jesus insists on these commandments being one only: so do St. Paul and St. John. This is the central point of the doctrine of Christ.

2. *Petition*: The grace to understand that for the Christian life and for the attainment of Christian perfection, "other foundation no man can lay, but that which is laid: which is Christ Jesus" (1 *Cor.* 3, 11).

I. "A New Commandment"

"A new commandment I give unto you, that you love one another, as I have loved you, that you also love one another" (*John* 13, 34).

In more ways than one this precept was new indeed, and after so many centuries of Christianity it still remains new.

For the Jews the precept was new. For Israel, just as for all other ancient nations, love of the neighbor did not go beyond love for one's own nation. Foreigners did not come within its purview, or were rated as enemies.

Against the *lex talionis,* the law of retribution,—an eye for an eye, and a tooth for a tooth; or against that other law, "Thou shalt love thy neighbor and hate thine enemy," Jesus sets His own commandment, "Thou shalt not take vengeance: love thy enemies, do good to them that hate thee, and pray for them that persecute and calumniate thee' (*Matt.* 5, 43-44).

When Jesus proclaimed it on the mountain, this precept was a stark innovation; and ever since it has sounded new, astounding, and unreal in the ears of the carnal man, who in us also is very much alive. The ancients said that every man is a wolf to his fellow man . . . and would tear him to pieces. St. Augustine uses milder language; still our daily experience shows that he does hit the nail on the head, "All of us," says he, "are frail and fragile human beings. With our earthen vessels, that is our self-love, we manage to hamper each other; we continually stand in one another's way. Love alone can provide room for all of us and freedom of movement."

II. "As I Have Loved You"

The commandment of Jesus was new, because it excluded no man. "For you are all children of God by faith in Christ Jesus. For as many of you as have been baptized in Christ, have put on Christ. There is neither Jew nor Greek: there is neither bond nor free: there is neither male nor female. For you are all one in Christ Jesus" (*Gal.* 3, 26-28). "As He has loved us!" How far beyond our reach is that ideal! And so is that other ideal, "Be you therefore perfect, as also your heavenly Father is perfect" (*Matt.* 5, 48). He was the first to love us, with a spontaneous love: it could not have been otherwise: ours can only be love given in return and, alas, how cold it is and how devoid of gratitude!

He loved us unto the end, to the extreme limit. He being God's only-begotten Son, became man for our sake; He laid down His life for our salvation. St. John dares to say, "And we ought to lay down our lives for the brethren" (1 *John* 3, 16).

So did the Saints, not only the canonized Saints, but those too that have not yet been raised to our altars. Father Kolbe in the notorious Auschwitz concentration camp freely entered the "starvation shed" and chose death, taking the place of a poor man who had a wife and children.

Those are the heroes of Charity. God be praised, their name is legion, theirs are shining examples, for which we thank God and which, in the measure of the grace granted us, and the opportunities offered, we are determined to emulate in our daily lives. We implore the Father to give us a new heart, and to put a new spirit within us; we pray him to take away the stony heart out of our flesh, and to give us a heart of flesh (*Ezech.* 36, 26). Unless God grants that prayer, we shall fail to observe the "new commandment".

III. "By This Shall All Men Know. . ."

"By this shall all men know that you are my disciples, if you have love one for another" (*John* 13, 35). This is the distinguishing mark of the Christian, chosen by Jesus Himself, and pointing straight to Him: "This is my commandment that you love one another, as I have loved you" (*John* 15, 12). All the commandments are the commandments of Christ, but this one He specially calls His own. He that faithfully observes it gives proof that he is Christ's disciple.

The sign of the cross also is a distinguishing mark of the Christian: an outward sign and a symbol, whereby we profess our faith in the Blessed Trinity, and in our redemption by Christ our Lord. We may doubt whether many non-Christians understand that sign or are attracted by it to our Savior. But concerning fraternal charity, practiced with His grace, and for His sake, He Himself has said, "By this shall all men know that you are my disciples."

Perhaps we may remember here how St. John, the disciple whom Jesus loved, in his old age, could speak of nothing but of fraternal charity.

If we are determined to bear witness to Christ, both in our immediate surroundings and before all the world, and give a testimony which all men understand, and which can draw all men to Jesus, then before all other things we must observe that commandment, which on earth remains ever new, and which in a most special manner is our Lord's own commandment.

Prayer: Fill us, O Lord, with the spirit of Thy love, that refreshed by the Paschal Sacraments, we may under Thy loving care be of one mind. Through Jesus Christ, Thy Son (Postcommunion, Easter).

FRIDAY: THIRD SUNDAY AFTER EASTER

THE INFLUENCE OF A HOLY LIFE (1 Peter 2, 11-17)

1. The Epistle of the Mass of last Sunday is taken from the letter which St. Peter wrote from Rome, (which he calls Babylon) to the faithful of Asia Minor. Nearly all of them were converts from paganism; their neighbors held them in contempt, and calumniated them, saying they were enemies of the state and criminals. St. Peter exhorts them to lead holy lives: thus they will silence calumny, and earn the regard of all (1 *Peter* 2, 11-19).

2. *Petition*: May our lives be without reproach, so that, in the midst of a de-christianized world, they may bear convincing witness to Christ, to His doctrine, to His Church.

I. In the Midst of Non-Christians

St. Peter speaks of the daily behavior of Christians, which of necessity falls under the observation of their pagan neighbors. "Dearly beloved, I beseech you as strangers and pilgrims, to refrain yourselves from carnal desires, which are against the soul, conducting yourselves well among the Gentiles that, whereas they speak against you as evil-doers, they may, by the good works which they shall behold in you, glorify God in the day of visitation. Be ye subject therefore to every human creature for God's sake, whether it be to the king as excelling; or to governors as sent by him for the punishment of evil-doers and for the praise of the good; for so is the will of God, that by doing well you may put to silence the ignorance of foolish men: as free, and not as making liberty a cloak for malice, but as the servants of God. Honor all men, love the brotherhood, fear God. Honor the king. . ." (1 *Peter* 2, 11-17) and that was Nero!

The virtues recommended by the Apostles are those which every man esteems and values: general honesty, submission to lawful authority, uprightness, forbearance, respect for one's fellow men. These virtues all men see and admire. Surely a Christian ought to lead a better life than an unbeliever; a person dedicated to the service of God, a priest, a religious, must lead a better life than a layman: even laymen are strongly convinced of this, for to that priests are religious are called and do have special graces. Let us then strive after perfection, not by the practice of extraordinary virtues, but by practicing the common virtues more diligently and more perfectly.

II. "As the Servants of God"

They should live thus, not to earn the approval of men, but because "so is the will of God", "because they are servants of God", so that the Gentiles "may, by the good works which they behold in you glorify God". How pure, how noble, how true is this description of the conduct of the genuine Christian, entirely conformed to what the Master said, "Let your light shine before men, that they may see your good works, and glorify your Father who is in heaven" (*Matt.* 5, 16). But He also said, "Take heed that you do not your justice before men, to be seen by them. . . ." (*Matt.* 6, 1).

"Before men," but not because we are before them, out of vanity or for personal gain. Edification of one's neighbor should be a result, which one may desire, rather than an aim which one pursues. Dedicated, self-sacrificing love will at all times and in all places give the greatest edification.

How did the Church survive the fiercest persecutions? How did she live through contempt and calumny? Not through the eloquence of her preachers, nor by the shattering argumentation of her apologists, but by her own internal vitality, by the holiness, the love, the faith of her heroic children in all ages. These things drew the pagans to Christ.

III. The Light of Truth

The Collect at last Sunday's Mass speaks of "the light of God's truth, which He shows to those that have gone astray, that they may return to the path of justice". And active in spreading this light, are all those that profess the faith of Christ, that is all true Christians, more so those whose very habit proclaims to the world that they are disciples of Christ, and representatives of the Church. If they desire to be a light, shining before all men, and to lead to the path of justice those that have gone astray and that grope in the dark, then "they must repudiate whatever would sully the name of Christian, and strive worthily to bear that name".

It is necessary that the priest should announce the Gospel from the pulpit; but how many never set foot in a church! The light of truth, to which no man can close his eyes, is the upright life of Christians in the world, the saintly life of legions of priests, the wonderful love and devotion of thousands of brothers and nuns, who, everywhere on the broad face of the earth, serve the poor, the sick, the little ones, the lepers, and all those from whom the world turns away.

No Catholic Action bears more fruit than the upright life of the good Christian. "What you *are*, thunders so I can't hear what you say." (Emerson)

Prayer: O God, who sheddest the light of Thy truth to guide back to the path of justice those who have gone astray; grant unto all those that bear the name of Christian, not only to reject whatever is unworthy of that name, but also to seek after all things that may add luster to it. Through our Lord (Collect, third Sunday after Easter).

OUR ALL-POWERFUL INTERCESSOR

1. During the month of May a mighty wave of devotion seems to sweep over the entire Church. Not only in countries where Christ has reigned for centuries, but also in lands where the name of Jesus was preached only yesterday, whole cities and villages are astir to proclaim their love for, and their confidence in, the Mother of their Savior, who is their own Mother. Remember Lourdes, and Fatima, and Loreto, and so many other hallowed sanctuaries in every part of the world, where Christians gather to honor the Queen of heaven.

2. *Petition*: O God, may we dearly love our Mother, and place our trust in her intercession. May she be Queen, wherever Christ is King.

I. Close to Our Mother

Really and truly Mary is Mother of God. This is her most glorious title. We may call her "Queen of heaven and earth", and thus proclaim that she has been raised high above all other creatures; but that title does not express how closely she has approached the Deity. She is the masterpiec of God's creative power: in Mary the Divinity has, in a mysterious and most incomprehensible manner, established contact with our world of matter. Through Mary the Word of God became One of our race. At the Council of Ephesus, in the first part of the fifth century, after mature deliberation and fervent prayer, the Church defined that "the Holy", that was born of Mary, is true God as well as true Man, and that, therefore, Mary is indeed the Mother of God.

Still, notwithstanding this supreme dignity bestowed on her, Mary remains human, a mere human being, just as we are: and by the will of Jesus, expressed by His dying lips on the cross, she is our Mother. This double truth—that Mary is Mother of God, and Mother of all believers, the Christian professes when he has recourse to "our Blessed Lady", our Mother! "Behold thy mother":

these words were spoken by Jesus to all those who were to believe in Him. "All of you are her children": He seems to say, "love her, place your trust in her, as little children love and trust their mother."

Children love both their father and their mother; they know by instinct that through their mother, they readily find a way to the heart of their father. For the mother is closest to the children, and at the same time closest to the father. She stands between the father and the children, not as though she would usurp the father's place in the affection of the children, nor as though love for their mother would make the children forget their father.

The father is delighted to grant every request made by the mother in the children's name, for thus he tastes a double pleasure: he is glad to pay homage to her power with him, and he is delighted to give happiness to his children, who are as well her children.

However different these purely human relations may be from those that obtain in the divine and supernatural order, yet the comparison is right, and guaranteed by God Himself. One day St. Gertrude felt a scruple about her immense love for Mary. Was she not preferring the Mother, a mere human being, above the Son, who is God? Jesus Himself enlightened and consoled her. "Be not anxious, my daughter. Thine is the way I want things: when thou payest honor to my Mother, thou payest honor to Me."

II. Mary's Power

The Gospel tells us how incomprehensibly far Mary's power reaches. At her request, and because she was insistent, Jesus performed His first miracle. At a wedding feast, in order to spare poor people a painful humiliation, she obtains that Jesus should change a decision He had taken—that is a human way of putting it. Theologians and exegetes are faced here with one or two knotty problems, but the fact remains: Mary prayed, she insisted, she won! And that, even though "His hour was not yet come".

To scripture scholars, "His hour" signifies the hour of His death and of His triumph over death, the hour also when, just as at Cana, Jesus solemnly addressed His Mother as "Woman", and appointed her Mother of all the living, thus making her play a part in the great work of salvation.

The history of the Church, the progressive development of

the Christian doctrine of Mary's motherhood, the lives of all the Saints, and the daily experience of all those who invoke her, bear witness to her power, now that she is enthroned in heaven in the glory of her divine Son.

III. What Do They Ask?

Why are children drawn to their mother? Because with her they are always welcome, because to her they can unburden themselves of whatever is in their hearts, because from her they may ask everything: the very little ones ask for sweets, the older ones want counsel; those that are in trouble seek solace; those who are in need crave for help. As long as she is on earth, they carry all their troubles to her, and all their needs. A mother's blessing is God's blessing.

Mary is our heavenly Mother, most powerful, most bountiful, most merciful. Into her heart we pour all our desires, all our needs of body and soul.

Little Therese of Lisieux, with the childlike simplicity that was so natural to her, said, shortly before her death, "I would love to die a beautiful death. I have prayed for that favor from our Lady. You know, it is not the same thing to ask something from our Lady and to ask it from our Lord. She knows so well what to do with my requests, which of them she should pass on to Jesus, and which she should keep back." And so we pray that "by the glorious intercession of the Blessed Mary, ever Virgin, we may enjoy perpetual health of soul and body". But when we ask her for the conversion of sinners, the spread of God's kingdom, peace among nations, the sanctification of priests and of all those that are consecrated to God, then she "passes on" our prayers to Jesus, because we ask what is most pleasing to her Son.

As from the Father we ask all things "through Christ our Lord, His Son", so from Jesus we ask all things through Mary, our Lady, His Mother and our Mother! Above all we ask her that "after this our exile she show unto us the blessed Fruit of her womb, Jesus".

Prayer: Still as on we journey,
Help our weak endeavor,
Till with thee and Jesus
We rejoice forever.—*Ave Maris Stella*

SUPPORTED BY FAITH

1. No man, who looks back over all the years of his life, will listen unmoved to the prayer, which on this day our holy Mother the Church addresses to the Father in the name of her children. We see ourselves, kneeling as one of the congregation in one of our parish churches, surrounded by men and women who year after year have been buffeted by the storms of life. In the name of all, the Pastor addresses the following prayer to God:

2. *Petition*: O God, who givest to Thy people to be of one heart and will, grant them to love Thy commandments, and to cling in hope to Thy promises: so that amid this fickle world our hearts may be anchored to the joys that never deceive, through our Lord (Collect, 4th Sunday after Easter).

I. Amid This Fickle World

A most common topic of conversation, and a thing which all men have felt very keenly, are the frequent and profound changes that occur in the life of every man, of families, of governments, of States, of the whole world. Governments rise to power and collapse, dictators bestride the world and are overthrown, empires grow mighty and perish, the world is ever in turmoil. We all know days when "fortune" smiles on us, and others when it frowns; we pass through seasons of prosperity and of adversity; we meet with agreeable surprises and with sad disappointments.

Man's spiritual life also has its periods of bright sunshine and of murky darkness, hours of sweet solace and hours of dismal aridity. Everything on earth, within man and without him, is ever changing, becoming, dying: and in the midst of that fickle world and of those unexpected vicissitudes the Christian fashions his soul under God's eye, guided by a paternal and all-powerful Providence. For Jesus said: Not one sparrow shall fall to the ground without your Father (*Matt.* 10, 29). And St. Paul told his Christians: "We know that to them that love God, all things work together unto good" (*Rom.* 8, 28).

We need not worry to ask ourselves beforehand through what troubles and changes God is going to lead us: He knows best and His ways are the safest. Possibly to our shortsightedness those ways may seem by-ways and blind alleys; seen from on high they lead straight to the goal.

> And lead us safe through life,
> By ways which Thou dost choose,
> To gain in heaven the light,
> Wherein Thou dwellest, Lord.—*Sacris Solemniis*

II. "That Our Hearts May Be Anchored"

Where can man, tossed on the storm-swept ocean of the world, find an anchorage that will save him from the fury of the tempest?

A recent convert was asked, "Why did you renounce your freedom of thought?" His answer was, "I stood in need of a solid anchorage."

Our faith alone offers us that safe anchorage in the stormy ocean of life. The anchor keeps the ship from drifting with the current or from being swept on the rocks by the rolling waves; but the anchor itself must be held on something that does not yield. St. Paul says, "Faith is the substance of things to be hoped for, the evidence of things that appear not" (*Heb.* 11, 1). After saying these words the Apostle appeals to the great men of the Old Covenant, the patriarchs, who saw not but believed the word of God. "All these died according to faith, not having received the promises, but beholding them afar off, and saluting them, and confessing that they are pilgrims and strangers, on the earth" (*Heb.* 11, 13). "And therefore we also, having so great a crowd of witnesses . . . let us run by patience to the fight proposed to us, looking on Jesus, the author and finisher of faith. . . ." (*Heb.* 12, 1-2). The only safe anchorage of our hearts and our minds is our faith, our faith in Jesus, our Savior who said to us, "Have confidence, I have overcome the world" (*John* 16, 33). He has overcome the world, "which passeth away and the concupiscence thereof", while Jesus Christ is the same, "yesterday and today, and forever" (*Heb.* 13, 8).

III. In Our Spiritual Life

In the *Imitation of Christ*, chap. 23 of Book III, Jesus says to the soul, "My child, be careful not to trust to thy feelings; whatever they may be now, they will very soon be changed. As long as you live you are subject to change, even against your will; so that you are sometimes troubled; today fervent, tomorrow careless; at one time diligent, at another lazy; now heavy and now full of spirit. But the man who is wise and truly learned in spiritual things stands above all the changes of feelings, not heeding what he feels within himself, or from what quarter the wind of change blows; but taking care only to keep his whole mind set on the one necessary and wished-for end. For so a man can remain one and the same, absolutely unshaken, through all the changes of his life, keeping his eye fixed steadfastly on Me, by purity of intention. And the simpler the eye of the intention is, the more steadily will you make your way through the midst of the storms of life."

Whatever may happen, whether in the world around us, or in our own spiritual life, let us with a pure intention, and with bare faith (as St. John of the Cross puts it), look up to Christ, "the author of our faith", and the "finisher" when we shall see Him face to face.

Prayer: O God, Father of light, in whom there is neither change nor shadow of alteration, grant us in the midst of the vicissitudes of this life ever to abide by our faith, where Thou givest true joy. Through Christ our Lord.

MONDAY: FOURTH SUNDAY AFTER EASTER

"OF ONE HEART AND ONE WILL"

1. Owing to our accelerated means of communication the world is becoming more and more unified. The "United Nations" meets and deliberates about common interests. It seeks for greater unity and tries to foster world peace. But "the way of peace they have not known; there is no fear of God before their eyes" (*Rom.* 3, 17-18). Meanwhile we hear the Church praying thus:

2. *Petition*: "O God, who givest to Thy People to be of one heart and will, grant them to love Thy commandments, and to cling in hope to Thy promises: so that amid this fickle world our hearts may be anchored to the joys that never deceive. Through our Lord...."

I. "Of One Heart and Will"

Unless there be oneness of heart and will, there can be no unity, no peace, no happiness, either in the family, or in the community, in the State, among the nations.

How can there be a sense of "brotherhood" among men, unless all acknowledge the same Father, of whom all are children? In order to reveal to men that the God they were seeking, "if happily they may feel after Him, or find Him" (*Act.* 17, 27), is truly their Father, the Almighty sent His only-begotten Son, to make His Name known to mankind. The Son of God made Himself Son of man, made Himself our Brother, and before dying prayed to His Father in heaven, "that they all may be one, as thou, Father in me, and I in thee" (*John* 17, 21). Always that same comparison, which is so bewildering to us: "Be you therefore perfect *as also* your heavenly Father is perfect" (*Matt.* 5, 48). "Love one another as the Father loves you." "Be you one as the Father and the Son are one." He, who utters those words, knows the Father and He knows man; and yet that is the ideal He dares to set before us.

In the Collect of the Mass of yesterday the Church addressed supplication to God, "who gives to His people to be one of heart and will": God indeed does give grace, but only too often men spurn it. "And they said, peace, peace; and there is no peace" (*Ezech.* 8, 15). They seek for peace, but they fail to find the way to peace.

Alas, how difficult it is to establish and to maintain peace even among "the faithful", "His people", "those of His household"! Even those who are dedicated to God humbly confess that they sadly fall short of the standard set by their Lord.

II. "To Love Thy Commandments"

There lies the way to unity! Our heavenly Father seeks nothing but our good. What He commands, what He desires, is that which will benefit us most of all. He is infinitely wise, infinitely good, faithful, immutable, no respecter of persons. Unity and peace must come to us from above, through the faithful observance of God's holy Will. Then God's commandments will no longer appear as something arbitrary, as a burden laid on our shoulders and as a galling constraint from which one tries to escape. God's holy Will becomes a thing worthy of all love. "The law of God is in his heart, and his steps shall not be supplanted," that is, shall not falter (*Ps.* 36, 31). What we bear in our heart does not weigh down but urges us forward. Where all have learnt to love what God commands, there is unity of will and of heart, there is peace, there is true happiness. "Grant to Thy people, O Lord, grant to thy faithful, grant to those who are consecrated to Thee, to love thy commandments." "He that hath my commandments, and keepeth them, he it is that loveth me. And he that loveth me, shall be loved of my Father, and I will love him, and will manifest myself to him" (*John* 14, 21).

III. "Cling in Hope to Thy Promises"

By this path also, which runs parallel to the other, men will find unity and peace.

God does not promise mere temporal goods. Because they covet and grab these, individuals and nations fight and slaughter one another. God promises us true joy and true happiness: eternal bliss, to behold Him face to face, to love and praise Him. Men never quarrel, nor do they fight against each other, for the acquisition of those eternal joys: they pray and they toil that all men may secure the enjoyment of them. "Eye hath not seen, nor ear heard, neither hath it entered into the heart of man, what things God hath prepared for them that love him" (1 *Cor.* 2, 8). But that bliss is a thing so overwhelming, it is so different from what our senses can apprehend, so far above our earthly notions, that only those "that mind the things of the spirit, not those of the flesh" can desire them.

Just now the liturgy of the Church strives to prepare our hearts for the feast of the Ascension of our Lord: on that day at Mass we pray "that we who believe that our Savior ascended into heaven, may in spirit make our dwelling in heaven".

The more we divest ourselves of all selfish desires, the more we allow our Lord to wean us from earthly pleasures, so much more ardently shall we long for what God promises; if our hearts securely abide where there is true joy, then there shall be unity of heart and will, concord and peace among the nations, among the faithful, and above all among those whom Jesus Himself deigned to gather in His name.

Prayer: O God, who givest to Thy people to be of one heart and will, grant them to love Thy commandments, and to cling in hope to Thy promises: so that, amid this fickle world, our hearts may be anchored to the joys that never deceive.

THE FATHER, FOUNTAIN OF ALL GOOD

1. We hear Jesus saying to His Apostles in His farewell discourse after the Last Supper, "I say not to you that I will ask the Father for you, for the Father Himself loveth you" (*John* 16, 26-27). This is the gladdest of glad tidings, vouched for by Jesus Himself; and yet how readily we doubt this love!

2. *Petition*: The grace always "to know and believe the charity which God has given to us" (1 *John* 4, 16).

I. God May Try Us: "He Tempts no Man"

St. James, in the first chapter of his Epistle, tells us that evil cannot come from God. Moral evil, that is sin, entered the world in spite of God's will. In a manner, it is the very negation of God, and so cannot have its origin in Him.

God is love, divine love; that love would not be divine if our human mind could comprehend its manner of acting. God tries man because He loves him. He tried even His Son made man, in the way He tries us. "For whom the Lord loveth, he chastiseth, and as a father in the son he pleaseth himself" (*Prov.* 3, 12). He sends us—or He permits—sickness, difficulties of all sorts, humiliation. But "sickness is a gift of God, no less than health", says St. Ignatius. Difficulties are a challenge to greater effort. How many have gratefully exclaimed with the Prophet, "It is good for me that thou hast humbled me" (*Ps.* 118, 71). "Blessed is the man that endureth temptation; for when he hath been proved, he shall receive the crown of life, which God hath promised to them that love him" (*Jas.* 1, 12).

It is true that a trial, owing to our frailty and to our inclination to sin, may turn into a temptation, an occasion of sin. "But let no man, when he is tempted, say that he is tempted by God. For God is not a tempter of evils, and he tempteth no man. But every man is tempted by his own concupiscence, being drawn away and allured" (*Jas.* 1, 13-14).

Our Father, who loves us, offers us the opportunity for spiritual growth, He never lays snares for the feet of His children. "All is grace" said St. Therese of Lisieux, our trials most of all.

II. "Every Best Gift Comes From the Father"

After proclaiming that it is not God who tempts us, St. James continues, "Every best gift, and every perfect gift is from above, coming down from the Father of lights, with whom there is no change, nor shadow of alteration" (*Jas.* 1, 17).

These solemn words of the Apostle mean that not only does every good thing come from God, but also that whatever comes from God is a perfect gift, and that from God only good can come.

Health, prosperity, learning, success, earthly goods, are gifts from God's hand. Yes, even atomic energy. But man, bent on crossing the will of God, has power to make a wrong use of those good gifts. Therefore we may say that they are "perfect" gifts inasmuch as they are God's gifts; in the hands of man they are good, provided he uses them rightly.

God alone is the giver of supernatural gifts: the best and most perfect gift comes from on high, bestowed by the Father of lights. "For, of his own will (that is, out of sheer goodness) hath he begotten us by the word of truth" (*Jas.* 1, 18).

"The word of truth", the word that will save our souls, is the revelation, the glad tidings, that we have been made children of the Father. "Behold what manner of charity the Father hath bestowed upon us, that we should be called and should be the sons of God.... Dearly beloved, we are now the sons of God; and it hath not yet appeared what we shall be. We know that, when we shall appear, we shall be like to him because we shall see him as he is. And every one that hath this hope in him, sanctifieth himself, as he also is holy" (1 *John* 3, 1-3).

III. "The Gift of the Most High"

During these days the Church, through the liturgy, prepares our hearts for the coming of the Holy Ghost, whose proper name is "Gift". As the proper name of the Second Person is Logos, "Word", an expression of the Father's thought, so the proper name of the Third Person is "Gift", an expression of the Will and the Love of the Father and the Son. This love itself is the first gift, *the* Gift, whence proceed all others. "Tu septiformis munere, Thou who art sevenfold in Thy grace", we say to the Holy Ghost in the *Veni Creator*. The seven gifts of the Holy Ghost contain all other gifts. The "word of truth", which will save our souls, was first spoken by the Son, but "when he, the spirit of truth is come, he will teach you all truth" (*John* 16, 13).

In order to allow the "grafted word", that is the life of grace, to blossom forth and with the help of the Spirit to bear fruit, we must cast out all uncleanness and abundance of wickedness, receive it with meekness, and be doers of the word, and not hearers only, lest we deceive our own selves (*Jas.* 1, 21-22).

Prayer: O God, before whom every heart lies open, to whom every will is eloquent, and from whom nothing is hidden, we beseech Thee, cleanse the thoughts of our hearts by the gift of the Holy Ghost, so that we may love Thee perfectly, and praise Thee worthily, through Christ our Lord (Collect of the Mass to obtain the grace of the Holy Ghost).

WEDNESDAY: FOURTH SUNDAY AFTER EASTER

GRADUALLY (John 16, 12-13)

1. Towards the end of His earthly ministry, Jesus said to the Twelve, "All things whatsoever I have heard of my Father, I have made known to you" (*John* 15, 15). That is, all things which it was good for them to know at the time, and which they might grasp. His going away would assist them to gain a deeper insight into those things; so would His death and resurrection. His apparitions and His altogether new manner of being present to them before He ascended to His Father, and finally the coming of the Holy Ghost, would complete their enlightenment. But at that moment Jesus could say truly, "I have yet many things to say to you, but you cannot bear them now" (*John* 16, 12). Those words show how deeply the Master loved them, and how wisely He guided them.

2. *Petition*: The grace to trust the love and the wisdom of Him to whom we have dedicated ourselves, and who, in due time, will give us the light and strength we need.

I. "I Have Yet Many Things to Say to You"

During the forty days that intervened between the resurrection and the ascension, Jesus further initiated the Apostles into the mysteries of the Kingdom. In the light of the resurrection He led them to understand the scriptures, and "all things which the prophets have spoken of him". Now it became clear to them that the life was manifested ... that they have seen with their eyes, and looked upon, and that their hands have handled the word of life (1 *John* 1, 1).

Many things He still has to say to them, but this He will do through the Holy Ghost: "He shall glorify me, because he shall receive of mine, and shall show it to you" (*John* 16, 14).

The Holy Ghost will abide with the Apostles until their death. God's revelation is complete, and closes, with the death of the last Apostle. However, the Holy Ghost will always guide the Church into the full truth, and help her to gain a more perfect understanding of what has been revealed. And He will preserve her from error.

What Jesus has to say to us, He says by the mouth of His Church. St. Ignatius, in his Rules to Feel with the Church, says, "We must believe that Christ our Lord who is the Bridegroom, and the hierarchical Church, who is the Bride, have the same Spirit, who rules us and guides us to the salvation of our souls. For our Holy Mother the Church is led and ruled by the same Spirit and Lord, who gave us the Ten Commandments."

II. "But You Cannot Bear Them Now"

He is "the Way, the Truth and the Life"; no less is He the ideal Teacher and Master; He knows what is in man, and He was well aware of the erroneous notions that filled the minds of His disciples. With divine wisdom and infinite patience He labored to set right their distorted ideas, and gradually to prepare their minds for the acceptance of the stupendous mystery of the Holy Trinity: how He and the Father are One; and how He is One with a Third, whom He and the Father will send them.

Yet even what He deemed opportune and necessary to impart to them, for instance concerning His passion and death and resurrection, was a cause of scandal to them. To his clumsy request, "Show us the Father", Philip receives an answer which betrays a sense of painful disappointment in the Master's Heart: "Have I been so long a time with you and have you not known me? Philip, he that seeth me, seeth the Father also. How sayest thou, Show us the Father?" (*John* 14, 9.) It is a mild rebuke, because Jesus knows that they are men of good will, but the trouble lies with their human frailty.

In the same manner God deals with each of us: gradually and with divine patience, He endeavors to make us penetrate deeper into the knowledge of His being and of His words; He is immensely considerate, never loads us with a burden which we cannot bear, ever tempers the light so that its excessive brightness may not blind us. It behoves us to have confidence in His goodness and His knowledge of our soul. Whatever He sends us, all things He permits to happen, have been carefully weighed by Him; the burdens He lays on us will never be too heavy for our strength with His grace. Therefore we pray with the author of the *Imitation*, "Lord, Thou knowest what is best: do this or that as Thou wilt. Give what Thou wilt, and as much as Thou wilt, and when Thou wilt. Do with me what Thou knowest to be best, what pleases Thee most, and is most for Thy glory" (Bk. III, 15, 1-2).

III. "The Spirit of Truth"

"But when he, the Spirit of truth, is come, he will teach you all truth. For he shall not speak of himself, but what things soever he shall hear, he shall speak" (*John* 16, 13).

"All truth", as far as we can apprehend it as long as we are in the flesh: truth, which the natural man could not have discovered by the force of his own intelligence; which has been revealed to us by the Son in the Father's name; which through the intervention of the Holy Ghost is preserved faithfully in the Church; the fullness of which will be understood better in the course of the centuries. A task most important and delicate of our Holy Mother the Church, especially at this juncture which craves for novelty and adaptation to new conditions. So often do we pray "Come, O Holy Spirit, fill the hearts of Thy faithful. ...", and ask to be enlightened and to be granted the possession of true wisdom. Let us on such occasions be mindful of our Pastors, whose duty it is to lead us, above all of the Supreme Pastor, who has to solve so many delicate and intricate problems.

All truth, not as we see it now through a glass, in a dark manner, but face to face, even as we are known (1 *Cor*. 13, 12) and seen without any veil, will then be our blissful possession, world without end.

Prayer: We beseech Thee, O Lord, that the Holy Spirit, the Comforter, who proceedeth from Thee, may enlighten our minds, and communicate to them all truth, according to the promise of Thy Son, who liveth and reigneth... (Collect, Wednesday of Pentecost, Ember week).

THURSDAY: FOURTH SUNDAY AFTER EASTER

"MY FATHER AND YOUR FATHER" (John 20, 17)

1. Every word spoken by Jesus is "a word of life", a word that gives life to our soul, and that will never pass away. The words, which Jesus spoke to Magdalen immediately after the resurrection, proceeded from the very depths of His divine and human consciousness, "Go to my brethren and say to them, I ascend to my Father and to your Father, to my God and to your God" (*John* 20, 17).

2. The grace to understand better those simple words of Jesus, so consoling, yet so unfathomable. If we but knew the gift of God!

I. The Lord's Words

The words of Jesus are utterances of the God-Man. He reveals to us what He has heard from the Father. Through human concepts and human language, He has to bring to our knowledge what is beyond our comprehension—the ineffable mysteries of the divine Nature Itself, and of God's relations with man. Never did man speak like this man (*John* 7, 46), said the ministers of the Pharisees, who had been deputed to apprehend Him: they had been fascinated by His words, and they dared not lay hands on Him.

It has been said that "words should be the flower that grows out of silence". A beautiful saying. The words of Jesus are the most beautiful flower, which has grown out of the profoundest silence. In the Old Covenant Jahve dwelt in the silence of the heavens, but "at sundry times and in diverse manners He spoke to the fathers by the prophets; last of all in these days hath he spoken to us by his Son... who is the brightness of his glory and the figure of his substance" (*Heb.* 1, 1-3).

For thirty years, during the hidden life at Nazareth, Jesus preserved silence, while He prepared Himself in solitude to fulfill the mission that had been entrusted to Him—to reveal to man the Name of His Father. On mount Thabor we heard the Father's voice saying, "This is my beloved Son; hear ye him" (*Matt.* 17, 5). With what profound reverence ought we to listen to the Gospel, wherein the words of Jesus are set down and addressed to us!

II. "My Father and Your Father, My God and Your God"

The Father in heaven, of whom Jesus speaks so often, is called here in the same breath "My Father and your Father, My God and your God"; yet even the words used by Jesus suggest a profound difference. We are so intimately connected with Jesus that He can call us "brethren": so are we, for we have the same Father. Before He suffered, He said to the Apostles, "I will not now call you servants: for the servant knoweth not what his lord doth; but I have called you friends: because all things whatsoever I have heard from my Father, I have made known to you" (*John* 15, 15). And now He calls them His "brethren"; and really and truly, in the full sense, they are His brethren: in the full sense, not in the fullest. They are indeed children of the same Father; but He is the Only-begotten Son, who is One with the Father; they are sons by grace, adopted sons in Christ and through Christ. And yet they are His brothers, for whom He pleaded with the Father thus, "And the glory, which thou hast given me, I have given to them, that they may be one, as we also are one: I in them and thou in me; that they may be made perfect in one; and the world may know that thou hast sent me, and hast loved them as thou hast also loved me" (*John* 17, 22-23).

Simple words, "words of life", "words that shall never pass away"; words spoken in our own human language, and therefore intelligible to us; words also spoken by the God-Man, and therefore pregnant with an unfathomable meaning. "For this cause", said St. Paul, "I bow my knees to the Father of our Lord Jesus Christ, of whom all paternity in heaven and earth is named, that he would grant you, according to the riches of his glory, to be strengthened by his Spirit with might unto the inward man, that Christ may dwell by faith in your hearts; that being rooted and founded in charity, you may be able to comprehend, with all the saints, what is the breadth and length and height and depth: to know also the charity of Christ, which surpasseth all knowledge, that you may be filled unto the fullness of God" (*Eph.* 3, 14-19).

St. Paul feels overwhelmed by the grandeur of the mystery which he is trying to express; his solemn language is in striking contrast with the quiet simplicity of Christ's words. Jesus is not at a loss for words to express the mystery: He 'represents,' nay, He is, the Truth; through Him the whole Divinity speaks, using human terms.

Our Lord's words ought to arouse in our hearts profound gratitude, as well as childlike confidence: "In obedience to Thy life-giving commandments, and instructed by Thy divine teaching, we make bold to say, Our Brother; and through Thee we go to Thy Father, who is also our Father.

Prayer: Our Father, who art in heaven. . . .

"WONDROUS EXCHANGE"

1. In the "Secret", that is the prayer over the oblations, of the Mass of last Sunday, the sacrifice of the Mass is called "veneranda commercia", which words mean "sacred intercourse" or "wondrous exchange". The same expression is used at the Midnight Mass at Christmas. In the "Sacred Mysteries", which we celebrate in the Mass, man and God come close together: man offers something to God, and in return God bestows something on man.

2. *Petition*: The grace to admire God's wisdom and goodness in this "wondrous exchange", and to celebrate the Sacred Mysteries with devotion and gratitude.

I. The "Wondrous Exchange"

"O God, who by the wondrous exchange of this Sacrifice, hast brought us to partake of the one sovereign divine Nature. . . ."

"Every best gift and every perfect gift is from above": thus speaks the Apostle St. James in the Epistle of the Mass (1, 17). The best, the most perfect, the most incomprehensible gift is God Himeslf: through that gift we are made to partake of the one sovereign, divine Nature! The incarnation of the only-begotten Son, His death, His resurrection, and His ascent into heaven, have made this partaking possible. The Word became flesh in the holy Virgin's womb: she negotiated the "wondrous exchange", and gave Him His human Body: He gave the Divinity to that human nature. Here began that "sacred intercourse", or "wondrous exchange", which, thanks to the great mystery of our salvation and to the institution of the Holy Eucharist, will last throughout the ages, till the end of time.

But in this exchange we are struck, on the one hand, by our own extreme weakness and poverty, and on the other by God's infinite power and overwhelming liberality. What can we offer to Him that is not His own gift to us? And what proportion is there between what we offer Him, and what He gives in exchange? The things we offer are bread and wine, the food by which our body lives. In a mysterious manner He transforms our material offerings, and under the appearances of bread and wine He gives us His Body and His Blood, to be the food of our souls. And thus we become partakers of the one sovereign divine Nature. These are sacred mysteries of the most intimate intercourse between God and the soul, through which He abides in us and we in Him. All this is accomplished on the spiritual plane, as beseems God, who is a pure spirit, and who chooses to adapt Himself to our nature by acting through material channels.

Since in this "wondrous exchange" God gives us His own Self, it behoves us to offer Him, not only bread and wine, but our whole selves with all we have and all we are.

II. "To Have Knowledge of Thy Truth"

"Grant, we beseech Thee, that we may not merely have knowledge of Thy truth. . . ." The truth here referred to is the reality of the "Mysterium fidei", the "secret of our faith", viz. that Christ, under the appearances of bread and wine is here present; that through the ministry of the priest, and of the entire congregation of the faithful, He offers Himself to the Father, and offers Himself as food to His own! That truth we know, as we sing in the "Adoro Te",

> Sight, touch and taste in Thee are each deceived:
> The ear alone most safely is believed:
> I believe all the Son of God has spoken,
> Than Truth's own word there is no truer token.

Faith *is* knowledge, partial because knowledge through a veil; but knowledge vouched for by God, and by which our soul must live.

III. "Attain the Full Possession of Truth"

"Grant, we beg Thee, that we may not merely have knowledge of Thy truth, but by a worthy life attain the full possession of it. . ."

Faith is knowledge, but that knowledge is not acquired by study; it is a supernatural gift of God, which God has bestowed on us that we might live by it. It is light, but it shines through a veil, yet sheds brightness enough on our pilgrims' path to direct our feet to the heavenly fatherland. If we want to preserve that light, if we desire here on earth to see the veil growing thinner, we must let our faith permeate more and more our thoughts and our actions. The stronger our faith, the holier our life; the holier our life, the brighter the light of faith. Everything is God's gift; therefore we pray "that by a worthy life we may attain the full possession of his truth", which is, of Himself. Yes, everything is grace, and yet everything calls for our cooperation.

The partaking of the one sovereign divine Nature, which began here on earth and was fostered by the "wondrous exchange" of the Holy Sacrifice of the Mass and by Holy Communion, will one day be consummated in the most glorious manner.

Prayer: Jesus, whom for the present veiled I see
What I so thirst for, Oh! vouchsafe to me:
That I may see Thy countenance unfolding,
And may be blest Thy glory in beholding.
Amen.

Adoro Te

SATURDAY: FOURTH SUNDAY AFTER EASTER

A PRAYER TO MARY

1. The prayer which forms the subject of this meditation was composed by the French writer and theologian L. de Grandmaison, in 1888 when he was twenty years old and was a Jesuit novice. Throughout a long and fruitful life he used to say that prayer frequently, and he induced many others to recite it. It is the prayer of a generous, upright, pious young man. What he asks from the Mother of God can be summed up thus: a childlike heart, a generous heart, a valiant heart.

2. *Petition*: Fixing our gaze on the immaculate Virgin, Mother of God, with humility and confidence we beg of her to obtain for us those graces.

I. A Childlike Heart

Holy Mary, Mother of God,
Preserve in me a childlike heart;

> Pure and sparking as the fountain.
> Obtain for me a simple heart,
> That does not relish being sad.

"Unless you become like little children, you shall not enter into the kingdom of God." By those words our Savior warned the Apostles against ambition. They had asked Him, "Who thinkest thou is the greatest in the kingdom of heaven? And Jesus, calling unto him a little child, set him in the midst of them" (*Matt.* 18, 1-3) and proposed him to them as an example.

A little child is by nature simple, devoid of ambition and not inclined to envy. It is innocent and has nothing to hide; a child-like heart knows no secrets nor dark corners, and therefore a child's eye is clear and transparent.

Someone said, "If I owned all the world's wealth, gladly would I barter it for a child's heart."

The Heart of the Mother of Jesus is the purest and the most sinless that ever beat: she was conceived without sin, and full of grace. Of her the liturgy sings, "When I was little I was pleasing in the sight of the Most High." Everything in her was directed to God; she gladly received every grace that was offered her, she believed every word that was spoken to her in the name of the Lord; she said "Yea" to whatever God asked of her, and her *Fiat* knew neither limits nor reservation; in her wise and faithful childlike Heart she preserved and pondered over all that God had done to her.

Holy Mary, Mother of God, preserve in us a childlike heart.

II. A Generous Heart

> A heart that royally can give itself,
> That tenderly feels others' pain,
> A loyal heart, and prompt to give,
> That ne'er forgets a favor received,
> Nor ever resents an injury.
> Make my heart meek and humble,
> Loving, wanting no return.
> Ready to yield its place in another's heart,
> So that Thy Son may take that place.

A generous heart abhors all petty selfishness; it gives itself without counting, without seeking profit for itself.

Mary is the Mother of fair and generous love (*Ecclus.* 24, 24).

Her *Fiat* was a complete, loving, self-forgetting surrender to God. When the hour had come, she saw Jesus leaving her for good. From her watchful and generous heart sprang her request at Cana, "They have no wine." When on a certain occasion she desired to speak to Jesus, who was indoors, teaching a group of people, she heard Him say, "Who is my Mother and who are my brethren?" And stretching forth his hand towards his disciples he said, "Behold my mother and my brethren; for whosoever shall do the will of my Father that is in heaven, he is my brother, and sister and mother" (*Matt.* 46-50). Possibly those words caused her pain; they did not humiliate her, for she gladly gave way to the brethren of her divine Son.

Even like Jesus, she forgave from the bottom of her heart: Peter, who three times had denied her Son; the apostles who during the awful night had deserted Him; the executioners who had nailed Him to the cross.

Most generous Heart of Mary, make our hearts like unto thine.

III. A Valiant Heart

> A great heart, and undaunted,
> Which no ingratitude can close;
> By no unkindness hardened
> A heart aflame for the Master's glory,
> A heart where bleeds the wound of love,
> That only can be healed in heaven.

A stout, or valiant, heart is not cast down even by severe trials; it fearlessly faces all troubles; it perseveres silently; it needs no witnesses to be valiant. Mary's Heart was a valiant Heart, as was evident at the time of the Angel's message, and when Simeon spoke to her in prophecy. She always had before her eyes the sword which the old man said would pierce her heart. The prophecy was fulfilled on Calvary, when she stood by the cross of her dying Son. After having seen Him gloriously ascending into heaven, Mary still lived for some years, the support and solace of the new-born Church, bearing in her Heart a wound that love had made, and which heaven alone could heal.

Mary, Queen of martyrs, pray for us.

Prayer: Fully conscious of our frailty and our cowardice, we pray with confidence to the Mother of Mercy: Holy Mary, Mother of God. . . .

"DOERS OF THE WORD" (Jas. 1, 23-24)

1. In the Epistle of the Mass of this day, the Apostle St. James gives us a salutary warning, "Be ye doers of the word and not hearers only, deceiving yourselves" (*Jas.* 1, 22). These words should be treasured by every Christian, by every religious, most of all by every priest, who not only hears the word but even preaches it.

2. *Petition*: With Holy Church we pray, O God, from whom all good things do proceed: grant unto Thy suppliant, that by Thine inspiration we may think those things that are right, and under Thy guidance perform them. Through our Lord (Collect, 5th Sunday after Easter).

I. "Doers of the Word, not Hearers Only"; nor Preachers Only

That we were privileged to hear the word of truth is a first and very great grace indeed. Of the word of truth St. James says that it is "ingrafted": it is not of the nature of the original tree; it is an absolutely gratuitous gift, the glad tidings, which God in His infinite goodness vouchsafed to announce to us; by these tidings He announced to us that out of goodness and mercy He has delivered us through His own Son, that He has raised us to the state of His adopted children, and predestined us to share His own bliss for ever.

"The word of truth" teaches us what we have to believe and what we must do. Throughout eternity we shall praise the Lord and thank Him because He has deigned to let us hear this word: that is, hear and live in accordance with it. "For if a man be a hearer of the word, and not a doer, he shall be compared to a man beholding his own countenance in a glass. For he beheld himself and went his way, and presently forgot what manner of man he was" (*Jas.* 1, 23-24). That man did indeed hear, but he did not listen; it is the seed that fell on the rock. "Now they upon the rock, are they, who, when they hear, receive the word with joy: and these have no roots; for they believe for a while, and in time of temptation they fall away" (*Luke* 8, 13).

To be a doer is to persevere, and to persevere is to carry into execution: for the layman in the world, who has heard the word, it means that he believes and that he lives according to his faith;

for the priest, who has heard the call and has followed it, it means that he has become "a fellow-helper of the truth" with Christ (3 *John* 8); for the religious, who has accepted the Lord's invitation to follow Him, it means perfect detachment from all that is earthly. Every man's personal experience is that he is slow to hear the word, and still more slow to be a doer of the word. Let that be a salutary humiliation but not a cause of discouragement. We pray, and every day we make a new start.

II. "Think Those Things That Are Right"

In the Collect of the Mass today the Church asks God, "From whom all good things do proceed", that, by His inspiration, "we may think those things that are right".

Whatever is right, "the engrafted word", is God's gift. When the soul listens, it will hear the Lord's whispering voice, which enlightens, invites, comforts, encourages. But let us be careful to preserve in our hearts the divine inspirations and urgings; we should in silence ponder over them, and with generosity follow them.

God will give us the grace to heed His promptings. "Men write the commandments, but Thou helpest us to carry them out. They show the way, but Thou givest strength to walk in it. They do only the outward part, but Thou pourest light into our inmost hearts. They water indeed, but Thou givest the increase. They cry aloud in human words, but Thou alone canst give us to understand them" (3 *Imit. of Christ*, 2, 2).

And therefore we pray, "O God, grant to Thy suppliants, that, by Thine inspiration, we may think what is right." Whatever God wants us to do, that is right, that is best.

III. "And Under Thy Guidance Perform Them"

Every right thought proceeds from God's inspiration: we must accept it, and under His guidance put it into execution. "He, who hath begun a good work in you, will perfect it" (*Phil.* 1, 6). As a rule God's guidance is given silently, discreetly, often through events of our daily life, or through the directions of our Superiors, or through the inward promptings of the Spirit. In order that we may be aware of the divine invitations, in order to understand them and to follow them, it is necessary that peace and quiet should prevail in the soul; that we divest ourselves of all disorderly affections; that we be responsive and prompt to follow the way by which God wants to lead us, even when God's ways are not our ways.

Then shall we be able "to perform the things that are right", or rather, in St. Paul's words, "not we, but the grace of God in us" (1 *Cor.* 15, 10).

Everything comes from God, and everything is grace:therefore must we pray and have confidence. All despondency is from the evil one. But we must play our part as well: it is we that must do the thinking and also the performing, not we in virtue of our own strength but we together with God's grace. Therefore we must give our assent and our whole-hearted co-operation to God's inspirations. Cowardice, no less than despondency, comes from the evil one.

Prayer: Direct, we beseech Thee O Lord, all our actions by Thy holy inspiration, and carry them on by Thy gracious assistance; that every prayer and work of ours may always begin from Thee and through Thee be happily ended (Litany of all Saints).

TRUE PIETY (Jas. 1, 26-27)

1. All Christians, especially all religious, ought to keep in mind the words of St. James, which we read yesterday in the Epistle at the Mass, about true and false piety, or "religion clean and undefiled". More than once had Jesus addressed similar warnings to His disciples, "Not every one that saith to me Lord, Lord, shall enter into the kingdom of heaven: but he that doth the will of my Father who is in heaven" (*Matt.* 7, 21).

2. *Petition*: May God grant us the grace not "to deceive ourselves" in matters pertaining to God's service; may we be doers, and not mere hearers of the word.

I. True and False Religion

The Apostle did not intend to give a full description of true piety. He considers this virtue in connection with the whole Christian rule of life, and points to a few marks of genuine piety.

Religion and piety are what is noblest and highest in man: they are the embodiment of his internal attitude towards his Maker. "God is a spirit, and they that adore him must adore him in spirit and in truth" (*John* 4, 24). The nobler and the more valuable a thing is, the more we require that it should be genuine, and the more we are on our guard against adulteration. Gold must be pure and unalloyed, but who ever speaks of unalloyed lead? Hypocritical sanctimoniousness and faked devotion are despicable; neither God nor man can tolerate them. "If any man think himself to be religious, not bridling his tongue, but deceiving his own heart, this man's religion is vain. Religion clean and undefiled before God and the Father, is this: to visit the fatherless and widows in their tribulation: and to keep oneself unspotted from this world" (*Jas.* 1, 26-27). Hence today more than ever it is incumbent on every man that calls himself a Christian to live as a true Christian, and to be upright in all his dealings. Those that have consecrated themselves to God must be truly supernatural men. All of us should feel a profound sense of responsibility in this matter: before the world we are the representatives of Christ. At the same time we place our trust in God's grace and mercy.

II. False Piety

We might feel inclined to wonder why St. James establishes such a strong connection between genuine piety and the control of the tongue. St. James spoke of certain Christians and certain teachers who, misled by their zeal, had given free rein to their tongue, and hurt the feelings of their opponents by using biting words.

We may consider the matter in a more general manner, as does the Apostle in the rest of his letter. He says, "If any man offend not in word, the same is a perfect man" (3, 2). Long and painful experience has taught us all how many virtues we have to practice in order not to offend in word, not to give pain, not to flatter, not to offend against perfect truthfulness, not to sin by vanity or not to boast.

Furthermore St. James says, "If then you fulfill the royal law, according to the Scriptures 'Thou shalt love thy neighbor as thyself', you do well. But if you have respect to persons you commit sin. . . ." (2, 8-9). "If there shall come into your assembly a man having a golden ring, in fine apparel, and there shall come in also a poor man in mean attire; and you have respect to him that is clothed with the fine apparel, and you shall say to him, Sit thou here well; but say to the poor man, Stand thou there, or sit under my footstool, do you not judge within yourselves, and are become judges of unjust thought?" (2, 3-4.)

He that fails to observe "the royal law", that is, he who does not observe fraternal charity, is not truly pious; he is not a genuine disciple of Jesus Christ.

III. True Piety

"Religion clean and undefiled before God and the Father is this: to visit the fatherless and widows in their tribulation and to keep oneself unspotted from this world" (*Jas.* 1, 27).

In the Old Covenant God had said, "God in his holy place is the father of orphans, and the judge of widows (doing them justice)" (*Ps.* 67, 6). "Blessed is he who executeth judgment for them that suffer wrong; who giveth food to the hungry. The Lord keepeth the strangers, he will support the fatherless and the widow; and the ways of sinners he will destroy" (*Ps.* 145, 5-9).

Jesus did not abolish the old "royal law", but He perfected it. In the parable of the Good Samaritan, He drew for us a striking picture of the truly religious man, as well as of the man whose piety is not genuine. Kindness to the weak and the needy, that is "religion clean and undefiled before God". Those words of the Apostle ought to bring joy to the hearts of thousands of religious, men and women: even contemplatives practice "religion clean and undefiled"; for the motive that makes them lead lives of prayer and penance is to assist souls in need, and, God be praised, "they have kept themselves unspotted from this world." And "active" religious, who do "take care of widows and orphans", have a right to rely on the prayer of Him who sent them and who prayed thus to the Father, "I pray not that thou shouldst take them out of the world, but that thou shouldst keep them from evil" (*John* 17, 15).

Prayer: O God of hosts, to whom belongeth all that is perfect, engraft in our hearts the love of Thy Name, and grant us an increase of religion; that what is good in us thou mayest nourish, and in Thy loving-kindness preserve in us what Thou hast nourished. Through our Lord (Collect, 6th Sunday after Pentecost).

"ASK IN MY NAME" (John 16, 23-27)

1. In the Gospel of the Mass of last Sunday, we heard these solemn words of Jesus, "Amen, amen, I say to you, if you ask the Father anything in my name, He will give it you. Hitherto you have not asked anything in my name. Ask, and you shall receive, that your joy may be full" (*John* 16, 23-24).

2. *Petition*: In the name of Jesus we ask the Father that this solemn promise of Christ may strengthen our confidence; also that we may grasp and feel the full sense of the words with which we conclude nearly all our liturgical prayers, "Through Christ our Lord."

I. "Ask and You Shall Receive"

Very often we read in the Gospel that Jesus encouraged His Apostles to pray, "Ask and you shall receive." Here our Lord speaks of "prayer of impetration", in which we beg for favors. We are aware that prayer of adoration is more acceptable to God. The Our Father—the Lord's Prayer—is both a prayer of adoration and of impetration. The first part is a prayer of adoration, asking that God may be glorified, "Thy will be done on earth as it is in heaven." The second part is a prayer of impetration, begging for temporal and spiritual favors, "Give us this day our daily bread, and forgive us our trespasses."

It would be wrong to underestimate the prayer of impetration, which implies a humble confession of our misery before God, and which renders homage to the power and goodness of our heavenly Father. Nothing is more befitting to the creature nor more salutary, than that it should confess its indigence. What can be more pleasing to our heavenly Father than that we should approach Him as little children?

Do we have any needs? Which are these needs? Salutary questions, which we ought to ask ourselves, which compel us to search the recesses of our soul. They are a fitting preparation for prayer. *The Imitation of Christ* says, "Because of our countless external occupations, we fail to take notice of the needs of our soul." "Lord, teach us to pray," said the Apostles. So that we may pray well, O Lord, make us see the needs of our soul.

II. "In My Name"

"Hitherto you have not asked anything in my name" (*John* 16, 24). As long as Jesus was with them, and as long as they heard Him pray to His Father, the thought of "praying in his name" did not occur to them. The Son of man had first to be glorified, to rise from the grave, to ascend unto heaven, and to take His seat at the right hand of God the Father Almighty. Then they would ask the Father in His name.

Then they also would know better what to ask in His name; the spirit would suggest it to them. The day the sons of Zebedee, James and John, petitioned for the first seats in the Kingdom, Jesus had felt constrained to tell them, You know not what you ask (*Matt.* 20, 24).

It is quite proper to pray for health and for temporal prosperity; even the Church, in her liturgy, asks for those things; but then we always have a proviso in our minds, "provided such things are conducive towards salvation". Then "the Spirit helpeth our infirmity. For we know not what we should pray for as we ought; but the Spirit himself asketh for us with unspeakable groanings. And he that searcheth the hearts knoweth what the Spirit desireth, because he asketh for the saints according to God" (*Rom.* 8, 26-27).

From the words with which we conclude nearly all our liturgical prayers we see how perfectly the Church, the Lord's Bride, under the inspiration of the Holy Ghost, has understood the Master's behest, "Per Dominum nostrum, Jesum Christum, Filium tuum." This conclusion is a consecrated formula, borrowed by the Church from the style of the official petitions current in olden days. When a citizen petitioned for a favor, he would invoke the name of a patron, who was supposed to enjoy the favor of the prince and who supported the petitioner's request. The Patron whose support we invoke is "Our Lord Jesus Christ, Thy Son . . . " in whom the Father is well pleased. It is a formula we utter so frequently; and daily use may be the cause why it no longer makes an impression. Yet these words are replete with spiritual meaning. Let us utter them truly from the heart.

III. "The Father Gives of Himself"

"In that day you shall ask in my name; and I say not to you that I will ask the Father for you. For the Father himself loveth you, because you have loved me and have believed that I came out from God" (*John* 16, 26-27).

Here again we cannot fail to notice how Jesus is ever bent on putting the Father first: He, as it were, seeks to disappear; He wants His disciples to have their minds fixed on the Father, from whom comes all that is good, and to place their full trust in the Father. "Your Father knoweth that you have need of all those things" (*Matt.* 6, 32). "The Father himself loveth you." "If you then, being evil, know how to give good gifts to your children, how much more will your Father from heaven give the good spirit to them that ask him?" (*Luke* 11, 13.)

"Then your joy shall be full." The Holy Ghost will bring us that joy. "The fruit of the Spirit is charity, joy, peace" (*Gal.* 5, 22). And that fruit is loving conformity of our will with the will of the Father, of the Son, of the Holy Ghost, here on earth at the price of struggle and effort, but one day in the undisturbed bliss of heaven for ever.

Prayer: Having abundantly nourished us by means of this heavenly banquet, O Lord, make us not merely desire what is right, but obtain also the fulfillment of our desires. Through our Lord (Postcommunion, 5th Sunday after Easter).

THE VIGIL OF THE ASCENSION: ROGATION DAY

OUR LORD'S PRIESTLY PRAYER (John 17, 1-11)

1. The Gospel of the Mass this day, as nearly all the Gospels of the Sundays after Easter, is taken from the touching discourse, which, after the institution of the Holy Eucharist, Jesus according to St. John addressed to the Apostles. Just as this Sacred Mystery is a reminder that Jesus, though He went away, still abides with us; so is this moving farewell address an assertion of continued presence and intimate union. This last discourse ends with a solemn prayer, "These things Jesus spoke, and lifting up his eyes to heaven, he said, Father, the hour is come . . ." (*John* 17, 1). We are in the midst of the Apostles, we see the Lord's radiant countenance, eyes lifted up to heaven; we hear every word.

2. *Petition*: The grace to hear and relish this priestly prayer of Jesus, to draw close to His Heart, a "glowing furnace of love".

I. The Prayer of Jesus

"Prayer is the very breath of the soul," is an old and true saying. Surely, for no soul was prayer so indispensable, so spontaneous, so uninterrupted, as for the soul of Christ. He prayed continuously, fervently, most often in silence and solitude. We know the contents of our Lord's prayer from this soul-stirring priestly prayer, preserved for us in St. John's Gospel, as also from certain spontaneous cries of the soul, which are recorded in the Scriptures. "Yea, Father, I praise thee", "I thank thee, O Father", "I know that thou always hearest me." These cries express the complete, fervent, calm conformity of the will of Jesus with the will of His Father.

One day during His public ministry, the Twelve had reverently observed Him while He was absorbed in prayer; "When he ceased, one of the disciples said to him: Lord, teach us to pray." The prayer, which Jesus taught them on that occasion—at least the first part—contained the sum and substance of His own prayer: "Thy will be done on earth as it is in heaven." This is still the essential theme of His prayer when we behold Him, a sharer of our own human weakness, engaged in a deadly struggle to maintain intact the conformity of His will with that of the Father, "Not my will, but thine be done" (*Luke* 22, 42).

Lord Jesus, teach us to pray. Teach us, whatever may befall us, always to say, and with our whole heart, "Thy will be done on earth, as it is in heaven."

II. For Whom Does Jesus Pray?

First Jesus prays for Himself, that He may glorify the Father. "Father, the hour is come, glorify thy Son, that thy Son may glorify thee. As thou hast given him power over all flesh, that he may give eternal life to all whom thou hast given him."

Everything is for the glory of the Father, and for our salvation. "I have glorified thee on the earth, I have finished the work thou gavest me to do. And now, glorify thou me, O Father, with thyself, with the glory which I had, before the world was, with thee." This glory He will obtain by suffering and death, by His resurrection and ascent into heaven. "And he is the head of the body, the Church, who is the beginning, the first-born from the dead; that in all things he may hold the primacy. For in him it hath pleased the Father, that all fullness should dwell; and through the blood of his cross; both as to the things that are on earth and the things that are in heaven" (*Col.* 1, 18-20).

Thus Jesus prayed for Himself as the servant of the Father and, because of the Father's good pleasure, our servant also.

Jesus prays for His Apostles. Now that the hour of His going away has come, the Father shall keep them. "I pray not that thou shouldst take them out of the world, but that thou shouldst keep them from evil." Jesus knows them so well, frail men, and not very courageous. He knows the world too, in which He leaves them, which will hate them as it also has hated Him. He knows the weight of the burden, which He will lay on their shoulders, and how much it surpasses their strength. "Going therefore, teach ye all nations" (*Matt.* 28, 19).

"Sanctify them in truth. Thy word is truth. As thou hast sent me into the world, I also have sent them into the world. And for them I sanctify myself, that they may be sanctified in truth"; so that, sanctified by Him, they may dedicate themselves completely to their mission. They shall indeed "drink the chalice", and fortified by the Holy Ghost witness to Him with their blood.

And Jesus offered a special prayer, and even now offers it, for all those that have consecrated their life to the establishment and the spread of His Kingdom on earth. Let them put their firm trust in Him, who has vanquished the world, and who still pleads for them with the Father.

Jesus prays for all that believe in Him: "And not for them only do I pray, but for them also, who through their word shall believe in me; that they may be one, as thou, Father, in me, and I in thee; that they also may be one in us, that the world may believe that thou hast sent me" (*John* 17, 20-21).

The last preoccupation of the Savior before He goes away from them, and His most urgent prayer to the Father, is that all those that believe in Him—all Christians that bear His name—may be one, as He and the Father are one, "that the world may believe that thou hast sent me". And therefore He made us say *"Our Father, who art in heaven."* Therefore the Church recites the Our Father in her highest and most sacred prayer, the Holy Eucharist, as a preparation for the reception of Holy Communion, the sign and efficient cause of our union in Him, and with one another.

Prayer: O Lord Jesus Christ, teach us to pray as Thou hast prayed in every circumstance of Thy life, "Thy will be done on earth, as it is in heaven." And since this is the most ardent desire of Thine own Heart, teach us to implore heaven that all who believe in Thee, and strive to serve Thee, may be one, as Thou art one with the Father.

THE ASCENSION OF OUR LORD—I (Act. 1, 1-11)

1. Let us hear our Lord speaking with His Apostles for the last time. We are one of the group that accompanies the Savior as He goes to the Mount of Olives; we see Him slowly, majestically rise to heaven, "and a cloud received him out of their sight" (*Act.* 1, 9).

2. *Petition*: The grace that the "wonderful and glorious ascension" of Jesus may fill our hearts with joy; that our faith may be confirmed, our confidence strengthened, our love rendered more ardent.

I. The Last Conversations

The last apparition took place in the holy city of Jerusalem, in the Cenacle, where He had instituted the Blessed Sacrament. "And he said to them: Go ye into the whole world, and preach the gospel to every creature" (*Mark* 16, 15).

"All power is given to me in heaven and in earth. Going therefore teach ye all nations, baptizing them in the name of the Father, and of the Son, and of the Holy Ghost; teaching them to observe all things whatsoever I have commanded you: and behold I am with you all days even to the consummation of the world" (*Matt.* 28, 18-20).

"Without me you can do nothing" (*John* 115, 5). With Him they can overcome the world and convert the nations—not they but Jesus through them. Nor should they expect immediate success, or spectacular results: they will have to face persecution, and many trials shall befall them; but slowly the Kingdom will be established.

We are rather astonished to hear one of the disciples, at this moment (as we read in the Epistle of the Mass), ask Jesus, "Lord, wilt thou at this time restore again the kingdom to Israel?" (*Act.*

1, 6.) Poor men, it was so hard to let go the dreams of national power and greatness that had fascinated the mind of the chosen people all these centuries, and to give their allegiance to a universal Kingdom, which Jesus had inaugurated. Our Lord, patient as He had always been with them, did not rebuke them, "but he opened their understanding that they might understand the scriptures"; and He bade them stay in the city until He "sent upon them the promise of His Father, and that they should be endowed with power from on high" (*Luke* 24, 45-49).

Heart of Jesus, patient and rich in mercy, have mercy on us.

II. The Ascension

"And he led them out as far as Bethania; and lifting up his hands, he blessed them. And it came to pass, whilst he blessed them, he departed from them and was carried up to heaven" (*Luke* 24, 50-51). And the Acts (1, 9) add, "and a cloud received him out of their sight".

In all the other apparitions Jesus disappeared suddenly, but here he departs gradually. In its simplicity the scene is solemn and impressive. The prophet Elias had been taken to heaven in a fiery chariot, drawn by fiery steeds, in the midst of a whirlwind (4 *Kgs.* 2, 11).

"And while he blessed them, he departed from them." His farewell to His disciples and to our earth was a blessing. "Peace on earth" was the song of the angels when He was born at Bethlehem and when the heavenly messengers brought tidings of great joy, that a Savior had been born, And on this day, we too, with a full heart, say, "Glory to God in the highest, and on earth peace to men of good will."

Be Thou our guide, be Thou our goal;
Be Thou our pathway to the skies;
Our joy when sorrow fills the soul:
In death our everlasting prize.—*Salutis Humanae Sator*

III. Back to Jerusalem

"And while they were beholding him going up to heaven, behold two men stood by them in white garments, who said to them, Ye men of Galilee, why stand you looking up to heaven? This Jesus, who is taken up from you into heaven, shall so come, as you have seen him going into heaven" (*Act.* 1, 10-11).

It may be noted that in the work of our salvation on every

important occasion, God was pleased to use the ministry of angels. The Archangel Gabriel is sent as a messenger to Mary: "Behold, thou shalt conceive in thy womb, and bring forth a son." At Bethlehem angels announce the tidings of great joy: "This day is born to you a savior. You shall find him wrapped in swaddling clothes, and laid in a manger." After the resurrection the women at the sepulchre meet an angel, who says to them, "Why seek you the living with the dead? He is not here, but he is risen." And on Mount Olivet two heavenly spirits tell the Apostles, "This Jesus, who is taken up from you into heaven, shall so come, as you have seen him going into heaven": this will be His final solemn return in power and majesty, of which Jesus had said before the high priest, "I say to you, hereafter you shall see the Son of man, sitting on the right hand of the power of God, and coming in the clouds of heaven" (*Matt.* 26, 64).

"And they went back to Jerusalem with great joy." In this parting there was neither sadness nor distress; neither did they feel that here was the end of a glorious day and of a thrilling experience. With joy in their hearts they came down from the mountain, remembering His words, "If you loved me, you would indeed be glad because I go to the Father" (*John* 14, 28). His presence with them had been a glorious day, followed now by a still more glorious one, because He was now with the Father and would send them the Paraclete, who would forever abide with them. Soon they would see Him again, in the glory of heaven. The final triumph was assured.

Prayer: Grant, we beseech Thee, Almighty God, that just as we believe in the Ascension into heaven on this day of Thine only-begotten Son, our Savior, so we too in spirit may make our dwelling in heaven. Through the same Lord (Collect, Mass of today).

FRIDAY AFTER THE ASCENSION

THE ASCENSION OF OUR LORD—II

1. The Gospel and the Acts of the Apostles tell us only those things about the Ascension that were perceptible by the senses, except one word of St. Mark, "He sitteth at the right hand of God" (*Mark* 16, 19). This reticence is no reason why we should

abstain from trying to realize through human concepts and images, and to describe in human language, the solemn entry of Jesus into heaven. The liturgy itself represents the glorified Savior as ascending to the highest heaven, and being seated in glory at the Father's right hand.

2. *Petition*: The grace to rejoice because of the great honor done to our human nature, which in the Son has become partaker of the Divine Nature.

I. The Triumphal Entry

Jesus had said, "I came forth from the Father, and am come into the world: again I leave the world, and I go to the Father" (*John* 16, 28). In order to come into the world, he had emptied himself, taking the form of a servant, being made into the likeness of man, and in habit found as a man. And he humbled himself, becoming obedient unto death, even to the death of the cross" (*Phil.* 2, 7-8).

With the resurrection His glorification had begun; but, as He said to Mary Magdalen, He had not yet ascended to the Father and now after forty days, He does ascend to the Father, and triumphantly enters into His Father's Kingdom. "God hath exalted him, and hath given him a name which is above all names, that in the name of Jesus every knee should bow, of those that are in heaven, on earth and under the earth" (*Phil.* 2, 9-10).

St. Leo thus describes our Lord's triumphant entry into heaven, "In truth it was a great and unspeakable cause for rejoicing when, in the sight of a holy multitude, human nature ascended above the dignity of all celestial creatures, to pass above the ranks of the Angels, to be raised beyond the heights of the Archangels, and not to have any degree of loftiness set as a limit to its advancement, short of the right hand of the eternal Father, where it would be associated with his royal glory, to whose nature it was united in the Son." May we not hear the Father, greeting His Son with the words He had spoken from the cloud, "This is my only-begotten Son, in whom I am well pleased."

> Thou, through the starry orbs this day,
>   Didst to Thy throne ascend;
> Thenceforth to reign in sovereign power
>   And glory without end.
> There, seated in Thy Majesty,
>   To Thee submissive bow

The heaven of heavens, the earth beneath,
    The realms of hell below.
With trembling there the angels see
    The changed estate of men;
The flesh which sinn'd by Flesh redeem'd;
    Man in the Godhead reign.
                    —*Aeterne Rex Altissime*

II. Sursum Corda, Hearts on High

St. Leo says that our Lord's ascension is our own ascension.
Therefore we must keep our hearts and minds raised on high.
With the whole heavenly court we offer our homage to Jesus,
and sing with the Church,

To Christ returning gloriously
    With victory to heaven,
Praise with the Father evermore
    And Holy Ghost be given.

We rejoice at His happiness: He as man is the first to enter
into the glory of His Lord, and now His joy in the Father is full.

We are glad and grateful, because one day He will make us
partakers of this fullness; He has opened the way for us, He has
gone before to prepare a place for us; or perhaps more truly, we
all, in Him who is our Head, have entered into eternal bliss.
"God, who is rich in mercy, hath quickened us together in Christ;
and hath raised us up together, and hath made us sit together
in the heavenly places, through Christ Jesus" (*Eph.* 2, 4-6).

It is not possible for us to understand fully how intimately we
are united with Christ, and words fail us to express the nature
of this close union. Our soul is not merely the temple where He
abides: its very being is sanctified, permeated, as it were with
the Divinity.

We ought to feel the most absolute confidence. In Jesus, our
exalted High Priest who has entered into heaven, we have "an
anchor of the soul, sure and firm; and which entereth in, even
within the veil, where the forerunner Jesus is entered for us"
(*Heb.* 6, 19-20).

"Therefore, if you be risen with Christ, seek the things that are
above, where Christ is sitting at the right hand of God. Mind the
things that are above, not the things that are upon the earth"
(*Col.* 3, 1-2). Earthly things, if we do not see God in them, do
hurt the soul; if we use them as God has ordained, if we enjoy

them or make a holocaust of them according to His holy will, they will bring us closer to God.

Let us hear the prayer of Jesus, "And now I am not in the world, and these are in the world, and I come to thee. Holy Father, keep them in thy name, whom thou hast given me; that they may be one as we also are" (*John* 17, 11).

Prayer: Grant, we pray Thee, Almighty God, that just as we believe in the Ascension into heaven on this day of Thine only-begotten Son, our Savior, so we too in spirit may make our dwelling in heaven. Through the same Lord (Collect, Mass of the Ascension).

SATURDAY AFTER THE ASCENSION

WITH MARY IN THE CENACLE

1. Before parting from them Jesus had commanded the Apostles not to return to Galilee, but to stay at Jerusalem, until He would "send the promise of the Father upon them" (*Luke* 24, 49). The Eleven "were persevering with one mind in prayer, with the women, and Mary the mother of Jesus, and with his brethren". They had gone up into an upper room, the Cenacle.

2. *Petition*: The grace, that we may, as the disciples with Mary, prepare our souls by prayer and recollection for the coming of the Holy Ghost. *Veni Sancte Spiritus,* Come, O Holy Spirit, Come!

I. In the Cenacle

The last reference to Mary in the Gospels is in St. John; "Now there stood by the cross of Jesus his mother" (*John* 19, 25). In St. John's Gospel also, we read the last recorded words of Jesus to His Mother, "Woman, behold thy son." Her presence at that moment on Calvary, and the words of our dying Savior, bear a deep meaning for us. This is the last time Mary's name is mentioned in the Gospels; it will occur once again in the Acts of the Apostles, "Then they returned to Jerusalem from the mount that is called Olivet, which is nigh Jerusalem, within a sabbath day's journey (less than a mile). And when they were come in, they went up into an upper room, where abode Peter and John....

All these were persevering with one mind in prayer, with the women, and Mary the mother of Jesus, and with his brethren" (*Act.* 1, 12-14).

Did Mary assist at the Ascension? Scripture makes no mention of her presence; perhaps we may remember the words of St. Ignatius, that the sacred writer supposes that we have commonsense. Let us prayerfully meditate on what were the feelings of Mary when she saw Jesus raise His hands in blessing and slowly rise on high, till He was hidden by the cloud.

Now that Jesus is no more visibly with them, they naturally gather around His holy Mother. During thirty years she had lived with Him in the closest intimacy; everything she had kept and pondered in her heart. It was heavenly rapture for the Apostles to hear from her lips so many details about His hidden life at Nazareth, and about the marvellous events connected with His birth and childhood. She is the chief witness to the reality of His human nature. In the Litany we salute her as Mother of Good Counsel, Seat of Wisdom. Her wisdom and her counsel were infinitely precious to the Apostles during those days of fervent prayer and silent waiting.

II. Persevering Prayer

It has been truly said that this was the first "retreat" made by Christians, and organized by Jesus Himself. "He commanded them that they should not depart from Jerusalem", the Holy City, whence the preaching of the Gospel was to begin. During ten days, in obedience to His command, they remain together, persevering with one mind in prayer, waiting and preparing their hearts for the coming of the Promise of the Father.

In this little community, composed of those that had been closest to Jesus, we see the most perfect unity and a deep spirit of prayer, the very spirit of Jesus, in whose name and by whose command they are gathered to "be endued with power from on high" (*Luke* 24, 49).

Every year we ought to pass those ten hallowed days "persevering with one mind in prayer", preparing ourselves and opening the gates of our souls for the coming of the Holy Ghost, "the power from on high". Each one of us, and the whole Church, stands in need of that power in our days of corroding doubt and of militant unbelief.

Holy Church commands—it is a privilege rather than a command—that all those who are consecrated to God should spend every year a few days in the solitude of a spiritual retreat. Especially during those precious days we should "persevere with one mind in prayer". How badly do we stand in need of power from on high to bear testimony to the light in a world filled with darkness and despair.

III. With Mary

Mary was not an official witness to her Son, nor did she have any share in the apostolic ministry. But in the Cenacle she had a role to play, when the Mystical Body of her Son was about to be born. Long ago the Power of the Most High had overshadowed her to fashion in her womb the human body of the Son of God. In the Cenacle too her role is an essential one, hidden but necessary, as formerly at Nazareth when she became the Mother of God. Now at Jerusalem she once again must become Mother, when the Holy Ghost will come down on the first members of the Mystical Body, gathered around her. She is the Mother of Jesus and the Mother of all the living.

This last mention of Mary's name in our Sacred Books is suggestive of very important truths. Mary plays a necessary role—subordinate to Jesus, of course—in the work of our salvation. Mary gave us Jesus, and with Him she gave us all things.

Prayer: O Lord Jesus, who hast filled the Heart of the Blessed Virgin Mary, Thy Mother, with the gifts of the Holy Ghost, when with the Apostles she persevered in prayer in the solitude of the Cenacle, grant us, we beseech Thee, love of silence and solitude: so that praying more reverently we may obtain that the Holy Ghost also fill our hearts with His gifts, Thou, who livest and reignest world without end (Collect, Mass of our Lady of the Cenacle).

SUNDAY AFTER THE ASCENSION

THE SERVICE OF THE DIVINE MAJESTY

1. The subject of this meditation will be the Collect of the Mass. No man ever served the Divine Majesty more perfectly than Jesus, whose whole life can be summed up in these words, "Yea Father", which welled up from the very depths of His Heart.

2. *Petition*: The grace that, through loving surrender to the will of the Father, we may make our hearts, or rather, allow them to be made, like unto the Heart of Jesus. "Almighty and Everlasting God, grant us, ever to have a will devoted to Thee, and to serve Thy Majesty with a sincere heart. Through our Lord."

I. The Wording of the Prayer

"Almighty and Everlasting God": these words are very frequently used in the liturgy to address God.

When a man prays, he enters the divine presence, and it behoves him to recollect who God is, and who he is himself. When we are in the presence of God we cannot help feeling that we are powerless, ephemeral creatures.

God alone is almighty and everlasting, changeless, and in no way like unto us. Who dare approach Him without the deepest awe and reverence? When a man enters the presence of the great or the powerful of this world to beg for a favor, his first care is to show regard for the dignity and position of him whose favor he seeks.

Then we pray, "Grant us". We plead no merit on our part, allege no claim, assert no right; we place no reliance on what efforts we have made: we humbly beg God's favor! But we know that the Almighty is our Father, and we address Him with the confidence of little children, "Grant, O Lord!": it all depends on Thy good pleasure.

Nor do we forget that He has endowed us with free will and that He always respects the freedom He has bestowed on us; and that He expects us to co-operate with His grace. But we are aware that divine Wisdom and divine Omnipotence, without using compulsion, or without interfering with man's freedom, have many ways, unknown to us, to lead us to our goal. Many a time we read in Holy Writ, "Convert me, and I shall be converted, for thou art the Lord, my God" (*Jer.* 31, 18). When in all our human misery we stand face to face with the Almighty and Everlasting God, what else can we say but, Thou art "the First and the Last, the beginning and the end"? (*Apoc.* 22, 13.)

II. "A Will Devoted to Thee"

The first favor we ask God to grant us is to have always a will devoted to Him, that is, a will which makes us lovingly and wholly surrender ourselves to Him and to His service. A will devoted to God's service, excludes all resistance, all dissension, all opposition, all selfishness. God's service no longer appears as a burden that might weigh down; to us it has become a fascinating ideal, that lifts up and beckons us on. Such devotion is the fruit of love, and it also generates greater love. "The law of God is in his heart, and his steps shall not be supplanted" says the Psalmist (*Ps.* 36, 31).

Every soul that has dedicated itself to God ought to pray for this great grace. We are preparing our hearts for the advent of the Holy Ghost; with the Church we sing to Him,

> Bend the stubborn heart and will,
> Melt the frozen, warm the chill,
> Guide the steps that go astray.

III. "A Sincere Heart"

In the second part of the Collect, we ask our Lord to grant us the grace of serving His Majesty "with a sincere heart".

"To serve His Majesty": these two words fit together perfectly, even in the world, where "Majesties" are so ephemeral and at the same time so capricious. The Divine Majesty has a claim to service rendered with a devoted will and with a sincere heart. To serve God is man's first duty, as well as his greatest privilege. "To serve God is to rule". And that is a very old and very wise saying. To rule, indeed in subjection to Him, but in subjection because thus we freely will it out of love; but in subjection to Him alone; independent, and masters of ourselves, with regard to whatever is not God.

The service of the Divine Majesty excludes the service of any other master: it brooks no reservation, no insincerity, no pretence, no mean or selfish calculation. Alas, painful experience has shown us that we are negligent and thoughtless and fickle servants of the Divine Majesty. With a sincere heart we desire and resolve to serve God, but selfishness and a host of petty, human frailties manage stealthily to creep into our hearts. None the less we refuse to be discouraged or to yield to impatience.

"How pure must our zeal be, if it is to be gentle!" God's zeal is perfecty pure, and therefore infinitely gentle.

Heart of Jesus, patient and rich in mercy, have mercy on us!

Prayer: Almighty and Everlasting God, grant us both ever to have a will devoted to Thee, and to serve Thy Majesty with a sincere heart. Through our Lord (Collect, Sunday afetr Ascension).

MONDAY BEFORE PENTECOST

THE HEART OF JESUS IN HIS FAREWELL DISCOURSE

1. In His farewell discourse after the last Supper, Jesus lays bare the most intimate feelings of His Heart. St. John, the disciple whom Jesus loved, had kept His Lord's words in his heart, had pondered over them during long years, ever gaining a deeper insight into their meaning; finally, in his old age, prompted by the Holy Ghost, he set them down in his Gospel. In this meditation we shall try to understand what Jesus gave us in this last conversation with His own, what He promised us, what He asked of us. Hence we shall come to realize that truly He loved us unto the end.

2. *Petition*: The grace to understand better the Heart of our Savior, which "has made us partakers of His infinite riches".

I. What Does Jesus Give Us?

He gives us peace. "Peace I leave with you, my peace I give unto you" (*John* 14, 27). No one can give what he does not have; and therefore the world cannot give the peace which it does not possess. "And they healed the breach of the daughter of my people disgracefully saying peace, peace; and there was no peace" (*Jer.* 6, 14). "For all that is in the world is the concupiscence of the flesh, and the concupiscence of the eyes, and the pride of life" (1 *John* 2, 16). These are the never-failing sources of strife and discord among men.

Jesus gives us peace: At His cradle the angels sang "Peace to men of good will"; and Zacharias prophesied that He would "direct our feet into the way of peace". He is the "Lamb of God, who taketh away the sins of the world" (*John* 1, 29). He Himself is our Peace. Among the Jews the customary greeting was "Peace be to you". Coming from the lips of Jesus, these were not mere words: they issued from the depths of His Heart, in which dwells all the fullness of peace; and of this fullness He gives us generously. We must carefully preserve that peace and foster its growth around us. "And the peace of God, which surpasseth all understanding, keep your hearts and minds in Christ Jesus" (*Phil.* 4, 7).

Jesus gives us joy. "That my joy may be in you" (*John* 15, 11). His joy also is a joy that the world knows not and cannot give; for it is the result of true peace, a peace so secure that nothing on earth can disturb it. Here again we come face to face with that "gigantic secret of the Christian", who may suffer trial and temptation, but ever remembers that his hope will not be disappointed.

Jesus gives us love. "That the love, wherewith thou hast loved me, may be in them, and I in them" (*John* 17, 26), these are the concluding words of our Lord's priestly prayer to His Father, imploring the Father to love us with the love with which He loves the Son. This is His parting gift. St. John is the only Evangelist who does not record the institution of the Eucharist: instead he has preserved for us the burning words spoken by Jesus after He had given them His Body and His Blood as a pledge of His love, words that flowed straight from Christ's Heart, the "glowing furnace of charity".

These three gifts of Jesus are also fruits of the Holy Ghost, for whose coming we are at present preparing our hearts. "But the fruit of the Spirit is charity, joy, peace" (*Gal.* 5, 22).

II. What Does Jesus Promise Us?

"I will not leave you orphans" (*John* 14, 18). He will send them an Advocate, a Consoler, "the Spirit of truth, who will teach them all truth" and who will abide with them.

But He also remains with them, not only through His Spirit who will enlighten their minds, but sacramentally, whenever they do what He asks them to do "for a commemoration of Him"; truly will He be present with them, within them, and will be their food unto eternal life.

"And if you shall ask me anything in my name that I will do" (*John* 14, 14).

All this Jesus promised to His Apostles when He bade them farewell; all this He promises to those who, through the ministry of the Apostles, will believe in Him.

He gives us divine gifts, divine promises, coming straight from His Heart which is "full of goodness and love".

III. What Does Jesus Ask of Us?

It all can be summed up in one word, "Abide in me." And we abide in Him when we observe His commandment that we "love one another as he has loved us" (*John* 13, 34); and secondly, when we do what He bade us do in commemoration of Him, namely when, with the whole Church, we offer Him to the Father and, partaking of His Flesh and His Blood, we become one with Him and with each other.

Prayer: Unto Thy Church, we beseech Thee, O Lord, do Thou graciously grant the gifts of unity and peace, which in the gifts offered are mystically signified, through our Lord (Secret, Corpus Christi).

TUESDAY BEFORE PENTECOST

THE LAST QUSTION AND THE LAST ANSWER
BEFORE THE ASCENSION (Act. 1, 6-8)

1. In the Epistle of the Mass of the Ascension we read the last question which the disciples, on the way to the Mount of Olivet, addressed to their Lord, and the answer which Jesus gave them. We are struck once more by the sharp contrast between the pettiness and the lack of vision of the Apostles, and the divine patience of the Master. "Lord, wilt thou at this time restore again the kingdom to Israel? But he said to them, It is not for you to know the times or moments which the Father hath put in his own power: But you shall receive the power of the Holy Ghost coming upon you and you shall be witnesses unto me in Jerusalem and in all Judea and Samaria, and even to the uttermost part of the earth" (*Act* 1, 6-8).

2. *Petition*: The grace to have trust in our Lord's patience with us, and in His readiness to straighten out our warped ideas.

I. Human Pettiness

"Lord, wilt thou at this time restore again the kingdom to Israel?" We naturally hark back to that day, when the sons of Zebedee petitioned to be allotted the first seats in the kingdom that was coming. Maybe that occurred shortly after John and

James had become disciples? But now, when during three years Jesus had endeavored to correct and to purify the Messianic expectations of these devout men! And the question is asked at the very moment when He is about to ascend to His Father. Has his teaching ended in failure?

The exhilarating experiences of these forty days, the rising from the grave, the successive apparitions, the miracle by the lake of Tiberias, had wiped out the memory of the tragedy of Good Friday; and all the idle dreams of the olden days had rushed back into their minds again.

We also find it very hard to give up our long cherished ideas, and plans. So often we imagine that we know so much better than He, how and where He ought to make use of us in the building of His Kingdom. And if He is pleased to let our plans be wrecked and to allow our calculations to be defeated, we are sorely disappointed, and perhaps yield to discouragement.

Perhaps we have little right to be astonished at the lack of understanding of the Apostles, after they had been in close intercourse with Jesus for two years. Our Lord Himself does not seem to be highly astonished. To the sons of Zebedee He had said, "You know not what you ask" (*Matt.* 20, 21). And when Philip had clumsily butted in with the words, "Lord, show us the Father", Jesus said, "Philip, have I been so long a time with you, and have you not known me?" (*John* 14, 9). Jesus knows our human frailty, and His patience is divine.

II. God's Greatness

From the merely human point of view we may say that the question of the disciples painfully affected the Heart of Jesus. Yet the answer is calm and gentle.

"It is not for you to know the times or moments which the Father hath put in his own power." Here it is the Heart of Christ Himself that speaks, a "Heart patient and rich in mercy". On that Heart we also rely, we who are so slow to learn.

Another thing in the Lord's answer should draw our attention. Even now, after the resurrection, Jesus is bent on attributing all power and glory to the Father, and on putting the Father in the first place. "The times and moments the Father has put in His power." We do not forget that the Father and He are one, and that whatever is of the Father is also of the Son (*John* 14, 10). But as the Messiah, He is the One that is sent by the Father; He speaks and acts as the Father commands, while the Father speaks and acts in the plenitude of His power. And so, even here we learn that Jesus is "meek and humble of heart".

III. Superhuman Greatness

Then Jesus said to them, "But you shall receive the power of the Holy Ghost, coming upon you, and you shall witness to me in Jerusalem, and in all Judea, and Samaria, and even to the uttermost part of the Earth" (*Act.* 1, 8). These words show what a superhuman task Jesus is imposing on His Apostles.

He does not commision them to establish a small, national kingdom; their task is infinitely higher; it is also utterly different, nor can it be achieved by force of arms. It can be accomplished only by the power of the Holy Ghost, who will transform them into new men. Then they will stand, having their loins girt about with truth, and having on the breastplate of justice, and their feet shod with the preparation of the gospel of peace; in all things taking the shield of faith, by which they may be able to extinguish all the fiery darts of the most wicked one. They shall take unto them the helmet of salvation and the sword of the Spirit, which is the word of God (*Eph.* 6, 14-17).

Having put on "the armor of light" (*Rom.* 12, 12), they and their successors will go unto the extremities of the earth till the end of time: in the battle which they will wage against evil, they will shed no blood, except their own in testimony to their Lord.

May the power of the Spirit be poured forth on the universal Church, on all Christians, on all those who are consecrated to God, so that by word and deed, by suffering and death, they may be witnesses of Christ Jesus, our Lord.

Prayer: O guide our minds with Thy bless'd light,
With love our hearts inflame,
And with Thy strength, which ne'er decays,
Confirm our mortal frame.

WEDNESDAY BEFORE PENTECOST

"BEFORE ALL THINGS HAVE A CONSTANT MUTUAL CHARITY" (1 Peter 4, 8)

1. The Apostles, initiated by the Holy Ghost into "the fullness of the truth", penetrated the very fundamentals of Christ's

doctrine: that He is one with the Father who sent Him; that they themselves in Him and through Him must be one; one with Him, and one among themselves. And by this shall all men know that they truly are His disciples. This oneness is the hallmark of a truly Christian life. Jesus made the commandment of fraternal charity His own commandment; and St. Paul said, "He that loveth his neighbor hath fulfilled the law" (*Rom.* 13, 8). In the Epistle of last Sunday we heard St. Peter saying, "Before all things have a constant mutual charity among yourselves" (1 *Peter* 4, 8).

2. *Petition*: The grace that, in our Christian life and in our striving after perfection, the "royal commandment" may always be our guiding star.

I. "Before All Things Have a Constant Mutual Charity"

To grasp the meaning of "before all things" we should read these words in their context. The Apostle had just written, "Be prudent therefore and watch in prayers". Whatever be the exact and complete meaning of those words, there is certainly question of prayers and religious exercises. Then St. Peter says, "But before all things have a constant mutual charity among you." This preference cannot astonish us when we remember what Jesus taught in the Sermon on the Mountain, "If therefore thou offer thy gift at the altar, and there thou remember that thy brother hath anything against thee, leave there thy offering before the altar, and go first to be reconciled to thy brother, and then coming thou shalt offer thy gift" (*Matt.* 5, 23-24).

It is a thousand pities that we so readily forget, or neglect, this solemn injunction of our Savior. And, if Jesus laid down that rule when there was question of the material offerings which the Jews brought to the Temple, what ought we to do, when we offer to God the sacred Victim, His own Son? Surely the liturgy is guided by the spirit of Christ, when by word and gesture it reminds us before Holy Communion of the necessity of peace and mutual love. The best preparation for Holy Communion is to expel from our hearts every feeling that offends against fraternal charity.

"Have a constant mutual charity among yourselves; for charity covereth a multitude of sins", that is, refuses to see, or overlooks the neighbor's shortcomings and does not allow these to chill the fervor of our charity. In the same sense St. Paul said, "Charity thinketh no evil, beareth all things, endureth all things" (1 *Cor.* 13, 5-7).

Did not Jesus, "before all things", treat us with a charity that "covereth a multitude of sins"? If thus He treated us, we must do the same to our neighbor, for He said "Love one another as I have loved you."

II. Liberality

St. Peter says further, "Using hospitality one towards another without murmuring." Hospitality was universally practiced in Oriental lands. That Christians should zealously practice it is all the more reasonable. Let us remember what the Judge will say on the last day, "I was a stranger and you took me in" (*Matt.* 25, 35). Ours seems to be an age "of displaced persons": literally millions of people have been mercilessly torn up by the roots, cast adrift, and compelled to beg for food and shelter. It is good to think that so many Christian families, and religious houses, have nobly obeyed the "royal commandment". Still all around us there is so much spiritual and temporal misery; and surely we all long to extend a helping hand in whatever manner we are able.

"Without murmuring". Yes, the practice of charity does cost; without sacrifice there is no charity. But Christ's words resound in our ears, "Amen, amen, I say to you, as long as you did it to one of these my least brethren, you did it to me" (*Matt.* 25, 40).

"Charity covereth a multitude of sins." Do not these words say more than what is contained in the literal sense, and are we not justified in interpreting them a little more broadly? Charity, practiced for the sake of Christ, does draw a veil over many sins, by helping us to repent sincerely and to obtain full pardon.

III. Good Stewards of the Manifold Grace of God

"As every man hath received grace, ministering the same one to another; as good stewards of the manifold grace of God" (1 *Peter* 4, 10). Here St. Peter touches the very basis of the Christian life: we are in communion with one another, we form a closely-knit community. The bond that unites us is something even more intimate than blood relationship: we neither see it, nor feel it, nor are we naturally aware of it. It is a matter of faith; we must believe it, and then we can live by it.

Whatever we have received from God, and most of all the special graces bestowed on us, as for instance, a religious or a priestly vocation, must contribute to the welfare of all. We are stewards, not proprietors, still less profiteers, of "the manifold grace of God". Every Christian, every priest and religious who faithfully does his duty, walks in the presence of the Lord and is a faithful steward of the gifts of God. These gifts are of many different kinds, just as in the body every member differs from the other and has its own peculiar function. "But all these things one and the same Spirit worketh, dividing to every one according as he will" (1 *Cor.* 12, 11).

"If any man speak, let him speak as the words of God. If any man minister, let him do it as of the power which God administereth, that in all things God may be honored through Jesus Christ: to whom is glory and empire, for ever and ever. Amen" (1 *Peter* 4, 11). Whosoever in the spirit of faith does look up so high and so far, whatever be his calling and wherever his lot may be cast, stands in the full Light and in the fullness of Truth.

Prayer: Almighty and Everlasting God, grant us both ever to have a will devoted to Thee, and to serve Thy Majesty with a sincere heart. Through our Lord (Collect, Sunday after Ascension).

THURSDAY BEFORE PENTECOST

PERSECUTED, NOT SCANDALIZED

1. In the Gospel of last Sunday we heard Jesus telling the Apostles that they would be persecuted in many ways. Pretty often Jesus had warned them, and even in His farewell discourse He said to them: "These things I have told you, that when the hour shall come, you may remember that I told you of them" (*John* 16, 4).

2. *Petition*: The grace not to take scandal when we see evil stalking victoriously across the world; but to trust Him who has overcome the world, and whom we have seen ascending to His Father, that He might send us the Paraclete.

I. That You May Not Be Scandalized

Jesus sees into the future, and He fully knows what awaits His Apostles. Israel has rejected its Messiah and has condemned Him as a blasphemer. The disciples will be treated no better than the

Master. "They will put you out of the synagogues: yea, the hour cometh, that whosoever killeth you, will think that he doth a service to God" (*John* 16, 2). So the Jews did to Stephen and James, at Jerusalem. All the Apostles would shed their blood in testimony to Christ, except John, though he too faced a violent death. In every land and in every age the Prince of darkness has readily found hirelings prepared to oppress the Church and anxious to persecute its loyal members. "If the world hate you, know that it hath hated me before you" (*John* 15, 18).

Nor should we be scandalized, or discouraged, if we meet with what we deem opposition from our own brethren or sisters, who—so we fancy—fail to understand us. We are all frail, limited, human beings, carrying with us the weight of our many shortcomings; we have to live and labor so very close to one another; and so readily mutual relations may become encounters or degenerate into clashes. "God uses one diamond to polish another." However painful all this may be, let us never be scandalized, still less disheartened. Patience is a virtue that is most pleasing to our Lord. When we behold the fierce battle that is being fought in the world between Christ and Satan, a battle in which we ourselves are engaged and in which immortal souls are at stake, our own petty squabbles will appear what they are, small things and of the slightest importance. Then it ought to be easy just to drop them.

II. "But These Things I Have Told You"

If Jesus had not told them before, possibly they might have thought that the Master had not foreseen all their troubles and trials; and that, had He known what was implied in the charge He laid on them, He would never have commissioned them to undertake it. "But these things I have told you, that when the hour shall come, you may remember that I told you of them" (*John* 16, 4).

"When the hour shall come": in the fullness of His wisdom and His power the Father has appointed that hour, and we need not be anxious about it. "Enough for the day is the evil thereof!" When the hour does come, we know that a loving Providence has foreseen everything, disposed everything in such a manner that all things will work towards God's glory and our own greater good. "What shall we then say to these things? If God be for us, who is against us?" (*Rom.* 8, 31.) He knows all things, He rules all things, He orders all things, and He loves us dearly.

His last act on earth, before He ascended to heaven, was to

bless the Apostles, and us too. In that blessing and in His love we place our trust.

III. "Have Confidence"

Those were the Lord's last words: "Have confidence; I have overcome the world" (*John* 16, 33). What Jesus most insistently asked for from all was faith and confidence in Himself. Lack of faith and of confidence hurt His Heart most keenly. A lively faith and a firm trust always gave Him pleasure and drew from Him praise and reward.

"In the world you shall have distress, but have confidence; I have overcome the world", and in Me you have overcome it. His ascension to heaven and His triumphal return to the Father are to us a pledge of what Jesus has asked, and is still asking, the Father for us, "Father, I will that where I am, they also whom thou hast given me, may be with me; that they may see my glory, which thou hast given me, because thou hast loved me before the creation of the world" (*John* 17, 24).

Generally God has regard to our weakness, and the distress we have in the world is very light and easy to bear. Yet it is good that we remember the solemn words of St. Paul, "Who shall separate us from the love of Christ? Shall tribulation, or distress, or famine, or nakedness, or danger, or persecutions, or the sword? But in all these things we overcome, because of him that hath loved us. . . . Nothing shall be able to separate us from the love of God, which is in Christ Jesus our Lord" (*Rom.* 8, 35-39).

Prayer: Accept, O Lord, the gifts we offer for the glorious Ascension of Thy Son, and graciously grant that, delivered from the dangers of this life, we may attain to life eternal. Through our Lord (Secret, Mass of the Ascension).

FRIDAY BEFORE PENTECOST

OUR FRAIL NATURE AT THE RIGHT HAND OF GOD'S GLORY

1. On the feast of our Lord's Ascension we commemorate, as is said in the Canon of the Mass, "the most holy day on which Thine only-begotten Son our Lord placed our frail human nature at the right hand of Thy glory". These words are an

attempt to express in human language how intimately our human nature has been united with the Divine Word, and how it has been elevated and made a sharer in the Divine nature: "ut nos divinitatis suae tribueret esse participes".

2. *Petition*: The grace to believe with a lively faith that Jesus ascended into heaven "so that He might make us also sharers in His Divine Nature". If we have that faith "our souls will be drawn to heavenly desires".

I. Our Frail Human Nature

At Bethlehem we have seen the frailty of the Body that has now gloriously ascended into heaven: an "infant, wrapped in swaddling clothes and laid in a manger". "the body of our lowness", as St. Paul says (*Phil.* 3, 21). Like unto us in all things, we have seen the Son of man "advance in wisdom, age and grace with God and men" (*Luke* 2, 52). Mary and Joseph knew the truth; but no one at Nazareth ever suspected Him to be anything more than the "carpenter's son".

He felt the pangs of hunger in the desert, and in the boat He fell asleep out of sheer fatigue; that frail Body trembeled with fear and its "sweat became as drops of blood" during the agony at Gethsemane; we have beheld that Body on the cross, and seen it, stiff in death, carried to the grave.

Thus far we behold "our frail human nature", but at this point begins the glorification. "By dying He has destroyed death, and by rising again He has restored us unto life" (Easter Preface). But before that He had destroyed His own death, and restored His own life. The last proof of man's frailty—the death and the grave of Christ—proclaim the power and true glory of Jesus.

As He ascends unto heaven, we acclaim Him, "Hail, true Body, born of Mary, ever Virgin"—*Ave Verum*.

II. At the Right Hand of the Father

On earth we are happy and proud when a member of our family is raised to high position. And now, One of our race, One who called us "brethren", has been raised to the heaven of heavens, and is seated in glory at the right hand of the Father.

St. Gregory, alluding to the bridegroom of the Canticle, who with huge strides hastens over the mountains, thus describes the humiliations and the triumphs of the Word of God: "Do you desire, dear brethren, to know those strides? From heaven He descended into the womb of His Mother; then He went to the manger and thence to the cross, and from the cross to the grave. But from the grave to the glory of heaven." And we may add: and into heaven He carried in His Body the shining scars of His human frailty, the sacred wounds, which He preserved even in His glorified Body.

If a member of our family holds an office of power, we naturally hope that his influence will be to our advantage. Rightly we trust that Jesus, who through His Humanity is our Brother, will use His influence to our advantage, now that in heaven He is seated at the Father's right hand. But there is an important difference: that office was entrusted to our relative not primarily to assist us and to grant us favors; Jesus ascended into heaven and took His seat at the right hand of the Father "that He might make us sharers in His Divine Nature".

III. "I Go to Prepare a Place For You"

In Jesus everything is for our benefit: He became man not to gain aught for Himself, but for our sakes. Writes Ruysbroeck: "The wherefore of Christ's becoming man lies in His unfathomable love and in our dire need." He shows us the way, rather He *is* the Way to the Father. He is our Intercessor with the Father: "always living to make intercession for us" (*Heb.* 7, 25). He prepares a place for us; He sends His Spirit to abide with us. Being equal to the Father, He dares pray thus, "Father, I will that, where I am, there also whom thou hast given me may be with me, that they may see my glory" (*John* 17, 24). He is the Head of the Body: and the office of the Head is to make sure that the entire Body is hale and sound and to obtain that everlasting bliss for which the Creator "did so wonderfully fashion it, and still more wonderfully restore it".

He prepares a place for us in the house of His Father. To comfort and strengthen us during our earthly pilgrimage He has provided us with food better than manna from heaven: that same glorified Body, which is seated at the right hand of the Father in glory, is the nourishment of our soul to strengthen it unto life eternal.

Prayer: *O Sacrum convivium*: O sacred banquet, in which Christ is our food; in which we celebrate the remembrance of His passion; in which our soul is pervaded with grace; and in which we receive a pledge of the glory that shall be ours.

NEED AND DESIRE

1. In olden days it was customary to keep a Night Vigil on the eve of Pentecost, just as on the eve of Easter; it ended with the celebration of the Holy Eucharist. During that same night the Baptismal Font was blest and catechumens received Baptism.

   The Introit of the Mass alludes to that solemnity, when it says, "I will pour cleansing streams over you, and breathe a new spirit into you." When we celebrate the feast of Pentecost, the words "I will breathe a new spirit into you" are applicable to the whole Church, as well as to each individual Christian.

2. *Petition*: The grace to enter into the spirit of the Church, to feel deeply the needs of the Church, and our own; and to long ardently for the Spirit who will cleanse, enlighten and strengthen our soul. "Come, O Holy Spirit, come!"

I. "I Will Breathe a New Spirit Into You"

This was the message which Jahve addressed to His people: they had forsaken their God and gone after idols, but severe chastisement had helped them to return to the right path. God, ever faithful to His word, renews the promises He had made them: He will give them a new spirit, "And I will give you a new heart, and put a new spirit in you; and I will cause you to walk in my commandments, and to keep my judgments and do them" (*Ezech.* 36, 26-27).

"God, who at sundry times and in divers manners spoke in times past to the fathers by the prophets, last of all in these days hath spoken to us by his Son. Making purgation of sins, he sitteth at the right hand of the majesty on high" (*Heb.* 1, 1-3).

This Son, our Lord Jesus Christ, now that He has entered into His glory, can send them the Promised of His Father, who will give them a new spirit, that is, He will produce in them a thorough internal change; "He will teach them all truth," "for he shall not speak of himself, but whatsoever he shall hear, ... He shall receive of mine and show it to you" (*John* 16, 13-14).

He is the Gift of the Father, whom the Son will send, that He may pour the spirit of Jesus in their hearts, and give them a deeper insight into the teachings of their Lord.

II. Dire Need

"I have yet many things to say to you, but you cannot bear them now (*John* 16, 12). Till the very last day they showed how slow of understanding they were. Mary herself bears witness that even she did not always understand everything. The Apostles were well aware of their own weakness; and now Jesus had entrusted them with a task that demanded more than human strength: "Going therefore, teach ye all nations; be ye witnesses unto me even to the uttermost part of the earth." How could they fail to realize that they had real need of the strength of the Holy Ghost?

Now, as ever, Holy Church needs the assistance of the Holy Ghost "to teach her all truth", to preserve this truth pure from all error, to preach it and defend it in a world enamored of novelty and infatuated with its own wisdom.

And we also need the grace of the Holy Ghost, that we may be aware of, and follow, His inspirations; that we may "possess and preserve true wisdom", which will help us to judge rightly, and strengthen us to act courageously in doubt and temptation. We need His help lest we should grow weary and tepid, his help to remain open-minded and yet staunchly loyal to Christ. "Extinguish not the spirit . . . prove all things, hold fast that which is good" (1 *Thes.* 5, 19-21).

III. Ardent Desire

Jesus had told the Apostles most wonderful things about the "Advocate" He would send them. He was the "Other", yet One so like Jesus that they would not feel that they were orphans. He would teach them all truth, give them a better understanding of their Master and His doctrine, and make them love Him more ardently; He would endow them with the strength to bear witness to their Lord.

The Apostles, with Mary in their midst, spent those ten days in fervent prayer and holy expectation, ardently longing for the coming of the Promise of the Father.

To the Church the Holy Ghost is the "breath of life", by which she "became a living Body" and continues to live. What breath is to our material bodies, that the Holy Ghost is to the Church, which is Christ's Mystical Body.

Pentecost is to the Church more than the commemoration of the marvellous event that occurred at Jerusalem hundreds of years ago. Year after year the Church exults at the actual coming of the Holy Ghost into the depths of her own being, and into the souls of her children. When we listen to the ardent supplications contained in every prayer of the Mass on Pentecost day, we cannot fail to realize that the Church is not merely celebrating the remembrance of something: she is actually imploring the Holy Ghost to come down.

Every soul that lives united to God, and that knows its needs, yearns for the Spirit and for the fruits He gives: charity, joy, peace. Does man's heart need aught but true charity, pure joy, profound peace? "Come, Holy Spirit, Come."

Prayer: Grant, we implore Thee, Almighty God, that we, who celebrate this feast of the giving of the Holy Ghost, may be inflamed by heavenly desires, and long for the waters of life. Through our Lord (Prayer for the former blessing of the Font).

PENTECOST SUNDAY

THE DESCENT OF THE HOLY GHOST (Act. 2, 1-4)

1. On the fiftieth day (Pentecost) after the flight of the Israelites from Egypt (the Jewish Pasch) God promulgated His Law on Mount Sinai. Before His ascension into heaven Jesus had commanded the Apostles, Do not depart from Jerusalem. . . . You shall be baptized with the Holy Ghost not many days hence.

   "And when the days of the Pentecost were accomplished, they were all together in one place; and suddenly at about the third hour of the day (nine o'clock for us) there came a sound from heaven, as of a mighty wind coming and it filled the whole house where they were sitting. And there appeared to them parted tongues as it were of fire: and it sat upon every one of them. And they were all filled with the Holy Ghost: and they began to speak with diverse tongues, according as the Holy Ghost gave them to speak" (*Act.* 2, 1-4).

2. *Petition*: That we may, together with the whole Church, experience the invisible but mighty reality of this solemn and ever "fresh creation."

I. The Third Person of the Blessed Trinity

Jesus frequently spoke about His Father; His first recorded word is, "Did you not know that I must be about my Father's business?" and the last, "Father, into thy hands I commend my spirit." But no one has seen the Father except the Son, who is "the image of the invisible God" (*Col.* 1, 15). But "he that seeth me, seeth the Father also" (*John* 14, 9).

Only towards the close of His public ministry did Jesus mention clearly "Another", distinct from Himself and from the Father, whom He and the Father will send. This Other "shall not speak of himself": but He is indispensable so that "the mystery which hath been hidden from ages and generations be accomplished and manifested to God's saints" (*Col.* 1, 26). He comes last, but He will abide with us. He is sent by the Father and by the Son, but He sends no other. "If I go not, the Paraclete will not come to you: but if I go, I will send him to you" (*John* 16, 7).

And now, when Jesus has gone to His Father, and when the disciples, in obedience to the Master's command, "are persevering with one mind in prayer," and their souls are ready, the Third Person can come down.

II. The Descent of the Holy Ghost

We may remember here that other coming down of the Holy Ghost, on the Blessed Virgin Mary, in the hallowed secrecy and silence of Nazareth. Gabriel said, "The Holy Ghost shall come upon thee"; and when Mary had uttered her Fiat, "the power of the Most High overshadowed her", and the Son of God became man, as the Word assumed a human Body in the womb of Mary.

And now, by the power of the same Spirit the mystical Body of the glorified Christ is being formed. The little community of disciples, gathered around the Mother of Jesus, are made into a Church, in which the Creator-Spirit has come to abide. But this tremendous event does not occur in profound silence, as at Nazareth: because this day Christ's visible Church is being born, the Spirit comes with power and with impressive outward signs, which remind us of the proclamation of the Law on Sinai. These signs are symbols of the awe-inspiring event, which is taking place in the invisible world of the work of man's salvation.

The "sound from heaven, as a mighty wind" signifies the irresistible, yet absolutely free, power of the Holy Spirit, "who breatheth where he will" (*John* 3, 8): the Holy Spirit is *like* the air, which penetrates everywhere, and fills every place. Fire is the symbol of love, of the consuming power of love; (in another revelation of the Trinity, the Holy Ghost appeared in the form of a dove, which is the symbol of gentle love); a flame, "parted tongues, as it were of fire" appeared to them, and sat upon every one of them; they shall speak and bear testimony, as the Master has foretold.

We are struck with awe and wonder at this marvellous manifestation of the divine power. God, who is invisible, and whom our senses fail to apprehend, deigns to use material manifestations to make us grasp how He mysteriously achieves His work of salvation amongst us. "Truly it is meet and just, right and conducive to salvation, for us at all times and in all places, to give thanks to Thee, O Holy Lord, Father Almighty, eternal God through Christ our Lord ... who this day sent forth the Holy Ghost on Thy adopted children" (Preface).

III. The Effects of the Coming of the Holy Ghost

"And when this was noised abroad, the multitude came together and were confounded in mind." The Apostles came forth, and spoke to the multitude, "and every man heard them speak in his own tongue.... But Peter, standing up, with the Eleven, lifted up his voice and spoke to them." This Peter, who once had quailed before a servant maid, is a new man and boldly bears witness to Jesus, "Therefore let all the house of Israel know most certainly, that God hath made both Lord and Christ, this same Jesus, whom you have crucified" (*Act.* 2, 36). And three thousand men received his word and were baptized that day!

The Church of Christ is born! That very day she begins to fulfill her mission. This day, scattered throughout the world, triumphant here and persecuted elsewhere, passionately loved or bitterly hated, she prays with all her children:

Prayer: "Send forth Thy Spirit and they shall be created; and Thou shalt renew the face of the earth. Come, O Holy Ghost, fill the hearts of thy faithful, and kindle in them the fire of Thy love" (Gradual of today's Mass).

THE GIFT OF GOD

1. It is a moving spectacle, at High Mass on Pentecost day, to see the celebrant, the sacred ministers, the acolytes, and the whole congregation, falling on their knees, when the choir intones the *Veni Sancte Spiritus*: with burning hearts and ardent desire all listen to the hallowed melody and the pleading alleluias, "Come, O Holy Ghost, fill the hearts of Thy faithful."

2. *Petition*: That the Holy Ghost may fill our hearts and kindle in them divine love.

I. The Gift of God

"Donum Dei" the Gift of God: this is the proper name of the Third Person of the Blessed Trinity, who is the bond of love between the Father and the Son, and "the charity of God, poured forth in our hearts by the Holy Ghost, who is given to us" (*Rom.* 5, 5). Every gift is a pure token of love, not due from the giver, not merited by the recipient. This is true of "every best gift, and every perfect gift from above, coming from the Father of lights" (*Jas.* 1, 17); it is true most of all of Charity Itself, the primordial gift, whence all others flow. God's love was poured into our souls in holy Baptism. In this Sacrament the Holy Ghost was given to us, "poured forth into our hearts" as St. Paul says, like a rushing flood that pervades our whole being. The gift of sanctifying grace accomplishes a fundamental change in the soul, a new creation; we cease to be slaves, imbued with the spirit of fear and servitude. "You have received the spirit of adoption of sons, whereby we cry, Abba (Father). For the Spirit giveth testimony to our spirit that we are the sons of God" (*Rom.* 15-16). This is the spontaneous cry from the child's heart, into which the Holy Ghost has entered, dwells, works and prays.

II. The Gifts of the Holy Ghost

The influence of the Holy Ghost on the soul is profound and subtle. Through His seven gifts—wisdom, understanding, counsel, fortitude, knowledge, piety, the fear of the Lord—He pervades our every faculty, our intellect, our will, and renders them fit to receive God's grace.

So often we pray that we may *recta sapere,* that is, relish what is right in things spiritual and supernatural. The gifts of the Holy Ghost—wisdom, understanding, counsel and knowledge—give keenness and insight to the intellect. The Saints possess this relish: the holy Cure of Ars was well known not as a man of learning; his fellow priests were aware of this and expressed to the Bishop their doubts as to his fitness to hear confession and to preach the word of God. "I do not know," answered the Pastor, "whether he has much learning, but I know that he is enlightened." *The Imitation of Christ* points out this difference: "There is a great difference between the wisdom of a devout and enlightened servant of God, and the learning of a cultured and studious scholar. Far nobler is that knowledge which flows from above, from God Himself, than that which is painfully acquired by human intellect" (*Bk.* III; 31, 2).

The gifts of understanding, wisdom, counsel and knowledge enlighten the mind and give it supernatural intuition; the gifts of fortitude, piety and the fear of the Lord strengthen the will, and enable it to obey readily God's will and to persevere therein.

The gifts of the Holy Ghost are of many kinds; but He Himself is *the* Gift of the Father and of the Son to us: and in bestowing that Gift on us they have given us all things. That Gift is "the charity of God, poured forth in our hearts" (*Rom.* 5, 5).

While the entire congregation, kneeling before the altar prays, "Come, O Holy Ghost; fill the hearts of Thy faithful, and kindle in them the fire of Thy love," the Spirit Himself prays in us, according to the words of St. Paul, "The Spirit also helpeth our infirmity. For we know not what we should pray for as we ought; but the Spirit himself asketh for us with unspeakable groanings. And he that searcheth the hearts (the Father) knoweth what the Spirit desireth: because he asketh for the saints according to God" (*Rom.* 8, 26-27).

These words of the Apostle show what a profound mystery the Church and her children commemorate this day. They make us realize that the Spirit animates the Mystical Body, gives life to every member and to the entire Body, abides in it, is active in it, and will be active until the last day.

Prayer to the Father: "Send forth Thy Spirit, and they shall be created, and Thou shalt renew the face of the earth."

Prayer to the Holy Ghost: "Come, O Holy Ghost; fill the hearts of Thy faithful, and kindle in them the fire of Thy love."

THE HOLY GHOST AS PURIFIER

1. Before the priest administers the Sacrament of Baptism, he
    breathes on the child, and pronounces the following exorcism,
    "Depart from him, thou unclean spirit, and make room for the
    Holy Ghost, the Consoler." Through holy Baptism the Holy
    Ghost has come into our soul, and abiding there has made it
    His temple.

2. *Petition*: The grace never to desecrate this temple of the Holy
    Ghost, but to allow Him to complete the work of cleansing
    our soul.

I. The First Cleansing

By his own unaided natural strength man cannot achieve this
first cleansing: this work can be performed by God alone. "I will
pour upon you clean water, and you shall be cleansed.... And
I will give you a new heart, and put a new spirit within you"
(*Ezech.* 36, 25-26).

When after His resurrection Jesus appeared to His Apostles,
"He breathed over them, and he said to them, Receive ye the
Holy Ghost. Whose sins you shall forgive, they are forgiven them;
and whose sins you shall retain, they are retained" (*John* 20,
22-23). Original sin, and those offences by which, after Baptism,
we "have grieved the Holy Spirit of God" (*Eph.* 4, 30), are forgiven us by the power of the Holy Ghost. In the Postcommunion
of today's Mass we pray, "We beseech Thee, O Lord, that the
Holy Ghost, by these divine mysteries, may renew our souls, for
He is the remission of sins." He loved us first; and as He took the
first step in our first justification, so He still takes the initiative
whenever, after turning away from Him, we are brought back
to Him.

We render Him thanks for His goodness and mercy, and we
firmly resolve never again to grieve Him.

II. Daily Cleansing

The Holy Ghost has power, and is wont, to work in the very
depths of our soul, and there to continue and perfect His work
of cleansing. The unclean spirit has indeed been cast out to make

room for the Holy Ghost, but "on earth he goeth about seeking whom he may devour" (1 *Peter* 5, 8); "and the flesh lusteth against the spirit, and the spirit against the flesh" (*Gal.* 5, 17). The light and the strength of the Holy Ghost enable us to discover the snares of the devil and to resist his onslaughts; and His grace wipes out whatever stain or spot may have adhered to the soul in the course of the struggle. In the prayer to secure the grace of the Holy Ghost we say, "O God, before whom every heart is manifest, and every will is eloquent, and from whom nothing lies hidden; by the infusion of the Holy Ghost purify the thoughts of our hearts." The Holy Spirit, who poured charity into our hearts, which is the principle of supernatural life, abides in us, "fills our hearts," and purifies them by chastening their most hidden motives. Therefore the Church prays in the Sequence of the Mass,

> *Heal our wounds, our strength renew;*
> *On our dryness pour Thy dew;*
> *Wash the stains of guilt away;*
> *Bend the stubborn heart and will,*
> *Melt the frozen, warm the chill,*
> *Guide the steps that go astray.*

We must be careful not to put any obstacles to the work of the Spirit, who so graciously and so thoroughly cleanses our souls. Not seldom in His work of purification will He make use of external events, which should correct, detach and purify us inwardly. The impact of these things comes from without; but the *dulcis hospes animae*, "the soul's most welcome guest," uses them to complete in us His work of purification.

III. The Final Cleansing

Whenever God wishes to draw a soul entirely to Himself, and to prepare it for the most intimate intercourse with Himself already here below, the Holy Ghost cleanses it from the least traces of imperfection: a passive purification similar to the purification of the souls in purgatory. Spiritual aridity which nothing can refresh, a deep sense of desolation, heroic adherence to God whilst the soul is shrouded in utter darkness: these things burn out the last vestiges of self-love in the soul. God alone can do this. Only the Holy Ghost, "He that searcheth the reins and the hearts," can, without hurting or paralyzing, thus penetrate to the very depth of the soul.

If a ray of light happens to penetrate into the inmost recesses of our being, revealing unto us how much self-love insinuates itself even into our holiest actions, we should not lose courage: that light comes from God; it may humble us, it ought not to discourage us. It is most salutary, for it brings us closer to the truth, and so disposes us to receive further grace.

Prayer: May the infusion of the Holy Ghost cleanse our hearts, O Lord, and make them fruitful by the sprinkling of the dew of His grace (Postcommunion, Whit Sunday).

WEDNESDAY OF PENTECOST: EMBER WEEK

THE SPIRIT OF LIGHT

1. The Holy Ghost cleanses and enlightens. "Blessed are the clean of heart, for they shall see God" (*Matt.* 5, 8) and see all things in the light of God. The Church implores the light of the Holy Ghost before every important action, for instance before the Bishop confers holy orders. Pope Pius XII, before infallibly declaring that the Assumption of our Blessed Lady is a revealed dogma, knelt down with all the bishops who surrounded him, and said, "We desire that, before we define this most important matter, all of you here present should pray that the light of the Spirit may shine ever more brightly before our eyes." In our ordinary life, we often ask for the light of the Holy Ghost: before a retreat, before a profession, before study, etc.

2. *Petition*: That we may have firm faith and implicit trust in the light of the Holy Ghost, which guides the Church of Christ, her pastors and every Christian. "Your Father from heaven will give the good Spirit to them that ask him" (*Luke* 11, 13).

I. The Holy Ghost Teaches Us the Truth

"I will ask the Father, and he shall give you another Paraclete, the Spirit of truth. . . . He will teach you all things, and bring all things to your mind, whatsoever I shall have said to you. . . . He will teach you all truth. He will abide with you" (*John* 14: 16-17; 26: 16, 13).

In these words Jesus indicates the way in which the Spirit of light acts: "He shall not speak of himself" (*John* 16, 13), for He is the Spirit of Jesus; He enlightens the mind of the Apostles, reminding them of whatever the Master had said to them, unfolding to them the innermost meaning of the Lord's doctrine, and thus leading them to the possession of the fullness of truth. And He will abide with them; in a most special manner, indeed, with the Twelve, who are to be the founders of the Church, but also with the Church until the end of time.

A truth, which has not been discovered by man's intellect, but which has been revealed by God, cannot be preserved in all its purity, unless God Himself watches over its preservation: only the special assistance of the Spirit of Truth will safeguard against all deviation the deposit of faith which, while always remaining the same, is ever to be better understood.

We should frequently pray for the Pastors of the Church, and firmly believe that "whosoever followeth the Church walketh not in darkness".

II. The Holy Ghost Makes Us Love the Truth

A truth that gives life must be loved. We should embrace it with "our whole soul". A geometrical theorem appeals merely to cold reason, and bears no relation to the life of man's soul. God's words are addressed to the whole man, also to his will and to his liberty; and the whole man must respond: he must accept what God offers, believe what God reveals. The inward disposition and readiness to dedicate oneself heart and soul to God is the work of the Holy Ghost, who is Charity; He makes us long for "true Wisdom", which we neither know nor "relish" unless we love it. This is so, above all, when a truth is not a mere abstract idea, but a real Person, our Lord Jesus Christ, through whom the Father spoke to us, and who said, "I am the truth" (*John* 14, 6). None better than the Spirit of Jesus can make us know the Lord more intimately and love Him more ardently. "Come, O Holy Ghost; pour into our hearts ardent love for Him, whose Spirit Thou art."

III. The Holy Ghost Helps Us to "Do" the Truth

We cannot possess the truth unless we "do" the truth. Words of life must be embodied in deeds. "If any one wishes thoroughly to understand and relish the words of Christ, he must first of all endeavor to live a Christ-like life" (1 *Imit. of Christ*, 1, 2).

"To do" the truth is not easy: we may feel weak and inconstant; and we grow weary; and are inclined to yield to doubt and discouragement. In that hour it behoves us to remember our Lord's promise, "I will send you another Paraclete: he will abide with you." He is the "Creator Spirit"; He abides in us, is active in us ever exerting His power, mostly in silence and in a hidden manner, at the point where our thoughts and decisions take shape. "He helpeth our infirmity; himself asketh for us with unspeakable groanings . . . and the Father knoweth what the Spirit desireth" (*Rom.* 8, 26-27).

Prayer: Thou, of all consolers best,
Thou, the soul's most welcome guest
Sweet refreshment here below:
In our labor rest most sweet,
Grateful coolness in the heat,
Solace in the midst of woe.—*Sequence*

WHIT THURSDAY

THE HOLY GHOST AS BOND OF UNION

1.   We have considered how the Holy Ghost cleanses the soul and enlightens the mind; in His most inward being He is the mutual love of the Father and the Son; in our souls He is the Father's outpouring Charity, which unites us with the three Divine Persons, and forges the Bond that binds us all together. We prostrate ourselves before the Divine Majesty together with the whole Church.

2.   *Petition*: That Charity may enkindle our hearts.

I. The Holy Ghost, the Bond of Love Between the Father and the Son

In the divine unity of the Three Persons of the Blessed Trinity the Father is the first, whence the two Others are, the Son being the perfect Image of the Father, and the Holy Ghost being the mutual Love of the Father and the Son. "The Father and I are one" said Jesus. They are one through the Holy Ghost, who is the unifying Bond of love between Both. The marvellous immanent fertility of the Deity reaches its perfection in the Holy

Ghost. When Divine Omnipotence is externally active in creation, the Father acts first but through the Son, in the Spirit, who in this case also completes and makes perfect the divine operation. In the Gospel Jesus says, "If any one love me, he will keep my word, and my Father will love him, and we will come to him, and will make our abode with him" (*John* 14, 23). And with the Father and the Son also comes the Third Person, the Holy Ghost, who is the Substantial Bond of love between the Father and the Son.

About the unfathomable mystery of the Blessed Trinity we can but stammer: that we can do so and that our stammering language should express an absolutely sure knowledge is the most admirable proof of God's merciful love for man. Glory be to the Father, and to the Son, and to the Holy Ghost.

II. The Spirit Kindles in Us the Flame of Divine Love

"The charity of God is poured forth in our hearts by the Holy Ghost, who is given to us" (*Rom.* 5, 5). "You have received not the spirit of bondage in fear" (that is, the spirit that animates slaves when they face their masters), "but you have received the spirit of adoption of sons, whereby we cry, Abba, Father" (*Rom.* 8, 15). Since God has made us His adopted children, it behoves us to cultivate towards Him the sentiments of true sons, as St. John says, "Behold what manner of charity the Father hath bestowed upon us, that we should be called and should be the sons of God" (*John* 3, 1). And to the Romans St. Paul wrote: "For the Spirit himself giveth testimony to our spirit that we are the sons of God" (8, 16), and thus He Himself cries out in us, and we in Him, "Abba, Father."

No human heart could utter this cry, unless the Spirit did abide in it, and had kindled in it the flame of divine love. Divine love is a noble love, a love that urges to action. "He that hath my commandments, and keepeth them, he it is that loveth me" (*John* 14, 21); it is a burning love, that consumes utterly all self-love.

III. The Holy Ghost Enkindles in Us Fraternal Charity

The Holy Ghost is the Spirit of Christ. "He shall not speak of himself; but what things soever he shall hear, he shall speak; he shall glorify me, because he shall receive of mine, and shall show it to you" (*John* 16, 13-14). Since according to St. Augustine, Jesus made of the love of God and the love of the neighbor "two commandments but only one love," we may rest assured that the Spirit, who urges us to cry "Abba, Father," also prompts us to love all the children of that Father. The love of the Father, which He kindles in our hearts, is proved to be genuine by our love of the neighbor.

He is the Spirit of Truth; and St. John says, "If any man say, I love God, and hateth his brother, he is a liar" (1 *John* 4, 20), just as he who denies that Jesus is the Christ.

"He that hath the substance of this world, and shall see his brother in need, and shall shut up his heart from him: how doth the charity of God abide in him? My little children, let us not love in word, nor in tongue, but in deed and in truth" (1 *John* 3, 17-18).

After the Last Supper, Jesus concluded His sacerdotal prayer to the Father with these words, "I have made known thy name to them and will make it known; that the love wherewith thou hast loved me may be in them, and I in them" (*John* 17, 26). That love, with which the Father has loved the Son, and which must be in us, is the Holy Ghost, who unites the Father with the Son, and draws us into that Unity.

Prayer: Grant us, O Lord, the spirit of Thy love, that, through Thy fatherly mercy being one in Thee, we also may be united with one another. Through Christ our Lord.

FRIDAY OF PENTECOST: EMBER WEEK

THE SPIRIT OF FORTITUDE AND MEEKNESS

1. When the Bishop confers the sacrament of Confirmation, he gives the young Christian a gentle slap on the cheek: this symbolical gesture is reminiscent of the ceremony in which the king dubbed some one a knight by touching him on the shoulder with the sword. The sacrament of Confirmation bestows on the disciple of Christ the strength to withstand the enemies of his Faith: the sacred unction, and the sacramental words bestow on him the grace of the Holy Ghost, and the Bishop sends him into battle with these words (which may surprise us), *Pax tecum*, peace be to thee. This gesture and these words perfectly express the whole conception of Christianity.

2. *Petition*: The grace to understand that the life of the Christian is a sacred war to be fought in the spirit of peace.

I. The Spirit of Fortitude

Shortly before His ascension into heaven Jesus said to the Apostles, "You shall receive the power of the Holy Ghost coming upon you" (*Act.* 1, 8). This power was poured into their hearts to the accompaniment of outward signs: "a sound from heaven, as of a mighty wind ... and parted tongues, as it were of fire." These faint indications of the creative, all-pervading, irresistible, consuming power of the Most High. The Creator Spirit transformed those timorous, faint-hearted fishermen into doughty champions and bold apostles, who sailed forth to the conquest of the world and with their blood bore witness that Christ is the Son of God. Now they "can drink the chalice that I shall drink" (*Matt.* 20, 22), as Jesus had foretold.

Even in our times this Spirit of Fortitude animates and sustains all those who have to suffer for the faith. Never, throughout the centuries, were there as many as in our time who, in their struggle for Christ and against sin, "have resisted unto blood" (*Heb.* 12, 4), even unto greater sufferings.

To this Spirit of Fortitude the Church appeals, saying:

"And with Thy strength, which ne'er decays,
Confirm our mortal frame."

In the sacrament of Confirmation the Christian is anointed: the athletes of old used to anoint their bodies to make their limbs strong and nimble. The holy chrism, and the grace it confers, must fortify us in the spiritual strife of every day. As a rule this strife occurs in a hidden manner and hardly attracts attention. But we do need the strength of the Holy Ghost lest we should yield to sloth, to discouragement, to false shame; we need it so that in every place and on every occasion we may play our part in securing the victory of good over evil. For we are all responsible for the issue of the fierce contest between good and evil. The Church has sore need of valiant champions, fortified by the Holy Ghost. St. Paul thus describes the soldier of Christ, "Stand therefore, having your loins girt about with truth and having on the breastplate of justice: and your feet shod with the preparation of the gospel of peace; in all things taking the shield of faith, wherewith you may be able to extinguish all the fiery darts of the most wicked one. And take unto you the helmet of salvation and the sword of the Spirit, (which is the word of God)" (*Eph.* 6, 14-17).

II. The Spirit of Peace

The Spirit of Fortitude is also the Spirit of Peace. "A good soldier of Christ Jesus" (2 *Tim.* 2, 3) preaches the Gospel of peace. On the day of Pentecost the Holy Ghost appeared in the form of fiery tongues: but at the Baptism of Jesus He showed Himself in the guise of a dove, the symbol of peace and meekness. The Spirit of Christ is at once strong and gentle. Jesus is the "Lion of Juda", but also the "Lamb of God". The Church praises the martyrs as being "victorum genus optimum", the best sort of conquerors. St. Thomas More with these words took leave of the judges, who had sentenced him to death: "Gentlemen, I fervently hope that you, who here on earth have contributed to my execution, may one day meet me in heaven, where we shall enjoy eternal bliss together."

In the "school of Christ" we learn to be at the same time bold and meek: the essence of each of these virtues is love, love of God and love of the neighbor, but love "to the end".

III. The Spirit of Counsel

The same Spirit will teach us how, in the ever changing circumstances of real life, we are to practice both fortitude and meekness without permitting either of these virtues to tarnish the brightness of the other. For He is the Spirit of Counsel, who abides in us, and who guides and directs our thoughts and feelings at their very source, provided we ask Him and are inwardly free. This is "that true wisdom", and that "right relish", for which we so often pray. St. Ignatius called it "wise love": love which ignores measure and limit, but which is supernaturally discreet and prudent.

Prayer: Deign, we beseech Thee, O Lord, to pour into our souls Thy Holy Ghost, whose wisdom has created us, and whose providence governs us. Through our Lord ... (Collect, Saturday after **Pentecost**).

THE SOUL'S MOST WELCOME GUEST (John 14: 13, 16)

1. This is the last day of the Octave of Pentecost and of the Paschal season. As subject of this meditation we take the comforting words spoken by Jesus shortly before He left us, "I go to the Father, and I will ask the Father: and he shall give you another Paraclete, that he may abide with you for ever" (*John* 14: 13, 16). During these eight days we have commemorated the descent of the Holy Ghost. He does not leave us, He remains with us, in the Church, and in every soul.

2. *Petition*: The grace always to pay due reverence to the "Soul's most welcome Guest", and ever to heed His inspirations.

I. The Holy Ghost Abides in Us

Sanctifying grace is a partaking of the divine life which is indivisibly proper to the Three Divine Persons. "If any one love me, he will keep my word; and my Father will love him: and we will come to him and make our abode with him" (*John* 14, 23). It is the common opinion of theologians that all external operations of the Deity, are the joint act of the Three Divine Persons; but in the Great Mystery of God's plan for the salvation of man they generally ascribe to the Father our adoption as children of God; to the Son our incorporation into His Mystical Body; and to the Holy Ghost our sanctification, by His indwelling in our soul. These distinctions, or appropriations, are simply human attempts to help our minds grasp something of the ineffable working of God.

However, Holy Writ and the liturgy so often and so clearly speak of the indwelling of the Holy Ghost in our souls that, even though we know that the Three persons act together, yet we are justified in conceiving a special relation between the Holy Ghost and the soul that is in the state of grace: "And I will ask the Father: and he shall give you another Paraclete, that he may abide with you for ever" (*John* 14, 16).

"The charity of God, poured forth in our hearts by the Holy Ghost who is given to us" (*Rom.* 5, 5). "Or know you not that your members are the temple of the Holy Ghost who is in you, whom you have from God?" (1 *Cor.* 6, 19.)

In the same sense the liturgy says that "the Holy Ghost by dwelling in us, makes us perfect; that He cleanses, illumines and guides our souls; that by "the inward sprinkling of His dew he may render our souls fruitful" (Postcommunion, Whit Sunday).

He is the "dulcis hospes animae", the soul's most welcome guest.

II. Grieve Not the Holy Spirit of God

As the Paraclete deigns to abide in us as our Divine Guest and desires to enrich us with His gifts, we have a grave duty towards Him.

With love and gratitude we must be mindful of His presence. Indeed we are mindful of Him, and pay Him homage whenever we make the sign of the cross, or say the Glory be to the Father. . . . Would to God that we always said these prayers with due reverence!

We have the power to "grieve the Holy Spirit of God" (*Eph.* 4, 30). By uttering an untruth we grieve "the Spirit of Truth"; by "bitterness, anger and indignation", and by calumny we grieve the Spirit of God, who is the Spirit of Love; if we wish to please Him, "be ye kind to one another, merciful, forgiving one another, even as God hath forgiven you in Christ" (*Eph.* 4, 32).

And St. Paul tells us that we also can "extinguish the spirit" (1 *Thess.* 5, 19); He is light and He is fire; "the Spirit breatheth where he will . . . thou knowest not whence he cometh and whither he goeth" (*John* 3, 8). "Extinguish not the Spirit: but prove all things, and hold fast to that which is good" (1 *Thess.* 5, 19-21). We extinguish the Spirit when, through lack of faith and confidence, or through cowardice, we fail to heed the promptings of His grace; or when, through faintheartedness we cease to strive after better things. "But prove all things: hold fast to that which is good;" in order that we may do so we ask the Holy Ghost to grant us true wisdom, and we seek the counsel of an experienced director.

By sin we violate the temple where the Holy Ghost abides. "Know you not that you are the temple of God, and that the Spirit of God dwelleth in you? But if any man violate the temple of God, him shall God destroy. For the temple of God is holy, which you are" (1 *Cor.* 3, 16-17). And after exhorting the Corinthians to shun all impure sin, St. Paul adds, "Or know you not that your members are the temple of the Holy Ghost, who is in you, whom you have from God: and you are not your own?" (1 Cor. 6, 19.)

The most grievous sin, that "which shall not be forgiven", is the sin against the Holy Ghost, committed out of sheer malice, by which man shuts his heart to God's grace and God's mercy. This is the sin "against the Light" (Matt. 12, 31-32).

With hearts filled with awe and aflame with love, we adore the Paraclete, whom through the Son the Father has given to us, who abides in us, cleanses and illumines us, unites us together. "For the Spirit himself giveth testimony to our spirit that we are the sons of God ... groaning within ourselves, waiting for the adoption of the sons of God.... Likewise the Spirit also helpeth our infirmity. For we know not what we should pray for as we ought; but the Spirit himself asketh for us with unspeakable groaning. And he that searcheth the hearts knoweth what the Spirit desireth because he asketh for the saints according to God" (Rom. 8, 16-27).

Prayers We beseech Thee, O Lord, that the Holy Ghost inflame us with that fire which our Lord sent upon earth, and which He earnestly desires to be enkindled: who with Thee liveth and reigneth in the unity of the same Holy Ghost ... (Collect of todays's Mass).

MEDITATIONS FOR FEAST DAYS

DECEMBER 3
ST. FRANCIS XAVIER

1. St. Francis Xavier, the greatest apostle of modern times, died at the age of 46, after ten years of heroic labor in India, the Islands of the Far East and Japan. His last and most daring expedition ended in failure, and he died on December 3, 1552, on the barren island of Sancian, in sight of the Chinese coast. His ambition was to carry the Cross into the great Empire; but he died, struck down at the farthest outpost of the Church Militant. One of his most recent biographers, James Broderick, S.J., concludes the account of his tragic death with the following considerations, which give us ample matter for meditation.

"It was a poor and humble death, not unperplexed, such as befitted a poor and humble man who had no notion whatever that the world would want to remember him. He had brought thousands of others the comforts of the Church in their last moments, but he died himself without anointing or Viaticum. When they packed his frail exhausted body in lime and put it in the unconsecrated Chinese earth, there was no one to read over it the Church's last farewell to her children. Had he ever been so far untrue to his character as to give a thought to his obsequies, he would surely have been well content that his bones should remain there, as it were, keeping watch until the end of the world, if indeed he would not have prayed to God with all his heart to be allowed the last privilege of the lowly, an unknown and forgotten grave."

2. *Petition*: As we stand by Xavier's grave may we be granted the grace to realize how God did great things through one whose humility and selflessness were pleasing in His sight.

I. Gained to Christ by St. Ignatius

Francis, the youngest son of a noble but impoverished Basque family, had come to Paris University in 1525, when he was only nineteen years of age; his ambition was to gain learning and thus to rise to fame and fortune. Accidentally—so we would say—he happened to meet another Basque nobleman, fifteen years his senior, Ignatius of Loyola, who had been converted from worldliness a few years before. Ignatius was then trying to enlist young men into a Company that prepared itself to labor strenuously for the greater glory of God. With much patience and no less tact, Ignatius, who knew the secrets of the human heart, endeavored to persuade the wordly-minded and ambitious young doctor, to resign his chair of philosophy to which he had been promoted, and to enter into the "school of Christ", where he would strive to attain the highest degree of humility. In order to follow more effectively Christ our Lord, and to be more like to Him, Francis chose to have poverty with Christ poor, rather than riches; humiliation with Christ humiliated, rather than honor.

Until his death Xavier remained deeply grateful to Ignatius, who had opened to him the way to true glory. In his letters from the East, he called Ignatius his "true and only father"; and with deep emotion, which even now moves our hearts, he signs his letters, "the least and most distant of your sons, Francisco".

II. Heroic and Humble to the End

It seemed a sheer accident that Xavier was sent to the Indian Mission; in fact it happened by the special disposition of Providence. In March 1540 he was acting as secretary to St. Ignatius, and the only one of the Company then present at Rome with the founder. A priest was needed who could leave immediately for Lisbon, whence he would sail for the eastern territories of King John III of Portugal. And so Francis had his opportunity. He started at once, armed with a papal document that bestowed on him the office and powers of Papal Nuncio. On board ship he washed his clothes and prepared his food like the poorest voyager; above all he took care of the sick and dying; while being the most cheerful on board, he made himself the servant of all.

There is no need of mentioning here what Francis achieved in ten years' time, 1542 to 1552, as a pioneer and founder of missions. His real greatness does not lie there. What strikes and edifies us, is to see in him true greatness together with deep humility. On his arrival at Goa, he immediately called on the Bishop, and showing him his papal credentials he informed the prelate that, without his consent, he would not use the powers with which he was invested. And indeed, only once did he make use of them, and that was against the Portuguese commander at Malacca, who tried to prevent his journey to China. Whenever something went amiss or failed, he blamed none but himself, and his own sins. To Gaspar Berze, who in his absence exercised the powers of Provincial, he wrote, "For the love of Christ our Lord and because of all that you owe to our Father Ignatius, I beseech you, once, twice, thrice, as often as I can, continually apply yourself to the practice of humility. I have seen more than one perishing because of lack of humility."

We read in the *Imitation of Christ*, "Generous love of Jesus urges man to do great things", and these great things he does with perfect humility and simplicity. Xavier's death was the death of a hero. Yet the young Chinese who was with him heard him continually repeating these words, "Jesus, Son of David, have mercy on me; O Virgin Mother of God, remember me."

He wrote his letters to Ignatius, kneeling on the ground and he constantly asked for prayers and begged for advice.

Prayer: O God, who didst bring the peoples of the Indies within the fold of Thy Church by means of the preaching and miracles of blessed Francis; mercifully grant that we may both honor his glorious merits and imitate his virtuous example. Through our Lord (Collect, Mass of today).

JANUARY 18-25

THE CHURCH UNITY OCTAVE: "THAT THEY ALL MAY BE ONE"

1. The first "Octave of Prayers for unity" was organized by two Episcopalian ministers in the United States, from the 18th to the 25th of January 1908. Their aim was to draw closer together all those that believe in Christ, and to pave the way for the so ardently desired reunion of all Christians. It may appear natural that this yearning for unity found expression first among those who had wandered away from the fold; but almost immediately their cry was heard by Mother Church. In 1909 Pius X approved the octave of prayers; his successor Benedict XV bestowed on it high praise, and Pius XI encouraged the celebration of the Octave at Rome, and himself daily offered holy Mass for the proposed intentions. Nowadays the Octave is held all over the world; and the prayer "that they may be one" more agreeable

to Christ's Heart than any other, rises up to heaven from thousands of churches and oratories, and from millions of souls, that feel their brotherhood in Christ.

2. *Petition:* With Jesus we pray "That they all may be one, as thou, Father, in me, and I in Thee; that they also may be one in us, that the world may believe that thou hast sent me" (*John* 17, 21).

I. The Lord's Ardent Wish and Last Prayer

In His priestly prayer after the Last Supper, when He is on the point of going away from them, Jesus reveals to the Apostles what is the dearest wish of His Heart: He prays for "all who through the word of the Apostles (and of their successors) will believe in Him, that they may be one."

Long ago He had told them that there ought to be but one flock and one Shepherd. How close that union can be and must be Jesus shows us by pointing, as He always does when speaking of perfection, to the most ineffable union that ever can be: "that they all may be one, as thou, Father, in me, and I in thee, that they also be one in us".

How is it possible that this most ardent wish of the beloved Son has not been fulfilled? When Jesus stood before the grave of Lazarus we heard Him say, "Father, I give thee thanks that thou hast heard me. And I knew that thou hearest me always, but because of the people who stand about have I said it, that they may believe that thou hast sent me" (*John* 11, 41-42). And for that same reason He asks the Father that they may be one.

Indeed, "the Father always heareth" the Son, "as long as man's perversity and free will does not come in the way to thwart the holy will of the Father and of the Son", as St. Bernard very aptly puts it.

II. Man's Frailty and Wickedness

Jesus desired that there should be one flock and one shepherd, one Church, "not having spot or wrinkle" (*Eph.* 5, 27). He had sown good seed in His field, but soon "his enemy came and oversowed cockle among the wheat" (*Matt.* 13, 25). St. Luke writes in the Acts, "And the multitude of believers had but one heart and one soul" (4, 32). Alas, this did not last very long. He that "knows what is in man" had foreseen it, when He said, "It must needs be that scandals come" (*Matt.* 18, 7). The Lord's Heart bled when

He spoke those words. When at Ephesus St. Paul was told that internal strife was tearing asunder the Church at Corinth, he wrote, "For there must be also heresies: that they also who are approved may be made manifest among you" (1 *Cor.* 11, 19). And so we too must prove our fidelity to Christ.

The preservation of harmony in groups of men is always a thorny problem: each one's selfishness clashes with that of his neighbor. And in the case of the Church we are dealing with men of all races and of all times; and what is at stake is God's revealed truth, divine mysteries hard to grasp by the human mind. These truths must be preserved unaltered, and ought to be understood ever more perfectly. The Holy Ghost, whom Jesus sent down on the Apostles, still abides in the Church, guides her and enlightens her. But at the same time another spirit, an evil one, is active among men, also among believers. In the course of the centuries he has managed to enlist into his service every human passion to besmirch the Mystical Body of Christ, to weaken it, to tear it asunder.

The Church has known dark periods, when scandal and abuses poisoned the conduct of her children, which brought in their wake darkness and confusion in the minds of people, schism and apostasy. In the XVIth century, a major part of Europe broke away from Rome: a fatal calamity followed by centuries of enmity and estrangement, mutual distrust and misunderstanding.

The Church did possess and teach Christ's revealed truth; but her face was not without wrinkle, and the conduct of her children was not spotless. The so-called reformers departed from the rock, on which Christ had built His Church, and took the "pure Evangel" as their standard; but lacking divine guidance, they strayed further and further from the straight road, and were in their turn rent to shreds by recurring internal schisms. We may humbly admit that at the beginning, and even now, all the guilt was not on one side. "The charity of Christ presseth us" (2 *Cor.* 5, 14) "that doing the truth in charity, we may in all things grow up in him who is the head, even Christ" (*Eph.* 4, 15).

III. Back to Unity

Therefore, during these days, together with all our separated brethren, we shall pray fervently and offer our sacrifices generously for the restoration of unity; or rather, we shall pray and offer together with Jesus Himself, whose fervent prayer ever remains "that they all may be one". As symbol of that unity, and as its perfect realization, He has given us the holy Eucharist: "For we being many are one bread, one body, all that partake of one bread" (1 *Cor.* 10, 17).

We truly possess the spirit of Christ when, with this intention, we lead lives "worthy of the Gospel" (*Phil.* 1, 17), and endeavor to make our own communities one, as Jesus and the Father are one.

Prayer: The prayer of the Octave, or the Collect of the Mass for the Unity of the Church: "O God, who settest straight what has gone astray, and gatherest together what has been scattered, and keepest what Thou hast gathered together, we beseech Thee, in Thy mercy to pour down on Christian people the grace of union with Thee: that putting aside disunion, and attaching themselves to the true shepherd of Thy Church, they may be able to render Thee true service. Through our Lord."

JANUARY 25

CONVERSION OF ST. PAUL

"BY THE GRACE OF GOD I AM WHAT I AM"
(1 *Cor.* 15, 10)

1. After the resurrection of Jesus and the miracle of Pentecost, the conversion of St. Paul was the most striking event in the life of the youthful Church. In this case the Lord did not stand at the gate, knocking until it was opened (*Apoc.* 3, 20); He entered by sheer force, and transformed a raving enemy into an ardent apostle.

2. *Petition*: We thank God and praise Him, "who alone doth great things and unsearchable, wonderful things without number" (*Job.* 5, 9). We pray that we may ever have confidence in the power of grace.

I. Saul, the Persecutor

To Timothy, his dearest disciple and youthful collaborator, St. Paul wrote that formerly he "was blasphemer and persecutor, and contumelious" (*Tim.* 1, 13). He was born ten years after Christ, at Tarsus, a port on the southern coast of Asia Minor; he had received a Greek education, and had acquired Roman citizenship. His background, therefore, differed greatly from that of the other Apostles.

He was a Jew, even a rabbi, passionately devoted to the Law of Moses; and adhered to the strictest sect of the Pharisees. He had never seen Jesus of Nazareth, whom he regarded as the founder of a detestable sect; and he found pleasure in blaspheming the Lord's name and making others do the same. It was now six years since he had, under the direction of the high priest, set afoot a violent campaign against the followers of the Nazarene, with the aim of destroying them to the last man. He had witnessed and applauded the stoning of Stephen.

And yet, it had pleased God to separate him, and to call him by His grace from his mother's womb (*Gal.* 1, 15). He was certainly a man of talent, of broad culture, and above all deeply religious. He himself tells us that he persecuted the Church of God unwittingly. He had never sinned against the light, the full light. The *Lumen Christi* had not yet shone before his eyes. Soon, as in a flash of lightning, it would strike him to the ground. God is wonderful in His works!

II. Paul Apprehended by Christ

One morning, in the spring of the year 36, Saul had ridden forth from Jerusalem "that if he found any men or women of this way (disciples of Jesus) in the synagogues of Damascus, he might bring them bound to Jerusalem. And as he went on his journey, it came to pass that he drew nigh to Damascus; and suddenly a light from heaven shined round about him. And falling to the ground, he heard a voice saying to him, Saul, Saul, why persecutest thou me? Who said, Who art thou, Lord? And he, I am Jesus whom thou persecutest. It is hard for thee to kick against the goad. And he trembling and astonished said, Lord what wilt thou have me to do?" (*Act.* 9, 2-6.)

This was indeed an unexpected and a crushing blow: that Jesus of Nazareth, in whose resurrection he had refused to believe, stood there before him, alive and glorious. He addressed him by name, and asked, not why he was persecuting His disciples, but more directly, Why persecutest thou Me?

Was Saul perhaps inclined to resist, and is that why Jesus said, "It is hard for thee (thou canst not) to kick against the goad"? Trembling and astounded he said, "Lord, what wilt thou have me to do?" Paul's response to the proffered grace is striking: he offers no apologies, he asks no clarification; but as a true man of action he there and then surrenders himself completely to the Lord. He had been "apprehended by Christ" as later he will say to the Philippians (3, 12). At one stroke he is entirely won over to Christ, and his whole life will be "a following after Christ, that he may apprehend Christ, as he also has been apprehended by Christ Jesus".

III. "Paul, an Apostle of Jesus Christ"

In this first meeting with Jesus Saul asked, "What wilt thou have me to do?", and the answer was, "Arise, and go into the city, and there it shall be told thee what thou must do." He was to receive Baptism, and then, by the imposition of hands, be filled with the Holy Ghost. Then Jesus will show him how much he must suffer for his name's sake (*Act.* 9, 16).

After receiving Baptism, for more than a year he retired to Arabia, where in silence and solitude Jesus personally and gradually formed His Apostle, and poured in his soul that profound understanding of Christ's person and doctrine.

Paul is an "Apostle of Jesus Christ", not like Matthias, by the choice of the other Apostles; Christ Himself has called him, "a vessel of election, to carry his name before the Gentiles and Kings". Of this Paul is fully aware: and when the need arises, he sharply defends his right, or rather the right of Jesus, whose Apostle he is. Yet he never forgot that among the Apostles he was the last comer: "And last of all he was seen also by me, as by one born out of due time. For I am the least of the apostles, who am not worthy to be called an apostle because I persecuted the church of God. But by the grace of God I am what I am" (1 *Cor.* 15, 8-10).

Paul had learnt by experience that everything he was and had was sheer grace; as he readily confessed, by himself he was a persecutor of Christ: and if he did not remain a persecutor, he owed it exclusively to Christ, "the Son of God, who loved me and delivered himself for me" (*Gal.* 2, 20). And therefore Paul can remain truly humble, even when he bears witness that "his grace in me has not been void, but I have labored more abundantly than all they; yet not I, but the grace of God with me" (1 *Cor.* 15, 10).

Both God's gracious preventing love, and Paul's generous return, that is, his tireless apostolic labors, ought to foster in us confidence and generosity.

Prayer: O God, who hast shown the marvellous power of Thy grace in the conversion of Paul, Thine Apostle, grant, by his intercession, that we may have confidence in Thy grace, and imitate his fidelity in Thy service. Through Christ our Lord.

JANUARY 29

ST. FRANCIS OF SALES

1. Among canonized Saints St. Francis of Sales is one of the most human and most lovable. Without shock or hurt grace sanctified all his human talents, purified and ennobled them, made them blossom forth and bear "good fruit". Among the disciples of Him, who said: "Learn of me, because I am meek and humble of heart, and you shall find rest to your souls" (*Matt*. 11, 29), Francis was one of the most proficient, and most highly favored by heaven.

"Had ther been aught better than large-heartedness, our Lord would have told us", he used to say.

2. *Petition*: The grace to admire God in this Saint, of whom his best friend, St. Jane de Chantal, said that "in all things, he trod the ordinary way".

I. Meek of Heart

Nature had endowed him with a gentle disposition: that was God's gift. When he informs us that he had struggled during twenty-four years to acquire this virtue, the holy man in his humility meant that it took him that length of time to gain perfect control of his internal sensibility. Although by temperament he was meek and gentle, he had a most sensitive soul, which was easily ruffled and perturbed. He had to control himself to maintain his internal composure. Once he said to St. Jane de Chantal, "Mine is a weak nature; yet, by God's grace, since I am a bishop, I have never uttered a harsh word to a single member of my flock."

A halo of charity and kindness surrounds the entire personality of this Saint: his features, his entire demeanor, his doctrine, his spirituality, all breathe gentleness and goodness. Not that he was a weakling or lacked grit. He said, "I love independent and energetic characters." From his spiritual daughter, St. Jane, he required painful sacrifices. He told her "you will cry out, O my Father, how is it that suddenly you have grown so severe? No, my daughter, not suddenly; for since I received the grace of understanding something of the fruits of the cross, this feeling (of the necessity of sacrifice) has sunk ever deeper and deeper into my soul, and has never gone out of it. Have I not told you that I would free you from all bonds?" And stronger still, "We must persuade a man that there is something gravely amiss with his soul, then hand him the knife, that with his own hand he may cut it out." In reality he is as straightforward and sincere as St. John of the Cross or as St. Ignatius; but his manner is gentle, and his utterance always amiable. Did he not say to his nuns, "Live joyfully in the midst of the thorns of Christ's crown, and as the nightingale in his coppice, sing aloud, Long live Jesus"?

II. Humble of Heart

Francis was born of a noble family, the son of an influential magistrate; he had obtained theological degrees; he was a distinguished orator; and his manners were pleasing, his demeanor courteous: the road lay open to high preferment in the Church. He was a very youg man when he was appointed Bishop, that is, Bishop of a minor see, Geneva: he never set foot in his episcopal city, where the Calvinists ruled supreme; he lived in the small mountain town of Annecy, in Savoy, far from Paris. At Annecy he lived for twenty years, well pleased that he never was promoted to a larger see. In the same manner did St. Augustine remain the pastor of his unimportant diocese of Hippo.

St. Francis was the pastor of a small flock, extremely devoted to his people, accessible to all, ever ready to help, kind and amiable to all comers, and never averse to enjoying a good joke. An impoverished nobleman insisted on borrowing 100 francs from him. The Bishop knew the man and answered, "No, my friend, not a loan of 100 francs; but I make you a gift of 50 francs, and so we shall both be gainers by 50 francs."

This gentle and humble man proved to be a pioneer and a leader in the religious life of his day. For men and women in the world desirous of leading a holy life, he wrote his great work An Introduction to the Devout Life—that is, to the truly Christian life. Its originality does not lie in its contents, but in its method and its presentation. "What," he writes, "here am I writing about the devout life, and I myself am far from being truly devout; but then, how I long to reach that ideal!"

For young women and widows whose health was unable to bear the strain of the cloistered life, as it was understood in those days, with the help of St. Jane de Chantal, he founded a new "congregation". The rules were less severe, and every day the nuns were permitted to spend a few hours outside the enclosure to nurse the sick and to work among the poor: hence the name of Sisters of the Visitation. In the *Treatise on Divine Love* which he wrote for their use, he says, "I shall say nothing in this book which I have not learnt from others." Indeed, he was humble of heart.

When the Archbishop of Lyons, who was his friend and his ecclesiastical superior, informed him that he did not see his way to sanction this new form of religious life, and that the sisters must submit to strict enclosure and be really cloistered nuns, he wrote, "Gladly, and with real joy, have I obeyed this decision. God alone is competent to found such Institutes." We can gauge the importance he attached to humility from the following words which, perhaps not without a malicious smile, he once addressed to his Sisters, "It is better for you to have a little more humility and fewer virtues, than more virtues and less humility."

Here we are really in the "School of Christ", and he, who speaks, is one of the most proficient and most lovable disciples of the Master.

III. "Rest to Your Souls"

To them that take Jesus as their Master, and learn of Him to be meek and humble of heart, our Lord promises rest to their souls. No one comes to Jesus, no one remains for long His disciple, no one grasps the doctrine He teaches, unless he be led and enlightened by love. To such as love Him and the virtues dear to His Heart, He gives "His peace". The meek and humble heart of Saint Francis enjoyed the most exquisite peace; for he had mastered those passions that wreck the peace of our fickle hearts— pride, jealousy, impatience, susceptibility. This peace of soul, Francis found and preserved undisturbed. Yet love knows no rest: it blossoms forth into restless zeal, a restlessness that does not perturb. Truly he toiled restlessly to help devout souls that yearn for perfection, in acquiring "love, joy and peace" in the service of God and of immortal souls.

Prayer: O God, who hast willed that Thy blessed Confessor and Bishop, Francis, should make himself all things to all men for the saving of their souls; grant that, guided by his counsels, and aided by his prayers, we may be permeated by the sweetness of Thy charity, and so attain everlasting joy. Through our Lord (Collect of the Feast).

FEBRUARY 2

THE PURIFICATION OF THE BLESSED VIRGIN

1. The several names, by which this feast is called, point to a Mystery, which offers many aspects for pious meditation: "Candlemas", because on this day the Church blesses wax-candles in honor of Him whom the old man Simeon greeted as "a light to the revelation of the gentiles"; also the "Presentation of Jesus in the Temple", the "Meeting of Simeon and the Child", the "Purification of Mary" (the only feast in honor of Mary preserved in the Anglican liturgy).

   Forty days after the Nativity Mary and Joseph "carried the child to Jerusalem, to present him to the Lord" (*Luke* 2, 22). The onlookers saw a young couple with a child, differing in no way from scores of other pious Jews, who entered every day the House of God.

2. *Petition*: We ask to join Mary and Joseph; may our soul grasp and savor this mystery: and may we offer ourselves to the Father together with the Infant Christ.

I. Obedience

In a few lines St. Luke says five times that all these things were done "according to the law of Moses", "as it is written in the law". It was ordained that every Jewish mother who had borne a child should, after forty days, submit to a rite of purification; when this was possible, she would proceed to the Temple, where she received the priest's blessing. Another Law prescribed that the first male child of every mother should be consecrated to God. Lastly, to complete the ceremony, the parents had to offer a sacrifice: in the case of poor people, like Joseph and Mary, "a pair of turtle doves, or two young pigeons" would suffice.

If St. Luke lays so much stress on the fact that they "did everything according to the custom of the law", it is probably because
he wants us to understand that Mary did not deem herself ex-
empted from the prescriptions of the Law. She, so highly favored
by God, the Virgin Mother of the Son of God, goes to the
Temple with the Child; she appears before the priest to receive
his blessing, and to be declared purified; she places the Infant
in his hands, that he may dedicate It to God, that Child who,
when He came into the world, had said, Behold, I come to do
thy will, O God (*Heb.* 10: 5, 9). And before departing she made
her little oblation.

Then two other persons appear on the scene: it is not the Law
that brings them at this hour; but they come in obedience to the
promptings of the Holy Ghost, who enlightened their mind; and
rewarded their long and faithful service of God and their ardent
yearning for the Messiah. Below the veil of poverty, they discovered the divine, and with their whole heart they praised
the Lord.

II. Simeon's Prophecy

Simeon, "a man just and devout", who was waiting for the consolation of Israel, "came by the Spirit into the temple." And when
his parents brought in the child Jesus, to do for him according
to the custom of the law, he also took him into his arms, and
blessed God and said,

> Now thou dost dismiss thy servant, O Lord,
> According to thy word in peace;
> Because my eyes have seen thy salvation
> Which thou hast prepared before the face of all peoples;
> A light to the revelation of the Gentiles,
> And the glory of thy people, Israel.

"And his father and mother were wondering at those things
which were spoken concerning him" (*Luke* 2, 33).

Simeon had taken the Infant into his arms, for Mary could not
deny the venerable man's ardent desire; and what he says to her
in rapt ecstasy, whilst he holds the Child, fills her soul with
wonder. Gabriel had said, "He shall be great ... the Lord God
shall give unto him the throne of David his father, and he shall
reign in the house of Jacob forever, and of his kingdom there shall
be no end" (*Luke* 1, 32-33). But Simeon's canticle opens far
vaster horizons: Israel is still in the picture, but Simeon salutes

in her Child "the Savior of all peoples, a light for the revelation
of the gentiles"! Does this aged servant of Jahve know more about
her Child than she herself? And he also knows what the future
holds in store for Him and for His Mother. "And Simeon blessed
them," (surely he had a right to do so, as "the Holy Ghost was
in him"), "and said to Mary his mother, Behold this child is set
for the fall and for the resurrection of many in Israel, and for a
sign that shall be contradicted; and thy own soul a sword shall
pierce: that out of many hearts thoughts may be revealed" (*Luke*
2, 34-35). Gabriel had not said a word about all this, and here for
the first time God deigned to remove a small portion of the
veil that shrouded, even for Mary, the mystery of our salvation.
Surely, at these words Mary wondered, and once again she spoke
her *Fiat*, and humbly submitted to God's will. That will was
that she should bear a large share in the sufferings which
Jesus would endure to save us. "But Mary kept all those words,
pondering them in her heart" (*Luke* 2, 19).

"And after they had performed all things according to the law
of the Lord, they returned". . . "into Galilee to their city of Nazareth", says St. Luke (2, 39), who omits the adoration of the
Magi and the flight into Egypt. They went back to Bethlehem,
where they soon beheld how the double prophecy of Simeon was
fulfilled for the first time: Wise men from the East, Gentiles,
came to adore "the light to the revelation of the gentiles"; Herod
endeavored to quench that Light, and thus this Child is become
"a sign that shall be contradicted: that out of many hearts
thoughts may be revealed". That light still shines, and Christ still
is a sign that is being contradicted!

Prayer: Almighty and Eternal God, we humbly implore Thy
Majesty that, like Thine only-begotten Son who, clad in our flesh,
was on this day presented in the Temple, we also, purified in soul,
may likewise be presented to Thee. Through the same Lord
(Collect, today's Mass).

OUR LADY'S APPARITION TO BERNADETTE

1.   "The Fact of Lourdes", which had its beginning on the 11th
of February, 1858 without pomp or show, must be reckoned as

one of the most striking events in the religious history of our time. "This day the glorious Queen of heaven appeared on earth; this day she spoke to her people words of salvation, and granted them a pledge of peace" (Antiphon of the feast).

We try to see Bernadette, in ecstasy before the "little white Lady" who appeared in a niche of the grotto. We join the huge throng of pilgrims who daily kneel in prayer at that same place and who go home, perhaps not cured, but certainly consoled and strengthened in their faith.

2. *Petition*: The grace to see the Lord's hand in all these events, and to make "the message of Lourdes"—prayer and penance— our rule of life.

I. Mary's Solicitude

On the 25th of March, during the sixteenth apparition, the "little white Lady" said to Bernadette, "I am the Immaculate Conception." So it was true that the Virgin Mother of God and, by Christ's will and testament, our own Mother, had come to urge this poor shepherd girl to pray and do penance for sinners. The Kingdom of her Son on earth, always the butt of the violent onslaughts of the Prince of this world, and the imminent danger which many of her children run to lose their souls, fill her Mother's Heart with solicitude.

From our Lady's apparitions during the last century, [at La Salette (1844), at Lourdes (1858), at Fatima (1917)] we must conclude that Mary wants to give our modern world a special message; in each case she insistently asks that we should pray and do penance for sinners. Mary, Help of Christians, is so familiar with our needs! From heaven she sees how faith is growing fainter and fainter in broad layers of modern society, how world-liness is invading the souls even of professing Christians, how numerous are those who either forget, or deny, that God reigns in heaven. She knows the fearful dangers which threaten the human race, if it throws to the wind belief in God and in His law, at the very moment when scientific progress is placing in our hands means of destruction undreamt of in previous ages.

It is God's unfathomable mystery, how in the accomplishment of the work of our salvation He deigns to use the ministry of His holy Mother, also our Mother, to help us, and save us from peril. And Mary herself chooses those to whom she will communicate the will of her divine Son.

II. Mary's Choice

This choice ought not to make us wonder; for we know that it is determined by the spirit of Jesus, and that this spirit was revealed to us when Jesus exclaimed: "I confess to thee O Father, Lord of heaven and earth, because thou hast hid these things from the wise and prudent, and hast revealed them to little ones. Yea Father, for so it hath seemed good in thy sight" (*Matt.* 11, 25-26).

Bernadette is a child of fourteen, belonging to an impoverished family in the country town of Lourdes, in the South of France. She has had very little schooling and has not yet received her first Holy Communion. She is an ordinary child, with childish shortcomings, a little capricious and not quite devoid of childish vanity. But she was far from being a good-for-nothing; such people God does not choose. She was a healthy, straightforward, even pious girl; in her home they used to say the rosary every night, with the little prayer, "Mary, conceived without sin, pray for us". Simple and humble, without the faintest sign of self-consciousness, her heart had been prepared for God, to receive the confidences of her who called herself the handmaid of the Lord.

Such was Bernadette, when Mary appeared to her; and such she remained till her death, even when her name was on the lips of millions of men throughout the world, and when bishops and Cardinals vied with each other for the privilege of an interview with her at the convent of Nevers. "Because he that is mighty hath done great things to me. He hath regarded the humility of his handmaid and hath exalted the humble."

Other privileged children of Mary, for instance those of La Salette, did not become saints. Man remains free, and even great graces may be thrown to the wind. The last words spoken by Bernadette on her deathbed are touching: "Holy Mary, Mother of God, pray for me, poor sinner, poor sinner." We do not wonder at those words: she had seen the Immaculate, the Virgin Mother of God.

III. Mary's Message

All through the first two apparitions, Bernadette simply gazed ecstatically at the "little white Lady"; during the third apparition Mary asked her, "Would you give me the pleasure of coming here during fourteen days?" The polite form of address deeply struck the poor child; "She called me 'you'!" During these fourteen days Mary explained to the child what was to be her mission: "Pray to God for sinners"; and taught her to make the sign of the cross and to recite the rosary. On one occasion the bystanders heard her repeat, while tears flowed from her eyes, "penance, penance". And, at the bidding of the Lady, she kissed the ground, and drank from the muddy water of the spring, that had welled up close at hand; and she ate some of the herbs that grew close to the rock. These were symbolical actions, signifying penance and humility.

"Go, tell the priest that I desire that a chapel be built here, and that people should come here in procession." In the face of fierce opposition, the humble girl delivered her message, and fulfilled her mission with the utmost simplicity and sincerity, yet with remarkable courage, constancy and patience. In 1866 the task, laid on her, had been accomplished: she had borne testimony; and that testimony, together with Mary's call to prayer and to penance, had re-echoed throughout the universal Church. Then she went and hid herself in a monastery at Nevers, where, by physical and mental suffering she sanctified her soul for the conversion of sinners. God alone knows how many millions since then have knelt in prayer before that grotto, how many have received pardon of their sins, and have been strengthened in the faith, or have found back the sacred treasure they had lost. In the course of one hundred years 54 cures were officially certified as miraculous. Every year thousands of sufferers come to Lourdes to pray for healing; their bodily ailments are not cured, but they receive a more precious grace—peace and joy, and a ready will to carry their cross for the love of Jesus and for the conversion of sinners.

At Lourdes Mary leads all her children that approach her, either back to Jesus or closer to Him: her call to prayer, penance and repentance makes all feel they are brothers and sisters in the communion of Saints.

We thank and praise the divine Goodness and Mercy for the wonderful "Fact of Lourdes". He works through the intervention of His holy Mother; she in turn found a humble handmaid in St. Bernadette.

Prayer: O God, who didst prepare a worthy dwelling for Thy Son by the Immaculate Conception of the blessed Virgin; we humbly ask of Thee that by celebrating the appearance of the same Virgin we may obtain health of soul and body. Through the same Lord (Collect of the day).

O God, Protector and Lover of the humble, who didst strengthen thy handmaid Mary Bernard by the apparition and intercourse of the Immaculate Virgin Mary, grant, we beseech Thee,
that by treading the paths of faith without dissimulation we may
merit to behold Thy face in heaven. Through Christ our Lord
(Collect, Mass of St. Bernadette).

ST. THOMAS AQUINAS

1. St. Thomas is universally acknowledged as the Prince of
    theologians. His fellow Dominican, Fra Angelico, has painted
    him absorbed in ecstatic adoration before the Savior hanging
    high on the cross. His eyes are fixed on Christ, and gaze intently on the dying Redeemer. On his chest he bears a jewel,
    shining with the brightness of the sun: the painter wanted to
    impress on us that in the Angelic Doctor the highest holiness
    goes hand in hand with the most sublime knowledge.

    Or we might contemplate Thomas in adoration before the
    Blessed Sacrament. At the request of the Pope, St. Thomas
    composed both the Mass and the Office of the Blessed Sacrament. Here he had the opportunity to give expression to the
    ardent love that devoured his heart.

2. Kneeling with St. Thomas before the altar, we pray,
    > Jesus, whom for the present veil'd I see,
    > What I so thirst for, Oh! vouchsafe to me:
    > That I may see Thy countenance unfolding,
    > And may be blest Thy glory in beholding.

I. Love of Truth

St. Thomas was profoundly enamored of Truth, the full Truth,
for which we are born, and which is God Himself. With all his
powers and with his whole heart he searched for truth, reverently,
humbly, devotedly, convinced that truth is greater than our
human mind, that we must serve the truth with all our power,
and never make the truth subservient to our own opinions or
vain conceits.

As a thinker, and as a searcher after truth, he is absolutely honest. He loves the truth because it is the truth; nor does he ever ask who propounded it, whether friend or foe. He made his own the pithy saying of St. Ambrose, "Whatever is true, by whomsoever it may have been spoken, is the word of the Spirit." He knows that "we can do nothing against the truth, but for the truth" (2 *Cor.* 13, 8). "He rejoiceth with the truth" (1 *Cor.* 13, 6).

St. Thomas sought after truth, not merely in his studies, but even more in all he said and did, every day of his life. Uprightness and absolute sincerity are fundamental features in every noble character. One of his earliest biographers, using medieval imagery, tried to convey the impression which the Saint made on his contemporaries: "His whole life was as silver; his speech was white and bright as silver; pure and unalloyed as silver was his conduct; clear as the sound of silver was his doctrine." Like St. Paul, he knew how to "do the truth in charity" (*Eph.* 4, 15), that is, to pay homage to the truth without giving offence to our neighbor. Such tact is an art known to, and practiced by, the Saints.

In all things and everywhere St. Thomas was the servant of the truth. With complete forgetfulness of self, and with faithful love, he served Him who said, "I am the truth."

II. Yet One of the Little Ones

St. Thomas was aware of his mental powers and learning. That did not make him self-complacent: he was far too wise for that, and had his eyes steadfastly fixed on God. Therefore he cannot be reckoned with "the wise and the prudent, from whom the Father, Lord of heaven and earth, hath hid these things"; but with the little ones to whom He hath revealed them (*Matt.* 11, 25). Never did the Saint compare himself with others, whether to despise them or to envy them; he did not fancy himself, never strove for fame; he *was* great, and ingenious, and childlike; and served God with every talent that had been given him.

Learning, authority, and whatever makes a man distinguished above his fellows, readily degenerate into pride. In the measure in which this happens to a man, he loses what St. Thomas calls "devotion", that is, readiness to devote oneself wholly to God's service. But if learning goes together with perfect surrender of self to God, then devotion grows all the more genuine and all the more pure. The study of St. Thomas was like that of St. Augustine, a "devout search", with the eyes of the mind ever

"looking on Jesus the author and finisher of faith" (*Heb.* 12, 2).
There is a story that, on a certain occasion, Jesus appearing
to him said, "Thomas, thou hast written well about Me. What reward dost thou desire?" Thomas answered, "None other than
Thyself, O Lord."

> To Thee my heart I bow with bended knee
> As failing quite in contemplating Thee.

III.   "Knowledge Shall Be Destroyed"

Thomas died in 1279 at the early age of 49. He was on his way
to the Council of Lyons, whither the Pope had summoned him,
when he was suddenly taken ill. With his fellow traveller Raynald, also a Friar Preacher, he was hospitably received in the
Cistercian monastery at Naples. His monumental work, the
Summa Theologica, lay unfinished, and Raynald urged him to
put the finishing touches to it. "O Raynald," he said, "all my
writings appear to me as chaff, compared with what I have seen
and what was revealed to me." Thus the greatest theologians had
learnt by experience what St. Paul had written in his hymn of
praise on charity: "Charity never falleth away.... Knowledge
shall be destroyed, for we know in part. But when that which is
perfect is come, that which is in part shall be put away" (1 *Cor.*
13, 8-10). He died in the Cistercian monastery on the 7th of
March 1279.

He had written, "God alone can satisfy our desires. And He
surpasses them all; therefore there is no rest for man, but in God."

Prayer: Jesus, whom for the present veil'd I see,
        What I so thirst for, Oh! vouchsafe to me;
        That I may see Thy countenance unfolding,
        And may be blest Thy glory in beholding.

THE FEAST OF ST. JOSEPH, SPOUSE OF MARY

1.   St. Joseph, Spouse of Mary, most unexpectedly found himself playing a part in the drama of the incarnation. At a moment of great perplexity God sent him an angel to enlighten

and comfort him. "Joseph, son of David, fear not to take unto thee Mary, thy wife; for that which is conceived in her, is of the Holy Ghost. And she shall bring forth a son; and thou shalt call his name Jesus" (*Matt.* 1, 20-21).

2. *Petition*: The grace to understand better the dignity and the holiness of our Lord's foster father, and to have confidence in his powerful intercession.

I. St. Joseph's Important, Though Indirect, Role

The cult of St. Joseph spread in the Church rather late: it is only in the 17th century that the liturgy began to honor him. We need not say that St. Joseph had been forgotten, or perhaps ignored. In earlier times the main preoccupation of the Church, in preaching the good tidings, was to emphasize who was her Founder and the Savior of the human race: Jesus Christ, the second Person of the Blessed Trinity, true God and true man.

The preaching of this message necessarily implied that Mary was really and truly the Mother of God and, as emphatically declared by the Gospel, the Virginal Mother of Christ. The intervention of St. Joseph in the scheme of our salvation was indirect, though of great importance. By God's own choice he was the protector and the witness of the virginal motherhood, the Child's legal father, and the head of the Holy Family.

In a unique and most sublime manner St. Joseph was connected with those we rightly call our Blessed Lady and our Blessed Lord. Yet those ties were not so fundamental that, from the beginning, in formulating her dogma and fixing her liturgical prayer, the Church should have found it necessary to determine which was the precise place of St. Joseph in the divine economy. So it happened that, for centuries, he received scant notice; but gradually the Church, that is the Christian people, the supreme Pontiffs, the doctors and theologians, paid more heed to him whom the Gospel called "a just man", and found solace in paying him the homage he deserved.

What St. Joseph was to Mary and to Jesus while he was on earth, their protector and guardian, that he is now acknowledged to be to our Lord's family: the protector of the Church, the guardian of virgins, the patron of Christian families, and the patron of the interior life.

II. Joseph, a Faithful Steward

Above all Joseph had to be faithful. To him God had deigned to entrust His most precious treasures in heaven and on earth and His most intimate secret; His only-begotten Son in whom He was well pleased, that Son's holy, immaculate, virginal Mother and the ineffable mystery wrought in the womb of the Virgin through the power of the Most High.

We can read in the Gospel how he fulfilled his task of God's trusted steward. We admire his absolute uprightness and, at the same time, his most delicate charity in the painful circumstances that had arisen before God's angel came down to reveal the mystery to him. Indeed, he was worthy of the Lord's confidence. In St. Luke's sober account of the events at Bethlehem we read between the lines how he took counsel with Mary, when there was no room for them in the inn; then how he guarded and protected Mary and the Child during the flight into Egypt, in the land of exile, and during the return journey; how he deliberated whither they ought to go after their return.

At Nazareth he is the bread-winner of the family. We love to think with what intense joy he labored to support Jesus and Mary, and how he devoted himself to their welfare. It was his privilege to assist in the education of the Child, Wisdom Incarnate.

We do not know the time of his death. Most probably it occurred before the beginning of the public ministry of Jesus. He entered into the joy of his Lord, for he had been faithful, not over a few things, but over the most precious treasure God could entrust to a man.

III. St. Joseph Is Humble

In truth he was the head of the Holy Family, and the husband of Mary; in law he was the father of the divine Child; he had given him His name. The angel had said, "Thou shalt call his name Jesus." God deigned to communicate His will to Mary and to Jesus through Joseph. Legally it is because of him that Jesus is the Son of David.

And yet how modest he was: he was aware that, though he was the head of the household, still he was the least. He served Mary and the Child. He loved Mary with his whole heart, and revered her for what she was; Mary loved Joseph and revered him too. Never was there such sublime love between two human beings.

o Mary he yields the honor to form and fashion and train their holy Child. When at the age of twelve Jesus is lost in Jerusalem, and found again in the Temple, Joseph lets Mary speak; that was the Mother's right. And Mary, vying, as it were, in delicacy and tact with Joseph, says, "Son, why hast thou done so to us? Behold thy father and I have sought thee sorrowing" (*Luke* 2, 48). The Mother speaks, but she first names the father.

And now the humble foster father of Jesus is the protector of Holy Church. In the Litany of All Saints his name is invoked after that of John the Baptist, even before those of the Apostles and the patriarchs. St. Teresa of Avila often said that she had never asked a favor from St. Joseph without obtaining it through his intercession. And she exhorted her Carmelites to ask the gift of prayer from him, who had been so familiar with Jesus and Mary.

Prayer: We beseech Thee, O Lord, to help us through the merits of the Spouse of Thy most holy Mother; and what our own efforts cannot obtain, do Thou grant us through his intercession. Who livest... (Collect of the Feast).

MARCH 25

THE ANNUNCIATION OF THE BLESSED VIRGIN

1. On this day the Church commemorates the most mysterious and the most solemn event in the history of mankind and of the universe. God, whom neither time nor eternity can encompass, enters our created world; He becomes man in the virginal womb of her that is blessed amongst women. This is the central mystery of our faith. Whatever went before was merely a preparation for this sublime mystery, which links what is highest with what is lowest; whatever comes after is the result, till "the end when he (Christ) shall have delivered up the kingdom to God and the Father, when he shall have brought to nought all principality, and power, and virtue" (1 *Cor.* 15, 24). We may behold Mary in converse with the angel.

2. *Petition*: The grace "to rise to the contemplation of God made man; to approach this sanctuary in a spirit of humble devotion, striving to gain spiritual knowledge through reverence and love, rather than to gain love through knowledge."

I. Mary, God's Ultimate Instrument

The first step towards the Incarnation of the Son of God was creation itself. For the Son is the "first-born of every creature ... for in him were all things created in heaven and on earth ... all things were created by him and in him" (*Col.* 1, 15-16).

After He had created our material universe, God created man, who is both matter and spirit. "And when the fullness of time was come", the Son of God would unite with the Divinity man's nature composed of matter and spirit. Then came sin into the world, but man's sin could not make void the divine decree; because of sin God's plan was realized in a manner even more sublime. Not only will God's only-begotten Son become man, but He will also be the Savior and restorer of all things.

Another step towards the implementation of God's inscrutable design was the election of the Jewish people. Its mission was to preserve faith in the one true God, when all nations had lapsed into idolatry, and to keep alive the expectation of a Savior: the Messiah was to be born in the house of Abraham. It is noteworthy that the genealogy of Jesus Christ, Son of David, son of Abraham, which we read in the first chapter of St. Matthew, contains the names of not a few that were sinners (how could it be otherwise?), till we come to the name of "Joseph, the husband of Mary, of whom was born Jesus, who is called Christ" (*Matt.* 1, 16).

We admire the delicate attention with which divine Wisdom prepares the last stage for the Incarnation of the Son. God preserves her who is to be His Son's Mother, from every stain of sin. Mary was conceived without sin, redeemed in a sublime manner in prevision of Christ's merits. The fullness of grace, which God had bestowed on her in the beginning, could and did grow steadily. That she had resolved to remain a virgin, and yet to espouse Joseph, we may attribute to a special guidance of the Spirit. Such guidance seems appropriate in the case of one that had been preserved from original sin, and chosen to become the Mother of God.

And thus Mary, though she was not aware of it, became God's ultimate instrument in the consummation of His great design.

II. The Angel's Message

On that memorable day, the "Angel Gabriel was sent from God into a city of Galilee, called Nazareth". The account of St. Luke (1, 26-37), the details of which he must have received from Mary herself, records the most important, the most confidential, the most sacred colloquy that ever took place on earth between two created beings. Let us, with reverence and devotion, read once again those "words", which Mary kept in her heart, even more religiously than anything else, connected with those sacred events.

The angel salutes her, allays her fears, does not *ask* whether she consents, but *tells* her she will bear a Son and yet remain a virgin, "because no word shall be impossible with God".

Mary hears the message from heaven, thinks it right to ask a question; the angel gives her the answer, which removes every difficulty; and then she gives her consent. We admire her prudence, her wisdom, her sincerity, her humility.

III.   Mary's Answer

"Behold the handmaid of the Lord; be it done to me according to thy word" (*Luke* 1, 38). Mary's *Fiat* was the most powerful word ever uttered by created lips. It was not a command, as when the Creator said, *Fiat Lux;* it was a *Fiat* spoken in acceptance of God's will, a humble *Fiat,* befitting a creature, even a creature who has been chosen to be the Mother of God and Queen of heaven and earth. And yet it was a mighty word, for which God waited to become man. And it was uttered in the fullness of her liberty. "Thou shalt bear a son", said the angel; freely Mary gave her assent. God has been pleased to endow us with free will: that freedom He respects in every man, also in Mary, the holiest and most exalted of all His creatures.

Her *Fiat* implied the absolute and unlimited acceptance of God's plan for man's salvation, and of the part that was reserved for her in that plan. Did God, at that hour, vouchsafe unto her further light as to the manner in which our salvation was to be wrought: through suffering, death, and resurrection? About this, revelation is silent. But we know that, whatever light God was pleased to give her, she still had to walk by faith. "Blessed art thou that hast believed," said Elizabeth. She was and remained the humble "handmaid of the Lord", abiding by her *Fiat* all her life, till she stood at the foot of the cross.

Prayer: O God, by whose will Thy Word took flesh in the womb of the Blessed Virgin Mary at the message of Thy angel; grant us, we implore Thee, that we may enjoy the intercession before Thee of her whom we truly believe to be the Mother of God. Through the same Lord (Collect of the Feast).

ST. JOSEPH THE WORKER

"SEEK YE FIRST THE KINGDOM OF GOD" (*Matt.* 6, 33)

1. The institution of the feast of St. Joseph the Worker was announced by Pope Pius XII on the 1st of May 1955, in an address to the Italian Catholic Labor Unions. The Father of all the faithful desired to give a proof of his deep concern for the lot of the Catholic workers. If they lose the faith, dark days are in store for the Church and for the world. So far the 1st of May had been "May Day", a purely secular festival. The institution of this feast has christened May Day, and placed it in the Church's calendar. God grant that it may be not merely a day of liturgical ceremonies, but also a day of prayer for our brothers, on whose loyalty to Christ the future depends.

2. *Petition*: We behold Joseph in his workshop at Nazareth, in the sweat of his brow earning the daily bread for his family. We pray that we may recognize in this village carpenter the holiest laborer that ever bent over a tool-bench. May we imitate his virtues.

> Hail mightiest of Saints,
> To whom submissive bent
> He, whose creator-hand outstretched
> The starry firmament.

I. Joseph Had to Work

In Genesis it is said that God made man "and put him in a paradise of pleasure, to dress it and to keep it" (*Gen.* 2, 15). This was before the fall; but even then man had to use his mental and his physical faculties to discover, as it were, and to develop the riches of God's creation, to perfect his own personality, and to give praise to the Creator.

After the fall, he himself, as well as nature, has lost his pristine integrity, and now labor becomes toil. "Thorns and thistles shall the earth bring forth. In the sweat of thy face shalt thou eat bread" (*Gen.* 3, 18-19). It is a law of nature, therefore of God, that man shall work, and every man must obey that law; he that does evade it thereby becomes a parasite, and a source of disorder.

Joseph was a manual laborer, probably a carpenter, who with his daily earnings supported his family. It was rough, monotonous work, with fairly primitive tools. He was a village carpenter, not a cabinet-maker. Many years he stood alone in his shop; but later he taught the trade to his Son, and had His help. When Joseph died, Jesus continued His father's work, until He began His public ministry.

Therefore Joseph, and also Jesus, shared the lot of the vast majority of men, and lived by the labor of their hands. But the Patron of workers will be, not Jesus, who is "the way, the truth and the life", but His foster father St. Joseph, the bridegroom of the Virgin Mother of God.

II. St. Joseph Happy in His Work

In those days there did not exist at Nazareth those crying scandalous, social and economic maladjustments of our modern world.

The village carpenter at Nazareth was not a pauper, and managed to make both ends meet. But he was not rich, which is proved by the fact that, at the time of the Presentation of Jesus in the Temple, he offered two turtle doves. Surely all around him there were people that were more comfortable, people that worked less and earned more. Inequality has always existed and always will exist. It existed in the day of Cain; and then "shall sin forthwith be present at the door" of man's heart, as God told Cain before he slew his brother Abel (Gen. 4, 7).

Joseph was perfectly happy in his humble avocation: did he not enjoy domestic happiness, hardly less intense than the bliss of heaven? To this healthy, wise, upright man it was an immense joy to labor for the support of such a family. He was about "his Father's business"; He was the guardian of the Father's only-begotten Son, and of that Son's Mother.

Our Holy Father the Pope, who declared St. Joseph patron and model of the modern workman, knew only too well that many workers today have to fulfill their Christian duties in conditions and surroundings far less favorable than those in which St. Joseph worked; he therefore exhorted all his children to bear a compassionate heart and, whenever possible, to contribute by prayer and sacrifice to a better understanding among men, and to the practice of brotherly love in our society.

III. Seek Ye First the Kingdom of God (Matt. 6, 33)

Social, economic, political conditions are in perpetual flux. "Seek ye therefore first the kingdom of God, and his justice" is one of the words of which Jesus said, "Heaven and earth shall pass, but my words shall not pass" (*Matt.* 24, 35). St. Joseph, the just man, in all things sought to fulfill his duty perfectly, that is, to do the will of the Father. And in this manner did the carpenter of Nazareth contribute to the establishment of the Kingdom of God, of which Jesus, the carpenter's Son, was to be the Founder and the King.

The Kingdom of Christ, the future of which so largely depends on the faith of the working classes, is a "kingdom of justice, love and peace". First of all of justice: for God's Kingdom cannot be based on injustice. But even justice is not the supreme quality of God's Kingdom. "God is love", and love, which never runs counter to justice goes far beyond it. Love never divides, it always unites, reconciles, spreads peace and harmony.

Let us strive to maintain in our religious communities Christ's Kingdom of justice, love and peace: each "doing from the heart what he does", content and happy to be permitted to serve God in the place and office which He has allotted to us. In this way we shall, like St. Joseph, help "to re-establish all things in Christ" (*Eph.* 2, 10).

Prayer: O God, Creator of all things, who hast laid the obligation to work upon the human race; mercifully grant that through the example and patronage of St. Joseph we may accomplish the works that Thou dost command, and obtain the rewards Thou dost promise. Through our Lord (Collect of the Feast).

MAY 31

THE QUEENSHIP OF THE BLESSED VIRGIN MARY

1. The Liturgical feast of Mary's Queenship was established during the Marian year 1954, on the 11th of October. In this manner the Vicar of Christ solemnly sanctioned a title, which the Christian people had given to Mary during centuries. In the 15th century the devout Dominican painter, Fra Angelico, many a time painted on the walls of his monastery at Florence,

the coronation of Mary as Queen of Heaven. We behold our Lady, on bended knees, with folded hands, bowing slightly before her divine Son, who places a crown on His Mother's brow. Even at the moment when she is being crowned Queen of heaven and earth, her attitude is as humble and as meek as when she said to the angel, "Behold the handmaid of the Lord."

2. *Petition*: The grace to join the heavenly court in paying homage to our Queen.

> Hail, Queen of heaven enthroned,
> Hail by angels Mistress owned.

I. Mary Our Queen

In the Litany of Loreto Christian piety has, with the exception of the middle group of invocations, divided Mary's titles into three groups; Mother, Virgin, Queen. These are the most exalted and the most honorable titles one can give to a woman: and all three together, in the worthiest sense, belong only to one Woman, our Blessed Lady.

The first two, Mother and Virgin, refer to what is most sacred about a woman; and here, where Mary is concerned, they are ranked in the order of their dignity. These two titles are at the head of the entire series, and will be enlarged upon in various ways: "Holy Mother of God, and Holy Virgin of Virgins." Kind as a mother, but more than any other mother, because she is Mother of God; inviolate as a virgin, but more than any other virgin, because she is the Virgin Mother of the Son of God.

In the third series we salute her as Queen: her "style and title", her rank and office in the Kingdom of her Son. We salute her as Queen of every angelic choir, and of every group of Saints. To these titles several have been added during the last century, as shining jewels in her royal diadem—the last: Queen assumed into heaven!

II. Mary's Right to the Title

No earthly title is glorious enough to express Mary's exalted dignity. Queen, princess, sovereign, refer to social relations among men. Mary is in all truth Mother of God, and this implies a natural relation between her, and Him who is God and man. Her dignity is unique, immeasurable and, as St. Thomas says, in a certain sense infinite. "The Humanity of Jesus, which is united with the

Deity; the bliss of the Saints, which is the possession of God; the Blessed Virgin Mary, who is Mother of God; all these, because of the infinite Good which is God, are in a certain sense infinite."

When the angel had delivered his message, and Mary had given her consent, Mary became the Mother of the Son of the Most High. "The Lord God shall give him the throne of his father, and he shall reign in the house of Jacob for ever, and of his kingdom there shall be no end." And to His Mother He gives a royal dignity, of which likewise there shall be no end.

Mary furthermore deserves this title, because as Mother of the Savior she received from Him a most intimate and unique share in the work of our salvation. The Encyclical of Oct. 11, 1954 said, "It is true that, in the real and strictest sense, the title of King belongs exclusively to Christ, God and man. However Mary, in a limited sense, shares His royal dignity; because she is the Mother of Christ, our God, and because she was associated with Christ's work of salvation."

And therefore in the liturgical office of this day the Church sings:

"By the cross of Christ His Mother stood,
Sharing in His sufferings, of all the world Queen;
The Virgin Mary was taken up to heaven;
She reigns with Christ for all eternity...."
Together with her Son in the glory of His Father.

III. Our Queen's Power

The King, at times, is obliged to use His power to chastise; not so the Queen. She uses her influence and her power only to scatter favors, to intercede, to plead, to obtain mercy, to save. Painters of the Last Judgment were wont to represent this in the following manner: Christ, the Supreme Judge, appears in the clouds with a stern countenance; close to Him, but a little lower, in the attitude of a suppliant, Mary looks up to her divine Son. This is not an inappropriate way to represent to our senses how our Queen, Mother of Mercy, deigns to use her "omnipotentia supplex", her boundless power of intercession, to plead for us, poor banished children of Eve, to whom she longs to show one day the blessed fruit of her womb.

Prayer: On Nov. 1, 1954, in his address on the Queenship of Mary, Pope Pius XII said, "Anxious to interpret the feelings of

. Christians, we thus pray fervently to the Blessed Mary, ever irgin:

"To thee, O Mary, most dear Mother, we raise our hearts from the depths of this vale of tears, where distressed mankind struggles against the rising waves of an ocean lashed into fury by the violent tempest of our passions; we hope to be strengthened by the contemplation of thy glory; we salute thee as Queen and Ruler of heaven and earth, as our Queen and Mistress.... Be thou indeed our Queen, and show us the way to holiness.... Reign thou over the whole human race, and lead into the fold those that do not yet know the name of thy Son. Reign over the Church, especially in those lands where the Church suffers persecution. Reign over each one of us, over families, over realms and nations. Grant that all those who this day acclaim thee as their Queen and their Mistress, may one day enjoy the plenitude of bliss in thy Kingdom, where they shall behold thy Son, who with the Father and the Holy Ghost, liveth and reigneth for ever, world without end. Amen."